THIRD EDITION

Fundamentals of
BUSINESS MATHEMATICS
in Canada

F. ERNEST JEROME

JACKIE SHEMKO
Durham College

McGraw Hill Education

Fundamentals of Business Mathematics in Canada Third Edition

Statistics Canada information is used with the permission of Statistics Canada. Users are forbidden to copy this material and/or redisseminate the data, in an original or modified form, for commercial purposes, without the expressed permission of Statistics Canada. Information on the availability of the wide range of data from Statistics Canada can be obtained from Statistics Canada's Regional Offices, its website at www.statcan.gc.ca and its toll-free access number 1-800-263-1136.

The Internet addresses listed in the text were accurate at the time of publication. The inclusion of a website does not indicate an endorsement by the authors or McGraw-Hill Ryerson, and McGraw-Hill Ryerson does not guarantee the accuracy of information presented at these sites.

ISBN-13: 978-1-25-937015-1
ISBN-10: 1-25-937015-1

3 4 5 6 7 8 TCP 22 21 20

Printed and bound in Canada

Care has been taken to trace ownership of copyright material contained in this text; however, the publisher will welcome any information that enables it to rectify any reference or credit for subsequent editions.

Portfolio and Program Manager: *Karen Fozard*
Product Manager: *Sara Braithwaite*
Marketing Manager: *Cathie Lefebvre*
Product Developer: *Erin Catto*
Supervising Editor: *Janie Deneau*
Senior Product Team Associate: *Marina Seguin*
Photo/Permissions Researcher: *Photo Affairs, Inc.*
Copy Editor: *Rodney Rawlings*
Proofreader: *Rodney Rawlings*
Plant Production Coordinator: *Sarah Strynatka*
Manufacturing Production Coordinator: *Sheryl MacAdam*
Inside Design: *Michelle Losier*
Cover Design: *Lightbox Visual Communications Inc.*
Composition: *Aptara®, Inc.*
Cover Photo: *Yagi Studio/Getty Images*
Printer: *Transcontinental Printing Group*

About the Authors

F. Ernest Jerome received a B.Sc. degree in Honours Physics from McMaster University, where he was that university's first undergraduate to be a prize-winner in the annual Canadian Association of Physicists' Examination national competition. After earning a graduate degree in Oceanography at the University of British Columbia, he was appointed head of the Physics Department at Vancouver Island University (VIU) in Nanaimo, B.C. Professor Jerome later obtained an MBA in finance from UBC, where he was awarded the Schulich Fellowship for Entrepreneurship. He subsequently taught courses in business mathematics, corporate finance, personal financial planning, mutual funds, and securities analysis in VIU's Faculty of Business. He holds a Chartered Financial Planner designation, and received the 1987 Outstanding Achievement Award from the Canadian Institute of Financial Planning.

Jackie Shemko teaches in the School of Business, I.T. & Management at Durham College in Oshawa, Ontario. Over the course of 20 years of teaching at the college level, Jackie has taught a wide range of courses, including Business Mathematics, Operations Management, and Economics. She holds a Bachelor of Business Administration from Wilfrid Laurier University and a Bachelor of Education from Nipissing University. Prior to beginning her teaching career, Jackie worked in corporate banking with the Canadian Imperial Bank of Commerce.

Brief Contents

Contents

CHAPTER 11

CHAPTER 12

CHAPTER 13

LIST OF FIGURES

LIST OF TABLES

MATH APPS BOXES

Preface

Business mathematics continues to be an important foundational course in most business administration programs in Canadian colleges. The business mathematics curriculum helps students build the mathematics skills they will need as they progress through their studies in accounting, marketing, operations management, human resources management, and business information systems.

Fundamentals of Business Mathematics in Canada, Third Edition is a comprehensive yet accessible text designed primarily for one-semester business mathematics courses. In recognition of the time pressures inherent in single-semester mathematics courses, the content and chapter features have been selected to support the development of essential learning outcomes. The focus is on clear exposition, with careful consideration given to the topic areas for which, based on the authors' and reviewers' experience, students need additional support. The text presents a carefully selected suite of categorized problems—basic, intermediate, and advanced—allowing faculty to easily tailor in-class examples and homework assignments by level of difficulty. All topics typically addressed in business mathematics courses are presented. The structure of the text allows faculty to customize their delivery as they decide how far into each topic they wish to take their students.

Jerome/Shemko is suitable for courses that emphasize either an algebraic approach or a preprogrammed financial calculator approach to compound interest problems. Both algebraic solutions and financial calculator solutions are presented in most Example problems for compound-interest topics.

NEW TO THIS EDITION

This edition incorporates suggestions from users and reviewers of the previous editions. The aim is to continue to present an accessible and flexible resource that encourages students to build skills and apply those skills with confidence to real-world problems.

- **Updated problems:** Although low interest rates persist in Canada, it is important that students appreciate how individuals and businesses are affected when rates climb. While the majority of Exercise and Example problems use rates that are in line with our current low interest rate environment, we have provided many examples with slightly higher interest rates, to help reinforce the idea that businesses, consumers and investors should appreciate the impact that higher rates could have on their own finances and the economy as a whole.

- **New Math Apps features:** Six new Math Apps boxes have been written to help illustrate the "real-world" application of chapter concepts. "Striking the Balance with Provincial Sales Taxes" in Chapter 1 compares the provincial sales tax frameworks in British Columbia, Alberta, and Nova Scotia, showing how provincial governments have struggled to balance consumer preferences with their own fiscal challenges. In Chapter 4, "The Cost of a 'Cash-less' Society" provides an update about a Competition Bureau investigation into credit card merchant fees, and how that prompted Visa and MasterCard to commit to a voluntary schedule of fee reductions. In Chapter 7, "What to Do with a Small Amount of Savings in a Low Interest Rate Environment?" helps reinforce the idea that while low interest rates are a boon for borrowers, they pose significant challenges for investors, especially those with only small amounts to work with. Also in Chapter 7, "Canada Student Loans: How to Manage Your Debt

After Graduation" provides updates about federal government attempts to improve collections of student debt, and provides tips about responsible management of student loan repayment. "Beware of Payday Loans!" in Chapter 9 helps students understand that the convenience of so-called "payday loans" comes at a significant cost. Finally, in Chapter 13, "Mortgage Choices: Understanding the Options" introduces students to the decision making they will face when shopping for a residential mortgage, including fixed versus floating rates and shorter versus longer terms.

- **Updated rates and statistics:** This edition incorporates the most recent data available at the time of writing, including foreign exchange rates, Canada Savings bond rates, strip bond pricing, and current treatment of HST in Ontario, Prince Edward Island, New Brunswick, Nova Scotia, and Newfoundland and Labrador.

FEATURES

- **Check your Understanding feature:** Students are highly encouraged to maximize the utility of the Example problems throughout the text. At the end of each worked Example problem, a feature called "Check your Understanding" encourages students to *rework the question* using a slightly different set of parameters. The bottom-line answer is provided right in the feature, making it easy for students to check their work and accurately assess whether they understand the concept and are ready to move on. This feature is designed to help students become more *actively engaged* in the material as they make their way through the text.

- **Related problem:** Each worked Example problem directs students to a related problem in the end-of-section Exercise. Having read the worked example and reworked it using the "Check your Understanding" feature, students are then pointed to a problem in the Exercise that requires them to use the concept that they have just studied. This "read, do, and do again" approach will help students use the worked Example problems to support their learning.

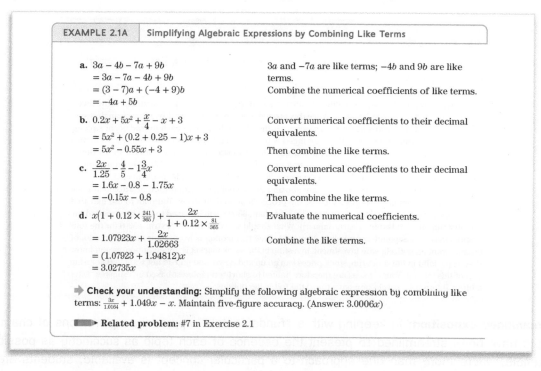

EXAMPLE 2.1A	Simplifying Algebraic Expressions by Combining Like Terms

a. $3a - 4b - 7a + 9b$

$= 3a - 7a - 4b + 9b$

$= (3 - 7)a + (-4 + 9)b$

$= -4a + 5b$

$3a$ and $-7a$ are like terms; $-4b$ and $9b$ are like terms.
Combine the numerical coefficients of like terms.

b. $0.2x + 5x^2 + \frac{x}{4} - x + 3$

$= 5x^2 + (0.2 + 0.25 - 1)x + 3$

$= 5x^2 - 0.55x + 3$

Convert numerical coefficients to their decimal equivalents.
Then combine the like terms.

c. $\frac{2x}{1.25} - \frac{4}{5} - 1\frac{3}{4}x$

$= 1.6x - 0.8 - 1.75x$

$= -0.15x - 0.8$

Convert numerical coefficients to their decimal equivalents.
Then combine the like terms.

d. $x\left(1 + 0.12 \times \frac{241}{365}\right) + \frac{2x}{1 + 0.12 \times \frac{81}{365}}$

$= 1.07923x + \frac{2x}{1.02663}$

$= (1.07923 + 1.94812)x$

$= 3.02735x$

Evaluate the numerical coefficients.

Combine the like terms.

➡ **Check your understanding:** Simplify the following algebraic expression by combining like terms: $\frac{3x}{1.0164} + 1.049x - x$. Maintain five-figure accuracy. (Answer: $3.0006x$)

▶ **Related problem:** #7 in Exercise 2.1

- **Categorized exercise problems:** Each section of the text provides a rich bank of practice problems for in-class or homework use. These problems are grouped into Basic, Intermediate, and Advanced sections. This will help instructors to present a "scaffolded" approach to each concept. Where time permits, faculty can use the advanced problems to illustrate extensions of the chapter concepts or, alternatively, to provide enrichment problems for students who seek extra challenge. A full set of end-of-chapter Review Problems is similarly categorized.

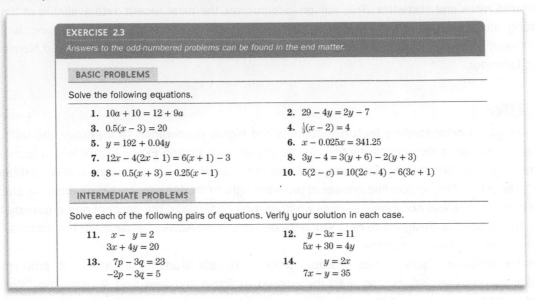

EXERCISE 2.3

Answers to the odd-numbered problems can be found in the end matter.

BASIC PROBLEMS

Solve the following equations.

1. $10a + 10 = 12 + 9a$
2. $29 - 4y = 2y - 7$
3. $0.5(x - 3) = 20$
4. $\frac{1}{3}(x - 2) = 4$
5. $y = 192 + 0.04y$
6. $x - 0.025x = 341.25$
7. $12x - 4(2x - 1) = 6(x + 1) - 3$
8. $3y - 4 = 3(y + 6) - 2(y + 3)$
9. $8 - 0.5(x + 3) = 0.25(x - 1)$
10. $5(2 - c) = 10(2c - 4) - 6(3c + 1)$

INTERMEDIATE PROBLEMS

Solve each of the following pairs of equations. Verify your solution in each case.

11. $x - y = 2$
    $3x + 4y = 20$
12. $y - 3x = 11$
    $5x + 30 = 4y$
13. $7p - 3q = 23$
    $-2p - 3q = 5$
14. $y = 2x$
    $7x - y = 35$

- **Math Apps:** These boxes, found in selected chapters, illustrate the application or misapplication of mathematics to business and personal finance.

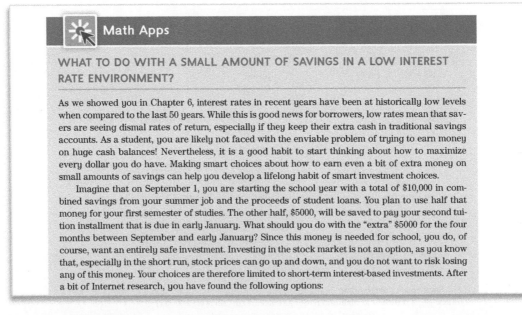

Math Apps

WHAT TO DO WITH A SMALL AMOUNT OF SAVINGS IN A LOW INTEREST RATE ENVIRONMENT?

As we showed you in Chapter 6, interest rates in recent years have been at historically low levels when compared to the last 50 years. While this is good news for borrowers, low rates mean that savers are seeing dismal rates of return, especially if they keep their extra cash in traditional savings accounts. As a student, you are likely not faced with the enviable problem of trying to earn money on huge cash balances! Nevertheless, it is a good habit to start thinking about how to maximize every dollar you do have. Making smart choices about how to earn even a bit of extra money on small amounts of savings can help you develop a lifelong habit of smart investment choices.

Imagine that on September 1, you are starting the school year with a total of $10,000 in combined savings from your summer job and the proceeds of student loans. You plan to use half that money for your first semester of studies. The other half, $5000, will be saved to pay your second tuition installment that is due in early January. What should you do with the "extra" $5000 for the four months between September and early January? Since this money is needed for school, you do, of course, want an entirely safe investment. Investing in the stock market is not an option, as you know that, especially in the short run, stock prices can go up and down, and you do not want to risk losing any of this money. Your choices are therefore limited to short-term interest-based investments. After a bit of Internet research, you have found the following options:

- **Streamlined exposition:** In keeping with a "fundamentals" approach, explanations of chapter concepts have been streamlined to present the essence of each topic as succinctly as possible. For example, where more than one approach to a particular concept is available, students are made aware of both approaches but the "preferred" approach (as directed by reviewers) is the one that is expanded upon. This helps students to focus on the essential learning outcomes and avoid confusion that often results when multiple approaches are emphasized equally.

TECHNOLOGY

LEARN WITHOUT LIMITS

McGraw-Hill Connect® is an award-winning digital teaching and learning platform that gives students the means to better connect with their coursework, with their instructors, and with the important concepts that they will need to know for success now and in the future. With Connect, instructors can take advantage of McGraw-Hill's trusted content to seamlessly deliver assignments, quizzes, and tests online. McGraw-Hill Connect is a learning platform that continually adapts to each student, delivering precisely what they need, when they need it, so class time is more engaging and effective. Connect makes teaching and learning personal, easy, and proven.

CONNECT KEY FEATURES

SMARTBOOK®

As the first and only adaptive reading experience, SmartBook is changing the way students read and learn. SmartBook creates a personalized reading experience by highlighting the most important concepts a student needs to learn at that moment in time. As a student engages with SmartBook, the reading experience continuously adapts by highlighting content based on what each student knows and doesn't know. This ensures that he or she is focused on the content needed to close specific knowledge gaps, while it simultaneously promotes long-term learning.

CONNECT INSIGHT®

Connect Insight is a new, one-of-a-kind visual analytics dashboard—now available for instructors—that provides at-a-glance information regarding student performance that is immediately actionable. By presenting assignment, assessment, and topical performance results together with a time metric easily visible for aggregate or individual results, Connect Insight gives instructors the ability to take a just-in-time approach to teaching and learning, which was never before available. It presents data that helps instructors improve class performance in a way that is efficient and effective.

SIMPLE ASSIGNMENT MANAGEMENT

With Connect, creating assignments is easier than ever, so instructors can spend more time teaching and less time managing.

- Assign SmartBook learning modules.
- Instructors can edit existing questions and create their own questions.
- Draw from a variety of text specific questions, resources, and test bank material to assign online.
- Streamline lesson planning, student progress reporting, and assignment grading to make classroom management more efficient than ever.

SMART GRADING

When it comes to studying, time is precious. Connect helps students learn more efficiently by providing feedback and practice material when they need it, where they need it.

- Automatically score assignments, giving students immediate feedback on their work and comparisons with correct answers.
- Access and review each response; manually change grades or leave comments for students to review.
- Track individual student performance—by question, by assignment, or in relation to the class overall—with detailed grade reports.
- Reinforce classroom concepts with practice tests and instant quizzes.
- Integrate grade reports easily with Learning Management Systems including Blackboard, D2L, and Moodle.

INSTRUCTOR LIBRARY

The Connect Instructor Library is a repository for additional resources to improve student engagement in and out of the class. It provides all the critical resources instructors need to build their course.

- Access instructor resources.
- View assignments and resources created for past sections.
- Post your own resources for students to use.

INSTRUCTOR RESOURCES

- **Instructor's Solutions Manual:** Prepared by the author, with a technical review by Mariana Ionescu of George Brown College.
- **Computerized Test Bank:** Prepared by Julie Howse of St. Lawrence College.
- **Microsoft® PowerPoint® Lecture Slides:** Prepared by Sarah Chan.

SUPERIOR LEARNING SOLUTIONS AND SUPPORT

The McGraw-Hill Education team is ready to help instructors assess and integrate any of our products, technology, and services into your course for optimal teaching and learning performance. Whether it's helping your students improve their grades or putting your entire course online, the McGraw-Hill Education team is here to help you do it. Contact your Learning Solutions Consultant today to learn how to maximize all of McGraw-Hill Education's resources.

For more information, please visit us online at http://www.mheducation.ca/he/solutions.

ACKNOWLEDGEMENTS

Business mathematics faculty across Canada are constantly adapting their course content and delivery to best serve their students. In this third edition of *Fundamentals of Business Mathematics in Canada*, we have been assisted by many of those faculty who have shared their insights through thoughtful reviews and suggestions. We appreciate their ideas and applaud their tireless commitment to their students.

We would also like to thank the many professionals at McGraw-Hill Ryerson who strive to produce content that will best support students in their learning: Rhondda McNabb (Director of Product), Karen Fozard (Portfolio and Program Manager), Sara Braithwaite (Product Manager), Erin Catto (Product Developer), Cathie Lefebvre (Marketing Manager), Janie Deneau (Supervising Editor), Rodney Rawlings (Copy Editor and Proofreader), Mariana Ionescu (Technical Checker), and others involved in the development and production of this edition. This team is a deep well of knowledge, and we appreciate their dedication to their craft.

Ernie Jerome & Jackie Shemko

CHAPTER 1

Review and Applications of Basic Mathematics

LEARNING OBJECTIVES

After completing this chapter, you will be able to:

LO1 Perform arithmetic operations in their proper order

LO2 Convert fractions to their percent and decimal equivalents

LO3 Maintain the proper number of digits in calculations

LO4 Given any two of the three quantities percent rate, portion, and base, solve for the third

LO5 Calculate the gross earnings of employees paid a salary, an hourly wage, or commissions

LO6 Calculate the simple average or weighted average (as appropriate) of a set of values

LO7 Perform basic calculations for the Goods and Services Tax, Harmonized Sales Tax, provincial sales tax, and real property tax

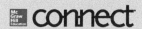 Throughout this chapter interactive charts and Help Me Solve It videos are marked with a ⬈.

MOST ROUTINE CALCULATIONS IN BUSINESS are now performed electronically. Does this mean that mathematical skills are less important or less valued than in the past? Definitely not—the mathematics and statistics you study in your business program are more widely expected and more highly valued in business than ever before. Technology has empowered us to access more information more readily, and to perform more sophisticated analysis of the information. To take full advantage of technology, you must know which information is relevant, which analyses or calculations should be performed, how to interpret the results, and how to explain the outcome in terms that others can understand.

Employers and clients now expect higher education and performance standards from middle managers and advisors than in the past. Increasingly, employers also expect managers and management trainees to undertake a program of study leading to a credential recognized in their industry. These programs usually have a significant mathematics component.

Naturally, a college course in business mathematics or statistics will cover a broader range of topics (often in greater depth) than you might need for a particular industry. This broader education opens more career options to you and provides a stronger set of mathematical skills for your chosen career.

TIP

How to Succeed in Business Mathematics

In Connect, there are a guide and a video entitled "How to Succeed in Business Mathematics." These can be found in Library Resources under Course-wide Content.

1.1   Order of Operations

LO1   When evaluating an expression such as

$$5 + 3^2 \times 2 - 4 \div 6$$

there is potential for confusion about the sequence of mathematical steps. Do we just perform the indicated operations in a strict left-to-right sequence, or is some other order intended? To eliminate any possible confusion, mathematicians have agreed on the use of brackets and a set of rules for the order of mathematical operations. The rules are:

Rules for Order of Operations
1. Perform operations within brackets (in the order of Steps 2, 3, and 4 below).
2. Evaluate the powers.[1]
3. Perform multiplication and division in order from left to right.
4. Perform addition and subtraction in order from left to right.

---

[1]   A power is a quantity such as 3^2 or 5^3 (which are shorthand methods for representing 3×3 and $5 \times 5 \times 5$, respectively). Section 2.2 includes a review of powers and exponents.

TIP

Using "BEDMAS"

To help remember the order of operations, you can use the acronym "BEDMAS" representing the sequence:

Brackets, **E**xponents, **D**ivision and **M**ultiplication, **A**ddition and **S**ubtraction.

TIP

Signs of Numbers

Pay careful attention to the signs associated with numbers. For example, in the expression $3 + (-4)$, the first term, 3, has a positive sign, while the term (-4) has a negative sign. We can simplify the expression by recognizing that adding a negative number is mathematically the same as subtracting that number. That is,

$$3 + (-4) = 3 - 4$$
$$= -1$$

When a positive number and a negative number are multiplied or divided, the result will be negative. For example, $3 \times (-1) = -3$. Similarly, $-14 \div 2 = -7$. However, when two negative numbers are multiplied or divided, the result will be positive. For example, $(-3) \times (-2) = 6$ and $(-18) \div (-9) = 2$.

EXAMPLE 1.1A	Exercises Illustrating the Order of Mathematical Operations

a. $30 - 6 \div 3 + 5 = 30 - 2 + 5$
$\qquad = 33$

Do division before subtraction and addition.

b. $(30 - 6) \div 3 + 5 = 24 \div 3 + 5$
$\qquad = 8 + 5$
$\qquad = 13$

Do operations within brackets first; then do division before addition.

c. $\dfrac{30 - 6}{3 + 5} = \dfrac{24}{8} = 3$

Brackets are implied in the numerator and the denominator.

d. $72 \div (3 \times 2) - 6 = 72 \div 6 - 6$
$\qquad = 12 - 6$
$\qquad = 6$

Do operations within brackets first; then do division before subtraction.

e. $72 \div (3 \times 2^2) - 6 = 72 \div (3 \times 4) - 6$
$\qquad = 72 \div 12 - 6$
$\qquad = 6 - 6$
$\qquad = 0$

Do operations within brackets (the power before the multiplication); then do division before subtraction.

f. $72 \div (3 \times 2)^2 - 6 = 72 \div 6^2 - 6$
$\qquad = 72 \div 36 - 6$
$\qquad = 2 - 6$
$\qquad = -4$

Do operations within brackets first, then the power, then divide, then subtract.

g. $\left(\dfrac{32 + 8^2}{2 \times 3}\right) - 4 = \left(\dfrac{32 + 64}{2 \times 3}\right) - 4$

$\qquad\qquad\quad = \left(\dfrac{96}{6}\right) - 4$

$\qquad\qquad\quad = 16 - 4$

$\qquad\qquad\quad = 12$

Do operations within brackets first, starting with the power. Brackets are implied in the numerator and the denominator. Divide, then subtract.

h. $3 \times \left(\dfrac{21 + 43}{2 \times 2}\right)^2 = 3 \times \left(\dfrac{64}{4}\right)^2$

$\qquad\qquad\qquad = 3 \times 16^2$

$\qquad\qquad\qquad = 3 \times 256$

$\qquad\qquad\qquad = 768$

Evaluate the numerator and denominator within the bracket. Then divide within the bracket. Evaluate the power. Then multiply.

➡ **Check your understanding:** Evaluate the following: $4(2 - 5) - 4(5 - 2)$. (Answer: -24)

▰▶ **Related problem:** #1 in Exercise 1.1

EXERCISE 1.1

Answers to the odd-numbered problems can be found in the end matter.

BASIC PROBLEMS

Evaluate each of the following. In Problems 24–28, evaluate the answers accurate to the cent.

1. $20 - 4 \times 2 - 8$
2. $18 \div 3 + 6 \times 2$
3. $(20 - 4) \times 2 - 8$
4. $18 \div (3 + 6) \times 2$
5. $20 - (4 \times 2 - 8)$
6. $(18 \div 3 + 6) \times 2$
7. $54 - 36 \div 4 + 2^2$
8. $(5 + 3)^2 - 3^2 \div 9 + 3$
9. $(54 - 36) \div (4 + 2)^2$
10. $5 + (3^2 - 3)^2 \div (9 + 3)$
11. $\dfrac{8^2 - 4^2}{(4 - 2)^3}$
12. $1000(1 + 0.02)^3$
13. $(-1)(-3) + 7 - 6^2$
14. $15(37 - 3^2)$

INTERMEDIATE PROBLEMS

15. $3(6 + 4)^2 - 5(17 - 20)^2$
16. $(4 \times 3 - 2)^2 \div (4 - 3 \times 2^2)$
17. $[(20 + 8 \times 5) - 7 \times (-3)] \div 9$
18. $5[19 + (5^2 - 16)^2]^2$
19. $(9 \times 3 + 32 \div 2^2)^3$
20. $180 - 2[(-3 \times 2^3 + 128 \div 4^2) + 6(-3 + 7)]$
21. $\dfrac{[8 \times 6 \div 4 + (-3) \times 2]^2}{4 + 2}$
22. $\dfrac{3^4 - 7 \times 2 - 6 \times 4}{5}$
23. $7^2 - \dfrac{13(-4) + 7}{(-9)}$
24. $\$2000\left[\dfrac{(1 + 0.08)^4 - (1 + 0.02)^4}{0.08 - 0.02}\right]$
25. $\$100\left(1 + 0.06 \times \tfrac{45}{365}\right)$
26. $\dfrac{\$200}{1 + 0.09 \times \tfrac{4}{12}}$

ADVANCED PROBLEMS

27. $\dfrac{\$600}{1 + 0.075 \times \tfrac{250}{365}}$
28. $\$300\left[\dfrac{1 - \tfrac{1}{(1 + 0.03)^2}}{0.03}\right]$
29. $\dfrac{28 - 2(3 + 2^2 - 2)}{6} + 3\left(\dfrac{3 \times 6^2}{4}\right)$
30. $\dfrac{4^2 - 2(-3 + 5)}{[(-6) \times 4 + 3(-1) + 7] \div (-5)}$

1.2   Fractions

Definitions

In a fraction, the upper number and lower number are given the following labels:

$$\frac{\textbf{numerator}}{\textbf{denominator}}$$

Fractions can be labelled using the following categories:

Category	Examples	Description
Proper fraction	$\frac{3}{4}, \frac{1}{2}, \frac{3}{5}$	Numerator is smaller than denominator
Improper fraction	$\frac{6}{5}, \frac{3}{2}, \frac{11}{9}$	Numerator is larger than denominator
Mixed number	$2\frac{1}{3}, 8\frac{3}{5}, 13\frac{5}{8}$	A whole number plus a fraction
Equivalent fractions	$\frac{1}{2} = \frac{5}{10} = \frac{15}{30}$	Fractions that are equal in value, even though their respective numerators and denominators differ

---

EXAMPLE 1.2A | **Calculating an Equivalent Fraction**

Find the missing numbers that make the following three fractions equivalent.

$$\frac{7}{12} = \frac{56}{?} = \frac{?}{300}$$

SOLUTION

To create a fraction equivalent to $\frac{7}{12}$, *both* the numerator and the denominator must be multiplied by the same number. To obtain 56 in the numerator of the second equivalent fraction, 7 was multiplied by 8. Hence, the denominator must also be multiplied by 8. Therefore,

$$\frac{7}{12} = \frac{7 \times 8}{12 \times 8} = \frac{56}{96}$$

To obtain the denominator (300) in the third equivalent fraction, 12 was multiplied by $\frac{300}{12} = 25$. The numerator must also be multiplied by 25. Hence, the equivalent fraction is

$$\frac{7 \times 25}{12 \times 25} = \frac{175}{300}$$

In summary,

$$\frac{7}{12} = \frac{56}{96} = \frac{175}{300}$$

➡ **Check your understanding:** Find the missing number that makes the following fractions equivalent. $\frac{7}{12} = \frac{420}{?}$ (Answer: $\frac{7}{12} = \frac{420}{720}$)

▸ **Related problem:** #1 in Exercise 1.2

LO2 Decimal and Percent Equivalents

To find the *decimal equivalent* value of a fraction, divide the numerator by the denominator. To express the fraction in *percent equivalent* form, shift the decimal point two places to the right (or multiply by 100) and add the % symbol.

EXAMPLE 1.2B | **Finding the Decimal and Percent Equivalents of Fractions and Mixed Number**

Convert each of the following fractions and mixed numbers to its decimal equivalent and percent equivalent values.

a. $\frac{2}{5} = 0.4 = 40\%$ **b.** $\frac{5}{2} = 2.5 = 250\%$

c. $1\frac{3}{16} = 1.1875 = 118.75\%$ **d.** $\frac{3}{1500} = 0.002 = 0.2\%$

➡ **Check your understanding:** Convert $3\frac{4}{5}$ to its decimal equivalent and percent equivalent values. (Answer: 3.8 and 380%)

▰▶ **Related problem:** #4 in Exercise 1.2

TIP

Adding or Subtracting Fractions

To add or subtract fractions, the easiest approach is to first convert each fraction to its decimal equivalent value. Then add or subtract the decimal equivalents as required. For example, $\frac{2}{7} + \frac{252}{365} = 0.28571 + 0.69041 = 0.9761$ to four-figure accuracy.

LO3 Rounding of Decimal and Percent Equivalents

For some fractions, the decimal equivalent has an endless series of digits. Such a number is called a *non-terminating decimal*. In some cases, a nonterminating decimal contains a repeating digit or a repeating group of digits. This particular type of nonterminating decimal is called a *repeating decimal*. A shorthand notation for repeating decimals is to put a horizontal bar over the first occurrence of the repeating digit or group of digits. For example,

$$\frac{2}{9} = 0.222222 = 0.\overline{2} \quad \text{and} \quad 2\frac{4}{11} = 2.36363636 = 2.\overline{36}$$

When a nonterminating decimal or its percent equivalent is used in a calculation, the question arises: How many figures or digits should be retained? The following rules provide sufficient accuracy for the vast majority of our calculations.

Rules for Rounding Numbers
1. In intermediate results, keep at least one more figure than the number of figures required in the final result. (When counting figures for the purpose of rounding, do not count leading zeros[2] used only to properly position the decimal point.)
2. If the first digit dropped is 5 or greater, increase the last retained digit by 1.
3. If the first digit dropped is less than 5, leave the last retained digit unchanged.

---

[2] The following example illustrates the reasoning behind this instruction. A length of 6 mm is neither more nor less precise than a length of 0.006 m. (Recall that there are 1000 mm in 1 m.) The leading zeros in 0.006 m do not add precision to the measurement. They are inserted to properly position the decimal point. Both measurements have one-figure accuracy. Contrast this case with measurements of 1007 mm and 1.007 m. Here each zero comes from a decision about *what the digit should be* (rather than *where the decimal point should be*). These measurements both have four-figure accuracy. This rule applies to the total number of figures (other than leading zeros) in a value. It does not apply to the number of decimal places.

Suppose, for example, the answer to a calculation is expected to be a few hundred dollars and you want the answer accurate to the cent. In other words, you require five-figure accuracy in your answer. To achieve this accuracy, the first rule says you should retain (at least) six figures in values[3] used in the calculations. The rule also applies to intermediate results that you carry forward to subsequent calculations. The consequence of rounding can be stated in another way—if, for example, you use a number rounded to four figures in your calculations, you can expect only three-figure accuracy in your final answer.

TRAP

"Rounding Then Rounding"

Suppose you were asked to round 7.4999 to the nearest whole number. Avoid the trap of "rounding then rounding." For example, some students will begin by rounding 7.4999 to the nearest tenth, to give 7.5. Then they will round that *already rounded* number to the nearest whole, which is 8. This approach is incorrect. When asked to round any number, look only at the first digit beyond the required degree of accuracy. Rounding 7.4999 to the nearest whole number, we should look only at the *first* digit after the decimal sign. Since the first digit being dropped (in this case, the first digit after the decimal) is less than 5, leave the last retained digit unchanged. Some people refer to this as "rounding down." Therefore, 7.4999 rounded to the nearest whole is 7, not 8.

EXAMPLE 1.2C	Fractions Having Repeating Decimal Equivalents

Convert each of the following fractions to its decimal equivalent value expressed in the repeating decimal notation.

a. $\frac{14}{9} = 1.555\cdots = 1.\overline{5}$

b. $3\frac{2}{11} = 3.181818\cdots = 3.\overline{18}$

c. $5\frac{2}{27} = 5.074074\cdots = 5.\overline{074}$

d. $\frac{5}{7} = 0.714285714285\cdots = 0.\overline{714285}$

➡️ **Check your understanding:** Convert the fraction $\frac{11}{12}$ to its decimal equivalent form in the repeating decimal notation. (Answer: $0.91\overline{6}$)

▶ **Related problem:** #13 in Exercise 1.2

EXAMPLE 1.2D	Calculating and Rounding the Decimal Equivalents of Fractions

Convert each of the following fractions and mixed numbers to its decimal equivalent value rounded to four-figure accuracy.

a. $\frac{2}{3} = 0.6667$

b. $6\frac{1}{12} = 6.083$

c. $\frac{173}{11} = 15.73$

d. $\frac{2}{1071} = 0.001867$

e. $\frac{17,816}{3} = 5939$

➡️ **Check your understanding:** Convert the fraction $\frac{3}{365}$ to its decimal equivalent value rounded to *five-figure* accuracy. (Answer: 0.0082192)

▶ **Related problem:** #25 in Exercise 1.2

---

[3] Some values may be known and written with perfect accuracy in less than five figures. For example, a year has exactly 12 months, or an interest rate may be exactly 6%.

EXAMPLE 1.2E	Demonstrating the Consequences of Too Much Rounding

Accurate to the cent, evaluate

$$\$140\left(1 + 0.11 \times \tfrac{113}{365}\right) + \$74\left(1 + 0.09 \times \tfrac{276}{365}\right)$$

SOLUTION

If we first evaluate the contents of the brackets, we obtain

$$\$140(1.0340548) + \$74(1.0680548)$$

With just a crude estimation, we can say that the first product will be a little greater than $140 and the second product will be a little greater than $74. Therefore, the answer will be between $200 and $300. If you want the answer to be accurate to the cent, then you are seeking *five-figure* accuracy. If you wish to round the values used, Rule 1 says that you must keep at least *six* figures in intermediate values. That is, you should round no further than

$$\$140(1.03405) + \$74(1.06805) = \$144.767 + \$79.0357$$
$$= \$223.8027$$
$$= \$223.80 \text{ (rounded to the cent)}$$

Suppose instead that you round to three figures, perhaps thinking that keeping two decimal places will give you an answer correct to two decimal places (that is, accurate to the cent.) You will obtain

$$\$140(1.03) + \$74(1.07) = \$144.20 + \$79.18$$
$$= \$223.38$$

This answer is in error by $0.42.

What if you keep five figures (in the hope that the answer will be as accurate as the values used to calculate it)? Your result will be

$$\$140(1.0341) + \$74(1.0681) = \$144.774 + \$79.0394$$
$$= \$223.8134$$
$$= \$223.81 \text{ (rounded to the cent)}$$

This answer is in error by $0.01. The trend we observe here is typical—the more figures you keep in intermediate steps of a calculation, the smaller the error in your final answer.

There is one more point worth noting. Consider the first line in the initial calculation where you properly maintained six-figure accuracy. That is,

$$\$140(1.03405) + \$74(1.06805) = \$144.767 + \$79.0357$$

Suppose you round the two amounts on the right side to the nearest cent *before* you add them. The sum is then

$$\$144.77 + \$79.04 = \$223.81$$

which is $0.01 larger than the correct answer. The error arises because, just at the final addition, you failed to maintain six-figure accuracy (to ensure five-figure accuracy in the final answer).

In summary, if you want five-figure accuracy in your answer, you cannot round to less than six figures *at any stage* of the calculations. (You can verify that keeping more than six figures will not change the answer at the fifth figure.)

➡ **Check your understanding:** Accurate to the cent, evaluate $\$1388\left(1 + 0.05 \times \tfrac{112}{365}\right) + \$50\left(1 + 0.04 \times \tfrac{90}{365}\right)$. (Answer: $1459.79)

◼▶ **Related problem:** #33 in Exercise 1.2

> ## TIP
>
> ### Optimal Use of Your Calculator
>
> Whenever possible, use your calculator's memory registers to save intermediate results. This will save time and reduce keystroke errors during data re-entry. It also virtually eliminates the introduction of rounding errors, since most calculators internally retain two or three more figures than are shown in the display. Example 1.2F illustrates this approach.

EXAMPLE 1.2F	Optimal Use of Your Calculator

We will again evaluate (accurate to the cent) the same expression as in Example 1.2E,

$$\$140\left(1 + 0.11 \times \tfrac{113}{365}\right) + \$74\left(1 + 0.09 \times \tfrac{276}{365}\right)$$

This time we will use our financial calculator in a way that (1) avoids manual re-entry of intermediate results and (2) maintains maximum precision by avoiding rounding (other than rounding imposed by the inherent limitation of the calculator).

SOLUTION

We assume the Texas Instruments BA II PLUS calculator is set for a floating-decimal format and for the algebraic operating system (AOS) calculation method. (Refer to Appendix 1A for instructions on making these settings.) In the AOS mode, we can enter numbers, brackets, and operations in the same left-to-right sequence as they are written in. The calculator performs the calculations according to the proper order of operations.

$$140 \boxed{\times} \boxed{(} 1 \boxed{+} 0.11 \boxed{\times} 113 \boxed{\div} 365 \boxed{)}$$
$$\boxed{+} 74 \boxed{\times} \boxed{(} 1 \boxed{+} 0.09 \boxed{\times} 276 \boxed{\div} 365 \boxed{)} \boxed{=} \ 223.80$$

The result is $223.80.

You see that it is possible to evaluate quite complex expressions without writing down intermediate results. However, if someone is going to read and readily understand your solution, you should present enough detail and intermediate results to reveal the steps in your solution.

➡ **Check your understanding:** Accurate to the cent, evaluate
$\$398\left(1 + 0.09 \times \tfrac{5}{12}\right) + \$50\left(1 + 0.04 \times \tfrac{11}{12}\right)$. (Answer: $464.76)

▰▰▶ **Related problem:** #35 in Exercise 1.2

Evaluating Complex Fractions

A **complex fraction** is a fraction containing one or more other fractions in its numerator or denominator. In simplifying complex fractions, pay particular attention to the correct order of mathematical operations, as discussed in Section 1.1.

EXAMPLE 1.2G	Evaluating Complex Fractions

Evaluate each of the following complex fractions accurate to the cent.

a. $\dfrac{\$425}{\left(1 + \frac{0.09}{12}\right)^{24}}$ b. $\dfrac{\$1265\left(1 + 0.115 \times \frac{87}{365}\right)}{1 + 0.125 \times \frac{43}{365}}$

SOLUTION

We assume the Texas Instruments BA II PLUS calculator is set for a floating-decimal format and for the algebraic operating system (AOS) calculation method. (Refer to Appendix 1A for instructions on making these settings.)

a. 425 ÷ (1 + 0.09 ÷ 12) y^x 24 = 355.23

    The result is $355.23.

b. 1265 × (1 + 0.115 × 87 ÷ 365)

    ÷ (1 + 0.125 × 43 ÷ 365) = 1280.81

    The result is $1280.81.

➡ **Check your understanding:** Evaluate $\dfrac{\$200\left(1 + 0.07 \times \frac{30}{365}\right)}{1 + 0.085 \times \frac{225}{365}}$ with accuracy to the nearest cent.

(Answer: $191.14)

▶ **Related problem:** #39 in Exercise 1.2

? Checkpoint Questions

1. Circle "True" or "False" for each of the following:

    a. The number 0.00312 has five-figure accuracy.   True   False

    b. The number 1.000047 has seven-figure accuracy.   True   False

    c. The number 100.38 has two-figure accuracy.   True   False

    d. The fraction $\frac{12}{49}$ is equivalent to the fraction $\frac{156}{637}$.   True   False

    e. The fraction $\frac{6}{16}$ is equivalent to the fraction $\frac{126}{240}$.   True   False

    f. The fraction $\frac{8}{3}$ is a proper fraction.   True   False

    g. The value $2\frac{1}{3}$ is a mixed number.   True   False

2. If you want four-figure accuracy in your final result, what minimum number of figures must be retained in the values used in the calculations?

3. For a final result of approximately $7000 to be accurate to the cent, what minimum number of figures must be retained in the values used in the calculations?

4. If a final result on the order of five million dollars is to be accurate to the nearest dollar, what minimum number of figures must be retained in the calculations?

5. If an interest rate (which might be greater than 10%) is to be calculated to the nearest 0.01%, what minimum number of digits must be retained in the numbers used to calculate the interest rate?

EXERCISE 1.2

Answers to the odd-numbered problems can be found in the end matter.

BASIC PROBLEMS

Fill in the missing numbers to create sets of equivalent fractions.

1. $\frac{3}{8} = \frac{12}{?} = \frac{?}{120}$ **2.** $\frac{9}{13} = \frac{54}{?} = \frac{?}{143}$ **3.** $\frac{8}{9} = \frac{?}{279} = \frac{488}{?}$

The following fractions and mixed numbers have *terminating* decimal equivalent forms. Express their decimal and percent equivalent forms to five-figure accuracy.

4. $\frac{7}{8}$ **5.** $\frac{47}{20}$ **6.** $-\frac{9}{16}$ **7.** $\frac{-35}{25}$

8. $1\frac{7}{25}$ **9.** $\frac{25}{1000}$ **10.** $-1\frac{11}{32}$ **11.** $12\frac{5}{8}$

The following fractions and mixed numbers have *repeating* decimal equivalent forms. Express their decimal and percent equivalent forms in the repeating decimal notation. Show just the minimum number of decimal places needed to display the repeating digit or group of digits.

12. $\frac{5}{6}$ **13.** $-\frac{8}{3}$ **14.** $1\frac{1}{11}$ **15.** $\frac{37}{27}$

INTERMEDIATE PROBLEMS

Round each of the following to four-figure accuracy.

16. 11.3845 **17.** 9.6455 **18.** 0.5545454 **19.** 1000.49

20. 1.0023456 **21.** 0.030405 **22.** 40.09515 **23.** 0.0090909

Convert each of the following fractions and mixed numbers to its decimal equivalent and percent equivalent values, rounded to five-figure accuracy.

24. $\frac{7}{6}$ **25.** $\frac{1}{60}$ **26.** $\frac{15}{365}$ **27.** $\frac{0.095}{12}$

28. $3\frac{12}{19}$ **29.** $6\frac{1}{17}$ **30.** $\frac{3}{7}$ **31.** $1\frac{0.035}{12}$

Evaluate each of the following, accurate to the nearest cent.

32. $\$92\left(1 + 0.095 \times \frac{112}{365}\right)$

33. $\$100\left(1 + 0.11 \times \frac{5}{12}\right) + \$87\left(1 + 0.08 \times \frac{7}{12}\right)$

34. $\$454.76\left(1 - 0.105 \times \frac{11}{12}\right)$

35. $\dfrac{\$3490}{1 + 0.125 \times \frac{91}{365}}$

36. $\dfrac{\$10,000}{1 - 0.10 \times \frac{182}{365}}$

37. $\$650\left(1 + \dfrac{0.105}{2}\right)^2$

38. $\dfrac{\$15,400}{\left(1 + \frac{0.13}{12}\right)^6}$

39. $\dfrac{\$550}{\left(1 + \frac{0.115}{2}\right)^4}$

ADVANCED PROBLEMS

40. $\dfrac{\$6600\left(1 + 0.085 \times \frac{153}{365}\right)}{1 + 0.125 \times \frac{82}{365}}$

41. $\$1000\left[\dfrac{\left(1 + \frac{0.09}{12}\right)^7 - 1}{\frac{0.09}{12}}\right]$

42. $\$475\left[\dfrac{\left(1 + \frac{0.075}{12}\right)^{2\frac{1}{2}} - 1}{\frac{0.075}{12}}\right]$

43. $\dfrac{\$17,500\left(1 + 0.0475 \times 2\frac{187}{365}\right)}{1 + 0.0875 \times \frac{197}{365}}$

1.3   The Basic Percentage Problem

 LO4   Often we wish to compare a portion, or part of a quantity, to the whole amount. One measure of the relative size is the fraction

$$\frac{Portion}{Base}$$

where the term *Base* is used to represent the whole or entire amount. The fraction is called the *Rate*. That is,

THE BASIC PERCENTAGE FORMULA $\text{Rate} = \dfrac{\text{Portion}}{\text{Base}}$ **(1-1)**

This relation is also used in a more general way to compare a quantity (the *Portion*) to some other standard or benchmark (the *Base*). In these cases the *Portion* may be larger than the *Base*. Then the *Rate* will be greater than 1 and the percent equivalent *Rate* will be more than 100%.

TRAP

Decimal Equivalent of Rates Smaller Than 1%

When a *Rate* is less than 1%, students sometimes forget to move the decimal two places to the left in order to obtain the decimal equivalent *Rate*. For example, be clear on the distinction between 0.25% and 25%. The former is just $\frac{1}{4}$ of 1%—the latter is 25 *times* 1%. Their decimal equivalents are 0.0025 and 0.25, respectively.

Given any two of the three quantities: *Portion*, *Base*, and *Rate*, you can calculate the unknown quantity by using formula (1-1). *First* substitute the known values, and *then* rearrange the equation to solve for the unknown.

TIP

The Portion, Rate, Base Triangle

In the examples in this section, we will substitute known values into formula (1-1) and rearrange to solve for the unknown. It is important to become comfortable with rearranging formulas, and we encourage you to practise this important basic skill. Then, you may find it saves time to use the diagram shown here when solving problems involving rate, portion, and base.

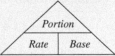

When you have determined which variable you are being asked to find, cover up that variable in the triangle. The remaining variables will appear in the correct order to help you solve for the unknown value you are seeking. For example, if a question requires you to solve for *Portion*, covering the word *Portion* in the triangle leaves the words *Rate* and *Base* side by side, which indicates those two values must be multiplied. If another question requires you to solve for *Base*, covering up the word *Base* in the triangle leaves *Portion* above the word *Rate*, which indicates that you must use the fraction $\frac{Portion}{Rate}$ to solve for *Base*. Finally, if asked to solve for *Rate*, covering that word in the triangle reveals the word *Portion* above the word *Base*, which indicates you must use the fraction $\frac{Portion}{Base}$ to solve for *Rate*.

TIP

Using the Word "Of" to Distinguish Between the Base and the Portion

The key to solving percentage problems is to distinguish between the *Base* and the *Portion*. The *Base* is always the standard or benchmark to which the *Portion* is being compared. In the wording of problems, the quantity following the word "of" is almost always the *Base*. For example, consider the following questions:

"What is 12% of $993?"   The value after the word "of" is $993, which is the *Base*. We are being asked to solve for the *Portion*.

"75 is 8% of what number?"   The words "what number" come after the word "of," so we are being asked to solve for the *Base*. The value 75 represents the *Portion*.

EXAMPLE 1.3A	Using the Basic Percentage Formula

a. What is $40\frac{1}{4}\%$ of $140.25?

b. How much is $0.08\overline{3}\%$ of $5000?

c. What percentage is 7.38 kg of 4.39 kg?

SOLUTION

a. The question asks us to calculate a part (*Portion*) of a given whole (*Base*). The value $140.25 appears after the word "of," and is the base—the benchmark to which the unknown value, *Portion*, is being compared. The rate is $40\frac{1}{4}\%$, which, when written in its decimal equivalent form, is 0.4025. Substituting the known values into formula (1-1):

$$\text{Rate} = \frac{\text{Portion}}{\text{Base}}$$

we obtain

$$0.4025 = \frac{\text{Portion}}{\$140.25}$$

Multiply both sides by $140.25 to get rid of the fraction on the right side of the equation:

$$0.4025 \times \$140.25 = \frac{\text{Portion}}{\$140.25} \times \$140.25$$
$$\$56.4506 = \text{Portion}$$

Switching the left and right sides, and then rounding to the cent, we get Portion = $56.45. That is, $40\frac{1}{4}\%$ of $140.25 is $56.45.

b. This question asks us to calculate a part (Portion) given the whole (Base) and rate. As in Part (a), we must substitute the known values into formula (1-1):

$$\text{Rate} = \frac{\text{Portion}}{\text{Base}}$$

Note that when writing a rate or percentage in a formula, we must first convert it to its decimal equivalent. Divide the percentage, $0.08\overline{3}\%$, by 100 to arrive at its decimal equivalent, $0.0008\overline{3}$. Substituting into formula (1-1) we obtain

$$0.0008\overline{3} = \frac{\text{Portion}}{\$5000}$$
$$Portion = 0.0008\overline{3} \times \$5000 = 0.0008333 \times \$5000 = \$4.17$$

Here is the line of self-questioning and thinking behind rounding the repeating decimal at the fourth figure. (Remember not to count the three leading zeros in 0.0008333, because they serve only to position the decimal point.)

Question, Q: What accuracy do we want in the answer?

Answer, A: We want the answer to be accurate to the cent. (This is the normal understanding in financial calculations.)

Q: How many digits or figures of accuracy does the preceding answer imply?

A: This number of digits depends on the size of the answer. So we must first estimate that size. 0.083% is a little less than 0.1% (one-tenth of one percent). Since 1% of $5000 is $50, then 0.1% of $5000 is only $5. Therefore, the answer will be a little less than $5. For the answer to be accurate to the cent, we seek *three-figure* accuracy.

Q: How many figures of accuracy must we maintain throughout the calculations?

A: The fundamental rule is to keep at least one more figure of accuracy than is required in the final answer. Therefore, we must maintain at least four-figure accuracy in the calculations.

In conclusion, $4.17 is 0.08$\overline{3}$% of $5000.

c. We are given both the *Portion* and the *Base* for a comparison. Here 7.38 kg is being compared to the reference amount (Base) of 4.39 kg. The answer will be greater than 100%, since the Portion is larger than the Base.

$$\text{Rate} = \frac{\text{Portion}}{\text{Base}} = \frac{7.38}{4.39} = 1.681 = 168.1\%$$

Thus, 7.38 kg is 168.1% of 4.39 kg.

➡ **Check your understanding:** 250% of what amount is $10? (Answer: $4)

▬▶ **Related problem:** #3 in Exercise 1.3

EXAMPLE 1.3B	A Word Problem Requiring the Basic Percentage Formula

A battery manufacturer encloses a 50-cent rebate coupon in a package of two AAA batteries retailing for $4.29. What percent rebate does the coupon represent?

SOLUTION

In effect, the question is asking you to compare the rebate to the retail price. Therefore, the retail price is the *Base* in the comparison.

$$\text{Rate} = \frac{\text{Portion}}{\text{Base}} = \frac{\$0.50}{\$4.29} = 0.117 = 11.7\%$$

The manufacturer's percent rebate on the batteries is 11.7%.

➡ **Check your understanding:** If a 75-cent rebate coupon represents a savings of 4% of the regular retail price, what was the retail price of the item before the rebate? (Answer: $18.75)

▬▶ **Related problem:** #23 in Exercise 1.3

TIP

Units of Portion and Base

The preceding example demonstrates that the *Portion* and the *Base* must have the same units when calculating *Rate*. (In other words, both quantities in Example 1.3B must be in dollars, or both must be in cents.)

EXERCISE 1.3

Answers to the odd-numbered problems can be found in the end matter.

Calculate dollar amounts accurate to the cent and percent amounts to three-figure accuracy.

BASIC PROBLEMS

1. Calculate $6.\overline{6}\%$ of $666.66.

2. What percent is $1.50 of $11.50?

3. What percent is 88¢ of $44?

4. $45 is 60% of what amount?

5. $134 is what percent of $67?

6. $69 is 30% of what amount?

7. What amount is 0.075% of $1650?

8. 150% of $60 is what amount?

9. $12\frac{3}{4}\%$ of what amount is $27.50?

10. 0.75% of $100 is what amount?

11. What percent of $950 is $590?

12. $8\frac{1}{2}\%$ of what amount is $10?

13. 500 g is what percent of 2.8 kg?

14. $130\frac{1}{2}\%$ of $455 is what amount?

15. $559.35 is 113% of what amount?

16. 350% of what amount is $1000?

17. $10 is 0.5% of what amount?

18. $1.25 is $\frac{3}{4}\%$ of what amount?

INTERMEDIATE PROBLEMS

19. Cecilia and Nathan estimate their total cost for a vacation in Australia to be $14,775.

    a. What percentage is this cost of their combined gross monthly income of $8775?

    b. If 72% of their gross monthly income is already consumed by rent, taxes, car payments, and other regular living expenses, what percentage is the trip's cost of their remaining annual disposable income?

20. In a one-month period, a convenience store had sales of $65,560 from its gas pumps and sales of $36,740 from other in-store products. What percent of total sales were from gasoline?

21. In a basketball game, the Langara College Falcons scored $54.\overline{54}\%$ of 33 shots from the 2-point zone, $46.\overline{6}\%$ of 15 attempts from the 3-point distance, and 79.3% of 29 free throws (1 point each). How many points did the Falcons score?

22. A provincial minister of education recently announced that his government's forecasted expenditure of $31.8 billion on education next year represents 25.04% of the provincial budget. Rounded to the nearest million dollars, what is the province's total budget for the next year?

23. Unusually high snowfall in January caused the City of Winnipeg to exceed its January snow removal budget. In January, the city spent $11.3 million dollars, which represented 179.37% of its snow removal budget for the month. Rounded to the nearest $100,000, what amount did Winnipeg budget for January's snow clearance?

24. A performing artist who is under contract with a record label has determined that the royalty rate he receives for songs downloaded from Apple iTunes is 5.7%. If this artist received royalties from Apple of $99,736.41 for a year, how many song downloads at $0.99 each did his band have for that year?

25. In August, Canada's exports to the United States were $33.7 billion, which were 97% of July's exports to the United States. Rounded to the nearest $0.1 billion, what was the value of Canada's exports to the United States in July?

26. The Canada Mortgage and Housing Corporation (CMHC) recommends that monthly housing costs, including monthly mortgage payments, property taxes, and heating expenses, should not exceed 32% of a family's gross monthly income. Using this guideline, Marina and Salvatore have determined that their monthly housing costs should not exceed $2323. To the nearest dollar, what is Marina and Salvatore's combined gross monthly income?

27. A property sold for 250% of what the vendors originally paid for it. What was that original price if the recent selling price was $210,000?

28. An online discount broker charges a transaction fee of $30 plus an additional 3 cents per share. A full-service broker charges a commission rate of 2.4% of the total dollar value of a stock transaction. Suppose you purchase 200 shares of the Bank of Nova Scotia at $55.40 per share. What percentage are the total fees charged by the online discount broker of the commission you would pay the full-service broker?

ADVANCED PROBLEMS

29. A province's progressive income tax rates are structured as follows: 5.05% tax on the first $39,723 of taxable income; 9.15% on the next $39,725; 11.16% on the next $429,552; and 13.16% on any additional taxable income. Rounded to the nearest 0.01%, what percentage is an individual's total income tax of his (taxable) income if his taxable income for a year is:

   a. $33,000?

   b. $66,000?

   c. $185,000?

30. The Calgary Flames sold approximately 14,000 seats to season's ticket holders. If season tickets represent 72.5% of the Scotiabank Saddledome's seating capacity, how many seats were not sold to season's ticket holders? Round to the nearest 100.

31. The maximum amount an individual can contribute to his or her registered retirement savings plan (RRSP) for a year is set by the regulations of the *Income Tax Act*. For the year 2015, the maximum contribution was the lesser of $24,930 or 18% of the individual's "earned income" during 2014. What was the lowest amount of earned income for 2014 at which an individual could make a full $24,930 contribution in 2015? (Round to the nearest dollar.)

32. A stockbroker is paid 45% of the commission her firm charges her clients. If she personally receives $134.55 on an $11,500 transaction, what is the firm's commission rate?

33. A mortality rate indicates the fraction of individuals in a population who are expected to die in the next year.

   a. If the mortality rate among 35-year-old males is 0.34%, what is the expected number of deaths per year among a province's total of 50,000 males of this age?

   b. If 35-year-old males constitute 0.83% of the overall population in a city of 1.45 million, how many deaths of males of this age are expected in that city in a year?

1.4 | Payroll

LO5 An employee's earnings may be based on an hourly wage, a salary, a piecework rate, or a rate of commission. In some cases, earnings are based on a combination of a commission with a wage or a salary. This section deals only with the calculation of *gross earnings*—the amount earned before any deductions.[4]

Salaries

Where employment tends to be predictable and steady, an employee typically receives a salary quoted in terms of a biweekly, a monthly, or an annual amount. A monthly salary is usually paid on a monthly or semimonthly basis. An annual salary may be paid at monthly, semimonthly, biweekly, or weekly intervals. For monthly and semimonthly pay periods, the gross earnings per pay are calculated by dividing the annual salary by 12 and 24, respectively.

For purposes of this section, we assume there are exactly 52 weeks in a year. Therefore, we can divide an annual salary by 26 or by 52 to obtain the gross earnings per biweekly or weekly pay period, respectively.[5]

If a salaried employee has a specified length of regular pay period and he is eligible for an overtime rate of pay, the usual hourly overtime rate is

$$1.5 \times \frac{\text{Gross earnings for a regular pay period}}{\text{Hours in a regular pay period}}$$

Because of the factor 1.5, this overtime rate is usually referred to as "time and a half."

EXAMPLE 1.4A	Calculating Biweekly and Weekly Earnings and Hourly Overtime Rate from an Annual Salary

Benazir's annual salary is $45,000. Her regular workweek consists of four 10-hour workdays. She is eligible for overtime at time and a half on time worked in excess of 10 hours per day or 40 hours per week. Determine her gross earnings in a pay period if

a. she is paid semimonthly.

b. she is paid biweekly.

c. she works 6 hours of overtime in a biweekly pay period.

SOLUTION

a. "Semimonthly" means twice per month, so Benazir's annual salary would be paid in 24 installments.

$$\text{Semimonthly gross pay} = \frac{\text{Annual salary}}{24} = \frac{\$45,000}{24} = \$1875$$

---

[4] Employers are required by law to withhold income tax and the employee's share of Canada Pension Plan contributions and employment insurance premiums. By agreement with the employees or their union, an employer may also deduct and remit various insurance premiums, union dues, and pension plan contributions.

[5] A 365-day year contains 52 weeks plus one day; a leap year contains 52 weeks plus two days. As an approximate average, one year in six will have 53 Fridays, the customary payday for weekly and biweekly payrolls. Accordingly, approximately one year in six will have 53 weekly paydays, and one year in twelve will have 27 biweekly paydays. Employers must take this into account when converting annual salaries to weekly or biweekly rates of pay.

b. "Biweekly" means once every two weeks, or 26 times per year.

$$\text{Biweekly gross pay} = \frac{\text{Annual salary}}{26} = \frac{\$45,000}{24} = \$1730.77$$

c. Regular hourly rate $= \dfrac{\text{Regular biweekly gross pay}}{\text{Regular hours in biweekly period}} = \dfrac{\$1730.77}{2 \times 4 \times 10} = \$21.635$

Overtime hourly rate $=$ Overtime factor $\times$ Regular hourly rate $= 1.5 \times \$21.635 = \$32.453$

Total gross earnings $=$ Regular pay $+$ Overtime pay $= \$1730.77 + 6(\$32.453) = \$1925.49$

⮕ **Check your understanding:** Determine Benazir's gross earnings in a pay period if she is paid weekly and works no overtime hours. (Answer: $865.38 per week)

▰▰▰▶ **Related problem:** #1 in Exercise 1.4

Hourly Wages

In jobs where the amount of work available is irregular or unpredictable, or where overtime is a common occurrence, employees are typically paid an hourly wage. Sometimes, a collective agreement between the employer and employees sets the number of hours per day (typically $7\frac{1}{2}$ or 8) and hours per week (typically $37\frac{1}{2}$ or 40) beyond which higher overtime rates apply. If no such agreement exists, federal or provincial employment standards laws apply. The most common overtime rate is 1.5 times the regular hourly rate ("time and a half"). Some unions have negotiated more favourable overtime rates (such as "double time").

Each province recognizes certain holidays that, depending on the province, are called "statutory holidays," "public holidays," or "general holidays." New Year's Day, Good Friday, Canada Day, Labour Day, Thanksgiving Day, and Christmas Day are holidays common to all provinces. With a few exceptions, provincial employment standards require that employees receive their usual rate of pay for a statutory holiday *not* worked. If employees are required to work on a "stat" holiday, they must be paid an *additional premium* rate of 1.5 times their regular rate of pay.

You calculate the gross earnings for a pay period by adding overtime pay, "stat" holiday pay, and "stat" holiday premium pay to the regular pay. That is,

$$
\begin{array}{rl}
 & \text{Regular hourly rate} \times \text{Regular hours} \\
+ & \text{Overtime hourly rate} \times \text{Overtime hours} \\
+ & \text{"Stat" holiday pay} \\
+ & \underline{\text{"Stat" holiday premium hourly rate} \times \text{"Stat" holiday hours worked}} \\
= & \text{Gross earnings}
\end{array}
$$

In calculations in this section, time worked on a "stat" holiday does *not* count toward the threshold for overtime hours in a week.[6]

Sometimes wages in production and manufacturing jobs are structured to create an incentive for higher productivity. A *piecework rate* is based on the unit of production, such as $1 per garment sewn, or 7 cents per tree planted, or $15 per tonne of output.

$$\binom{\text{Piecework}}{\text{earnings}} = \binom{\text{Number of}}{\text{units produced}} \times \binom{\text{Piecework}}{\text{rate}}$$

---

[6] This is the basic standard established by employment standards legislation in some provinces, including Ontario and Alberta. As with many employment standards set by provincial legislation and regulations, unions typically negotiate more favourable remuneration and working conditions in their collective agreements.

EXAMPLE 1.4B	Calculating the Gross Earnings of an Hourly Paid Employee

Steve is paid $29.60 an hour for his work as an electrician. The regular workweek is 37.5 hours (five 7.5-hour shifts). In the most recent biweekly pay period (midnight Friday to midnight of the second following Friday), he worked full shifts from Monday to Friday of both weeks. The first Monday of the pay period was a statutory holiday. In addition, he worked 6 hours on each Saturday. Overtime is paid at $1\frac{1}{2}$ times the regular rate and the statutory holiday time premium is 1.5 times the regular rate. What was Steve's gross pay for the period?

SOLUTION

In addition to "stat" holiday pay for the first Monday, Steve will be paid a holiday premium rate of 1.5 times his regular rate for hours actually worked on that Monday. (These hours do not count toward the 37.5 hours-per-week threshold for overtime eligibility.) Steve's hourly rate for overtime is $1.5 \times \$29.60 = \$44.40$.

The given information is summarized in the following table.

	Week 1				Week 2		
Day	**Hours**	**Rate of pay**		**Day**	**Hours**	**Rate of pay**	
Sat	6	Regular		Sat	6	Regular	
Sun	0			Sun	0		
Mon	7.5	Holiday premium		Mon	7.5	Regular	
Tues	7.5	Regular		Tues	7.5	Regular	
Wed	7.5	Regular		Wed	7.5	Regular	
Thur	7.5	Regular		Thur	7.5	Regular	
Fri	7.5	Regular		Fri	7.5	1.5 hours regular; 6 hours overtime	

In week 1, Steve worked a total of 43.5 hours. Since the 7.5 hours worked on the holiday Monday do not count toward any overtime calculations, Steve worked only $43.5 - 7.5 = 36$ "regular" hours. He earns no overtime pay for week 1. In week 2, Steve worked a total of 43.5 "regular" hours, which is $43.5 - 37.5 = 6$ hours above the overtime threshold. The last 6 hours of the Friday shift in week 2, therefore, are paid at the time and a half overtime rate.

The components of Steve's gross pay are:

Regular pay:	$[6 + 4(7.5) + 6 + 4(7.5) + 1.5]\$29.60 =$	$2175.60
Overtime pay:	$6(\$44.40) =$	$266.40
Holiday pay:	$7.5(\$29.60) =$	$222.00
Holiday premium pay:	$7.5(\$44.40) =$	$333.00
Total:		$2997.00

Steve's gross pay for the two-week period was $2997.

➡ **Check your understanding:** Recalculate Steve's gross pay for this period if he worked the same hours as above, but this time the Monday of week 1 was not a statutory holiday. (Answer: $2752.80)

▮▮▶ **Related problem:** #5 in Exercise 1.4

EXAMPLE 1.4C	Calculating Gross Earnings Including a Piecework Wage

An orchardist pays apple pickers $10 per hour plus $8 per 100 kg of apples picked. If a worker picks, on average, 180 kg of apples per hour for a 40-hour workweek, what are the gross earnings for the week?

SOLUTION

$$\begin{pmatrix} \text{Gross} \\ \text{earnings} \end{pmatrix} = \begin{pmatrix} \text{Hourly} \\ \text{rate} \end{pmatrix} \times \begin{pmatrix} \text{Number} \\ \text{of hours} \end{pmatrix} + \begin{pmatrix} \text{Piecework} \\ \text{rate} \end{pmatrix} \times \begin{pmatrix} \text{Number} \\ \text{of units} \end{pmatrix}$$

$$= (\$10.00 \times 40) + \$8.00\left(\frac{180}{100} \times 40\right)$$

$$= \$400 + \$576$$

$$= \$976$$

The worker's gross earnings for the week are $976.

➡ **Check your understanding:** Calculate the worker's gross earnings for a 40-hour workweek during which she picked, on average, 120 kg of apples per hour. (Answer: $784)

▮▮▮▶ **Related problem:** #7 in Exercise 1.4

Commissions

For sales positions, it is standard practice to base at least a portion of the salesperson's earnings on sales volume. If earnings are calculated strictly as a percent of sales, the salesperson is working on *straight commission*. A *graduated commission* structure pays progressively higher commission rates at higher levels of sales. A salesperson who receives a base salary and a commission on sales is working on a *salary plus commission* basis. In some arrangements, the commission is paid only on sales exceeding a minimum level called the *quota*.

EXAMPLE 1.4D	Calculating Gross Earnings Based on a Salary Plus Commission

James manages a men's clothing store for a national chain. His monthly remuneration has three components: a $1500 base salary, plus 2% of the amount by which the store's total sales volume for the month exceeds $40,000, plus 8% of the amount by which his personal sales exceed $4000. Calculate his gross compensation for a month in which his sales totalled $9900 and other staff had sales amounting to $109,260.

SOLUTION

Base salary	$1500.00
Commission on total store's volume:	
0.02($109,260 + $9900 − $40,000)	1583.20
Commission on personal sales:	
0.08($9900 − $4000)	472.00
Total compensation	$3555.20

James's gross earnings for the month are $3555.20.

➡ **Check your understanding:** Calculate James's gross compensation for a month in which his sales totalled $8500 and other staff had sales amounting to $125,900. (Answer: $3748)

▮▮▮▶ **Related problem:** #4 in Exercise 1.4

EXAMPLE 1.4E	Calculating Gross Earnings Based on a Graduated Commission

Tanya sells mutual funds for Pacific Financial Services Ltd. On mutual fund sales, Pacific Financial Services charges a "front-end load" or gross commission rate of 6%. Tanya is paid on a graduated commission structure. She receives 40% of the gross commission on the first $100,000 worth of mutual funds she sells in a month, and 60% of the gross commission on all additional sales in the same month. What are her earnings for a month in which she sells $180,000 worth of mutual funds?

SOLUTION

Commission on first $100,000:	
$0.40 \times 0.06 \times \$100,000$	$2400
Commission on next $80,000:	
$0.60 \times 0.06 \times \$80,000$	2880
Total earnings	$5280

Tanya's earnings are $5280 from her total mutual funds sales of $180,000 in the month.

➡ **Check your understanding:** Calculate Tanya's earnings for a month in which she sells $225,000 worth of mutual funds. (Answer: $6900)

▰▰▷ **Related problem:** #12 in Exercise 1.4

EXERCISE 1.4

Answers to the odd-numbered problems can be found in the end matter.

In this exercise, assume there are exactly 52 weeks in a year.

BASIC PROBLEMS

1. Aletta's annual salary of $33,500 is paid weekly. She is paid at time and a half for any over-time beyond her regular workweek of 35 hours. What is her gross pay for a week in which she works 39 hours?

2. Lucille receives an annual salary of $37,500, paid biweekly. She works 37.5 hours in a nor-mal workweek. What are her gross earnings for a two-week pay period in which she works 9 hours of overtime at $1\frac{1}{2}$ times her regular rate of pay?

3. Hasad is paid an annual salary of $54,600 based on a 40-hour workweek. He is paid biweekly. What is his gross pay for a biweekly pay period if he works 43 hours in the first week and 46.5 hours in the second week? Overtime is paid at time and a half.

4. Hillary sells jewellery from her part-time home-based business. She receives a straight com-mission of 21% from her supplier. At the year-end, she also receives a 7% bonus on sales exceeding her annual quota of $50,000. What will her gross annual earnings be for a year in which her sales are $66,000?

INTERMEDIATE PROBLEMS

5. Allison's regular hourly rate of pay is $13.70. She is paid time and a half for all work on weekends and for any time over 7.5 hours on weekdays. Calculate her gross earnings for a week in which she works 4.5, 0, 7.5, 8.5, 6, 6, and 9 hours on Saturday to Friday, respectively.

6. Sam is paid $34.50 per hour as a power plant engineer. He is paid $1\frac{1}{2}$ times the regular rate for all time exceeding 8 hours in a day or 40 hours in a week. Statutory holidays worked are paid at double time (in addition to holiday pay). What are his gross earnings for a week in which he clocks 8, 9.5, 8, 8, 10, 0, and 8 hours on Saturday to Friday, respectively, where Monday is a statutory holiday?

7. Mary sews for a clothing manufacturer. She is paid $10.75 per hour plus a piecework rate that depends on the type of garment in production. The current production run is men's shirts, for which she is paid $4 for each unit exceeding her quota of 30 shirts in an 8-hour shift. What is her total pay for a regular workweek in which her output on successive days is 34, 36, 37, 38, and 30 shirts?

8. Herb packs fish in 0.5 kilogram cans on a processing line. He is paid $12.25 per hour plus $0.18 per kilogram for production in excess of 500 kilograms in a 7.5-hour shift. How much will he earn per day if he packs 250 cans per hour?

9. Svetlana is an independent insurance broker placing various clients with any of several insurance companies. On homeowner insurance policies, each month she receives
   • $20 for each renewal of an existing policy;
   • $35 for each policy placed with a new client; and
   • 5.5% of the annual premiums on all policies (new and renewed) written in the month.

   In October, she placed 37 new-client policies representing $14,375 in annual premiums and 126 policy renewals representing $47,880 in annual premiums. What amount did Svetlana earn in October?

10. A shoe salesperson is paid the greater of $600 per week or 11% of sales.
    a. What are his earnings for a week in which sales are $5636?
    b. At what volume of sales per week will he start to earn more from the commission-based compensation?

11. Manfred is considering job offers of the same type of sales position from two retailers with similar product lines:
    • Supreme Audio & Video is offering a base salary of $2000 per month plus a 4% commission rate on sales.
    • Buy-Right Electronics will pay a base salary of $1500 per month plus commission rates of 3% on the first $25,000 of sales and 6% on additional sales in a month.

    Based on past experience, Manfred is confident he can attain average monthly sales of $55,000. At this level of sales, what would be his average gross earnings per month from each retailer?

12. Tom sells mutual funds on a graduated commission structure. He receives 3.3% on the first $50,000 of sales in a month, 4.4% on the next $50,000, and 5.5% on all further sales. What are his gross earnings for a month in which he sells $140,000 worth of mutual funds?

ADVANCED PROBLEMS

13. Sharon is a manufacturer's representative selling office furniture directly to businesses. She receives a monthly salary of $2000 plus a 2.2% commission on sales exceeding her quota of $150,000 per month.
    a. What are her earnings for a month in which she has $227,000 in sales?
    b. If her average monthly sales are $235,000, what straight commission rate would generate the same average monthly earnings as her current basis of remuneration?

14. Karen works in a retail electronics store. She receives a weekly base salary of $400 plus a commission of 3% of sales exceeding her quota of $20,000 per week. What is her sales total for a week in which she earns $630.38?

15. Daniella's gross monthly earnings are based on commission rates of 4% on the first $40,000 of sales, 5% on the next $50,000, and 6% on all additional sales for the month. What is her sales total for a month in which she earns $5350?

16. Karim is paid a gross monthly salary of $2600 in his current job. He is considering taking a new sales position that would pay a gross salary of $1200 per month, plus a 4% commission on sales in excess of his monthly quota of $18,000. How much would Karim need to sell per month in the new job in order to match his monthly earnings in his current job?

1.5   Simple and Weighted Averages

 LO6   Simple Average

The type of average initially encountered in basic mathematics is called the *simple average*. To calculate the simple average, simply (of course) add the values for all items and then divide by the number of items. That is,

SIMPLE AVERAGE FORMULA $\text{Simple average} = \dfrac{\text{Sum of the values}}{\text{Total number of items}}$ **(1-2)**

This average should be used in cases where each item has the *same* importance or each value occurs the *same* number of times.

Weighted Average

We will now consider a situation requiring a different approach to averaging. Suppose you operate a seasonal business that employs 10 people during the peak period of July, August, and September. Only 2 employees are retained during the rest of the year. Is the average number of people employed during the year $\frac{10+2}{2} = 6$? No—a simple average of "10" and "2" is not appropriate, because these two employment levels lasted for different lengths of time. The value "2" should influence the average more than the value "10." More precisely, each employment value should influence the average in proportion to the length of time at the level of employment. Mathematicians express this idea by saying: "Each employment level should be *weighted* by the time period for which it lasted." Consequently, we assign a *weighting factor* of 3 months to the value "10" and a weighting factor of 9 months to the value "2." Then the *weighted average* number of employees during the year is calculated as follows:

$$\frac{(3 \times 10) + (9 \times 2)}{3 + 9} = 4.0$$

In the numerator, each of the two employment values (10 and 2) is multiplied by its weighting factor (3 months and 9 months, respectively). The two products are then added. Finally, this sum is divided by the sum of the weighting factors.

In general, *a weighted average should be calculated when the values being averaged have differing relative importance, or when some values occur more often than others.*

WEIGHTED AVERAGE FORMULA $\text{Weighted average} = \dfrac{\text{Sum of (Weighting factor} \times \text{Value)}}{\text{Sum of weighting factors}}$ **(1-3)**

The preceding word equation[7] implies three steps for calculating a weighted average:

1. First multiply each of the "Values" by its "Weighting factor." The weighting factors represent the relative importance of each value, or the number of times each value occurs.
2. Add all of the products calculated in Step 1.
3. Finally, divide the Step 2 result by the sum of the "Weighting factors."

Weighted averages are frequently encountered in business. For example, the Toronto Stock Exchange's S&P/TSX Composite Index is based on a weighted average price of the shares of over 200 companies. Accountants sometimes use the weighted average price paid for goods to determine the overall value of a firm's inventory. Several more examples are presented in this section's Example problems and Exercise problems. When calculating weighted averages, you need to make careful decisions about which values should be averaged and which numbers should be used for the weighting factors. The following flowchart suggests questions you should ask yourself before the "number crunching" begins.

FIGURE 1.1   Approach for Problems on Averages

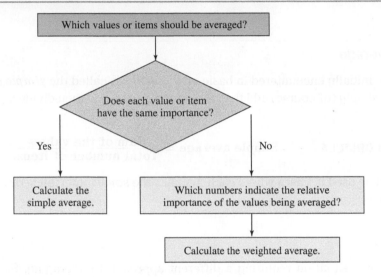

| EXAMPLE 1.5A | Calculation of Simple and Weighted Averages |

Northern Transport has 86 drivers each earning $23.85 per hour, 14 clerical staff members each earning $18.50 per hour, and 8 mechanics each earning $35.50 per hour.

a. What is the simple average of the three hourly rates?

b. Calculate the weighted average hourly rate earned by the three categories of employees.

SOLUTION

a. Simple average $= \dfrac{\$23.85 + \$18.50 + \$35.50}{3} = \$25.95$

b. Each hourly rate should be assigned a weighting factor reflecting the relative importance of that rate. The greater the number of employees receiving a particular wage rate, the more importance should be given to that rate. It is natural, then, to use the number of employees receiving each hourly rate as the weighting factors.

---

[7]   Note that if each of the "Values" has the same importance, then each weighting factor is "1." The "Weighted average" formula then reduces to the "Simple average" formula.

$$\text{Weighted average} = \frac{(86 \times \$23.85) + (14 \times \$18.50) + (8 \times \$35.50)}{86 + 14 + 8}$$

$$= \frac{\$2051.10 + \$259 + \$284}{108}$$

$$= \$24.02$$

The weighted average is less than the simple average because a high proportion of the employees earn the two lower hourly rates.

⇨ **Check your understanding:** What is the new weighted average hourly rate earned by the three categories of employees if there are 50 drivers, 18 clerical staff, and 12 mechanics? (Answer: $24.39)

▰▰▶ **Related problem:** #14 in Exercise 1.5

EXAMPLE 1.5B	Calculating the Weighted-Average Rate of Return for an Investment Portfolio

One year ago, Mrs. Boyd divided her savings among four mutual funds as follows: 20% was invested in a bond fund, 15% in a money market fund, 40% in a Canadian equity fund, and 25% in a global equity fund. During the past year, the rates of return on the individual mutual funds were 3%, 1.75%, −2%, and 4.5%, respectively. What was the overall rate of return on her portfolio?

SOLUTION

A simple average of the four rates of return is not the appropriate calculation, because Mrs. Boyd invested different amounts of money in each mutual fund. The −2% return on the Canadian equity fund should have twice the influence of the 3% return on the bond fund, because she invested twice as much money in the Canadian equity fund as in the bond fund. Therefore, we should choose weighting factors that reflect the relative amount of money invested in each mutual fund.

Mutual fund	Fraction of money invested (Weighting factor)	Rate of return (Value)
Bond fund	0.20	3%
Money market fund	0.15	1.75%
Canadian equity fund	0.40	−2%
Global equity fund	0.25	4.5%
Total:	1.00	

$$\text{Weighted average} = \frac{(0.2 \times 3\%) + (0.15 \times 1.75\%) + [0.40 \times (-2\%)] + (0.25 \times 4.5\%)}{0.20 + 0.15 + 0.40 + 0.25}$$

$$= \frac{0.6\% + 0.2625\% - 0.8\% + 1.125\%}{1}$$

$$= 1.1875\%$$

Mrs. Boyd's portfolio increased in value by 1.1875%.

⇨ **Check your understanding:** Calculate Mrs. Boyd's overall rate of return if she had divided her savings as follows: 40% was invested in the bond fund, 10% was invested in the money market fund, 30% was invested in the Canadian equity fund, and 20% was invested in the global equity fund. (Answer: 1.675%)

▰▰▶ **Related problem:** #11 in Exercise 1.5

EXAMPLE 1.5C | Calculating the Weighted Average of a Varying Investment in a Business

As of January 1, Alan had already invested $63,000 in his business. On February 1 he invested another $5000. Alan withdrew $12,000 on June 1 and injected $3000 on November 1. What was his average cumulative investment in the business during the year? (Assume that all months have the same length, or weighting.)

SOLUTION

A common error made in this type of problem is to attempt, in some way, to average the amounts that are contributed to or withdrawn from the business. We should instead average the cumulative balance of the invested funds. The amounts contributed and withdrawn from time to time are used only to revise the cumulative investment. A weighted average should be calculated, since the various amounts are invested for *differing* lengths of time. Each cumulative investment should be weighted by the number of months for which it lasted.

Period	Cumulative investment	Number of months
Jan. 1–Jan. 31	$63,000	1
Feb. 1–May 31	$63,000 + $5000 = $68,000	4
June 1–Oct. 31	$68,000 − $12,000 = $56,000	5
Nov. 1–Dec. 31	$56,000 + $3000 = $59,000	2

$$\text{Average investment} = \frac{(1 \times \$63,000) + (4 \times \$68,000) + (5 \times \$56,000) + (2 \times \$59,000)}{12}$$

$$= \$61,083.33$$

Alan's average investment in the business was $61,083.33.

➡ **Check your understanding:** What is Alan's average cumulative investment in the business during the year if he had already invested $75,000 as of January 1, invested another $24,000 on April 1, and withdrew $10,000 on October 1? (Answer: $90,500)

▐▌▶ **Related problem:** #15 in Exercise 1.5

EXAMPLE 1.5D | Calculating a (Weighted) Grade Point Average

Most colleges compute a grade point average (GPA) as the measure of a student's overall academic achievement. To compute the GPA, each letter grade is first converted to a grade point value. Each course's grade point value is then weighted by the number of credits the course carries.

The first table below gives City College's scale for converting letter grades to grade point values. The next table presents Louise's courses and grades. Calculate her GPA.

Letter grade	Grade point value
A	4.0
A−	3.7
B+	3.3
B	3.0
B−	2.7
C+	2.3
C	2.0
C−	1.7
D	1.0

Course	Credits	Grade
English 100	3	B+
Math 100	4	B
Business 100	2	A
Economics 120	3	B−
Accounting 100	4	C+
Marketing 140	2	A−
Computing 110	3	C
Total	21	

SOLUTION

The values to be averaged are the grade point scores Louise has achieved on her seven courses. However, these values are not given in a ready-to-use list. A new table should be constructed, showing the grade points earned on each course. (See the first three columns in the next table.)

Course	Grade	Grade points	Credits	Grade points × Credits
English 100	B+	3.3	3	9.9
Math 100	B	3.0	4	12.0
Business 100	A	4.0	2	8.0
Economics 120	B–	2.7	3	8.1
Accounting 100	C+	2.3	4	9.2
Marketing 140	A–	3.7	2	7.4
Computing 110	C	2.0	3	6.0
Total:			21	60.6

A simple average of the grade point values is not appropriate because some courses carry more credits than others. A 4-credit course should count twice as much in the average as a 2-credit course. Therefore, each course's grade point score should be weighted by the number of credits that course carries (Column 4). The first step in the calculation of the weighted average is to multiply each grade point value by its weighting factor, as shown in Column 5. In the second step, the products in Column 5 are added.

The third and last step is to divide the total in Column 5 by the total in Column 4. Hence,

$$\text{GPA} = \frac{60.6}{21} = 2.89$$

Louise's grade point average is 2.89.

➡ **Check your understanding:** What would Louise's GPA have been if her grades in English 100 and Accounting 100 had been A's? (Answer: 3.31)

▰▰▶ **Related problem:** #8 in Exercise 1.5

Checkpoint Questions

1. Circle "True" or "False" for each of the following:

    a. In a weighted average question, the sum of the weighting factors must equal 1.   True   False

    b. A company purchased 6 trucks for $28,000 each, 4 trucks for $32,000 each, and   True   False
    10 trucks for $46,000 each. The weighted average price per truck is $37,800.

    c. Shelley's car consumes 6.8 litres per 100 kilometres in the city, and 4.9 litres   True   False
    per 100 kilometres on the highway. Shelley has calculated her weighted average
    gasoline consumption to be 5.7 litres per 100 kilometres. Based on these facts,
    we can conclude that Shelley drives more kilometres in the city than on the highway.

2. In what circumstance should you calculate a weighted average instead of a simple average?

3. In what circumstance is the weighted average equal to the simple average?

4. How must you allocate your money among a number of investments so that your portfolio's overall rate of return will be the same as the simple average of the rates of return on individual investments?

EXERCISE 1.5

Answers to the odd-numbered problems can be found in the end matter.

BASIC PROBLEMS

1. A survey of 254 randomly chosen residences in a city revealed that 2 had four computers, 6 had three computers, 43 had two computers, 176 had one computer, and 27 had no computer at all. Based on the survey, what would you estimate to be the average number of computers per household?

2. An investor accumulated 1800 shares of Microtel Corporation over a period of several months. She bought 1000 shares at $15.63, 500 shares at $19, and 300 shares at $21.75. What was her average cost per share?

3. Tim currently owes $37,500 to a private lender. The rate of interest on this debt is 8%. If he borrows an additional $20,000 at a rate of 7% from the same lender, what average rate of interest is Tim paying on his accumulated debt?

4. Serge's graduated commission scale pays him 3% on his first $30,000 in sales, 4% on the next $20,000, and 6% on all additional sales in a month. What is his average commission rate on sales for a month totalling

   a. $60,000?   **b.** $100,000?

5. A hockey goalie's "goals against average" (GAA) is the average number of goals scored against him or her per (complete) game. In his first 20 games in goal, O. U. Sieve had one shutout, two 1-goal games, three 2-goal games, four 3-goal games, seven 4-goal games, two 6-goal games, and one 10-goal disaster. Calculate his GAA.

6. During a recent math test, 37 students finished the test in forty-five minutes, 12 students finished in fifty minutes, and 18 students finished in fifty-five minutes. Rounded to the nearest 0.1 minute, what was the average completion time for the test?

7. A restaurant owner buys peaches from a local farmer. Prices fluctuate weekly based on supply. The restaurant owner bought 60 litres of peaches at $2.25 per litre in the first week of August, 40 litres at $2.50 per litre in the second week of August, and 110 litres of peaches at $2.10 per litre in the third week of August. What average price per litre did the restaurant owner pay?

INTERMEDIATE PROBLEMS

8. Margot's grades and course credits in her first semester at college are shown below. Using the table in Example 1.5D for converting letter grades to grade point values, calculate Margot's grade point average for the semester.

Course	Credits	Grade
Marketing	3	B−
Business Math	5	C+
Accounting	4	B+
Human Resource Management	3	B
Computer Applications	2	C−
Business Communications	4	C

9. Alihan's transcript shows the following academic record for four semesters of part-time college studies. Calculate his cumulative GPA at the end of his fourth semester.

Semester	Credits	GPA
1	6	3.5
2	9	3.0
3	12	2.75
4	7.5	3.2

10. An account receivable is an outstanding debt owed to a business by a customer. The "age" of an account receivable is the length of time that it has been outstanding. At the end of October, a firm has $12,570 in receivables that are 30 days old, $6850 in receivables that are 60 days old, and $1325 in receivables that are 90 days old. What is the average age of its accounts receivable at the end of October?

11. One year ago, Sook-Yin allocated the funds in her portfolio among five securities in the proportions listed below. The rate of return on each security for the year is given in the third column of the table.

Security	Proportion invested (%)	Rate of return for the year (%)
Company A shares	15	6
Province B bonds	20	3
Company C shares	10	−13
Units in Fund D	35	2
Company E shares	20	7

Calculate the rate of return for the entire portfolio.

12. Suppose a group of consumers spends 30% of its disposable income on food, 20% on clothing, and 50% on rent. If over the course of a year the price of food rose 10%, the price of clothing dropped 5%, and rent rose 15%, what was the average price increase experienced by these consumers?

13. One of the methods permitted by International Financial Reporting Standards (IFRS) for reporting the value of a firm's inventory is *weighted-average inventory pricing*. The Boswell Corporation began its fiscal year with an inventory of 156 units valued at $10.55 per unit. During the year it made the purchases listed in the following table.

	Units purchased	Unit cost ($)
Order #1	300	10.86
Order #2	1000	10.47
Order #3	500	10.97

At the end of the year, 239 units remained in inventory. Determine:

a. The weighted-average cost of the units purchased during the year.

b. The weighted-average cost of the beginning inventory and all units purchased during the year.

c. The value of the ending inventory based on the weighted-average cost calculated in Part (b).

14. Preston bought gasoline for his truck four times last month. He bought 74 litres at $1.25 per litre, 45 litres at $1.32 per litre, 88 litres at $1.28 per litre, and 20 litres at $1.39 per litre.

a. What simple average price per litre did Preston pay for gasoline last month?

b. What weighted average price per litre did Preston pay for gasoline last month? Round to the cent.

c. Which averaging method is the better reflection of Preston's gasoline cost last month? Why?

ADVANCED PROBLEMS

15. As of January 1, Rheal had already invested $172,000 in her business. On April 1 she invested another $12,000. Rheal withdrew $15,000 on June 1 and withdrew another $5000 on August 1. Rounded to the nearest dollar, what was her average cumulative investment in the business during the year? (Assume that all months have the same length, or weighting.)

16. The balance on Nucorp's revolving loan began the month at $35,000. On the eighth of the month another $10,000 was borrowed. Nucorp was able to repay $20,000 on the 25th of the 31-day month. What was the average balance on the loan during the month? (Use each day's closing balance as the loan balance for the day.)

17. A seasonal manufacturing operation began the calendar year with 14 employees. During the year, employees were hired or laid off on various dates as presented in the table below.

Date	Employee changes
April 1	7 hired
May 1	8 hired
June 1	11 hired
Sept. 1	6 laid off
Oct. 1	14 laid off

What was the average number of employees on the payroll during the calendar year? (Assume that each month has the same length.)

18. Lien, the owner of a grocery store, prepares her Deluxe Nut Combo by mixing various ingredients she buys in bulk. The table below presents the amount of each ingredient that Lien uses to make a batch of her combo mix, as well as the per-kilogram cost of each ingredient.

Ingredient	Amount	Cost per kg
Peanuts	5 kg	$2.95
Cashews	2 kg	$9.50
Almonds	1 kg	$11.50
Sunflower seeds	500 g	$2.75
Raisins	400 g	$3.60
Smarties	300 g	$6.40

a. What is Lien's average cost per kilogram of her Deluxe Nut Combo? Per 100 grams?

b. If Lien sets the retail price of the Deluxe Nut Combo equal to 150% of her cost, what is her retail price per 100 grams?

1.6 | Taxes

LO7   A **tax rate** is the percentage of a price or taxable amount that must be paid in tax. The dollar amount of the tax payable is

$$\text{Tax payable} = \text{Tax rate} \times \text{Taxable amount}$$

This word equation is really just a variation of formula (1-1):

$$\text{Portion} = \text{Rate} \times \text{Base}$$

Goods and Services Tax (GST); Harmonized Sales Tax (HST)

The Goods and Services Tax (GST) is a federal sales tax charged on the vast majority of goods and services. The tax is paid by the purchaser of the good or service to the seller. Consequently, a business collects the GST on the goods and services it sells, and pays the GST on the goods and services it purchases. When the business files its GST return with the Canada Revenue Agency (CRA), it remits only the amount by which the tax collected from sales exceeds the tax paid on purchases. If, in a reporting period, the GST collected from sales happens to be less than the GST paid by the business on its purchases, the CRA will refund the difference to the business.

The tax rate for the GST is 5% in every province and territory. The provinces of Newfoundland and Labrador, New Brunswick, Nova Scotia, Prince Edward Island, and Ontario have agreed with the federal government to blend their respective provincial sales taxes with the GST in a single Harmonized Sales Tax (HST). The HST is administered by the federal government through the CRA. The HST applies to the same base of goods and services as the GST. The HST rate varies by province, as shown in Table 1.1.

TABLE 1.1 HST Rates by Province (as of October 1, 2016)

Province	Provincial tax portion	Federal tax portion	Total HST rate
Newfoundland and Labrador	10%	5%	15%
New Brunswick	10%	5%	15%
Nova Scotia	10%	5%	15%*
Prince Edward Island	10%	5%	15%
Ontario	8%	5%	13%

EXAMPLE 1.6A | **Calculation of the GST or the HST Payable by a Business**

Ace Appliance Repair files GST returns quarterly. During the first quarter of the year, Ace billed its customers $17,650 for labour and $4960 for parts, and then added the GST. In the same period, Ace paid $3250 to suppliers for parts, $1800 for rent, $673 for utilities, and $594 for truck repairs, plus the GST on these goods and services.

a. What GST must be remitted by Ace (or refunded by the CRA) for the first quarter?

b. Repeat Part (a) for the case where Ace also bought a new truck for $36,000 on the last day of the quarter.

c. Repeat Part (a) for the case where Ace pays HST (at the rate of 13%) instead of GST.

SOLUTION

---

a. GST collected = 0.05($17,650 + $4960) = $1130.50

GST paid = 0.05($3250 + $1800 + $673 + $594) = $315.85

GST remittance payable = $1130.50 − $315.85 = $814.65

b. GST paid on the truck purchase = 0.05 × $36,000 = $1800

With the truck purchase, Ace paid total GST of $315.85 + $1800 = $2115.85. GST collected for the period was $1130.50. Since Ace paid more GST than it collected, Ace qualifies for a refund.

GST refund receivable = $2115.85 − $1130.50 = $985.35

c. HST collected = 0.13($17,650 + $4960) = $2939.30

HST paid = 0.13($3250 + $1800 + $673 + $594) = $821.21

HST remittance payable = $2939.30 − $821.21 = $2118.09

➡ **Check your understanding:** Suppose Ace pays HST at a rate of 13%, and its payment to suppliers for parts was $9250 (instead of $3250). Ace also bought the new $36,000 truck during this period. What HST must be remitted by Ace (or refunded by the CRA) for the first quarter? Assume all other information remains the same as above. (Answer: Ace will receive an HST rebate of $3341.91.)

▰▰▶ **Related problem:** #1 in Exercise 1.6

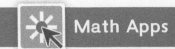 **Math Apps**

STRIKING THE BALANCE WITH PROVINCIAL SALES TAXES

While policies related to the collection of the GST are made by the federal government and applied consistently across the country, decisions about provincial sales taxes rest solely with each provincial government. As illustrated in Tables 1.1 and 1.2, the provincial tax rate varies from as low as 0% in Alberta to as high as 10% in Newfoundland and Labrador and the Maritime provinces. While most consumers across the country would prefer a 0% sales tax rate, the economics of balancing multi-billion-dollar provincial budgets are complex, and the sales taxes collected at the provincial level represent revenues that fund many important services. While sales tax rates have long been stable in most provinces, some provincial governments have, in recent years, shone the spotlight on the provincial tax structure as they struggle to strike a balance between keeping taxpayers happy while maintaining service levels for provincial responsibilities such as health care, education, and roads.

In 2010, the province of British Columbia introduced a 12% harmonized sales tax (HST) to replace the 7% provincial sales tax (PST) and 5% federal goods and services tax (GST). While, on the surface, this move would seem to be mathematically equivalent and not worthy of much attention on the part of consumers, the issue became a political minefield for then-Premier Gordon Campbell. Although the single HST is considered more efficient for businesses to administer than the separate PST and GST systems, many British Columbians vocally opposed the HST implementation. Because the 12% HST was applied to many categories of purchases that were previously PST-exempt, taxpayers argued that the HST implementation would result in an increased tax burden, particularly on "big ticket" items. In the face of extreme political pressure, a referendum was held in August 2011, with 55% of votes cast in favour of scrapping the HST. While the referendum was seen by many as a win for the average taxpayer, the return to the separate PST and GST systems was seen as a costly change for small businesses, who had already made the transition to the HST, and resulted in the provincial government having to repay $1.6 billion in HST transition assistance that had been provided by the federal government.

In Nova Scotia, where the 15% HST is one of the highest consumption taxes in the country, citizens have seen promised tax cuts cancelled in provincial budget announcements. The 15% rate (made up of the 10% PST portion and the 5% federal GST portion) was set in 2010 by the newly elected NDP government led by Premier Darrell Dexter. The 2% tax hike was, Dexter claimed, a short-term strategy necessary to get the province's budget in order. In early 2012, Dexter announced that the province would reduce the HST rate to 14% starting July 1, 2014, then to 13% starting July 1, 2015, a move that he said was affordable, since the province's budget was projected to be in surplus. By October 2013, however, the promised tax cuts were cancelled, deemed not affordable by the newly elected Liberal government led by Stephen McNeil.

Even Alberta, with its long history of plentiful oil revenues and a 0% provincial tax rate, has grappled with balancing its provincial books. In the midst of declining provincial revenues caused by record-low oil prices in 2015, the province's economy was on shaky ground. Then-Premier Jim Prentice warned Albertans to brace for change. Some analysts recommended that introduction of a PST might be a valuable item in the premier's toolkit for striking a balance in the faltering economy. Prentice himself promised that all options were on the table. In the October 2015 provincial election, NDP leader Rachel Notley led her party to a majority government and introduced her first budget later that month, firmly slamming the door on any talk of a PST implementation. Of her government's first budget, Notley stated, "That budget nor any other budget in the term of this government will not and does not include a PST."

While PST is only one way for provincial governments to bring in revenue, the fact that it is so visible to average consumers as they make everyday purchases makes it an area ripe for debate. All business students should get into the habit of reading the business section of at least one national newspaper. Take note of what is happening in your province around the issue of PST reform, especially during provincial election campaigns!

Provincial Sales Tax (PST)

Rather than participating in the HST, Quebec, Manitoba, Saskatchewan, and British Columbia charge a sales tax at the *retail* level. This tax typically applies to a somewhat narrower range of goods and services than the GST and HST. The provincial sales tax (PST) rates for these provinces are shown in Table 1.2. The provincial tax rate is applied to the retail price. That is,

$$PST = \text{Sales tax rate} \times \text{Retail price}$$

TABLE 1.2   Provincial Sales Tax Rates (as of October 1, 2016)

Province	Tax rate
Quebec	9.975%
Manitoba	8%
Saskatchewan	5%
Alberta	0%
British Columbia	7%

Note that only the 5% GST applies in Canada's three territories, as the territorial governments do not impose a territorial equivalent of the PST.

EXAMPLE 1.6B | **Calculating the PST**

Calculate the PST on a $100 item in

a. Saskatchewan

b. Quebec

SOLUTION

a. $PST = 0.05 \times \$100 = \$5$

b. $PST = 0.09975 \times \$100 = \$9.98$

➡ **Check your understanding:** Calculate the PST on a $100 item in Manitoba. (Answer: $7)

✏➤ **Related problem:** #3 in Exercise 1.6

Property Tax

Real estate property tax is not a sales tax, but rather an annual tax paid by the owners of real estate. Property taxes are paid to municipal and regional governments to cover costs of municipal services, public schools, policing, and so on. Tax rates are set by municipal and regional governments, and by other agencies (such as school boards) authorized by the provincial government to levy property taxes. The taxable value (usually called the *assessed value*) of each property is set by a provincial agency. Assessed values are periodically revised to keep them in line with market values.

Property tax rates in most provinces east of Manitoba are quoted in terms of dollars of tax per $100 of assessed value. For example, if the rate for a municipality is $1.55 per $100 of assessed value, the property tax on a home assessed at $200,000 will be

$$\frac{\$1.55}{\$100} \times \$200,000 = \$3100$$

A tax rate of $1.55 per $100 of assessed value is equal to 1.55% of assessed value. Most municipalities in Ontario now specify property tax rates simply as a percentage of the assessed value.

Provinces west of Ontario quote property tax rates as mill rates. A **mill rate** indicates the amount of tax per $1000 of assessed value. For example, a mill rate of 13.732 means a tax of $13.732 per $1000 of assessed value. The percent equivalent of this mill rate is 1.3732%. If you choose to work with a mill rate rather than its percent equivalent, then

PROPERTY TAX FORMULA
$$\text{Property tax} = \frac{\text{Mill rate}}{1000} \times \text{Assessed value of the property} \qquad (1\text{-}4)$$

EXAMPLE 1.6C	Calculating the Property Tax on a Residential Property

A homeowner's tax notice lists the following mill rates for various local services and capital developments. If the assessed value of the property is $264,500, calculate each tax levy and the current year's total property taxes.

Tax category	Mill rate
Schools	6.7496
General city	7.8137
Water	0.8023
Sewer and sanitation	0.7468

SOLUTION

$$\text{School tax levy} = \frac{\text{School mill rate}}{1000} \times \text{Assessed value}$$
$$= \frac{6.7496}{1000} \times \$264,500$$
$$= \$1785.269$$

Similarly

$$\text{General city levy} = \frac{7.8137}{1000} \times \$264,500 = \$2066.724$$

$$\text{Water levy} = \frac{0.8023}{1000} \times \$264,500 = \$212.208$$

$$\text{Sewer levy} = \frac{0.7468}{1000} \times \$264,500 = \$197.529$$

$$\text{Total property taxes} = \$1785.269 + \$2066.724 + \$212.208 + \$197.529$$
$$= \$4261.73$$

➡ **Check your understanding:** Calculate the total annual property taxes owing for a property assessed at $374,000. (Answer: $6026.04)

▥▶ **Related problem:** #5 in Exercise 1.6

EXAMPLE 1.6D	Calculating a Property Tax Rate

The town council of Concord has approved a new capital levy component of the property tax to pay for a new recreation complex. The levy must raise $400,000 in each of the next 10 years.

a. If the total assessed value of properties within Concord's jurisdiction is $738 million, what tax rate (to five-figure accuracy) must be set for the capital levy? Determine the rate both as a mill rate and as dollars per $100.

b. As a result of the capital levy, what additional tax will be paid each year by the owner of a property assessed at $200,000?

SOLUTION

a. Let us first calculate the tax rate as a percentage.

$$\text{Capital levy tax rate} = \frac{\text{Required total tax}}{\text{Total assessed value}} \times \$100\%$$

$$= \frac{\$400,000}{\$738,000,000} \times 100\%$$

$$= 0.054201\%$$

Therefore, the tax rate for the extra capital levy is $0.054201 per $100 of assessed value. This corresponds to $0.54201 per $1000 of assessed value. Hence, the mill rate is 0.54201.

b. With the tax levy quoted as $0.054201 per $100 of assessed value,

$$\text{Additional tax} = \frac{\$0.054201}{\$100} \times \$200,000 = \$108.40$$

With the tax levy quoted as 0.54201 mill,

$$\text{Additional tax} = \frac{\$0.54201}{\$1000} \times \$200,000 = \$108.40$$

➡ **Check your understanding:** Redo Parts (a) and (b). This time, the new levy must raise $850,000 in each of the next 10 years. (Answer: **a.** $0.11518 per $100 of assessed value or mill rate of 1.1518; **b.** $230.36)

▰▰▶ **Related problem:** #11 in Exercise 1.6

EXERCISE 1.6

Answers to the odd-numbered problems can be found in the end matter.

BASIC PROBLEMS

1. Johnston Distributing, Inc. files quarterly GST returns. The purchases on which it paid the GST and the sales on which it collected the GST for the last four quarters were as follows:

Quarter	Purchases ($)	Sales ($)
1	596,476	751,841
2	967,679	627,374
3	823,268	1,231,916
4	829,804	994,622

Calculate the GST remittance or refund due for each quarter.

2. Sawchuk's Home and Garden Centre in Toronto files monthly HST returns. The purchases on which it paid the HST and the sales on which it collected the HST for the past four months were as follows:

Month	Purchases ($)	Sales ($)
March	135,650	57,890
April	213,425	205,170
May	176,730	313,245
June	153,715	268,590

Based on an HST rate of 13%, calculate the HST remittance or refund due for each month.

3. Calculate the total amount, including both GST and PST, that an individual will pay for a car priced at $39,500 in:

   a. Alberta

   b. Quebec

   c. British Columbia

4. How much more will a consumer pay for an item listed at $1000 (pretax) in Quebec than in Ontario?

5. What are the taxes on a property assessed at $227,000 if the mill rate is 16.8629?

INTERMEDIATE PROBLEMS

6. a. What percentage is the HST of an HST-inclusive price in New Brunswick?

   b. The total price including HST of an item in New Brunswick is $171.35. What is the amount of HST included in the price?

7. To attract shoppers, retailers occasionally advertise something like "Pay no HST!" Needless to say, neither the federal nor the provincial government is willing to forgo its sales tax. In this situation, the retailer must calculate and remit the HST as though the "ticket" price already includes these sales taxes. How much HST must a retailer in Prince Edward Island report on a $495 item that he sells on a pay-no-HST basis? (*Hint:* What percentage is the HST of an HST-inclusive price?)

8. The assessment on a farm consists of $143,000 for the house and $467,000 for the land and farm buildings. A mill rate of 15.0294 applies to residences, and a rate of 4.6423 applies to agricultural land and buildings. What are the total property taxes payable on the farm?

9. a. Express a property tax rate increase of 0.1 mill in terms of dollars per $100 of assessed value.

   b. If the mill rate increases by 0.1 mill, what is the dollar increase in property taxes on a $300,000 home?

10. The assessed value on a property increased from $285,000 last year to $298,000 in the current year. Last year's property tax rate was $1.56324 per $100 of assessed value.

    a. What will be the change in the property tax from last year if the new tax rate is set at $1.52193 per $100?

    b. What would the new tax rate have to be for the dollar amount of the property taxes to be unchanged?

ADVANCED PROBLEMS

11. The school board in a municipality will require an extra $2,430,000 for its operating budget next year. The current mill rate for the school tax component of property taxes is 7.1253.

    a. If the total of the assessed values of properties in the municipality remains at the current figure of $6.78 billion, at what value must next year's school mill rate be set?

    b. If the total of all assessed values rises by 5% over this year's aggregate assessment, at what value must next year's school mill rate be set?

12. The total assessed value of property in Brockton has risen by $97 million from last year's figure of $1.563 billion. The property tax rate last year for city services was $0.94181 per $100 of assessed value. If the city's budget has increased by $750,000, what tax rate should it set for the current year?

Key Terms

Complex fraction

Denominator

Equivalent fractions

Improper fraction

Mill rate

Mixed number

Numerator

Proper fraction

Tax rate

Summary of Notation and Key Formulas

FORMULA (1-1) $\text{Rate} = \dfrac{\text{Portion}}{\text{Base}}$

FORMULA (1-2) $\text{Simple average} = \dfrac{\text{Sum of the values}}{\text{Total number of items}}$

FORMULA (1-3) $\text{Weighted average} = \dfrac{\text{Sum of (Weighting factor} \times \text{Value)}}{\text{Sum of weighting factors}}$

FORMULA (1-4) $\text{Property tax} = \dfrac{\text{Mill rate}}{1000} \times \text{Assessed value of the property}$

Review Problems

Answers to the odd-numbered review problems can be found in the end matter.

BASIC PROBLEMS

1. **LO1** Evaluate each of the following:

   a. $(2^3 - 3)^2 - 20 \div (2 + 2^3)$

   b. $4(2 \times 3^2 - 2^3)^2 \div (10 - 4 \times 5)$

   c. $81 \div (5^2 - 16) - 4(2^3 - 13)$

   d. $\$213.85\left(1 - 0.095 \times \frac{5}{12}\right)$

2. **LO4** What percent of $6.39 is $16.39?

3. **LO4** 80% of what amount is $100?

4. **LO4** 167.5% of what amount is $100?

5. **LO5** Jessica's $40,885 annual salary is paid weekly. She is paid at time and a half for any overtime beyond her regular workweek of 37 hours. What is her gross pay for a week in which she works 42 hours? Assume there are exactly 52 weeks in a year.

6. **LO6** An investor accumulated 750 common shares of Bank of Nova Scotia over a period of several months. He bought 200 shares at $50.26, 400 shares at $58.42, and 150 shares at $61.84. What was the investor's average cost per share?

INTERMEDIATE PROBLEMS

7. **LO1** Evaluate each of the following:

   a. $\dfrac{\$2315}{1 + 0.0825 \times \frac{77}{365}}$

   b. $\$325.75\left(1 + \dfrac{0.105}{4}\right)^2$

   c. $\dfrac{\$170}{\left(1 + \frac{0.0925}{2}\right)^3}$

8.   **LO4** The actual profit of $23,400 for the most recent fiscal quarter is 90% of the forecast profit. What was the forecast profit?

9.   **LO4** Renalda sold Westel stock that she purchased at $2.20 per share one year ago for 135% of the original price. At what price did she sell the stock?

10. **LO4** Through a calculation (on Canadian Individual Tax Returns) known as the "Old Age Security clawback," an individual receiving Old Age Security (OAS) benefits must repay an increasing portion of these benefits to the federal government as the individual's net income rises beyond a certain threshold. If the OAS clawback is 15% of net income exceeding $72,809, at what amount of net income must a taxpayer repay all $6839 of OAS benefits received in the year?

11. **LO5** Havel signed a listing agreement with a realtor. The commission rate is 4% on the first $200,000 of the selling price, and 2.5% on the remainder.

     a. What commission will Havel pay if he sells his home for $289,000?

     b. What is the average commission rate on the selling price?

12. **LO5** Luther is paid an annual salary of $56,600 based on a $37\frac{1}{2}$-hour workweek.

     a. What is his equivalent hourly wage? (Assume that a year has exactly 52 weeks.)

     b. What would be his total remuneration for a biweekly pay period of that year if he worked 4.5 hours of overtime at time and a half?

13. **LO5** Sonja is paid $42.50 per hour as a veterinarian. She is paid $1\frac{1}{2}$ times the regular rate for all time exceeding $7\frac{1}{2}$ hours in a day or $37\frac{1}{2}$ hours per week. Work on a statutory holiday is paid at double time. What were her gross earnings for a week in which she worked 6, 0, 3, $7\frac{1}{2}$, 9, $7\frac{1}{2}$, and 8 hours on Saturday to Friday, respectively, and the Monday was a statutory holiday?

14. **LO5** Istvan earns an annual salary of $61,000 as a manager with a provincial utility. He is paid biweekly. During a strike, he worked 33 hours more than the regular 75 hours for a 2-week pay period. What was his gross pay for that period if the company agreed to pay 1.5 times his equivalent hourly rate for overtime? (Assume that a year has exactly 52 weeks.)

15. **LO5** Marion receives a monthly base salary of $1000. On the first $10,000 of sales above her monthly quota of $20,000, she is paid a commission of 8%. On any additional sales, the commission rate is 10%. What were her gross earnings for the month of August, in which she had sales amounting to $38,670?

16. **LO6** One year ago Helga allocated the funds in her portfolio among five securities in the amounts listed in the following table. The rate of return on each security for the year is given in the third column of the table.

Security	Amount invested ($)	Rate of return for the year (%)
Company U shares	5000	30
Province V bonds	20,000	−3
Company W shares	8000	−15
Units in Fund X	25,000	13
Company Y shares	4500	45

Calculate the average rate of return for the entire portfolio.

ADVANCED PROBLEMS

17. **LO1** Evaluate each of the following.

    a. $\dfrac{\$827.69}{1 + 0.125 \times \frac{273}{365}} + \$531.49\left(1 + 0.125 \times \frac{41}{365}\right)$

    b. $\$550.45\left(1 + 0.0875 \times \frac{195}{365}\right) - \dfrac{\$376.29}{1 + 0.0875 \times \frac{99}{365}}$

    c. $\$1137\left(1 + \frac{0.0975}{12}\right)^2 + \dfrac{\$2643}{\left(1 + \frac{0.0975}{12}\right)^3}$

18. **LO5** Lauren's gross pay for July was $3188.35 on net sales totalling $88,630. If her base salary is $1000 per month, what is her rate of commission on sales exceeding her monthly quota of $40,000?

19. **LO6** Anthony began the year with $96,400 already invested in his Snow 'n Ice retail store. He withdrew $14,200 on March 1 and another $21,800 on April 1. On August 1, he invested $23,700, and on November 1, he contributed another $19,300. What was his average cumulative investment during the year? (Assume that each month has the same length.)

Appendix 1A: The Texas Instruments BA II PLUS Format Settings

The BA II PLUS calculator allows you to control some aspects of how values are displayed. Here we explain how you gain access to and make changes to a list of format settings.

    Immediately above the decimal key (in the bottom row of keys) you will find the word FORMAT. This position means that the "format" settings are the secondary function of the key. To access the list of settings, press the 2nd key followed by the decimal key. Hereafter, we will represent this keystroke sequence as 2nd Format .

    Press as 2nd Format . The calculator's display now shows

DEC =	n

where n is one of the digits, 0 to 9. Before we discuss this particular display, you should know that the display is revealing just the first item in the following vertical list:

DEC =	n
DEG	
US	mm-dd-yyyy
US	1,000.
Chn	

    You can move down the list using the scroll-down key ↓ . Scroll through the entire list by pressing ↓ four times. Return to the top of the list by pressing ↑ four times or by pressing ↓ one more time.

    The first item in the list indicates the number, n, of decimal places that will be shown in your display. A setting of "9" gives you a floating-decimal display. This means you will see either the *actual* number of decimal places for a terminating decimal, or *nine* decimal places for a nonterminating decimal. (Both alternatives are subject to the limit of 10 digits in the display.) The floating-decimal display is the best general-purpose setting for us. If the current setting is not "9," change it to "9" by pressing

9 Enter

Scroll down to the second item in the list (probably appearing as *DEG*). It does not concern us in business math. Scroll down to the third item. The factory setting is

$$US \quad 12\text{-}31\text{-}1990$$

This means that the format for calendar dates is the American format of mm-dd-yyyy (rather than the European format of dd-mm-yyyy.) Leave the calculator in the American format and scroll down to the fourth item. The factory setting is

$$US \quad 1,000.$$

This means that the calculator is using the American and British convention of employing commas for separators in numbers (rather than the continental European convention of using dots).

Scroll down to the fifth and last item. In the display you will see either "*Chn*" or "*AOS*." These are alternatives for how the calculator handles the sequence of mathematical operations you enter on the keypad. In the "*Chn*" (chain) calculation method, operations are performed in the sequence in which you enter them. That is, if you enter

$$5 \boxed{+} 4 \boxed{\times} 2 \boxed{=}$$

the calculator does the $5 + 4$ addition before the multiplication, giving a result of 18. (Don't try it while you are still in the Format list.)

In the "*AOS*" (Algebraic Operating System) calculation method, the calculator performs operations according to the standard order of operations presented in Section 1.1. The same calculation then yields the result 13, because the calculator does the multiplication before the addition.

With either "*Chn*" or "*AOS*" in the display, you can switch to the other calculation method by pressing $\boxed{\text{2nd}}$ $\boxed{\text{SET}}$. By the $\boxed{\text{SET}}$ key, we mean the key having SET as its secondary function. The setting you choose is a matter of personal preference. In either case, you can use the calculator's bracket keys to provide further control over the order of calculations.

Now close and exit from the settings list by pressing $\boxed{\text{2nd}}$ $\boxed{\text{QUIT}}$. By the $\boxed{\text{QUIT}}$ key, we mean the key having QUIT as its secondary function. The settings you have made will remain (even after the calculator is turned off) until you change them.

© JGI/Jamie Grill/Blend Images RF

CHAPTER 2

Review and Applications of Algebra

LEARNING OBJECTIVES

After completing this chapter, you will be able to:

LO1 Simplify algebraic expressions by extracting common factors and applying rules of exponents

LO2 Rearrange a formula or equation to isolate a particular variable

LO3 Solve a linear equation in one variable, and two linear equations in two variables

LO4 Graph a linear equation in two variables

LO5 Express a linear equation in slope-intercept form

LO6 Solve two equations in two unknowns by a graphical method

LO7 Solve "word problems" that lead to a linear equation in one unknown, or two linear equations in two unknowns

LO8 Solve problems involving percent change

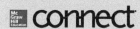 **connect** Throughout this chapter interactive charts and Help Me Solve It videos are marked with a ↗.

ALGEBRA IS A BRANCH OF mathematics in which letters or symbols are used to represent various items (variables). Quantitative relationships (equations) can then be expressed in a concise manner. Algebra has rules and procedures for working with these equations. The rules enable us to calculate values of unknown variables and to derive new relationships among variables.

Algebra is vital for the application of mathematics to business. If your algebraic skills are rusty, devote some extra time to exercises in this chapter.

We begin by reviewing basic terminology, techniques for simplifying algebraic expressions, procedures for solving linear equations, and the use of graphs to demonstrate the relationship between variables. Our refurbished skills will then be used in word problems and in applications of percent change.

TIP

How to Succeed in Business Mathematics

In Connect, there are a guide and a video entitled "How to Succeed in Business Mathematics." These can be found in Library Resources under Course-wide Content.

2.1   Operations with Algebraic Expressions

LO1   Definitions

We will use a simple example to illustrate some basic language of algebra. Suppose you work in the payroll department of a large retail store. Every month you must calculate each employee's gross earnings. The sales people are paid a base salary of $2500 per month plus a commission of 4% of sales. The gross earnings of a salesperson in a month are calculated using

$$\$2500 + 0.04 \times (\text{Sales for the month})$$

The only quantity that varies from one salesperson to another, and from one month to another, is the amount of each individual's sales. "Sales for the month" is therefore the mathematical *variable* in this calculation. In algebra we use a letter or symbol to represent a mathematical variable. Using s to represent "sales for the month," we can write the following algebraic expression to represent each salesperson's gross monthly earnings:

$$\$2500 + 0.04s$$

An **algebraic expression** indicates the mathematical operations to be carried out on a combination of numbers and variables. To obtain any salesperson's gross earnings, we substitute that person's sales for the month as the value for s. Following the rules for order of operations, we must first multiply the sales by 0.04 and then add $2500.

The components of an algebraic expression that are separated by addition or subtraction signs are called **terms**. This particular expression has two terms: $2500 and $0.04s$. An expression containing only one term is called a **monomial**. A **binomial** expression has two terms, and a **trinomial** has three terms. The name **polynomial** may be used for any expression with more than one term.

Each term in an expression consists of one or more **factors** separated by multiplication or division signs. (Multiplication is implied by writing factors side by side with no multiplication symbol between them.) The numerical factor in a term is called the **numerical coefficient**, and the variable factors together are called the **literal coefficient**. The first term in our sample binomial contains only one factor: $2500. The second term contains two factors: the numerical coefficient 0.04 and the literal coefficient s. To summarize:

Term	Factor(s)	Numerical coefficient	Literal coefficient
$2500	$2500	$2500	None
$0.04s$	$0.04, s$	0.04	s

As a further example, consider the trinomial expression $3x^2 + xy - 6y^2$. The following chart identifies the factors, and numerical and literal coefficients for each of the three terms in the expression.

Term	Factors	Numerical coefficient	Literal coefficient
$3x^2$	$3, x, x$	3	x^2
xy	x, y	1	xy
$-6y^2$	$-6, y, y$	-6	y^2

Addition and Subtraction

Sometimes an algebraic expression may be simplified by adding or subtracting certain terms before any values are substituted for the variables. Terms with the same *literal* coefficients are called **like terms**. Only like terms may be directly added or subtracted. Addition or subtraction of like terms is performed by adding or subtracting their numerical coefficients while keeping their common literal coefficient, for example $2xy + 3xy = 5xy$. Adding or subtracting like terms is often referred to as *collecting* or *combining* like terms.

EXAMPLE 2.1A | Simplifying Algebraic Expressions by Combining Like Terms

a. $3a - 4b - 7a + 9b$

$= 3a - 7a - 4b + 9b$

$= (3 - 7)a + (-4 + 9)b$

$= -4a + 5b$

$3a$ and $-7a$ are like terms; $-4b$ and $9b$ are like terms.

Combine the numerical coefficients of like terms.

b. $0.2x + 5x^2 + \dfrac{x}{4} - x + 3$

$= 5x^2 + (0.2 + 0.25 - 1)x + 3$

$= 5x^2 - 0.55x + 3$

Convert numerical coefficients to their decimal equivalents.

Then combine the like terms.

c. $\dfrac{2x}{1.25} - \dfrac{4}{5} - 1\dfrac{3}{4}x$

$= 1.6x - 0.8 - 1.75x$

$= -0.15x - 0.8$

Convert numerical coefficients to their decimal equivalents.

Then combine the like terms.

d. $x\left(1 + 0.12 \times \frac{241}{365}\right) + \dfrac{2x}{1 + 0.12 \times \frac{81}{365}}$

$= 1.07923x + \dfrac{2x}{1.02663}$

$= (1.07923 + 1.94812)x$

$= 3.02735x$

Evaluate the numerical coefficients.

Combine the like terms.

➡ **Check your understanding:** Simplify the following algebraic expression by combining like terms: $\frac{3x}{1.0164} + 1.049x - x$. Maintain five-figure accuracy. (Answer: $3.0006x$)

▮▮▶ **Related problem:** #7 in Exercise 2.1

b.
$$0.5x - 0.75 + 7x = 3x + 1.5$$
$$0.5x - 0.75 + 7x - 3x = 1.5 \qquad \text{Transpose } 3x \text{ to the LHS and change its sign.}$$
$$4.5x - 0.75 = 1.5$$
$$4.5x = 1.5 + 0.75 \qquad \text{Transpose } -0.75 \text{ to the RHS and change its sign.}$$
$$4.5x = 2.25$$
$$x = \frac{2.25}{4.5} \qquad \text{Divide both sides by the numerical coefficient of } x.$$
$$x = 0.5$$

Verification:
LHS $= 0.5(0.5) - 0.75 + 7(0.5) = 0.25 - 0.75 + 3.5 = 3.0$
RHS $= 3(0.5) + 1.5 = 1.5 + 1.5 = 3.0$

Since LHS $=$ RHS, $x = 0.5$ is the root, or solution.

➡ **Check your understanding:** Solve the following equation and verify the solution.
$6x + 0.75x - 73.5 = 2x + 12$. (Answer: $x = 18$, LHS $= 48$, RHS $= 48$)

▮▮▶ **Related problem:** #1 in Exercise 2.3

EXAMPLE 2.3B	Solving a Linear Equation Having Decimal-Fraction Coefficients

Solve the following equation for x (accurate to the cent). Verify the solution.

$$\frac{x}{1 + 0.11 \times \frac{75}{365}} + 2x\left(1 + 0.11 \times \frac{92}{365}\right) = \$1150.96$$

SOLUTION

In this equation, the numerical coefficients are not simple numbers as in the previous example. These coefficients should be reduced to a single number (which may not be an integer) by performing the indicated operations. Then carry on with the usual three-step procedure for solving a linear equation in one unknown.

$$\frac{x}{1.0226027} + 2x(1.0277260) = \$1150.96$$
$$0.9778969x + 2.055452x = \$1150.96$$
$$3.033349x = \$1150.96$$
$$x = \frac{\$1150.96}{3.033349}$$
$$= \$379.44$$

Verification:
$$\text{LHS} = \frac{\$379.44}{1 + 0.11 \times \frac{75}{365}} + 2(\$379.44)\left(1 + 0.11 \times \frac{92}{365}\right)$$
$$= \frac{\$379.44}{1.0226027} + 2(\$379.44)(1.0277260)$$
$$= \$371.053 + \$779.921$$
$$= \$1150.97$$
$$= \text{RHS}$$

The $0.01 difference between the LHS and the RHS arises from rounding the solution $x = \$379.4354$ to the nearest cent and then using the rounded value for the verification.

BA II PLUS Keystrokes
(when set for "*AOS*" calculations)

Step 1: Obtain the coefficient of x in the first term and save in memory.

1 [+] 0.11 [×] 75 [÷] 365
[=] [1/x] [STO] [1]

Step 2: Obtain the coefficient of x in the second term.

2 [×] [( ] 1 [+] 0.11 [×]
92 [÷] 365 [ )] [=]

Step 3: Recall and add the first term's coefficient. Save this sum.

[+] [RCL] [1] [=] [STO] [2]

Step 4: Divide the right side by this saved combined coefficient of x.

1150.96 [÷] [RCL] [2] [=]

Ans: 379.44

➡ **Check your understanding:** Solve the following equation for x (accurate to the cent). Verify the solution. $3x(1 + 0.18 \times \frac{7}{12}) + \dfrac{x}{1 + 0.18 \times \frac{119}{365}} = \$2755.47$ (Answer: $x = \$646.89$)

▰▶ **Related problem:** #25 in Exercise 2.3

Solving Two Linear Equations in Two Unknowns

A single linear equation in one unknown has only one solution. In contrast, a single linear equation in two variables has an *infinite* number of solutions. For example, the equation $y = x + 2$ has solutions $(x, y) = (0, 2)$, $(1, 3)$, $(2, 4)$, and so on.

If, however, *two* linear equations in two unknowns must be satisfied *at the same time*, there is *only one solution*. In other words, only one pair of values will satisfy *both* equations.

To find this solution, we will combine the two equations in a way that will eliminate one variable, leaving a single linear equation in the other variable. We will illustrate a technique using the following pair of equations. The equations are numbered for ease of reference.

$$2x - 3y = -6 \qquad ①$$
$$x + y = 2 \qquad ②$$

It is legitimate to add the respective sides of two equations, or to subtract the respective sides of two equations. For example, let us add equations ① and ②.

$$
\begin{array}{ll}
2x - 3y = -6 & ① \\
\underline{x + y = 2} & ② \\
3x - 2y = -4 & ① + ②
\end{array}
$$

If we subtract equation ② from equation ①, we have:

$$
\begin{array}{ll}
2x - 3y = -6 & ① \\
\underline{x + y = 2} & ② \\
x - 4y = -8 & ① - ②
\end{array}
$$

Although both procedures are legal, neither the addition nor the subtraction of the two equations has moved us closer to a solution—we have merely produced more equations containing two unknowns.

The following observations suggest a technique for solving the equations. If the numerical coefficient of x in equation ② had been 2, the subtraction ① − ② would produce an equation without a term in x. Furthermore, you can achieve this outcome if you multiply both sides of equation ② by 2 *before* the subtraction. Then the equations before subtraction are

$$
\begin{array}{ll}
① & 2x - 3y = -6 \\
② \times 2: & \underline{2x + 2y = 4} \\
\text{Subtraction gives:} & -5y = -10 \\
& y = \dfrac{-10}{-5} = 2
\end{array}
$$

You can now obtain the solution for the other variable by substituting $y = 2$ into either of the original equations. Substitution into equation ① gives

$$
\begin{array}{ll}
2x - 3(2) = -6 \\
2x = -6 + 6 \\
x = 0
\end{array}
$$

The solution is $x = 0$, $y = 2$ or $(x, y) = (0, 2)$. You may verify this solution by substituting $(x, y) = (0, 2)$ into the equation that was not used in the preceding step. That is, substitute $x = 0$ and $y = 2$ into the left side of equation ② giving

$$x + y = 0 + 2 = 2$$

Since the value obtained for the left side of equation ② equals the value of the right side, we have verified that $(x, y) = (0, 2)$ is the solution to the pair of equations.

Alternatively, you can solve the two equations by eliminating y instead of x. To eliminate y, multiply equation ② by 3, and then *add* it to the original equation ①.

In general, it may be necessary to multiply *each* equation by a different number to set up the elimination of one variable. Suppose the objective is to eliminate x. You can always obtain identical coefficients for x in both equations by

1. Multiplying the first equation by the coefficient of x from the second equation, and then
2. Multiplying the second equation by the coefficient of x from the first equation (in its original form).

Finally, subtract either one of the revised equations from the other equation to eliminate x.

TIP

Treat Both Sides of an Equation in the Same Way

In the preceding Steps 1 and 2, remember to multiply *every term* on *both sides* of the equation by the chosen number.

The following examples demonstrate the technique.

EXAMPLE 2.3C	Solving Two Equations Having Integer Coefficients

Solve the following pair of equations to three-figure accuracy. Check the solution.

$$7x - 5y = 3 \quad ①$$
$$5x + 2y = 9 \quad ②$$

SOLUTION

We begin by manipulating equations ① and ② to eliminate one of the variables—either x or y. In this example, we will choose to eliminate y. To eliminate y, first make the numerical coefficients of y the same in both equations:

$$① \times 2: \qquad 14x - 10y = 6$$
$$② \times -5: \qquad -25x - 10y = -45$$

Then, subtract to give

$$39x = 51$$
$$x = \frac{51}{39} = 1.308$$

We must now substitute this value for x into one of the original equations. We will choose to substitute this value for x into equation ②. Solving for y we have

$$5(1.308) + 2y = 9$$
$$2y = 9 - 6.540$$
$$y = 1.230$$

To three figures, the solution is $x = 1.31$, $y = 1.23$.

Check:

Since we chose to substitute $x = 1.308$ into equation ② to solve for y, we must use the *other* equation, equation ①, when verifying the solution. Substitute $x = 1.308$ and $y = 1.230$ into equation ①:

$$\text{LHS of ①} = 7(1.308) - 5(1.230)$$
$$= 3.006$$
$$= \text{RHS of ① to two figures.}$$

This is one of a small minority of cases wherein four-figure accuracy in intermediate calculations does not give three-figure accuracy in the final result.

➡ **Check your understanding:** Solve the following pair of equations to three-figure accuracy. Check the solution. $24a - 44b = -160.0$ ①
$$13a + 16b = \;\;\; 399.3 \quad ② \text{ (Answer: } a = 15.7, b = 12.2)$$

▰▰▶ **Related problem:** #11 in Exercise 2.3

EXAMPLE 2.3D	Solving Two Equations Having Decimal-Fraction Coefficients

Solve the following pair of equations to three-figure accuracy. Check the solution.

$$1.9a + 3.8b = 85.5 \quad ①$$
$$3.4a - 5.1b = -49.3 \quad ②$$

SOLUTION

We have the choice to plan to eliminate either a or b. In this case, we will choose to eliminate a. To begin, make the coefficient of a the same in both equations.

$$\begin{array}{llr}
① \times 3.4\text{:} & 6.46a + 12.92b = & 290.7 \\
② \times 1.9\text{:} & 6.46a - \;\;\;9.69b = & -93.67 \\
\hline
\text{Subtract:} & 22.61b = & 384.37 \\
& b = & 17.00
\end{array}$$

Substitute $b = 17.00$ into either equation ① or ②. We will opt to substitute into equation ①:

$$1.9a + 3.8(17.00) = 85.5$$
$$a = \frac{85.5 - 3.8(17.00)}{1.9}$$
$$= 11.00$$

To three figures, the solution is $a = 11.0$, $b = 17.0$.

Check:

Since we solved for a by substituting $b = 17.00$ into equation ①, we must now use equation ② to verify our answer. Substitute $a = 11.0$ and $b = 17.0$ into equation ②:

$$\text{LHS of ②} = 3.4(11.0) - 5.1(17.0)$$
$$= 37.4 - 86.7$$
$$= -49.3$$
$$= \text{RHS of ②}$$

➡ **Check your understanding:** Solve the following pair of equations to five-figure accuracy. Check the solution. $0.33e + 1.67f = 292$ ①
$$1.2e + 0.61f = 377 \quad ② \text{ (Answer: } e = 250.45, f = 125.36)$$

▰▰▶ **Related problem:** #16 in Exercise 2.3

EXERCISE 2.3

Answers to the odd-numbered problems can be found in the end matter.

BASIC PROBLEMS

Solve the following equations.

1. $10a + 10 = 12 + 9a$
2. $29 - 4y = 2y - 7$
3. $0.5(x - 3) = 20$
4. $\frac{1}{3}(x - 2) = 4$
5. $y = 192 + 0.04y$
6. $x - 0.025x = 341.25$
7. $12x - 4(2x - 1) = 6(x + 1) - 3$
8. $3y - 4 = 3(y + 6) - 2(y + 3)$
9. $8 - 0.5(x + 3) = 0.25(x - 1)$
10. $5(2 - c) = 10(2c - 4) - 6(3c + 1)$

INTERMEDIATE PROBLEMS

Solve each of the following pairs of equations. Verify your solution in each case.

11. $x - y = 2$
    $3x + 4y = 20$
12. $y - 3x = 11$
    $5x + 30 = 4y$
13. $7p - 3q = 23$
    $-2p - 3q = 5$
14. $y = 2x$
    $7x - y = 35$

Solve each of the following pairs of equations to three-figure accuracy. Verify your solution in each case.

15. $-3c + d = -500$
    $0.7c + 0.2d = 550$
16. $0.03x + 0.05y = 51$
    $0.8x - 0.7y = 140$
17. $2v + 6w = 1$
    $-9w + 10v = 18$
18. $2.5a + 2b = 11$
    $8a + 3.5b = 13$
19. $37x - 63y = 235$
    $18x + 26y = 468$
20. $68.9n - 38.5m = 57$
    $45.1n - 79.4m = -658$

ADVANCED PROBLEMS

Solve the following equations. The solutions should be accurate to the cent.

21. $\dfrac{x}{1.1^2} + 2x(1.1)^3 = \$1000$

22. $\dfrac{3x}{1.025^6} + x(1.025)^8 = \$2641.35$

23. $\dfrac{2x}{1.03^7} + x + x(1.03)^{10} = \$1000 + \dfrac{\$2000}{1.03^4}$

24. $x(1.05)^3 + \$1000 + \dfrac{x}{1.05^7} = \dfrac{\$5000}{1.05^2}$

25. $x\left(1 + 0.095 \times \frac{84}{365}\right) + \dfrac{2x}{1 + 0.095 \times \frac{108}{365}} = \$1160.20$

2.4   Solving Linear Equations Graphically

The relationship between two variables may be presented in a variety of ways. Three common methods are

- A table listing pairs of values of the two variables
- An algebraic equation involving the two variables
- A graph depicting the relationship between the two variables

So far in this chapter we have limited ourselves to expressing the relationship between variables using algebraic equations. We will now turn our attention to the use of graphs to represent that relationship. The graphical presentation is best for quickly giving an impression of the nature of the relationship between the two variables. It also allows a user to *quickly estimate* the value of one variable that corresponds to any selected value of the other variable.

An algebraic equation has the advantage of expressing the relationship with the greatest degree of precision. Graphical analysis is usually limited to three-figure precision.

LO4   Graphing a Linear Equation in Two Unknowns

The notation used to indicate that a mathematical relationship exists between two variables, x and y, is

$$y = f(x)$$

which is read "y is a function of x." A pair of numerical values of the variables, customarily written in the order (x, y), is said to *satisfy* the equation if the two sides of the equation are equal after substitution of the values.

A single pair of (x, y) values gives a point when plotted on graph paper. In the context of graphing, this pair of values is called the *coordinates* of the point. A graph of the equation $y = f(x)$ is a plot of all pairs of (x, y) values within a certain range that satisfy the equation. If the x-coordinate and the y-coordinate of *any* point on a plotted curve are substituted into the corresponding algebraic equation, the two sides of the equation will have the same numerical value.

In practice, we obtain the graph of an equation through the following steps:

1. Construct a *table of values* consisting of pairs of (x, y) values that satisfy the equation. Each pair is obtained by assigning a value to one variable and then solving the resulting equation in one unknown for the other variable.

2. Construct and label the x-axis and the y-axis to accommodate the range of values in the table. By convention, the horizontal axis is the x-axis and the vertical axis is the y-axis, like this:

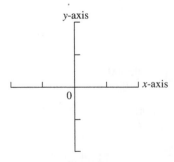

3. Plot the (x, y) pairs from the table as the (x, y) coordinates of points on the graph.

4. Connect the plotted points with a *smooth* curve.

EXAMPLE 2.4A	Graphing a Linear Equation in Two Variables

Graph the equation $2x - 3y = -6$ over the range $x = -6$ to $x = 6$.

SOLUTION

The first step listed above is to construct a table of values. Since the range over which the graph is to be plotted is specified in terms of x, it is natural to assign to x a series of values (such as $x = -6, -3, 0, 3, 6$) covering the range. Since we will be repeatedly solving the equation for y, we should rearrange the equation so that y is isolated on one side.

Transposing $2x$ to the right side and dividing both sides by -3, we obtain

$$y = \tfrac{2}{3}x + 2$$

Now substitute a few values for x over the range $x = -6$ to $x = 6$:

$$x = -6: \qquad y = \tfrac{2}{3}(-6) + 2 = -2$$
$$x = -3: \qquad y = \tfrac{2}{3}(-3) + 2 = 0$$
$$x = 0: \qquad y = \tfrac{2}{3}(0) + 2 = 2$$
$$x = 3: \qquad y = \tfrac{2}{3}(3) + 2 = 4$$
$$x = 6: \qquad y = \tfrac{2}{3}(6) + 2 = 6$$

The table of values summarizing these (x, y) pairs is:

x:	−6	−3	0	3	6	← Assigned x values
y:	−2	0	2	4	6	← Calculated y values

The next step is to draw the two axes, with the x-axis including the range from −6 to +6 and the y-axis encompassing the range from −2 to +6. The five points can then be plotted and a smooth line drawn to connect the points.

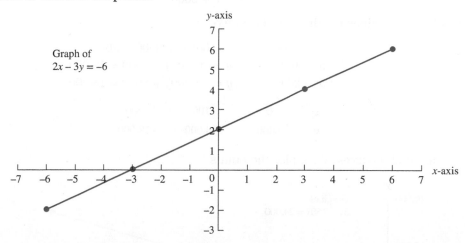

Graph of
$2x - 3y = -6$

The most notable feature about the graph is that the plotted points lie on a straight line. This is a general outcome for linear equations in two variables and is the reason they are called *linear* equations.

▶ **Check your understanding:** What two additional points of (x, y) pairs would be helpful to find if the original instructions had been to graph the equation over the range $x = -9$ to $x = 9$? (Answer: $x = -9, y = -4$ and $x = 9, y = 8$)

▶ **Related problem:** #1 in Exercise 2.4

TIP

Suggestions and Shortcuts

- To construct the graph of a *linear* equation, it is sufficient to have just two (x, y) pairs in the table of values. Plotting a third point provides a check of your calculations. If all three points do not lie on a straight line, then you have made an error in calculating the coordinates of the points or in plotting the points.

- For the best precision in constructing the graph of a linear equation, you should use the two points near the ends of the range over which the graph is to be drawn.

- The easiest (x, y) pair to determine comes from assigning the value 0 to x.

- If x has a fractional coefficient, assign values to x that are a multiple of the coefficient's denominator. This makes the calculations easier and is likely to yield "nicer" values to plot for y. In the preceding example, because the coefficient of x was $\frac{2}{3}$, we used values for x that were multiples of 3.

EXAMPLE 2.4B	Graphing a Linear Equation in Two Variables

Graph the equation $3y - 150x = 24,000$ over the range $x = 0$ to $x = 200$.

SOLUTION

Manipulate the equation to isolate y on the left side. To begin, transpose $-150x$, with a change of sign, from the left side to the right side of the equation:

$$3y = 150x + 24,000$$

Divide both sides by 3 to isolate y on the left side of the equation:

$$y = 50x + 8000$$

Construct a table of values for the stated range of x:

$$x = \quad 0: \qquad y = 50(0) + 8000 = 8000$$
$$x = 100: \qquad y = 50(100) + 8000 = 13,000$$
$$x = 200: \qquad y = 50(200) + 8000 = 18,000$$

x:	0	100	200
y:	8000	13,000	18,000

Construct and label the axes. Then plot the points.

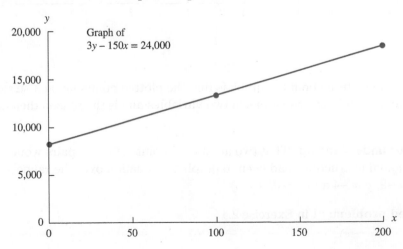

> ➡ **Check your understanding:** How would your table of values change if you had been asked to graph the equation over the range $x = -200$ to $x = 200$? (Answer: Solving the equation for $x = -200$, would provide the (x, y) pair $x = -200$, $y = -2000$. Plotting this point, together with the points $x = 0$, $y = 8000$ and $x = 200$, $y = 18{,}000$ would provide the outermost points and midpoint of the line.)
>
> ▰▰▸ **Related problem:** #4 in Exercise 2.4

LO5   The Slope-Intercept Form of a Linear Equation

In Examples 2.4A and 2.4B we rearranged the given linear equations so as to isolate y on the left side. Accordingly,

$$2x - 3y = -6 \qquad \text{was expressed as} \quad y = \tfrac{2}{3}x + 2$$

and

$$3y - 150x = 24{,}000 \quad \text{was expressed as} \quad y = 50x + 8000$$

We did this to simplify the calculations for creating tables of values to plot. A further benefit of expressing a linear equation in this form is that we can predict two important characteristics of the equation's straight-line graph.

First note that when $x = 0$, the first equation gives $y = 2$ and the second gives $y = 8000$. As you can see if you look back to their graphs, these are the values for y where the straight lines cross the y-axis. We call such a value the **y-intercept** of a straight line.

The second property we can predict is a measure of the steepness of the line. To understand this, consider the following table of values for $y = 50x + 8000$ over the range $x = 0$ to $x = 4$.

x:	0	1	2	3	4
y:	8000	8050	8100	8150	8200

Note that every time x increases by 1, y increases by 50 because 50 is the coefficient of x in the rearranged equation. The change in the y-coordinate per unit change in the x-coordinate is called the **slope** of the straight line. The steeper the line, the greater the value of the slope.

It is a general result that, if you express a linear equation in the form

$$y = mx + b$$

where m and b represent constants, then

$$\text{slope} = m \quad \text{and} \quad y\text{-intercept} = b$$

Consequently, it is referred to as the *slope-intercept form* of the equation of a straight line.

This knowledge enables us to write an equation corresponding to a given straight-line graph. Consider the linear relationship displayed below. The y-intercept is clearly $b = 4$. To obtain the slope, first select any two points lying near opposite ends of the straight line. We have chosen the points $(-2, 8)$ and $(5, -6)$.

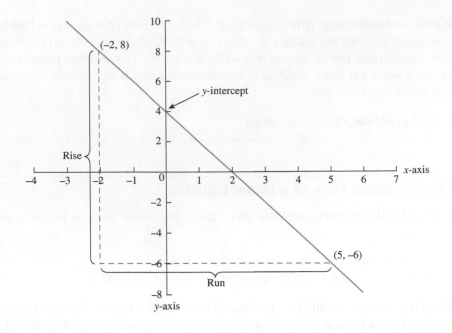

In general,

$$\text{Slope, } m = \frac{\text{Rise}}{\text{Run}} = \frac{\text{Vertical distance between the points}}{\text{Horizontal distance between the points}} = \frac{y_2 - y_1}{x_2 - x_1}$$

where (x_1, y_1) and (x_2, y_2) represent the coordinates of the two points. In this case,

$$m = \frac{(-6) - (8)}{(5) - (-2)} = \frac{-14}{7} = -2$$

Any line that slopes downward to the right has a negative slope. Any line sloping upward to the right has a positive slope.

The final step is to substitute the values for m and b in the general form $y = mx + b$. The equation of the straight line in the graph is

$$y = -2x + 4$$

LO6   **Solving Two Equations in Two Unknowns Graphically**

Let us plot on the same set of axes both of the following linear equations over the range $x = -4$ to $x = 4$.

$$x - 2y = -2 \quad ①$$
$$x + y = \quad 4 \quad ②$$

For each equation, we will first obtain the coordinates of the two points at opposite ends of the graphing range. Rearranging both equations to isolate y on the left side, we obtain

$$y = 1 + 0.5x \quad ①$$
$$y = 4 - \quad x \quad ②$$

For each equation, calculate the y-coordinates when $x = -4$ and $x = 4$.

$y = 1 + 0.5x$ ①

x:	−4	4
y:	−1	3

$y = 4 - x$ ②

x:	−4	4
y:	8	0

Plot the two points for each equation and connect them by a straight line. The resulting graph is shown as follows. The coordinates of any point on a line satisfy that line's equation. But there is only one point that satisfies *both* equations, because there is only one point that lies on *both* lines—the intersection point. In the present case, $(x, y) = (2, 2)$ is the *solution* to equations ① and ②.

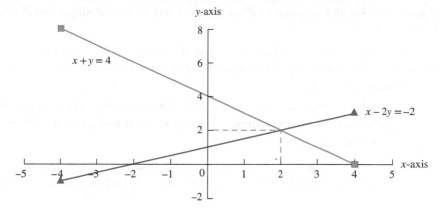

You can solve any two linear equations in two unknowns by this approach. However, when the coefficients in the equations are not small integers or simple fractions, this method can be time-consuming and "messy." The solution is limited to three-figure accuracy (at best) because of the imprecision of plotting points and reading the graph to find the coordinates of the intersection point.

EXERCISE 2.4

Answers to the odd-numbered problems can be found in the end matter.

BASIC PROBLEMS

Graph each of the equations in Problems 1 to 5. Visit Connect and use the Graph Templates found under the Student Resources for Chapter 2.

1. $-2x + y = 0$ over the range $x = -3$ to $x = 6$
2. $2x + y = 4$ over the range $x = -3$ to $x = 6$
3. $3x - 4y + 12 = 0$ over the range $x = -8$ to $x = 12$
4. $y = 60x + 6000$ over the range $x = 0$ to $x = 50$
5. $y = 4.5x + 5000$ over the range $x = 0$ to $x = 6000$
6. Determine the slope and y-intercept of each of the following equations.
   a. $2x = 3y + 4$
   b. $8 - 3x = 2y$
   c. $8x - 2y - 3 = 0$
   d. $6x = 9y$

INTERMEDIATE PROBLEMS

7. A plumber charges a flat $100 for a home service call plus $20 per 15 minutes of labour. Write an equation for calculating the total charges, C, in terms of the hours of labour, H. If you were to plot a graph of C vs. H, what would be the slope and C-intercept of the line?
8. In his sales job, Ehud earns a base salary of $1500 per month plus a commission of 5% on sales revenue. Write an equation for calculating his gross earnings, E, for a month in terms of his sales revenue, R. If you were to plot a graph of E vs. R, what would be the slope and E-intercept of the line?

9. The formula for converting from Celsius temperatures, C, to Fahrenheit temperatures, F, is $F = \frac{9}{5}C + 32$.

   a. If you were to plot a graph of F vs. C, what would be the slope and F-intercept of the line?

   b. The slope represents the change in F per unit change in C. Use the value of the slope to determine the increase in Fahrenheit temperature corresponding to a 10 Celsius–degree temperature increase.

   c. Rearrange the given formula to obtain a formula for converting from Fahrenheit temperatures to Celsius temperatures. What would be the slope and C-intercept if C vs. F were plotted on a graph?

Use the graphical method to solve each of the pairs of equations in Problems 10 to 13. Visit Connect and use the Graph Templates found under the Student Resources for Chapter 2.

10. $x + y = 2$
    $x = 5$

11. $x - 3y = 3$
    $y = -2$

12. $x + y = 4$
    $2x - y = 8$

13. $y - 3x = 11$
    $5x + 30 = 4y$

INTERMEDIATE PROBLEM

14. Funshade Corp. manufactures and sells sunglasses for a wholesale price of $6 each. Therefore, its total revenue, TR, from the sale of X pairs of sunglasses in a year is

$$TR = \$6X$$

It costs Funshade Corp. $2 for materials and labour to produce each pair of glasses. In addition, Funshade expects to incur $80,000 of other costs during a year. Therefore, Funshade's total costs for the year, TC, are expected to be

$$TC = \$2X + \$80,000$$

Net income, NI, is found by subtracting total costs, TC, from total revenue, TR. Funshade's expected net income, NI, for the year will be

$$NI = TR - TC$$
$$= \$6X - (\$2X + \$80,000)$$
$$= \$4X - \$80,000$$

   a. What is the slope and TR-intercept of a TR vs. X plot?

   b. What is the slope and TC-intercept of a TC vs. X plot?

   c. What is the slope and NI-intercept of an NI vs. X plot?

   d. Which of the three plotted lines is steepest?

   e. How much does NI increase for each pair of sunglasses sold?

   f. If Funshade were able to reduce its materials and labour cost to $1.75 per pair of sunglasses, state for each plotted line whether its slope would increase, decrease, or remain unchanged.

2.5 Solving Word Problems

LO4   In the preceding two sections, we reviewed procedures for solving linear equations. With practice, solving linear equations becomes a mechanical procedure that follows a fairly routine series of steps. However, *practical* applications of mathematics rarely come as given equations that need only to be solved. Instead, a problem is presented to us in a more informal descriptive manner. We must deduce mathematical relationships from the given information and from our broader knowledge of general concepts and principles.

It is a large step to go from just solving *given* equations to *creating* one or more equations from a word problem and then solving them. Constructing algebraic equations from given information cannot be reduced to mechanical steps (such as those previously listed for solving linear equations). We can, however, outline a *general approach* for solving word problems.

A General Approach for Solving Problems

Particularly if you are having difficulty with a word problem, use the following procedure to reduce the solution to small steps. Let us assume for now that there is only one unknown in the problem.

Step 1: *Read the entire problem* to gain a sense of the topic involved and what is being asked. For example, you might find that the problem involves a loan repayment and you are asked to determine the size of the monthly payment.

Step 2: Now take pencil and paper in hand. On a second reading, *extract and label the given data. Identify the unknown quantity and choose a symbol for it. Draw and label a diagram if appropriate.* There are standard symbols for many quantities. These should be used to label numerical values as they are extracted. Otherwise, use one or two words to identify each value. Choose a symbol to represent the unknown quantity. Diagrams are particularly useful in problems involving multiple payments over a period of time. Incorporate as much data as possible in the diagram.

Step 3: *Create a word equation* that relates what you know (the data) to what you want to know (the unknown quantity). The word equation may be based on a fundamental principle of broad application, or it may be a unique relationship stated or implied in the problem itself. An example of a word equation is

$$\text{Profit} = \text{Revenues} - \text{Expenses}$$

This equation would typically *not* be given to you in the question. It would be assumed that you know the fundamental relationship among revenues, expenses, and profit. When solving word problems, think about the situation being described and consider whether there are any broad principles that you can apply to that situation. Take the time to write that principle in full words. For example, in a problem involving a price reduction, a fundamental relationship that you could draw upon would be

$$\text{Reduced selling price} = \text{Regular selling price} - \text{Amount of the price reduction}$$

In other problems, there may not be any broad principles that you are expected to use. In these cases, the relationships among the variables will be given to you in the problem. For example, if you are told that a bookstore sells twice as many softcover books as hardcover books, the relationship might be written

$$\text{Number of softcover books sold} = 2(\text{Number of hardcover books sold})$$

Step 4: *Convert the word equation to an algebraic equation.* Express the words and phrases in the word equation in terms of the unknown quantity's symbol and the numerical values extracted in Step 2.

Step 5: *Solve the equation.* Check that the answer is reasonable. Write a concluding statement that directly responds to the question asked.

Summary of the Steps for Solving Word Problems

1. Read the entire problem.

2. Extract and label the data. Identify the unknown quantity and specify its symbol. Draw and label a diagram if appropriate.

3. Create a word equation that relates the given data to the unknown quantity.

4. Convert the word equation to an algebraic equation.

5. Solve the equation.

To remember the steps, think of "REDWAS" representing **R**ead, **E**xtract & **D**raw, **W**ord equation, **A**lgebraic equation, and **S**olve.

TIP

Overcoming That Old "I Just Can't Seem to Get Started" Feeling

Have you ever stared and stared at a word problem without getting anywhere? (If you have, you belong to a rather large club.) Think about how you have approached word problems in the past. Did you begin by trying to find a formula in which to substitute the given numbers? If so, you were really trying to do Steps 1, 2, 3, and 4 all at once! It's not surprising that you became stumped on problems of even moderate difficulty. Even if you happen to hit on the right formula and calculate the right answer, the "formula browsing" approach is not an effective way to "do" mathematics. It omits Step 3, wherein you bring mathematical ideas and concepts to bear on a particular situation. For problems of any complexity, you should use our five-step ladder instead of trying to leap tall problems in a single bound.

The following examples illustrate the five-step approach for solving word problems. It is very important that you take the time to actively read the following examples. Many word problems share common patterns. By taking the time to study these examples, you will learn approaches that you can apply to many of the problems in the Exercise at the end of this section, and improve your fluency with word problems in general.

EXAMPLE 2.5A | **Calculating the Base or Initial Value**

A retailer reduced his prices by 15% for a holiday sale. What was the regular price of an item on sale at $123.25?

SOLUTION

Step 1: Read the problem. (This step is assumed hereafter.)

Step 2: Extract and label the data. Identify the unknown and define its symbol.

$$\text{Discount rate} = 15\% \quad \text{Sale price} = \$123.25$$

Let P represent the regular price.

Step 3: Create a word equation that relates the given data to the unknown quantity.

$$\text{Sale price} = \text{Regular price} - \text{Price reduction}$$
$$= \text{Regular price} - (\text{Discount rate} \times \text{Regular price})$$

Step 4: Convert the word equation to an algebraic equation.

$$\$123.25 = P - 0.15P$$

Step 5: Solve the equation.

$$\$123.25 = 0.85P$$

$$P = \frac{\$123.25}{0.85} = \$145$$

The original price of the item was $145.

➡ **Check your understanding:** If a retailer reduced his prices by 35% for a winter sale, what would the regular price be for an item that is now reduced to $175? (Answer: $269.23)

▮▮▮▷ **Related problem:** #1 in Exercise 2.5

EXAMPLE 2.5B	A Problem on Mixtures

Biko Confectionery intends to prepare and sell a Premier Nut Mix consisting of almonds and cashews. The manager obtains almonds at a wholesale cost of $10.38 per kilogram and cashews at a cost of $15.50 per kilogram. He wants to mix the nuts in a proportion that produces 12 kilograms of Premier Mix having an effective wholesale cost no greater than $12.30 per kilogram. What is the maximum weight of cashews that can be put in the mix?

SOLUTION

Step 2: Let C represent the weight of cashews in a 12-kilogram batch.

Type of nut	Cost per kg	Weight (kg)
Cashews	$15.50	C
Almonds	$10.38	$12 - C$
Premier Mix	$12.30 (maximum)	12

Step 3: The maximum cost of the mix will be reached when the maximum proportion of the more expensive component (cashews) is used.

Total cost of Premier mix = Total cost of cashews + Total cost of almonds

where each total cost is the product of the number of kilograms and the cost per kilogram.

Step 4: $\$12.30(12) = \$15.50C + \$10.38(12 - C)$

Step 5:
$$\$147.60 = \$15.50C + \$124.56 - \$10.38C$$
$$\$147.60 - \$124.56 = \$15.50C - \$10.38C$$
$$\$23.04 = \$5.12C$$
$$C = \frac{\$23.04}{\$5.12}$$
$$C = 4.50 \text{ kg}$$

The maximum weight of cashews in the batch of Premier Nut Mix is 4.5 kilograms.

▶ **Check your understanding:** Biko Confectionary decides to change its Premier Mix so that the nuts are mixed in a proportion that produces 23 kilograms of Premier Mix having an effective wholesale cost of no more than $11.49 per kilogram. If the per-kilogram cost of almonds and cashews has not changed, what is the maximum weight of cashews that can be put in the mix? (Answer: 4.99 kg)

▶ **Related problem:** #18 in Exercise 2.5

EXAMPLE 2.5C	An Allocation Problem

Digitech Inc. has a stock option incentive program for its employees. A stock option is a contract between a company and its employees that gives the employees the right to buy shares of the company's stock at a predetermined price. If the market price of the stock increases above the option price, employees can make a profit by "exercising" their option—buying shares at the lower contract price and then selling them in the open market. At Digitech Inc., in any allocation of options, each of 8 senior managers receives twice as many stock options as each of 31 supervisors. Each supervisor receives 2.5 times as many stock options as each of 348 front-line employees. The board of directors has just approved the issue of a total of 500,000 stock options. Rounded to the nearest whole number, how many options will each senior manager, supervisor, and front-line employee receive?

SOLUTION

Step 2: Let F represent the number of options each front-line employee will receive.

Position	Number of individuals	Options per individual
Front-line employee	348	F
Supervisor	31	$2.5F$
Senior manager	8	$2(2.5F) = 5F$

Total number of options = 500,000

Step 3: Total number of options = (Number given to front-line employees) + (Number given to supervisors) + (Number given to senior managers)

Step 4:
$$500,000 = 348F + 31(2.5F) + 8(5F)$$

Step 5:
$$500,000 = 348F + 77.5F + 40F$$
$$= 465.5F$$
$$F = \frac{500,000}{465.5} = 1074.11$$

Each front-line employee will receive 1074 options, each supervisor will receive $2.5(1074.11) = 2685$ options, and each senior manager will receive $5(1074.11) = 5371$ options.

▶ **Check your understanding:** Meridian Inc.'s board of directors just approved the issue of 455,000 stock options. Each of the 25 middle managers will receive 1.5 as many options as each of the 200 regular employees. Each of 5 senior managers receives three times as many options as each of the middle managers. How many options will each senior manager, middle manager, and regular employee receive? (Answer: Each regular employee will receive 1750 options, each middle manager will receive 2625 options, and each senior manager will receive 7875 options.)

▶ **Related problem:** #13 in Exercise 2.5

| EXAMPLE 2.5D | A Problem Involving Successive Partitioning of a Whole |

Getty Oil and Gas has a 47% ownership stake in an oil well. Paliser Energy owns a 29% stake in the same well. Suppose Getty sells $\frac{5}{8}$ of its stake for \$470,000. If Paliser uses that transaction as the basis for calculating the value of its own 29% position, what value will Paliser obtain?

SOLUTION

Step 2: The pie chart below presents the ownership stakes in pictorial form. Getty is selling $\frac{5}{8}$ of the 47% portion it owns for \$470,000.

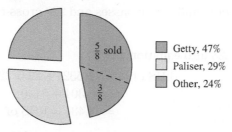

Step 3: If we can determine what a 1% ownership stake is worth, then Paliser's 29% is worth 29 times as much. Let v represent the value of a 1% stake.

Step 4: Getty is selling $\frac{5}{8}$ of its 47% for \$470,000. Then

$$\frac{5}{8}(47v) = \$470,000$$

$$v = \frac{8}{5} \times \frac{\$470,000}{47} = \$16,000$$

Step 5: and Paliser's 29% stake is worth

$$29v = 29(\$16,000) = \$464,000$$

➡ **Check your understanding:** Suppose Getty Oil and Gas had only 36% ownership in the oil well. Further suppose Getty sold $\frac{2}{9}$ of its stake for \$185,000. If Paliser uses that transaction as the basis for calculating the value of its own 29% position, what value will Paliser obtain? (Answer: \$670,625)

▬▶ **Related problem:** #24 in Exercise 2.5

| EXAMPLE 2.5E | A Solution Involving Two Equations in Two Unknowns |

Whistling Mountain charges \$72 for a day pass for downhill skiing and \$22.50 for a day pass for cross-country skiing. If a day's total revenue from the sale of 760 passes was \$43,434, how many of each type of pass were sold?

SOLUTION

Step 2: Price of downhill pass = \$72; Price of cross-country pass = \$22.50.
Total passes sold = 760; Total revenue = \$43,434
Let d represent the number of downhill passes sold, and
let c represent the number of cross-country passes sold.[1]

Step 3:   Total passes sold = 760   ①
          Total revenue = \$43,434   ②

---

[1] The solution to this problem can also be developed in terms of a single variable, say d for the number of downhill passes sold. Then the number of cross-country passes sold is $760 - d$.

Step 4:
$$d + c = 760 \quad \text{①}$$
$$72d + 22.5c = 43{,}434 \quad \text{②}$$

Step 5: Now eliminate c.

① × 22.5:	$22.5d + 22.5c = 17{,}100$
②:	$72d + 22.5c = 43{,}434$
Subtract:	$-49.5d = -26{,}334$
	$d = 532$

Substitute $d = 532$ into ①:
$$532 + c = 760$$
$$c = 760 - 532 = 228$$

On this particular day, 532 downhill skiing passes and 228 cross-country skiing passes were sold.

Check:

Substitute $d = 532$ and $c = 228$ into equation ②:
$$\text{LHS of ②} = 72(532) + 22.5(228)$$
$$= 38{,}304 + 5130$$
$$= 43{,}434 = \text{RHS of ②}$$

➡ **Check your understanding:** An amusement park charges $45 for a day pass that allows full access to all rides. For customers who do not want to go on rides, the admission price is $18. If the daily revenue from the sale of 1430 passes was $56,358, how many of each type of pass were sold? (Answer: 1134 full-access passes, 296 no-ride passes)

▮▮▶ **Related problem:** #23 in Exercise 2.5

EXAMPLE 2.5F	A Word Problem Giving Two Equations with Large Coefficients

SOLUTION

Westwood Orchard received $3843.90 for its first shipment of 1530 kilograms of McIntosh apples and 945 kilograms of Delicious apples to the processing plant. Its second shipment, consisting of 2485 kilograms of McIntosh and 2370 kilograms of Delicious, resulted in a payment of $7395.70. What was Westwood Orchard paid per kilogram for each variety of apple?

SOLUTION

Shipment	McIntosh (kg)	Delicious (kg)	Total revenue ($)
1	1530	945	3843.90
2	2485	2370	7395.70

The details of each shipment are summarized in the table. Let M and D represent the price per kilogram that Westwood received for McIntosh and Delicious apples, respectively. The idea in words that provides the basis for constructing algebraic equations in terms of M and D is

Revenue from McIntosh apples + Revenue from Delicious apples = Total revenue

Expressing this idea in algebraic terms for each shipment gives

$$1530M + 945D = \$3843.90 \quad \text{①}$$
$$2485M + 2370D = \$7395.70 \quad \text{②}$$

Since multiplication by the numerical coefficient of either M or D will result in large unwieldy numbers, divide each equation by its own coefficient of M. This will make the coefficient of M equal to 1 in both equations and permit the elimination of M by subtraction. We want a price per kilogram that is accurate to the cent. Since the orchardist will receive (at most) a few dollars per kilogram, we need three-figure accuracy in our final answer. Therefore, we must maintain four-figure accuracy if we round any intermediate results.

$$
\begin{array}{rl}
① \div 1530: & M + 0.6176D = \quad \$2.512 \\
② \div 2485: & \underline{M + 0.9537D = \quad \$2.976} \\
\text{Subtract:} & -0.3361D = -\$0.4640
\end{array}
$$

$$
D = \frac{\$0.4640}{0.3361} = \$1.381
$$

To solve for M with the least amount of work, substitute $D = \$1.381$ into one of the modified equations.

$$
M = \$2.512 - 0.6176 \times \$1.381 = \$1.659
$$

Westwood Orchard receives $1.38 per kilogram for Delicious apples and $1.66 per kilogram for McIntosh apples.

Check:

Substitute $D = \$1.38$ and $M = \$1.66$ into equation ②:

$$
\begin{aligned}
\text{LHS of } ② &= 2485(\$1.66) + 2370(\$1.38) \\
&= \$4125.10 + \$3270.60 \\
&= \$7395.70
\end{aligned}
$$

➡ **Check your understanding:** Vineland Orchards received $8031.20 for its first shipment of 2742 kilograms of Empire apples and 1921 kilograms of Spartan apples. Its second shipment, consisting of 3475 kilograms of Empire and 2265 kilograms of Spartan, resulted in a payment of $9900.10. What was Vineland Orchard paid per kilogram for each variety of apple? (Answer: $1.78 per kg for Empire apples, $1.64 per kg for Spartan apples)

▮▮▮▷ **Related problem:** #27 in Exercise 2.5

EXERCISE 2.5

Answers to the odd-numbered problems can be found in the end matter.

BASIC PROBLEMS

1. A Web site had $\frac{2}{7}$ more hits last month than in the same month of the preceding year. If there were 2655 hits last month, how many were there one year earlier?

2. The retail price of a pair of skis consists of the wholesale cost to the retailer plus the retailer's markup. If skis retailing for $712 are marked up by 60% of the wholesale cost, what is that wholesale cost?

3. The prices in Angie's Garden Centre include the 13% Harmonized Sales Tax (HST). How much HST will she report for a plant sold at $39.95?

4. A stockbroker's commission on a transaction is 2.5% of the first $5000 of the transaction amount and 1.5% of the remainder. What was the amount of a transaction that generated a total commission of $227?

5. A caterer has the following price structure for banquets. The first 20 meals are charged the basic price per meal. The next 20 meals are discounted by $2 each and all additional meals are each reduced by $3. If the total cost for 73 meals comes to $1686, what is the basic price per meal?

6. Econocar offers two plans for one-week rentals of a compact car. A rate of $295 per week includes the first 1000 kilometres. Extra distance costs 15 cents per kilometre. A weekly rate of $389 allows unlimited driving. Rounded to the nearest kilometre, beyond what driving distance is the unlimited driving plan cheaper?

7. Alicia pays 38% income tax on any additional earnings. She has an opportunity to work overtime at 1.5 times her base wage of $23.50 per hour. Rounded to the nearest quarter-hour, how much overtime must she work to earn enough money (after tax) to buy a canoe that costs $2750 including sales taxes?

8. Product X requires 30 minutes of machining on a lathe, and Product Y requires 45 minutes of machining on the same lathe. If the lathe was operated for 60.5 hours last week for machining a combined total of 93 units of Products X and Y, how many units of each product were produced?

9. Marichka bought 5 litres of milk and four dozen eggs for $19.51. Lonnie purchased 9 litres of milk and three dozen eggs for $22.98. What were the prices for a litre of milk and a dozen eggs?

10. Victoria Hills Preschool purchases a consistent amount of milk and orange juice every week. After price increases from $1.50 to $1.60 per litre of milk and from $1.30 to $1.39 per can of frozen orange juice, the weekly bill rose from $57 to $60.85. How many litres of milk and cans of orange juice are purchased every week?

INTERMEDIATE PROBLEMS

11. Classic Homes has found from experience that there should be 40% as many two-bedroom homes as three-bedroom homes in a subdivision, and twice as many two-bedroom homes as four-bedroom homes. How many homes of each type should Classic build in a new 96-home subdivision?

12. Broadway Mazda usually spends half as much on radio advertising as on Internet-based advertising, and 60% as much on television advertising as on radio advertising. If next year's total advertising budget is $160,000, how much (rounded to the nearest dollar) should be allocated to each form of advertising?

13. A city's commercial construction bylaws require five parking spaces for every 100 square metres of retail rental space in a shopping centre. Four percent of the parking spaces must be accessible spaces for customers with physical disabilities. Of the remainder, there must be 40% more regular-size spaces than "small car" spaces. How many parking spaces of each type are required for a 27,500 square metre shopping centre?

14. Erin has invested in both an equity mutual fund and a bond mutual fund. Her financial advisor told her that her overall portfolio rose in value by 1.1% last year. Erin noted in the newspaper that the equity fund lost 3.3% last year while the bond fund rose 7.7%. To the nearest 0.1%, what percentage of her portfolio was in the equity fund at the beginning of the year?

15. Steel is an alloy of iron and nickel. A steel recycling company has two piles of scrap steel. Pile A contains steel with 5.25% nickel content. Pile B contains steel with 2.84% nickel. The company has an order for 32.5 tonnes of steel containing 4.15% nickel. How much scrap steel should be taken from each pile for reprocessing?

16. The board of directors of Meditronics Inc. has designated 100,000 stock options for distribution to employees and management of the company. Each of 3 executives is to receive 2000 more options than each of 8 engineers. Each engineer is to receive 50% more options than each of 14 technicians. How many options will a person in each position receive?

17. Janil is researching "pay as you go" cell phone plans for his mother, who does not want to lock into a fixed,- term contract and has no need for data or text plans. Plan A charges 20 cents per minute for local calls and 40 cents per minute for long-distance calls in Canada. Plan B charges a flat rate of 35 cents per minute for calls anywhere in Canada. Both plans can be cancelled at any time with no penalty. Above what percentage would her usage need to be long-distance in order for Plan B to be the better choice for Janil's mother?

18. Quality Grocer makes its own bulk "trail mix" by mixing raisins and peanuts. The whole-sale cost of raisins is $3.75 per kilogram and the cost of peanuts is $2.89 per kilogram. To the nearest 0.1 kilogram, what amounts of peanuts and raisins should be mixed to produce 50 kilograms of trail mix with an effective wholesale cost of $3.20 per kilogram?

19. A firm received a bill from its accountant for $3310, representing a combined total of 41 "billable" hours for both the Certified General Accountant (CGA) and her accounting clerk, for conducting the firm's audit. If the CGA charges her time at $120 per hour and the clerk's time at $50 per hour, how many hours did each work on the audit?

20. Joan, Stella, and Sue have agreed to form a partnership. For the original capital investment of $32,760, Sue agrees to contribute 20% more than Joan, and Joan agrees to contribute 20% more than Stella. How much will each contribute?

21. The annual net income of the SGR partnership is to be distributed so that Sven receives 30% less than George, and Robert receives 25% more than George. If the past year's net income was $88,880, what amount should be allocated to each partner?

22. It takes 20 minutes of machine time to manufacture Product X and 30 minutes of machine time to manufacture Product Y. If the machine operated 47 hours last week to produce a combined total of 120 units of the two products, how many units of Y were manufactured?

23. The tickets for a junior hockey game cost $19 for the blue section and $25.50 for the red section. If 4460 tickets were sold for a total of $93,450, how many seats were sold in each section?

24. Regal Resources owns a 58% interest in a mineral claim. Yukon Explorations owns the remainder. If Regal sells one-fifth of its interest for $1.2 million, what is the implied value of Yukon's interest?

25. The statistics for a professional accounting program indicate that five-sevenths of those who enter the program complete Level 1. Two-ninths of Level 1 completers do not finish Level 2. If 587 students completed Level 2 last year, how many (including this group of 587) began Level 1?

26. Hastings Marine Supplies sold four-sevenths of its inventory at cost in a bankruptcy sale. The remainder was sold at 45% of cost to liquidators for $6700.

    a. What was the original cost of the inventory that was sold to the liquidators?

    b. What were the proceeds from the bankruptcy sale?

27. The annual dues for the Southern Pines Golf Club are $2140 for regular members and $856 for student members. If the total revenue from the dues of 583 members for the past year was $942,028, how many members did the club have in each category?

28. Mr. and Mrs. Chudnowski paid $1050 to fly with their three children from Winnipeg to Regina. Mrs. Ramsey paid a total of $610 for herself and two children on the same flight, and at the same rate structure as the Chudnowski family. What were the airfares per adult and per child?

29. Budget Truck Rentals offers short-term truck rentals consisting of an hourly rate plus a per-kilometre charge. Vratislav paid $54.45 for a two-hour rental during which he drove 47 kilometres. Bryn paid $127.55 for five hours and 93 kilometres driven. What rate did Budget charge per hour and per kilometre?

ADVANCED PROBLEMS

30. Mr. Parker structured his will so that each of his four children will receive half as much from the proceeds of his estate as his wife, and each of 13 grandchildren will receive one-third as much as each child. After his death, $759,000 remains after expenses and taxes for distribution among his heirs. How much will each child and grandchild receive?

31. To coordinate production in a three-stage manufacturing process, Stage B must be assigned 60% more workers than Stage A. Stage C requires three-quarters as many workers as Stage B. How should the scheduler allocate 114 workers to the three stages?

32. Fred has centralized the purchasing and record-keeping functions for his 3 restaurants in a single office. The annual costs of the office are allocated to the 3 locations. The Hillside restaurant is charged $1000 less than twice the charge to the Barnett restaurant. The Westside restaurant is charged $2000 more than the Hillside location. What is the charge to the Westside location if the cost of operating the central office for a year is $27,600?

2.6 | Application: Percent Change

LO8 When a quantity changes, the amount of the change is often expressed as a percentage of the initial value. That is,

$$\text{Percent change} = \frac{\text{Final value} - \text{Initial value}}{\text{Initial value}} \times 100$$

We can write a more compact formula if we define the following symbols:

$$V_i = \text{Initial (or beginning or original or old) value}$$
$$V_f = \text{Final (or ending or new) value}$$
$$c = \text{Percent change (or its decimal equivalent)}$$

Then

PERCENT CHANGE $$c = \frac{V_f - V_i}{V_i} \times 100 \qquad \text{(2-1)}$$

Note that when a quantity doubles, the percent change is 100%. If a quantity triples, the percent change is 200%, and so on.

TIP ✔

Order Matters, Language Matters

The order of the final and initial values in the numerator is important—it determines the sign of the percent change. If a quantity decreases in size, its percent change is negative.

To illustrate a point on language, consider the example of a company whose sales declined from $4 million in Year 1 to $3 million in Year 2. The percent change in sales is

$$\frac{\text{Year 2 sales} - \text{Year 1 sales}}{\text{Year 1 sales}} \times 100 = \frac{\$3 \text{ million} - \$4 \text{ million}}{\$4 \text{ million}} \times 100$$
$$= \frac{-1}{4} \times 100$$
$$= -25\%$$

We can say either "The sales changed by −25%" or "The sales decreased by 25%" from Year 1 to Year 2. The direction of the change may be indicated either by an algebraic sign or by a descriptive word such as "rose," "fell," "increased," or "decreased." However, it would be incorrect and potentially confusing to say that "the sales decreased by −25%."

EXAMPLE 2.6A	Calculating the Percent Change

The share price of Klondike Resources rose from \$2 on January 1, 2014 to \$4 on December 31, 2014. It fell back to \$2 by December 31, 2015. Calculate the percent change in share price during 2014, during 2015, and during the entire two-year period.

SOLUTION

For 2014,

$$c = \frac{\text{Dec. 31, 2014 price} - \text{Jan. 1, 2014 price}}{\text{Jan. 1, 2014 price}} \times 100 = \frac{\$4 - \$2}{\$2} \times 100 = 100\%$$

Similarly, for 2015,

$$c = \frac{\$2 - \$4}{\$4} \times 100 = -50\%$$

For the entire two years,

$$c = \frac{\$2 - \$2}{\$2} \times 100 = 0\%$$

The share price increased by 100% in 2014 and then decreased by 50% in 2015. For the entire two-year period, there was no net price change.

➡ **Check your understanding:** You bought Klondike Resources shares on January 1, 2013 when they were priced at \$1.15 per share. Calculate the percentage change in share price for the entire three-year period if you sold the shares for \$2 each on December 31, 2015. (Answer: The share price increased by 73.91% during the three-year period.)

▰▰▷ **Related problem:** #27 in Exercise 2.6

TRAP

Percent Changes Are Not Additive

As the preceding example demonstrates, the overall percent change for a series of intervals cannot be obtained simply by adding the percent changes for the individual intervals. The reason is that the initial value for the percent change calculation is different in each interval.

EXAMPLE 2.6B	Calculating the Percent Change in a Percentage

A chartered bank raises the interest rate on its Visa card from 14% to 18%. What is the percent increase in the interest charges on a given balance?

SOLUTION

The interest charges increase proportionately with the rise in the interest rate. The interest rate change must be calculated in relative terms (using formula (2-1)), not in absolute terms (18% − 14% = 4%). Therefore, the percent change in interest charges is

$$c = \frac{V_f - V_i}{V_i} \times 100 = \frac{18\% - 14\%}{14\%} \times 100 = \frac{4}{14} \times 100 = 28.57\%$$

⮕ **Check your understanding:** The peak prime rate in the recent past occurred in the latter half of 2007 when the prime rate was 6.25%. By the latter half of 2015, the prime rate had fallen to 2.7%. What is the percentage decrease in the interest cost for a given loan balance being charged the prime rate in 2007 versus 2015? (Answer: 56.8% reduction in interest costs)

▬▶ **Related problem:** #35 in Exercise 2.6

 ## Math Apps

PRICEJACKS

If you are an observant shopper, you have noticed that the standard or regular package size of many consumer items (toothpaste, facial tissue, cereal, bar soap, detergent, chocolate bars, etc.) changes from time to time for no apparent reason. For example, at one point or another during the past few years, each of 130, 100, and 75 millilitres has been the "regular" size of toothpaste tubes.

This is an example of the pricejack cycle. As *Consumer Reports* has noted, "Manufacturers often try to avoid a straightforward price increase for fear that consumers may think the product is not worth any more than they have been paying. One way to avoid the appearance of a price increase is to reduce the size of the package while holding the price steady." An even sneakier ploy is to reduce the price by a smaller percentage than the size reduction. The unit price (price per gram or per millilitre) ends up higher.

The other part of the pricejack cycle—increasing both the unit price and the product volume or weight—is a little more problematic for manufacturers. Often the packaging points out that it is the "New Economy Size!" or "Contains $\frac{1}{3}$ more!" so that consumers will expect to pay a higher package price. The former size is, of course, no longer available on store shelves for the consumer to compare unit prices and note the increase in the unit price.

If you have a good memory for prices, some straightforward calculations can help you evaluate whether a particular product's true pricing has increased or decreased. For example, suppose a bag of potato chips that weighed 200 grams was sold for $3. If the size of the bag increases to 250 grams and the price increases to $3.90, we can calculate the percentage change in the per-gram unit price. Before the price and size change, we were paying $\frac{\$3}{200}$ or $0.015 per gram. After the size and price change, we are paying $\frac{\$3.90}{250}$ or $0.0156 per gram. The percentage change in price per gram is

$$c = \frac{V_f - V_i}{V_i} \times 100 = \frac{\$0.0156 - \$0.015}{\$0.015} \times 100$$
$$= 4.00\%$$

This means we are paying 4% more per gram than we did before the pricejacking occurred.

| EXAMPLE 2.6C | Calculating the Percent Change in the Unit Price |

Suppose the price of Colgate toothpaste drops from $2.99 to $2.77 when the tube size is reduced from 100 to 75 millilitres. Calculate

a. The percent change in the tube volume

b. The percent change in the tube price

c. The percent change in the unit price per millilitre

SOLUTION

a. The percent change in the tube's volume is

$$c = \frac{V_f - V_i}{V_i} \times 100 = \frac{75 \text{ ml} - 100 \text{ ml}}{100 \text{ ml}} \times 100 = -25.00\%$$

b. The percent change in the tube's price is

$$c = \frac{\$2.77 - \$2.99}{\$2.99} \times 100 = -7.36\%$$

c. The initial unit price is

$$\frac{\text{Price}}{\text{Volume}} = \frac{\$2.99}{100 \text{ ml}} = \$0.02990 \text{ per ml or } 2.990\text{¢ per ml}$$

The final unit price is

$$\frac{\$2.77}{75 \text{ ml}} = \$0.03693 \text{ per ml or } 3.693\text{¢ per ml}$$

The percent change in the unit price is

$$c = \frac{3.693 - 2.990}{2.990} \times 100 = 23.51\%$$

➡ **Check your understanding:** The price of a box of crackers drops from $3.50 to $3 when the product weight is reduced from 500 grams to 400 grams. Calculate the percent change in box weight, box price, and unit price. (Answer: The box weight was reduced by 20%, the box price fell by 14.29%, and the unit price rose by 7.14%.)

▮▮▮➡ **Related problem:** #29 in Exercise 2.6

Calculating V_i or V_f When C Is Known

Sometimes the percent change and either the initial or the final value are known. To calculate the remaining unknown, first substitute the known values into formula (2-1) and then manipulate the resulting equation to solve for the unknown.

TIP

Signs Matter

Whenever the percent change represents a decrease, a negative value must be substituted for c in formula (2-1).

EXAMPLE 2.6D | Calculating V_i Given V_f and C

What amount when increased by 230% equals $495?

SOLUTION

We are given c = 230% and V_f = $495. Note that the decimal equivalent of c is c = 2.3.
Substituting in formula (2-1),

$$230\% = \frac{\$495 - V_i}{V_i} \times 100$$

After dividing both sides by 100%, we have

$$2.3 = \frac{\$495 - V_i}{V_i}$$

Cross-multiply to obtain

$$2.3\,V_i = \$495 - V_i$$
$$2.3\,V_i + V_i = \$495$$
$$3.3\,V_i = \$495$$

Initial amount,

$$V_i = \frac{\$495}{3.3} = \$150$$

Therefore, $150 increased by 230% equals $495.

➡ **Check your understanding:** What amount when increased by 84% equals $920?
(Answer: $500)

▮▮▮▶ **Related problem:** #19 in Exercise 2.6

EXAMPLE 2.6E | Calculating V_f Given V_i and C

If $9550 is decreased by 0.75%, what remains?

SOLUTION

The initial amount is $9550, and we need to calculate the final amount after a decrease of 0.75%
(c = −0.0075).

Substituting in formula (2-1),

$$-0.0075 = \frac{V_f - \$9550}{\$9550}$$

Cross-multiplying,

$$-0.0075(\$9550) = V_f - \$9550$$

After transposing terms to isolate V_f on the left side,

Final amount, $$V_f = \$9550 - \$71.625 = \$9478.38$$

$9550 after a decrease of 0.75% leaves $9478.38.

➡ **Check your understanding:** If $257.50 is reduced by 1.25%, what remains? (Answer: $254.28)

▮▮▮▶ **Related problem:** #17 in Exercise 2.6

EXAMPLE 2.6F	Calculating V_i Given V_f and C

For the fiscal year just completed, a company had sales of $157,500. This represents a 5% increase over the prior year. What were the sales in the prior year?[2]

SOLUTION

We are given the "final" sales and need to calculate the "initial" sales.

Substituting in formula (2-1),

$$0.05 = \frac{\$157{,}500 - V_i}{V_i}$$

Cross-multiplying,

$$0.05\, V_i = \$157{,}500 - V_i$$
$$0.05\, V_i + V_i = \$157{,}500$$
$$1.05\, V_i = \$157{,}500$$

Prior year's sales,

$$V_i = \frac{\$157{,}500}{1.05} = \$150{,}000$$

The sales in the prior year totalled $150,000.

➡ **Check your understanding:** Suppose sales of $157,500 for the year just completed represented a 40% increase over sales for the prior year. What were the sales in the prior year? (Answer: $112,500)

✏️▶ **Related problem:** #32 in Exercise 2.6

Reversing a Percent Difference

If x is 10% less than y, by what percentage is y greater than x? (The answer is *not* 10%.) Before we deal further with this question, let us be very clear on the interpretation of certain comparisons.

$$\text{"}A \text{ is 40\% } of\ B\text{"}\quad \text{means that}\quad A = 0.40B$$

but

$$\text{"}A \text{ is 40\% } greater\ than\ B\text{"}\quad \text{means that}\quad A = B + 0.40B = 1.40B$$

Note also that: "A is 40% *greater than* B" has the same meaning as "A is 140% *of* B."

Returning now to the original question,

$$\text{"}x \text{ is 10\% less than } y\text{"}\quad \text{means that}\quad x = y - 0.10y = 0.90y$$

Hence,

$$y = \frac{x}{0.90} = 1.11\overline{1}x = x + 0.11\overline{1}x$$

Therefore, if x is 10% less than y, then y is $11.\overline{1}$% greater than x.

---

[2] It is tempting, but incorrect, to reason that the prior year's sales must be $100\% - 5\% = 95\%$ of $157,500 (which is $149,625). The 5% increase in sales means that

Most recent year's sales = 105% of (Prior year's sales)

rather than

Prior year's sales = 95% of (Most recent year's sales)

EXAMPLE 2.6G | **Reversing a Percent Difference**

If C is 120% more than D, by what percentage is D less than C?

SOLUTION

If C is 120% more than D, then

$$C = D + 1.20D = 2.20D$$

Hence,

$$D = \frac{C}{2.20} = 0.45\overline{45}C$$

That is,

D is $45.\overline{45}$% of C

which makes D

$100\% - 45.\overline{45}\% = 54.\overline{54}\%$ less than C

➡ **Check your understanding:** If C is 175% more than D, by what percentage is D less than C? (Answer: D is $63.\overline{63}$% less than C.)

✏▶ **Related problem:** #37 in Exercise 2.6

EXAMPLE 2.6H | **Reversing a Percent Difference**

During a clearance sale, a merchant advertised: "You will pay 50% more elsewhere!" By what percentage are the merchant's prices lower than her competitors' prices?

SOLUTION

If competitors' prices are 50% higher, then

$$\text{Competitors' prices} = 1.5(\text{Merchant's prices})$$

Hence,

$$\text{Merchant's prices} = \frac{\text{Competitors' prices}}{1.5} = 0.6667 \,(\text{Competitors' prices})$$

Therefore, the merchant's prices are $100\% - 66.67\% = 33.33\%$ less than her competitors' prices. (Commentary: "You will pay 50% more elsewhere!" is a more eyecatching slogan than "You will pay 33.3% less here!" However, many customers are likely to interpret the advertisement as "50% off" rather than "33.3% off." Imagine trying to explain to customers that the effective 33.3% in-store discount is equivalent to paying 50% more elsewhere.)

➡ **Check your understanding:** If the merchant advertised "You will pay 60% more elsewhere," by what percentage are the merchant's prices lower than her competitors' prices? (Answer: 37.5%)

✏▶ **Related problem:** #39 in Exercise 2.6

In all problems, calculate dollar amounts accurate to the cent, and percent amounts accurate to the nearest 0.01%.

BASIC PROBLEMS

Calculate the missing value for Problems 1 through 8.

Problem	Initial value	Final value	Percent change (%)
1.	$95	$100	?
2.	135 kg	35 kg	?
3.	0.11	0.13	?
4.	0.095	0.085	?
5.	$134.39	?	−12
6.	112 g	?	112
7.	?	$75	200
8.	?	$75	−50

9. $100 is what percent more than $90?

10. $100 is what percent less than $110?

11. What amount when increased by 25% equals $100?

12. $75 is 75% more than what amount?

13. $754.30 is what percent less than $759?

14. How much is $75 after an increase of 75%?

15. $100 is 10% less than what amount?

16. What amount after a reduction of 20% equals $100?

17. How much is $900 after a decrease of 90%?

18. How much is $10,000 after an increase of $\frac{3}{4}$%?

19. What amount after being increased by 210% equals $465?

INTERMEDIATE PROBLEMS

20. The total cost of a leather jacket (including HST of 13% on the retail price) is $281.37. What is the retail price of the jacket?

21. Enrollment in the Business Administration program at a community college in September 2015 was 1200 students. This represented a 5.26% increase from the previous year. How many students were enrolled in the program in September 2014?

22. Nykita achieved jewellery sales of $18,400 in her home-based business last year. She is projecting a 12% increase for next year due to an improved marketing campaign. What level of sales is Nykita projecting for next year?

23. The market value of Amir's downtown condominium is estimated to have grown from $285,000 to $334,000 in one calendar year. By what percentage increase did Amir's real estate investment grow?

24. Due to reduced commissions, Jamal's earnings this year fell by 6.5% from last year's level of $87,650. Rounded to the nearest dollar, how much did Jamal earn this year?

25. On July 1, 2015, Canada's population was 35,851,800. This represented a 4.39% increase over a 4-year period. Rounded to the nearest 1000, what was Canada's population on July 1, 2011?

26. Becker Tools sold 32,400 hammers at an average price of $15.10 in Year 1 and 27,450 hammers at an average price of $15.50 in Year 2. What was the percent change from Year 1 to Year 2 in

    a. The number of hammers sold?
    b. The average selling price?
    c. The revenue from the sale of hammers?

27. An investor purchased shares of Digger Resources at a price of $0.55 per share. One year later, the shares traded at $1.55, but they fell back to $0.75 by the end of the second year after the date of purchase. Calculate the percent change in the share price

    a. In the first year
    b. In the second year
    c. Over both years

28. After Island Farms increased the container size for its premium ice cream from 1.65 to 2.2 litres, the retail price increased from $5.49 to $7.98. What was the percent change in the unit price?

29. The retail price of Paradise Island cheddar cheese dropped from $10.98 to $9.98 when the package size was reduced from 700 to 600 grams. What was the percent change in the unit price? Use five-figure accuracy in intermediate calculations.

30. The Edmonton Real Estate Board reports that the average selling price of homes this month in the greater Edmonton area was $348,535, a decrease of 1.8% from last month. Rounded to the nearest $100, what was the average selling price of a home last month?

31. Mountain Sports is advertising "30% Off All Skiing Equipment" in its Spring Clearance Sale. On ski boots marked down to $348.60, what is the regular price?

32. Apple's worldwide sales of iPhones were 231.2 million in 2015. This represented a 3.66% increase over 2014's unit sales. Rounded to the nearest 1000, how many iPhones did Apple sell in 2014?

33. In September 2015, the research company Emarketer estimated that Twitter's worldwide advertising revenues for 2015 would hit $2.03 billion. This figure represents a 241% increase from the company's 2013 advertising revenues. Rounded to the nearest $1000, what were Twitter's advertising revenues in 2013?

34. Mutual Fund A charges an annual management fee of 2.38% of money under management. The corresponding management fee for Mutual Fund B is 1.65%. On the same invested amount, what percentage more fees will you pay to Fund A than to Fund B?

35. In January of 2008, the federal government reduced the GST rate from 6% to 5%. What was the resulting percent reduction in the dollar amount of GST consumers paid on any item?

36. The price of the shares of Nadir Explorations Ltd. fell by 76% in the past year, to the current price of $0.45 per share. In dollars and cents, how much did the price of a share drop in the past year?

37. If the Canadian dollar is worth 1.5% less than the U.S. dollar, by what percentage does the U.S. dollar exceed the value of the Canadian dollar?

38. The manufacturer of Caramalt chocolate bars wants to implement a 7.5% increase in the unit retail price along with a reduction in the bar size from 100 to 80 grams. If the current retail price of a 100-gram bar is $1.15, what should be the price of an 80-gram bar?

39. Last year, Canada's exports to the U.S. exceeded imports from the U.S. by 14.1%. By what percentage were the United States' exports to Canada less than its imports from Canada?

40. Sears Canada reported that its annual sales revenue fell 14.2% in 2014 as compared to 2013. What percentage were 2013 sales of 2014 sales?

ADVANCED PROBLEMS

41. An owner listed a property for 140% more than she paid for it 12 years ago. After receiving no offers during the first three months of market exposure, she dropped the list price by 10%, to $172,800. What was the original price that the owner paid for the property?

42. A car dealer normally lists new cars at 22% above cost. A demonstrator model was sold for $17,568 after a 10% reduction from the list price. What amount did the dealer pay for this car?

43. The Hampton District school board decided to reduce the number of students per teacher next year by 15%. If the number of students does not change, by what percentage must the number of teachers be increased?

44. The Lightning laser printer prints 30% more pages per minute than the Reliable laser printer. What percentage less time than the Reliable will the Lightning require for long print jobs?

45. If the euro is worth 32% more than the Canadian dollar, how much less (in percentage terms) is the Canadian dollar worth than the euro?

46. A hospital can increase the dollar amount budgeted for nurses' overtime wages during the next year by only 3%. The nurses' union has just won a 5% hourly rate increase for the next year. By what percentage must the hospital cut the number of overtime hours in order to stay within budget?

Key Terms

Algebraic expression	Linear equation	Root
Base	Literal coefficient	Slope
Binomial	Monomial	Substitution
Equation	Nonlinear equation	Terms
Exponent	Numerical coefficient	Trinomial
Factors	Polynomial	y-intercept
Like terms	Power	

Summary of Notation and Key Formulas

V_i = Initial (or beginning or original or old) value
V_f = Final (or ending or new) value
c = Percent change (or its decimal equivalent)

FORMULA (2-1) $c = \dfrac{V_f - V_i}{V_i} \times 100\%$ Finding the percent change in a quantity

Review Problems

Answers to the odd-numbered review problems can be found in the end matter.

BASIC PROBLEMS

1.   **LO1** Simplify each of the following and collect the like terms.

   a. $2(7x - 3y) - 3(2x - 3y)$

   b. $15x - (4 - 10x + 12)$

2.   **LO2** Use formula (5-5), $NI = (CM)X - FC$, to calculate FC if $NI = \$200{,}000$, $CM = \$8$, and $X = 40{,}000$.

3.   **LO3** Use formula (6-2), $S = P(1 + rt)$, to calculate r if $S = \$1243.75$, $P = \$1200$, and $t = \frac{7}{12}$.

4.   **LO3** Solve the following equations:

   a. $3.1t + 145 = 10 + 7.6t$

   b. $1.25y - 20.5 = 0.5y - 11.5$

5.   **LO4** Graph the equation $-2x + y = 4$ over the range $x = -3$ to $x = 6$. Visit Connect and use the Graph Templates found under the Student Resources for Chapter 2.

6.   **LO5** Determine the slope and b-intercept of each of the following equations:

   a. $2b + 3 = 5a$ **b.** $3a - 4b = 12$ **c.** $7a = -8b$

7.   **LO7** At a local public swimming pool, an afternoon of public swimming resulted in revenues totalling $240.75. Adults were charged $3.50 and children were charged $1.25. If records show that a total of 126 swimmers attended during the afternoon, how many were adults and how many were children?

8.   **LO7** A local paving company paved an 11.5 kilometre section of highway over the course of two days. The crew paved 4.25 kilometres more on the second day than on the first day. How many kilometres of highway were paved on each day?

9.   **LO8** Solve each of the following:

   a. What amount is 17.5% more than $29.43?

   b. What amount reduced by 80% leaves $100?

   c. What amount reduced by 15% equals $100?

   d. What is $47.50 after an increase of 320%?

   e. What amount when decreased by 62% equals $213.56?

   f. What amount when increased by 125% equals $787.50?

   g. What amount is 30% less than $300?

INTERMEDIATE PROBLEMS

10.   **LO1** Simplify and collect the like terms: $\dfrac{9y - 7}{3} - 2.3(y - 2)$

11.   **LO1** Multiply and collect the like terms: $4(3a + 2b)(2b - a) - 5a(2a - b)$

12.   **LO1** Evaluate each of the following expressions for the given values of the variables. The answer should be accurate to the cent.

   a. $L(1 - d_1)(1 - d_2)(1 - d_3)$ for $L = \$340$, $d_1 = 0.15$, $d_2 = 0.08$, $d_3 = 0.05$

   b. $\dfrac{R}{i}\left[1 - \dfrac{1}{(1 + i)^n}\right]$ for $R = \$575$, $i = 0.085$, $n = 3$

13. **LO2** Use formula (4-4), $N = L(1 - d_1)(1 - d_2)(1 - d_3)$, to calculate d_2 if $N = \$324.30$, $L = \$498$, $d_1 = 0.20$, and $d_3 = 0.075$.

14. **LO1** Perform the indicated multiplication and division, and combine the like terms.

    a. $6(4y - 3)(2 - 3y) - 3(5 - y)(1 + 4y)$

    b. $\dfrac{5b - 4}{4} - \dfrac{25 - b}{1.25} + \dfrac{7}{8}b$

    c. $\dfrac{96nm^2 - 72n^2m^2}{48n^2m}$

15. **LO1** Simplify: $\dfrac{(-3x^2)^3(2x^{-2})}{6x^5}$

16. **LO1** Evaluate the following expressions to six-figure accuracy.

    a. $(1.0075)^{24}$ **b.** $(1.05)^{\frac{1}{6}} - 1$ **c.** $\dfrac{(1 + 0.0075)^{36} - 1}{0.0075}$

17. **LO3** Solve each of the following pairs of equations to three-figure accuracy.

    a. $4a - 5b = 30$
       $2a - 6b = 22$

    b. $76x - 29y = 1050$
       $-13x - 63y = 250$

18. **LO3** Solve the following pair of equations.

    $3x + 5y = 11$
    $2x - \ y = 16$

19. **LO5** A homeowner pays a flat "customer charge" of \$28 per month for municipal water services, plus an additional \$2.75 per cubic metre of water consumed. Write an equation for calculating the total water bill, B, for a month in terms of water consumption, C. If you were to plot a graph of B vs. C, what would be the slope and B-intercept of the line?

20. **LO6** Use the graphical method to solve the following pair of equations. Visit Connect and use the Graph Templates found under the Student Resources for Chapter 2.

    $y + 3x = 18$
    $5x + 10 = 5y$

21. **LO7** The profits from a partnership are to be distributed so that Grace receives 20% more than Kajsa, and Mary Anne receives five-eighths as much as Grace. How much should each receive from a total distribution of \$36,000?

22. **LO7** Rory invested a total of \$7800 in shares of ABC Ltd. and XYZ Inc. One year later the investment was worth \$9310, after the shares of ABC had increased in value by 15% and the shares of XYZ were up 25%. How much did Rory invest in each company?

23. **LO7** Nguyen fishes for red snapper and lingcod off the coast of British Columbia, and delivers his catch each week to a fish buyer. On one delivery, he received \$2454.20 for 370 kilograms of red snapper and 264 kilograms of lingcod. On another occasion he was paid \$2124.70 for 304 kilograms of lingcod and 255 kilograms of red snapper. What price per kilogram was Nguyen paid for each type of fish?

24. **LO8** Yellowknife Mining sold 34,300 ounces of gold in Year 1 at an average price of \$1160 per ounce. Production was down to 23,750 ounces in Year 2 because of a strike by the miners, but the average price obtained was \$1280 per ounce. What was the percent change from Year 1 to Year 2 in

    a. The amount of gold produced?

    b. The average selling price per ounce?

    c. The revenue from the sale of gold?

25. **LO8** Two years ago the shares of Diamond Strike Resources traded at a price of $3.40 per share. One year later the shares were at $11.50, but then they declined in value by 35% during the subsequent year. Calculate

   a. The percent change in the share price during the first year

   b. The current share price

26. **LO8** Barry recently sold some stock after holding it for two years. The stock's price rose 150% during the first year, but fell 40% in the second year. At what price did he buy the stock if he sold it for $24 per share?

27. **LO8** Albion Distributors' revenues and expenses for the fiscal year just completed were $2,347,000 and $2,189,000, respectively.

   a. If in the current year revenues rise by 10% but expense increases are held to 5%, what will be the percent increase in profit?

   b. If, instead, revenues decline by 10% and expenses are reduced by 5%, what will be the percent change in profit?

28. **LO1** Evaluate the following expressions to six-figure accuracy.

   a. $\dfrac{(1.00\overline{6})^{240} - 1}{0.00\overline{6}}$
                         b. $(1 + 0.025)^{1/3} - 1$

ADVANCED PROBLEMS

---

29. **LO1** Simplify

$$\left(-\frac{2x^2}{3}\right)^{-2}\left(\frac{5^2}{6x^3}\right)\left(-\frac{15}{x^5}\right)^{-1}$$

30. **LO1** Solve the following equations for x to five-figure accuracy and verify the solution.

   a. $\dfrac{x}{1.08^3} + \dfrac{x}{2}(1.08)^4 = \$850$

   b. $2x(1 + 0.085 \times \frac{77}{365}) + \dfrac{x}{1 + 0.085 \times \frac{132}{365}} = \$1565.70$

31. **LO1** Evaluate $P(1 + i)^n + \dfrac{S}{1 + rt}$ accurate to the cent for $P = \$2500$, $i = 0.1025$, $n = 2$, $S = \$1500$, $r = 0.09$, and $t = \frac{93}{365}$.

32. **LO1** Solve the following equations for x to six-figure accuracy.

   a. $\dfrac{2x}{1 + 0.13 \times \frac{92}{365}} + x\left(1 + 0.13 \times \frac{59}{365}\right) = \$831$

   b. $3x(1.03^5) + \dfrac{x}{1.03^3} + x = \dfrac{\$2500}{1.03^2}$

33. **LO7** Bart purchased 60% of a three-eighths interest in a ski chalet for $65,000. Rounded to the nearest dollar, what was the implied value of the chalet?

34. **LO7** Deanna is paid a base salary plus commission. On sales of $27,000 and $35,500 in two successive months, her gross pay was $2815.00 and $3197.50, respectively. What are her base salary and commission rate (in percent)?

35. **LO7** A hockey arena has 2500 seats in the preferred red sections near centre ice and 4500 seats in the less desirable blue sections. At regular season prices, a sell-out would generate ticket revenue of $50,250 for a single game. Ticket prices are raised by 20% in the "blues" and 30% in the "reds" for the playoffs. Ticket revenue from a playoff sell-out would be $62,400. What are the ticket prices for the playoffs?

© Veer RF

CHAPTER 3

Ratios and Proportions

LEARNING OBJECTIVES

After completing this chapter, you will be able to:

LO1 Set up and manipulate ratios

LO2 Set up and solve proportions

LO3 Use proportions to allocate or prorate an amount on a proportionate basis

LO4 Use quoted exchange rates to convert between currencies

LO5 Relate currency exchange rate movement to currency appreciation or depreciation

LO6 Interpret and use index numbers

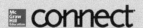 **connect** Throughout this chapter interactive charts and Help Me Solve It videos are marked with a ⬈.

RAW BUSINESS DATA CAN TAKE on greater meaning when comparisons are made between associated quantities. For example, a firm's profit for a year is an important figure in itself. However, comparing profit to invested capital, total sales, or last year's profit can provide useful insights into the firm's performance. Ratios are widely used to make such comparisons. In accounting and finance, a technique for the interpretation of financial statements is known as *ratio analysis*. Each financial statement ratio compares the size of one balance sheet or income statement figure to another. Each ratio provides an indication of a financial strength or weakness of the business. Managers compare ratios from one period to the next, to detect early-warning signs that the financial health of the company may be changing.

Ratios and proportions are also employed when resources, costs, profits, and so on, must be allocated on a pro rata or proportionate basis. For example, a partnership's profits are commonly distributed among the partners in proportion to each partner's capital investment. Many quantities we encounter in economics and finance are ratios in disguise. Late in the chapter, we will discuss two examples—currency exchange rates and index numbers.

TIP

How to Succeed in Business Mathematics

In Connect, there are a guide and a video entitled "How to Succeed in Business Mathematics." These can be found in Library Resources under Course-wide Content.

3.1   Ratios

LO1   A **ratio** is a comparison of two or more quantities. Suppose that a store sells $2000 worth of Product X and $1500 worth of Product Y in a particular month. The ratio of the sales of Product X to the sales of Product Y may be expressed in any of the following ways:

- Using a colon, as in "2000:1500," which is read "2000 to 1500."
- As a common fraction, $\frac{2000}{1500}$.
- As the decimal equivalent of the common fraction, $1.3\overline{3}$.
- As the percent equivalent of the common fraction, $133\frac{1}{3}\%$.

In the first two forms, the components of the ratio separated by division are called the **terms of a ratio**.[1] Each of the terms in a ratio may be multiplied or divided by the same number to give an **equivalent ratio**. For example, both terms in the ratio 2000:1500 may be divided by 100 to give the equivalent ratio 20:15 or $\frac{20}{15}$.

Ratios may have as many terms as there are quantities being compared. If, in our example, the store sold $2500 worth of Product Z in the same month, the ratio of the sales of Products X, Y, and Z is 2000:1500:2500.

Reducing a Ratio to Its Lowest Terms

It is customary to express a ratio in its **lowest terms**, that is, as the equivalent ratio having the smallest integers possible for its terms. The relative size of the terms is then more apparent. Three cases require somewhat different procedures to reduce a ratio to its lowest terms.

1. If all terms in the given ratio are integers, divide every term by the common factors of all terms. A **common factor** is an integer that divides two or more other integers evenly. For example, the terms in 2000:1500:2500 have 100 and 5 as common factors. After dividing by 100 then by 5 (or by their product, 500), the ratio becomes 4:3:5.

---

[1] The word *term* has two quite different uses in basic algebra. In Chapter 2, *term* referred to a component of an algebraic expression separated from other components by addition or subtraction signs. In this chapter, *term* refers to a component of a ratio set apart by division. The meaning of *term* must be inferred from the context in which it is used.

2. If one or more terms are decimal numbers, make all terms integers by moving the decimal point in *every* term to the right by the *same* number of places. Then reduce the ratio to its lowest terms as in the previous case. For an example, see Part (b) of Example 3.1B.

3. If one or more terms contain a fraction, the terms should first be cleared of the fractions. Start by multiplying every term in the ratio by the denominator of any one of the fractions. Repeat this process using the denominator of any fraction that remains. When the ratio contains only integers, reduce the ratio to its lowest terms as in the first case. See Part (c) of Example 3.1B.

EXAMPLE 3.1A	Expressing a Ratio in Equivalent Forms

a. A hospital ward has 10 nurses caring for 60 patients. The ratio of nurses to patients can be expressed as:

$10:60$	Using the colon notation
$1:6$	Using the colon notation with the lowest terms (each term divided by 10)
$\dfrac{1}{6}$	As a common fraction
$0.1\overline{6}$	As a decimal equivalent
$16.\overline{6}\%$	As a percent equivalent

b. A survey of cars in a parking lot indicated that two-fifths of the cars were North American brands and one-third were Japanese brands. The ratio of North American to Japanese cars was:

$\dfrac{2}{5}:\dfrac{1}{3}$	Ratio with given terms in the colon notation
$6:5$	As an equivalent ratio obtained by multiplying both terms by 5 and by 3 to clear the terms of fractions
$\dfrac{6}{5}$	As a common fraction
1.2	As a decimal equivalent
120%	As a percent equivalent

c. The costs of manufacturing an item are $150 for materials and $225 for labour. The ratio of labour cost to materials cost is:

$225:150$	Ratio with the given terms in the colon notation
$9:6$	Equivalent ratio (each term divided by 25)
$3:2$	Equivalent ratio with lowest terms (after division by 3)
$\dfrac{3}{2}$	As a common fraction
1.5	As a decimal equivalent
150%	As a percent equivalent

➡ **Check your understanding:** Recalculate the ratio of labour cost to materials cost in Part (c) if the costs of manufacturing an item are $840 for materials and $200 for labour. (Answer: The ratio of labour cost to materials cost is $200:840$. After dividing by the common factors 10 and 4, the ratio is $5:21$. The relationship can also be expressed as the common fraction $\frac{5}{21}$, as the decimal equivalent 0.238, and as the percentage equivalent 23.8%.)

▮▮▶ **Related problem:** #1 in Exercise 3.1

EXAMPLE 3.1B	Reducing a Ratio to Its Lowest Terms

Reduce the following ratios to their lowest terms.

a. $105:63:84$

b. $1.2:1.68:0.72$

c. $\frac{3}{8}:\frac{5}{6}:\frac{1}{3}$

SOLUTION

a. $105:63:84 = 35:21:28$	Divide each term by 3.
$= 5:3:4$	Divide each term by 7.
b. $1.2:1.68:0.72 = 120:168:72$	Move all decimals 2 spaces to the right.
$= 30:42:18$	Divide each term by 4.
$= 5:7:3$	Divide each term by 6.
c. $\frac{3}{8}:\frac{5}{6}:\frac{1}{3} = \frac{9}{8}:\frac{15}{6}:\frac{3}{3}$	Multiply each term by 3.
$= \frac{9}{8}:\frac{5}{2}:1$	Reduce each term.
$= \frac{18}{8}:\frac{10}{2}:2$	Multiply each term by 2.
$= \frac{9}{4}:5:2$	Reduce each term.
$= 9:20:8$	Multiply each term by 4.

➡ **Check your understanding:** Using Part (c) as a guide, reduce the following ratio to its lowest terms: $\frac{3}{8}:\frac{5}{6}:\frac{3}{4}$. (Answer: $9:20:18$)

▰▰▶ **Related problem:** #29 in Exercise 3.1

Converting a Ratio to an Equivalent Ratio Whose Smallest Term Is 1

The ratio $179:97:29$ is already in its lowest terms, but still contains rather large integers. In this situation, many people prefer to express the ratio as the equivalent ratio whose *smallest* term has the value 1. If we divide all terms by the smallest term, we obtain

$$\frac{179}{29}:\frac{97}{29}:\frac{29}{29} \quad \text{or} \quad 6.17:3.34:1$$

where the terms have been rounded to three figures. The relative size of the terms is more apparent in $6.17:3.34:1$ than in $179:97:29$.

EXAMPLE 3.1C	Determining an Equivalent Ratio Having 1 as the Smallest Term

Convert each of the following ratios to an equivalent ratio having 1 as the smallest term. Round the resulting terms to three figures.

a. $117:79:167$

b. $1.05:8.1:2.2$

c. $\frac{18}{19}:1\frac{13}{14}$

SOLUTION

a. $117:79:167 = \frac{117}{79}:\frac{79}{79}:\frac{167}{79}$ Divide each term by the smallest term, 79.

$= 1.48:1:2.11$

b. $1.05:8.1:2.2 = \frac{1.05}{1.05}:\frac{8.1}{1.05}:\frac{2.2}{1.05}$ Divide each term by the smallest term, 1.05.

$= 1:7.71:2.10$

c. $\frac{18}{19}:1\frac{13}{14} = 0.947:1.929$ Convert the fractions to decimal equivalents.

$= 1:2.04$ Divide by the smaller term, 0.947.

Convert the fractions to decimal equivalents. Divide by the smaller term, 0.947.

➡ **Check your understanding:** Using Part (c) as a guide, convert $\frac{13}{19}:3\frac{6}{7}$ to an equivalent ratio having 1 as the smallest term. (Answer: 1:5.64)

▰▰▶ **Related problem:** #24 in Exercise 3.1

EXERCISE 3.1

Answers to the odd-numbered problems can be found in the end matter.

BASIC PROBLEMS

1. A daycare centre has 3 employees caring for 45 children. Express the ratio of employees to children using:

   a. Colon notation

   b. Colon notation with the lowest terms

   c. A common fraction with the lowest terms

   d. A decimal equivalent

   e. A percent equivalent

2. You saved $50 of last week's paycheque of $380. Express the ratio of savings to income using:

   a. Colon notation

   b. Colon notation with the lowest terms

   c. A common fraction with the lowest terms

   d. A decimal equivalent

   e. A percent equivalent

Express each of the following ratios in its lowest terms.

3. 12:64	**4.** 56:21	**5.** 45:15:30
6. 26:130:65	**7.** 0.08:0.12	**8.** 2.5:3.5:3
9. 0.84:1.4:1.96	**10.** 11.7:7.8:3.9	**11.** 0.24:0.39:0.15
12. 0.091:0.021:0.042	**13.** $\frac{1}{8}:\frac{3}{4}$	**14.** $\frac{11}{3}:\frac{11}{7}$
15. $2\frac{1}{2}:\frac{5}{8}$	**16.** $4\frac{1}{8}:2\frac{1}{5}$	**17.** $\frac{2}{3}:\frac{3}{4}:\frac{5}{6}$
18. $10\frac{1}{2}:7:4\frac{1}{5}$		

Express each of the following ratios as an equivalent ratio whose smallest term is 1. Maintain three-figure accuracy.

19. $7.6:3$

20. $1.41:8.22$

21. $0.177:0.81$

22. $0.0131:0.0086$

23. $\frac{3}{7}:\frac{19}{17}$

24. $4\frac{3}{13}:\frac{27}{17}$

25. $77:23:41$

26. $11:38:27$

27. $3.5:5.4:8$

28. $0.47:0.15:0.26$

29. $\frac{5}{8}:\frac{17}{11}:\frac{6}{7}$

30. $5\frac{1}{2}:3\frac{3}{4}:8\frac{1}{3}$

INTERMEDIATE PROBLEMS

Set up a ratio in each of Problems 31 to 37. If the ratio cannot be reduced to an equivalent ratio in terms of small integers, then express it as a ratio of decimal equivalents with the smallest term set at 1. Maintain three-figure accuracy.

31. During the past three months, Mako Distributing made 25% of its sales in Region A, 35% in Region B, and 40% in Region C. What is the ratio of the sales in Region A to the sales in Region B to the sales in Region C?

32. Don, Bob, and Ron Maloney's partnership interests in Maloney Bros. Contracting are in the ratio of their capital contributions of $78,000, $52,000, and $65,000, respectively. What is the ratio of Bob's to Ron's to Don's partnership interest?

33. Victoria Developments has obtained $3.6 million of total capital from three sources. Preferred shareholders contributed $550,000 (preferred equity), common shareholders contributed $1.2 million (common equity), and the remainder was borrowed (debt). What is the firm's ratio of debt to preferred equity to common equity?

34. The cost to manufacture a fibreglass boat consists of $4480 for materials, $6330 for direct labour, and $2650 for overhead. Express the three cost components as a ratio.

ADVANCED PROBLEMS

35. A provincial government budget forecasts expenditures of $1.56 billion on education, $1.365 billion on health services, and $975 million on social services. Express the three budget items as a ratio.

36. The brine used in an industrial process is 12.5% salt by weight. What is the ratio (by weights) of salt to water in the brine?

37. The instructions for preparing the fuel mix for a two-cycle engine are to add 250 millilitres of oil to 5 millilitres of gasoline. What is the ratio (by volumes) of gasoline to oil in the fuel mix?

3.2 Proportions

LO2 In Section 3.1 we introduced ratios using an example in which sales of Products X, Y, and Z in a month were $2000, $1500, and $2500, respectively. We will extend the same example to illustrate proportions. Mathematics has a special notation for a compact version of the statement "The ratio of the sales of X to the sales of Y is 4:3":

$$\text{Sales of X}:\text{Sales of Y} = 4:3$$

If we let x represent "sales of Product X" and y represent "sales of Product Y," a still more compact statement is

$$x:y = 4:3$$

The diagram above illustrates what this equation is saying. It shows two columns having known heights "4" and "3," and two other columns of unknown heights "x" and "y." The equation provides the following additional information about columns "x" and "y"—they have the same relative height as the known columns. That is, although we do not know x or y individually, we do know that x is $33\frac{1}{3}\%$ larger than y because 4 is $33\frac{1}{3}\%$ larger than 3. With this extra information we recognize that, given a value for either x or y, we can then calculate the value of the other variable.

The equation "$x:y = 4:3$" is an example of a proportion. In general, a **proportion** is a statement of the equality of two ratios. The language we use to express this proportion is

"x is to y, as 4 is to 3"

When using proportions to solve problems, first convert each ratio to its equivalent fraction. In the current example, we can rewrite the proportion as

$$\frac{x}{y} = \frac{4}{3}$$

Given either x or y, you can solve for the other variable. For example, suppose that the sales of Product X in the next month are forecast to be \$1800. What will be the sales of Product Y if the sales of the two products maintain the same ratio? You can answer this question by substituting $x = \$1800$ and solving for y:

$$\frac{\$1800}{y} = \frac{4}{3}$$

You can clear the equation of fractions by using cross-multiplication. Simply multiply each numerator by the denominator from the other side. This gives

$$1800 \times 3 = 4y$$

$$y = \frac{\$1800 \times 3}{4} = \$1350$$

The projected sales of Product Y in the next month are \$1350.

TIP ✔

Cross-Multiplication Shortcut

It is valid to perform just one of the two cross-multiplications. For example, to solve for w in

$$\frac{w}{\$1400} = \frac{7}{5}$$

just cross-multiply \$1400 by 7 giving

$$w = \frac{7 \times \$1400}{5} = \$1960$$

EXAMPLE 3.2A | **Solving a Proportion**

Solve the proportion: $3:5 = 9:x$

SOLUTION

$\frac{3}{5} = \frac{9}{x}$ Express each ratio as a fraction.

$3x = 45$ Cross-multiply.

$x = \frac{45}{3} = 15$ Divide both sides by the coefficient of x.

➡ **Check your understanding:** Solve the proportion: $2.5:y = 4:7$. (Answer: $y = 4.375$)

◗▶ **Related problem:** #1 in Exercise 3.2

EXAMPLE 3.2B | **Solving a Word Problem Using a Proportion**

Monica and Avni have already invested $8960 and $6880, respectively, in their partnership. If Monica invests another $5000, what amount should Avni contribute to maintain their investments in the original ratio?

SOLUTION

Avni and Monica's additional investments must be in the same ratio as their initial investments. That is,

$$\text{Avni's investment}:\text{Monica's investment} = \$6880:\$8960$$

Let Avni's additional investment be represented by x. Then

$$x:\$5000 = \$6880:\$8960$$

Writing the ratios as fractions,

$$\frac{x}{\$5000} = \frac{\$6880}{\$8960}$$

Therefore,

$$x = \frac{\$6880 \times \$5000}{\$8960} = \$3839.29$$

Avni should contribute $3839.29 to maintain the same ratio of investment in the partnership.

➡ **Check your understanding:** Redo the problem. This time, instead of the additional $5000, Monica invests an additional $6000. (Answer: Avni's additional investment = $4607.14)

◗▶ **Related problem:** #11 in Exercise 3.2

Proportions with Three Variables

From Section 3.1, the value of the ratio

$$\text{Sales of X}:\text{Sales of Y}:\text{Sales of Z}$$

was $4:3:5$ in the base month. That is,

$$x:y:z = 4:3:5$$

where x, y, and z represent the monthly sales of products X, Y, and Z, respectively. Read the proportion as follows:

"x is to y is to z, as 4 is to 3 is to 5"

This proportion implies a separate proportion for each pair of terms. That is,

$$x:y = 4:3 \quad \text{and} \quad y:z = 3:5 \quad \text{and} \quad x:z = 4:5$$

We can construct the following three equations from them:

$$\frac{x}{y} = \frac{4}{3} \quad \text{and} \quad \frac{y}{z} = \frac{3}{5} \quad \text{and} \quad \frac{x}{z} = \frac{4}{5}$$

If we know just one of the three variables x, y, and z, these equations allow us to solve for the other two. Example 3.2C provides an illustration.

TIP

Maintain Terms in a Consistent Order

When you extract a simple proportion from a more complex proportion, keep the proportion's terms in the same order on both sides of the simple proportion (and its corresponding equation). For example, if $a:5:7 = 4:3:c$, then you may write

$a:5 = 4:3$ or $5:a = 3:4$ but *not* $a:5 = 3:4$.

Furthermore, you may write

$$\frac{a}{5} = \frac{4}{3} \quad \text{or} \quad \frac{5}{a} = \frac{3}{4} \quad \text{but } not \quad \frac{a}{5} = \frac{3}{4}$$

EXAMPLE 3.2C | Solving a Proportion Having Two Unknowns

Solve the following proportion for x and y.

$$2:5:3 = 7:x:y$$

SOLUTION

Based on the given proportion, we can construct two simpler proportions, each of which contains only one unknown:

$$2:5 = 7:x \qquad \text{and} \qquad 2:3 = 7:y$$

Then

$$\frac{2}{5} = \frac{7}{x} \qquad \text{and} \qquad \frac{2}{3} = \frac{7}{y}$$

After cross-multiplication, these equations become

$$2x = 35 \qquad \text{and} \qquad 2y = 21$$

Hence,

$$x = \frac{35}{2} = 17.5 \qquad \text{and} \qquad y = \frac{21}{2} = 10.5$$

➡ **Check your understanding:** Solve the following proportion for x and y. $3:5:2 = 4:x:y$. (Answer: $x = 6.\overline{6}$ and $y = 2.\overline{6}$)

▶ **Related problem:** #21 in Exercise 3.2

EXAMPLE 3.2D	Solving a Problem Using a Proportion

A 560-bed hospital is staffed with 232 registered nurses and 185 other support staff. The hospital is about to open a new 86-bed wing. Assuming the same proportionate staffing levels, how many more nurses and support staff will need to be hired?

SOLUTION

Let n represent the number of additional nurses and s the number of additional staff. Then n and s must satisfy the proportion

$$\text{Beds:Nurses:Staff} = 560:232:185 = 86:n:s$$

Therefore,

$$\frac{560}{232} = \frac{86}{n} \qquad \text{and} \qquad \frac{560}{185} = \frac{86}{s}$$

$$560n = 86 \times 232 \qquad\qquad 560s = 86 \times 185$$

$$n = \frac{86 \times 232}{560} \qquad\qquad s = \frac{86 \times 185}{560}$$

$$= 35.6 \qquad\qquad\qquad = 28.4$$

Rounding the calculated values to the nearest integer, the hospital should hire 36 nurses and 28 support staff for the new wing.

➡ **Check your understanding:** Redo the problem. This time, the new wing will have 110 beds instead of 86. (Answer: Rounded to the nearest integer, hire 46 nurses, 36 support staff.)

▬▶ **Related problem:** #23 in Exercise 3.2

 ## Math Apps

BIGGER IS NOT ALWAYS BETTER

For designers of advertising copy, creative flair may be more important than mathematical proficiency. However, mathematical incompetence can lead to embarrassing, if not harmful, results.

One famous story concerns a slick advertisement for a particular computer that appeared in several trade publications. The ad presented a bar chart highlighting the fact that the advertised computer had a *higher* price-to-performance ratio than any of its competitors! (Particularly in the electronics area, the price-to-performance ratio is used to compare competing devices.)

People in the computer industry immediately recognized that the price-to-performance ratio comparison presented in the advertisement actually provided a reason *not* to purchase the advertised computer. Think about what, at a basic mathematical level, will make the price-to-performance ratio high. A large numerator (*high* price) and/or a small denominator (*low* performance) will make the ratio high. Therefore, a higher ratio represents a *lower* "bang for your buck."

EXERCISE 3.2

Answers to the odd-numbered problems can be found in the end matter.

BASIC PROBLEMS

Solve the following proportions for the unknown quantities. Maintain three-figure accuracy.

1. $9:7 = 54:b$	**2.** $17:q = 119:91$	**3.** $88:17 = a:45$
4. $d:13.2 = 16:31$	**5.** $1.89:0.31 = 175:k$	**6.** $1.56:h = 56.2:31.7$
7. $0.043:y = 550:198$	**8.** $0.057:0.149 = z:0.05$	**9.** $m:\dfrac{3}{4} = \dfrac{1}{2}:\dfrac{9}{8}$

10. $\dfrac{10}{3}:\dfrac{12}{7} = \dfrac{5}{18}:r$

Solve the following problems using proportions.

11. The Khans wish to purchase a larger house to accommodate their growing family. The current year's property tax on their home amounts to $3545 based on its assessed value of $328,000. The assessed value of a property they are seriously considering is $437,000. What property tax can the Khans expect to pay on this home if property taxes are in the same ratio as assessed values?

12. The West Essex School Board employs 348 teachers for the 7412 students registered in the district's schools in the current year. The enrolment forecast for next year is 7780 students. Assuming the same student–teacher ratio for the next year, how many additional teaching positions must the board fill?

13. A high-definition movie lasting 1 hour and 45 minutes consumed 3.5 GB of memory on the hard drive of a personal video recorder (PVR). Rounded to the nearest minute, what is the maximum duration of high-definition recording that could be saved on the PVR's 80-GB hard drive?

14. Viraj's neighbour sold 14.5 hectares of land for $328,000. If Viraj were to sell his 23.25-hectare parcel at a proportionate price, what amount would he receive? Round your answer to the nearest dollar.

15. Based on past experience, a manufacturing process requires 2.3 hours of direct labour for each $174 worth of raw materials processed. If the company is planning to consume $78,300 worth of raw materials, what total amount should it budget for labour at $31.50 per hour?

INTERMEDIATE PROBLEMS

Solve the following proportions for the unknown quantities. Maintain three-figure accuracy.

16. $6:7:5 = n:105:m$	**17.** $3:4:13 = x:y:6.5$	**18.** $625:f:500 = g:3:4$
19. $a:58:132 = 38:27:b$	**20.** $0.69:1.17:0.4 = r:s:6.5$	**21.** $8500:x:y = 1.\overline{3}:1:1.\overline{6}$

Solve the following problems using proportions.

22. An international equity mutual fund includes American stocks, Japanese stocks, German stocks, and British stocks in the ratio $27:19:14:11$ respectively. If its current holdings of German stocks are valued at US$238 million, what are the values of its holdings in the securities of the other three countries?

23. Last year, the worldwide vehicle sales of General Motors, Toyota, and Ford, respectively, were in the ratio $124:128:79$. Toyota has just announced sales of 5.02 million vehicles for the first half of the current fiscal year. If the three companies have maintained the same market share as they had last year, how many vehicles did General Motors and Ford sell in the first half of this year? (Round answers to the nearest 0.01 million vehicles.)

24. A punch recipe calls for cranberry juice, ginger ale, and pineapple juice to be mixed in the ratio $6:2.5:1$. How much cranberry juice and pineapple juice should be mixed with a 2-litre bottle of ginger ale?

25. A business consultant is analyzing the cost structure of two firms in the grocery business. On sales of $3.66 million, Thrifty's had wholesale costs of $2.15 million and overhead expenses of $1.13 million. If Economart had the same proportionate costs on its sales of $5.03 million, what would its wholesale costs and overhead expenses have been?

ADVANCED PROBLEMS

26. The Ministry of Education reported that the average school board in the province has 31,900 students in kindergarten-to-grade-12 programs, an annual budget of $288 million, and 1916 full-time-equivalent teachers. The Northern School District (NSD), with an annual budget of $80.1 million and 545 teachers, serves 9350 students. What adjustments would have to be made to NSD's budget and staffing to have them in the same proportion to enrolment as the provincial average? (Round dollar amounts to the nearest $0.01 million, and teachers to the nearest whole number.)

27. Tom Nortons Donuts considers the Hamilton area to be one of its most mature, fully exploited markets. The 59 outlets in the metropolitan area serve a population of 675,000 and generate annual sales of $66.67 million. The management of Tom Nortons views its Calgary market as under-exploited. The 65 outlets generate annual sales of $63.05 million from a population of 1,075,000. If Tom Nortons had penetrated the Calgary market to the same degree and success as the Hamilton market, how many additional outlets would it have, and how much higher (rounded to the nearest $0.01 million) would its annual sales be?

3.3 | Application: Proration

 LO3 There are many instances in business where an amount of money must be allocated among partners, departments, cost centres, and so on. In a procedure called **proration**, the allocation is made on a proportionate basis.

We will illustrate the formal approach to proration using the following example. Connor and Kristen invested $45,000 and $72,000, respectively, to start up CK Partners. The partnership's profit is to be allocated in proportion to their respective investments. In the first year, the profit was $58,500. What amounts should be allocated to Connor and Kristen?[2]

The situation is represented pictorially below. The profit of $58,500 must be split into two parts so that Connor's portion, C, relative to Kristen's portion, K, is the same as 45 relative to 72 ($45,000 relative to $72,000). In mathematics,

$$C:K = 45:72$$

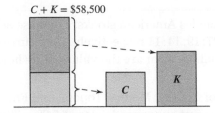

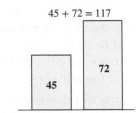

---

[2] A more intuitive approach may occur to you for doing this profit allocation. But your intuition may fail you in situations that are more complex than this simple two-way split. The formal approach presented here will pay dividends when you encounter more complex scenarios.

We can make the proportion more complete. The size of C relative to $58,500 (the sum of the two terms in the first ratio) is the same as 45 relative to 117 (the sum of the two terms in the second ratio). A corresponding statement can be made for K. This additional information can be included in the proportion as follows:

$$C:K:\$58,\!500 = 45:72:117$$

Now we can determine C and K by solving two equations based on this proportion:

$$\frac{C}{\$58,\!500} = \frac{45}{117} \quad \text{and} \quad \frac{K}{\$58,\!500} = \frac{72}{117}$$

After cross-multiplication, we obtain Connor's share, $C = \$22,\!500$, and Kristen's share, $K = \$36,\!000$.

In general, if we have a proportion such as

$$x:y = a:b$$

then we can also write the proportion

$$x:y:(x+y) = a:b:(a+b)$$

and construct the equations

$$\frac{x}{y} = \frac{a}{b}, \quad \frac{x}{x+y} = \frac{a}{a+b}, \quad \text{and} \quad \frac{y}{x+y} = \frac{b}{a+b}$$

Many more applications of proration are presented in the following examples and in the problems of Exercise 3.3.

EXAMPLE 3.3A	**Prorating a Refund Based on the Unused Time Period**

Franco paid $2116 for his automobile insurance coverage for the period July 1 to June 30 of the following year. He sold his car and cancelled the insurance on March 8. The insurer's procedure is to calculate a refund prorated to the exact number of days remaining in the period of coverage. (March 8 is not included in the refundable days.) A $20 service charge is then deducted. What refund will Franco receive?

SOLUTION

The basis for calculating the refund (before the service charge) is

$$\frac{\text{Refund}}{\text{Annual premium}} = \frac{\text{Number of remaining days of coverage}}{365 \text{ days}}$$

The "unused" days in the July 1 to June 30 period are the 23 days remaining in March plus all of April, May, and June. (See Section 6.2 for a method of determining the number of days in each month.) Hence,

$$\frac{\text{Refund}}{\$2116} = \frac{23 + 30 + 31 + 30}{365}$$

$$\text{Refund} = \frac{114 \times \$2116}{365}$$

$$= \$660.89$$

After deduction of the service charge, the net refund will be $660.89 − $20 = $640.89.

➡ **Check your understanding:** Redo the problem, this time assuming Franco sold his car and cancelled the insurance on April 4. (Answer: Net refund = $484.36)

▪▭▶ **Related problem:** #1 in Exercise 3.3

EXAMPLE 3.3B	Allocating Profits Based on the Amount Invested by Each Owner

The partnership of Mr. X, Mr. Y, and Ms. Z has agreed to distribute profits in the same proportion as their respective capital investments in the partnership. How will the recent period's profit of $28,780 be allocated if Mr. X's capital account shows a balance of $34,000, Mr. Y's shows $49,000, and Ms. Z's shows $54,500?

SOLUTION

The ratio of a partner's share of the profit to the total profit will equal the ratio of that partner's capital investment to the total investment.

$$\text{Total investment} = \$34,000 + \$49,000 + \$54,500 = \$137,500$$

$$\frac{\text{Mr. X's share}}{\text{Total profit}} = \frac{\text{Mr. X's investment}}{\text{Total investment}}$$

$$\frac{\text{Mr. X's share}}{\$28,780} = \frac{\$34,000}{\$137,500}$$

$$\text{Mr. X's share} = \frac{\$34,000}{\$137,500} \times \$28,780 = \$7116.51$$

Similarly,

$$\text{Mr. Y's share} = \frac{\$49,000}{\$137,500} \times \$28,780 = \$10,256.15$$

Either of two approaches may now be employed to calculate Ms. Z's share. The longer approach has the advantage of providing a means of checking the answers. In it we calculate Ms. Z's share in the same manner as the other two shares:

$$\text{Ms. Z's share} = \frac{\$54,500}{\$137,500} \times \$28,780 = \$11,407.35$$

The allocations can be checked by verifying that their total, within rounding error, is $28,780:

$$\$7116.51 + \$10,256.15 + \$11,407.35 = \$28,780.01$$

The shorter method for calculating Ms. Z's share is to calculate the balance left from the $28,780 after Mr. X's and Mr. Y's shares have been paid out:

$$\text{Ms. Z's share} = \$28,780.00 - \$7116.51 - \$10,256.15$$
$$= \$11,407.34$$

However, with this method we do not have a means of checking the calculations since, in effect, we have forced Ms. Z's share to be the balance of the $28,780 (whether Mr. X's and Mr. Y's shares were calculated correctly or not).

➡ **Check your understanding:** Redo the problem. This time, the period's profit was $47,495. (Answer: Mr. X's share = $11,744.22, Mr. Y's share = $16,925.49, Ms. Z's share = $18,825.29)

▮▶ **Related problem:** #5 in Exercise 3.3

EXAMPLE 3.3C	Allocating a Firm's Shared Costs

The Quebec plant of a manufacturing company produced 10,000 units of a product during the last fiscal quarter using 5000 hours of direct labour. In the same period, the Ontario plant produced 20,000 units using 9000 hours of direct labour. How will shared managerial costs of $49,000 for the period be allocated between the two plants if the allocation is based on

a. Direct labour hours?

b. Units of output?

SOLUTION

a.
$$\frac{\text{Quebec's share}}{\text{Total overhead}} = \frac{\text{Quebec's labour hours}}{\text{Total labour hours}}$$

$$\text{Quebec's share} = \frac{5000}{14,000} \times \$49,000 = \$17,500.00$$

Similarly,

$$\text{Ontario's share} = \frac{9000}{14,000} \times \$49,000 = \$31,500.00$$

b.
$$\frac{\text{Quebec's share}}{\text{Total overhead}} = \frac{\text{Quebec's output}}{\text{Total output}}$$

$$\text{Quebec's share} = \frac{10,000}{30,000} \times \$49,000 = \$16,333.33$$

Similarly,

$$\text{Ontario's share} = \frac{20,000}{30,000} \times \$49,000 = \$32,666.67$$

➡ **Check your understanding:** At Edmonton Distribution Inc., the marketing department employs 12 people and the accounting department employs 7 people. How will shared costs of $122,000 be allocated between the two departments if the allocation is based on number of employees? (Answer: $77,052.63 allocated to the marketing department; $44,947.37 allocated to the accounting department)

▮▮▷ **Related problem:** #9 in Exercise 3.3

EXERCISE 3.3

Answers to the odd-numbered problems can be found in the end matter.

BASIC PROBLEMS

1. The Morrison family settled a warranty claim with the manufacturer of their roof shingles. The shingles were guaranteed for 15 years, but required replacement after just 9.5 years on their home. If the shingles were originally purchased for $3850, and the manufacturer has agreed to a prorated refund based on the length of time the shingles were used, how much will the Morrison family receive as settlement of their claim?

2. A three-year magazine subscription costing $136 may be cancelled at any time, and a prorated refund will be made for the remaining weekly issues. If Juanita cancels her subscription after receiving 17 issues in the second year, what refund should she get? Assume there are exactly 52 weeks in a year.

3. When real estate is sold, the year's property taxes are allocated to the vendor and the purchaser in proportion to the number of days that each party owns the property during the year. If the purchaser took possession of a property effective August 8 (of a 365-day year), how will the year's property taxes of $2849 be allocated to the vendor and purchaser?

4. If you use your car for both business and pleasure, the Canada Revenue Agency will usually allow you to report a portion of the costs of operating the vehicle as a business expense. This portion is determined by the ratio of the distance travelled on business to the total distance travelled in the year. Last year, Harjap spent a total of $11,348 on gasoline, oil, repairs and maintenance, and insurance. His travel log shows that he drove 14,488 kilometres on business and 8329 kilometres on personal use. What vehicle expense can Harjap report for the year?

5. If you operate a home-based business, the Canada Revenue Agency (CRA) will usually allow you to report certain "office-in-home" expenses. The portion of heat, insurance, electricity, property taxes, and mortgage interest that you may report must be (in the language of the CRA) "reasonable under the circumstances."

    Rose uses 2 of the 11 rooms in her home for her real estate appraisal business. The combined floor area of the 2 rooms is 36 square metres. The remainder of the house has an area of 147 square metres. Rose's total expenses in the home-related categories were $17,512 for the year. What amount will qualify as "office-in-home" expenses if the proration is based on

    a. The number of rooms used for the business?

    b. The floor area devoted to business use?

INTERMEDIATE PROBLEMS

6. The leases in multiple-unit commercial developments commonly permit the landlord to allocate to the tenants various common area and general costs such as property taxes, janitorial services, security services, and snow removal. These costs are usually prorated on the basis of the floor area leased to each tenant. Sunseekers Tanning Salon, Avanti Pizza, and Pine Tree Pharmacy are the three tenants in Pine Tree Square. They lease 172 square metres, 136 square metres, and 420 square metres, respectively. How should common costs totalling $9872 for the past year be allocated?

7. Three insurance companies agree to jointly insure a cargo ship for $38.6 million. If insurers A, B, and C allocate premiums received and accept the risk in the ratio 3:8:5, respectively,

    a. How will the annual premium of $900,000 be distributed?

    b. What is the maximum claim exposure of each insurer?

8. Mr. Subhani's will specified that, upon liquidation of any asset, the proceeds be divided among his wife, his son, and his sister in the ratio of 7:5:3.

    a. If the son received $9500 from the sale of securities, what amounts did Mr. Subhani's wife and sister receive?

    b. What amount would the sister receive from the sale of the deceased's car for $27,000?

9. Their partnership agreement requires Harry, Draco, and Hermione to provide capital "when and as required" by the partnership in the ratio 1:1.35:0.85, respectively.

    a. The total initial capital requirement was $256,000. How much did each partner contribute?

    b. One year later, Hermione's share of an additional injection of capital was $16,320. What was Draco's share?

10. The X-ray department of a hospital served 934 patients last month and uses 185 square metres of space. The ultrasound department of the hospital served 1800 patients last month and uses 275 square metres of space. How will overhead costs of $85,000 for the month be allocated between the two departments if the allocation is based on

    a. Number of patients served?

    b. Space used?

ADVANCED PROBLEMS

11. Kevin, Lyle, and Marnie operate Food Country as a partnership. Their agreement provides that half of the profit in each calendar quarter be distributed in proportion to each partner's investment in the partnership, and that the other half be distributed in proportion to the total number of hours that each partner works in the business. The following table presents each partner's investment, and the hours worked during the most recent quarter. Rounded to the nearest cent, how should the quarter's profit of $112,460 be allocated?

Partner	Amount invested ($)	Hours worked
Kevin	130,000	210
Lyle	86,000	365
Marnie	29,000	632

12. The following table shows National Paper Products's capital investment in each of its three divisions, and the most recent year's gross sales for each division. The operating costs of the head office for the year were $839,000. These costs are allocated to the divisions before each division's profit is determined. How much (rounded to the nearest dollar) should be allocated to each division if the costs are prorated on the basis of

    a. The capital investment in each division?

    b. The sales of each division?

Division	Investment ($)	Gross sales ($)
Industrial products	25,300,000	21,200,000
Fine paper	17,250,000	8,350,000
Containers and packaging	11,900,000	7,450,000

13. Geological Consultants Ltd. is a private company with four shareholders: W, X, Y, and Z. Their respective shareholdings are shown in the table below. X is retiring and has come to an agreement with the other three shareholders to sell his shares to them for $175,000. The agreement calls for the 500 shares to be purchased and allocated among W, Y, and Z in the same ratio as their present shareholdings. Because the shares are indivisible, the share allocation must be rounded to integer values.

Partner	Number of shares owned
W	300
X	500
Y	350
Z	400

    a. What implied value does the transaction place on the entire company?

    b. How many shares will W, Y, and Z each own after the buyout?

    c. What amount will each of the continuing shareholders contribute toward the $175,000 purchase price? Prorate the $175,000 on the basis of the allocation of the shares in Part (b).

3.4 Application: Exchange Rates and Currency Conversion

LO4 International trade and tourism are important components of commercial activity in Canada. Also, Canadians are increasingly investing in foreign securities. The vast majority of these transactions involve a conversion from Canadian dollars to a foreign currency, or vice versa. In this section, we will study the mathematics of currency conversion.

Suppose that

$$\$1.00 \text{ Canadian} = \$0.85 \text{ American}$$

In finance, this is usually written

$$C\$1.00 = US\$0.85$$

To get the C$ equivalent of US$1.00, divide both sides of the equation by 0.85, giving

$$C\$1.17647 = US\$1.00$$

The **exchange rate** between two currencies is defined as the amount of one currency required to purchase one unit of the other currency. Consequently, the exchange rate for a pair of currencies has two equivalent forms, depending on which currency is being purchased. For the C$ and US$, the exchange rate may be quoted as either

$$\frac{US\$0.85}{C\$1.00} \quad \text{or} \quad \frac{C\$1.17647}{US\$1.00}$$

You should employ a formal approach for currency conversion in order to handle cases in which you do not have a feel for the relative values of two currencies. Using the preceding exchange rates, let us calculate the cost in C$ to purchase US$600. It does not matter which version of the two exchange rates you pick. Suppose you choose $\frac{US\$0.85}{C\$1.00}$. Set up an equation stating that the ratio of the actual amounts of money in the exchange transaction equals the exchange rate. That is,

$$\frac{US\$600}{C\$x} = \frac{US\$0.85}{C\$1.00}$$

Note that the currencies must be in the *same order* in both ratios. Now solve for the unknown amount of money, C$x. In this case, cross-multiplication gives

$$C\$1.00 \times US\$600 = US\$0.85 \times C\$x$$

Then

$$C\$x = \frac{C\$1.00 \times US\$600}{US\$0.85} = C\$705.88$$

Financial institutions usually charge for their currency exchange services. Some charge a fee or commission. A majority of them take the approach employed in retailing where inventory is purchased and then sold at a higher price. These financial institutions buy a foreign currency at one "price" and sell it at a higher "price." For example, a bank might pay you C$195 to buy the £100 you have left over after your trip to Great Britain. But a person immediately after you wanting to obtain £100 would have to pay something like C$205. The bank thereby makes a C$10 profit from the two transactions. Operationally, the bank uses a different exchange rate for buying a currency (the "buy rate") than for selling the same currency (the "sell rate").

While you are becoming familiar with currency exchange calculations, we will assume that a foreign currency may be bought and sold at the same exchange rate (perhaps with a commission involved). Later in this section, we will deal with situations involving differing "buy" and "sell" exchange rates.

EXAMPLE 3.4A	Currency Conversion Including a Commission

After spending a week in London, you are travelling on to France. Before departure from Gatwick Airport, you convert your remaining 87 British pounds (£) to euros (€) at the exchange rate £0.715 per € (that is, $\frac{£0.715}{€1.00}$). How many euros will you receive if the currency shop charges a 5% commission on transactions of this small size?

SOLUTION

Before any commission, equivalent currency amounts have a ratio equal to the exchange rate. Let €x represent the equivalent number of euros before deduction of the commission. Then,

$$\frac{£87.00}{€x} = \frac{£0.715}{€1.00}$$

Cross-multiplication gives

$$£87.00 \times €1.00 = £0.715 \times €x$$

Therefore,

$$€x = \frac{£87.00 \times €1.00}{£0.715} = €121.68$$

The commission charge is

$$0.05 \times €121.68 = €6.08$$

The net amount you will receive is €121.68 - €6.08 = €115.60

➡ **Check your understanding:** Redo the problem. This time, you convert 47 British pounds (£) to euros (€) at an exchange rate £0.721 per € at a currency shop that charges a 6% commission. (Answer: €61.28)

▐▬▶ **Related problem:** #7 in Exercise 3.4

Using Exchange Rate Tables

Each day, the financial pages of major Canadian daily newspapers present tables of currency exchange rates. Since most exchange rates change from hour to hour in foreign exchange markets, a table of exchange rates usually specifies the time on the preceding day when the quotations were obtained.

Exchange rates are normally presented in two formats. The less commonly traded currencies are listed in a table similar to Table 3.1. Exchange rates are reported in terms of "C$ per unit of foreign currency" and "US$ per unit of foreign currency." A few of them are presented in Table 3.1.

TABLE 3.1   Foreign Exchange Rates (noon, Toronto, October 30, 2015)

Country	Currency	C$ per unit	US$ per unit
Brazil	real	0.3403	0.2601
China	yuan	0.2071	0.1583
Hong Kong	dollar	0.1688	0.1290
India	rupee	0.02000	0.01529
Indonesia	rupiah	0.000096	0.000073
Mexico	peso	0.07914	0.06049
New Zealand	dollar	0.8849	0.6764
Philippines	peso	0.02799	0.02139
Poland	zloty	0.3396	0.2596
Russia	ruble	0.02050	0.01567
South Korea	won	0.001147	0.000877
Sweden	krona	0.1540	0.1177
Thailand	baht	0.03674	0.02808

Source: Bank of Canada.

The major currencies of international trade are usually presented in a Currency Cross Rate table such as Table 3.2. The figure in any cell of the table is the number of units of the currency in the *row* heading per unit of the currency in the *column* heading. For example, in the top row we see that it required C$1.3083 to purchase US$1.00, C$1.4446 to purchase €1.00, C$0.01084 to purchase ¥1.00, and so on. Expressed as ratios, these exchange rates are

$$\frac{C\$1.3083}{US\$1.00}, \quad \frac{C\$1.4446}{€1.00}, \quad \text{and} \quad \frac{C\$0.01084}{¥1.00}$$

TABLE 3.2   Currency Cross Rates (noon, Toronto, October 30, 2015)

	Per C$	Per US$	Per €	Per ¥	Per £	Per Sw fr	Per A$
Canadian dollar (C$)	•	1.3083	1.4446	0.01084	2.0203	1.3269	0.9332
U.S. dollar (US$)	0.7644	•	1.1042	0.008286	1.5442	1.0142	0.7133
Euro (€)	0.6922	0.9056	•	0.007504	1.3985	0.9185	0.646
Japaense yen (¥)	92.2509	120.6919	133.2657	•	186.3745	122.4077	86.0886
British pound (£)	0.4950	0.6476	0.7150	0.005366	•	0.6568	0.4619
Swiss franc (Sw fr)	0.7536	0.986	1.0887	0.008169	1.5226	•	0.7033
Australian dollar (A$)	1.0716	1.402	1.548	0.01162	2.1649	1.4219	•

Source: Bank of Canada.

Along the diagonal of the table, the obvious value 1.0000 has been omitted to avoid clutter. Note that each exchange rate below the diagonal is the reciprocal of its counterpart above the diagonal. For example,

$$US\$0.7644 \text{ per C\$} = US\$\frac{1}{1.3083} \text{ per C\$}$$

and

$$£0.6476 \text{ per US\$} = £\frac{1}{1.5442} \text{ per US\$}$$

Consequently, half of the values in the table are not really needed. It would be sufficient to have just the values above the diagonal or just the values below the diagonal.

EXAMPLE 3.4B | **Currency Conversion Using a Currency Cross Rate Table**

Using an exchange rate from Table 3.2, calculate the number of yen that C$650 could purchase at noon (Toronto time) on October 30, 2015. Round answer to the nearest yen.

SOLUTION

Let the number of yen be ¥y. From Table 3.2, we can work with either

$$\frac{C\$0.01084}{¥1.00} \quad \text{or} \quad \frac{¥92.2509}{C\$1.00}$$

If we choose the second version, then

$$\frac{¥y}{C\$650} = \frac{¥92.2509}{C\$1.00}$$

Cross-multiplication gives

$$¥y = \frac{¥92.2509}{C\$1.00} \times C\$650 = ¥59,963.09$$

Rounded to the nearest yen, C$650 could purchase ¥59,963 at noon (Toronto time) on October 30, 2015.

➡ **Check your understanding:** Redo the problem. This time, calculate the number of yen that C$1,500 could purchase. (Answer: ¥138,376)

▶ **Related problem:** #3 in Exercise 3.4

Sell and Buy Rates for Currency Exchange

The exchange rates quoted in Tables 3.1 and 3.2 are known technically as mid-rates. A **mid-rate** is the exchange rate if there is no charge for providing the currency conversion service. But if you go to a bank to purchase a foreign currency, you will pay more (in terms of C$ per unit of foreign currency) than the mid-rate. The difference represents the bank's charge for providing this service. The bank calls this rate (at which it will *sell* you the foreign currency) the **sell rate**. When you return from a vacation with left-over foreign currency, the bank will *buy* the currency from you at its **buy rate**. This rate will be lower (in terms of C$ per unit of foreign currency) than the prevailing mid-rate. Again, the difference is the bank's charge for the service.

The percentage **spread** or difference between the sell and buy rates depends on many factors. Three important factors are:

- The overall volume of trading in the currency. For example, the percentage spread is smaller on the more heavily traded US$ than on the lower volume British £.
- The form of the exchange transaction. For example, the spread is less on travellers' cheques than on cash.
- The type of business handling the exchange. For example, the spread is smaller at domestic chartered banks than at airport currency-exchange kiosks. As some of the Exercise problems will demonstrate, it is very costly for you to conduct currency-exchange transactions at airport currency-exchange businesses.

EXAMPLE 3.4C | **Currency Conversion at Sell and Buy Rates**

The following table shows the buy and sell rates for US$ quoted by the RBC Royal Bank and a currency exchange kiosk at Toronto's Pearson International Airport on the same date that the mid-rate was C$1.335 per US$. The kiosk also charges an additional flat fee of C$3.50 on every buy or sell transaction.

RBC Royal Bank		Currency exchange kiosk	
Buy rate	**Sell rate**	**Buy rate**	**Sell rate**
C$1.2946 / US$1	C$1.3647 / US$1	C$1.2669 / US$1	C$1.4035 / US$1

On a purchase of US$100, what was the percent transaction cost in each case? (The transaction cost includes the difference between the sell or buy rate and the mid-rate, plus any other fees charged.)

SOLUTION

At the mid-rate, the purchase of US$100 would have required

$$\text{US}\$100 \times \frac{\text{C}\$1.335}{\text{US}\$1.00} = \text{C}\$133.50$$

Both the Royal Bank and the airport kiosk are *selling* you US$, so you must use the quoted "sell rate." At the Royal Bank, you would have paid

$$\text{US}\$100 \times \frac{\text{C}\$1.3647}{\text{US}\$1.00} = \text{C}\$136.47$$

At the airport kiosk, you would have paid

$$\text{US}\$100 \times \frac{\text{C}\$1.4035}{\text{US}\$1.00} = \text{C}\$140.35 + \text{C}\$3.50 = \text{C}\$143.85$$

The percent transaction cost at the Royal Bank was

$$\frac{\text{C}\$136.47 - \text{C}\$133.50}{\text{C}\$133.50} \times 100 = 2.22\%.$$

SOLUTION

a. Amounts with the same purchasing power will be in the same ratio as the CPIs on the respective dates. That is,

$$\frac{2010\ amount}{2012\ amount} = \frac{2010\ CPI}{2012\ CPI}$$

$$\frac{2010\ amount}{\$1000} = \frac{116.5}{121.7}$$

$$2010\ amount = 0.957272 \times \$1000 = \$957.27$$

b. The usual measure of inflation is the percent increase in the CPI. Hence,

$$Percent\ inflation = \frac{2014\ CPI - 2010\ CPI}{2010\ CPI} \times 100$$

$$= \frac{125.2 - 116.5}{116.5} \times 100$$

$$= 7.47\%$$

In 2014, consumer prices were, on average, 7.47% higher than prices in 2010.

c. To keep pace with inflation, salaries must be in the same ratio as the corresponding CPIs.

$$\frac{2014\ salary}{2012\ salary} = \frac{2014\ CPI}{2012\ CPI}$$

$$\frac{2014\ salary}{\$55,000} = \frac{125.2}{121.7}$$

$$2014\ salary = 1.028759 \times \$55,000 = \$56,581.76$$

Rounded to the nearest dollar, Kay had to earn $56,582 in 2014 to keep pace with inflation.

➡ **Check your understanding:** Using the CPI values provided above, answer the following questions: **a.** What amount in 2014 had the same purchasing power as $500 in 2012? **b.** What was the overall percent inflation from 2012 to 2014? **c.** If Kay earned $60,000 in 2014, what amount would she have been earning in 2010 if her earnings had kept pace with inflation? Round your answer to the nearest dollar. (Answer: **a.** $514.38 **b.** 2.88% **c.** $55,831)

▮▮▶ **Related problem:** #7 in Exercise 3.6

EXERCISE 3.6

Answers to the odd-numbered problems can be found in the end matter.

BASIC PROBLEMS

1. Suppose the S&P/TSX Composite portfolio cost $134,590 in 1975 (when the base value of the index was set at 1000). What value was quoted for the S&P/TSX Composite Index on a later date when the same portfolio had a value of $859,700?

2. An item cost $3278 on the base date, when the Consumer Price Index was set at 100. Currently, the same item costs $4961. If the cost of the item has exactly matched inflation, what is the current CPI value?

3. The basket of goods and services included in the Consumer Price Index cost $21,350 on the base date. Eight years later, the same basket cost $26,090. What was the CPI on the latter date?

4. A basket of goods and services representative of the CPI cost $2750 when the CPI stood at 127.2.

   a. What did the basket of goods cost 10 years earlier, when the CPI was at 107.9?

   b. What was the overall percent inflation experienced by consumers for the entire 10-year period?

5. In one year, the CPI increased from 125.9 to 127.2. How much money was required at the end of the year in order to have the same purchasing power as $1000 at the beginning?

INTERMEDIATE PROBLEMS

6. A college student wishes to compare tuition fee increases during the period 2000 to 2015 to the general increase in the cost of living. Tuition increased from $225 per course in the 2000/01 academic year to $375 per course in the 2014/15 academic year. The average CPI rose from 96.1 in 2000 to 127.1 in 2015. What would the tuition fee per course have been in the 2014/15 year if tuition increases had merely kept pace with inflation during the 15 years?

7. Statistics Canada calculates separate subindexes of the CPI for goods and for services. The goods index rose from 96.8 to 112.0 over a 10-year period. During the same period, the services index rose from 95.2 to 115.1.

   a. How much did representative goods, worth $1000 at the beginning, cost at the end of the 10-year period?

   b. How much did representative services, worth $1000 at the beginning, cost at the end of the 10-year period?

   c. What is the difference between the percent increase in the price level of services and the percent increase in the price level of goods during the decade?

8. From the end of 2000 to the end of 2014, the S&P/TSX Composite Index rose from 8934 to 14,632. If you had invested $50,000 in a portfolio of the shares of the companies in the Index at the end of 2000, what would the value of those shares have been at the end of 2014? (This calculation considers only the price appreciation of the original shares. It does not include additional growth in the portfolio's value resulting from the receipt and reinvestment of dividends.)

ADVANCED PROBLEMS

9. We want to compare the increase in value of the stock portfolio represented by the S&P/TSX Composite Index during the 14-year period described in Problem 8 to the general increase in prices of goods and services during the same period. The CPI rose from 96.7 at the end of 2000 to 124.5 at the end of 2014. Calculate the percent increase in the value of the portfolio and the percent increase in the general price level during the 14-year period.

10. Canada has had relatively low inflation rates since the 1990s. The CPI was at 115.1, 117.8, 120.7, 121.3, 123.1, and 124.3 at the beginning of 2010, 2011, 2012, 2013, 2014, and 2015, respectively. These numbers are quoted in terms of a base value of 100 in 2002.

    a. What amount was required at the beginning of 2015 in order to have the same purchasing power as $100 five years earlier, at the beginning of 2010?

    b. What were the inflation rates for each of the years 2010 to 2014 inclusive?

11. The late 1970s and early 1980s were years of historically high rates of inflation in Canada. The CPI was at 35.1, 38.1, 41.8, 46.9, 52.2, and 56.5 at the beginning of 1978, 1979, 1980, 1981, 1982, and 1983, respectively. These numbers are quoted in terms of a base value of 100 in mid-2002.

    a. What amount was required at the beginning of 1983 in order to have the same purchasing power as $100 just five years earlier?

    b. What were the inflation rates for each of the years 1978 to 1982 inclusive?

12. The 1970s were years of high inflation in Canada. By the 1990s, inflation rates had fallen, and have been held to lower levels ever since. Use the Bank of Canada's Inflation Calculator to answer the following questions:

    a. Obtain the cumulative percent inflation for each of four decades: 1975 to 1985, 1985 to 1995, 1995 to 2005, and 2005 to 2015.

    b. How much money was needed in 1995 to have the same purchasing power as $100 in 1985?

    c. How much money was needed in 1975 to have the same purchasing power as $100 in 1985?

    d. How much money was needed in 2015 to have the same purchasing power as $100 in 1975?

Key Terms

Buy rate	Lowest terms	Ratio
Common factor	Mid-rate	Sell rate
Equivalent ratio	Proportion	Spread
Exchange rate	Proration	Terms of a ratio

Summary of Notation and Key Formulas

$$\text{Index number} = \frac{\text{Price or value on the selected date}}{\text{Price or value on the base date}} \times \text{Base value}$$

Review Problems

Answers to the odd-numbered review problems can be found in the end matter.

BASIC PROBLEMS

1. **LO1** Express each of the following ratios in its lowest terms.

    a. $0.18:0.60:0.45$ **b.** $\frac{9}{8}:\frac{3}{4}:\frac{3}{2}$

    c. $\frac{1}{6}:\frac{1}{3}:\frac{1}{9}$ **d.** $6\frac{1}{4}:5:8\frac{3}{4}$

2. **LO2** Solve the following proportions for the unknown quantities.

    a. $t:26:10 = 24:39:s$ **b.** $x:3600:y = 48:40:105$

3. **LO2** Solve the following proportions to four-figure accuracy.

    a. $65:43 = 27.3:x$ **b.** $1410:2330:870 = a:550:b$

4. `LO1` Mark, Ben, and Tanya own 4250, 2550, and 5950 shares, respectively, of MBT Inc. Expressed in its lowest terms, what is the ratio of their share holdings?

5. `LO2` A test-marketing of a newly released video game in a representative Canadian city, with a population of 120,000, resulted in sales of 543 units in a three-month period. If the game sells at the same rate in the rest of the country, where 21,000,000 Canadians have access to retail outlets, what three-month sales may be forecast for the game?

6. `LO4` If Indonesian rupiah 1.00 = C$0.000098, how many rupiah can be purchased with C$1500?

7. `LO4` Before Mr. and Mrs. Percival left for Great Britain, they purchased British pounds at an exchange rate of C$1.8797 = £1.00. When they returned to Canada eight weeks later they converted their remaining £242 back to Canadian currency at the rate of C$1.9035 = £1.00. How much did they gain or lose in Canadian dollars on the round-trip transaction involving the £242?

8. `LO6` Three years ago, when the CPI was at 122.0, the members of a union were earning $22.25 per hour. Now, with the current CPI at 127.1, they are negotiating for a new hourly rate that will restore their former purchasing power. What hourly rate are they seeking?

INTERMEDIATE PROBLEMS

9. `LO2` The new University Hospital is scheduled to have 436 beds. The ratio of nurses to beds to nurses' aides for staffing the hospital is $4:9:2$. Rounded to the nearest person, how many nurses and aides will need to be hired?

10. `LO2` For the last five years the sales of Departments D, E, and F have maintained a relatively stable ratio of $13:17:21$. Department E is forecasting sales of $478,000 for next year. Based on the past sales ratio, what sales would be expected for Departments D and F? Round to the nearest dollar.

11. `LO3` Mr. Nolan's will specifies that the proceeds from his estate be divided among his wife, son, and stepson in the ratio of $\frac{7}{5}:1\frac{5}{7}$, respectively. How much will each receive from the distribution of his $331,000 estate?

12. `LO3` Wendy, Simone, and Leif share the costs of their coffee fund in the ratio $\frac{3}{2}:\frac{2}{3}:\frac{5}{3}$. How will costs of $55 be allocated among them?

13. `LO3` How should common area costs totalling $28,600 be allocated among commercial tenants A, B, C, and D if the costs are prorated based on leased areas of 1260, 3800, 1550, and 2930 square metres, respectively?

14. `LO3` Milan, Katka, and Shoshanna started their partnership with a total investment of $135,000 contributed in the ratio of $3:4:2$. If each partner contributes another $10,000, what will be the ratio of their total contributions?

15. `LO2` A provincial government allocates 25% of its budget to education, 39% to health care, and 11% to social services. If the dollar amount budgeted for education is $22.6 billion, how much is budgeted for health care and for social services? Round to the nearest $0.01 billion.

16. `LO2` A profit-sharing bonus was divided among four employees—Ms. L, Mr. M, Ms. N, and Mr. P—in the ratio of $1.5:1:0.75:0.5$, respectively. If Ms. N received $2000, how much did each of the others receive?

17. `LO5` The exchange rate between the US$ and the C$ declines from US$0.8105 to US$0.7995 per C$. What will be the change in the C$ price to an importer of a US$2000 item?

18. `LO5` If C$1.00 rises from ¥87.94 to ¥89.78, what will be the change in the C$ price to an importer of a ¥2,965,000 car?

19. **LO6** The CPI stood at 114.6. Five years later the CPI was 125.9.

    a. What was the inflation rate for the five-year period?

    b. What amount was required at the end in order to have the same purchasing power as $100 five years earlier?

ADVANCED PROBLEMS

20. **LO3** A partnership agreement provides that half of the annual profit be distributed in proportion to each partner's investment in the partnership, and that the other half be distributed in proportion to the total number of hours that each partner worked in the business during the year. How should the most recent year's profit of $84,780 be allocated if the amounts invested by Alan, Byron, and Carol are $70,000, $30,000, and $45,000, and their hours of work for the year were 425, 1680, and 1440, respectively?

21. **LO4** A steel company in Hamilton can purchase Alberta coal at C$85 per metric ton (1000 kg) or West Virginia coal at US$65 per ton (2000 lb)(1 kg = 2.205 lb). How much cheaper in C$ per metric ton is the less expensive source if US$0.785 = C$1.00?

22. **LO5** The exchange rate between Currencies X and Y is currently Y0.05614 = X1.00. If X weakens by 1.5% relative to Y, what will be the new values for the exchange rates per unit of X and per unit of Y?

© Hero/Corbis/Glow Images RF

CHAPTER 4
Mathematics of Merchandising

LEARNING OBJECTIVES

After completing this chapter, you will be able to:

LO1 Calculate the net price of an item after single or multiple trade discounts

LO2 Calculate a single discount rate that is equivalent to a series of discounts

LO3 Apply ordinary, end-of-month, and receipt-of-goods dating notation to problems involving terms of payment of an invoice

LO4 Calculate the amount of the cash discount for which a payment qualifies

LO5 Solve merchandise pricing problems involving markup and markdown

 **connect**   Throughout this chapter interactive charts and Help Me Solve It videos are marked with a ↗.

MATHEMATICS TOUCHES ALMOST EVERY STAGE of product distribution and merchandising. Consider a retailer who buys goods from her suppliers, marks up the price, and sells the goods to her customers. The cost of the goods to the retailer is usually determined by deducting a "trade discount" from the supplier's "list price." The invoice she receives may offer a "cash discount" for prompt payment of the invoice. The amount of "markup" the retailer adds to the cost price must cover part of her overhead costs, and also generate a suitable profit. For a sale or special promotion, the retailer may offer a discount or "markdown" from the regular selling price.

In this chapter, we will learn the terminology and procedures for these calculations. We will also explore the mathematical relationships among pricing variables. This will help us understand how a change in one variable affects the other variables.

TIP

How to Succeed in Business Mathematics

In Connect, there are a guide and a video entitled "How to Succeed in Business Mathematics." These can be found in Library Resources under Course-wide Content.

4.1 | Trade Discounts

LO1 Goods move from a manufacturer to the ultimate consumer through the *distribution chain* or *merchandising chain*. In the chain illustrated by Figure 4.1, a product is first sold by a *manufacturer* to one or more *distributors*. The agreement between a manufacturer and a distributor usually gives the distributor the *exclusive* right to distribute the product in a fairly large geographic region, but prohibits the distributor from handling competing products. Typically, a distributor also has marketing responsibilities in the region. The distributor then resells the goods to a number of *wholesalers*. A wholesaler carries a wider range of products within a general category or theme. All are for resale to *retailers* within a smaller geographic area. Retailers sell mainly to the ultimate consumers of the goods.

FIGURE 4.1 The Distribution Chain

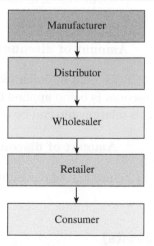

In many cases, one or more of the intermediate links may be absent. Large national retailers and *buying groups* of smaller retailers may have enough buying power to purchase directly from manufacturers. "Cutting out" members of the distribution chain may allow large retailers to set lower prices than their smaller competitors who generally do not have enough purchasing power to buy directly from the manufacturers of the goods they sell.

To understand how prices are usually established within the distribution chain, imagine that you are a wholesaler buying from a distributor. The distributor is likely to have a catalogue of list prices. A **list price** is commonly chosen to reflect the ultimate retail selling price. (No doubt you have noticed terms such as "manufacturer's suggested retail price" or "recommended selling price" on the packaging or in advertisements for certain products.) The distributor will offer you a percent discount from the list price[1] called the **trade discount** rate. The word "trade" signifies that the discount applies only to a transaction within the "trade," that is, within the merchandising chain (but not including the consumer). There may be some negotiating room for setting the rate of trade discount.

The resulting price after deducting the amount of the trade discount from the list price is called the **net price**. That is,

$$\text{Net price} = \text{List price} - \text{Amount of trade discount}$$
$$= \text{List price} - (\text{Rate of trade discount} \times \text{List price})$$

The following symbols will be used to convert the preceding word equation to an algebraic equation.

$$N = \text{Net price}$$
$$L = \text{List price}$$
$$d = \text{Rate of trade discount}$$

Replacing the quantities in the word equation by these symbols, we obtain

$$N = L - dL$$

Since L is a common factor on the right side, we can write the basic discounting formula as

NET PRICE AFTER A DISCOUNT $N = L(1 - d)$ **(4-1)**

Finding the Amount of Discount in Dollars

The net price, N, is the price *after* a discount has been applied. Therefore, N will always be a smaller value than the list price, L. The amount of the discount in dollars is the difference between the list price and the net price. For example, if an item with a list price of $150 sells for a net price of $125, it is being discounted by $25. This relationship can be expressed as

Amount of discount = $L - N$ **(4-2)**

Another way to determine the amount of a discount in dollars is by multiplying the list price, L, by the discount rate, d. For example, if a 40% discount is being applied to an item that lists for $250, the amount of the discount is $250 × 0.40, or $100. This relationship can be expressed as

Amount of discount = dL   **(4-3)**

The choice of formula for calculating the amount of discount is dependent upon which variables are provided in any given question.

Multiple Discounts (or Series Discounts)

In the past, it was common for a seller/vendor in the merchandising chain to offer more than one discount. For example, in addition to the basic trade discount offered to a member of the distribution chain, the seller might also offer discounts for large volume purchases, for special promotions and cooperative advertising, and for early orders of seasonal items.

---

[1]   The use of trade discounts in conjunction with fixed list prices makes it easier for the seller to set different prices for various categories of customers. For example, a manufacturer might offer one discount rate to a distributor in one part of the country, another discount rate to "big box" retailers, and yet another rate to smaller buying groups. Every customer sees the same upfront list price. Price flexibility is achieved in the setting of the trade discount rate.

If a purchaser qualifies for more than one discount, the understanding is that the discounts should be compounded rather than added. This means that we use a formula similar to formula (4-1) but with a $(1 - d)$ factor for each discount. If there are three discounts, d_1, d_2, and d_3, then the net price is

NET PRICE AFTER
THREE DISCOUNTS
$$N = L(1 - d_1)(1 - d_2)(1 - d_3) \qquad\qquad \textbf{(4-4)}$$

The granting of separate multiple discounts has been largely abandoned. It is now more typical for buyers and sellers to negotiate a single discount rate that can be adjusted over time as the business relationship evolves. Rather than offering a volume discount on individual orders, vendors increasingly pay a year-end discount (in the 2% to 5% range) dependent on a customer's total purchases during the year.

Single Discount Rate Equivalent to Multiple Discounts

LO2   An **equivalent discount rate** is the single discount rate that gives the same net price as the combined effect of the multiple discounts. Suppose, for example, that the net amount after applying three discounts to a list price of $100 is $74. Then the dollar amount of the discount is $100 − $74 = $26. Substituting the known values into formula (4-3), we obtain

$$\text{Amount of discount} = dL$$
$$\$26 = d(\$100)$$

Rearranging to solving for d we obtain

$$d = \frac{\$26}{\$100}$$
$$d = 0.26$$

Converting the d value to a percentage requires that we multiply by 100. Therefore, the discount rate is $0.26 \times 100 = 26\%$.

This example suggests the most straightforward approach for calculating an equivalent discount rate. First, determine the net price after applying the given multiple discounts to a list price of $100. Then calculate the dollar amount of the discount—the percent equivalent discount rate is *numerically* equal to the amount of the discount. See Example 4.1E.

TRAP   ⚠

Do Not Add Series Discounts

The single rate that is equivalent to two or more discounts *cannot* be obtained by adding the individual discounts. For example, if a retailer offers a 40% discount and another 15% discount on an item, the customer is *not* saving a total of 55%. The equivalent discount rate will always be smaller than the sum of the discounts. This happens because the second and third individual discounts are applied to amounts smaller than the list price, whereas the equivalent rate is applied to the full list price.

Other Applications

Although formula (4-1) was derived in the context of trade discounts, it may be used in any discount or "% off" calculation. Indeed, formula (4-1) applies to any situation in which an amount (L) is reduced by d percent. Such applications include the calculation of the "sale" price after a percentage markdown, the value of an investment after a percentage loss, and budget amounts after a percentage cut.

Similarly, formula (4-4) may be employed in any situation where a beginning amount, L, undergoes a series of compound percent decreases. N represents the amount left after the decreases. For example, suppose a product's sales are forecast to decline from the past year's sales of $200,000 by 10%, 20%, and 15% in the next three successive years. Substituting into formula (4-4), we can calculate sales in the third year as follows:

$$
\begin{aligned}
N &= L(1 - d_1)(1 - d_2)(1 - d_3) \\
&= \$200,000(1 - 0.10)(1 - 0.20)(1 - 0.15) \\
&= \$200,000(0.90)(0.80)(0.85) \\
&= \$122,400
\end{aligned}
$$

Note that the three decreases result in an overall sales reduction of $200,000 − $122,400 = $77,600. As a percentage this is $\frac{\$77,600}{\$200,000}$ or 38.8%. This is less than the sum (10% + 20% + 15% = 45%) of the three percentage decreases.

| EXAMPLE 4.1A | Calculating the Discount Amount and Net Price |

A wholesaler lists an item at $117 less 20%. What is the amount of the discount and the net price to a retailer?

SOLUTION

Given: $L = \$117$, $d = 0.20$

Substituting these values into formula (4-3), we have

$$
\begin{aligned}
\text{Amount of discount} &= dL \\
&= (0.20)(\$117) \\
&= \$23.40
\end{aligned}
$$

Now, substitute known values for L and *Amount of discount* into formula (4-2) to solve for N.

$$
\begin{aligned}
\text{Amount of discount} &= L - N \\
\$23.40 &= \$117 - N
\end{aligned}
$$

Subtract $117 from both sides:
$$
\begin{aligned}
\$23.40 - \$117 &= -N \\
-\$93.60 &= -N
\end{aligned}
$$

Multiply both sides by −1 and transpose:
$$
N = \$93.60
$$

The discount was $23.40 and the retailer's net price was $93.60.

➡ **Check your understanding:** What is the amount of discount and net price if the list price changes to $198 and all other information remains the same?
(Answer: Amount of discount = $39.60 and Net price = $158.40)

▪▪▶ **Related problem:** #1 in Exercise 4.1

| EXAMPLE 4.1B | Calculating the List Price |

After a trade discount of 30%, a service station is able to purchase windshield wiper blades for a net price of $19.46. What is the list price of the blades?

SOLUTION

Given: $d = 0.30$, $N = \$19.46$

Substituting these values into formula (4-1), we have

$$N = L(1 - d)$$
$$\$19.46 = L(1 - 0.30)$$

Solving for L, we obtain

$$L = \frac{\$19.46}{0.70} = \$27.80$$

The list price of the blades is $27.80.

➡ **Check your understanding:** What is the list price of the blades if the trade discount is 40% and all other information remains the same? (Answer: $32.43)

▮▮▶ **Related problem:** #7 in Exercise 4.1

| EXAMPLE 4.1C | Calculating the Trade Discount Rate |

A sporting goods store is able to purchase men's down-filled jackets at a net price of $173.40 after a discount of $115.60. What rate of trade discount was obtained?

SOLUTION

Given: Net price, $N = \$173.40$, Amount of discount = $115.60

Substituting into formula (4-3) we have

$$\text{Amount of discount} = dL$$
$$\$115.60 = dL$$

At this point, we can see that we must calculate L, the "List price" before we can solve for d. This is a good illustration of the fact that solving a problem sometimes requires you to take a "detour," to go back and find another variable before you can proceed to solve for the variable you are really seeking.

To find L, substitute known values into formula (4-2) and solve:

$$\text{Amount of discount} = L - N$$
$$\$115.60 = L - \$173.40$$
$$L = \$115.60 + \$173.40$$
$$L = \$289$$

Remember that the reason we needed the value for L was to allow us to solve for d in formula (4-3) above. We can retrace our steps back to where we left off at

$$\$115.60 = dL$$

Substituting $L = \$289$ we have: $\quad \$115.60 = d(\$289)$

Solving for d we have: $\quad d = \dfrac{\$115.60}{\$289} = 0.40$

The trade discount rate is 40%.

➡ **Check your understanding:** What is the rate of trade discount if the net price of the coat is $346.80 and all other information remains the same? (Answer: 25%)

▮▮▶ **Related problem:** #11 in Exercise 4.1

EXAMPLE 4.1D	Calculating the Net Price After Multiple Discounts

Western Sports Inc. and Central Athletic Apparel both produce branded team jerseys for schools and clubs. Each supplier offers jerseys that are very similar in quality and popularity. Both manufacturers quote a list price of $46 for a jersey. Western Sports Inc. offers a regular trade discount of 25% plus an additional volume discount of 10% on orders of at least 1000 jerseys. Central Athletic Apparel offers a standard discount of 30% and a further 5% discount on orders exceeding 500 jerseys. Which source will give the lower net price on an order for 1000 jerseys? How much lower per jersey?

SOLUTION

Given: For Western Sports, $L = \$46$, $d_1 = 25\%$, $d_2 = 10\%$;
       for Central Athletic, $L = \$46$, $d_1 = 30\%$, $d_2 = 5\%$

The net price per jersey from Western Sports is

$$N = L(1 - d_1)(1 - d_2) = \$46(1 - 0.25)(1 - 0.10)$$
$$= \$46(0.75)(0.90)$$
$$= \$31.05$$

The net price per jersey from Central Athletic is

$$N = L(1 - d_1)(1 - d_2) = \$46(1 - 0.30)(1 - 0.05)$$
$$= \$46(0.70)(0.95)$$
$$= \$30.59$$

Therefore, Central Athletic's net price is $31.05 − $30.59 = $0.46 per jersey lower. (Note that the sum of the two discount rates in each case is 35%. However, the combined discounts do not have the same effect. This reinforces the point that series discounts cannot simply be added together.)

➡ **Check your understanding:** Redo the question assuming that, this time, both manufacturers quote a list price of $32 per jersey. All other information remains the same. (Answer: Central Athletic's net price is lower by 32 cents per jersey.)

▮▮▶ **Related problem:** #17 in Exercise 4.1

EXAMPLE 4.1E	Calculating an Equivalent Discount Rate

What single discount rate is equivalent to multiple discounts of 20% and 10%?

SOLUTION

Let us apply the two discounts to a beginning value of $100. (Although any beginning value could be used, the choice of $100 allows for easy conversion from dollars to a rate of discount.)

$$N = L(1 - d_1)(1 - d_2) = \$100(1 - 0.20)(1 - 0.10) = \$100(0.80)(0.90) = \$72$$

The amount of the discount is $100 − $72 = $28. Then $\frac{\$28}{\$100} = 0.28$ which, after converting to a percentage by multiplying by 100, means the single discount rate is 28%. Therefore, a single discount rate of 28.0% is equivalent to multiple discount rates of 20% and 10%.

➡ **Check your understanding:** What single discount rate is equivalent to multiple discounts of 30% and 20%? (Answer: 44.0%)

▮▮▶ **Related problem:** #23 in Exercise 4.1

EXAMPLE 4.1F	Calculating One of a Series of Discounts

A provincial government recently tabled a budget in which agricultural subsidies will be reduced by 10% in each of the next three years. Subsidies in the current fiscal year total $11,000,000. What will be the amount of the reduction in the third year?

SOLUTION

The third 10% reduction will apply to the amount left after the first two reductions. The subsidies paid in the second year will be

$$N = L(1 - d_1)(1 - d_2) = \$11,000,000(1 - 0.10)(1 - 0.10)$$
$$= \$11,000,000(0.90)(0.90)$$
$$= \$8,910,000$$

Reduction in the third year $= d_3 \times \$8,910,000 = 0.10(\$8,910,000) = \$891,000$

➡ **Check your understanding:** Redo the question. This time, the subsidies are being reduced by 12% in each of the next three years. All other information remains the same. (Answer: $1,022,208 reduction in the third year)

▮▮▶ **Related problem:** #31 in Exercise 4.1

EXERCISE 4.1

Answers to the odd-numbered problems can be found in the end matter.

In the following questions, round dollar values to the nearest $0.01 and percentages to the nearest 0.01%.

BASIC PROBLEMS

1. An electronics distributor is eligible for a 33.$\overline{3}$% trade discount. What net price will the distributor pay for a tablet device that lists for $249? What is the amount of the discount?

2. A retailer is eligible for a 16% discount. How much will the retailer pay for an item that lists for $995? What is the amount of the discount?

3. An automotive parts distributor paid $106.65 for a part that lists for $127.98. What is the amount of the discount? What discount rate was applied to the purchase?

4. If an item that lists for $49.95 is sold to a member of the distribution chain for $34.97, what is the amount of the discount? What discount rate is being applied?

5. The distributor of Nikita power tools is offering a trade discount of 38% to hardware stores. What will be the stores' cost to purchase a rotary saw listed at $135?

6. Best Buy Entertainment can obtain Panasonic digital media players for $134 less a trade discount of 35%. A comparable Samsung model is available for $127 less a discount of 30%. Which media player has the lower net cost? How much lower?

7. After a discount of 12.5%, a home improvement retailer paid $2849 to buy a riding lawn mower from a supplier. What is the lawn mower's list price? What is the discount amount?

8. Mark's Wholesale Supply Co. is eligible for a 27.25% discount from its supplier. Mark's Wholesale paid $413.05 for an item. What is the list price of that item? What is the amount of the discount?

9. A 37.5% trade discount on a Nikon digital camera represents a discount of $223.14 from the suggested retail price. What is the net price to the buyer?

10. After a trade discount of 27.5%, a jeweller can obtain half-carat Canadian Polar Bear diamonds for $2138.75. What is the amount of the trade discount in dollars?

11. The net price to a car dealer of a model with a manufacturer's list price of $34,900 is $28,687.80. What trade discount rate is the dealer being given?

12. Green Thumb Garden Centre sells spreading junipers to the garden departments of local grocery stores. The net price per tree is $27.06 after a trade discount of $22.14. What rate of trade discount is the nursery giving to the stores?

13. After a discount of $258.75, a distributor paid $891.25 to purchase an item from a manufacturer. What rate of discount was applied to the purchase?

14. Benedict's Restaurant Supply paid $390.45 to buy an industrial mixer from a wholesaler. Benedict's was eligible for a discount of $179.55. What rate of discount was applied to the purchase?

15. A college bookstore buys back good-condition textbooks for 45% off the retail price of new books. What will a student receive for a book currently selling at $104.50 new?

16. The net proceeds to the vendor of a house after payment of a 5.5% real estate commission were $321,111. What price did the house sell for?

17. How much will a wholesaler pay for an item that lists for $99 if she is eligible for a trade discount of 30% and a special promotional discount of 18.75%. What is the total amount of the discount in dollars?

18. Durham Distributors buys an item from a supplier that lists for $595. Durham is eligible for a trade discount of 20%, a volume discount of 12.5% and a special promotional discount of 8%. How much does Durham Distributors pay for the item? What is the total discount amount in dollars?

19. Janeth is selling a cottage property that is currently listed for $299,900. Her real estate agent has convinced her that the price needs to be discounted by 3.2% to take into account the poor condition of the roof. Rounded to the nearest dollar, what new price has Janeth agreed to place on this property?

INTERMEDIATE PROBLEMS

20. Marina found a purse that regularly sells for $100 on the sale rack of her favourite store. The purse was marked down by 40%. A sign on the sale rack said "Take an additional 50% off sale prices today only." Marina is convinced that she will be saving $90 on this purchase.

   a. How much will Marina actually pay for the purse?

   b. If the retailer had really meant to sell the purse for $10, what discount rate would it have needed to advertise in the "today only" sale?

21. Niagara Dairies gives convenience stores a trade discount of 24% on butter listed at $72.00 per case. Silverwood Milk Products has a list price of $74.50 per case of butter. What rate of discount will Silverwood have to offer to match Niagara's price to convenience stores?

22. At its current price of $0.80 per kilogram, the wholesale price of a commodity is down 73% from its price one year ago. What was that price?

23. An invoice shows a net price of $176.72 after trade discounts of 30%, 10%, and 2% have been deducted.

   a. What was the list price of the goods?

   b. What single rate of trade discount would be equivalent to the discount series?

24. A national "big box" retailer is able to purchase automotive tires directly from the manufacturer. The retailer pays $172.35 for a performance tire that lists for $382.99. A small local tire shop does not have sufficient purchasing power to deal directly with the manufacturer, and must purchase the same tire from a distributor for $248.94.

   a. What rate of trade discount is the national retailer eligible for?

   b. What rate of trade discount is the local tire shop eligible for?

   c. The local tire shop approached its distributor and negotiated a "seasonal" discount that would bring the price of the tire down to the same price currently being paid by the "big box" retailer. What additional "seasonal" discount did the local tire shop negotiate?

25. A wholesaler lists an item for $48.75 less 20%. What additional "special promotion" discount must be offered to retailers to get the net price down to $36.66?

Problems 26 through 29 illustrate that the concepts of "discount" or "percentage off" can be applied to non-merchandising scenarios.

26. A merchant pays a 3.5% fee to the Bank of Montreal on all MasterCard sales.

   a. What amount will she pay on sales of $17,564 for a month?

   b. What were her gross sales for a month in which the bank charged total fees of $732.88?

27. Cynthia and Byron sell mutual funds for Syndicated Investors. Purchasers of mutual funds from agents of Syndicated Investors pay a front-end commission of 5.5%. The commission is paid on the total amount paid to Syndicated Investors, not on just the net amount actually invested in mutual funds.

   a. Mr. and Mrs. Stevens placed $5500 through Cynthia. What amount was actually invested in mutual funds after the commission was paid?

   b. If the net amount invested in mutual funds as a result of Byron's sale to Mrs. Stocker was $6426, what amount of commission was paid on the sale?

28. a. Mirabai's income tax rate on additional income is 42%. She has just received a wage increase of $1.25 per hour. What is her after-tax increase in hourly pay?

   b. Shira's tax rate on additional income is 47%. How much extra must he earn to keep an additional $1000 after tax?

29. The evening news reports that the S&P/TSX Composite Index dropped 1.7% on the day to close at 13,646 points. Rounded to the nearest integer, how many points did the index fall on the day?

ADVANCED PROBLEMS

30. A retailer is offered a regular discount of 25%, a further discount of 7.5% if she places an order exceeding $10,000 (at list prices), and another 5% promotional allowance (discount) for participating in a joint promotion with the distributor.

   a. If the retailer is eligible for all three trade discounts, what will be the net price of an order totalling $11,500?

   b. What is the dollar amount of the saving from the quantity discount (assuming that she does not participate in the joint promotion)?

   c. What is the dollar amount of the joint promotional allowance?

31. In addition to the basic trade discount of 20%, an outboard engine manufacturer gives a boat dealer an additional discount of 12.5% for providing follow-up warranty service, and a 5% discount for cooperative advertising and boat-show promotions.

   a. After the basic trade discount, what further price reduction (in dollars) does the 12.5% discount represent on an engine with a list price of $3000?

   b. After the first two discounts, what price reduction does the 5% discount give on the $3000 engine?

32. The representative for a European ski manufacturer offers Snow 'n Surf Sporting Goods a regular discount of 25%, a volume discount of 10% for an order of at least 100 pairs of skis, and an early booking discount of 5% for orders placed before July 1.

   a. If Snow 'n Surf is eligible for all three trade discounts on skis listed at a suggested retail price of $890, what is the net price per pair of skis?

   b. Assuming that Snow 'n Surf qualifies for the volume discount, what is the dollar amount of the early-order discount per pair of skis?

c. The net price after all three trade discounts on a less expensive model of skis is $410.40. What is the suggested retail price?

d. What single trade discount rate would be equivalent to the three trade discounts?

33. The makers of Sea-Fun Jet Skis offer their dealers a series discount of 20% and 10%. In order to encourage the dealers to hold inventory during the slow winter months, Sea-Fun would like to increase the overall discount to 35%. What third discount should Sea-Fun offer to have their dealers receiving a total discount of 35%?

34. Ever-rest sells its mattresses for $960 less 25%. Posture-Perfect mattresses are listed at $880 less 20% and 5%. What second trade discount would Ever-rest need to offer to match Posture-Perfect's net price?

4.2   Cash Discounts and Terms of Payment

LO3   Other than the final sale to the consumer, transactions within the merchandising chain commonly involve "trade credit." Under this arrangement, the vendor does not require payment for goods during a "credit period" that can range from a few days to a few weeks. No interest is charged during this interval. Following a transaction, the vendor sends the buyer an invoice, such as the sample shown in Figure 4.2. The invoice presents details of the "terms of payment," items purchased, unit prices, applicable trade discount rates, shipping cost, Nova Scotia's 15% Harmonized Sales Tax (HST), and the amount due.

FIGURE 4.2   A Sample Sales Invoice

ATLANTIC ATHLETIC WHOLESALE LTD.

177 Main Avenue
Halifax, Nova Scotia B3M 1B4

Sold to:
McGarrigle Sports
725 Kings Road
Sydney, NS B1S 1C2

Date: July 17, 2016
Terms: 2/10, n/30

Invoice No: 3498
Via: Beatty Trucking

Quantity	Product number	Description	Unit list price	Discount	Net amount
5	W-32	Universal Gymnasium	$2300	30%	$8050.00
150	S-4	Soccer balls	$56.00	25%, 15%	5355.00
1000	H-8a	Hockey pucks	$2.20	35%, 10%, 7%	1196.91

Invoice total:	$14,601.91
Shipping charges:	546.00
HST:	2272.19
Total amount due:	$17,420.10

1.5% per month on overdue accounts

Terms of Payment

An invoice normally provides information about any discount for prompt payment and the duration of credit extended to the customer. These **terms of payment** include:

- The length of the **credit period**. The credit period is the length of time for which trade credit is granted. The invoice amount is due at the end of the credit period. Normally, interest is not charged for the credit period. It is common practice to charge a penalty on overdue amounts. The "1.5% per month" indicated on the sample invoice means that any portion of the invoice amount that goes overdue (anywhere from one day to one month) is liable for a 1.5% penalty. How strictly a vendor enforces the penalty is a judgement call.

- The **cash discount** rate offered (if any) and the length of the **discount period**. A cash discount is a deduction allowed for prompt payment[2] of the invoice amount (or any portion thereof). The time period within which a payment qualifies for the cash discount is called the *discount period*.

• The date on which both the credit period and the discount period begin.

The most common system for presenting the terms of payment is known as Section 4.3.) With ordinary dating, both the credit period and the discount period are measured from the invoice date (Day "0"). For example, if an invoice dated July 3 has a 30-day credit period, then July 4 is counted as "Day 1," July 5 as "Day 2," and so on. August 2 will be "Day 30," the final day of the credit period. A payment received on August 2 falls within the credit period, but a payment received on August 3 is liable for the overdue-account penalty.

A shorthand notation is normally used on an invoice to present the terms of payment. Figure 4.3 illustrates the ordinary dating notation in the particular case of a 2% cash discount offered during a 10-day discount period, and a 30-day credit period. The abbreviation "2/10, n/30" is read "Two ten, net thirty."

FIGURE 4.3   Interpreting the Terms of Payment in Ordinary Dating

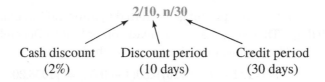

In Figure 4.4 the invoice date, discount period, and credit period for the example 2/10, n/30 are plotted on a time axis. The 2% cash discount is credited on *either partial payments or full payment* made *on or before* the last day of the discount period. The balance is due by the end of the 30-day credit period.

FIGURE 4.4   Discount and Credit Periods for the Ordinary Dating Case 2/10, n/30

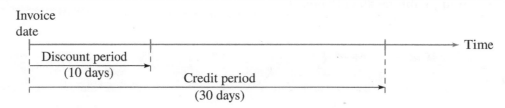

A variation of the ordinary dating notation is "2/10, 1/30, n/60." In this case, a reduced cash discount of 1% is offered on payments made any time from the 11th to the 30th day after the invoice date.

Formula (4-1), $N = L(1 - d)$, may be used to calculate the amount required to settle an invoice if the cash discount is taken. Substitute the invoice amount for L and the cash discount rate for d. The value calculated for N is the full payment that will settle the invoice within the discount period.

TIP

L is Larger, *N* is Smaller

For questions involving discounts for early payment, it is helpful to remember that L is always a *larger* amount than N. If we are taking advantage of the discount for early payment, the *larger* invoice amount, L, can be settled by a *smaller* cash payment, N. A smaller amount of actual cash, N, will receive credit for a larger amount, L, because we are paying within the discount period.

---

[2] It is generally advisable for the purchaser to take advantage of a cash discount. Forgoing the discount is usually equivalent to paying a high interest rate for trade credit during the remainder of the credit period. Therefore, failure of a customer to take advantage of a cash discount provides an early warning signal that the customer may, at least temporarily, be in a weak financial condition. In recent years, there has been a trend away from offering cash discounts. Vendors find that many customers pay after the discount period but still deduct the cash discount from their remittance. Enforcement of the discount period cut-off gives rise to too many hassles with customers.

Partial Payments

LO4 A **partial payment** is any payment smaller than the amount required to fully satisfy the invoice. Unless otherwise indicated on the invoice, partial payments made within the discount period are eligible for the cash discount. The basic discount formula (4-1) may be used to calculate the amount credited to the customer's account. But you must be careful how you use it. See the Trap box that follows the Math Apps below.

EXAMPLE 4.2A	Invoice Settlement with Ordinary Dating

An invoice for $1079.80 with terms 2/10, n/30 is dated November 25. It was received in the mail on November 27. What payment will settle the invoice if payment is made on

a. December 1? **b.** December 5? **c.** December 7?

SOLUTION

a. b. The last day of the discount period is the 10th day after the November 25 invoice date. November has 30 days. Therefore, payments made on or before December 5 are eligible for the 2% cash discount. The payment required to settle the invoice is

$$N = L(1 - d) = \$1079.80(1 - 0.02) = \$1058.20$$

c. After December 5, the full amount must be paid to settle the invoice. The payment required is $1079.80.

⇒ **Check your understanding:** Redo the question assuming the terms are now 3/7, 1/15, n/30. All other information remains the same. (Answers: **a.** $1047.41, **b.** and **c.** $1069)

◼▶ **Related problem:** #5 in Exercise 4.2

 Math Apps

THE COST OF A "CASH-LESS" SOCIETY

Think back to the last thing you bought. Was it your morning coffee? A music download? A tank of gas? Now, think about how you paid for that purchase. Did you use cash? A debit card? A credit card? According to a report by the Canadian Payments Association (CPA), it is increasingly likely you used some form of "plastic"—a debit or credit card. While cash is still the most popular form of payment, the report's author, Michael Tompkins, describes cash as being "still on top but losing speed." In fact, as the following table shows, while cash accounted for 35% of transactions in 2014, the volume of cash transactions was down by 16% since 2011. The number of transactions involving the use of debit and credit cards, on the other hand, is growing significantly, as are transactions involving electronic funds transfers and online transfers.

CANADIAN PAYMENT METHODS			
Rank	Payment method	% of total volume in 2014	Change since 2011 (total %)
1	Cash	35%	−16%
2	Debit cards	24%	+18%
3	Credit cards	21%	+26%
4	Electronic funds transfers	12%	+17%
5	Cheques and paper	5%	−20%
6	Online transfers	1%	+184%

Source: Canadian Payments Association.

While consumers enjoy the convenience of a wide variety of payment options, business owners have become concerned about the increasing use of "plastic"—particularly credit cards. Every time a consumer uses a credit card, the merchant is charged a "merchant fee" or "interchange fee" that, in the past, might have been between 1.5% and 3% of the total transaction amount. These fees are charged by the banks and credit card companies who provide transaction processing services and associated point-of-sale hardware and software. The Canadian Federation of Independent Business (CFIB), a small business advocacy group, estimates that these interchange fees might be costing merchants across Canada between $5 billion and $7 billion per year! While merchants are also charged fees for debit transactions, these fees tend to be much lower, generally in the range of 6 cents per transaction, instead of a percentage of the entire purchase.

In 2012, credit card interchange fees came under scrutiny at a federal Competition Bureau tribunal. Kent Thomson, lead counsel for the Bureau, argued that interchange or merchant fees amount to billions of dollars in hidden costs in Canada every year—"hidden" because credit card companies have historically prohibited merchants from putting a surcharge on credit card transactions to recoup these costs. Thomson argued that Canada's credit card system is a "perverse" place, where shoppers who pay with cash or debit subsidize purchases made with credit cards. Increased costs are passed along to all customers, regardless of which form of payment they use. The Bureau argued that "without changes to Visa's and MasterCard's rules, merchants will continue to pay excessively high card acceptance fees, and these fees will continue to be passed along to consumers in the form of higher prices for goods and services."

While the Competition Tribunal eventually dismissed the case, the attention given to interchange fees contributed to some significant changes in the credit card landscape in Canada. Both Visa and MasterCard voluntarily agreed to reduce and freeze their interchange fees to an average of 1.5% for a five-year period, spanning 2015 to 2020. This reduction will result in some businesses paying lower fees, and provide a five-year window of stable pricing. This stability will be a welcome change from the annual increases most merchants faced in the years leading up to the freeze. Joe Oliver, federal finance minister at the time the agreement was announced, has stated that the commitments made by Visa and MasterCard "represent a meaningful long-term reduction in costs for merchants that should ultimately result in lower prices for consumers."

Some predict more change on the horizon for the credit card industry in Canada. Even with the voluntary fee reduction and freeze announced by Visa and MasterCard, the federal government is still facing pressure to impose regulations that would provide additional relief to merchants. Likely it is only a matter of time before Canada joins the United States, Australia, and some European countries in allowing business owners to put a surcharge on credit card purchases, placing the burden of interchange fees squarely on the shoulders of the customers who use credit cards to make purchases. In theory, if merchants were allowed to pass those costs along directly to credit-card-wielding customers, prices might come down for everyone else, since those fees are currently built into the current price structure and subsidized by all customers. Bank analyst John Aiken is not so sure. "In 2003," he said, "the Reserve Bank of Australia cut interchange fees by roughly half, believing that the cost savings to merchants would be passed on to consumers in the form of lower prices." In reality, "to offset reduced interchange fees, [credit card] issuers increased annual fees, revised reward programs, hiked interest rates on credit cards and related fees for credit card services, and reduced spending on technology innovations. In the end, it appears consumers bear the brunt of the change."

TRAP

This One Catches a Majority of Students!

Suppose a vendor sends you an invoice for $1000 with the offer of a 2% cash discount. You are unable to pay the entire amount, but you do have enough funds to make a $500 partial payment. How much will you still owe toward the invoice after making the $500 partial payment?

Mistake 1: One common mistake is to start by applying a 2% discount to the entire $1000 account balance. Students will say that $1000(1 − 0.02) = $980, so a $500 payment brings the balance down to $980 − $500 = $480. The problem with this approach is that the vendor would not give you a discount on the entire invoice amount if you are only paying *part* of that invoice.

Mistake 2: A second mistake is to apply the 2% discount to the payment by calculating $500(1 − 0.02) = $490, leaving a remaining balance outstanding of $1000 − $490 = $510. This is incorrect. If you pay $500 of actual cash and are only given credit for $490, this represents a *penalty* for paying early, not a reward!

Mistake 3: A final mistake is to say that the $500 cash payment is treated as $500 × 102% = $510 credited to your account, leaving a balance of $1000 − $510 = $490. This is incorrect. To understand why, suppose that instead of a partial payment, you wanted to settle the entire $1000 invoice within the discount period. You would need to pay $1000(1 − 0.02) = $980 of cash, and you would receive additional credit of $20 in the form of the cash discount. The $20 represents 2% of $1000 (the larger amount credited) not 2% of the smaller $980 of cash actually paid. So by applying 2% to our $500 partial payment, we are applying the percentage to the wrong number—the smaller amount paid instead of the larger amount actually credited.

Correct approach: To get the right answer, begin with the basic discount formula (4-1) and put the following interpretation on the variables:

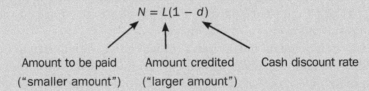

When you make a cash payment of $500, you will receive credit for a larger amount, *L*. The value of that larger amount is currently unknown, so we need to solve for it using

$$N = L(1 − d)$$
$$\$500 = L(1 − 0.02)$$

The larger amount credited to your account will be *L* = $500 ⁄ 0.98 = $510.20.

So by paying $500 of actual cash, you will receive additional credit of $10.20 in the form of a discount or "reward" for early payment. $10.20 represents 2% of the $510.20 of total credit we received. This leaves $1000 − $510.20 = $489.80 still owing toward the invoice.

EXAMPLE 4.2B	**Partial Payments with Ordinary Dating**

Roland Electric received an invoice for $3845 dated March 25 with terms 3/10, 1/20, n/60. Roland paid $1500 on April 4, $600 on April 12, and $500 on April 30. What balance was still owed after April 30?

SOLUTION

The 3% discount applies to any payment made on or before April 4 (March 25 + 10 days.) The 1% discount applies to any payment made in the period April 5 to April 14 inclusive. Therefore, the $1500 payment qualifies for the 3% discount, the $600 payment qualifies for the 1% discount, and the $500 payment does not qualify for any discount. To determine the amount credited for each partial payment, solve for L in formula (4-1). For the $1500 payment,

$$\$1500 = L(1 - 0.03) \text{ giving } L = \frac{\$1500}{0.97} = \$1546.39$$

For the $600 payment,

$$\$600 = L(1 - 0.01) \text{ giving } L = \frac{\$600}{0.99} = \$606.06$$

The balance owed after April 30 was

$$\$3845 - (\$1546.39 + \$606.06 + \$500) = \$1192.55$$

➡ **Check your understanding:** Redo the question assuming that, this time, Roland paid $1800 on April 8, $900 on April 13, and $200 on April 28. All other information remains the same. (Answer: $917.73 still owing after April 30)

▰▱▶ **Related problem:** #13 in Exercise 4.2

EXERCISE 4.2

Answers to the odd-numbered problems can be found in the end matter.

BASIC PROBLEMS

1. An invoice for $2365 is dated September 25 and has credit terms 2/10, n/30. What payment is required on October 5 to settle the invoice?

2. A $2365 invoice dated October 25 has credit terms $1\frac{1}{2}$/15, n/45. How much must be paid on November 10 to settle the invoice?

3. How much would be required on July 7 to settle an invoice of $815.49 dated June 27 with credit terms 2/10, 1/20, n/60?

4. How much would be required on April 13 to settle a $5445 invoice dated March 23 with credit terms 3/10, $1\frac{1}{2}$/20, n/60?

5. On May 25, Morris Hardware received an invoice from Precision Tools Inc. for $5076.64. The invoice was dated May 22 and offered terms of 2/10, 1/20, n/30. What payment will settle the invoice on

    a. June 1?   b. June 2?   c. June 5?

6. River Run Restaurant received an electronic invoice from Canadian Food Supply Inc. dated February 27 of a leap year. The amount of the invoice is $2896.77 with terms $2\frac{1}{2}$/10, 1/30, n/60.

    a. What is the last date on which River Run is eligible for the $2\frac{1}{2}$% discount?

    b. What amount will be required on that date to settle the invoice?

    c. Instead of the payment in (b), what amount must be paid on March 29 to settle the invoice?

7. Central College received an invoice on April 18 from Lakeside Glass for the installation of a glass partition wall. The invoice for $18,976.45 was dated April 16 with terms 2/15, 1/30, n/45.

   a. What is the balance after a payment of $10,000 on May 1?

   b. What additional payment on May 15 will settle the account?

8. An invoice for $2345 has terms 2/10, n/30. As a result of a partial payment that was made within the discount period, the account was credited with $1365. How much was the partial payment? What is the balance remaining on the account?

9. An invoice dated November 18 for $5445 has terms 3/10, n/90. If a $3000 cash payment is made on November 27, how much will be credited to the account? What is the balance owing on the account?

10. An invoice dated March 28 for $3765.25 has terms $1\frac{1}{3}$/15, n/45. A payment was made on April 11 which brought the balance owing on the account down to $2042.28. How much was the payment?

11. An invoice for $775.50 has terms $1\frac{1}{4}$/15, n/60. A payment was made within the discount period to bring the balance owing on the account down to $293.98. How much was the payment?

INTERMEDIATE PROBLEMS

12. Mayfair Distributors sent Bed 'n Bath an invoice dated December 23 for $5344.90 with terms 2/10, 1/20, n/30. The penalty on overdue accounts is $1\frac{1}{2}$% of the overdue balance.

    a. What is the balance after a payment of $3000 on January 3?

    b. What additional payment on January 30 will settle the account?

13. Ristorante Italiano made payments of $5000 on March 29 and $3000 on April 7 to General Restaurant Supplies on an invoice for $11,870. The invoice was dated March 21 and carried terms of $1\frac{1}{2}$/10, $\frac{1}{2}$/20, n/30.

    a. What is the balance after the second payment?

    b. On what date is the balance due?

14. Northern Outfitters's invoice to Whitewater Outdoor Adventures for $2463.80 was dated October 22 with terms 2/10, n/30. Late payments are charged a 1% penalty on the overdue balance. Whitewater made payments of $1000 on October 31 and $800 on November 20. What amount will pay off the balance on December 8?

15. What total amount must be paid on July 4 to settle invoices dated June 20 for $485, June 24 for $367, and June 30 for $722, all with terms $1\frac{1}{2}$/10, n/30?

16. The Simcoe School Board has three invoices from Johnston Transport, all with terms 2/10, 1/20, n/60. Invoice 277, dated October 22, is for $14,200; Invoice 327, dated November 2, is for $8600; and Invoice 341, dated November 3, is for $11,500. What total payment to Johnston on November 12 will settle all three invoices?

17. Harris Manufacturing waited until the last day of the discount period—June 12—to settle an invoice from its supplier, Edwards Electrical Products. The terms were 3/15, n/30. The June 12 payment was $4074, and resulted in full settlement of the debt.

    a. What was the date of the invoice?

    b. What was the full invoice amount?

18. A college club hosted a "Welcome back" barbecue for its student members. The college food service department presented the club with an invoice dated September 15 for $875.75 with terms 2/7, 1/15, n/30. The club made one payment on September 22. A second payment of $429.33 on September 30 fully settled the debt. How much was the September 22 payment?

ADVANCED PROBLEMS

19. Ballard Jewellers received an invoice dated August 22 from Safeguard Security Systems for $2856.57 with terms $2\frac{1}{2}$/10, 1/20, n/45. Ballard made payments of $900 on September 1, $850 on September 10, and $700 on September 30. What amount was still owed on October 1?

20. Peak Roofing sent Jensen Builders an invoice dated July 12 for $5400 with terms 3/10, $1\frac{1}{2}$/20, n/45. Jensen made a payment of $2000 on July 20, and a second payment on August 1 that reduced the balance owed to $1000. What was the size of the second payment?

21. On August 6, A&B Construction has three outstanding invoices payable to Excel Builder's Supply. Invoice 535, dated July 16, is for $3228.56; Invoice 598, dated July 24, is for $2945.31; and Invoice 678, dated August 3, is for $6217.69. All invoices have terms 4/10, 2/20, n/60. If A&B makes a $10,000 payment to Excel on August 6, what further payment on August 15 will settle the account? Note that Excel applies payments to the oldest invoices first.

4.3 Other Terms of Payment

End-of-Month (EOM) Dating

In Figure 4.5 plots the invoice date, the end-of-month date, the discount period, and the credit period on a time axis for the example 2/10, n/30, EOM. In this case the 2% cash discount may be taken in the first 10 days of the next month. If no credit period is explicitly stated, it is understood that the credit period ends 20 days after the discount period. Therefore, n/30 is implied in the notation 2/10, EOM.

FIGURE 4.5 Discount and Credit Periods for the EOM Dating Case 2/10, n/30, EOM

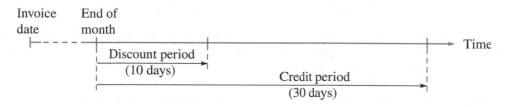

EXAMPLE 4.3A | **Invoice Settlement with EOM Dating**

An invoice for $650.48 with terms $1\frac{1}{2}$/10, EOM is dated November 25. What payment will settle the invoice on

a. November 28?

b. December 6?

c. December 10?

d. December 11?

SOLUTION

a. b.c. The discount period ends at the end of the tenth day after the month's end. Therefore, payments made on or before December 10 qualify for the $1\frac{1}{2}$% cash discount. The payment required to settle the invoice is
$$N = L(1 - d) = \$650.48(1 - 0.015) = \$640.72$$

d. Payment of the full $650.48 is required.

➡ **Check your understanding:** Redo the question assuming the terms are 2/5, EOM. All other information remains the same. (Answers: **a.** $637.47, **b., c.,** and **d.** $650.48)

■■■▶ **Related problem:** #1 in Exercise 4.3

Receipt-of-Goods (ROG) Dating

When the goods being purchased are to be shipped over a long distance with an uncertain delivery date, **receipt-of-goods dating** is sometimes used. Payment terms quoted in the form "2/10, n/30, ROG" mean that the discount and credit periods start on the date of receipt of the goods. Figure 4.6 plots the invoice date, the date of receipt of the goods, the discount period, and the credit period on a time axis for the ROG dating example 2/10, n/30, ROG.

FIGURE 4.6   Discount and Credit Periods for the ROG Dating Case 2/10, n/30, ROG

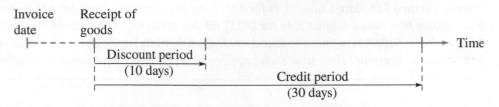

EXAMPLE 4.3B | **ROG Dating**

An invoice dated November 25 for $5340 with terms 1/15, ROG was received on December 1. The merchandise was shipped from Vancouver on December 15 and was received by the purchaser in Goose Bay on January 8.

a. What is the last day of the discount period?   **b.** What is the last day of the credit period?

SOLUTION

a. The last day of the discount period is the 15th day after the date of receipt of the goods. Therefore, January 23 is the last day of the discount period.

b. When a net period is not stated, the understanding is that the credit period ends 20 days after the end of the discount period. This makes February 12 the last day of the credit period. Any unpaid balance is due on that date.

➡ **Check your understanding:** Redo the question assuming the shipment was received by the purchaser in Goose Bay on January 17. All other information remains the same. (Answers: **a.** February 1, **b.** February 21)

▰▰▶ **Related problem:** #3 in Exercise 4.3

EXAMPLE 4.3C | **Partial Payments with EOM Dating**

Counter Culture Microbiological Labs received an invoice for $3000 dated October 20 with terms 2/10, EOM.

a. What amount must Counter Culture pay on November 10 to reduce the balance owed by $1000?

b. What will be the balance owed if Counter Culture instead pays $1000 on November 10?

SOLUTION

a. November 10 is the last day of the discount period. Any partial payment within the discount period qualifies for the cash discount. Using formula (4-1), the $1000 credited is a larger amount, L, than the actual cash paid, N.

$$N = L(1 - d)$$
$$= \$1000(1 - 0.02) = \$980$$

b. In this case, the $1000 represents the smaller amount, N. Counter Culture paid $1000 of cash but receives credit for a larger amount, L.

$$N = L(1 - d)$$
$$\$1000 = L(1 - 0.02)$$
$$L = \frac{\$1000}{1 - 0.02} = \frac{\$1000}{0.98} = \$1020.41 \text{ credited to the account}$$

Hence, balance owed = $3000 − $1020.41 = $1979.59.

⮕ **Check your understanding:** Redo the question assuming the terms are 4/10, EOM. All other information remains the same. (Answers: **a.** $960, **b.** $1041.67 credited, for a balance owed of $1958.33)

▮▮▶ **Related problem:** #5 in Exercise 4.3

EXERCISE 4.3

Answers to the odd-numbered problems can be found in the end matter.

BASIC PROBLEMS

1. An invoice dated December 24 for $3765.25 has terms $1\frac{1}{2}$/15, n/30, EOM. The customer received the goods on January 2. How much is required on January 17 to fully settle the account?

2. An invoice dated August 4 for $775.50 has terms 2/10, EOM. The customer received the shipment on July 30. How much would the customer need to pay on September 5 to fully settle the account?

3. An invoice for $1450.61 dated May 23 has credit terms 2/10, ROG. The customer received the goods on May 28. How much must be paid on June 8 to fully settle the account?

4. An invoice dated November 19 for $995 has credit terms $1\frac{1}{2}$/15, n/60, ROG. The buyer received the goods on December 2. How much must the buyer pay on December 16 to fully settle the account?

5. An invoice for $2678.50 dated April 15 has terms $1\frac{1}{2}$/15, EOM.
   a. When does the discount period end?
   b. When does the credit period end?
   c. What payment on April 30 will reduce the outstanding balance by $800?
   d. If an additional payment of $800 is made on May 5, what will be the new balance?
   e. What further payment on May 10 will reduce the outstanding balance to $800?

6. An invoice for $13,600 dated May 18 has terms 2/10, ROG. The goods were shipped on May 21 and received on May 28.
   a. When does the discount period end?
   b. When does the credit period end?
   c. What payment on May 30 will reduce the outstanding balance by $5000?
   d. Instead of the payment in (c), $5000 is paid on May 30. What will be the balance owed?
   e. Instead of the payments in (c) and (d), what payment on June 5 will reduce the outstanding balance to $5000?

7. Burlingame Carpets received a cheque for $8000 on December 10 from Sorenson Flooring as partial payment of Burlingame's invoice. The invoice, dated November 20, was for $14,772 with terms 2/10, 1/20, n/45, EOM.

   a. How much should Burlingame credit Sorenson's account?

   b. What is the balance still owed?

INTERMEDIATE PROBLEMS

Calculate the missing values in Problems 8 through 11. Assume in each case that the payment is made within the discount period.

Problem	Invoice amount ($)	Credit terms	Payment ($)	Amount credited ($)	Balance owed ($)
8.	2365.00	$1\frac{1}{2}$/10, EOM	?	1421.32	?
9.	815.49	2/10, n/45, ROG	500.00	?	?
10.	1450.61	?/15, n/60, ROG	500.00	?	943.00
11.	995.00	?/10, EOM	700.00	?	285.54

12. Lakeside Marine received an invoice from Osborne Boats dated March 26 with terms $1\frac{1}{2}$/15, n/45, ROG for four 19-foot Barracuda boats at $53,500 each, less 20%, 5%. The boats arrived on April 27. Lakeside made a payment of $120,000 on the account on May 10. How much does Lakeside still owe?

ADVANCED PROBLEM

13. McAfee Power Supply received an invoice dated September 14 from Brant Manufacturing with terms $2\frac{1}{2}$/10, EOM for the following items: four portable generators at $3900 each less 20%, 7%, and six electrical transformers at $4880 each less 25%, 5%. What amount paid on October 10 will cut the amount owed in half?

4.4   Markup

 LO5   The **markup** or **gross profit** is the amount added to the cost of an item to arrive at its selling price. Thus,

$$\text{Selling price} = \text{Cost} + \text{Markup}$$

The markup on each unit must be large enough to cover a portion of the overall operating expenses (such as wages, rent, and utilities) and also make a suitable contribution to the overall operating profit. Expressing this idea as a word equation,

$$\text{Markup} = \text{Overhead expenses per unit} + \text{Operating profit[3] per unit}$$

Let us define the following symbols:

$$S = \text{Selling price (per unit)}$$
$$C = \text{Cost (per unit)}$$
$$M = \text{Markup (per unit)}$$
$$E = \text{Overhead or operating expenses (per unit)}$$
$$P = \text{Operating profit (per unit)}$$

---

[3] In accounting, the "operating profit" on a Statement of Earnings is the profit from normal business operations. Unusual revenues from the sale of capital assets or other nonrecurring events are not included. The "operating profit" in our discussion of markup corresponds to the operating profit from a Statement of Earnings, but calculated on a per-unit basis.

The algebraic versions of the preceding word equations are

SELLING PRICE $S = C + M$ **(4-5)**

MARKUP $M = E + P$ **(4-6)**[4]

If we replace M in formula (4-5) by $E + P$, we obtain

SELLING PRICE $S = C + E + P$ **(4-7)**

Figure 4.7 is a pictorial representation of these relationships. It shows that S may be viewed as being composed of C and M or of C, E, and P. The boundary between E and P is shown as a dashed line because an *accurate* breakdown of M into its components may be done only at the *end* of an accounting period. Suppose, for example, that sales volume during a month is lower than normal. Then each unit's E must include a larger share of the fixed rent expense than it would in a month of higher sales. For a future operating period, a merchandiser can only estimate E based on his sales forecast and his experience in previous periods. (Managers prefer to think of each product line's E in terms of its percentage of C or its percentage of S.) The expected P based on an estimated E is also an approximation.

FIGURE 4.7   Markup Diagram

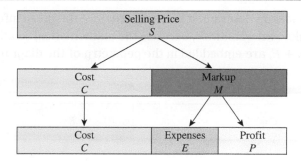

If a retailer is prepared to break even ($P = 0$) in order to clear out old stock, then the reduced price in a clearance sale needs to cover only the cost and the overhead expense. That is,

$$S_{\text{(break even)}} = C + E \text{ and } M_{\text{(break even)}} = E$$

Merchandisers prefer to think of an item's markup in terms of its *percentage* of cost and its *percentage* of selling price. In the "real world," the terminology in this respect is inconsistent. We will use

$$\textbf{Rate of markup on cost} = \frac{M}{C} \times 100\%$$

and

$$\textbf{Rate of markup on selling price*} = \frac{M}{S} \times 100\%$$

*Rate of markup on selling price is sometimes (especially in accounting terminology) called the *gross profit margin*.

When pricing merchandise, retailers usually first decide upon the **rate of markup on cost** for each product line. Then they calculate the corresponding dollar amount of the markup for each product and add it to the unit cost. As shown above, **rate of markup on selling price** can be calculated by dividing dollars of markup, M, by the selling price, S.

The Connection Between the Net Price, *N*, and the Cost, *C*

In Section 4.1, we calculated the net price, N, after one or more trade discounts. In this section we use C to represent an item's (unit) cost. In most cases that we will encounter, C will equal the value of N calculated for one unit.

---

[4] In applications of formulas (4-5), (4-6), and (4-7) in this chapter, we will assume that E and P are constant over the range of sales being considered. In practice, economies of scale usually result in the operating expenses per unit decreasing as the sales volume rises.

For example, suppose a retailer can purchase an item from a wholesaler for a list price of $59, less a trade discount of 15%. Using formula (4-1), $N = L(1 - d)$, we find that the retailer pays a net price of $N = 59(1 - 0.15)$ or $50.15. The per unit cost to the retailer is $C = \$50.15$.

EXAMPLE 4.4A	Calculating the Markup and Selling Price That Will Give a Desired Operating Profit

Coastal Marine is importing a new line of inflatable boats at a unit cost of $1860. Coastal estimates that operating expenses per unit will be 30% of cost.

a. What should the markup and selling price be if Coastal Marine's desired operating profit per unit is 25% of cost?

b. What are Coastal Marine's rate of markup on cost and rate of markup on selling price for the inflatable boats?

SOLUTION

a. Given: $C = \$1860$, $E = 0.30C$, $P = 0.25C$

First we sketch a markup diagram. It helps us organize the given information. It will also help us solve for the unknown quantities, because the mathematical relationships, $M = E + P$ and $S = C + M = C + E + P$, are embedded in the geometry of the diagram.

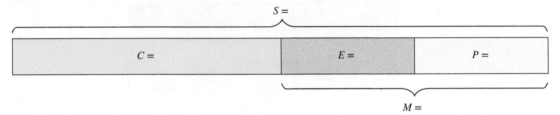

Next enter the given information. The diagram now looks like this:

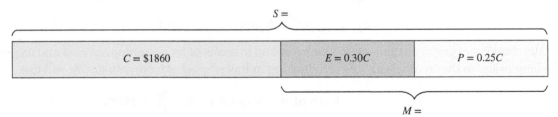

We can directly calculate E and P. That is,

$$E = 0.30C = 0.30(\$1860) = \$558$$

and

$$P = 0.25C = 0.25(\$1860) = \$465$$

After you obtain the numerical value for a variable, enter it on the diagram. This helps you keep track of the variables that are known, and makes it easier to identify the variable that may be calculated next. The diagram now looks like this:

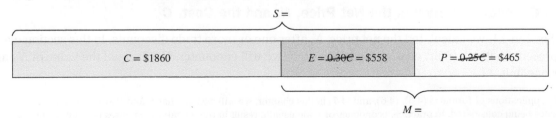

Since	$M = E + P$
then from the diagram, it is clear that	$M = \$558 + \$465 = \$1023$
Since	$S = C + M$
then	$S = \$1860 + \$1023 = \$2883$

Coastal Marine should apply a markup of $1023, resulting in a selling price of $2883.

b. Rate of markup on cost $= \dfrac{M}{C} \times 100 = \dfrac{\$1023}{\$1860} \times 100 = 55.0\%$

Rate of markup on selling price $= \dfrac{M}{S} \times 100 = \dfrac{\$1023}{\$2883} \times 100 = 35.5\%$

➡ **Check your understanding:** Redo the question assuming that Coastal Marine buys the inflatable boats at a unit cost of $2270. All other information remains the same. (Answers: **a.** Markup = $1248.50, Selling price = $3518.50, **b.** Rate of markup on cost = 55%, Rate of markup on selling price = 35.5%)

▰▰▶ **Related problem:** #1 in Exercise 4.4

EXAMPLE 4.4B | **Calculating the Operating Profit per Unit**

Kabir is the owner of Fredericton Cycle. He wants to estimate the operating profit per unit on a new line of bicycles he may add to his inventory. His cost for each bicycle will be $385. Kabir does financial projections based on operating expenses of 35% of cost. If he matches the competition's retail price of $649 on these bicycles, what will be his operating profit per unit?

SOLUTION

Enter the given information on a markup diagram:

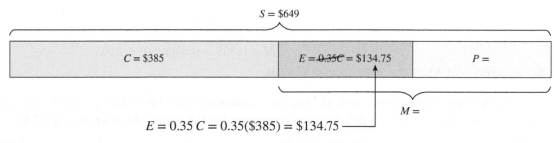

$$E = 0.35\,C = 0.35(\$385) = \$134.75$$

Since	$S = C + E + P$
It follows from the diagram that	$\$649 = \$385 + \$134.75 + P$
Therefore,	$P = \$649 - \$385 - \$134.75 = \$129.25$

Kabir's estimated operating profit will be $129.25 per bicycle.

➡ **Check your understanding:** Redo the question assuming that Kabir's cost for each bicycle is now $325. All other information remains the same. (Answer: $P = \$210.25$)

▰▰▶ **Related problem:** #3 in Exercise 4.4

EXAMPLE 4.4C	Calculating the Sellingc Price That Produces a Desired Markup on Selling Price

The cost of a gas barbecue to a retailer is $245. If the retailer wants a 30% rate of markup on selling price, determine the amount of the markup and the selling price.

SOLUTION

Enter the given information on a markup diagram. Since the rate of markup on selling price is 30%, then $\frac{M}{S} = 0.30$ and, after cross-multiplying, $M = 0.30S$.

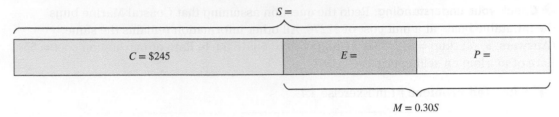

This problem is less straightforward than the preceding examples. If you can express a relationship (among some of the quantities portrayed on the diagram) in terms of a single unknown variable, then you can solve for that variable.

$$S = C + M$$
$$S = \$245 + 0.30S$$

Now solve this equation for S.

$$S - 0.30S = \$245$$
$$0.70S = \$245$$
$$S = \frac{\$245}{0.70} = \$350$$

Hence,

$$M = 0.30S = 0.30(\$350) = \$105$$

After a markup of $105, the selling price is $350.

➡ **Check your understanding:** Redo the question assuming that the retailer wants a 45% rate of markup on selling price. All other information remains the same. (Answer: $M = \$200.45$, $S = \$445.45$)

▮▮▮▶ **Related problem:** #18 in Exercise 4.4

EXAMPLE 4.4D	Using Relationships Among Pricing Variables

Cal-Tire sells its all-season tires at $175 each. Cal-Tire purchases the tires from the factory for $122. Overhead expenses are 20% of the selling price. Determine

a. The amount of markup

b. The rate of markup on cost

c. The rate of markup on selling price

d. The operating profit per tire

SOLUTION

Enter the given information on a markup diagram:

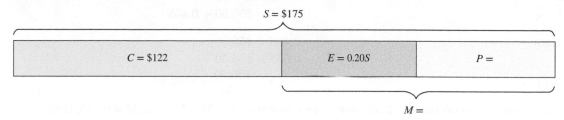

$S = \$175$

| C = \$122 | E = 0.20S | P = |

$M =$

a. $M = \$175 - \$122 = \$53$

The markup is \$53. Enter the markup amount on the diagram.

b. $\left(\begin{array}{c}\text{Rate of markup} \\ \text{on cost}\end{array}\right) = \dfrac{M}{C} \times 100$

$$= \dfrac{\$53}{\$122} \times 100 = 43.4\%$$

c. $\left(\begin{array}{c}\text{Rate of markup} \\ \text{on selling price}\end{array}\right) = \dfrac{M}{S} \times 100$

$$= \dfrac{\$53}{\$175} \times 100 = 30.3\%$$

d. $E = 0.20S = 0.20(\$175) = \$35$

After entering these amounts on the diagram, it is apparent that

$P = \$53 - \$35 = \$18$

➡ **Check your understanding:** Redo the question assuming that Cal-Tire retails the tires for \$225 each and purchases them from the factory for \$145. All other information remains the same. (Answers: **a.** Markup = \$80, **b.** Rate of markup on cost = 55.2%, **c.** Rate of markup on selling price = 35.6%, **d.** Operating profit per tire = \$35)

✏ **Related problem:** #16 in Exercise 4.4

| EXAMPLE 4.4E | Calculating the Markup and Selling Price That Will Give a Desired Operating Profit |

A sporting goods store sets the selling price of baseball gloves to include expected overhead expenses of 25% of the selling price and a desired profit of 20% of the selling price. Determine the selling price and the rate of markup on cost for a glove that costs the store \$56.50.

SOLUTION

Given: $E = 0.25S$, $P = 0.20S$, $C = \$56.50$

Enter the given information on a markup diagram. We can immediately see that $M = 0.45S$.

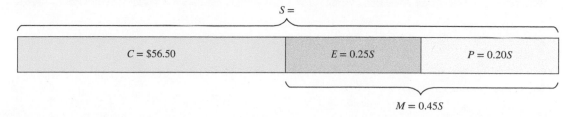

$S =$

| C = \$56.50 | E = 0.25S | P = 0.20S |

$M = 0.45S$

Since $M = 0.45S$ and, as we readily observe in the diagram,

$$S = C + M$$
$$S = \$56.50 + 0.45S$$

then

$$S - 0.45S = \$56.50$$
$$0.55S = \$56.50$$

and

$$S = \frac{\$56.50}{0.55} = \$102.73$$

Enter this value on the diagram. Since we know that $S = \$102.73$, and $M = 0.45S$, then

$$M = 0.45S$$
$$= 0.45(\$102.73)$$
$$= \$46.23$$

Hence,

$$\text{Rate of markup on cost} = \frac{M}{C} \times 100\% = \frac{\$46.23}{\$56.50} \times 100\% = 81.8\%$$

After a markup on cost of 81.8%, the selling price of the glove is $102.73.

▶ **Check your understanding:** Redo the question assuming that the store desires a profit of 35% of the selling price, and the glove now costs the store $75.50. All other information remains the same. (Answer: Selling price = $188.75, Rate of markup on cost = 150%)

▮▶ **Related problem:** #25 in Exercise 4.4

Checkpoint Questions

1. Circle true or false for each of the following statements:

   a. "Markup" and "profit" mean the same thing.   True   False

   b. If a retailer is prepared to break even to sell old stock, the clearance   True   False
   price should be set equal to the item's cost.

   c. Markup can exceed cost.   True   False

   d. If an item is selling at 100% markup on cost, it is selling for double its cost. True   False

2. For a given dollar amount of markup, which will be the larger number: the rate of markup on cost or the rate of markup on selling price? Explain.

3. Is it possible for the rate of markup on selling price to exceed 100%? Explain.

4. Is it possible for the rate of markup on cost to exceed 100%? Explain.

EXERCISE 4.4

Answers to the odd-numbered problems can be found in the end matter.

BASIC PROBLEMS

1. A car dealer buys a vehicle for $28,000. The dealer estimates that operating expenses per unit are 25% of cost. The dealer's desired operating profit is 15% of cost.

   a. What should the markup and selling price be for this vehicle?

   b. What is the dealer's rate of markup based on cost?

   c. What is the dealer's rate of markup based on selling price?

2. A home improvement centre buys a shop vacuum for $38. Operating expenses are estimated to be 35% of cost, and desired operating profit is 45% of cost.

   a. What price should be charged for the vacuum?

   b. What is the home improvement centre's rate of markup based on cost and based on selling price?

3. A college bookstore buys a textbook for $85. Operating expenses are estimated to be 15% of cost. If the book is sold for $125, what will be the bookstore's operating profit per unit?

4. A sporting goods store buys a hockey stick for $47.85 and sells it for $87. Operating expenses are estimated to be 20% of cost. What is the store's operating profit per unit? What is the rate of markup based on selling price?

5. Omega Restaurant buys Shiraz wine at $16.95 per bottle, and sells it to customers at $34.95 per bottle. Calculate Omega's rate of markup on cost and rate of markup on selling price of the wine.

6. A fashion retailer wants to break even on a clearance sale of end of season stock. What price should be set for a bathing suit that cost $38.50 if operating expenses are estimated to be 35% of cost?

7. The markup on movie cinema popcorn is estimated to be an astonishing 1275% based on cost. If a large bag of popcorn sells for $7.50, what is the cost of the popcorn to the cinema?

For Problems 8 through 11, determine:
   a. The amount of markup.
   b. The amount of operating (overhead) expenses.
   c. The operating profit or loss.
   d. The rate of markup on cost.
   e. The rate of markup on selling price.

Problem	Cost, C ($)	Selling price, S ($)	Operating expenses, E
8.	30.00	50.00	40% of cost
9.	64.00	96.00	25% of selling price
10.	55.65	79.50	30% of selling price
11.	17.50	29.75	50% of cost

INTERMEDIATE PROBLEMS

12. Loblaws purchases raisins at $85.75 per 25-kilogram box and then sells them in its bulk foods department for $0.59 per 100 grams. What are Loblaws's rate of markup on cost and rate of markup on selling price of the raisins?

13. Just Desserts buys cheesecakes from General Bakeries at $33.60 per cheesecake. It then cuts each cheesecake into 16 slices and sells them to customers at $6.50 per slice. Calculate the rate of markup on cost and the rate of markup on selling price.

14. The Annapolis Rotary Club sells hot dogs for $1.95 each at the annual Annapolis Fall Fair. The Rotary Club buys wieners at $3.95 per package of 10 wieners, and hot dog buns at $2.90 per dozen. It costs $78 for enough condiments for 1000 hot dogs. What are the Rotary Club's rate of markup on selling price and rate of markup on cost of the hot dogs?

15. Maritime Cellular purchases an Android phone for $595 less trade discounts of 20% and 10%. Maritime's overhead expenses are $59 per unit.
    a. What should be the selling price to generate a profit of $40 per phone?
    b. What is the rate of markup on cost?
    c. What is the rate of markup on selling price?
    d. What would be the break-even selling price for a clear-out sale in preparation for the launch of a new model?

16. A college bookstore orders sweatshirts branded with each program's logo at a suggested retail price of $58 less trade discounts of 30% and 7%. The bookstore manager intends to sell the sweatshirts at the suggested retail price. If overhead expenses are 25% of the selling price,
    a. What will be the operating profit on each sweatshirt?
    b. What is the rate of markup on cost?
    c. What is the rate of markup on selling price?
    d. What would be the break-even selling price for an inventory clearance sale?

17. The rate of markup on the cost of a badminton racquet selling at $54.95 is 45%.
    a. What was the cost of the racquet to the retailer?
    b. What is the rate of markup on selling price?

18. Pet Mart purchased a litter of six puppies from a reputable breeder for $121 each. If the rate of markup on selling price is 45%,
    a. What is the selling price of each puppy?
    b. What is the rate of markup on cost?

19. A florist buys a potted plant for $12 less trade discounts of 20% and 5%. If the florist applies a rate of markup based on cost of 90%:
    a. What is the selling price of the plant?
    b. What is the rate of markup based on selling price?

20. After applying a rate of markup of 50% based on selling price, a retailer prices a pair of gloves at $19.90.
    a. What is the cost of the gloves to the retailer?
    b. What is the rate of markup based on cost?

21. A vending machine company purchases bottled soft drinks for $0.80 per bottle. What will be the operating profit per bottle if the company estimates its operating expenses to be $0.85 per bottle and rate of markup based on cost is 150%?

22. Grocery and department stores sometimes offer items priced below cost (called "loss leaders") to attract customers to the store, in the hope that they will also purchase other, high margin goods that will generate profit. This week, a grocery chain is offering peanut butter as a loss leader. The peanut butter's cost is $2.65 per jar. Overhead expenses are 22% of cost. What selling price should the grocery chain set if it is willing to lose $0.25 per jar?

ADVANCED PROBLEMS

23. Workers World bought 250 pairs of rubber boots at $15 per pair. The manager applies a 90% rate of markup on cost when pricing footwear. What is the operating profit per pair if overhead expenses work out on average to be 20% of the selling price?

24. The owner of a hair salon buys shampoo for resale to her customers. She buys the product from a wholesaler for $15 a bottle, less series discounts of 40% and 10%. The salon owner prices her stock to allow for overhead of 55% of cost and an operating profit of 20% of the selling price. At what price should she sell the shampoo?

25. Beaver Building Supply obtains 4-by-8-foot sheets of half-inch plywood from Macmillan Forest Products at $34 per sheet less discounts of 30% and 5%. The trade price is to be set to cover Beaver's overhead of 20% of the selling price and to provide an operating profit of 12% of the selling price. What should be the trade price per sheet?

26. Village Foods employs a 35% rate of markup on the cost of all dairy products. The store's overhead averages out to 20% of sales each month. What is the operating profit on a 4-litre pail of ice cream for which the wholesale cost is $4.65?

27. Prestige Clothiers' regular prices for men's clothing are set to provide a 40% rate of markup on selling price. Overhead expenses are, on average, 30% of cost. What is the operating profit on a suit that sells for $495?

28. The rate of markup on the cost of fresh peaches in a grocery store is 125% because of the large losses from spoilage and bruising while the peaches are in storage and on display. What is the rate of markup on selling price?

4.5 | Markdown

LO5   A **markdown** is a reduction in the selling price of an item. Retailers use markdowns for many reasons: to reduce excess inventory, to clear out damaged or discontinued items, or to increase sales volume during special "sale" events. Sometimes retailers will mark down a few popular items to the break-even point, or even below it, just to attract additional customers who they hope will also purchase other items. Grocery stores do this on a regular basis.

$$\text{Amount of markdown} = \text{Regular selling price} - \text{Reduced selling price}$$

Using the symbols

$$D = \text{Amount of markdown in dollars}$$
$$S = \text{(Regular) selling price}$$
$$S_{(\text{reduced})} = \text{Reduced selling price (or Sale price)}$$

the word equation becomes

$$D = S - S_{(\text{reduced})} \tag{4-8}$$

The **rate of markdown** is the markdown calculated as a percentage of the regular selling price. That is,

$$\textbf{Rate of markdown} = \frac{D}{S} \times 100 \tag{4-9}$$

If the regular selling price and rate of markdown are given, you can calculate the reduced selling price using the basic discounting formula $N = L(1 - d)$ restated as

$$S_{(\text{reduced})} = S(1 - \textbf{Rate of markdown}) \tag{4-10}$$

EXAMPLE 4.5A | **Calculating the Reduced Selling Price**

Toby's Cycle Shop advertises a 20% markdown on an Alpine mountain bike regularly priced at $445. Cycle City's regular selling price for the same model of bike is $429.

a. What is the reduced price at Toby's?

b. What rate of markdown would Cycle City have to offer to match Toby's reduced price?

SOLUTION

a. The reduced or marked-down price may be calculated using formula (4-10):

$$S_{(reduced)} = S(1 - \text{Rate of markdown})$$
$$= \$445(1 - 0.20)$$
$$= \$356$$

The reduced price is $356.

b. In order to match Toby's reduced price, Cycle City must mark down its price by

$$D = S - S_{(reduced)} = \$429 - \$356 = \$73$$

The necessary rate of markdown is

$$\frac{D}{S} \times 100 = \frac{\$73}{\$429} \times 100 = 17.0\%$$

A markdown of 17.0% will enable Cycle City to match Toby's reduced price.

➡ **Check your understanding:** Redo the question assuming that Toby advertises a 35% markdown on the mountain bike. All other information remains the same. (Answers: **a.** Reduced price = $289.25, **b.** Rate of markdown = 32.6%)

▣▶ **Related problem:** #1 in Exercise 4.5

EXAMPLE 4.5B | **Calculating the Rate of Markdown**

An item costing $150 was marked up by 40% of the selling price. During the store's Tenth Anniversary Sale, the selling price was reduced to $175. What was the regular selling price, and what was the rate of markdown during the sale?

SOLUTION

For all but the easiest markdown problems, it pays to draw an expanded version of the markup diagram we employed in Section 4.4. Enter all known information on the diagram as follows.

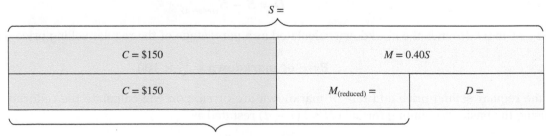

From the diagram, we note that

$$S = C + M$$
$$S = \$150 + 0.40S$$

Hence, $$0.60S = \$150$$

and $$S = \frac{\$150}{0.6} = \$250$$

Enter this value on the diagram. You can see from the diagram that

$$D = S - S_{(reduced)} = \$250 - \$175 = \$75$$

Therefore,

$$\text{Rate of markdown} = \frac{D}{S} \times 100 = \frac{\$75}{\$250} \times 100 = 30.0\%$$

The regular selling price was $250 and the rate of markdown was 30.0%.

▶ **Check your understanding:** Redo the question assuming that the item now costs $115. All other information remains the same. (Answers: Regular selling price = $191.67, Rate of markdown = 8.7%)

▮▮▶ **Related problem:** #3 in Exercise 4.5

Checkpoint Questions

1. Suppose an item that originally had a 40% rate of markup on cost is marked down 40%. Is its reduced selling price equal to C? Explain.

2. An item is marked down by the same percentage as the rate of markup on selling price. Will the reduced operating profit be positive, negative, or zero? Explain.

EXERCISE 4.5

Answers to the odd-numbered problems can be found in the end matter.

BASIC PROBLEMS

1. Banff Sporting Goods advertises a 40% markdown on a snowboard regularly priced at $475.
   a. What is the reduced selling price?
   b. A competitor's regular selling price for the same snowboard is $450. What rate of markdown would that competitor need to advertise in order to match Banff's reduced price?

2. Jets Away Airline offers a return flight from Edmonton to Tampa for $745. What rate of markdown would need to be offered in order to match a competitor's price of $675 for the same flight?

3. An item costing $185 was marked up by 50% of cost. The item was later marked down in an end-of-season clearance sale by $60.
   a. What was the regular selling price of the item?
   b. What rate of markdown did the store advertise in the end-of-season clearance?

4. An item that costs a retailer $58.50 is normally sold for $95. During a storewide sale, the item was marked down by 30%.

   a. What is the normal rate of markup based on cost?

   b. What was the reduced sale price?

   c. By how much was the item marked down in dollars?

5. Office Supply Depot plans to stop carrying the Casio FC-200 calculator. It normally marks up the calculator from the $31.50 wholesale cost to the regular selling price of $51.98.

   a. What is the normal rate of markup on selling price?

   b. What rate of markdown can be advertised if Office Supply Depot wishes to clear out the stock at $31.50, the wholesale cost?

6. The sign on a rack of running shoes reads: "All prices already marked down 30%!" What is the regular selling price of a pair of shoes marked at

   a. $100?   b. $196.49?

7. Morgan's Department Store emailed out 15%-off coupons for its 20th Anniversary Sale. The coupons may be used for any products in the store. For items already on sale, the coupon applies to the sale price.

   a. What price would a coupon holder pay for a duvet (regular price $295) already on sale at 20% off?

   b. What single rate of markdown would have the same effect as the two price reductions?

8. A bakery sells day-old loaves of bread for $1.25. This represents a markdown of 65% from the regular price. What is the regular selling price of the loaves?

9. Poles Apart obtains Nitro T1 snowboards at a cost of $345 and marks them up by 35% of the selling price. For its Annual Spring Sale, Poles Apart marks down prices by 25%. What is the sale price of the snowboards?

10. Merchants C and D sell the same article at $69.95 and $64.95, respectively. They both advertise that they will match the price offered by any other store on any product that they stock.

    a. What discount rate must C give to match D's price marked down by 20% during a sale?

    b. What discount rate must D give to match C's price marked down by 20% during a sale?

11. Sommerhill Sports buys a child's baseball glove for $24.99 and sells it for $49.98.

    a. What is the rate of markup on cost?

    b. What is the rate of markup on selling price?

    c. If the glove is reduced to $24.99 in a fall sale, what is the rate of markdown?

12. Future World buys a laptop computer for $580. The rate of markup is 30% of cost.

    a. What is the rate of markup on selling price?

    b. If the laptop is marked down by 30%, what is the reduced selling price?

13. A bottle of vitamins costs a pharmacy $19.25. The bottle is marked up by 35% of selling price.

    a. What is the selling price?

    b. What is the rate of markup on cost?

    c. If the vitamins are marked down by 25% as the expiration date approaches, calculate D, the dollars of markdown.

    d. What is the reduced selling price?

14. A two-person tent costs a retailer $249. The rate of markup is 25% of the selling price.

    a. What is the selling price?

    b. What is the rate of markup based on cost?

    c. If the tent is damaged while in the storeroom, and is marked down to a reduced selling price of $249, calculate the dollars of markdown and the rate of markdown.

15. The Canadian Code of Advertising Standards prohibits retailers from making false claims about the "savings" a customer is receiving when purchasing a marked-down product. The advertised "regular price" must be the true price at which the retailer actually sold a substantial volume of the product within a reasonable time (usually six months) before or after the advertised markdown. If a product that is marked down to $31.70 is advertised as providing a 55% discount, and the maximum price the product has actually been sold for during the last six months has been $60, is the retailer complying with the Code?

16. A GMC Sierra Crew Cab has a manufacturer's suggested retail price (MSRP) of $38,495. In a year-end promotion, dealers are offering an $11,000 rebate, and an additional $1000 "loyalty" rebate to buyers who currently own a GMC or Chevrolet truck, van, or SUV. What single percentage discount is a buyer receiving if she is eligible for both rebates?

ADVANCED PROBLEMS

17. Workwear Station uses a markup on cost of 60% to establish its retail prices. This pricing rule builds in a profit of 25% of cost. What rate of markdown can Workwear Station offer and just break even on the reduced price?

18. A pharmacy marks up its springtime shipment of sunscreen to provide for overhead expenses of 40% of cost and a profit of 70% of cost. At the end of the summer, what rate of markdown can the pharmacy apply to the remaining inventory of sunscreen and still break even on sales at this level?

4.6   Comprehensive Applications

LO1 to LO5   The problems in this section bring together elements from two or more sections of the chapter. Consequently, their solution usually requires several steps and has a higher degree of difficulty. The more complex the problem, the more benefit you will derive from using a diagram of the sort illustrated in the following examples.

The unit cost, C, and the operating (or overhead) expenses per unit, E, do not change when a retailer marks down the price. Therefore, the reduced operating profit, $P_{(reduced)}$, after a markdown is

$$P_{(reduced)} = S_{(reduced)} - C - E$$

A merchant breaks even on a particular item when $P_{(reduced)} = 0$, that is, when

$$S_{(reduced)} = S_{(break\ even)} = C + E$$

EXAMPLE 4.6A	**Using Relationships Among Pricing Variables**

The Electronics Warehouse purchased Samsung tablets at a discount of 45% from its supplier's suggested retail price of $480. The Electronics Warehouse's normal rate of markup on selling price is 40%. The manager wants to clear out the remaining units because a new model is soon to be released. What rate of markdown can The Electronics Warehouse offer and still break even on each unit? On average, operating expenses are 35% of cost.

SOLUTION

The first sentence tells us that $C = \$480(1 - 0.45)$. The second sentence tells us that $M = 0.40S$. The fourth sentence tells us that $P_{(reduced)} = 0$. The last sentence tells us that $E = 0.35C$. Enter this information on the following markup/markdown diagram.

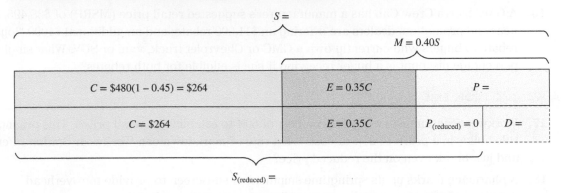

We need to obtain both D and S in order to calculate the rate of markdown. From the upper part of the diagram, we can write an equation containing S as the only unknown.

$$S = \$264 + 0.40S$$

Therefore,

$$S = \frac{\$264}{0.6} = \$440$$

As you obtain numerical values, enter them on the diagram. You can directly calculate

$$E = 0.35C = 0.35(\$264) = \$92.40$$

Then observe on the diagram that there is enough information to obtain $S_{(reduced)}$.

$$S_{(reduced)} = \$264 + \$92.40 + \$0 = \$356.40$$

With the value for $S_{(reduced)}$ entered on the diagram, notice that you can now calculate D.

$$D = S - S_{(reduced)} = \$440 - \$356.40 = \$83.60$$

Therefore,

$$\text{Rate of markdown} = \frac{D}{S} \times 100 - \frac{\$83.60}{\$440} \times 100 = 19.0\%$$

The Electronics Warehouse can offer a markdown of 19.0% and still break even.

▶ **Check your understanding:** Redo the question assuming that The Electronics Warehouse purchases the tablets at a discount of 35% from its supplier's suggested retail price of $520. The Electronics Warehouse's normal rate of markup on selling price is 45%. All other information remains the same. (Answer: Rate of markdown = 25.8%)

▶ **Related problem:** #5 in Exercise 4.6

EXAMPLE 4.6B	**Using Relationships Among Pricing Variables**

Standard Appliances obtains Frigid-Air refrigerators for $1460 less 30% and 5%. Standard's overhead works out to 18% of the regular selling price of $1495. A scratched demonstrator unit from their floor display was cleared out for $1195.

a. What is the regular rate of markup on cost?

b. What was the rate of markdown on the demonstrator unit?

c. What was the operating profit or loss on the demonstrator unit?

d. What rate of markup on cost was actually realized?

SOLUTION

Standard Appliances' cost for one refrigerator was

$$\begin{aligned}
C = N &= L(1 - d_1)(1 - d_2) \\
&= \$1460(1 - 0.30)(1 - 0.05) \\
&= \$970.90
\end{aligned}$$

Enter this value and the other given information on a markup/markdown diagram:

$S = \$1495$

		$M =$		
$C = \$970.90$	$E = 0.18S$	$P =$		
$C = \$970.90$	$E = 0.18S$	$P_{(reduced)} =$	$D =$	

$S_{(reduced)} = \$1195$

a. From the upper part of the diagram, we see that

$$M = \$1495 - \$970.90 = \$524.10$$

Hence,
$$\text{Rate of markup on cost} = \frac{M}{C} \times 100 = \frac{\$524.10}{\$970.90} \times 100 = 54.0\%$$

b. On the diagram, we note that both S and $S_{(reduced)}$ are known. Therefore,

$$D = \$1495 - \$1195 = \$300$$

and
$$\text{Rate of markdown} = \frac{D}{S} \times 100 = \frac{\$300}{\$1495} \times 100 = 20.1\%$$

c. Now we want $P_{(reduced)}$. First calculate E.

$$E = 0.18S = 0.18(\$1495) = \$269.10$$

Therefore,
$$P_{(reduced)} = \$1195 - \$970.90 - \$269.10 = -\$45$$

The negative sign means that the store suffered a loss of $45 on the demonstrator unit.

d. The actual markup at the reduced price was

$$M_{(reduced)} = E + P_{(reduced)} = \$269.10 + (-\$45) = \$224.10$$

The rate of markup on cost actually realized was

$$\frac{M_{(reduced)}}{C} \times 100 = \frac{\$224.10}{\$970.90} \times 100 = 23.1\%$$

⇒ **Check your understanding:** Redo the question assuming that Standard Appliances obtains the refrigerators for $1275 less 25% and 5%. Standard's overhead works out to 20% of the regular selling price of $1300. All other information remains the same. (Answers: **a.** Regular rate of markup on cost = 43.1%, **b.** Rate of markdown = 8.1%, **c.** Operating profit = $26.56, **d.** Rate of markup on cost = 31.5%)

▬▶ **Related problem:** #17 in Exercise 4.6

EXERCISE 4.6

Answers to the odd-numbered problems can be found in the end matter.

BASIC PROBLEMS

1. Computer World purchased a Toshiba netbook for $480 less 40% and 25%. The netbook was then marked up by 120% of cost. Overhead expenses are 55% of cost. In a sale, Computer World offered the netbook at 40% off. Determine

   a. The net cost of the netbook
   b. The amount of the markup
   c. The overhead expenses per netbook
   d. The regular selling price
   e. The sale price (reduced selling price)
   f. The rate of markup on cost at the sale price
   g. The operating profit or loss at the sale price

2. In February, Long Lake Nursery ordered lawn fertilizer at $18.60 less $33\frac{1}{3}$%, $12\frac{1}{2}$%, and 5% per 20-kilogram bag. The fertilizer is normally priced to provide a 55% rate of markup on selling price. Operating (overhead) expenses are 30% of cost. To clear out the remaining bags of fertilizer in July, they were marked down by 45%. Calculate

   a. The net cost per bag
   b. The operating expenses per bag
   c. The regular selling price
   d. The sale price (reduced selling price)
   e. The reduced markup at the sale price
   f. The operating profit or loss at the sale price
   g. The rate of markup on the sale price

INTERMEDIATE PROBLEMS

3. A retailer pays $81 to a wholesaler for an article. The retail price is set using a 40% rate of markup on selling price. To increase traffic to his store, the retailer marks the article down 20% during a sale. What is the sale price?

4. A built-in Kitchenaid refrigerator costs Morrison's Appliance Centre $5000 less 30% and 15%. The normal rate of markup on cost is 90%. The refrigerator is marked down 30% in a sale. What is the sale price?

5. The Shoe Shop's normal rate of markup on selling price is 45%. What rate of markdown can the store offer on a pair of shoes normally priced at $140, and still realize a 20% rate of markup on cost at the sale price?

6. Next Designs sets its regular prices based on overhead expenses at 50% of cost and an operating profit of 40% of cost. What will be the operating profit (as a percent of cost) for clothing sold at a 20% discount?

Calculate the missing values in Problems 7 through 10.

Problem	Cost, C ($)	Overhead, E	Markup, M	Regular price, S ($)	Rate of markdown	Sale price, $S_{(reduced)}$ ($)	Reduced profit, $P_{(reduced)}$ ($)
7.	37.25	20% of C	60% of C	?	?	41.72	?
8.	7.92	70% of C	?% of C	19.80	20%	?	?
9.	98.00	18% of S	?% of S	147.00	$16\frac{2}{3}$%	?	?
10.	115.70	20% of S	35% of S	?	?	133.50	?

11. Mountain Outfitters marked down a pair of snowshoes to $187 in a "60% off" spring sale. Mountain Outfitters originally bought the snowshoes from its supplier for $240 less a trade discount of 30% and a promotional discount of 5%. Mountain Outfitters' overhead expenses are 35% of cost.

    a. What was the regular selling price of the snowshoes before the markdown?

    b. What operating profit or loss will Mountain Outfitters realize when the snowshoes are sold for the reduced price of $187?

12. Sports Extreme advertised a Freestyle XL Stand Up Paddleboard for a regular price of $548. Sports Extreme bought the board from its supplier for $375 less a trade discount of 35%. The Sports Extreme's overhead expenses are 25% of cost.

    a. What operating profit or loss will Sports Extreme realize if the paddleboard is sold at the regular price?

    b. What operating profit or loss will Sports Extreme realize if the paddleboard is sold during a "30% off" weekend sale?

    c. What rate of markdown can Sports Extreme advertise if it is willing to just break even on the sale of the paddle board during an end of season sale?

ADVANCED PROBLEMS

13. Water Sports Ltd. pays $360 less 25% for a backyard above-ground pool kit. Overhead expenses are $16\frac{2}{3}$% of the regular selling price, and the operating profit is 15% of the selling price.

    a. What is the maximum rate of markdown the store can offer and still break even?

    b. What is the profit or loss per unit if Water Sports clears out its remaining stock at 20% off in a Hot August Bargains Sale?

14. A pair of noise-cancelling headphones retails for $349. The dealer's overhead is 25% of cost, and normal operating profit is $16\frac{2}{3}$% of cost.

    a. What is the largest amount of markdown (in dollars) that will allow the dealer to break even?

    b. What rate of markdown will price the headphones at cost?

15. Rainbow Paints is discontinuing a line of paint that it purchased at $30 less 45% and 10% per 4-litre pail. The store's overhead is 50% of cost, and normal operating profit is 30% of cost. If the manager of the store is prepared to accept a loss of one-quarter of the overhead expenses, what markdown rate can the store offer in order to clear out the paint?

16. The Cell Kiosk buys Android smartphones at $550 less 40% and 10%. The price is marked up to allow for overhead of 50% of cost and profit of 35% of cost. The unit on display in the store is scratched. What rate of markdown from the regular price can the store offer on the display unit if it is to recover only half of the unit overhead costs?

17. Sports Outfitters purchased hockey jerseys for $72 less 40% and 15%. The normal rate of markup on selling price is 40%, and overhead is 25% of the regular selling price. The jerseys were reduced to $45.90 for the store's Boxing Day Blowout.

    a. What was the rate of markdown for the sale?

    b. What was the profit or loss on each jersey at the sale price?

    c. At the sale price, what was the rate of markup on cost?

18. Home Workshop Supply obtains table saws for $720 less $33\frac{1}{3}$% and 15%. A saw regularly priced at $750 was sold for $450. The shop's overhead is 22% of cost.

    a. What was the markdown rate on the saw?

    b. What was the profit or loss on the sale of the saw?

    c. What rate of markup on cost was realized at the reduced price?

Key Terms

Cash discount	List price	Rate of markdown
Credit period	Markdown	Rate of markup on cost
Discount period	Markup	Rate of markup on selling price
End-of-month dating	Net price	
Equivalent discount rate	Ordinary dating	Receipt-of-goods dating
Gross profit	Partial payment	Terms of payment
		Trade discount

Summary of Notation and Key Formulas

$$L = \text{List price}$$
$$d = \text{Rate of trade discount}$$
$$N = \text{Net price}$$

In the broader context of calculating the final amount after a percentage reduction to a beginning amount:

$$L = \text{Beginning (larger) amount}$$
$$d = \text{Decimal equivalent of percentage reduction}$$
$$N = \text{Final (smaller) amount}$$

The variables used in pricing and profit calculations are:

$$S = \text{Selling price (per unit)}$$
$$C = \text{Cost (per unit)}$$
$$M = \text{Markup (per unit)}$$
$$E = \text{Overhead or operating expenses (per unit)}$$
$$P = \text{Operating profit (per unit)}$$
$$D = \text{(Amount of) Markdown}$$
$$S_{(reduced)} = \text{Reduced selling price (per unit)}$$
$$P_{(reduced)} = \text{Reduced operating profit (per unit)}$$

FORMULA (4-1)	$N = L(1 - d)$	Finding the net amount or net price after applying a single rate of discount to the original amount or list price.
FORMULA (4-2)	**Amount of discount** $= L - N$	Finding the dollars of discount when the original or list price, L, and the smaller, net price, N, are known.
FORMULA (4-3)	**Amount of discount** $= dL$	Finding the dollars of discount when the original or list price, L, and the rate of discount, d, are known.
FORMULA (4-4)	$N = L(1 - d_1)(1 - d_2)(1 - d_3)$	Finding the net price after a series of three compounding discount rates.
FORMULA (4-5)	$S = C + M$	Selling price is the sum of the cost and the markup.
FORMULA (4-6)	$M = E + P$	Markup is the sum of the overhead expenses and the operating profit.
FORMULA (4-7)	$S = C + E + P$	Selling price is the sum of the cost plus overhead expenses plus operating profit.
FORMULA (4-8)	$D = S - S_{(reduced)}$	Finding the dollars of markdown when S is marked down to $S_{(reduced)}$.
FORMULA (4-9)	**Rate of markdown** $= \dfrac{D}{S} \times 100\%$	To find rate of markdown, divide dollars of markdown, D, by regular selling price, S. Multiply by 100 to convert to a percentage.
FORMULA (4-10)	$S_{(reduced)} = S(1 - \text{rate of markdown})$	A restatement of formula (4-1) to solve for reduced selling price after a specified rate of markdown.

Review Problems

Answers to the odd-numbered review problems can be found in the end matter.

BASIC PROBLEMS

1. **LO1** Specialty Builders Supply has two sources for the same power saw. Source A sells the saw at $196 less 20%, and Source B offers it at $186.60 less $16\frac{2}{3}\%$. Which source is less expensive, and by how much?

2. **LO1** A trade discount of 22.5% from the suggested selling price for a line of computers translates to a $337.05 discount. What net price will a retailer pay?

3. **LO3** What total amount must be paid on May 4 to settle invoices dated April 20 for $650, April 24 for $790, and April 30 for $465, all with terms $1\frac{1}{2}/10$, n/30?

4. **LO1** **LO5** Nelson Hardware ordered a shipment of gas barbecues at a suggested retail price of $459 less trade discounts of 25% and 10%. The manager intends to sell the barbecues at the suggested retail price. If overhead expenses are 20% of the selling price,

   a. What will be the unit operating profit?

   b. What is the rate of markup on cost?

   c. What is the rate of markup on selling price?

   d. What would be the break-even selling price for an inventory clearance sale? (Remember that "break-even" means no profit or loss results from the sale.)

5. **LO1** A 28% trade discount on a digital camera represents a discount of $136.92 from the suggested retail price. What is the net price to the buyer?

6. **LO3** An invoice dated August 23 for $8382 carries terms 2/10, n/30, EOM. How much would the customer need to pay on September 3 in order to fully settle this invoice?

7. **LO1** **LO5** Bosley's Pet Foods buys dog food for $19.50 per bag, less 40%. The store's overhead is $33\frac{1}{3}$% of the selling price, and the desired profit is 10% of the selling price.

   a. At what price per bag should the dog food be sold?

   b. At this price, what is the rate of markup on cost?

   c. If Bosley decides to clear out remaining inventory at a break-even price, what will be the new price per bag?

8. **LO1** The net price of an item after a discount of 22% is $155.61. What is the amount of the discount?

9. **LO1** **LO5** An item that regularly sells for $85 is marked down in a 45% off sale.

   a. What is the reduced selling price?

   b. What is the amount of the markdown?

10. **LO1** A retailer is eligible for a trade discount of 35%, a volume discount of 10%, and a special promotional discount of 2%. What is the list price of an item for which the retailer paid $112.94?

11. **LO3** **LO4** Packard Brothers Roofing presented a customer with an invoice dated September 10 for $8452.75. Credit terms were 2/10, n/30. If the customer paid $5000 on September 20, how much is still owing on the customer's account?

INTERMEDIATE PROBLEMS

12. **LO5** Retail diamonds carry high rates of markup, especially when sold in jewellery stores located in malls, where overhead expenses are particularly high. Denali Diamonds's rate of markup on cost for its diamond engagement rings is 150%. If Denali advertises a one-carat diamond solitaire ring for $6299, and overhead expenses are 42% of cost, what operating profit is Denali earning on the sale of the ring?

13. **LO3** **LO4** An invoice dated January 17 for $10,388.84 carries terms 2/5, 1/10, n/30. A payment of $2000 was made on January 21. A second payment was made on January 26, which brought the balance owing on the account down to $5000. How much was the second payment?

14. **LO1** **LO2** An invoice shows a net price of $199.16 after trade discounts of 22%, 7%, and 5% are deducted.

   a. What was the list price of the goods?

   b. What single trade discount would be equivalent to the discount series?

15. `LO1` `LO2` In addition to the regular trade discount of 25% and a volume purchase discount of $8\frac{1}{3}$% from the manufacturer, Appliance Warehouse is offered a further 5% discount for orders placed in January.

   a. What is the net price after all three trade discounts on refrigerators listed at $1195?

   b. What is the list price on an electric range whose net price works out to be $470.25?

   c. What single trade discount rate is equivalent to the three trade discounts?

   d. After the regular and volume discounts are both taken, what dollar amount of savings does the extra discount for January orders represent on a $1000 list price item?

16. `LO1` The net proceeds to the vendor of a house after payment of a 4.5% real estate commission were $275,995. At what price did the house sell?

17. `LO5` What is the cost of an item that sells for $87.49 if

   a. The rate of markup on cost is 30%?

   b. The rate of markup on selling price is 30%?

18. `LO1` Mr. and Mrs. Ogrodnik want to list their house at a price that will net them a minimum of $320,000 after a real estate commission of 5.5% of the selling price. Rounded to the nearest dollar, what is the lowest offer they could accept on their home?

19. `LO5` Ski 'n Cycle purchased Elan 200 skis for $492 per pair and priced them to give a 40% rate of markup on selling price. When this model was discontinued, the store marked down its remaining stock by 30%. What was the sale price after the markdown?

20. `LO3` `LO4` Omega Restaurant received an invoice dated July 22 from Industrial Kitchen Equipment for $3691, with terms 2/10, 1/20, n/45. Omega made payments of $1100 on August 1, $900 on August 10, and $800 on August 31. What amount was still owed on September 1?

21. `LO3` `LO4` Custom Kitchens received an invoice dated November 17 from Idea Cabinets Ltd. for $7260 with terms 3/15, $1\frac{1}{2}$/30, n/60. If Custom Kitchens made a payment of $4000 on December 2, what further payment on December 16 will settle the account?

22. `LO1` Mapleview Poultry Farms gives convenience stores a trade discount of 25% on eggs listed at $43 per case. What trade discount will Sunnyside Farms have to give on its list price of $44.50 per case to match Mapleview's price to convenience stores?

23. `LO5` A pharmacy marked up its sunscreen to provide for overhead expenses of 40% of cost and a profit of 45% of cost. At the end of the summer, what rate of markdown can the pharmacy apply to the remaining inventory of sunscreen and still break even on sales at the reduced price?

24. `LO1` At its current price of $1.10 per share, the price of Apex Resources stock is down 78% from its price one year ago. What was that price?

25. `LO1` A merchant pays a 1.5% fee to the RBC Royal Bank on all Visa sales.

   a. What amount will he pay on sales of $28,476 for a month?

   b. What were his gross sales for a month in which the bank charged fees totalling $981.71?

26. `LO1` In three successive years the price of the common shares of Bedrock Resources Ltd. fell 40%, 60%, and 70%, ending the third year at 50 cents.

   a. What was the share price at the beginning of the three-year skid?

   b. How much (in dollars and cents) did the share price drop in the second year?

27. `LO4` A payment of $500 on an invoice for $887 reduced the balance owed to $378.09. What cash discount rate was allowed on the $500 payment?

28. `LO1` `LO5` Sunrise Building Supply obtains 4-by-8-foot sheets of wallboard from Canadian Gypsum at $30 per sheet less 30% and 10%. The price is to be set to cover Sunrise's overhead of 20% of the selling price and to provide an operating profit of 18% of the selling price. What should be the retail price per sheet?

29. `LO3` `LO4` An invoice for $8830 is dated March 24 and has credit terms 3/10, n/40, ROG. The customer received the goods on April 3. If a $3900 payment was made on April 8, what additional payment on April 13 would bring the balance owing down to $2000?

30. `LO3` `LO4` Regal Event Management received an invoice from a supplier of banquet tables dated November 18 for $8650. Regal received the tables on November 26. The credit terms are $1\frac{1}{2}$/10, n/30, EOM. If Regal made a payment of $5000 on December 9, what additional payment on December 20 would completely settle the account?

ADVANCED PROBLEMS

31. `LO1` The evening news reports that the S&P/TSX Composite Index dropped 0.9% on the day to close at 13,123 points. How many points did the index fall?

32. `LO1` `LO5` Central Ski and Cycle purchased 50 pairs of ski boots for $360 per pair less $33\frac{1}{3}$% and 10%. The regular rate of markup on selling price of the boots is 40%. The store's overhead is 22% of the selling price. During a January clearance sale, the price was reduced to $270 per pair.

   a. What was the rate of markdown for the sale?

   b. What was the profit or loss on each pair of boots at the sale price?

   c. At the sale price, what was the rate of markup on cost?

33. `LO5` A snowblower retails for $489. The dealer's overhead is 20% of cost, and normal operating profit is $16\frac{2}{3}$% of cost.

   a. What is the largest amount of markdown (in dollars) that can be offered and still allow the dealer to break even?

   b. What rate of markdown will price the snowblower at cost?

34. `LO5` If a grocery store's rate of markup on the selling price of tomatoes is 55%, what is the rate of markup on the cost of tomatoes?

35. `LO5` The Pro Shop at Sunny Lake Golf and Country Club prices its golf club sets to allow for overhead of $33\frac{1}{3}$% of cost and profit of 20% of cost.

   a. What is the regular selling price as a percentage of cost?

   b. What discount rate can the Pro Shop offer to club members if it will accept half of the normal profit on member purchases?

36. `LO1` A uranium mining town reported population declines of 3.2%, 5.2%, and 4.7% for the three successive five-year periods 2000–2005, 2005–2010, and 2010–2015. If the population at the end of 2015 was 9320,

   a. How many people lived in the town at the beginning of 2000?

   b. What was the population loss in each of the five-year periods?

© Image Source RF

CHAPTER 5
Cost-Volume-Profit Analysis

LEARNING OBJECTIVES
After completing this chapter, you will be able to:

LO1   Distinguish between fixed costs and variable costs

LO2   Use the revenue and cost function approach to perform cost-volume-profit analysis

LO3   Construct and use a break-even chart to perform cost-volume-profit analysis

LO4   Use the contribution margin approach to perform cost-volume-profit analysis

LO5   Use the contribution rate approach to perform cost-volume-profit analysis

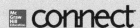 Throughout this chapter interactive charts and Help Me Solve It videos are marked with a ↗.

IMAGINE THAT YOU ARE CONSIDERING investing in a new business venture. Now, imagine that you had a way to look into the future and know whether your new venture would earn a profit or suffer a loss. How valuable would that ability to predict the future be to you? Would the ability to "see the future" help you make a better business decision today?

While we cannot, in fact, predict the future with certainty, we *do* have access to a tool that can help us better understand whether a business has a likelihood of generating a future profit. In Chapter 2, we reviewed the nature of linear equations. An important application of linear equations is forecasting a business's profit at various levels of sales. This application is known as **cost-volume-profit analysis** or

CVP analysis for short. In this chapter, you will learn how to perform CVP analysis using a number of different approaches. You will learn to use CVP analysis to answer a variety of "what if" questions that will help the leader of a new or existing business better understand what might happen to profit levels under various future scenarios. For example, you will use CVP analysis to answer questions such as: "How many units of sales does this business need to sell just to cover its costs?" "What will the business's profit or loss be at a given level of future sales?"

Performing cost-volume-profit analysis does not, of course, guarantee that a business will indeed generate a profit. There are many unknown variables that could affect our future business outcomes and even the best market research cannot guarantee that our product or service will be embraced by the market. However, cost-volume-profit analysis gives us the ability to predict profit levels under an endless number of "what if" scenarios. By performing CVP analysis using the "best case" and "worst case" possible scenarios, we can better anticipate the range of profit levels the business might experience in the future.

5.1 Introduction to Cost-Volume-Profit Analysis

LO1 Fixed Costs and Variable Costs

Many types of costs of an operating business can, with good approximation, be treated as being either fixed or variable. A strictly **fixed cost** does not change if sales increase or decrease. Examples include rent, management salaries, some forms of depreciation expense, and property taxes. A **variable cost** grows or declines in direct proportion to the volume of sales. This means that, if unit sales increase by 10%, total *variable* costs will increase by 10%. (Total *fixed* costs will not change in this example.) Variable costs typically include materials costs and direct labour costs in manufacturing, or the wholesale cost of goods in retailing.

The definitions of fixed costs and variable costs have important implications for the cost of producing an additional unit. To illustrate, consider a case where the number of units sold by a business doubles from one year to the next. By definition, *total fixed* costs do not change but *total variable* costs in the second year are double the total variable costs in the first year. Therefore, each *additional* unit produced in the second year adds *no* fixed costs, but each *additional* unit adds the *same* dollar amount of variable costs. We use the term **unit variable cost** for this cost of producing an additional unit. It can be calculated by dividing the total variable costs by the total units produced.

With a little thought, you can identify some costs that are neither strictly fixed nor purely variable. The compensation of sales personnel by a salary plus commission is an example of a *mixed cost* that has fixed and variable cost components. In such cases, the fixed and variable components may be separated and assigned to the respective fixed cost and variable cost categories.

In the following example, we describe a proposed business and analyze its costs. The following symbols will be used throughout the chapter.

$$S = \text{Selling price or revenue per unit}$$
$$VC = \text{Unit variable costs (or Variable costs per unit)}[1]$$
$$FC = \text{(Total) fixed costs}$$

---

[1] There are many instances in the textbook in which we use two- or three-character symbols to represent a quantity. There are two main reasons for this. Sometimes it's because the multiple-character symbol is widely used in accounting and finance textbooks. In other cases, the most obvious choice for a single-character symbol is used elsewhere in the book to represent another quantity. When writing the product of two symbols, we avoid confusion by placing one of the symbols within brackets. For example, we write the product of VC and X as $(VC)X$ rather than as VCX.

TRAP

Fixed Costs Can Change

Do not be tempted to define a fixed cost as "a cost that does not change." Fixed costs can (and do) change. For example, suppose a business pays $2000 a month to lease a space. Upon renewal of the lease, the owner of the building increases the lease fee to $2200 a month. The lease cost, although changing, is still a fixed cost for the business that is paying it. Why? Because the change in the lease cost is *not* due to a change in the business's sales levels. Fixed costs are costs that do not change if sales increase or decrease. Fixed costs can, however, change for other reasons.

EXAMPLE 5.1A	Classifying Costs

Chuck is considering the start-up of a furniture and equipment delivery service in his hometown. He can buy a used cube truck (1600-kilogram payload capacity) for $32,000. He will need to hire a helper to assist with loading and unloading. After conferring with the operator of a similar service in another town of similar size, Chuck feels he can charge $60 per delivery and that each delivery will require an average round-trip driving distance of 25 kilometres. He has estimated the following expenses:

Truck insurance and licence	$3000/year
Fuel	$100 every 400 km
Oil changes	$70 every 5000 km
Helper's wages	$2500/month
Chuck's wages	$3500/month
EI and CPP premiums	$300/month
Tires	$900 every 75,000 km
Cell phone	$75/month
Other truck repairs and maintenance	$1000 per 10,000 km
Business licence	$180/year
Depreciation*	$180 per 1000 km

* Chuck and his accountant estimate that the truck can be driven for another 150,000 kilometres, after which it can be sold for $5000. The $27,000 decrease in value spread over 150,000 kilometres represents a depreciation of $180 per 1000 kilometres.

a. Classify the costs into two categories—fixed costs and variable costs.

b. Determine values for *FC*, the (total) monthly fixed costs, and *VC*, the variable costs per delivery.

SOLUTION

a. Fixed costs are those costs that do not change as the number of deliveries per month changes. In the present case, costs expressed on a monthly or annual basis are fixed costs. Variable costs are costs that grow or decline in direction proportion to sales levels. In the present case, costs expressed on a per-kilometre basis are variable costs, as they increase or decrease based on the number of deliveries that Chuck's business makes.

Fixed costs:	*Variable costs:*
Truck insurance and licence	Fuel
Helper's wages	Oil changes
Owner's wages	Tires
EI and CPP premiums	Other truck repairs and maintenance
Cell phone	Depreciation
Business licence	

b. *Fixed costs:*

Truck insurance and licence = $3000/year		= $250/month
Helper's wages		= $2500/month
Owner's wages		= $3500/month
EI and CPP premiums		= $300/month
Cell phone		= $75/month
Business licence	= $180/year	= $15/month
Total *FC*		= $6640/month

Let us first calculate the variable costs per km. Then, based on Chuck's estimate for an average round-trip delivery, we will multiply by 25 to obtain the variable costs per delivery.

Fuel	= $100 every 400 km	$\Rightarrow \dfrac{10,000¢}{400 \text{ km}}$	= 25.0¢ per km
Oil changes	= $70 every 5000 km	$\Rightarrow \dfrac{7000¢}{5000 \text{ km}}$	= 1.4¢ per km
Tires	= $900 every 75,000 km	$\Rightarrow \dfrac{90,000¢}{75,000 \text{ km}}$	= 1.2¢ per km
Other repairs & maintenance	= $1000 per 10,000 km	$\Rightarrow \dfrac{100,000¢}{10,000 \text{ km}}$	= 10.0¢ per km
Depreciation	= $180 per 1000 km	$\Rightarrow \dfrac{18,000¢}{1000 \text{ km}}$	= 18.0¢ per km
Variable costs			= 55.6¢ per km

VC, the variable costs per delivery = 25(55.6¢) = 1390¢ = $13.90 per delivery.

Interpretation: Each delivery adds $13.90 to Chuck's costs. The remaining $46.10 of the $60 revenue from each delivery may be applied to the monthly fixed costs of $6640. Once the fixed costs are covered, $46.10 from each additional delivery provides Chuck with a profit on his $32,000 investment.

⮞ **Check your understanding:** What would be the new *VC*, variable costs per delivery, if fuel costs were estimated to be $120 every 400 kilometres, and tires were estimated to cost $1200 every 75,000 kilometres? All other costs remain the same as above. (Answer: *VC* = $15.25 per delivery)

◼▶ **Related problem:** #3 in Exercise 5.1

COST-VOLUME-PROFIT (CVP) ANALYSIS

Imagine that you are doing a feasibility study for a new business. You wish to examine the profitability of the business at various levels of sales. Entrepreneurs and potential investors/lenders commonly begin by calculating the **break-even point**. This is the number of units of product that must be sold just to cover all costs. At this particular sales volume, there is neither a profit nor a loss. For the business proposal to merit further consideration, the volume of sales needed to break even should be attainable within a reasonable time frame.

The break-even point is one of the key outcomes from a cost-volume-profit analysis. **Cost-volume-profit analysis** is a technique for estimating a firm's operating *profit* at any sales *volume*, given the firm's fixed *costs* and unit variable *costs*. "Operating profit" (or "net income") is the amount left over from sales revenue after all costs or expenses have been paid, and is expressed as

$$\text{Operating profit} = \text{Total revenue} - \text{Operating expenses}$$

At the break-even point, this difference is zero.

To begin a cost-volume-profit analysis, you must estimate *FC*, *VC*, and *S* (in a similar manner to Example 5.1A). Once you have values for *FC*, *VC*, and *S*, there are alternative methods for completing the cost-volume-profit analysis. We will present three approaches—there may be insufficient time in your curriculum for you to study all of them.

The revenue and cost function approach presented in Section 5.2 is rather mechanical. Two other approaches are more insightful. If you have good skills at constructing and interpreting graphs, the graphical approach in Section 5.3 provides a revealing "picture" of the cost-volume-profit relationships for a business. Many "what if?" questions can readily be answered. This approach is time-consuming and has limited precision; but these issues might not be significant given that some of the costs are usually estimates, and that the assumptions listed below for our CVP analyses are not strictly met in most situations.

The contribution margin approach in Section 5.4, as well as being efficient and precise, provides useful insights to the economics of operating a business. For these reasons, it is the method most commonly used by managers and accountants for CVP analysis.

The following assumptions apply to all three methods:

- Each operating expense can be treated as either a fixed cost or a variable cost.
- The selling price per unit remains the same regardless of sales volume. (The analysis does not, therefore, accommodate volume discounts or price reductions during a sale or promotion.)
- Production volume equals sales volume. (Consequently, all expenses in an operating period are incurred for sales made in the same period.)

EXAMPLE 5.1B	Calculating Total Costs at Different Sales Volumes

Yasmine has been running her small, home-based business, Green for Life, for one year. She sells individually packaged servings of natural ingredients that can be mixed with water to create a healthy drink. Yasmine sold 32,000 units last year. Her total costs last year were $39,200, which included $12,000 of fixed costs. If Yasmine's fixed and unit variable costs are expected to remain the same, what will her expected total costs be next year if she sells 50,000 units?

SOLUTION

A business's total costs can be separated into fixed costs and variable costs. Yasmine's total costs last year were $39,200, of which $12,000 were fixed costs. Therefore, total variable costs for all units sold last year were $39,200 − $12,000, or $27,200 of total variable costs. These were the total variable costs associated with the production and sale of 32,000 units. To find the variable costs per unit, or *VC*, divide last year's total variable costs by the number of units sold:

$$\text{Unit variable cost or } VC = \frac{\$27,200}{32,000 \text{ units}} = \$0.85 \text{ per unit}$$

If Yasmine expects to sell 50,000 units next year, she should expect

$$\text{Total variable costs for next year} = 50,000 \text{ units} \times \$0.85 \text{ per unit} = \$42,500$$

Fixed costs of $12,000 per year are not expected to change. Therefore, if Yasmine sells 50,000 units next year, her total costs are projected to be

$$\text{Total Costs} = \text{Total Fixed Costs} + \text{Total Variable Costs}$$
$$= \$12,000 + \$42,500$$
$$= \$54,500$$

Therefore, if Yasmine sells 50,000 units of her health mix product next year, she should expect to have total costs of $54,500.

➡️ **Check your understanding:** What would Yasmine's projected total costs be for next year if she expects to sell 75,000 units? (Answer: $75,750)

▰▰▶ **Related problem:** #4 in Exercise 5.1

EXERCISE 5.1

Answers to the odd-numbered problems can be found in the end matter.

BASIC PROBLEMS

1. Below is a list of costs. Classify each of them as variable, fixed, or mixed (a combination of variable and fixed components).
   a. Cost of raw materials used in producing a firm's products
   b. Property taxes
   c. Wages of sales staff paid on a salary plus commission basis
   d. Wages of hourly paid production-line workers
   e. Site licence for software
   f. Leasing costs for a delivery truck ($600 per month plus $0.40 per kilometre)
   g. Packaging materials for products
   h. Property insurance

2. A company's sales revenue decreased by 15% from one operating period to the next. Assuming no change in the prices of its inputs and outputs, by what percentage did
   a. Fixed costs change?   b. Unit variable costs change?
   c. Total variable costs change?

3. Sarah is considering the start-up of a residential cleaning business. She can buy a used car for $8000. She has a friend who will work for her. Based on her research, Sarah believes she can charge $90 to clean an average-sized family home. Sarah expects most of her clients will be local, and estimates that the round-trip driving distance associated with each job will average 10 kilometres. She has estimated the following expenses:

Cleaning supplies	$10/home
Cell phone	$80/month
Advertising	$75/month
Friend's wages	$30/home
Sarah's wages	$1500/month
Business licence	$150/year
Car insurance and licence	$1500/year
Fuel	$75 every 500 km
Oil changes	$50 every 5000 km
Tires	$500 every 100,000 km
Business liability insurance	$600/year
Depreciation	$150 per 1000 km

   a. Classify the costs into two categories—fixed costs and variable costs.
   b. Determine values for *FC*, the (total) monthly fixed costs, and *VC*, the variable costs per home.

4. Triax Corp. produced 50,000 units at a total cost of $1,600,000 (including $400,000 of fixed costs) in the fiscal year just completed. If fixed costs and unit variable costs do not change next year, how much will it cost to produce 60,000 units?

5. Lanark Industries produced 580,000 USB memory sticks last year. Total costs last year were $3,710,000, which included $3,335,000 of total variable costs. If fixed costs and unit variable costs do not change next year, how much will it cost to produce 650,000 USB memory sticks?

6. Treetop Trekking provided forest tours for 875 customers last month. Total costs last month were $4800, including $600 of fixed costs. Fixed costs are expected to increase by 10% next month, due to increased business insurance fees. Unit variable costs (costs per person per tour) are expected to remain the same. What will the expected total monthly costs be if the business expects to provide tours for 1000 customers next month?

7. Dynacan Ltd. manufactured 10,000 units of product last year and identified the following manufacturing and overhead costs. (V denotes "variable cost" and F denotes "fixed cost").

Materials used in manufacturing (V)	$50,400,000
Wages paid to production workers (V)	93,000,000
Wages paid to management and salaried employees (F)	22,200,000
Other materials and supplies (V)	16,000,000
Power to run plant equipment (V)	14,200,000
Other utilities (F)	19,200,000
Depreciation (straight line) on plant and equipment (F)	9,600,000
Property taxes (F)	5,000,000

If unit variable costs and fixed costs remain unchanged, calculate the total cost to produce 9700 units this year.

Math Apps

THE DRAGONS DO THE MATH

Dragons' Den is a reality television program that airs in over 20 countries around the world. The show's contestants present their business ideas before a panel of potential investors with the hope of getting investment capital from wealthy entrepreneurs. In return, the contestants must sell a percentage of their business to the investors.

Typically, successful contestants' pitches contain the same basic elements: an innovative or unique selling idea, a confident presentation, a clear business strategy based on research, and a concrete financial plan. People on the show often pitch their "million-dollar" business idea even though they have never made a sale. In one episode, the confident entrepreneur reported sales of $300,000, then admitted to an overall loss of $10,000. Contestants have to know their numbers as they relate to gross margins, fixed and variable costs, market size, and break-even points, and be able to demonstrate the confidence needed to secure the funds they are seeking.

Behind the scenes after each episode, the contestant's business plan still has to undergo the "due diligence" phase before the on-air promises become reality. Deals often fall apart once the numbers are crunched.

5.2 Revenue and Cost Function Approach to CVP analysis

LO2 In this approach, we first develop general formulas for the total revenue, total cost, and net income from the sale of X units of a product. We will use the following symbols:

$$TR = \text{Total revenue (from the sale of } X \text{ units)}$$
$$TC = \text{Total cost (of the } X \text{ units sold)}$$
$$NI = \text{Net income (from the sale of } X \text{ units)}$$

The total revenue from the sale of X units at a selling price of S per unit is simply

$$TR = (S)X$$

The total cost is the sum of the total variable costs plus the fixed costs. That is,

$$TC = (\text{Variable costs per unit} \times \text{Number of units sold}) + \text{Fixed costs}$$
$$TC = (VC)X + FC$$

The equation for TR is called the **revenue function** and the equation for TC is called the **cost function**. The net income (or profit) for a period is the total revenue minus the total cost. Hence,

$$
\begin{aligned}
NI &= TR - TC \\
&= (S)X - [(VC)X + FC] \\
&= (S)X - (VC)X - FC \\
&= (S - VC)X - FC
\end{aligned}
$$

In summary,

REVENUE FUNCTION	$TR = (S)X$	**(5-1)**
COST FUNCTION	$TC = (VC)X + FC$	**(5-2)**
NET INCOME	$NI = (S - VC)X - FC$	**(5-3)**

TIP

Total Revenue Versus Net Income

Don't confuse "total revenue" with "net income" or "profit." Total revenue is simply the dollars that flowed into the business from the sale of its goods or services. This does *not* represent money the owner can pocket, because all the costs associated with those sales have not yet been deducted. Net income or profit represents the dollars that are left over after all costs have been subtracted from the total revenue value.

We can obtain the break-even volume in this approach by setting $NI = 0$ in formula (5-3) for the special case $X =$ Break-even volume. That is,

$$
\begin{aligned}
NI &= (S - VC)X - FC \\
0 &= (S - VC)(\text{Break-even volume}) - FC \\
FC &= (S - VC)(\text{Break-even volume})
\end{aligned}
$$

BREAK-EVEN SALES VOLUME $\qquad$ $\text{Break-Even Volume} = \dfrac{FC}{S - VC}$ $\qquad$ **(5-3a)**

Although this is just a special case of formula (5-3), finding the number of sales units, X, required to break even is a very common question in CVP analysis questions. Therefore, when asked to solve for the number of units (or volume) required to break even, you might choose to start with this special-case rearrangement of the net income formula.

Breakeven Worksheet on the Texas Instruments BA II PLUS

With this worksheet, you can compute the value for any one of the five variables in formula (5-3), $NI = (S - VC)X - FC$ after entering values for the other four variables. Appendix 5A demonstrates the use of the Break-Even Worksheet.

EXAMPLE 5.2A	CVP Analysis (Revenue and Cost Function Approach)

In Example 5.1A concerning Chuck's delivery service, we found that

$$VC = \$13.90 \text{ per delivery and } FC = \$6640 \text{ per month}$$

The fixed costs included Chuck's personal wages in the amount of $3500/month. The unit variable costs, VC, assumed an average round-trip driving distance of 25 kilometres. The revenue per delivery, S, was a flat $60.

a. What is the break-even point in (i) deliveries per month? (ii) revenue per month?

b. Chuck can get by in the first year if he withdraws personal wages of only $2500 per month on average instead of $3500. What average number of deliveries per month is needed to reach this minimum income requirement?

c. What personal wages can Chuck withdraw if he makes 174 deliveries in a month?

d. If the average round-trip distance per delivery turns out to be 30 instead of 25 kilometres, how many deliveries per month are needed to break even?

SOLUTION

Substituting the known quantities into formulas (5-1), (5-2), and (5-3) gives

$$TR = (S)X = \$60X$$
$$TC = (VC)X + FC = \$13.90X + \$6640$$
$$NI = (S - VC)X - FC = \$46.10X - \$6640$$

a. (i) To calculate the break-even volume, solve for X in the net income formula (5-3) when $NI = 0$.

$$NI = \$46.10X - \$6640$$
$$0 = \$46.10(\text{Break-even volume}) - \$6640$$
$$0 + \$6640 = \$46.10(\text{Break-even volume})$$
$$\frac{\$6640}{\$46.10} = \text{Break-even volume}$$
$$\text{Break-even volume} = \frac{\$6640}{\$46.10} = 144.03 \approx 144 \text{ deliveries per month}$$

Notice the same answer would be found if we started with the rearranged formula (5-3a).

(ii) Since Chuck charges a flat price of $60 per delivery, the break-even sales revenue (from 144 deliveries) is 144($60) = $8640 per month.

b. Monthly wages of $3500 are already included in $FC = \$6640$. If Chuck reduces his monthly wage to only $2500, fixed costs are reduced by $1000. With $FC = \$6640 - \$1000 = \$5640$, we can calculate the new monthly break-even volume. Remember that, when solving for the break-even volume, we have the option of starting with the rearranged version of the net income formula as discussed above. Using that approach, formula (5-3a) we have

$$\text{Break-even volume} = \frac{FC}{S - VC} = \frac{\$5640}{\$60 - \$13.90} = \frac{\$5640}{\$46.10} = 122.34$$

An average of 122.34 deliveries per month will provide Chuck with an income of $2500 per month. (Note that since we cannot perform a "partial" delivery, the business owner would typically round this number *up* to 123 deliveries per month in order to break even. If only 122 deliveries are made in a month, the break-even threshold is not quite achieved, and the business would have a very slight loss. Only after 123 deliveries per month does the business actually cross the break-even threshold.)

c. The original $FC = \$6640$ included Chuck's wage of $3500 per month. In addition to that wage, Chuck can withdraw any available profit, NI. At $X = 174$ deliveries per month,

$$NI = \$46.10X - \$6640 = \$46.10(174) - \$6640 = \$1381.40$$

Therefore, Chuck can withdraw a total of

$$\$3500 + \$1381.40 = \$4881.40$$

d. Variable costs of $VC = \$13.90$ per delivery were based on an average round-trip distance of 25 kilometres per delivery. This corresponds to variable costs of $\frac{\$13.90}{25} = \$0.556$ per kilometre. At a 30-kilometre round-trip driving distance per delivery,

$$VC = 30(\$0.556) = \$16.68 \text{ per delivery}$$

Again solve for X in formula (5-3) when $NI = 0$.

$$NI = (S - VC)X - FC$$
$$0 = (\$60 - \$16.68)(\text{Break-even volume}) - \$6640$$
$$0 + \$6640 = \$43.22(\text{Break-even volume})$$
$$\text{Break-even volume} = \frac{\$6640}{\$43.32} = 153.28 \text{ deliveries per month}$$

An average of 153.28 deliveries per month are needed to break even if the average round-trip distance per delivery increases to 30 kilometres.

➡ **Check your understanding:** At the new VC of $16.68 per delivery, what is the maximum monthly personal wage Chuck can withdraw from the business if he makes 200 deliveries in a month? (Answer: $3500 + $2024 = $5524)

▮▮▶ **Related problem:** #5 in Exercise 5.2

EXAMPLE 5.2B	CVP Analysis (Revenue and Cost Function Approach)

A manufacturing company is studying the feasibility of producing a new product. A new production line could manufacture up to 800 units per month at a production cost of $50 per unit. Fixed costs would be $22,400 per month. Variable selling and shipping costs are estimated to be $20 per unit. Market research indicates that a unit price of $110 would be competitive.

a. What is the break-even point as a percent of capacity?

b. What would be the net income at 90% of capacity?

c. What would unit sales have to be to attain a net income of $9000 per month?

d. In a serious recession, sales might fall to 55% of capacity. What would be the resulting net income?

e. What dollar amount of sales would result in a loss of $2000 per month?

f. In the highest-cost scenario, fixed costs might be $25,000, production costs might be $55 per unit, and selling and shipping costs might be $22 per unit. What would the break-even point be in these circumstances?

SOLUTION

In the expected scenario, $S = \$110$, $VC = \$50 + \$20 = \$70$, and $FC = \$22,400$ per month. Hence,

$$TR = \$110X$$
$$TC = \$70X + \$22,400$$
$$NI = \$40X - \$22,400$$

a. At the break-even point, $NI = 0$. Hence

$$0 = \$40(\text{Break-even volume}) - \$22,400$$
$$0 + \$22,400 = \$40(\text{Break-even volume})$$
$$\text{Break-even volume} = \frac{\$22,400}{\$40} = 560 \text{ units per month}$$

Since the production line can produce up to 800 units per month, 560 units represents

$$\frac{560}{800} \times 100 = 70\% \text{ of capacity}$$

b. At 90% of capacity, production would be $0.9 \times 800 = 720$ units per month. Using formula (5-3),

$$NI = \$40(720) - \$22,400 = \$6400 \text{ per month}$$

c. Setting $NI = \$9000$ in the formula (5-3), we obtain

$$\$9000 = \$40X - \$22,400$$
$$\$9000 + \$22,400 = \$40X$$

Unit sales would have to be $X = \dfrac{\$9000 + \$22,400}{\$40} = 785 \text{ per month}$

d. In the recession scenario, unit sales would be $0.55 \times 800 = 440$ per month. Using formula (5-3),

$$NI = (\$40)440 - \$22,400 = -\$4800$$

The company would lose $4800 per month in the recession.

e. Substituting $NI = -\$2000$ per month in formula (5-3),

$$-\$2000 = \$40X - \$22,400$$
$$-\$2000 + \$22,400 = \$40X$$
$$X = \frac{-\$2000 + \$22,400}{\$40} = 510 \text{ units per month}$$

At sales of 510 units per month, the dollar amount of sales would be

$$TR = (\$110)X = (\$110)510 = \$56,100$$

f. In the highest-cost scenario, $FC = \$25,000$ per month and $VC = \$77$ per unit. The net income equation (5-3) becomes

$$NI = (\$110 - \$77)X - \$25,000 = \$33X - \$25,000$$

At the break-even point, $NI = 0$.

$$0 = \$33(\text{Break-even volume}) - \$25,000$$
$$0 + \$25,000 = \$33(\text{Break-even volume})$$
$$\text{Break-even volume} = \frac{\$25,000}{\$33} = 758 \text{ units per month}$$

The break-even point in this case would be 758 units per month. Sales of 758 units per month represents $\frac{758}{800} \times 100 = 94.75\%$ of capacity.

➡ **Check your understanding:** In the high-cost scenario in Part (f), what percentage of capacity would sales need to be in order for the company to limit its monthly loss to $2000? (Answer: 87.13% of capacity)

▮▮▶ **Related problem:** #9 in Exercise 5.2

EXAMPLE 5.2C | **CVP Analysis with Sales Volume in Dollars Instead of Units**

Last year Marconi Printing had total revenue of $375,000 while operating at 75% of capacity. The total of its variable costs was $150,000. Annual fixed costs were $180,000.

a. What is Marconi's break-even point expressed
   (i) in dollars of revenue?   (ii) as a percent of capacity?

b. If the current S, VC, and FC are the same as last year, what net income can be expected from revenue of $450,000 in the current year?

SOLUTION

In this situation, although we know that total sales were $375,000 for the year, we do not know the unit selling price, S. To solve this problem, we will let $S = \$1$. Then X represents the number of $1 units sold. The revenue function is simply

$$TR = \$1X$$

In the cost function, $TC = (VC)X + FC$, VC must be interpreted as the variable cost per $1 of revenue. In the present case,

$$VC = \frac{\text{Total variable cost}}{\text{Total unit sales}} = \frac{\$150,000}{375,000} = \$0.40$$

This means that, for every $1 of sales, the company has variable costs of $0.40. Then

$$TC = \$0.40X + \$180,000$$

and

$$NI = (\$1.00 - \$0.40)X - \$180,000 = \$0.60X - \$180,000$$

a. (i) Setting $NI = 0$ in the net income equation, formula (5-3), we obtain

$$\$0 = \$0.60(\text{Break-even volume}) - \$180,000$$

$$\text{Break-even volume} = \frac{\$180,000}{\$0.60} = 300,000 \text{ units}$$

Since each unit is deemed to sell at $1, Marconi will break even on revenue of $300,000.

(ii) If revenue of $375,000 represents 75% of capacity, then

$$\$375,000 = 0.75(\text{Full capacity})$$

$$\text{Full capacity} = \frac{\$375,000}{0.75} = \$500,000 \text{ of revenue}$$

The break-even point of $300,000 of revenue represents

$$\frac{\$300,000}{\$500,000} \times 100 = 60\% \text{ of capacity}$$

b. Substitute $X = 450,000$ in the net income equation, formula (5-3).

$$NI = \$0.60(450,000) - \$180,000 = \$90,000$$

Revenue of $450,000 in the current year should produce a net income of $90,000.

➡ **Check your understanding:** If the current S, VC, and FC are the same as last year, what net income would Marconi Printing expect if it operates at 50% of capacity? (Answer: $30,000 loss)

▮▮▮▶ **Related problem:** #11 in Exercise 5.2

Texas Instruments BA II PLUS Break-Even Worksheet: *We demonstrate the use of this worksheet in Appendix 5A. It provides another alternative for solving Problems 1 to 13 and 15 to 20.*

BASIC PROBLEMS

1. Toys-4-U manufactures a toy that it sells for $30 each. The variable cost per toy is $10 and the fixed costs for this product line are $100,000 per year.

   a. What is the break-even point in units?

   b. What is the break-even sales revenue?

2. Reliable Plastics makes containers that it sells for $2.55 each. Its fixed costs for this product are $2000 per month and the variable cost per unit is $1.30.

   a. What is the break-even point in units?

   b. What is the break-even sales revenue?

3. Ingrid processes and bottles jam in her home-based business. Her fixed costs are $250 per month and the variable cost for each jar produced is $1.20. She sells the jam to local specialty shops for $3.20 each.

   a. How many jars must she sell per year to break even?

   b. What will be her profit if she sells 3000 jars in a year?

4. Canada Bagel Company manufactures packages of bagels that it sells for $2.50. The variable costs per package are $1.

   a. To just break even, how many packages of bagels must be sold per month if the fixed costs are $60,000 per month?

   b. What must unit sales be in order to have a profit of $7500 per month?

5. A small manufacturing operation can produce up to 250 units per week of a product that it sells for $20 per unit. The variable cost per unit is $12, and the fixed cost per week is $1200.

   a. How many units must the business sell per week to break even?

   b. Determine the firm's weekly profit or loss if it sells:

   (i) 120 units per week

   (ii) 250 units per week

   c. At what level of sales will the net income be $400 per week?

INTERMEDIATE PROBLEMS

6. Valley Peat Ltd. sells peat moss for $10 per bag. Variable costs are $7.50 per bag and annual fixed costs are $100,000.

   a. How many bags of peat must be sold in a year to break even?

   b. What will be the net income for a year in which 60,000 bags of peat are sold?

   c. How many bags must be sold for a net income of $60,000 in a year?

   d. What annual sales in terms of bags and in terms of dollars would produce a loss of $10,000?

   e. How much do the break-even unit sales and break-even revenue increase per $1000 increase in annual fixed costs?

7. Huntsville Office Supplies (HOS) is evaluating the profitability of leasing a photocopier for its customers to use on a self-serve basis at 10¢ per copy. The copier may be leased for $300 per month plus 1.5¢ per copy on a full-service contract. HOS can purchase paper at $5 per 500-sheet ream. Toner costs $100 per bottle, which in normal use will last for 5000 pages. HOS is allowing for additional costs (including electricity) of 0.5¢ per copy.

   a. How many copies per month must be sold in order to break even?

   b. What will be the increase in monthly profit for each 1000 copies sold above the break-even point?

8. Home Security Specialists Inc. assembles and packages home security systems from standard components. Its basic home security system is sold to customers who prefer to install the system themselves in their own homes. Each system is assembled from components costing $1400 and sells for $2000. Labour costs for assembly are $100 per system. This product line's share of overhead costs is $10,000 per month.

   a. How many basic security systems must be sold each month to break even on this product line?

   b. What will be the profit or loss for a month in which 15 basic home security systems are sold?

9. Bentley Plastics Ltd. has annual fixed costs of $450,000 and variable costs of $15 per unit. The selling price per unit is $25. The production line can manufacture up to 60,000 units per year.

   a. What is the break-even point as a percentage of capacity?

   b. What annual revenue is required to break even?

   c. What will be the annual net income at annual sales of:

      (i) 50,000 units?   **(ii)** $1,000,000?   **(iii)** 90% of capacity?

   d. What minimum annual unit sales are required to limit the annual loss to $20,000?

   e. If the unit selling price and fixed costs remain the same, what are the changes in break-even unit sales and break-even revenue for a $1 increase in variable costs?

10. Jordan is developing a business plan for a residential building inspection service he may start. Rent and utilities for an office would cost $1000 per month. The fixed costs for a vehicle would be $450 per month. He estimates that the variable office costs (word processing and supplies) will be $50 per inspection and variable vehicle costs will be $25 per inspection. Jordan would also spend $200 per month to lease a computer, and $350 per month for advertising.

    a. If he charges $275 per inspection, how many inspections per month are required before he can "pay himself?"

    b. How many inspections per month are required for Jordan to be able to withdraw a salary of $4000 per month?

11. Beta Inc. has based its budget forecast for next year on the assumption it will operate at 90% of capacity. The budget is:

Sales revenue		$18,000,000
Fixed costs	$10,000,000	
Total variable costs	$6,000,000	
Total costs		$16,000,000
Net income		$2,000,000

    a. At what percentage of capacity would Beta break even?

    b. What would be Beta's net income if it operates at 70% of capacity?

12. Alpha Corp. expects to operate at 80% of capacity next year. Its forecast operating budget is:

Sales revenue		$1,200,000
Fixed costs	$300,000	
Total variable costs	$800,000	
Total costs		$1,100,000
Net income		$100,000

a. What is Alpha's break-even revenue?

b. What would be Alpha's net income if it operates at full capacity?

13. A farmer is trying to decide whether to rent his neighbour's land to grow additional hay for sale to feedlots at $180 per delivered tonne. The land can be rented at $400 per hectare for the season. Cultivation and planting will cost $600 per hectare; spraying and fertilizer will cost $450 per hectare. It will cost $42 per tonne to cut, condition, and bale the hay, and $24 per tonne to transport it to the feedlots.

a. How many tonnes per hectare must be produced to break even?

b. What is the profit or loss at the $180 per tonne price if the crop yield is:

   (i) 15 tonnes per hectare?

   (ii) 10 tonnes per hectare?

c. What is the new break-even tonnage if the selling price is increased to $190 per tonne?

ADVANCED PROBLEMS

14. In the past year, the Greenwood Corporation had sales of $1,200,000, fixed costs of $400,000, and total variable costs of $600,000.

a. At what sales figure would Greenwood have broken even last year?

b. If sales increase by 15% in the year ahead (but all prices remain the same), how much (in $) will the net income increase?

c. If fixed costs are 10% lower in the year ahead (but sales and variable costs remain the same as last year), how much (in $) will the net income increase?

d. If variable costs are 10% higher in the year ahead (but sales and fixed costs remain the same as last year), how much (in $) will the net income decrease?

15. A college ski club is planning a weekend package for its members. The members will each be charged $270. For a group of 15 or more, the club can purchase a two-day downhill pass and two nights' accommodation for $220 per person. A 36-passenger capacity bus can be chartered for $1400.

a. How many must sign up to break even?

b. If the bus is filled, how much profit will the club make?

c. If the student government agrees to cover any loss up to $400, what is the minimum number of participants required?

16. Genifax reported the following information for September:

Sales revenue	$180,000
Fixed manufacturing costs	22,000
Fixed marketing and overhead costs	14,000
Total variable costs	120,000
Unit price	9

a. Determine the unit sales required to break even.

b. What unit sales would generate a net income of $30,000?

    c. What unit sales would generate a profit of 20% of the sales revenue?

    d. What sales revenue is required to produce a profit of $20,000?

    e. If unit variable costs are reduced by 10% with no change in the fixed costs, what unit sales are required to break even?

17. In the year just ended, a small manufacturer sold its product at the wholesale price of $37.50. The unit variable costs were $13.25, and the monthly fixed costs were $5600.

    a. If unit variable costs are expected to rise to $15.00 and fixed costs to $6000 per month for the next year, at what amount should the product be priced in order to have the same break-even volume as last year?

    b. What should the product's price be in order to have the same profit as last year on sales of 300 units per month in both years?

18. Mickey's Restaurant had a net income last year of $40,000 after fixed costs of $130,000 and total variable costs of $80,000.

    a. What was the restaurant's break-even point in sales dollars?

    b. If fixed costs in the current year rise to $140,000 and variable costs remain at the same percentage of sales as for last year, what will be the break-even point?

    c. What sales in the current year will result in a profit of $50,000?

19. A sporting goods manufacturer lost $400,000 on sales of $3 million in a year during the last recession. The production lines operated at only 60% of capacity during the year. Variable costs represent one-third of the sales dollars.

    a. At what percent of capacity must the firm operate in order to break even?

    b. What would its net income be at 80% of capacity?

    c. What dollar sales would generate a net income of $700,000?

    d. How much does each additional dollar of sales increase the net income?

    e. How much does every $1 increase in fixed costs raise the break-even sales?

20. This problem is designed to illustrate how the relative proportions of fixed and variable costs affect a firm's net income when the sales volume changes.

Two hypothetical firms, Hi-Tech and Lo-Tech, manufacture and sell the same product at the same price of $50. Hi-Tech is highly mechanized with monthly fixed costs of $4000 and unit variable costs of $10. Lo-Tech is labour-intensive and can readily lay off or take on more workers as production requirements warrant. Lo-Tech's monthly fixed costs are $1000, and its unit variable costs are $40.

    a. Calculate the break-even volume for both firms.

    b. At each firm's break-even point, calculate the percentage of the firm's total costs that are fixed and the percentage that are variable.

    c. For a 10% increase in sales above the break-even point, calculate the dollar increase in each firm's net income. Explain the differing results.

    d. For a 10% decrease in sales below the break-even point, calculate the dollar decrease in each firm's net income. Explain the differing results.

    e. What is each firm's net income at sales of 150 units per month and each firm's loss at sales of 50 units per month?

21. The Woodstock plant of Goodstone Tires manufactures a single line of automobile tires. In its first fiscal quarter, the plant had total revenue of $4,500,000 and net income of $900,000 from the production and sale of 60,000 tires. In the subsequent quarter, the net income was $700,000 from the production and sale of 50,000 tires. Calculate the unit selling price, the total revenue in the second quarter, the variable costs per tire, and the total fixed costs per calendar quarter.

22. The Kelowna division of Windstream RVs builds the Wanderer model. The division had total revenue of $4,785,000 and a profit of $520,000 on the sale of 165 units in the first half of its financial year. Sales declined to 117 units in the second half of the year, resulting in a profit of only $136,000. Determine the selling price per unit, the total revenue in the second half, the unit variable costs, and the annual fixed costs.

5.3   Graphical Approach to CVP Analysis

LO3   The graphical approach to CVP analysis requires that both the cost function and the revenue function (defined in Section 5.2) be plotted on the same graph as illustrated in Figure 5.1. Such a graph is called a **break-even chart**, because the sales volume at which the business will break even is immediately apparent.

FIGURE 5.1   Break-Even Chart

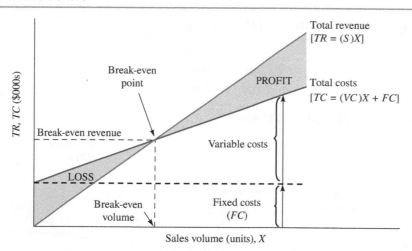

The intersection of the *TR* and *TC* lines is the only point at which total revenue equals total costs, and the firm breaks even. This intersection is therefore called the *break-even point*. The coordinates of the point give the sales volume and total revenue required for the firm to break even. At higher sales, the business will show a profit because the revenue line is above the total cost line. The profit equals the vertical separation of the lines. At any sales volume to the left of the break-even point, total costs exceed total revenue. The size of the loss is represented by the vertical distance between the two lines. At zero sales volume, there are no revenues or variable costs, but the business still incurs the fixed costs.

EXAMPLE 5.3A	Graphical CVP Analysis of the Business Described in Example 5.1A

We will use the data presented in Example 5.1A for Chuck's delivery service. We determined that

$$VC = \$13.90 \text{ per delivery} \quad \text{and} \quad FC = \$6640 \text{ per month}$$

The fixed costs included Chuck's personal wages and benefits in the amount of $3500/month. The revenue per delivery, S, was a flat $60.

a. What are the revenue and cost functions for this business?

b. Construct a break-even chart for the range 100 to 200 deliveries per month.

c. What is the break-even point in (i) deliveries per month? (ii) revenue per month?

d. Chuck can get by in the first year if he withdraws only $2500 of personal wages per month on average instead of $3500. What average number of deliveries per month is needed to reach this minimum income requirement?

e. How much in wages and benefits is Chuck able to withdraw if he makes 174 deliveries in a month?

SOLUTION

a. Let X represent the number of deliveries per month. Using formulas (5-1) and (5-2), we obtain

Revenue function: $\qquad\qquad\qquad\qquad TR = (S)X = \$60X$

Cost function: $\qquad\qquad\qquad\qquad TC = (VC)X + FC = \$13.90X + \$6640$

b. Construct a table of values for both the revenue function and the cost function. The two end points of the range for X are good choices to plot.

X:	100	200
TR:	$6000	$12,000
TC:	$8030	$9420

Now plot both the TR and the TC lines.

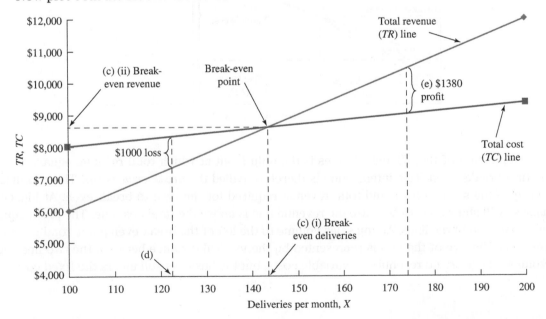

c. The break-even point is approximately (i) 144 deliveries per month and (ii) revenue of $8640 per month.

d. The point at which Chuck can withdraw only $2500 per month (instead of the $3500 per month already built into the *TC* function) is the point where a $1000 loss is indicated on the break-even chart. This occurs where the *TR* line is $1000 below the *TC* line, that is, at about 122 deliveries per month.

e. At 174 deliveries per month, the *TR* line is about $1380 per month above the *TC* line. Chuck can withdraw this $1380 profit in addition to the $3500 per month already included in the *TC* function. His total monthly withdrawal for wages and benefits would then be $1380 + $3500 = $4880 per month.

Note: There are small differences between these answers and those obtained by other methods in Example 5.2A and Example 5.4A, due to the imprecise nature of the graphical approach.

➧ **Check your understanding:** Suppose after additional research, Chuck discovers that his variable costs per delivery will be $20 instead of $13.90. Construct another break-even chart for the range of 100 to 200 deliveries per month. What is the new break-even point in **(a)** deliveries per month? **(b)** revenue per month? (Answer: Depending upon the scale and accuracy of your graph, you should conclude that Chuck will require approximately **(a)** 166 deliveries or **(b)** $9960 per month of sales to break even.)

▰▰▰▸ **Related problem:** #1 in Exercise 5.3

EXAMPLE 5.3B	Graphical Cost-Volume-Profit and Break-Even Analysis

The board of directors of a Tier 2 Junior A hockey team is preparing financial projections for the next season's operations. The team rents the city's 4000-seat arena for the entire season for $200,000 plus 25% of revenue from ticket sales. The city operates the food concessions at the games and pays the team one-third of the gross revenue.

The team will pay $200,000 for uniforms and equipment, $200,000 for travel costs, $100,000 for the coach's salary and benefits, $100,000 for housing subsidies for team members not living at home, and $40,000 for insurance. The average ticket price will be $16, and past experience shows that each fan spends an average of $6 on food and beverages at the games.

Use a break-even chart to answer the following questions.

a. What must the aggregate attendance for the 30 home games be for the team to just cover all of its costs for the season?

b. What will the profit or loss be if the attendance averages 75% of capacity?

c. The team has $280,000 in a contingency fund to absorb losses. What season attendance would just wipe out this fund?

SOLUTION

a. The total of the fixed costs is

$$FC = \$200,000 + \$200,000 + \$200,000 + \$100,000 + \$100,000 + \$40,000$$
$$= \$840,000$$

The unit variable cost is the 25% of the price of each ticket that the team must pay to the city as part of the rent.

$$VC = 0.25 \times \$16 = \$4 \text{ per ticket}$$

The cost function, formula (5-2), for the analysis is

$$TC = (VC)X + FC$$
$$= \$4X + \$840,000$$

Each ticket sold generates revenue for the team of $16 from the admission price and $2 from the team's share (one-third) of the concession revenue ($6 per fan). The revenue function, formula (5-1), is

$$TR = (\$16 + \$2)X$$
$$= \$18X$$

The cost and revenue functions should be plotted for the range from $X = 0$ to $X = 120,000$, which is full capacity (30×4000) for the season.

X:	0	120,000
TR:	$0	$2,160,000
TC:	$840,000	$1,320,000

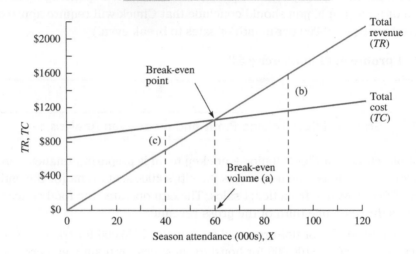

For the team to cover its costs, it must have the attendance figure at the break-even point. Therefore, the team will just cover all its expenses if the total season attendance is 60,000.

b. The season attendance at 75% of capacity is

$$0.75 \times 120,000 = 90,000$$

At an attendance of 90,000, the TR line is $420,000 above the TC line. The team will then have a profit of $420,000.

c. The answer will be the attendance at which the TC line is $280,000 above the TR line. This separation occurs at an attendance of 40,000.

➡ **Check your understanding:** Suppose market research suggests the team could increase the average ticket price to $22 without suffering a significant drop in attendance. Draw another break-even chart. What must the aggregate attendance for the 30 home games be for the team to break even for the season? Remember that a new ticket price will result in a new VC. (Answer: Depending upon the scale and accuracy of your graph, you should conclude that the break-even point is season attendance of approximately 45,405.)

■■▶ **Related problem:** #3 in Exercise 5.3

EXERCISE 5.3

INTERMEDIATE PROBLEMS

Use the graphical approach to CVP analysis to solve Problems 1 through 6. Visit Connect and use the Graph Templates found under the Student Resources for Chapter 5. The problems in this section are full or shortened versions of select problems from Exercise 5.2.

1. Canada Bagel Company manufactures packages of bagels that it sells for $2.50. The variable costs per package are $1.

   a. To just break even, how many packages of bagels must be sold per month if the fixed costs are $60,000 per month?

   b. What must unit sales be in order to have a profit of $7500 per month?

2. A small manufacturing operation can produce up to 250 units per week of a product that it sells for $20 per unit. The variable cost per unit is $12, and the fixed costs per week are $1200.

   a. How many units must the firm sell per week to break even?

   b. Determine the firm's weekly profit or loss if it sells: **(i)** 120 units per week. **(ii)** 250 units per week.

   c. At what level of sales will the net income be $400 per week?

3. Valley Peat Ltd. sells peat moss for $10 per bag. Variable costs are $7.50 per bag and annual fixed costs are $100,000.

   a. How many bags of peat must be sold per year to break even?

   b. What will be the net income for a year in which 60,000 bags of peat are sold?

   c. How many bags must be sold for a net income of $60,000 in a year?

   d. What volume of sales would produce a loss of $10,000 in a year?

4. Home Security Specialists Inc. assembles and packages home security systems from standard components. Its basic home security system is sold to customers who prefer to install the system themselves in their own homes. Each system is assembled from components costing $1400 and sells for $2000. Labour costs for assembly are $100 per system. This product line's share of overhead costs is $10,000 per month.

   a. How many basic security systems must be sold each month to break even on this product line?

   b. What will be the profit or loss for a month in which 15 basic home security systems are sold?

5. Huntsville Office Supplies (HOS) is evaluating the profitability of leasing a photocopier for its customers to use on a self-serve basis at 10¢ per copy. The copier may be leased for $300 per month plus 1.5¢ per copy on a full-service contract. HOS can purchase paper at $5 per 500-sheet ream. Toner costs $100 per bottle, which in normal use will last for 5000 pages. HOS is allowing for additional costs (including electricity) of 0.5¢ per copy.

   a. How many copies per month must be sold in order to break even?

   b. What will be the increase in monthly profit for each 1000 copies sold above the break-even point?

6. Jordan is developing a business plan for a residential building inspection service he wants to start up. Rent and utilities for an office would cost $1000 per month. The fixed costs for a vehicle would be $450 per month. He estimates that the variable office costs (word processing and supplies) will be $50 per inspection and variable vehicle costs will be $25 per inspection. Jordan would also spend $200 per month to lease a computer, and $350 per month for advertising.

   a. If he charges $275 per inspection, how many inspections per month are required before he can "pay himself?"

   b. How many inspections per month are required for Jordan to be able to withdraw a salary of $4000 per month?

ADVANCED PROBLEMS

To solve Problems 7 to 10, visit Connect and use the Break-Even Chart found in "Interactive Charts" under the Student Resources for Chapter 5.

7. Leaving other variables unchanged, what effect does increasing the value of VC have on

   a. The Fixed Cost (FC) line?

   b. The Total Cost (TC) line?

   c. The Total Revenue (TR) line?

   d. The break-even point?

8. Leaving other variables unchanged, what effect does increasing the value of S have on

   a. The Fixed Cost (FC) line?

   b. The Total Cost (TC) line?

   c. The Total Revenue (TR) line?

   d. The break-even point?

9. Leaving other variables unchanged, what effect does increasing the value of FC have on

   a. The Fixed Cost (FC) line?

   b. The Total Cost (TC) line?

   c. The Total Revenue (TR) line?

   d. The break-even point?

10. Solve Problems 4, 5, and 6 using the interactive chart and its accompanying report.

5.4 Contribution Margin Approach to CVP Analysis

LO4 Suppose we produce a product that sells for $5 each ($S = $5), and the associated variable costs are $3 per unit ($VC = $3). This means that each additional unit we produce and sell adds $3 to our total costs.

In the contribution margin approach to CVP analysis, we take the following point of view. Think of the $5 from the sale of each unit as having two components: (1) the $3 needed to pay the variable costs of producing that particular unit and (2) the remaining $2 available for other purposes.

For the early sales in a period, we put the $2 component toward the payment of fixed costs. Suppose our fixed costs are $1000 per month ($FC = $1000). Each unit contributes $2 toward paying fixed costs. These ideas are represented in the diagram below. The fixed costs will not be fully paid until we sell

$1000/$2 = 500 units in the month. This is our break-even point. If we fall 40 units short of 500, we will have a loss of $2(40) = $80 for the month.

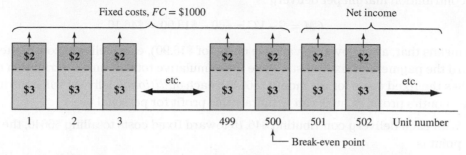

The 501st unit we sell in a month still costs an additional $VC = $3 to produce, but the extra $2 from its sale is "pure" profit. Each and every unit beyond the 500th contributes a full $2 to the net income or profit for the month. If we sell a total of 560 units in a month, our net income will be $2(560 − 500) = $120.

Let us now generalize this discussion. We have talked about each unit *contributing* $2 first toward the payment of fixed costs and then, after we pass the break-even point, *contributing* $2 toward our net income. In accounting and marketing, this $2 component of the selling price is called the **contribution margin**. It is simply the difference between the selling price and the variable costs per unit. Introducing the symbol *CM* to represent contribution margin, we have

CONTRIBUTION MARGIN $$CM = S - VC \qquad \text{(5-4)}$$

As we readily deduced in the numerical example, the number of units that must be sold just to pay the fixed costs (and break even) is

$$\text{Unit sales at the break-even point} = \frac{FC}{CM}$$

The total contribution margin from the sale of X units will be $(CM)X$. The net income for a period will be the amount left over after we subtract the fixed costs from $(CM)X$. That is,

NET INCOME $$NI = (CM)X - FC \qquad \text{(5-5)[2]}$$

EXAMPLE 5.4A | **CVP Analysis Using the Contribution Margin Approach**

In Example 5.1A concerning Chuck's delivery service, we found that

$$VC = $13.90 \text{ per delivery} \quad \text{and} \quad FC = $6640 \text{ per month}$$

The fixed costs included Chuck's personal wages in the amount of $3500/month. The unit variable costs, VC, assumed an average round-trip driving distance of 25 kilometres. The revenue per delivery, S, was a flat $60.

  a. Calculate and interpret the unit contribution margin (per delivery).

  b. What is the break-even point in **(i)** deliveries per month? **(ii)** revenue per month?

  c. Chuck can get by in the first year if he withdraws only $2500 per month on average instead of $3500. What average number of deliveries per month is needed to reach this minimum income requirement?

  d. What personal wage can Chuck withdraw if he makes 174 deliveries in a month?

  e. If the average round-trip distance per delivery turns out to be 30 instead of 25 kilometres, how many deliveries per month are needed to break even?

---

[2] Note that if you substitute definition (5-4) into formula (5-5), you end up with the net income formula (5-3),
$NI = (S - VC)X - FC$, which was derived in Section 5.2.

SOLUTION

a. The contribution margin per delivery is

$$CM = S - VC = \$60 - \$13.90 = \$46.10$$

This means that, after covering variable costs (of $13.90), each delivery contributes $46.10 toward the payment of fixed costs. Once the cumulative total of unit contribution margins reaches the fixed costs for the month ($6640), each *additional* delivery will contribute $46.10 to the month's profit. (Chuck can withdraw this profit for personal use.)

b. (i) With each delivery contributing $46.10 toward fixed costs totalling $6640, the break-even point is

$$\frac{FC}{CM} = \frac{\$6640}{\$46.10} = 144.03 \approx 144 \text{ deliveries per month}$$

(ii) The break-even revenue (from 144 deliveries) is 144($60) = $8640.

c. Since monthly wages and benefits of $3500 are already included in $FC = \$6640$, a monthly wage of only $2500 reduces the fixed costs by $1000 to $5640. The break-even point is then lowered to an average of

$$\frac{FC}{CM} = \frac{\$5640}{\$46.10} = 122.34 \text{ deliveries per month}$$

d. 174 deliveries in a month are 174 − 144 = 30 deliveries more than the break-even point calculated in Part (b). Of the $60 revenue from *each* of these extra deliveries, only $CM = \$46.10$ is available as profit that Chuck can withdraw for personal use. (The other $13.90 is required to pay the additional variable cost of each delivery.) Therefore, Chuck can withdraw a total of

$$\$3500 + 30(\$46.10) = \$4883.00 \text{ for that month}$$

e. Variable costs of $VC = \$13.90$ per delivery were based on an average distance of 25 kilometres per delivery. This corresponds to variable costs of $\frac{\$13.90}{25} = \$0.556$ per kilometre. At 30 kilometres of driving distance per delivery,

$$VC = 30(\$0.556) = \$16.68 \text{ per delivery}$$

The contribution margin becomes

$$CM = S - VC = \$60 - \$16.68 = \$43.32$$

and the break-even point becomes an average of

$$\frac{FC}{CM} = \frac{\$6640}{\$43.32} = 153.28 \text{ deliveries per month}$$

▶ **Check your understanding:** If the average round-trip distance per delivery turns out to be 30 instead of 25 kilometres, how many deliveries per month are needed for the business to generate a profit of $1000 per month? (Answer: 176.36 deliveries per month)

▶ **Related problem:** #5 in Exercise 5.4

EXAMPLE 5.4B	CVP Analysis Using the Contribution Margin Approach

A manufacturing company is studying the feasibility of producing a new product. A new production line could manufacture up to 800 units per month at a cost of $50 per unit. Fixed costs would be $22,400 per month. Variable selling and shipping costs are estimated to be $20 per unit. Market research indicates that a unit price of $110 would be competitive.

a. What is the break-even point as a percent of capacity?

b. What would be the net income at 90% of capacity?

c. What would unit sales have to be to attain a net income of $9000 per month?

d. In a serious recession sales might fall to 55% of capacity. What would be the resulting net income?

e. What dollar amount of sales would result in a loss of $2000 per month?

f. In the highest-cost scenario, fixed costs might be $25,000, production costs might be $55 per unit, and selling and shipping costs might be $22 per unit. What would the break-even point be in these circumstances?

SOLUTION

In the expected scenario, $S = \$110$, $VC = \$50 + \$20 = \$70$, and $FC = \$22,400$ per month.

Hence,
$$CM = S - VC = \$110 - \$70 = \$40$$

a. The break-even volume is

$$\frac{FC}{CM} = \frac{\$22,400}{40} = 560 \text{ units per month}$$

This represents $\frac{560}{800} = 0.70$ or, when multiplied by 100 to convert to a percentage, 70% of capacity.

b. At 90% of capacity, production would be $0.9 \times 800 = 720$ units per month. This is $720 - 560 = 160$ units above the break-even point. The contribution margin from these units goes entirely to net income. Therefore,

$$NI = 160(\$40) = \$6400 \text{ per month}$$

Note: This answer can also be obtained by substitution in formula (5-5).

c. For a net income of $9000 per month, the number of units sold *in excess* of the break-even point would have to be

$$\frac{NI}{CM} = \frac{\$9000}{\$40} = 225$$

Total unit sales would have to be $560 + 225 = 785$ per month.

d. In the recession scenario, sales would be only $0.55 \times 800 = 440$ units per month. This number is $560 - 440 = 120$ units short of the break-even point, resulting in a loss of

$$120(CM) = 120(\$40) = \$4800 \text{ per month}$$

e. Each unit that the company falls short of the break-even point will contribute a loss of $CM = \$40$. For a loss of $2000 in a month, the company must fall

$$\frac{NI}{CM} = \frac{\$2000}{\$40} = 50 \text{ units}$$

short of the break-even point. Total unit sales would be $560 - 50 = 510$ units per month. The dollar amount of sales would be

$$510(S) = 510(\$110) = \$56,100 \text{ per month}$$

f. In the highest-cost scenario, $FC = \$25,000$ per month and $VC = \$77$ per unit.

Then

$$CM = \$110 - \$77 = \$33$$

and

$$\text{Break-even volume} = \frac{FC}{CM} = \frac{\$25,000}{\$33} = 757.6 \text{ units}$$

The break-even point in this scenario would be an average of 757.6 units per month (which converts to $757.6/800 = 0.9470 \times 100 = 94.70\%$ of capacity).

➡ **Check your understanding:** In the highest-cost scenario in Part (f), what percentage of capacity would sales need to be in order for the company to limit its monthly loss to $2000? (Answer: 87.12% of capacity)

▰▰▷ **Related problem:** #7 in Exercise 5.4

EXAMPLE 5.4C | **Using the Contribution Margin Approach to CVP Analysis**

Alberta Oilseed Co. processes rapeseed to produce canola oil and rapeseed meal. The company can process up to 20,000 tonnes of rapeseed per year. The company pays growers $800 per tonne, and each tonne yields $2000 worth of oil and meal. Variable processing costs are $470 per tonne, and fixed processing costs are $3,400,000 per year at all production levels. Administrative overhead is $3,000,000 per year regardless of the volume of production. Marketing and transportation costs work out to $230 per tonne processed.

a. Determine the break-even volume in terms of

 (i) Tonnes of rapeseed processed per year

 (ii) Percent capacity utilization

 (iii) Dollar amount of product sales for the year

b. In order to attain a net income of $2,400,000 in a year,

 (i) How many tonnes of rapeseed must be processed and sold in the year?

 (ii) What dollar value of oil and meal must be sold?

c. What is the maximum price that the company can pay per tonne of rapeseed and still break even on a volume of 16,000 tonnes per year?

SOLUTION

From the given information,

$$\text{Full capacity} = 20,000 \text{ tonnes per year}$$
$$VC = \$800 + \$470 + \$230 = \$1500 \text{ per tonne}$$
$$S = \$2000 \text{ per (input) tonne}$$
$$FC = \$3,400,000 + \$3,000,000 = \$6,400,000 \text{ per year}$$

Hence,

$$CM = S - VC = \$2000 - \$1500 = \$500 \text{ per tonne}$$

a. (i) $\text{Break-even volume} = \dfrac{FC}{CM} = \dfrac{\$6,400,000}{\$500} = 12,800 \text{ tonnes per year}$

 (ii) 12,800 tonnes per year represent $\dfrac{12,800}{20,000} \times 100 = 64\%$ of capacity

 (iii) Sales revenue at the break-even point is $12,800(\$2000) = \$25,600,000$.

b. (i) Each tonne above the break-even point contributes $CM = \$500$ to the net income. A net income of $2,400,000 will require the sale of

$$\frac{\$2,400,000}{\$500} = 4800 \text{ tonnes more then the break-even point}$$

Total sales must be $12,800 + 4800 = 17,600$ tonnes in the year.

(ii) The sales revenue required to generate a net income of $2,400,000 is

$$17,600(\$2000) = \$35,200,000$$

c. In this scenario, S and FC are unchanged but VC is higher, raising the break-even point from 12,800 tonnes to 16,000 tonnes. Since

$$\text{Break-even volume} = \frac{FC}{CM}$$

then

$$CM = \frac{FC}{\text{Break-even volume}} = \frac{\$6,400,000}{16,000} = \$400 \text{ per tonne}$$

This is $100 per tonne less than the former CM. Therefore, the VC per tonne is $100 higher, representing the increase in the price paid to rapeseed growers. The maximum price that can be paid to growers and still break even at a volume of 16,000 tonnes is $800 + \$100 = \$900$ per tonne.

➡ **Check your understanding:** If growers are being paid $900 per tonne and fixed processing costs increase to $3,800,000, how many tonnes of rapeseed must be processed and sold in order to break even? (Answer: 17,000 tonnes)

▰▰▶ **Related problem:** #13 in Exercise 5.4

EXERCISE 5.4

Problems 1 to 22 in Exercise 5.2 may be solved using the Contribution Margin approach.

ADVANCED PROBLEMS

23. **Interactive Contribution Margin Chart** This chart presents a pictorial display of the components of total cost and total revenue from a contribution margin point of view.

    To improve your intuitive understanding of the contribution margin approach to CVP analysis, visit Connect and use the chart found in the "Interactive Charts" under the Student Resources for Chapter 5 to solve Problems 3 to 5 and 7 to 10 in Exercise 5.2.

5.5 | Contribution Rate Approach to CVP Analysis

LO5 The contribution margin expressed as a percentage of the unit selling price is called the **contribution rate**, CR. That is,

CONTRIBUTION RATE
$$CR = \frac{CM}{S} \times 100 \qquad \text{(5-6)}$$

You can think of the contribution rate as the percentage of the unit selling price that is available first to pay fixed costs and then to produce a profit.

It is also possible to calculate the contribution rate from a firm's total revenue and total variable costs in an operating period. To see how this can be done, substitute $CM = S - VC$ in the numerator above, and then multiply both the numerator and the denominator by X, the total units sold. We obtain

CONTRIBUTION RATE
$$CR = \frac{(S - VC)X}{(S)X} = \frac{(S)X - (VC)X}{(S)X}$$

$$= \frac{\text{Total revenue} - \text{Total variable costs}}{\text{Total revenue}} \times 100 \qquad \text{(5-7)}$$

Hence, the contribution rate may also be viewed as the percentage of total revenue available first to pay fixed costs and then to generate a profit. When revenue and cost information is available on an aggregate rather than on a per-unit basis, this approach must be used to calculate the contribution rate. At the break-even point, revenue will exceed total variable costs by the fixed costs exactly. Therefore,

$$CR = \frac{FC}{\text{Break-even revenue}}$$

If you already know the values for FC and CR, re-arrange this equation to obtain the break-even revenue. That is,

BREAK-EVEN REVENUE
$$\text{Break-even revenue} = \frac{FC}{CR} \qquad \text{(5-8)}$$

EXAMPLE 5.5A | **CVP Analysis with Sales Volume in Dollars Instead of Units**

Last year Marconi Printing had total revenue of $375,000 while operating at 75% of capacity. The total of its variable costs was $150,000. Fixed costs were $180,000.

a. What is Marconi's break-even point expressed:

  (i) in dollars of revenue?   (ii) as a percent of capacity?

b. If the current S, VC, and FC are the same as last year, what net income can be expected from revenue of $450,000 in the current year?

SOLUTION

When no information is provided about the unit price and unit variable cost, cost-volume-profit analysis may still be undertaken. The further assumption required is that the firm sells a single product or, if more than one product, the product mix does not change from one period to the next.

Although we do not have sufficient information to calculate the unit contribution margin, we can calculate the total contribution margin and the contribution rate. That is,

$$CR = \frac{\text{Total revenue} - \text{Total variable costs}}{\text{Total revenue}} \times 100$$

$$= \frac{\$375,000 - \$150,000}{\$375,000} \times 100$$

$$= 60\%$$

The most useful interpretation of this figure is that 60 cents from every dollar of revenue is the amount available to pay fixed costs. Once fixed costs are covered for the period, 60 cents of each additional dollar of revenue "flows through to the bottom line" (that is, becomes net income or operating profit for the period).

a. (i) The break-even point will occur when

$$\text{Revenue} = \frac{FC}{CR} = \frac{\$180,000}{0.60} = \$300,000$$

  (ii) If revenue of $375,000 represents 75% of capacity, then

$$\text{Full capacity} = \frac{\$375,000}{0.75} = \$500,000 \text{ of revenue}$$

The break-even point of $300,000 represents

$$\frac{\$300,000}{\$500,000} \times 100 = 60\% \text{ of capacity}$$

b. The new revenue level of $450,000 is $150,000 beyond the break-even point. Since $CR = 60\%$, then 60 cents of each dollar beyond the break-even point become net income. Hence,

$$\text{Net income} = 0.60 \times \$150,000 = \$90,000$$

Revenue of $450,000 in the current year should produce a net income of $90,000.

▶ **Check your understanding:** If the cost structure remains the same as last year, what net income would Marconi Printing expect if it operates at 50% of capacity? (Answer: $30,000 loss)

▮▮▶ **Related problem:** #1 in Exercise 5.5

 ## Checkpoint Questions

1. Circle "True" or "False" for each of the following statements:

   a. A fixed cost is a cost that never changes.   True   False

   b. "Net income" and "total revenue" mean the same thing.   True   False

   c. "Total revenue" and "total sales dollars" mean the same thing   True   False

   d. "Net income" and "operating profit" mean the same thing   True   False

   e. All else being equal, lower fixed costs will result in a higher break-even point.   True   False

2. What effect (if any) will each of the following have on a product's unit contribution margin? In each case, assume that all other variables remain unchanged.

   a. The business raises the selling price of the product.

   b. The prices of some raw materials used in manufacturing decrease.

   c. The local regional government increases the business's property tax.

   d. The company's president is given a raise.

   e. The production workers receive a raise in their hourly rate.

3. Once a business is operating beyond the break-even point, why doesn't each additional dollar of revenue add a dollar to net income?

4. What effect (if any) will each of the following have on a firm's break-even point? In each case, assume that all other variables remain unchanged.

   a. Fixed costs decrease.

   b. Variable costs increase.

   c. Sales volume increases.

   d. Unit selling price decreases.

   e. The contribution rate increases.

EXERCISE 5.5

Answers to the odd-numbered problems can be found in the end matter.

Use the contribution rate approach to CVP analysis to solve the following problems. Problems 3, 4, and 5 are repeated from Exercise 5.2, to help illustrate the fact that multiple approaches to CVP analysis can be used to solve a given problem.

BASIC PROBLEMS

1. Morgan is planning to run a small lawn care business this summer. He can rent a ride-on lawn tractor for $680 per month. He estimates that it will cost $5 in gasoline to cut the average lawn, and he intends to charge a flat rate of $25 per lawn.

   a. What is the contribution rate that Morgan's business is expected to generate?

   b. What is Morgan's break-even level of revenue per month?

   c. How many lawns per month must Morgan cut in order to break even?

2. A small business calculates that its monthly fixed costs are $3,200. If the business calculates its contribution rate to be 0.42, what level of monthly sales must be generated in order to break even?

INTERMEDIATE PROBLEMS

3. Beta Inc. has based its budget forecast for next year on the assumption it will operate at 90% of capacity. The budget is:

Sales revenue		$18,000,000
Fixed costs	$10,000,000	
Total variable costs	$6,000,000	
Total costs		$16,000,000
Net income		$2,000,000

   a. At what percentage of capacity would Beta break even?

   b. What would be Beta's net income if it operates at 70% of capacity?

4. Alpha Corp. expects to operate at 80% of capacity next year. Its forecast operating budget is:

Sales revenue		$1,200,000
Fixed costs	$300,000	
Total variable costs	$800,000	
Total costs		$1,100,000
Net income		$100,000

   a. What is Alpha's break-even revenue?

   b. What would be Alpha's net income if it operates at full capacity?

ADVANCED PROBLEMS

5. In the past year, the Greenwood Corporation had sales of $1,200,000, fixed costs of $400,000, and total variable costs of $600,000.

   a. At what sales figure would Greenwood have broken even last year?

   b. If sales increase by 15% in the year ahead (but all prices remain the same), how much (in $) will the net income increase?

   c. If fixed costs are 10% lower in the year ahead (but sales and variable costs remain the same as last year), how much (in $) will the net income increase?

    d. If variable costs are 10% higher in the year ahead (but sales and fixed costs remain the same as last year), how much (in $) will the net income decrease?

6. Canada Mills Corporation's annual fixed costs are $690,000. Variable costs are equal to 40% of sales revenue.

    a. What annual sales level must Canada Mills achieve in order to break even?

    b. What annual profit will Canada Mills earn on annual sales of $2,000,000?

    c. What annual sales level must be achieved in order to earn an annual income of $300,000?

Key Terms

Break-even chart	**Cost function**	**Unit variable cost**
Break-even point	**Cost-volume-profit analysis**	**Variable cost**
Contribution margin	**Fixed cost**	
Contribution rate	**Revenue function**	

Summary of Notation and Key Formulas

The following notation was introduced for cost-volume-profit analysis:

S = Selling price or revenue per unit
VC = Variable costs per unit
FC = Fixed costs
CM = Contribution margin per unit
TC = Total costs for the period

CR = Contribution rate
X = Total number of units sold in the period
NI = Net income (or operating profit) for the period
TR = Total revenue for the period

FORMULA (5-1) $TR = (S)X$ Finding the total revenue from the sale of X units

FORMULA (5-2) $TC = (VC)X + FC$ Finding the total costs from the sale of X units

FORMULA (5-3) $NI = (S - VC)X - FC$ Finding net income from the sale of X units

FORMULA (5-3a) $\text{Break-even volume} = \dfrac{FC}{S - VC}$ Finding the break-even level of sales volume

FORMULA (5-4) $CM = S - VC$ Finding the contribution margin

FORMULA (5-5) $NI = (CM)X - FC$ Finding the net income from the sale of X units

FORMULA (5-6) $CR = \dfrac{CM}{S} \times 100\%$ Finding the contribution rate

FORMULA (5-7) $CR = \dfrac{\text{Total revenue} - \text{Total variable costs}}{\text{Total revenue}} \times 100\%$ Finding the contribution rate

FORMULA (5-8) $\text{Break-even revenue} = \dfrac{FC}{CR}$ Finding break-even revenue using contribution rate

Review Problems

Answers to the odd-numbered review problems can be found in the end matter.

1. **LO1** Emma is launching a home-based business. She intends to make and sell gluten-free desserts. Emma has identified the following cost categories for her business. For each cost category, identify whether the cost would be considered a fixed or a variable cost.

   a. Sugar

   b. Weekly newspaper advertisement

   c. Lease of a delivery vehicle

   d. Cake boxes

2. **LO1** Sri has written his first novel, and has produced copies of his book that he plans to sell to independent bookstores for $16.50 a copy. Each copy of the book costs $8.75 to print at a local printing company. Sri estimates that his fixed costs for sales and promotion expenses will be $300 per month.

   a. What will Sri's total costs be if he sells 1500 copies of his book next month?

   b. What will Sri's total costs be if he sells 3000 copies of his book next month?

   c. Explain why the total in Part (b) above is not twice as much as the total in Part (a).

3. **LO1** Sabine owns and operates a part-time pet grooming business. She charges a flat rate of $40 to bathe and groom a dog. Last year, Sabine groomed 384 dogs. Her total costs were $4848, which included $3600 of fixed costs.

   a. What are Sabine's variable costs per dog groomed?

   b. Assuming her cost structure does not change, what would Sabine's total costs be in a year in which she groomed a total of 500 dogs?

4. **LO2 LO4** A heavy equipment manufacturing company has annual fixed costs of $14,000,000. Unit selling price is $15,000 and unit variable costs are $8,000.

   a. What is the company's break-even point in unit sales per year?

   b. What annual sales revenue must the company achieve in order to break even?

   c. What will be the annual profit or loss if annual sales are 3000 units?

   d. How many units must the company sell per year to generate an annual profit of $700,000?

5. **LO2 LO4** Memex Corp. manufactures memory expansion boards for laptop computers. The average selling price of its finished product is $180 per unit. The average variable cost per unit is $110. Memex incurs fixed costs of $1,260,000 per year.

   a. What is the break-even point in unit sales per year?

   b. What annual sales revenue must Memex achieve in order to break even?

   c. What will be the company's profit or loss at the following levels of sales for a year: 20,000 units? 17,500 units?

6. **LO3** Whitewater Industries sells a plastic one-piece kayak for $850. Unit variable costs are $400, and fixed costs for this product line are $20,000 per month.

   a. Construct a break-even chart for the range 0 to 80 kayaks per month. Visit Connect and use the Graph Templates found under the Student Resources for Chapter 5.

   b. Reading from your chart, what is the approximate number of kayaks that must be sold per month in order to break even?

   c. Reading from your chart, what is the approximate monthly net income or loss if monthly sales are 60 units?

7. **LO2 LO4** ChildCare Industries manufactures infant car seats that it sells to retailers for $155 each. The costs to manufacture each additional seat are $65, and the monthly fixed costs are $18,000.

   a. How many seats must be sold per year to break even?

   b. What will ChildCare's loss be if it sells 2000 seats in a year?

INTERMEDIATE PROBLEMS

8. **LO2 LO3 LO4** Performance Audio Corp. manufactures portable waterproof speakers at a unit variable cost of $43. It sells them for $70 each. It can produce a maximum of 3200 units per month. Annual fixed costs are $648,000.

   a. What is the break-even volume per month?

   b. What is the monthly net income at a volume of 2500 units per month?

   c. What is the monthly net income if Performance operates at 50% of capacity during a recession?

   d. At what percent utilization would the annual net income be $226,800?

   e. If fixed and variable costs remain the same, how much do the monthly break-even unit sales change for a $1 increase in the selling price?

   f. Use the graphical approach to CVP analysis to redo Parts (a), (b), and (c) above. Visit Connect and use the Graph Templates found under the Student Resources for Chapter 5.

9. **LO2 LO4** Fisher Publishing Inc. is doing a financial feasibility analysis for a new book. Editing and preproduction costs are estimated at $45,000. The printing costs are a flat $7000 for setup plus $8 per book. The author's royalty is 8% of the publisher's selling price to bookstores. Advertising and promotion costs are budgeted at $8000.

   a. If the price to bookstores is set at $35, how many books must be sold to break even?

   b. The marketing department is forecasting sales of 4800 books at the $35 price. What will be the net income from the project at this volume of sales?

   c. The marketing department is also forecasting that, if the price is reduced by 10%, unit sales will be 15% higher. Which price should be selected? (Show calculations that support your recommendation.)

   d. In a highest-cost scenario, fixed costs might be $5000 higher and the printing costs might be $9 per book. By how many books would the break-even volume be raised?

10. **LO2 LO4** The Armour Company had the following revenue and costs in the most recently completed fiscal year:

Total revenue	$10,000,000
Total fixed costs	$2,000,000
Total variable costs	$6,000,000
Total units produced and sold	1,000,000

   a. What is the unit sales volume at the break-even point?

   b. How many units must be produced and sold for the company to have a net income of $1,000,000 for the year?

11. **LO2 LO4** Cambridge Manufacturing is evaluating the introduction of a new product that would have a unit selling price of $100. The total annual fixed costs are estimated to be $200,000, and the unit variable costs are projected at $60. Forecast sales volume for the first year is 8000 units.

   a. What sales volume (in units) is required to break even?

   b. What volume is required to generate a net income of $100,000?

   c. What would be the net income at the forecast sales volume?

   d. At the forecast sales volume, what will be the change in the net income if fixed costs are

       (i) 5% higher than expected?

       (ii) 10% lower than expected?

   e. At the forecast sales volume, what will be the change in the net income if unit variable costs are

       (i) 10% higher than expected?

       (ii) 5% lower than expected?

   f. At the forecast sales volume, what will be the change in the net income if the unit selling price is

       (i) 5% higher?

       (ii) 10% lower?

   g. At the forecast sales volume, what will be the change in the net income if unit variable costs are 10% higher than expected and fixed costs are simultaneously 10% lower than expected?

ADVANCED PROBLEMS

12. `LO2` `LO4` The monthly fixed costs of operating a 30-unit motel are $28,000. The price per unit per night for next year is set at $110. Costs arising from rentals on a per-unit per-day basis are $12 for cleaning services, $6 for supplies and laundry, and $6 for heat and utilities.

   a. Based on a 30-day month, at what average occupancy rate will the motel break even?

   b. What will the motel's net income be at an occupancy rate of

       (i) 40%?

       (ii) 30%?

   c. Should the owner reduce the price from $110 to $94 per unit per night if it will result in an increase in the average occupancy rate from 40% to 50%? Present calculations that justify your answer.

13. `LO4` To raise funds for its community activities, a Lions Club chapter is negotiating with International Carnivals to bring its midway rides and games to town for a three-day opening. The event will be held on part of the parking lot of a local shopping centre, which is to receive 10% of the gross revenue. The Lions Club members will sell the ride and game tickets at the site. International Carnivals requires either $15,000 plus 30% of revenue or $10,000 plus 50% of revenue. The experience of other towns that have held the event is that customers spend an average of $10 per person on rides and games.

   a. What is the break-even attendance under each basis for remunerating International Carnivals?

   b. For each alternative, what will be the club's profit or loss if the attendance is

       (i) 3000?

       (ii) 2200?

   c. How would you briefly explain the advantages and disadvantages of the two alternatives to a club member?

14. `LO5` Norwood Industries has annual fixed costs of $1.8 million. Unit variable costs are currently 55% of the unit selling price.

   a. What annual revenue is required to break even?

   b. What revenue would result in a loss of $100,000 in a year?

   c. What annual revenue would produce a profit of $300,000?

   d. Market research indicates that if prices are increased by 10%, total revenue will remain at the Part (c) amount because the higher prices will be offset by reduced sales volume. Will the operating profit remain at $300,000? Present calculations to justify your answer.

Appendix 5A: The Texas Instruments BA II PLUS Break-Even Worksheet

The BA II PLUS's Owner's Manual uses the term "worksheet" to refer to a list of settings and functions designed for a particular application. Usually, a worksheet is the second function of a key. For example, the letters BRKEVN appear above the [6] key. These letters indicate that the Breakeven Worksheet is the second function of this key. You can access it by pressing [2nd] [6] in sequence (rather than at the same time). Hereafter, we will represent these keystrokes as [2nd] [BRKEVN]. The calculator's display then shows:

$FC =$	n,nnn.nn

where the n's represent numerical digits. (Your display may show more or fewer digits.)

You should think of a worksheet as a single column of items that you can view one at a time in the display. The Break-Even Worksheet's column consists of the following five items:

$FC =$	n,nnn.nn
$VC =$	nn.nn
$P =$	nn.nn
$PFT =$	nnn.nn
$Q =$	n,nnn

The solid line around the first item denotes that the calculator's display currently provides a "window" to the first item in the column. You can use the scroll keys [↑] and [↓] to move down or up the list. The five worksheet symbols are defined as follows. (Unfortunately, three of the five symbols differ from the symbols used in this textbook.)

$$FC = \text{(Total) fixed costs}$$
$$VC = \text{Variable costs per unit}$$
$$P = \text{Selling price per unit (S in the textbook)}$$
$$PFT = \text{Profit or Net income (NI in the textbook)}$$
$$Q = \text{Number of units sold (X in the textbook)}$$

The Break-Even Worksheet allows you to enter values for any four of these five variables and then compute the value of the remaining, fifth variable. We will use the worksheet to solve Problem 4 from Exercise 5.2. But first close the worksheet by pressing [2nd] [QUIT]. (By the [QUIT] key, we mean the key in the upper left corner of the keypad showing QUIT as its second function.)

EXAMPLE 5AA	Using the Breakeven Worksheet to Solve Problem 4 from Exercise 5.2

In terms of the textbook's notation, we are given $S = \$2.50$ and $VC = \$1$.

a. We want to determine the break-even volume if $FC = \$60,000$ per month.

[2nd] [BRKEVN] ⇒ Open the Breakeven Worksheet.

60000 [ENTER] ⇒ Key in and save the value for FC.

[↓] 1.00 [ENTER] ⇒ Scroll down to VC. Key in and save its value.

[↓] 2.50 [ENTER] ⇒ Scroll down to P. Key in and save its value.

[↓] 0 [ENTER] ⇒ Scroll down to PFT. Key in and save its value. (At the break-even point, $PFT = \$0$.)

[↓] [CPT] ⇒ Scroll down to Q. Compute its value.

The answer that appears is 40,000. That is, 40,000 bags of bagels per month must be sold to break even.

b. Now we want the number of units, X, that must be sold in order to have $NI = \$7500$ per month. If we do not clear the worksheet, the most recently entered and calculated values remain in memory. Therefore, we need only to change the value for "*PFT*" to $7500 and then re-calculate "*Q*."

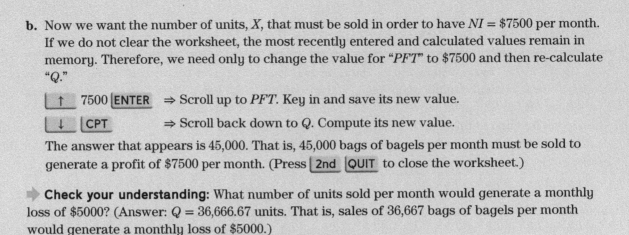

↑ 7500 ENTER   ⇒ Scroll up to *PFT*. Key in and save its new value.
↓ CPT   ⇒ Scroll back down to *Q*. Compute its new value.

The answer that appears is 45,000. That is, 45,000 bags of bagels per month must be sold to generate a profit of $7500 per month. (Press 2nd QUIT to close the worksheet.)

⟹ **Check your understanding:** What number of units sold per month would generate a monthly loss of $5000? (Answer: $Q = 36{,}666.67$ units. That is, sales of 36,667 bags of bagels per month would generate a monthly loss of $5000.)

© Fancy/Image Source RF

CHAPTER 6
Simple Interest

LEARNING OBJECTIVES
After completing this chapter, you will be able to:

LO1 Calculate interest, rate, term, maturity value (future value), and present value in a simple interest environment

LO2 Calculate the equivalent value on any date of a single payment or a stream of payments

LO3 Present details of the amount and timing of payments in a time diagram

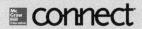 **connect** Throughout this chapter interactive charts and Help Me Solve It videos are marked with a ↗.

EVERY DAY MONEY IS BORROWED and loaned in tens of thousands of transactions. The transaction amounts range from a few dollars on credit-card purchases to multibillion-dollar refinancings of federal government debt.

Interest is the fee or rent that lenders charge for the use of their money. For many individuals and corporations, and for most provincial and federal governments, interest on debt is one of the largest expenditures in their annual budgets.

Clearly, debt plays a key role in our personal finances and our economic system. As a fundamental skill, you must be able to calculate interest on debt. But to be a truly effective participant in financial decision-making, you must be able to analyze the broader effects that prevailing interest rates have on the value of personal investments and business assets. The remainder of the text is devoted to developing these skills and techniques.

In this chapter you will first learn how to calculate interest in the simple-interest system. We will then take the first step toward answering a central question in finance: "What is an investment worth?" This step involves the concept of "equivalent value." It is a far-reaching idea that will carry forward to the compound-interest system in later chapters.

6.1 | Basic Concepts

LO1 Borrowing and lending are two sides of the same transaction. The amount borrowed/loaned is called the **principal**. To the borrower, the principal is a *debt*; to the lender, the principal represents an *investment*.

The interest paid by the borrower is the lender's investment income. There are two systems[1] for calculating interest.

- **Simple interest** is a system whereby interest is calculated and paid only on the principal amount. Simple interest is used mainly for short-term loans and investments. (By "short-term" we mean durations of up to one year.) Chapters 6 and 7 cover the mathematics and applications of simple interest.
- **Compound interest** is a system whereby interest is calculated and added to the original principal amount at regular intervals of time. For subsequent periods, interest is calculated on the combination of the original principal and the accumulated (or accrued) interest from previous periods. Compound interest is used mainly (but not exclusively) for loans and investments with durations longer than one year. Chapters 8 and beyond cover the mathematics and applications of compound interest.

The **rate of interest** is the amount of interest (expressed as a percentage of the principal) charged per period. Simple interest rates are usually calculated and quoted for a one-year period. Such a rate is often called a *per annum rate*. That is,

$$\text{Interest rate (per annum)} = \frac{\text{Annual interest}}{\text{Principal}} \times 100$$

Note: If a time interval (such as "per month") is not indicated for a quoted interest rate, assume the rate is an annual or per annum rate.

The rate of interest charged on a loan is the lender's rate of return on investment. (It seems more natural for us to take the borrower's point of view, because we usually become borrowers before we become lenders.)

If you "go with your intuition," you will probably correctly calculate the amount of simple interest. For example, how much interest will $1000 earn in six months if it earns an 8% rate of interest? Your thinking probably goes as follows: "In one year, $1000 will earn $80 (8% of $1000). In six months ($\frac{1}{2}$ year), $1000 will earn only $40 ($\frac{1}{2}$ of $80)."

Now write an equation for the preceding calculation, but in terms of the following symbols:

$$I = \text{Amount of interest paid or received}$$
$$P = \text{Principal amount of the loan or investment}$$
$$r = \text{Annual rate of simple interest}$$
$$t = \text{Time period (term), in years, of the loan or investment}$$

To obtain the $40 ($I$) amount, you multiplied $1000 ($P$) by 0.08 ($r$) and by $\frac{1}{2}$ year (t). In general,

AMOUNT OF SIMPLE INTEREST $I = Prt$ **(6-1)**

---

[1] We are *not* referring to two alternative methods for obtaining the same answer to an interest calculation. Rather, the two "systems" usually result in different amounts of interest being calculated.

TIP

Interest Rates in Algebraic Formulas

When substituting the numerical value for an interest rate into any equation or formula, you must use the decimal equivalent of the interest rate. For example, 9% would be expressed as 0.09 in an equation.

TIP

The $I = Prt$ Triangle

Don't try to memorize other versions of formula (6-1) that have different variables isolated on the left-hand side. In any problem requiring formula (6-1), just substitute the three known variables and then solve for the remaining unknown variable. Alternatively, you might use the $I = Prt$ triangle as a visual aid to help you solve for any of the variables.

To use the triangle method, cover up the variable that you are solving for. The remaining variables will appear in the correct arrangement to help you solve for the unknown value you are seeking. For example, if a question requires you to solve for P, covering the variable P in the triangle leaves I positioned above r and t, which is interpreted as $\frac{I}{rt}$. If a question requires that you solve for r, covering up the letter r in the diagram leaves I positioned above P and t, which is interpreted as $\frac{I}{Pt}$. Finally, if a question requires that you solve for t, covering the letter t reveals I positioned above P and r, which is read as $\frac{I}{Pr}$.

EXAMPLE 6.1A | **Calculating the Amount of Interest**

What amount of interest will be charged on $6500 borrowed for five months at a simple interest rate of 11%?

SOLUTION

Given: $P = \$6500$, $t = \frac{5}{12}$ year, $r = 11\%$

Since no time period is given for the 11% rate, we understand that the rate is per year.

The amount of interest payable at the end of the loan period is

$$I = Prt = \$6500(0.11)\left(\tfrac{5}{12}\right) = \$297.92$$

➡ **Check your understanding:** Redo the question, this time assuming the money is borrowed for eight months. (Answer: $I = \$476.67$)

◀▶ **Related problem:** #1 in Exercise 6.1

EXAMPLE 6.1B | **Calculating the Principal Amount**

If a three-month term deposit at a bank pays a simple interest rate of 4.5%, how much will have to be deposited to earn $100 of interest?

SOLUTION

a. The term will be calculated by three methods:

Method 1: Counting the number of days of each partial and full month within the interval (using Table 6.1).
Method 2: Using the serial numbers of the beginning date and the ending date (from Table 6.2).
Method 3: Using the "DATE" worksheet of the Texas Instruments BA II PLUS calculator.

Method 1 (using Table 6.1):

Loan #1		Loan #2		Loan #3	
Month	Days	Month	Days	Month	Days
March	1	January	21	November	2
April	30	February	29	December	31
May	31	March	31	January	31
June	30	April	30	February	28
July	31	May	31	March	31
August	31	June	3	April	0
September	3				
Total	157	Total	145	Total	123

Method 2: (using Table 6.2) Particularly when the term of the loan includes a year-end, it is helpful to draw a time line showing the dates on which the loan was advanced and repaid. Look up the serial numbers for these dates in Table 6.2, and write them on the time line.

Loan #1

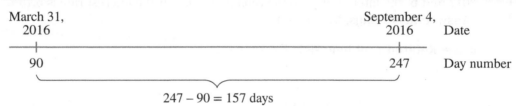

$247 - 90 = 157$ days

The term of the loan is 157 days.

Loan #2

When a date falls after February 29 of a leap year, you must add one day to the serial number obtained from Table 6.2.

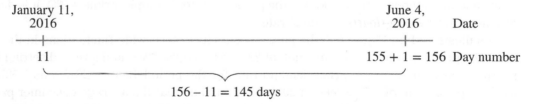

$156 - 11 = 145$ days

The term of the loan is 145 days.

Loan #3

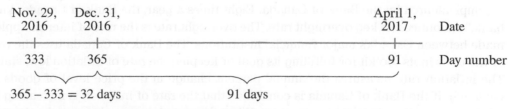

$365 - 333 = 32$ days 91 days

The term of the loan is $32 + 91 = 123$ days.

Method 3: Using the "Date" worksheet of the Texas Instruments BA II PLUS calculator as described in Appendix 6A.

Loan #1	**Loan #2**	**Loan #3**
2nd DATE	↑ ↑	↑ ↑
3.3116 ENTER ①	1.1116 ENTER	11.2916 ENTER
↓ 9.0416 ENTER ②	↓ 6.0416 ENTER	↓ 4.0117 ENTER
↓ CPT	↓ CPT	↓ CPT
Answer: DBD = 157	*Answer: DBD* = 145	*Answer: DBD* = 123
		2nd QUIT

① This enters March 31, 2016 as the beginning of the interval.

② This enters September 4, 2016 as the end of the interval.

b. Each loan's term should be expressed as a fraction of a year when substituted in formula (6-1).

Loan #1 $I = Prt = \$3000(0.0775)\left(\frac{157}{365}\right) = \$100.01$

Loan #2 $I = Prt = \$14{,}600(0.0925)\left(\frac{145}{365}\right) = \$536.50$

Loan #3 $I = Prt = \$23{,}000(0.069)\left(\frac{123}{365}\right) = \$534.80$

➡ **Check your understanding:** Select one of the methods presented above to calculate:
a. the term of a $6000 loan that was advanced on February 8, 2016 and repaid on January 4, 2017 and **b.** the interest due on the repayment date if the interest rate is 5.75%.
(Answer: **a.** 331 days, **b.** $312.86)

▰▰▶ **Related problem:** #9 in Exercise 6.2

Variable or Floating Interest Rates

The interest rate on short-term loans is often linked to the "prime rate" charged by the chartered banks. The **prime rate of interest** is a bank's lowest lending rate—it is available only on the most secure loans. Less secure loans are charged anywhere from $\frac{1}{2}$% to 5% more than the prime rate. The chartered banks change the prime rate from time to time in response to interest rate movements in the financial markets. When a loan's interest rate is linked to the prime rate (for example, prime + 2%), it is described as a *variable* interest rate or a *floating* interest rate.

As illustrated by Figure 6.2, the past 50 years have seen wide fluctuations in the prime borrowing rate. The prime rate hit an all-time high of 22.75% in August 1981, and a record-setting low of only 2.25% in April 2009. The average prime lending rate for the period 1960 to 2015 was 7.53%, well above the average prime rate of 2.78% seen in 2015. Keep in mind that the average consumer pays more than the prime rate, depending upon the nature of the loan, whether it is secured by real property, and the overall degree of risk perceived by the lender.

In Canada, the prime lending rate fluctuates with prevailing economic conditions and economic policy implemented by the Bank of Canada. Eight times a year, the Bank of Canada, known as the "central bank," announces its key overnight rate. The overnight rate is the rate of interest applied to one-day loans made between Canada's major financial institutions. The Bank of Canada uses the overnight rate as one of the tools in its toolkit for fulfilling its goal of keeping the rate of inflation low, stable, and predictable. The inflation rate measures the annual percent change in the price level of goods and services in the economy. If the Bank of Canada is concerned that the rate of inflation is increasing beyond its target, it might increase the overnight lending rate. When the overnight rate changes, the chartered banks typically follow suit with corresponding adjustments to their prime lending rate. Historically, the prime lending rate set by the "big banks" is about 2% higher than the overnight rate. A higher prime lending rate results in increased borrowing costs for businesses and consumers and, in theory, a reduction in overall spending in the economy. Less demand for goods and services would, in turn, bring the rate of inflation down, since reduced demand generally leads to lower prices. It is a complicated set of interrelated factors! You can read more about the influence of the Bank of Canada on interest rates at www.bankofcanada.ca.

FIGURE 6.2   Average Annual Prime Lending Rate in Canada, 1963 to 2015

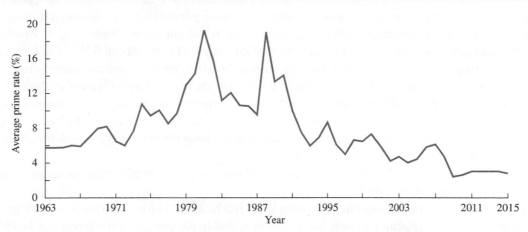

Source: Bank of Canada, Data and Statistics Office, www.bankofcanada.ca/wp-content/uploads/2010/09/selected_historical_page49_50_51.pdf.

EXAMPLE 6.2B	Floating Interest Rates

Lajos borrowed $5000 on April 7 at prime + 1%. The prime rate was initially 3.5%. It increased to 4% effective May 23, and 4.25% effective July 13. What amount was required to repay the loan on August 2?

SOLUTION

The statement that the interest rate "increased to 4% effective May 23" means that interest was charged for May 23 (and subsequent days) at the new 4% rate. We need to break the overall loan period into intervals within which the interest rate is constant.

In the following table, the beginning and ending dates have been given for each interval. Since we count the first day but not the last day in an interval, May 23 is counted only in the second interval and July 13 is counted only in the third interval. This is consistent with the new interest rates taking effect on May 23 and July 13.

Interval	Number of days	Interest rate	Interest ($)
April 7 to May 23	24 + 22 = 46	3.5 + 1 = 4.5%	28.356 ①
May 23 to July 13	9 + 30 + 12 = 51	4.0 + 1 = 5.0%	34.932 ②
July 13 to August 2	19 + 1 = 20	4.25 + 1 = 5.25%	14.384
		Total:	77.672

① Interest = Prt = $5000(0.045)$\left(\frac{46}{365}\right)$ = $28.356

② Interest = Prt = $5000(0.05)$\left(\frac{51}{365}\right)$ = $34.932

The amount required to repay the loan on August 2 was $5000 + $77.67 = $5077.67.

Check your understanding: Lajos borrowed $1200 on March 12 at prime + 0.75%. The prime rate was initially 4.25%. It dropped to 3.75% effective June 7, and 3% effective September 23. What amount was required to repay the loan on November 14? (Answer: $1236.69)

Related problem: #19 in Exercise 6.2

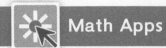

CARD TRICKS: TAKING MORE INTEREST

According to the Canadian Bankers Association, there are over 72 million Visa and MasterCard cards in circulation in Canada, and 89% of adult Canadians have at least one credit card. If you always pay your credit card balance in full during the *grace period* (the time between the statement date and the payment due date), you pay no interest on retail purchases made on your credit card. The minimum grace period (set by government regulations) is 21 days. About 60% of Canadian credit card holders pay off their balance in full every month. In effect, they receive an interest-free loan on each retail purchase from the date of purchase to the date on which the credit card's balance is paid.

The other 40% of Canadians who make only partial payments every month are usually aware of the interest rates charged by credit cards—9.4% to 14% on "low-rate" cards, 18% to 20% on "regular" cards. But most people are unaware of the details of how these rates are applied—details that make credit card debt more costly than consumers think.

Trick #1: *The Vanishing Interest-Free Period* There are a couple of scenarios under which the interest-free period will vanish.

Scenario A: After many months of paying your full balance before the due date, you pay only half the balance in a particular month. You might reasonably assume that no interest will be charged for the portion of your retail purchases covered by the partial payment. Wrong! In the following month's statement, you will be charged interest on all of the previous statement's purchases right from their purchase dates. Partial payments are not entitled to any interest-free period.

Scenario B: You have been making only partial payments for several months. You now have your financial act together and pay off the entire balance on the current October statement. You might reasonably expect that no interest charges will appear on your November statement for the purchases listed in the preceding October statement. Not necessarily so! Some credit card issuers require that the September statement *also* had to be paid in full for you not to be charged interest in the November statement for purchases appearing on the October statement. (You can obtain a vast amount of information about credit cards from the Web site of the Financial Consumer Agency of Canada (www.fcac-acfc.gc.ca). It describes two methods employed for determining interest-free status, and indicates the method used by each credit card.)

Trick #2: *The Vanishing Grace Period* If you withdraw cash from your credit card account, you will be charged interest (at your credit card's high rate) for *every* day from the date of withdrawal to the date of repayment. In addition, you may be charged a service fee and an ATM fee. The grace period does not apply to a cash advance even if you pay your balance in full.

Trick #3: *Fees Associated with Prepaid Cards* Some consumers attempt to eliminate the interest charges and fees associated with credit cards by switching to prepaid cards. Because these are not credit cards, and they are paid for up front, many consumers assume they are a way to eliminate the payment of fees altogether. While prepaid cards are indeed a way to avoid the risk of overspending, they are certainly not free. Most require that an activation fee be paid at the time of purchase, or before the card is used the first time. Additional fees may be charged for checking the balance on the card, making purchases, replacing the card if it is lost or stolen, or carrying a balance on the card beyond a certain date after the card is activated. In 2014, the Government of Canada enacted the "Prepaid Payment Products Regulations" to help ensure consumers who use prepaid cards are not taken advantage of by unfair practices or lack of disclosure of the rules associated with these products.

Other "card tricks" exist. Contact your credit card issuer to learn more about how convenience cheques, low introductory interest rates, and delays in processing your credit card payments may ultimately result in higher interest charges than you bargained for.

EXERCISE 6.2

Answers to the odd-numbered problems can be found in the end matter.

BASIC PROBLEMS

1. A loan was advanced on March 16 and repaid on October 29 of the same calendar year. How many days was the loan outstanding?

2. A deposit was made on November 18 and withdrawn on January 29 of the next calendar year. How many days was the investment on deposit?

3. A $6500 loan at 5.75% was advanced on June 17, 2013. How much interest was due when the loan was repaid on October 1, 2013?

4. How much interest accrued from November 30 to March 4 of the following calendar year on a $7350 loan at 7.5%? Assume February has 28 days.

5. On June 26 Laura put $2750 into a term deposit until September 3, when she needs the money for tuition, books, and other expenses to return to college. For term deposits in the 60 to 89-day range, her credit union pays an interest rate of 4.25%. How much interest will she earn on the term deposit?

6. Raimo borrowed $750 from Chris on October 30 and agreed to repay the debt with simple interest at the rate of 4.3% on May 10. How much interest was owed on May 10? Assume that February has 28 days.

7. Joyce had $2149 in her daily interest savings account for the entire month of June. Her account was credited with interest of $2.65 on June 30 (for the exact number of days in June). What annual rate of simple interest did her balance earn?

INTERMEDIATE PROBLEMS

8. A homeowner received an electricity bill for $218.83. The due date for payment was March 23. When she paid the bill in full on April 16, the homeowner was charged a late payment fee of $8. What annual rate of simple interest does the late payment fee represent?

9. Alysha borrowed money on November 4, 2015 and repaid it 84 days later. On what date did she repay the loan?

10. Elijah repaid a debt on March 16, 2016. The debt had been outstanding for 92 days. On what date did Elijah borrow the money?

11. $850 borrowed on January 7 was repaid with interest at an annual rate of 7% on July 1 of the same calendar year. What was the amount of interest? Assume February has 28 days.

12. The interest rate on $27,000 borrowed on October 16, 2016 was 8.7%. How much interest will be owed on the April 15, 2017 repayment date?

13. What was the principal amount of a loan at 9.5% if $67.78 of interest accrued from October 28, 2016 to April 14, 2017?

14. Maia's chequing account was $329 overdrawn beginning on September 24. On October 9 she made a deposit that restored a credit balance. If she was charged overdraft interest of $2.50, what annual rate of simple interest was charged?

15. In addition to a $2163 refund of her income tax overpayment, the Canada Revenue Agency (CRA) paid Raisa $13.36 of interest on the overpayment. If the simple interest rate paid by the CRA was 5.5%, how many days' interest was paid?

16. Megan was charged $124.83 interest on her bank loan for the period September 18 to October 18. If the rate of interest on her loan was 8.25%, what was the outstanding principal balance on the loan during the period?

17. On June 26, 2016, $1000 was borrowed at an interest rate of 10.75%. On what date was the loan repaid if the amount of accrued interest was $64.21?

18. On what date was a $1000 loan granted if the interest accrued as of November 16, 2016 was $50.05? The interest rate on the loan was 7.25%.

ADVANCED PROBLEMS
---

19. Mario borrowed $6000 on March 1 at a variable rate of interest. The interest rate began at 7.5%, increased to 8% effective April 17, and then fell by 0.25% effective June 30. How much interest will be owed on the August 1 repayment date?

20. How much will be required on February 1 to pay off a $3000 loan advanced on the previous September 30 if the variable interest rate began the interval at 10.7%, rose to 11.2% effective November 2, and then dropped back to 11% effective January 1?

21. The total accrued interest owed as of August 31 on a loan advanced the preceding June 3 was $169.66. If the variable interest rate started at 8.75%, rose to 9% effective July 1, and increased another 0.5% effective July 31, what was the principal amount of the loan?

6.3 | Maturity Value (Future Value) and Present Value of a Loan or Investment

When a loan or investment reaches the end of its term, we say it "matures." The last day of the term is called the **maturity date**. The **maturity value** (or **future value**) is the total of the original principal plus interest due on the maturity date. Using the symbol S to represent the maturity value (or future value), we have

$$S = P + I$$

Substituting $I = Prt$, we obtain

$$S = P + Prt$$

Extracting the common factor P yields

MATURITY VALUE (FUTURE VALUE) $$S = P(1 + rt)$$ (6-2)

EXAMPLE 6.3A	Calculating the Maturity Value

Celia invests $1500 by lending it to Adnan for 8 months at an interest rate of 9.25%. What is the maturity value of the loan?

SOLUTION

This problem reminds us that the borrower's debt is the lender's investment.

Given: $P = \$1500$, $t = \frac{8}{12}$ year, $r = 9.25\%$

The maturity value of the loan is
$$\begin{aligned} S &= P(1 + rt) \\ &= \$1500\left[1 + 0.0925\left(\tfrac{8}{12}\right)\right] \\ &= \$1500(1.061667) \\ &= \$1592.50 \end{aligned}$$

Note that this answer can be obtained just as easily by first calculating the interest due at maturity using $I = Prt$. Then simply add the principal to obtain the maturity value $(S = P + I)$. The choice of method is a matter of personal preference.

The maturity value that Adnan must pay to Celia at the end of the 8 months is $1592.50.

⇒ **Check your understanding:** What would be the maturity value of this loan if its term was 5 months instead of 8? (Answer: $1557.81)

▮▮▶ **Related problem:** #1 in Exercise 6.3

In some cases we are given a maturity value and asked to solve for the original or principal value of the loan or investment. It is useful to recognize that a rearrangement of formula (6-2), $S = P(1 + rt)$ can be used to solve for P, the beginning or principal value of a loan or investment. To isolate P, we need to divide both sides of formula (6-2) by $(1 + rt)$. This gives

PRINCIPAL VALUE $P = \dfrac{S}{(1 + rt)}$ or $P = S(1 + rt)^{-1}$ (6-3)

Although, in general, it is a good idea to avoid "formula clutter," starting with formula (6-3) when a question involves solving for P will help to avoid unnecessary computational errors.

| EXAMPLE 6.3B | Calculating the Principal |

What amount of money would have to be invested at 3.25% to grow to $10,000 after 91 days?

SOLUTION

Given: $r = 3.25\%$, $S = \$10,000$, $t = \frac{91}{365}$ year

Substitute the known values into formula (6-3) and solve for P.

$$P = \frac{S}{(1 + rt)}$$
$$P = \frac{\$10,000}{\left[1 + (0.0325)\left(\frac{91}{365}\right)\right]}$$
$$P = \$9919.62$$

If you prefer the alternate arrangement of formula (6-3) the solution would be

$$P = S(1 + rt)^{-1}$$
$$P = \$10,000\left[1 + (0.0325)\left(\frac{91}{365}\right)\right]^{-1}$$
$$P = \$9919.62$$

The required investment is $9919.62.

⇒ **Check your understanding:** What amount of money would have to be invested at 2.25% to grow to $5000 after 75 days? (Answer: $4976.99)

▮▮▶ **Related problem:** #3 in Exercise 6.3

When supplied with values for S, P, and either r or t, you may be tempted to use formula (6-2) or (6-3) to solve for the remaining unknown (either r or t). While this is mathematically possible, the manipulations required to solve for r or t are not trivial. In these cases, it is best to remember that if $S = P + I$, a simple rearrangement provides

AMOUNT OF INTEREST (IN DOLLARS) $I = S - P$ (6-4)

With I now known, we can solve $I = Prt$ for either r or t. The following example illustrates this approach.

EXAMPLE 6.3C | **Calculating the Interest Rate**

Liam put $9500 in a term deposit on May 22. It matured on September 4 at $9588.82. What interest rate did Liam earn on his term deposit?

SOLUTION

Given: $P = \$9500$; $S = \$9588.82$; the term runs from May 22 to September 4

Hence,

$$I = S - P = \$9588.82 - \$9500 = \$88.82$$

and, using Table 6.2,

$$t = (\text{September 4}) - (\text{May 22})$$
$$t = 247 - 142$$
$$t = 105 \text{ days}$$

The annual rate of simple interest is

$$r = \frac{I}{Pt} = \frac{\$88.82}{\$9500 \times \frac{105}{365}} = 0.03250 = 3.25\%$$

Liam earned an interest rate of 3.25% on his term deposit.

➡ **Check your understanding:** Liam invested $8300 on April 6. The investment matured on December 8 at $8593.68. What interest rate did he earn? (Answer: 5.25%)

▰▰▶ **Related problem:** #9 in Exercise 6.3

EXERCISE 6.3

Answers to the odd-numbered problems can be found in the end matter.

BASIC PROBLEMS

1. What will be the maturity value after seven months of $2950 earning interest at the rate of 4.5%?

2. $12,800 was invested in a 237-day term deposit earning 3.75%. What was its maturity value?

3. After a term of 23 days, a loan at 10.5% has a maturity value of $785.16. What was the principal value of the loan?

4. The maturity value of an investment earning 7.7% per annum for a 360-day term was $2291.01. What amount was originally invested?

5. Maclean borrowed $17,450 at a rate of 6.25% 285 days ago. What payment made today will settle the debt?

6. Yussef owes a total of $5878.78 to repay a loan that was advanced 10 months ago at a rate of 8.85%. What amount did Yussef originally borrow?

INTERMEDIATE PROBLEMS

7. The balance after 11 months, including interest, on a loan at 9.9% is $15,379.58. What are the principal and interest components of the balance?

8. $7348.25 was the amount required to pay off a loan after 14 months. If the loan was at 8.25% per annum simple interest, how much of the total was interest?

9. What was the interest rate on a $1750 loan if the amount required to pay off the loan after 5 months was $1828.02?

10. A $2875.40 investment grew to $3000 after eight months. What annual rate of simple interest did it earn?

11. Marliss made a $780.82 purchase on her Visa card. Including 45 days' interest, the amount billed on her credit card was $798.63. What annual interest rate does her card charge?

12. Janesh has savings of $9625.63. If he can invest this amount to earn 7.8%, how many days will it take for the investment to grow to $10,000?

13. A $7760 investment earning 6.25% matured at $8083.33. What was the term (in months) of the investment?

14. Sehar owed $5200 in tuition to her college admissions office. She missed the September 20 deadline, and now wishes to settle her account in full on October 9. If her college imposes a late fee equal to 5.5% per annum on late tuition payments made after the September 20 deadline, what total amount, including the late fee, will Sehar pay?

15. Abbey owed $162.50 to her town water department. The bill was due on November 8. When Abbey paid the bill on December 12, she paid a total of $171.50, including a late penalty. What annual simple rate of interest does the late fee represent?

16. The bookkeeper for Durham's Garage is trying to account for a payment that was made to settle a loan. He knows that a cheque for $3701.56 was written to settle the principal and 7 months' interest at 12.5%. What are the principal and interest components of the payment?

ADVANCED PROBLEMS

17. Today is March 25. Snow tires that you need are available today at a sale price of $89.95 each. If you wait until October 1 to buy the tires, you will pay the full price of $107.50 each. If you buy the tires today, you will need to borrow money at 12% per annum simple interest. Should you buy the tires today or wait until October 1? Explain.

18. The annual $3600 membership fee at the Oak Meadows Golf Club is due at the start of the year. A member can pay the full fee at the start of the year, or pay a $1600 deposit at the start of the year, and defer the remaining $2000 balance by 5 months. To take advantage of the deferral, the golf club requires a member to pay a $75 surcharge, which is added to the second payment. Effectively, what annual simple rate of interest is Oak Meadows charging on the $2000 deferred payment?

19. A&B Appliances sells a washer-dryer combination for $1535 cash. C&D Appliances offers the same combination for $1595 with no payments and no interest for 6 months. Therefore, you can pay $1535 now or invest the $1535 for 6 months and then pay $1595. What value would the annual rate of return have to exceed for the second alternative to be to your advantage?

20. Dominion Contracting invested surplus funds in term deposits. All were chosen to mature on April 1 when the firm intends to purchase a new excavator.

Investment date	Amount invested	Interest rate	Maturity date
November 16	$74,000	6.3%	April 1
December 30	$66,000	5.9%	April 1
February 8	$92,000	5.1%	April 1

What total amount will be available from the maturing term deposits on April 1 (of a leap year)?

> ## TIP
>
> **Invest Now ...**
>
> The concepts that will be developed in Sections 6.4 and 6.5 are fundamental to many other topics and applications in later chapters. If you invest extra effort at this stage to gain a thorough understanding of these concepts, it will pay substantial dividends later.

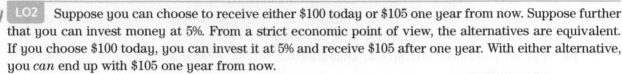

6.4 Equivalent Payments

LO2   Suppose you can choose to receive either $100 today or $105 one year from now. Suppose further that you can invest money at 5%. From a strict economic point of view, the alternatives are equivalent. If you choose $100 today, you can invest it at 5% and receive $105 after one year. With either alternative, you *can* end up with $105 one year from now.

This simple example illustrates the concept of *economically equivalent* payments (which we usually shorten to "equivalent payments"). Alternative payments that enable you to end up with the same dollar amount at a later date are called **equivalent payments**. Note the key role played by the interest rate at which money may be invested. If the interest rate had been 6% instead of 5% in our example, you would require $106 one year from now as the amount equivalent to $100 today.

In the terminology of Section 6.3, the later equivalent payment ($105) is just the future value of the alternative payment ($100) after one year. That is,

$$S = P(1 + rt) = \$100[1 + 0.05(1)] = \$100(1.05) = \$105$$

In Section 6.3, we used formula (6-2), $S = P(1 + rt)$, and formula (6-3), $P = \frac{S}{1 + rt}$, to solve for the maturity value and present value of loans and investments. We now see that these formulas also represent the relationship between a **P**rior equivalent payment (P) and a **S**ubsequent equivalent payment, (S). In this context, r represents the interest rate that invested funds can earn during the time interval, t, between the alternative payments. In our word problems, we use expressions such as "Money can earn x%" or "Money is worth x%" or "Money can be invested at x%" to specify this interest rate.[3]

The term **present value** is commonly used to refer to an economically equivalent amount at a *prior* date; future value is used for an equivalent amount at a *later* date.

EXAMPLE 6.4A	Calculating the Equivalent Payment at a Later Date

Herb is supposed to pay $1500 to Ranjit on September 20. Herb wishes to delay payment until December 1.

a. What amount should Herb expect to pay on December 1 if Ranjit can earn 3.25% on a low-risk investment?

b. Show why Ranjit should not care whether he receives the scheduled payment or the delayed payment.

---

[3] You might be thinking: "There are many different interest rates depending on the investment I choose. A savings account earns a very low interest rate, a guaranteed investment certificate earns a higher rate, Canada Savings Bonds earn yet another rate, and so on. What interest rate should I pick for equivalent-payment calculations in a 'real-world' situation?" In a real-world scenario, you should choose the interest rate on the basis of the following thinking. Normally, equivalent payments are viewed as *riskless* alternatives. In other words, you will definitely receive the later equivalent payment if you do not choose the earlier equivalent payment. Alternatively, if you choose the earlier payment, the outcome from investing it must be known with *certainty*. The investment question becomes: "What is the *best* interest rate I can earn with complete certainty during the time interval?" If you take a finance course, you will learn that this "risk-free rate" is the prevailing rate of return earned by federal government Treasury bills (Section 7.3) or bonds. Choose Treasury bills or bonds that have a term equal to the time interval between the equivalent payments.

SOLUTION

a. Herb is seeking a postponement of

$$11 \text{ days in September} + 31 \text{ days in October} + 30 \text{ days in November} = 72 \text{ days}$$

He should expect to pay an amount that is equivalent to $1500, 72 days later, allowing for a 3.25% rate of return. That is, he should expect to pay the future value of $1500, 72 days later.

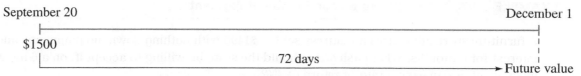

September 20   December 1

$1500

72 days

Future value

Substituting $P = \$1500$, $t = \frac{72}{365}$ and $r = 3.25\%$ into formula (6-2), the future value is

$$S = P(1 + rt) = \$1500\left[1 + 0.0325\left(\tfrac{72}{365}\right)\right] = \$1509.62$$

Herb should expect to pay $1509.62 on December 1 instead of $1500 on September 20.

b. Suppose that Herb makes the $1500 payment as scheduled on September 20. Since Ranjit can earn a 3.25% rate of return, by December 1 the $1500 will grow to

$$S = P(1 + rt) = \$1500\left[1 + 0.0325\left(\tfrac{72}{365}\right)\right] = \$1509.62$$

Ranjit should therefore be indifferent between receiving $1500 on September 20 or $1509.62 on December 1, because he can end up with $1509.62 on December 1 with either alternative.

➡ **Check your understanding:** What amount should Herb expect to pay if he wishes to delay payment until February 4 of the next calendar year? (Answer: $1518.30)

▶ **Related problem:** #7 in Exercise 6.4

EXAMPLE 6.4B	Calculating an Equivalent Payment at an Earlier Date

What payment on March 12 is equivalent to a $1000 payment on the subsequent July 6, if money is worth 6.8% per year?

SOLUTION

Since we want an equivalent payment at an earlier date, we should calculate the *present value* of $1000 on March 12.

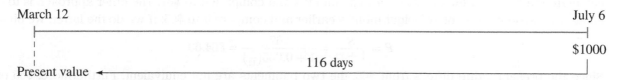

March 12   July 6

$1000

Present value ← 116 days

The number of days in the interval is

$$20 \text{ days in March} + 30 \text{ days in April} + 31 \text{ days in May} + 30 \text{ days in June} + 5 \text{ days in July} = 116 \text{ days}$$

Substituting $S = \$1000$, $r = 6.8\%$, and $t = \frac{116}{365}$ into formula (6-3), we obtain

$$P = \frac{S}{1 + rt} = \frac{\$1000}{1 + 0.068\left(\frac{116}{365}\right)} = \$978.85$$

$978.85 on March 12 is equivalent to $1000 on the subsequent July 6.

➡️ **Check your understanding:** What payment on April 12 is equivalent to a $3000 payment on the subsequent August 10 if money is worth 3.2% per year? (Answer: $2968.77)

▶ **Related problem:** #5 in Exercise 6.4

| EXAMPLE 6.4C | Calculating a Prior Equivalent Payment |

A furniture store advertises a mattress set for $1495 with nothing down, no payments, and no interest for 6 months. What cash price should the store be willing to accept if, on a 6-month investment, it can earn a rate of return of 4%?

SOLUTION

The store faces the choice between the cash offer and $1495 to be received 6 months from now (if a customer takes the credit terms). The store should be willing to accept a cash amount that is today's equivalent of $1495. In other words, the store should accept the present value of $1495.

If money can earn 4%,

$$P = \frac{S}{1 + rt} = \frac{\$1495}{1 + 0.04\left(\frac{6}{12}\right)} = \frac{\$1495}{1.02} = \$1465.69$$

The store should accept a cash offer of $1465.69.

➡️ **Check your understanding:** Redo the problem, assuming the store can earn a rate of 9%. (Answer: $1430.62)

▶ **Related problem:** #18 in Exercise 6.4

Comparing Payments

If money can earn 5.5%, is $65 today equivalent to $67 eight months from now?

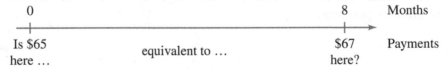

Trust your instincts. Two methods for answering this question may occur to you. One method is to calculate the future value of $65 after eight months and compare it to $67. The other approach is to calculate the present value of $67 eight months earlier and compare it to $65. If we do the latter, we obtain

$$P = \frac{S}{1 + rt} = \frac{\$67}{1 + 0.055\left(\frac{8}{12}\right)} = \$64.63$$

Since the present value differs from $65, the two payments are not equivalent. Furthermore, $65 paid today is worth

$$\$65 - \$64.63 = \$0.37$$

more than $67 paid eight months from now.

Suppose you are asked to compare the economic values of three or four or more alternative payments. What should you do? In general, you can compare the economic values of any number of alternative payments by calculating their equivalent values all at the *same* date. (The date at which the equivalent values are calculated is often referred to as the **focal date**.) The alternative payments can then be ranked on the basis of their equivalent values at the chosen focal date.

EXAMPLE 6.4D	Comparing the Economic Values of Alternative Payments

Marcus can purchase an airplane ticket now on the airline's Early Bird Sale for $459, or he can wait and pay $479 in 3 months. If he can earn a 6% rate of return on his money, which option should he choose?

SOLUTION

To compare today's economic values of the two alternatives, first calculate the present value of the regular price of $479.

$$P = \frac{S}{1 + rt} = \frac{\$479}{1 + 0.06\left(\frac{3}{12}\right)} = \$471.92$$

Marcus should choose the alternative having the *lower* economic value. That is, he should buy the ticket at the Early Bird price. However, his true saving is not $479 − $459 = $20, but rather $471.92 − $459 = $12.92.

➡ **Check your understanding:** Which option should Marcus choose if he can earn a rate of 2% on his money? (Answer: Marcus should still purchase the ticket today at the Early Bird price; doing so results in a savings of $17.62 in "today's" dollars.)

◼◼▶ **Related problem:** #16a in Exercise 6.4

EXAMPLE 6.4E	Finding the Rate of Return That Makes Two Payments Equivalent

Extending the problem in Example 6.4D, what rate of return would Marcus have to earn in order to be indifferent between the two prices?

SOLUTION

Marcus will be indifferent between the two prices if $459 invested for 3 months will grow to $479. In other words, he will be indifferent if $459 can earn $479 − $459 = $20 of interest in 3 months. The rate of return that would cause this to occur is

$$r = \frac{I}{Pt} = \frac{\$20}{\$459 \times \frac{3}{12}} = 0.174 = 17.4\%$$

If Marcus could earn a 17.4% rate of return, he could invest the $459 for 3 months and it would mature at $479, providing exactly the right amount to buy the ticket. If Marcus could earn more than 17.4%, it would be to his advantage to invest the $459 now and buy the ticket 3 months later. Because the $459 would have earned more than $20 of interest, he would be able to purchase the ticket for $479 and have some money left over. At any rate less than 17.4%, the $459 invested today would not earn sufficient interest to offset the $20 price difference, so Marcus would be financially better off to purchase the ticket today.

➡ **Check your understanding:** Suppose Marcus can choose between an Early Bird price of $475 and a regular price of $499 five months later. What rate of return would Marcus need to be earning in order to be indifferent between these two options? (Answer: 12.13%)

◼◼▶ **Related problem:** #16b in Exercise 6.4

Checkpoint Questions

1. What is meant by "equivalent payments"?

2. How can you determine whether two payments scheduled on different dates are equivalent to each other?

3. Circle "True" or "False" for each of the following:

   a. If the interest rate is positive, an earlier payment will always be smaller than its later equivalent payment.   True   False

   b. Using a rate of 6%, an investor has calculated that she will accept an equivalent payment of $1000 today in place of a scheduled future payment. If she changes the rate to 8%, the equivalent payment today would be higher than $1000.   True   False

   c. Using a rate of 9%, an investor has calculated that he will accept an equivalent payment of $1500 in 6 months from now, in place of a payment scheduled for today. If he adjusts the rate to 6%, the equivalent payment in 6 months from now would be smaller than $1500.   True   False

---

EXERCISE 6.4

Answers to the odd-numbered problems can be found in the end matter.

BASIC PROBLEMS

1. What amount of money paid today is equivalent to $560 paid 5 months from now if money can earn 1.75% per annum?

2. What amount, 7 months from now, is equivalent to $1215 today if money can be invested to earn 4.5%?

3. What payment, 174 days from now, is equivalent to $5230 paid today? Assume that money is worth 5.25% per annum.

4. Patrick is scheduled to receive $1480 in 60 days from now. How much should he accept today as an equivalent payment if his money can earn 6.75%?

5. What amount paid on September 24 is equivalent to $1000 paid on the following December 1 if money can earn 3%?

6. What amount received on January 13 is equivalent to $1000 received on the preceding August 12 if money can earn 5.5%?

7. Rasheed wishes to postpone for 90 days the payment of $450 that he owes to Roxanne. If money now earns 4.75%, what amount can he reasonably expect to pay at the later date?

8. Vivian is selling a cottage property. In the original agreement to purchase, the buyers were to pay $325,000 on September 1, 2015. If the buyers have proposed an earlier closing date, how much should Vivian be willing to accept for the property as an equivalent payment if it closes on June 15, 2015 and she can earn 3.85% on low-risk investments? Round your answer to the nearest dollar.

INTERMEDIATE PROBLEMS

9. What annual rate of return would money have to earn for $1975 to be equivalent to $1936.53 paid 100 days earlier?

10. At what rate can money be invested if $2370 is equivalent to $2508.79 paid 190 days later?

11. A late payment of $850.26 was considered equivalent to the originally scheduled payment of $830, allowing for interest at 9.9%. How many days late was the payment?

12. An early payment of $4574.73 was accepted instead of a scheduled payment of $4850, allowing for interest at the rate of 8.75%. How many days early was the payment?

13. Avril owes Value Furniture $1600, which is scheduled to be paid on August 15. Avril has surplus funds on June 15 and will settle the debt early if Value Furniture will make an adjustment reflecting the current short-term interest rate of 3.25%. What payment on June 15 should be acceptable to both parties?

14. Rashmi has the option of settling a debt by paying $5230 today, or waiting exactly 5 months and paying $5500.

    a. If her money can earn 8.2% per annum, which option should she choose?

    b. If her money can earn 13.5% per annum, which option should she choose?

    c. At what rate per annum would she be indifferent between the two alternatives?

15. To settle a $570 invoice, Anna can pay $560 now or the full amount 60 days later.

    a. Which alternative should she choose if money can earn 10.75%?

    b. What rate would money have to earn for Anna to be indifferent between the two alternatives?

16. Jonas recently purchased a one-year membership at Gold's Gym. He can add a second year to the membership now for $1215, or wait 11 months and pay the regular single-year price of $1280.

    a. Which is the better economic alternative if money is worth 8.5%?

    b. At what rate would the two alternatives be economically equivalent?

17. Nicholas can purchase the same furniture from Store A for $2495 cash or from Store B for $2560 with nothing down and no payments or interest for 8 months. Which option should Nicholas choose if he can pay for the furniture by cashing in Canada Savings Bonds currently earning 2.7% per annum?

18. During its 50-50 Sale, Marpole Furniture will sell its merchandise for 50% down, with the balance payable in 6 months. No interest is charged for the first 6 months. What 100% cash price should Marpole accept on a $1845 sofa and chair set if Marpole can earn a rate of return of 2.75% on its funds?

19. The Matheson family is having an in-ground backyard pool installed. Clearwater Pools will install the pool in the autumn for a cash payment of $28,000 due on September 30, 2014. Alternately, the Mathesons can wait for a spring installation and pay $30,000 on May 1, 2015.

    a. If the Mathesons earn 8% on their investments, which alternative should they select? In current dollars, how much will they save by selecting the preferred installation date?

    b. What rate of interest would the Mathesons need to earn on their funds to be indifferent between the fall and spring installation dates?

20. Ebe decided that he would accept an equivalent payment of $7472.71 on March 14, 2017 as full settlement of a scheduled $7500 payment. On what date was the $7500 scheduled payment due if Ebe used 2.15% as the rate of interest in his analysis?

21. Mr. and Mrs. Chan have listed for sale a residential building lot they own in a nearby town. They are considering two offers. The offer from the Smiths is for $145,000 consisting of $45,000 down and the balance to be paid in 6 months. The offer from the Kims is for $149,000 consisting of $29,000 down and $120,000 payable in one year. The Chans can earn an interest rate of 4.5% on low-risk short-term investments.

   a. What is the current economic value to the Chans of each offer?

   b. Other things being equal, which offer should the Chans accept? How much more is the better offer worth (in terms of current economic value)?

22. Westwood Homes is beginning work on its future College Park subdivision. Westwood is now pre-selling homes that will be ready for occupancy in nine months. Westwood is offering $5000 off the $295,000 selling price to anyone making an immediate $130,000 down payment (with the balance due in 9 months). The alternative is a $5000 deposit with the $290,000 balance due in 9 months. Mr. and Mrs. Symbaluk are trying to decide which option to choose. They currently earn 4.8% on low-risk short-term investments.

   a. What is the current economic cost of buying on the $130,000-down $5000-off option?

   b. What is the current economic cost of buying on the $5000-deposit full-price option?

   c. Which alternative should the Symbaluks choose? In current dollars, what is the economic advantage of the preferred alternative?

6.5 | The Equivalent Value of a Payment Stream

A **payment stream** is a series of two or more payments required by a single transaction or contract. For example, the terms of sale for a piece of land might stipulate that $100,000 be paid "up front," with an additional $75,000 payment required by the buyer in one year from the date of sale. To get their combined value, you might be inclined to add the payments and conclude that the value of the transaction is $175,000. If you do that, then every dollar, regardless of when it is paid, has an equal influence on the sum. In other words, the simple addition of payments occurring on different dates implies that a dollar on one date has the same economic value as a dollar on any other date. But we have seen that the *economic* value of a dollar depends on when it is paid. This characteristic of money is often referred to as the **time value of money**. The simple addition of the payments ignores the time value of money.

In Section 6.4, you learned how to calculate the equivalent value, on any date, of a *single* payment. A logical extension of this basic idea allows us to determine the equivalent value of a payment *stream*. We simply add the equivalent values (at the chosen focal date) of the individual payments. The following example illustrates the procedure.

Consider a payment stream consisting of three payments: $1000, $2000, and $3000, scheduled for March 1, May 1, and December 1 of the same year. Let us calculate the single payment on August 1 that is economically equivalent to the three scheduled payments. Suppose money can earn a simple interest rate of 4%.

 LO3 For problems involving multiple payments, a **time diagram** is virtually essential. It consists of a time axis or time line showing the dollar amounts and the dates of the payments. Figure 6.3 presents a time diagram for the problem at hand. The first benefit of a time line is that it helps you organize the data. Indicate the payment dates above the line and the amounts of the corresponding payments below the line. Do not make your diagram too small—use the full width of your page. Attempt to draw reasonably proportionate time intervals between the dates.

FIGURE 6.3   Entering Given Data on a Time Diagram

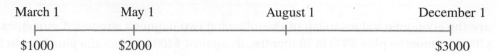

The solution idea for this problem is

$$\left(\begin{matrix}\text{The equivalent payment}\\ \text{on August 1}\end{matrix}\right) = \left(\begin{matrix}\text{The sum of the equivalent values on}\\ \text{August 1 of the individual payments}\end{matrix}\right)$$

The second benefit of a time diagram is that it allows you to indicate the steps needed to carry out the solution. In Figure 6.4, an arrow is drawn from each payment to the August 1 focal date (on which you want the equivalent value). On each arrow you can write the number of days in the time interval. An appropriate symbol (S for future value, P for present value) is entered for each equivalent value. Finally, you can indicate on the diagram that the three equivalent values are to be added. The written solution is now a matter of following the steps outlined in the diagram.

FIGURE 6.4   Showing the Solution Steps on a Time Diagram

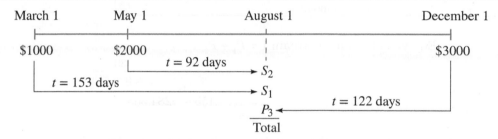

S_1 = Future value on August 1 of the $1000 payment
  = $1000\left[1 + 0.04\left(\frac{153}{365}\right)\right]$
  = 1016.767

S_2 = Future value on August 1 of the $2000 payment
  = $2000\left[1 + 0.04\left(\frac{92}{365}\right)\right]$
  = 2020.164

P_3 = Present value on August 1 of the $3000 payment
  = $\dfrac{\$3000}{1 + 0.04\left(\frac{122}{365}\right)}$
  = 2960.420

The equivalent value on August 1 of the payment stream is

$$S_1 + S_2 + P_3 = \$1016.767 + \$2020.164 + \$2960.420 = \$5997.35$$

The significance of this equivalent value is that a payment of $5997.35 on August 1 is economically equivalent to the three scheduled payments. The recipient will be in the same economic position whether he accepts $5997.35 on August 1 or receives the three payments as scheduled.

EXAMPLE 6.5A	Comparing the Economic Value of Two Payment Streams

Compare the economic values today of the following two payment streams if money can earn 6.5%: $700 in 4 months plus $300 in 10 months, as against $400 in 6 months plus $600 in 8 months.

SOLUTION

Construct a time line for each payment stream, indicating the scheduled payments and their equivalent values, P_1 to P_4, today. The stream with the larger total equivalent value today has the greater economic value.

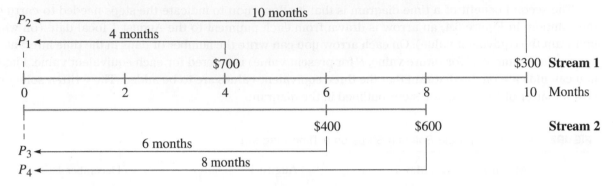

$$\text{Equivalent value of Stream } 1 = P_1 + P_2$$
$$= \frac{\$700}{1 + 0.065\left(\frac{4}{12}\right)} + \frac{\$300}{1 + 0.065\left(\frac{10}{12}\right)}$$
$$= \$685.155 + \$284.585$$
$$= \$969.74$$

Note that we keep six figures in the second-to-last line in order to obtain five-figure accuracy in the final result.

$$\text{Equivalent value of Stream } 2 = P_3 + P_4$$
$$= \frac{\$400}{1 + 0.065\left(\frac{6}{12}\right)} + \frac{\$600}{1 + 0.065\left(\frac{8}{12}\right)}$$
$$= \$387.409 + \$575.080$$
$$= \$962.49$$

Even though the sum of the nominal payments in each stream is $1000, the first stream's economic value today is $7.25 more than the second stream's value. This happens because, on average, the money in the first stream is received sooner.

Note: The date on which the economic values of the payment streams are calculated is commonly referred to as the *focal date*. The difference between the economic values of two payment streams depends, weakly, on the choice of the focal date. However, if asked to decide if one payment stream is worth more than an alternative payment stream, the choice of focal date will not influence the ultimate conclusion. If one payment stream is worth more than another payment stream, you will reach that same conclusion regardless of the focal date you choose.

➡ **Check your understanding:** Compare the economic values today of the following two payment streams if money can earn 4.75%: $800 in 3 months plus $1800 in 9 months, as against $100 in 1 month and $2700 in 11 months. (Answer: Equivalent value of stream 1 = $2528.69; Equivalent value of stream 2 = $2686.95)

▪▪▪▶ **Related problem:** #9 in Exercise 6.5

EXAMPLE 6.5B	Calculating an Unknown Payment in an Equivalent Payment Stream

Payments of $5000 due 4 months ago and $3000 due 2 months from now are to be replaced by a payment of $4000 today and a second payment in 6 months. What must the second payment be in order to make the replacement payment stream equivalent to the scheduled payment stream? Money in short-term investments can earn 5%. Use 6 months from now as the focal date.

SOLUTION

Each alternative payment stream is shown below on its own time line. We must determine the size of the payment x so that both payment streams have the same economic value 6 months from now. The equivalent values, at the focal date of the three known payments, are indicated by S_1, S_2, and S_3. The unknown payment, x, is already at the focal date.

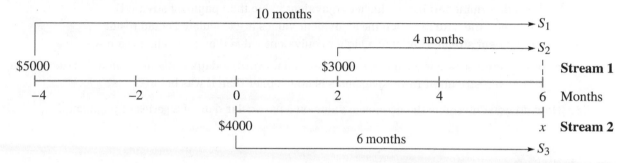

$$\text{Equivalent value of Stream 1} = S_1 + S_2$$
$$= \$5000\left[1 + 0.05\left(\tfrac{10}{12}\right)\right] + \$3000\left[1 + 0.05\left(\tfrac{4}{12}\right)\right]$$
$$= \$5208.333 + \$3050.000$$
$$= \$8258.333$$

$$\text{Equivalent value of Stream 2} = x + S_3$$
$$= x + \$4000\left[1 + 0.05\left(\tfrac{6}{12}\right)\right]$$
$$= x + \$4100.000$$

For the two streams to be economically equivalent,

$$x + \$4100.000 = \$8258.333$$

Hence, $$x = \$4158.33$$

For the two streams to be equivalent, the second payment must be $4158.33.

⇨ **Check your understanding:** Payments of $2000 due 3 months ago and $7000 due 4 months from now are to be replaced by a payment of $1000 today and a second payment in 5 months. What must the second payment be in order to make the new payment stream equivalent to the scheduled payment stream if money can earn 6%? Use 5 months from now as the focal date. (Answer: $8090)

▸ **Related problem:** #15 in Exercise 6.5

Checkpoint Questions

1. What is meant by "the time value of money"?

2. We frequently see a news item that reads something like: "Joe Superstar signed a five-year deal worth $25 million. Under the contract he will be paid $5 million in each of the next five years." In what respect is the statement incorrect? How should the value of the contract be calculated?

3. Circle "True" or "False" for each of the following:

   a. The date at which equivalent values of a payment stream are being compared   True   False
   is commonly referred to as the "focal date."

   b. When equivalent values at today's date are calculated, payment stream A has   True   False
   been determined to have a higher equivalent value than payment stream B.
   Changing the date at which the equivalent values are calculated could result
   in payment stream B having a higher equivalent value than payment stream A.

   c. If the interest rate money can earn is revised upward, today's economic value   True   False
   of a given stream of future payments is now higher than it was before.

4. How do you determine the economic value on a particular date of a series of payments?

EXERCISE 6.5

Answers to the odd-numbered problems can be found in the end matter.

BASIC PROBLEMS

1. Calculate the combined equivalent value today of $500 due today and $300 due in 3 months. Assume that money can earn 9.5%.

2. Calculate the combined equivalent value in 5 months from now of a payment stream consisting of $1000 payable today and $1500 payable in 5 months? Assume money can earn 5.5%.

3. Payments of $850 and $1140 were scheduled to be paid today and 9 months from now, respectively. What total payment today would place the payee in the same financial position as the scheduled payments? Money can earn 8.25%.

4. An agreement required that Joseph pay you $1000 six months ago, and an additional $500 today. Joseph missed the $1000 payment. What single payment today would you accept as full settlement of the entire debt if money can earn 4.25%?

INTERMEDIATE PROBLEMS

5. A payment stream consists of $1200 payable today and $1800 payable in 6 months. What is the equivalent value of the payment stream 2 months from now if money is worth 6.5%?

6. A hockey league requires parents to pay $500 on September 1 for the year's league fees, and an additional $250 fee on December 15 of the same year to cover costs associated with an annual Christmas hockey tournament.

   a. If a parent would like to write one cheque to cover all fees for the upcoming season, how much should the league be willing to accept as a single equivalent payment on September 1 if it can earn 3.2% on its money?

   b. If a parent would like to pay in advance to cover the upcoming hockey season fees, how much should the league be willing to accept as a single equivalent payment at a pre-registration event held on June 30 prior to the start of the hockey season?

7. On June 15, Dylan has obtained two quotes to have the roof of his home reshingled. Rocca Roofing will do the job for $8200 payable on June 15. Sylvestor Roofing will do the job for $5000 payable on June 15, an additional $2000 payable on July 15, and a final payment of $2000 payable on August 31. Based strictly on price, which company should Dylan select if his money is worth 4.5%? In current dollars, how much will Dylan save by selecting that company?

8. Payments of $900 and $1000 are due in 30 days and 210 days, respectively. If money can be invested at 7.75%, what single payment 90 days from now is equivalent to that payment stream?

9. A payment stream consists of three payments: $1000 today, $1500 in 70 days, and $2000 in 210 days. What single payment, 60 days from now, is economically equivalent to the payment stream if money can be invested at a rate of 8.5%?

10. What single payment, 45 days from now, is economically equivalent to the combination of three payments of $1750 each: one due 75 days ago, the second due today, and the third due in 75 days from now? Money is worth 9.9% per annum.

11. Two payments of $1300 and $1800 were scheduled to be paid 5 months ago and 3 months from now, respectively. The $1300 payment has not yet been made. What single payment at a focal date 1 month from now would be equivalent to the two scheduled payments if money can earn 4.5%?

12. If money earns 9.5%, calculate and compare the economic value today of the following payment streams:

    Stream 1: Payments of $900 and $1400 due 150 and 80 days ago, respectively.
    Stream 2: Payments of $800, $600, and $1000 due 30, 75, and 125 days from now, respectively.

13. What is the economic value today of each of the following payment streams if money can earn 7.5%? (Note that the two streams have the same total nominal value.)

    a. $1000, $3000, and $2000 due in 1, 3, and 5 months, respectively

    b. Two $3000 payments due 2 and 4 months from now

ADVANCED PROBLEMS

14. Eight months ago, Louise agreed to pay Thelma $750 and $950, six and 12 months respectively from the date of the agreement. With each payment, Louise agreed to pay interest on the respective principal amounts at the rate of 9.5% from the date of the agreement. Louise failed to make the first payment and now wishes to settle her obligations with a single payment 4 months from now. What payment should Thelma be willing to accept if money can earn 7.75%?

15. Payments of $2600, due 50 days ago, and $3100, due in 40 days, are to be replaced by $3000 today and another payment in 30 days. What must the second payment be if the payee is to end up in an equivalent financial position? Money now earns 8.25%. Use 30 days from now as the focal date.

16. Three payments of $2000 (originally due 6 months ago, today, and 6 months from now) have been renegotiated to two payments: $3000 1 month from now and a second payment due in 4 months. What must the second payment be for the replacement payments to be equivalent to the originally scheduled payments? Assume that money can earn an interest rate of 4%. Choose a focal date four months from now.

6.6   Loans: A Principle About Principal

In Section 8.3, we will develop (in the context of compound interest) an important relationship between the principal amount of a loan and the payments required to pay off the loan. The relationship applies to *all* compound interest loans and to *some* loans at simple interest. This topic is covered in depth in Section 8.3. Therefore, we will simply state the relationship at this point and demonstrate its use.

> **A General Principle Concerning Loans**
>
> The original principal amount of a loan is equal to the sum of the present values of all the payments required to pay off that loan. The interest rate used for the present-value calculations is the interest rate charged on the loan.

EXAMPLE 6.6A   Calculating the Size of the Final Loan Payment

A $5000 loan advanced on April 1 at a 10.5% interest rate requires payments of $1800 on each of June 1 and August 1, and a final payment on October 1. What must the final payment be to satisfy the loan in full?

SOLUTION

Let x represent the amount of the final payment. The payments and their equivalent (present) values, P_1, P_2, and P_3, are shown in the following time diagram.

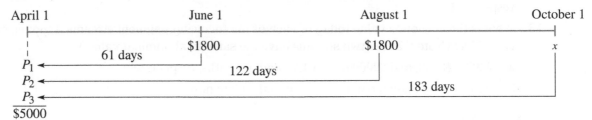

Since the original loan equals the combined present value of all of the payments, then

$$\$5000 = P_1 + P_2 + P_3$$

where

$$P_1 = \frac{\$1800}{1 + 0.105\left(\frac{61}{365}\right)} = \frac{\$1800}{1.0175479} = \$1768.958$$

$$P_2 = \frac{\$1800}{1 + 0.105\left(\frac{122}{365}\right)} = \frac{\$1800}{1.0350959} = \$1738.969$$

$$P_3 = \frac{x}{1 + 0.105\left(\frac{183}{365}\right)} = \frac{x}{1.0526438} = 0.9499889x$$

We maintain seven-figure precision in order to ensure six-figure accuracy in the final result.

Thus

$$\$5000 = \$1768.958 + \$1738.969 + 0.9499889x$$

$$\$1492.073 = 0.9499889x$$

$$x = \frac{\$1492.073}{0.9499889} = \$1570.62$$

The final payment on October 1 must be $1570.62.

⇒ **Check your understanding:** A $6000 loan advanced on March 8 at a 6.5% interest rate requires payments of $2000 on each of May 1 and September 1, and a final payment on November 15. What must the final payment be to satisfy the loan? (Answer: $2173.52)

▌▌▌▶ **Related problem:** #1 in Exercise 6.6

EXAMPLE 6.6B	Calculating the Size of Equal Loan Payments

A $4000 loan made at 11.75% is to be repaid in three equal payments, due 30, 90, and 150 days, respectively, after the date of the loan. Determine the size of the payments.

SOLUTION

Let the amount of each payment be represented by x. The payments and their equivalent (present) values are presented in the following time diagram.

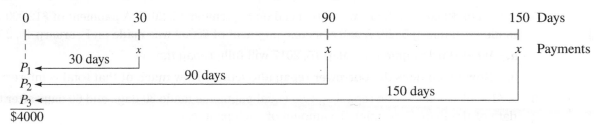

The original loan is equal to the sum of the present values of all of the payments. Therefore,

$$\$4000 = P_1 + P_2 + P_3$$

where

$$P_1 = \frac{x}{1 + 0.1175\left(\frac{30}{365}\right)} = \frac{x}{1.0096575} = 0.9904349x$$

$$P_2 = \frac{x}{1 + 0.1175\left(\frac{90}{365}\right)} = \frac{x}{1.0289726} = 0.9718432x$$

$$P_3 = \frac{x}{1 + 0.1175\left(\frac{150}{365}\right)} = \frac{x}{1.0482877} = 0.9539366x$$

Thus,

$$\$4000 = 0.9904349x + 0.9718432x + 0.9539366x$$
$$\$4000 = 2.916215x$$

$$x = \frac{\$4000}{2.916215} = \$1371.64$$

Each payment should be $1371.64.

⇒ **Check your understanding:** An $8000 loan made at 5.75% is to be repaid in three equal payments due 40, 80, and 120 days, respectively, after the date of the loan. Determine the size of the payments. (Answer: $2700.20)

▌▌▌▶ **Related problem:** #8 in Exercise 6.6

EXERCISE 6.6

Answers to the odd-numbered problems can be found in the end matter.

INTERMEDIATE PROBLEMS

1. A $3000 loan at 5% was made on March 1. Two payments of $1000 each were made on May 1 and June 1. What payment on July 1 will pay off the loan?

2. $5000 was borrowed at 2.5% on March 1. On April 1 and June 1, the borrower made payments of $2000 each. What payment was required on August 1 to pay off the loan's balance?

3. A $3000 loan on March 1 was repaid by payments of $500 on March 31, $1000 on June 15, and a final payment on August 31. How much was the third payment if the interest rate on the loan was 8.25%?

4. $10,000 was borrowed at 3.5% on July 17. The borrower repaid $5000 on August 12, and $2000 on September 18. What final payment is required on November 12 to fully repay the loan?

5. A loan of $25,000 at 4.25% was advanced on September 12, 2016. A payment of $12,000 was made on January 5, 2017, and a second payment of $8000 was made on February 18, 2017.

   a. What third payment on May 15, 2017 will fully repay the debt?

   b. How much does the borrower repay altogether? How much of that total is interest?

6. A $1000 loan at 3% was repaid by two equal payments made 30 days and 60 days after the date of the loan. Determine the amount of each payment.

7. Two equal payments, 50 days and 150 days after the date of the loan, paid off a $3000 loan at 8.25%. What was the amount of each payment?

ADVANCED PROBLEMS

8. What should be the amount of each payment if a $2500 loan at 8.75% is to be repaid by three equal payments due 2 months, 4 months, and 7 months following the date of the loan?

9. The simple interest rate on a $5000 loan is 7%. The loan is to be repaid by four equal payments on dates 100, 150, 200, and 250 days from the date on which the loan was advanced. What is the amount of each payment?

10. Anthony borrowed $7500 on September 15 and agreed to repay the loan by three equal payments on the following November 10, December 30, and February 28. Calculate the payment size if the interest rate on the loan was 8.75%. Use September 15 as the focal date.

Key Terms

Compound interest	Maturity date	Principal
Equivalent payments	Maturity value	Rate of interest
Focal date	Payment stream	Simple interest
Future value	Present value	Time diagram
Interest	Prime rate of interest	Time value of money

Summary of Notation and Key Formulas

P = Principal amount of the loan or investment; present value
r = Annual rate of simple interest
t = Time period (term), in years, of the loan or investment
I = Amount of interest paid or received
S = Maturity value of a loan or investment; future value

FORMULA (6-1)	$I = Prt$	Finding the amount of simple interest earned
FORMULA (6-2)	$S = P(1 + rt)$	Finding the maturity value or future value
FORMULA (6-3)	$P = \dfrac{S}{(1 + rt)}$ or $P = S(1 + rt)^{-1}$	Finding the principal or present value
FORMULA (6-4)	$I = S - P$	Finding the dollars of interest earned

Review Problems

Answers to the odd-numbered review problems can be found in the end matter.

BASIC PROBLEMS

1. **LO1** How much interest will be earned on a deposit of $42,000 if the funds are invested for 90 days at 6.15%?

2. **LO1** Martin invested $5500 for 10 months at 3.75%. How much will Martin have in total when the investment matures?

3. **LO1** How much would you need to deposit on March 10 into an account earning 5% if your goal is to have $7500 on December 1 of the same year?

4. **LO1** How many months would it take for an investment of $6800 to grow to be worth $6958.66 at 4%?

5. **LO1** Sylvie invested $17,000 at 4.65% on September 8, 2016.
   a. How much will her investment be worth on March 18, 2017?
   b. How much interest did Sylvie earn on the investment?

6. **LO1** If $3702.40 earned $212.45 interest from September 17, 2016 to March 11, 2017, what rate of interest was earned?

7. **LO1** Petra has forgotten the rate of simple interest she earned on a 120-day term deposit at Scotiabank. At the end of the 120 days, she received interest of $327.95 on her $21,000 deposit. What rate of simple interest did her deposit earn?

8. **LO2** What amount on January 23 is equivalent to $1000 on the preceding August 18 if money can earn 6.5%?

9. **LO1** What amount invested at 4.5% on November 19, 2016 had a maturity value of $10,000 on March 3, 2017?

10. **LO2** What payment in 2 months from now is equivalent to a $10,000 payment today if money can earn 3.95%?

11. **LO1** Marta borrowed $1750 from Jasper on November 15, 2016, and agreed to repay the debt with simple interest at the rate of 7.4% on June 3, 2017. How much interest was owed on June 3?

INTERMEDIATE PROBLEMS

12. **LO2** Brendyn was scheduled to pay $5000 in 8 months from now to settle a debt. If money can earn 4.5% on low-risk investments, how much should the lender be willing to accept today as an equivalent payment if Brendyn would like to eliminate the debt earlier than planned?

13. **LO1** A loan of $3300 at 9.25% simple interest was made on March 27. On what date was it repaid if the interest cost was $137.99?

14. **LO1** Jacques received the proceeds from an inheritance on March 15. He wants to set aside, in a term deposit on March 16, an amount sufficient to provide a $45,000 down payment for the purchase of a home on November 1. If the current interest rate on 181-day to 270-day deposits is 3.75%, what amount should he place in the term deposit?

15. **LO2** Sheldrick Contracting owes Western Equipment $60,000 payable on June 14. In late April, Sheldrick has surplus cash and wants to settle its debt. If Western can earn 3.6% on its money, how much should Western accept on April 29?

16. **LO2** Peter and Reesa can book their Horizon Holiday package at the early-booking price of $3900, or wait 4 months and pay the full price of $3995.

    a. Which option should they select if money can earn a 5.25% rate of return? In current dollars, how much do they save by selecting the preferred option?

    b. Which option should they select if money can earn a 9.75% rate of return? In current dollars, how much do they save by selecting the preferred option?

    c. At what interest rate would they be indifferent between the two prices?

17. **LO2 LO3** Payments of $1000 and $7500 were originally scheduled to be paid 5 months ago and 4 months from now, respectively. The first payment was not made. What single payment 2 months from now is equivalent to the scheduled payments if money can earn 6.25%?

18. **LO2 LO3** If money earns 7.5%, calculate and compare the economic value today of the following payment streams:

    Stream 1: Payments of $1800 and $2800 made 150 and 90 days ago, respectively.

    Stream 2: Payments of $1600, $1200, and $2000 due 30, 75, and 120 days from now, respectively.

19. **LO2 LO3** Thaya borrowed $17,000 on April 1. He repaid $8000 on June 1, and an additional $2000 on July 1. What final payment on September 1 will fully repay the debt if the loan carries interest at 8%?

20. **LO1** Jordan invested $3000 on September 8, 2014. When the investment matured on July 18, 2015, it was worth $3150.50. What rate of simple interest did Jordan earn?

ADVANCED PROBLEMS

21. **LO1** Salima borrowed $12,800 on May 12 at a variable rate of interest. The interest rate began at 5.5%, increased to 5.85% effective June 28, and then fell by 0.75% effective August 26. How much will be owed altogether on the October 18 repayment date?

22. **LO1** Evelyn put $15,000 into a 90-day term deposit at Laurentian Bank that paid a simple interest rate of 3.2%. When the term deposit matured, she invested the entire amount of the principal and interest from the first term deposit into a new 90-day term deposit that paid the same rate of interest. What total amount of interest did she earn on both term deposits?

23. **LO1** Umberto borrowed $7500 from Delores on November 7, 2016. When Umberto repaid the loan, Delores charged him $190.02 interest. If the rate of simple interest on the loan was 6.75%, on what date did Umberto repay the loan?

24. **LO2 LO3** Thad is planning to buy a rototiller next spring at an expected price of $579. In the current fall flyer from Evergreen Lawn and Garden, the model he wants is advertised at $499.95 in a Fall Clearance Special.

    a. If money can earn 4%, what is the economic value on the preceding September 15 of the $579 that Thad will pay to purchase the rototiller next April 1? (Assume that February has 28 days.)

    b. What are his true economic savings if he purchases the rototiller at the sale price of $499.95 on September 15?

    c. What interest rate would money have to earn for Thad to be indifferent between buying the rototiller at $499.95 on September 15 or buying it for $579 on the subsequent April 1?

25. **LO2 LO3** Mr. and Mrs. Parsons are considering two offers to purchase their summer cottage. Offer A is for $200,000 consisting of an immediate $40,000 down payment with the $160,000 balance payable 1 year later. Offer B is for $196,500 made up of a $30,000 down payment and the $166,500 balance payable in 6 months.

    a. If money can earn 4%, what is the current economic value of each offer?

    b. Other things being equal, which offer should the Parsons accept? What is the economic advantage of the preferred offer over the other offer?

    c. If money can earn 6%, which offer should the Parsons accept? What is the economic advantage of the preferred offer?

26. **LO2 LO3** Nine months ago, Muriel agreed to pay Aisha $1200 and $800 on dates 6 and 12 months, respectively, from the date of the agreement. With each payment Muriel agreed to pay interest at the rate of $8\frac{1}{2}$% from the date of the agreement. Muriel failed to make the first payment and now wishes to settle her obligations with a single payment 4 months from now. What payment should Aisha be willing to accept if money can earn 6.75%?

27. **LO2 LO3** A $9000 loan is to be repaid in three equal payments occurring 60, 180, and 300 days, respectively, after the date of the loan. Calculate the size of these payments if the interest rate on the loan is 7.25%. Use the loan date as the focal date.

Appendix 6A: The Texas Instruments BA II PLUS DATE Worksheet

The BA II PLUS's Owner's Manual uses the term "worksheet" to refer to a list of settings and functions designed for a particular application. Usually, a worksheet is the second function of a key. For example, the word **DATE** appears above the ⬚1⬚ key. You can access the **DATE** worksheet by pressing ⬚2nd⬚ ⬚1⬚ in sequence (rather than at the same time). Hereafter, we will represent these keystrokes as ⬚2nd⬚ ⬚DATE⬚. The calculator's display then has the form:[4]

> DT1 =   mm-dd-yyyy

The components of the display have the following meanings:

DT1 is the symbol used by the calculator for the *start* date (**DaTe 1**).
In place of "mm," you will see one or two digits representing the month.
In place of "dd," you will see two digits for the day of the month.
In place of "yyyy," you will see four digits for the year.

For example, the display

> DT1 =   12-31-2017

means that the start date of the interval is December 31, 2017.

You should think of a worksheet as a single column of items that you can view one at a time in the display. The DATE worksheet's column consists of the following four items:

> DT1 =   mm-dd-yyyy
> DT2 =   mm-dd-yyyy
> DBD =   nnn
> ACT

The solid line around the first item denotes that the display currently provides a "window" to the first item in the column. You can use the scroll keys ⬚↓⬚ and ⬚↑⬚ to move down or up the list. DT2 is the symbol used by the calculator for the *end* date (**DaTe 2**). DBD is the symbol for the number of **D**ays **B**etween **D**ates (that is, the number of days between DT1 and DT2, counting the start date but not the end date). ACT[6] is short for **ACT**ual. This means that calculations are based on the *actual* number of days in each month. This is the *only* method used in Canada. Some calculations in the United States treat all months as having 30 days.

The DATE worksheet allows you to enter values for any two of the three quantities—DT1, DT2, and DBD—and then compute the value of the third quantity. (The calculator automatically makes adjustments for leap years.) Examples 6AA and 6AB will demonstrate how to do this. But first close the worksheet by pressing ⬚2nd⬚ ⬚QUIT⬚. (By the ⬚QUIT⬚ key, we mean the key having **QUIT** as its second function.)

After reading Examples 6AA and 6AB, use the DATE worksheet to calculate your age in days, and then to calculate the calendar date on which you will be 20,000 days old.

---

[4]   This assumes that the calculator is using the default setting (US) for the date format. In the calculator's "Format" worksheet, you can change to the alternative "dd-mm-yyyy" format (EUR).

[5]   If your display shows "360" at this point, you should switch to "ACT" by pressing ⬚2nd⬚ ⬚SET⬚. By the ⬚SET⬚ key, we mean the key having **SET** as its second function.

EXAMPLE 6AA	Calculating "DBD" Given "DT1" and "DT2"

Calculate the number of days in the interval November 8, 2015 to April 23, 2016.

SOLUTION

Here are the keystrokes with brief explanations.

2nd DATE	⇒	Open the DATE worksheet.
11.0815 ENTER	⇒	Key in and save the value for *DT1*. Date information is entered in the format *mm.ddyy* where *mm* is the one- or two-digit number for the month, *dd* is the *two*-digit number for the day of the month, and *yy* is the *last* two digits of the year. Pressing the **ENTER** key saves this new value for *DT1*.
↓	⇒	Scroll down to *DT2*.
4.2316 ENTER	⇒	Key in and save the value for *DT2*.
↓	⇒	Scroll down to *DBD*.
CPT	⇒	Compute the value of *DBD*, the number of days in the interval. The answer that appears is 167 days. The calculator automatically handles leap years.
2nd QUIT	⇒	Close the worksheet.

➡ **Check your understanding:** Calculate the number of days in the interval September 7, 2015 to October 15, 2017. (Answer: 769 days)

EXAMPLE 6AB	Calculating "DT1" Given "DT2" and "DBD"

Determine the date that is 257 days before June 23, 2017.

SOLUTION

2nd DATE	⇒	Open the DATE worksheet.
↓	⇒	Scroll down to *DT2*.
6.2317 ENTER	⇒	Key in and save the value for *DT2*.
↓	⇒	Scroll down to *DBD*.
257 ENTER	⇒	Key in and save the value for *DBD*.
↑ ↑	⇒	Scroll up to *DT1*.
CPT	⇒	Compute the value of *DT1*. The answer "*SUN* = 10-09-2016" appears in the display. Hence, the beginning date of the interval is Thursday, October 9, 2016.
2nd QUIT	⇒	Close the worksheet.

➡ **Check your understanding:** Determine the date that is 184 days before February 12, 2016. (Answer: Wednesday, August 12, 2015)

© PhotoAlto/PunchStock RF

CHAPTER 7
Applications of Simple Interest

LEARNING OBJECTIVES

After completing this chapter, you will be able to:

LO1 Calculate the interest paid on savings accounts and short-term Guaranteed Investment Certificates

LO2 State the Valuation Principle and apply it to the calculation of the fair market value of an investment with known future cash flows

LO3 Calculate the market price and rate of return for Treasury bills and commercial paper

LO4 Describe typical terms, conditions, and repayment arrangements for revolving (demand) loans, fixed-payment (demand) loans, and Canada Student Loans

LO5 Prepare loan repayment schedules for revolving loans, fixed-payment loans, and Canada Student Loans

 **connect**   Throughout this chapter interactive charts and Help Me Solve It videos are marked with a ↗.

HAVE YOU HEARD OF TERM deposits, short-term Guaranteed Investment Certificates (GICs), and Treasury bills? Perhaps not, because these short-term simple-interest investments do not get the media attention received by more volatile and exciting long-term investments such as stocks and bonds. But short-term (or "money market") investments represent a much larger part of the investment "picture" than their low profile suggests. When a "bear" market hits stocks, many investors move their money from stocks to these low-risk short-term investments.

Our discussion of short-term investments raises the question: "How much should you pay for an investment?" Answering the question leads us to the Valuation Principle—a very important concept having broad application.

Next we will study arrangements and calculations for demand loans. Most businesses and many individuals have a line of credit or demand loan facility with a financial institution. Over half of college and university graduates face repayment of student loans. We conclude the chapter by describing the features and the calculation of interest on such loans.

7.1 | Savings Accounts and Short-Term GICs

LO1 Banks, trust companies, and credit unions use $I = Prt$ for calculating the interest on a variety of savings accounts and short-term investment products. Interest on most **savings accounts** is calculated on the daily closing balance and paid monthly. This means that you earn one day's interest on each day's closing balance, but the interest is not credited to your account until the last day of the month or the first day of the following month. Some savings accounts have a tiered scale of interest rates, with higher rates paid when the account's balance reaches certain higher levels. The interest rates on savings accounts are floating; they are adjusted to follow the trend of short-term rates in the financial markets. Interest on a few savings and chequing accounts is calculated on only the *minimum monthly* balance and paid monthly or semiannually.

Depositors can earn a higher interest rate if they are prepared to forgo access to their funds for at least 30 days. Banks, trust companies, life insurance companies, and credit unions offer **Guaranteed Investment Certificates**, usually referred to as "GICs" or "term deposits." Typically, a GIC is issued by a mortgage-lending subsidiary of a financial institution, and is *unconditionally guaranteed* by the parent company. The Canada Deposit Insurance Corporation also guarantees up to $100,000 per depositor. Short-term GICs are issued with maturities of 30 to 364 days. (Long-term GICs, with maturities of one to seven years, will be discussed in Section 8.5.)

Most banks, trust companies, and credit unions offer both *non-redeemable* and *redeemable* versions of short-term GICs. Redeemable GICs may be redeemed or "cashed in" before the scheduled maturity date. Non-redeemable GICs do not permit you to recover your money before the maturity date except under extraordinary circumstances.

Interest on short-term GICs is calculated on a simple-interest basis and is paid on the maturity date. Normally, the interest rates offered exhibit the following patterns:

- Higher rates are paid on non-redeemable GICs than on redeemable GICs.
- Higher rates are paid for longer terms (within the 30-to-364-day range).
- Higher rates are paid on larger principal amounts.

EXAMPLE 7.1A	Savings Account Interest Based on a Tiered Interest Rate

Mr. and Mrs. Hernandez have a Performance 55 bank account that pays a slightly higher rate to depositors aged 55 or older. Interest is calculated on the daily closing balance and received monthly as follows:

Portion of balance	Interest rate (%)
From 0 to $1000.00	0.25
From $1000.01 to $3000.00	0.30
Over $3000.00	0.35

On April 1, their balance was $1416.32. They withdrew $500 on April 9, deposited $1200 on April 15, and deposited another $1200 on April 29. Calculate the interest that they will receive for the month of April.

SOLUTION

The following table organizes the given information in preparation for the interest calculation:

Period	Number of days	Balance ($)	Amount ($) subject to a rate of: 0.25%	0.30%	0.35%
April 1–8	8	1416.32	1000.00	416.32	—
April 9–14	6	916.32	916.32	—	—
April 15–28	14	2116.32	1000.00	1116.32	—
April 29–30	2	3316.32	1000.00	2000.00	316.32

The interest earned for the period April 1 to 8 inclusive is

$$
\begin{aligned}
I(\text{April } 1-8) &= P_1 r_1 t + P_2 r_2 t \\
&= (P_1 r_1 + P_2 r_2)t \\
&= [\$1000(0.0025) + \$416.32(0.003)]\left(\tfrac{8}{365}\right) \\
&= (\$2.500 + \$1.249)(0.02192) \\
&= \$0.0822
\end{aligned}
$$

Note that we maintained four-figure precision to achieve three-figure accuracy in the final answer.

Similarly, $\qquad I(\text{April } 9-14) = \$916.32(0.0025)\left(\tfrac{6}{365}\right) = \$0.0377$

$$
\begin{aligned}
I(\text{April } 15-28) &= [\$1000(0.0025) + \$1116.32(0.003)]\left(\tfrac{14}{365}\right) \\
&= (\$2.50 + \$3.349)(0.03836) \\
&= \$0.224
\end{aligned}
$$

$$
\begin{aligned}
I(\text{April } 29-30) &= [\$1000(0.0025) + \$2000(0.003) + \$316.32(0.0035)]\left(\tfrac{2}{365}\right) \\
&= (\$2.50 + \$6.00 + \$1.107)(0.005479) \\
&= \$0.0526
\end{aligned}
$$

Mr. and Mrs. Hernandez will earn $0.40 interest in April.

➡ **Check your understanding:** If Mr. and Mrs. Hernandez have an account balance on April 1 of $2435.38 and all deposits and withdrawals remain the same as above, how much interest will they receive for the month of April? (Answer: $0.149 + $0.0872 + $0.344 + $0.0722 = $0.65)

▰▰▶ **Related problem:** #9 in Exercise 7.1

EXAMPLE 7.1B	Calculation of Interest on Short-Term GICs

For amounts of $25,000 to $99,999 and terms of 90 to 119 days, the CIBC pays an interest rate of 0.05% on redeemable GICs and 0.25% on non-redeemable GICs. In order to retain the redemption privilege, how much interest (in dollars) must Devan forgo on an investment of $25,000 for 119 days?

SOLUTION

On a non-redeemable GIC, Devan would earn

$$
I = Prt = \$25,000(0.0025)\left(\tfrac{119}{365}\right) = \$20.38
$$

On a redeemable GIC, he would earn

$$
I = Prt = \$25,000(0.0005)\left(\tfrac{119}{365}\right) = \$4.08
$$

Devan must forgo $20.38 − $4.08 = $16.30 of interest earnings to retain the redemption privilege.

> → **Check your understanding:** How much interest would Devan forgo on an investment of $85,000 for 100 days if he chooses to invest in a redeemable GIC at 0.04% instead of a non-redeemable GIC at 0.20%? (Answer: $37.26)
>
> ▮▮▮▶ **Related problem:** #5 in Exercise 7.1

 ## Math Apps

WHAT TO DO WITH A SMALL AMOUNT OF SAVINGS IN A LOW INTEREST RATE ENVIRONMENT?

As we showed you in Chapter 6, interest rates in recent years have been at historically low levels when compared to the last 50 years. While this is good news for borrowers, low rates mean that savers are seeing dismal rates of return, especially if they keep their extra cash in traditional savings accounts. As a student, you are likely not faced with the enviable problem of trying to earn money on huge cash balances! Nevertheless, it is a good habit to start thinking about how to maximize every dollar you do have. Making smart choices about how to earn even a bit of extra money on small amounts of savings can help you develop a lifelong habit of smart investment choices.

Imagine that on September 1, you are starting the school year with a total of $10,000 in combined savings from your summer job and the proceeds of student loans. You plan to use half that money for your first semester of studies. The other half, $5000, will be saved to pay your second tuition installment that is due in early January. What should you do with the "extra" $5000 for the four months between September and early January? Since this money is needed for school, you do, of course, want an entirely safe investment. Investing in the stock market is not an option, as you know that, especially in the short run, stock prices can go up and down, and you do not want to risk losing any of this money. Your choices are therefore limited to short-term interest-based investments. After a bit of Internet research, you have found the following options:

Investment option	Rate
"Smart Saver" account	0.45%
"Savings Builder" account	0.25% on the entire balance up to $250,000
Non-redeemable GIC	0.6% for 120- to 149-day terms, and balances between $5000 and $24,999
Redeemable GIC	0.05% for 120- to 179-day terms, and balances between $5000 and $99,999

Questions

Assuming you invest the $5000 for the period September 1 to the following January 1, calculate the total you will have on January 1 for each of the above four investment options. Assume that for the savings accounts, interest for each month will be deposited to your account on the first calendar day of the next month. Remember that the interest from the preceding month earns interest in the next month! For GICs, interest is paid only at maturity.

How much interest will you earn with each option? Which is the best option? How much better off are you by selecting the best of the four options, as compared to the worst of the four?

Answer

The total interest earned for each option is:

"Smart Saver" = $7.52
"Savings Builder" = $4.18
Non-redeemable GIC = $10.03
Redeemable GIC = $0.84

The non-redeemable GIC is the best option, offering you $10.03 of total interest, which is $10.03 − $0.84 = $9.19 better than the least attractive option, the redeemable GIC.

WHY BOTHER? While the difference between the best and the worst option is only $9.19, this example shows that simply by being aware of your options and knowing how to analyze them, you can make small improvements in the way you manage your money. The dollar amounts here are small, but notice that you earn $10.03/$0.84 = 11.9 times *more* interest with the best versus the worst of the investment options! Later in your life, you might have much larger sums of money to invest for short periods of time. Interest rates might rise, and the differences between "best-case" and "worst-case" options might be magnified. Imagine, for example, that you sell a car, a property, or another asset, and don't have to replace it right away. You might receive an annual bonus in your job, and you may want some time to think about how best to invest that money in the long term. You may find yourself, at times, with relatively large sums that need to be "parked" into a safe investment for short periods of time. Learn now how to examine your options, and later that $9.19 difference could be much larger!

EXERCISE 7.1

Answers to the odd-numbered problems can be found in the end matter.

BASIC PROBLEMS

1. Carol has a savings account balance of $2800 on September 1. On September 18, her balance increases to $3500 and remains there until the end of the month. Her account pays 1.05% per annum. Interest is calculated on the daily closing balance and paid on the first day of the next month. How much interest will be credited to Carol's account on October 1?

2. How much interest will be earned on a 91-day $15,000 term deposit that pays an interest rate of 0.2% per annum?

3. **a.** What will be the maturity value of $15,000 placed in a 120-day term deposit paying an interest rate of 1.25%?

   b. If, on the maturity date, the combined principal and interest are "rolled over" into a 90-day term deposit paying 1.15%, what amount will the depositor receive when the second term deposit matures?

INTERMEDIATE PROBLEMS

4. BMO Bank of Montreal advertises that it will pay an interest rate of 0.2% on a 30-to-59-day GIC, or 0.4% on a 60-to-89-day GIC. Janette has $12,000 to invest. How much more interest will she receive if she invests her money for 60 days instead of 59?

5. For investments between $100,000 and $249,999.99 and terms between 180 and 269 days, Royal Bank pays 1.00% on a non-redeemable GIC and 0.75% on a redeemable GIC. Julienne has $185,000 to invest for 195 days and is certain that she will not need earlier access to her money. How much more will she earn if she chooses the non-redeemable option instead of the redeemable?

6. For amounts between $10,000 and $24,999, a credit union pays a rate of 0.5% on term deposits with maturities in the 91-to-120-day range. However, early redemption will result in a rate of 0.2% being applied. How much more interest will a 91-day $20,000 term deposit earn if it is held until maturity than if it is redeemed after 80 days?

7. On a $10,000 principal investment, a bank offered interest rates of 0.65% on 270-to-364-day GICs and 0.6% on 180-to-269-day GICs. How much more will an investor earn from a 364-day GIC than from two consecutive 182-day GICs? (Assume that the interest rate on 180-to-269-day GICs will be the same on the renewal date as it is today. Remember that both the principal and the interest from the first 182-day GIC can be invested in the second 182-day GIC.)

8. A savings account pays interest of 1.5%. Interest is calculated on the daily closing balance and paid at the close of business on the last day of the month. A depositor who had a $2239 opening balance on September 1 deposited $734 on September 7 and $327 on September 21, and withdrew $300 on September 10. What interest will be credited to the account at the month's end?

9. The Moneybuilder account offered by a chartered bank calculates interest daily based on the daily closing balance as follows:

Interest rate (%)	Amount to which the rate applies
0.00	Balance when it is below $1000
0.10	Entire balance when it is between $1000 and $3000
0.15	Portion of balance above $3000

The balance at the beginning of March was $1678. On March 5, $700 was withdrawn. Then $2500 was deposited on March 15, and $900 was withdrawn on March 23. What interest will be credited to the account for the month of March?

ADVANCED PROBLEMS

10. An Investment Savings account offered by a trust company pays a rate of 0.25% on the first $1000 of daily closing balance, 0.5% on the portion of the balance between $1000 and $3000, and 0.75% on any balance in excess of $3000. What interest will be paid for the month of April if the opening balance was $2439, $950 was deposited on April 10, and $500 was withdrawn on April 23?

11. Joan has savings of $12,000 on June 1. Since she may need some of the money during the next three months, she is considering two options at her bank. (1) An Investment Builder account earns a 0.25% rate of interest. The interest is calculated on the daily closing balance and paid on the first day of the following month. (2) A 90-to-179-day cashable term deposit earns a rate of 0.8%, paid at maturity. If interest rates do not change and Joan does not withdraw any of the funds, how much more will she earn from the term deposit option up to September 1? (Keep in mind that savings account interest paid on the first day of the month will itself earn interest during the subsequent month.)

12. For principal amounts of $5000 to $49,999, a bank pays an interest rate of 0.65% on 180-to-269-day non-redeemable GICs, and 0.70% on 270-to-364-day non-redeemable GICs. Ranjit has $10,000 to invest for 364 days. Because he thinks interest rates will be higher six months from now, he is debating whether to choose a 182-day GIC now (and reinvest its maturity value in another 182-day GIC) or choose a 364-day GIC today. What would the interest rate on 182-day GICs have to be on the reinvestment date for both alternatives to yield the same maturity value 364 days from now?

7.2 The Valuation Principle

LO2 Consider an investment that will deliver a single payment of $110 one year from today. What is the most you should pay to buy the investment if you require a minimum rate of return of 10%? (In other words, what is the current value of the investment to you?) After a little thought, you probably answer "$100" for the following reason. The $10 difference between the amount you pay ($100) and the amount you will receive ($110) represents a 10% rate of return on your $100 investment.

But how would you calculate the price to pay if the given numbers are not so "nice?" For example, what maximum price should you pay for an investment that will pay you $129 after 247 days, if you require a rate of return of 5.5%? Let us think about where the $100 came from in the first example. Note that $100 invested for one year at 10% will grow to $110. Since $110 is the *future* value of $100, then $100 is the *present* value of $110. That is,

$$P = \frac{S}{1 + rt} = \frac{\$110}{1 + 0.10(1)} = \$100$$

This demonstrates that the present value calculation gives a price that "builds in" the required 10% rate of return. If your minimum required rate of return is only 8%, then you should be willing to pay up to

$$P = \frac{S}{1 + rt} = \frac{\$110}{1 + 0.08(1)} = \$101.85$$

The $8.15 ($110 − $101.85) you will earn during the next year provides a rate of return (on your $101.85 investment) of

$$\frac{\$8.15}{\$101.85} \times 100 = 8.00\%$$

The lower the rate of return you are prepared to accept, the higher the price you can pay now for a given future payment.

In the language of finance, the process of calculating a payment's present value is often called **discounting a payment**. (When you calculate the present value of a payment, you get a smaller number than the payment.) The interest rate used in the present value calculation is then called the **discount rate**.

To determine the price to pay for an investment that promises two or more future payments, we simply extend our basic idea. That is, first calculate the present value of each of the payments (using the required rate of return as the discount rate). Then add the present values.

For investments purchased privately, you have some flexibility to negotiate a *higher* rate of return by bargaining *down* the price. But for various types of investments available to the general public, the rates of return are determined by market forces of supply and demand. When an investment's price is established by competitive bidding among many buyers and sellers, we refer to the price as the **fair market value**. A particular fair market value corresponds to a specific rate of return from the investment. This rate of return is what we mean by the *market-determined rate of return*. For publicly traded investments, your only decision is whether or not to accept the prevailing price and the corresponding market-determined rate of return.

These ideas are so important and of such wide application in finance that they are formally embodied in the Valuation Principle.

Valuation Principle

The fair market value of an investment is the sum of the present values of the cash flows expected from the investment. The discount rate used in the present value calculations should be the prevailing market-determined rate of return on this type of investment.

If the expected cash flows are received as forecast, the investor's actual rate of return on the amount invested will be precisely the discount rate used in the fair market value calculation.

EXAMPLE 7.2A	Valuation of a Non-Interest-Bearing Obligation

An investment contract calls for a payment of $1000 five months from now and another payment, 10 months from now, of $1500.

a. What price will an investor be prepared to pay for the investment today if the required rate of return is 2%?

b. Demonstrate that the investor will realize a 2% rate of return on this price if the payments are received as expected.

SOLUTION

a. According to the Valuation Principle,

$$\text{Price} = \text{Present value of \$1000} + \text{Present value of \$1500}$$

$$= \frac{\$1000}{1 + 0.02\left(\frac{5}{12}\right)} + \frac{\$1500}{1 + 0.02\left(\frac{10}{12}\right)}$$

$$= \$991.736 + \$1475.410$$

$$= \$2467.15$$

An investor requiring a 2% rate of return should be willing to pay $2467.15 today for the contract.

b. Think of the $991.74 and $1475.41 components of the $2467.15 price as separately buying the future cash flows of $1000 and $1500, respectively.

$991.74 invested for five months at 2% will grow to

$$S = P(1 + rt) = \$991.74\left[1 + 0.02\left(\frac{5}{12}\right)\right] = \$1000$$

Therefore, the $1000 payment received after five months recovers the $991.74 investment along with five months' interest on $991.74 at 2%.

Similarly, it can be shown that the $1500 payment received after 10 months pays back the $1475.41 component of the initial investment plus 10 months' interest on $1475.41 at 2%.

➡ **Check your understanding:** What price will an investor be prepared to pay for the investment today if the required rate of return is 5%? (Answer: $979.592 + $1440.00 = $2419.59)

▮▬▶ **Related problem:** #1 in Exercise 7.2

EXAMPLE 7.2B	Valuation of an Interest-Bearing Obligation

On March 1, Murray signed a contract to pay Anton or his designate $2000 plus interest at 8% on June 1, and $3000 plus interest at 8% on September 1. Anton sold the contract to Randy on May 1 at a price negotiated to provide Randy with a 10% rate of return. What price did Randy pay?

SOLUTION

According to the Valuation Principle, the price paid by Randy should be the present value on May 1 of the two scheduled payments discounted at 10%. Unlike in Example 7.2A, we do not know at the outset the dollar amounts of the scheduled payments. As indicated in the following time diagram, we must first calculate the maturity value of each obligation using the contract's 8% interest rate. Then we can determine the present value of each scheduled payment using a discount rate of 10%. (The present value calculations thereby build in a 10% rate of return to Randy.)

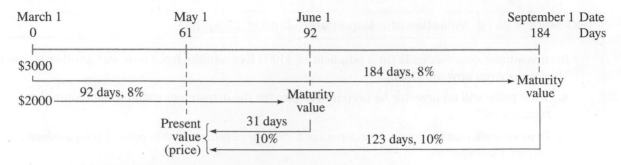

Payment due on June 1 = Maturity value of $2000 = 2000\left[1 + 0.08\left(\frac{92}{365}\right)\right]$ = $2040.33

Payment due on September 1 = Maturity value of $3000 = 3000\left[1 + 0.08\left(\frac{184}{365}\right)\right]$ = $3120.99

$$\begin{aligned} \text{Price} &= \text{Present value of scheduled payments} \\ &= \frac{\$2040.33}{1 + 0.10\left(\frac{31}{365}\right)} + \frac{\$3120.99}{1 + 0.10\left(\frac{123}{365}\right)} \\ &= \$2023.147 + \$3019.246 \\ &= \$5042.39 \end{aligned}$$

Randy paid $5042.39 for the contract.

⮕ **Check your understanding:** Suppose the original contract between Murray and Anton required an interest rate of 4.5% instead of 8%. How much would Randy pay for this contract on May 1 if he requires a rate of return of 12%? (Answer: $2002.273 + $2948.805 = $4951.08)

▬▬► **Related problem:** #10 in Exercise 7.2

Checkpoint Questions

1. Circle "True" or "False" for each of the following:

   a. An investor can achieve a higher rate of return by bargaining down the purchase price of an investment.   True   False

   b. An investment guarantees that an investor will receive future payments of $1000 and $2000. If an investor requires a 2% rate of return, the fair market value of this investment will be more than $3000.   True   False

   c. If the market determined rate of return on an investment declines, an investment's fair market value will also decline.   True   False

2. What do you need to know in order to be able to calculate the fair market value of an investment that will deliver two future payments?

3. If you purchase an investment privately, how do you determine the maximum price you are prepared to pay?

4. Assume that the expected cash flows from an investment and the market-determined rate of return do not change as time passes.

   a. What will happen to the investment's fair market value leading up to the first scheduled payment? Explain.

   b. If the first scheduled payment is $500, what will happen to the fair market value of the investment immediately after the payment is made? Explain.

EXERCISE 7.2

Answers to the odd-numbered problems can be found in the end matter.

BASIC PROBLEMS

1. Calculate the fair market value today of an investment that promises to pay $5250 in four months from now if the investor's required rate of return on the investment is 5%.

2. How much should an investor be willing to pay today for an investment that will pay $17,400 in nine months from now if the discount rate is 1.25%?

3. An investment promises two payments of $500, on dates three and six months from today. What is the value of the investment today if the required rate of return on the investment is 9%?

4. An investment promises two payments of $1000, on dates 60 and 90 days from today. What price will an investor pay today if her required rate of return is 3%?

INTERMEDIATE PROBLEMS

5. Certificate A pays $1000 in four months and another $1000 in eight months. Certificate B pays $1000 in five months and another $1000 in nine months. If the current rate of return required on this type of investment certificate is 2.75%, determine the current value of each of the certificates. Give an explanation for the lower value of B.

6. A contract requires payments of $1500, $2000, and $1000 in 100, 150, and 200 days, respectively, from today. What is the value of the contract today if the payments are discounted to yield a 10.5% rate of return?

7. An agreement stipulates payments of $4000, $2500, and $5000 in three, six, and nine months, respectively, from today. What is the highest price an investor will offer today to purchase the agreement if he requires a minimum rate of return of 6.25%?

8. An investor has determined that she is willing to pay $1951.62 today for an investment that will pay $2000 in seven months from now. What market rate of return has the investor used to determine the valuation of this investment?

9. An investment promises to pay a single future payment of $9000. At a market rate of return of 2.15%, the fair market value of this investment is $8872.82. How many months from today is the $9000 scheduled to be paid?

ADVANCED PROBLEMS

10. An assignable loan contract executed three months ago requires two payments to be paid five and ten months after the contract date. Each payment consists of a principal portion of $1800 plus interest at 5% on $1800 from the date of the contract. The payee is offering to sell the contract to a finance company in order to raise cash. If the finance company requires a return of 10%, what price will it be prepared to pay today for the contract?

11. Claude Scales, a commercial fisherman, bought a new navigation system for $10,000 from Coast Marine Electronics on March 20. He paid $2000 in cash and signed a conditional sale contract requiring a payment on July 1 of $3000 plus interest on the $3000 at a rate of 8%, and another payment on September 1 of $5000 plus interest on the $5000 at 8% from the date of the sale. Coast Marine immediately sold the contract to a finance company, which discounted the payments at its required return of 12%. What proceeds did Coast Marine receive from the sale of the contract?

7.3 Treasury Bills and Commercial Paper

LO3 **Treasury bills** (T-bills) are paper contracts issued to lenders by the federal government and several provincial governments when they borrow money for terms of less than one year. In March 2015, $135.7 billion of the Government of Canada's net federal debt of $612.3 billion was borrowed through T-bills.

The Bank of Canada conducts auctions of Government of Canada T-bills every second Tuesday. At each auction, the Government of Canada typically borrows between $10 billion and $15 billion. Some of this borrowing is "revolving" debt—the government is borrowing in order to have the funds needed to settle previously issued T-bills that are coming due. Three T-bill maturities are available at each auction—three-month, six-month, and one-year. Depending upon the date of the auction, the exact number of days for each maturity category varies slightly.[1]

The initial lenders (purchasers of the T-bills) are major investment dealers and chartered banks. In turn, these financial institutions sell most of the T-bills to their client-investors in multiples of $1000, typically with a minimum face value of $5000.

In everyday loan transactions, we normally stipulate the principal amount and then calculate the payment or payments required to repay the principal plus interest. With T-bills, the arrangement is different. The denomination or **face value** of a T-bill is the full amount, *including interest*, payable at maturity of the T-bill. The purchase price (or amount loaned) will be less than the face value—the difference represents the interest that will be earned on the loan. In investment language, T-bills are "issued at a discount to their face value."

How do you decide how much to pay (lend) for the right to receive a T-bill's face value on a known future date? This is the same type of question you were asked at the beginning of Section 7.2. You calculate the present value of the T-bill's face value, using your required rate of return as the discount rate.[2] For example, suppose you were considering the purchase of the $1,000,000 Government of Canada, 91-day T-bill illustrated below. On the T-bill's issue date, you would be willing to pay some amount less than the $1,000,000 maturity value. How much less would depend upon your required rate of return.

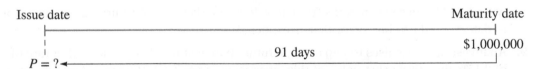

The purchaser of a T-bill is not required to hold it until it matures. There is an active market for the sale/purchase of T-bills that are partway through their terms. On any day, the price at which a T-bill may be bought or sold is the present value of its face value. The face value should be discounted at the *current* market-determined rate of return on T-bills over the *time remaining* until maturity. Typical market rates for a few maturities are listed online or in the financial pages of major newspapers each day. As illustrated by Table 7.1, historical T-bill rates have varied widely, depending upon prevailing economic conditions at the time.

---

[1] Three-month T-bills have either 91- or 98-day maturities; six-month T-bills have either 168- or 182-day maturities; one-year T-bills have either 350- or 364-day maturities.

[2] For the initial auction of T-bills, participating financial institutions submit price bids just prior to the auction. The institutions use their own required rate of return as the discount rate when determining the present value of the face value. An institution arrives at its required rate of return based on prevailing short-term interest rates in financial markets, and on the expected demand for T-bills from its clients. The Bank of Canada accepts bids in order of decreasing prices until the government's borrowing requirements for the week are met.

TABLE 7.1   Government of Canada T-Bill Rates (average monthly yield)

Issue date	Rate of return on 3-month T-bills	Rate of return on 6-month T-bills
January 1963	3.650%	3.770%
January 1973	3.900%	4.190%
January 1983	9.580%	9.600%
January 1993	6.562%	6.778%
January 2003	2.813%	3.000%
January 2013	0.930%	1.000%
January 2016	0.481%	0.465%

Source: Bank of Canada.

Some large corporations also borrow money for short periods by selling contracts called **commercial paper**. Commercial paper is essentially a corporation's version of T-bills. Common maturities are 30, 60, and 90 days (usually referred to as one-month, two-month, and three-month maturities). The minimum face value is usually $100,000. Like Treasury bills, commercial paper is priced at its discounted present value. The required rate of return (discount rate) on commercial paper is usually 0.4% to 0.8% higher than that on T-bills. The higher rate of return is required because of the small risk that the corporation might be unable to pay the face value on the due date.

EXAMPLE 7.3A	Valuation of a T-Bill on Its Issue Date

Suppose the average rate of return or yield on 168-day Government of Canada Treasury bills sold at a Tuesday auction was 1.38%. At this yield, what price was paid for a T-bill with a face value of $100,000?

SOLUTION

$$\text{Price} = \text{Present value of \$1000 discounted at 1.38\% for 168 days}$$
$$= \frac{\$100,000}{1 + 0.0138\left(\frac{168}{365}\right)}$$
$$= \$99,368.83$$

To obtain a yield of 1.38%, $99,368.83 was paid for the 168-day, $100,000 face value T-bill.

➡ **Check your understanding:** What price would be paid for this T-bill if the average rate of return or yield was 9.6%? (Answer: $95,768.35)

▮▮▮▶ **Related problem:** #1 in Exercise 7.3

EXAMPLE 7.3B	Valuation of a T-Bill

The institutional purchaser of the T-bill in Example 7.3A immediately sells it to a client at a higher price that represents a (lower) yield to the client of 1.18%. What profit did the institution make on the transaction?

SOLUTION

$$\text{Selling price to the client} = \frac{\$100,000}{1 + 0.0118\left(\frac{168}{365}\right)} = \$99,459.81$$

$$\text{Profit} = \text{Price charged to the client} - \text{Acquisition price}$$
$$= \$99,459.81 - \$99,368.83 = \$90.98$$

The institution's profit on the resale of the T-bill was $90.98.

➡️ **Check your understanding:** Suppose the T-bill was sold to yield the client a rate of return of 0.98% (instead of 1.18%). What profit would the institution make on the transaction? (Answer: $182.13)

▶️ **Related problem:** #9 in Exercise 7.3

EXAMPLE 7.3C	Calculation of the Rate of Return on a T-Bill Sold Before Maturity

Suppose the client who purchased the 168-day, $100,000 T-bill in Example 7.3B for $99,459.81 sold the T-bill after 73 days in order to invest the proceeds elsewhere.

a. What price would she receive if the short-term interest rate for this maturity had risen to 1.27% by the date of sale?

b. What rate of return (per annum) did the client realize while holding the T-bill?

SOLUTION

a. Days remaining to maturity = 168 − 73 = 95

$$\text{Selling price} = \text{Present value of \$100,000 discounted at 1.27\% for 95 days}$$
$$= \frac{\$100,000}{1 + 0.0127\left(\frac{95}{365}\right)}$$
$$= \$99,670.54$$

The client sold the T-bill for $99,670.54.

b. The client purchased an investment for $99,459.81 and sold it 73 days later for $99,670.54. We need to calculate the rate of return when $99,459.81 grows to $99,670.54 in 73 days. In effect, the initial investment of $99,459.81 earned interest amounting to

$$I = \$99,670.54 - \$99,459.81 = \$210.73$$

Formula (6-1) may now be used to obtain the corresponding rate of return.

$$r = \frac{I}{Pt} = \frac{\$210.73}{\$99,459.81\left(\frac{73}{365}\right)} = 0.01059 = 1.059\%$$

The client's rate of return during the 73-day holding period was 1.059%.

➡️ **Check your understanding:** Redo the question. This time, the short-term interest rate for this maturity had fallen to 0.90% by the date of the sale. **a.** What price will the client receive when she sells the T-bill after 73 days? **b.** What rate of return (per annum) did she realize while holding the T-bill? (Answer: **a.** $99,766.30, **b.** 1.541% per annum)

▶️ **Related problem:** #12 in Exercise 7.3

EXAMPLE 7.3D	Calculation of the Rate of Return on Commercial Paper

Sixty-day commercial paper with face value $100,000 was issued by Suncor Inc. for $99,765. What rate of return will be realized if the paper is held until maturity?

SOLUTION

In effect, the interest earned on an investment of $99,765 for 60 days is

$$\$100,000 - \$99,765 = \$235$$

Using formula (6-1) rearranged to solve for r, we have

$$r = \frac{I}{Pt} = \frac{\$235}{\$99,765\left(\frac{60}{365}\right)} = 0.01433 = 1.433\%$$

A 1.433% rate of return will be realized if the paper is held until it matures.

➡ **Check your understanding:** What rate of return would be realized if the commercial paper had been issued by Suncor Inc. for $99,450? (Answer: 3.364%)

▰▰▰▷ **Related problem:** #4 in Exercise 7.3

 Checkpoint Questions

1. Circle "True" or "False" for each of the following:

   a. Ninety-day commercial paper with face value $100,000 will typically sell for   True   False
       more than a Government of Canada T-bill with the same face value and
       maturity date.

   b. An investor must hold a T-bill until maturity.   True   False

   c. If short-term interest rates have increased during the past week, investors will   True   False
       pay less this week (than last week) for T-bills of the same term and face value.

   d. When it sells T-bills, the Government of Canada sets a price that reflects the   True   False
       rate of interest it is willing to pay to investors.

2. Is the price of a 98-day $100,000 T-bill higher or lower than the price of a 168-day
    $100,000 T-bill? Why?

3. If short-term interest rates do not change, what happens to a particular T-bill's fair
    market value as time passes?

EXERCISE 7.3

Answers to the odd-numbered problems can be found in the end matter.

Calculate prices accurate to the nearest cent and rates of return accurate to the nearest 0.001%.

BASIC PROBLEMS

1. Calculate the price of a $25,000, 91-day Province of British Columbia Treasury bill on its
    issue date if the current market rate of return is 1.672%.

2. Calculate the price on its issue date of $100,000 face value, 90-day commercial paper issued
    by GE Capital Canada if the prevailing market rate of return is 0.932%.

3. Calculate and compare the issue-date prices of $100,000 face value commercial paper invest-
    ments with 30-, 60-, and 90-day maturities, all priced to yield 3.5%.

4. A $100,000, 90-day commercial paper certificate issued by Wells Fargo Financial Canada was sold on its issue date for $99,250. What rate of return will it yield to the buyer?

5. On its issue date, an investor paid $99,760 for a $100,000 face value, 98-day Government of Canada T-bill. What was the investor's required rate of return?

INTERMEDIATE PROBLEMS

6. A $100,000, 91-day Province of Ontario Treasury bill was issued 37 days ago. What will be its purchase price today in order to yield the purchaser 1.14%?

7. An investor purchased $1 million face value of Honda Canada Finance Inc. 90-day commercial paper 28 days after its issue. What price was paid if the investor's required rate of return was 2.10%?

8. Calculate and compare the market values of a $100,000 face value Government of Canada Treasury bill on dates that are 91 days, 61 days, 31 days, and 1 day before maturity. Assume that the rate of return required in the market stays constant at 3% over the lifetime of the T-bill.

9. Over the past 35 years, the prevailing market yield or discount rate on 91-day T-bills has ranged from a low of 0.17% in February 2010 to a high of 20.82% in August 1981. (The period from 1979 to 1990 was a time of historically high inflation rates and interest rates.) How much more would you have paid for a $100,000 face value 91-day T-bill at the February 2010 discount rate than at the August 1981 discount rate?

10. Twenty-seven days ago, The Hatfield Corporation issued $300,000 face value 90-day commercial paper. How much will a investor pay for the commercial paper today if the required market rate of return is 2.15%?

ADVANCED PROBLEMS

11. An investor purchased a 182-day, $25,000 Province of Alberta Treasury bill on its date of issue for $24,812 and sold it 60 days later for $24,875.
    a. What rate of return was implied in the original price?
    b. What rate of return did the market require on the sale date?
    c. What rate of return did the original investor actually realize during the 60-day holding period?

12. A $100,000, 168-day Government of Canada Treasury bill was purchased on its date of issue to yield 2.1%.
    a. What price did the investor pay?
    b. Calculate the market value of the T-bill 85 days later if the rate of return then required by the market has
        (i) risen to 2.4%.
        (ii) remained at 2.1%.
        (iii) fallen to 1.8%.
    c. Calculate the rate of return actually realized by the investor if the T-bill is sold at each of the three prices calculated in Part (b).

13. A 168-day, $100,000 T-bill was initially issued at a price that would yield the buyer 0.446%. If the yield required by the market remains at 0.446%, how many days before its maturity date will the T-bill's market price first exceed $99,900?

7.4 | Demand Loans

Most businesses arrange demand loans or lines of credit to meet short-term financing requirements. Many individuals obtain personal lines of credit, set up on a demand basis, to meet their short-term borrowing needs.

LO4 Common Terms and Conditions

The name **demand loan** comes from the lender's right to demand full repayment of the loan at any time without notice. This rarely happens if the borrower fulfills the terms of the loan (unless the lender has reason to believe the borrower's financial condition is deteriorating). The borrower may repay any portion of the loan at any time without penalty.

The interest rate charged on demand loans is usually "floating." This means that the rate is linked to the prime rate of interest in the banking system. Interest rates are then quoted as "prime plus" some additional amount. For example, if a small business is viewed by the lender as a moderate risk, the business might be charged a rate of prime plus 2% or prime plus 3%.

Interest on a demand loan is paid on the same date each month. The most common approach is to calculate interest *from (and including)* the previous interest payment date *up to (but not including)* the current interest payment date. This procedure is consistent with the count-the-first-day-but-not-the-last-day rule for determining the length of the time interval in simple-interest calculations. The interest rate in effect each day is applied to each day's *closing* loan balance.

Arrangements for repaying the loan principal are negotiated between the borrower and lender. Acceptable terms will depend upon the purpose of the loan, the nature of the security given, and the seasonality of the borrower's income. The two most common demand loan arrangements are

- A revolving loan
- A fixed-payment loan

Revolving Loans

Revolving loans are preferred by businesses and individuals whose short-term borrowing requirements vary over the year. These loans give borrowers the flexibility to borrow additional funds at their discretion and to reduce their debt whenever extra funds are available. Most *lines of credit* and business *operating loans* are set up as revolving loans.

The borrower and the lending institution negotiate the terms and conditions of the loan—the credit limit, the security required, the interest rate, and so on. Subject to the credit limit and a few general guidelines, draws (or advances) of principal and repayments of principal are at the borrower's discretion.

For *fully-secured* revolving loans, the minimum monthly payment may be only the accrued interest on the outstanding loan balance. In most other cases, the minimum monthly payment is something like "the greater of $100 or 3% of the *current* balance." The "current balance" in this context includes accrued interest. The lender usually requires that the borrower have a chequing account (sometimes called a *current account* for a business) with the lending institution. The required monthly payment is then automatically withdrawn from the chequing account on the interest payment date.

EXAMPLE 7.4A | **Calculation of Interest on a Revolving Loan**

On March 20, Hank's Cycle Shop received an initial advance of $10,000 on its revolving demand loan. On the 15th of each month, interest is calculated (up to but not including the 15th) and deducted from Hank's bank account. The floating rate of interest started at 5.75% and dropped to 5.5% on April 5. On April 19, another $10,000 was drawn on the line of credit. What interest was charged to the bank account on April 15 and May 15?

SOLUTION

The one-month period ending on an interest payment date (April 15 and May 15) must be broken into intervals within which the balance on the loan *and* the interest rate are constant. In the following table, we should count the first day but not the last day in each interval. This will cause April 5 (the first day at the 5.5% interest rate) to be included in the second interval but not in the first interval.

Interval	Days	Principal ($)	Rate (%)	Amount of interest	
March 20–April 5	16	10,000	5.75	$10,000(0.0575)\left(\frac{16}{365}\right) =$	$25.205
April 5–April 15	10	10,000	5.5	$10,000(0.055)\left(\frac{10}{365}\right) =$	15.068
				Interest charged on April 15:	$40.27
April 15–April 19	4	10,000	5.5	$10,000(0.055)\left(\frac{4}{365}\right) =$	$6.027
April 19–May 15	26	20,000	5.5	$20,000(0.055)\left(\frac{26}{365}\right) =$	78.356
				Interest charged on May 15:	$84.38

The interest charged to Hank's bank account on April 15 was $40.27 and on May 15 was $84.38.

➡ **Check your understanding:** Suppose the initial advance on March 20 was $15,000. The floating interest rate started at 4.75% and increased to 5.25% on April 5. The additional draw on April 19 is, this time, $12,000. What interest will be charged to the bank account on April 15 and May 15? (Answer: $52.81 on April 15; $109.60 on May 15)

▰▰▷ **Related problem:** #1 in Exercise 7.4

LO5   Repayment Schedule for a Revolving Loan

A **loan repayment schedule** is a table in which interest charges, loan draws and payments, and outstanding balances are recorded. The schedule helps us organize our calculations and properly allocate payments to interest and principal.

Figure 7.1 presents a format for a demand loan repayment schedule. You enter a row in the schedule when any of the following three events takes place:
- A principal amount is advanced or repaid.
- The interest rate changes.
- Interest (and possibly principal) is paid on an interest payment date.

FIGURE 7.1   Demand Loan Repayment Schedule

(1)	(2)	(3)	(4)	(5)	(6)	(7)	(8)
Date	Number of days	Interest rate	Interest	Accrued interest	Payment (advance)	Principal portion	Balance

The columns in the table are used as follows. (Each item in the following list refers to the corresponding numbered column in Figure 7.1.)

1. In chronological order down Column (1), enter the *dates* on which payments are made, the interest rate changes, or principal amounts are advanced to the borrower.
2. Enter into Column (2) the *number of days* in the interval *ending* on each date in Column (1). In any particular row, record the number of days from (and including) the *previous* row's date to (but not including) the date in the row *at hand*.

3. Enter into Column (3) the ***interest rate*** that applies to each interval in Column (2). When the date in Column (1) is the date on which a new interest rate takes effect, the interest rate in Column (3) is still the *previous rate.* The reason is that the days in Column (2) are for the period *up to but not including* the date in Column (1).

4. In Column (4), enter the **interest** charge ($I = Prt$) for the number of days (t) in Column (2) at the interest rate (r) in Column (3) on the balance (P) from Column (8) of the *preceding* line.

5. In Column (5), enter the cumulative total of unpaid or ***accrued interest*** as of the current row's date. This amount is the interest just calculated in Column (4) plus any previously accrued but unpaid interest (from Column (5) in the *preceding* line).

6. In Column (6), enter the amount of any ***payment*** (of principal and/or interest). A loan ***advance*** is enclosed in brackets to distinguish it from a loan payment.

7. On an interest payment date, the accrued interest in Column (5) is deducted from the payment to obtain the ***principal portion*** of the payment. Put a single stroke through the accrued interest in Column (5) as a reminder that it has been paid and should not be carried forward to the next period. If an *unscheduled* payment is entered in Column (6), the entire amount is usually applied to principal. Enter it again in Column (7). Similarly, the amount of any loan advance in Column (6) should be duplicated in Column (7).

8. The new loan ***balance*** is the previous line's balance *less* any principal repaid or *plus* any principal advanced (the amount in Column (7)).

EXAMPLE 7.4B	Repayment Schedule for a Revolving Operating Loan

The Bank of Montreal approved a $50,000 line of credit on a demand basis to Tanya's Wardrobes to finance the store's inventory. Interest at the rate of prime plus 2% is charged to Tanya's chequing account at the bank on the 23rd of each month. The initial advance was $25,000 on September 23 when the prime rate stood at 3%. There were further advances of $8000 on October 30 and $10,000 on November 15. Payments of $7000 and $14,000 were applied against the principal on December 15 and January 15, respectively. The prime rate rose to 3.25% effective December 5. What was the total interest paid on the loan for the period September 23 to January 23?

SOLUTION

A large amount of information is given in the statement of the problem. The best way to organize the data is to construct a repayment schedule using the format in Figure 7.1. In the date column, list in chronological order all of the dates on which a transaction or an event affecting the loan occurs. These are the dates of advances, payments of principal or interest, and interest rate changes. Next, enter the information that is given for each transaction or event. At this point the schedule has the following entries:

Date	Number of days	Interest rate (%)	Interest ($)	Accrued interest ($)	Payment (advance) ($)	Principal portion ($)	Balance ($)
Sep. 23	—	5	—	—	(25,000)	(25,000)	25,000
Oct. 23		5				0	
Oct. 30		5			(8,000)	(8,000)	
Nov. 15		5			(10,000)	(10,000)	
Nov. 23		5				0	
Dec. 5		5				0	
Dec. 15		5.25			7,000	7,000	
Dec. 23		5.25				0	
Jan. 15		5.25			14,000	14,000	
Jan. 23		5.25				0	

Note that 5% (3% + 2%) has been entered on the December 5 line. Although the interest rate changes to 5.25% *effective* December 5, the "Number of days" entry on this line will be the number of days from (and including) November 23 to (but not including) December 5. These 12 days are still charged interest at the 5% rate. The 5.25% rate will first apply to the December 5 to December 15 period, which is handled on the December 15 line.

The "Number of days" column may be completed next. Then the calculations can proceed row by row to obtain the full schedule. The circled numbers (①, ②, etc.) in the following schedule refer to sample calculations listed after the schedule. Draw a stroke through an accrued interest figure when the interest is paid on the 23rd of each month.

Date	Number of days	Interest rate (%)	Interest ($)	Accrued interest ($)	Payment (advance) ($)	Principal portion ($)	Balance ($)
Sep. 23	—	5	—	—	(25,000)	(25,000)	25,000
Oct. 23	30	5	102.74 ①	~~102.74~~	102.74	0	25,000
Oct. 30	7	5	23.97	23.97	(8,000)	(8,000)	33,000
Nov. 15	16	5	72.33 ②	96.30 ③	(10,000)	(10,000)	43,000
Nov. 23	8	5	47.12 ④	~~143.42~~ ⑤	143.42	0	43,000
Dec. 5	12	5	70.68	70.68			43,000
Dec. 15	10	5.25	61.85	132.53	7,000	7,000	36,000
Dec. 23	8	5.25	41.42	~~173.95~~	173.95	0	36,000
Jan. 15	23	5.25	119.10	119.10	14,000	14,000	22,000
Jan. 23	8	5.25	25.32	~~144.42~~	144.42	0	22,000

① $I = Prt = \$25,000(0.05)\left(\frac{30}{365}\right) = \$102.74.$
② $I = Prt = \$33,000(0.05)\left(\frac{16}{365}\right) = \$72.33.$
③ Accrued interest = $\$23.97 + \$72.33 = \$96.30.$
④ $I = \$43,000(0.05)\left(\frac{8}{365}\right) = \$47.12.$
⑤ Accrued interest = $\$96.30 + \$47.12 = \$143.42.$

The total interest paid on the loan for the period September 23 to January 23 was

$$\$102.74 + \$143.42 + \$173.95 + \$144.42 = \$564.53$$

▶ **Check your understanding:** What would be the total interest paid on the loan for the period September 23 to January 23 if the prime rate had stood at 1.25% on September 23 and rose to 1.50% effective December 5? All other details about the loan remain the same.
(Answer: $\$66.78 + \$93.22 + \$114.80 + \$96.28 = \$371.08$ total interest paid)

▬▶ **Related problem:** #2 in Exercise 7.4

EXAMPLE 7.4C	Repayment Schedule for a Revolving Personal Line of Credit

Warren Bitenko has a $20,000 personal line of credit with the RBC Royal Bank. The interest rate is prime + 3.5%. On the last day of each month, a payment equal to the greater of $100 or 3% of the current balance (including the current month's accrued interest) is deducted from his chequing account.

On July 6, he took his first advance of $2000. On August 15, he took another draw of $7500. The prime rate started at 2.75%, and rose to 3% on September 9. Prepare a loan repayment schedule up to and including September 30.

SOLUTION

Begin a schedule by entering, in chronological order, the dates of advances, interest rate changes, and payments. Information known about these events should also be entered. At this point, the schedule has the following entries and you are ready to begin the calculations.

Date	Number of days	Interest rate (%)	Interest ($)	Accrued interest ($)	Payment (advance) ($)	Principal portion ($)	Balance ($)
July 6	—	6.25	—	—	(2,000)	(2,000)	2,000
July 31		6.25					
Aug. 15		6.25			(7,500)	(7,500)	
Aug. 31		6.25					
Sep. 9		6.25					
Sep. 30		6.5					

Now proceed row by row to construct the loan schedule. The circled numbers (①,②, etc.) in the following schedule refer to the sample calculations listed immediately after the schedule.

Date	Number of days	Interest rate (%)	Interest ($)	Accrued interest ($)	Payment (advance) ($)	Principal portion ($)	Balance ($)
July 6	—	6.25	—	—	(2,000.00)	(2,000.00)	2,000.00
July 31	25	6.25	8.56 ①	8.56	100.00 ②	91.44 ③	1,908.56
Aug. 15	15	6.25	4.90	4.90	(7,500.00)	(7,500.00)	9,408.56
Aug. 31	16	6.25	25.78	30.68	283.18 ④	252.50 ⑤	9,156.06
Sep. 9	9	6.25	14.11	14.11			9,156.06
Sep. 30	21	6.5	34.24	48.35	276.13	227.78	8,928.28

① $I = Prt = \$2000(0.0625)(\frac{25}{365}) = \$8.56$.
② The payment is the greater of $100 or $0.03 \times \$2008.56 = \$60.26$. The larger amount is $100.
③ Principal repaid = $100 − $8.56 = $91.44.
④ Required payment = $0.03 \times$ Current balance = $0.03 \times (\$9408.56 + \$30.68) = \$283.18$.
⑤ Principal repaid = $283.18 − $30.68 = $252.50.

➡ **Check your understanding:** How much total interest would Warren pay on this line of credit if the prime rate had started at 2.5% on July 6 and fallen to 2% on September 9? All other details about the loan remain the same. *Hint:* Redo the entire repayment schedule, as the values in the "Balance" column will change. (Answer: $8.22 + $29.45 + $42.51 = $80.18 total interest paid)

▰▰▷ **Related problem:** #7 in Exercise 7.4

Fixed-Payment Loans

A fixed-payment loan requires *equal* monthly payments. The interest component of each payment is the interest that has accrued on the outstanding principal balance since the preceding payment. As the outstanding loan balance declines, each successive payment has a smaller interest component and a larger principal component.

EXAMPLE 7.4D	Repayment Schedule for a Fixed-Payment Loan

The early 1990s were a time of relatively high interest rates as compared to current rates. Bailey & Co. borrowed $4000 at prime plus $1\frac{1}{2}$% from its bank on January 5, 1990 to purchase a piece of equipment. The floating-rate demand loan requires fixed monthly payments of $1000 on the first day of each month, beginning February 1. The prime rate was at 13.5% on January 5 and increased to 14.25% effective February 15, and 14.75% effective April 23. Construct a full repayment schedule showing details of the allocation of each payment to interest and principal.

SOLUTION

On a loan repayment schedule, enter the dates of payments and interest rate changes in chronological order. Information known about these events can also be entered. We can anticipate that a fifth payment (of less than $1000) on June 1 will pay off the loan. At this point, the schedule has the following entries:

Date	Number of days	Interest rate (%)	Interest ($)	Accrued interest ($)	Payment (advance) ($)	Principal portion ($)	Balance ($)
Jan. 5	—	15	—	—	(4,000)	(4,000.00)	4,000.00
Feb. 1		15			1,000		
Feb. 15		15					
Mar. 1		15.75			1,000		
Apr. 1		15.75			1,000		
Apr. 23		15.75					
May 1		16.25			1,000		
June 1		16.25					

Proceed with the calculations row by row. The circled numbers (①, ②, etc.) in the following schedule refer to sample calculations listed after the schedule. Draw a stroke through an accrued interest figure when the interest has been paid.

Date	Number of days	Interest rate (%)	Interest ($)	Accrued interest ($)	Payment (advance) ($)	Principal portion ($)	Balance ($)
Jan. 5	—	15	—	—	(4,000)	(4,000.00)	4,000.00
Feb. 1	27	15	44.38 ①	~~44.38~~	1,000	955.62 ②	3,044.38
Feb. 15	14	15	17.52	17.52			3,044.38
Mar. 1	14	15.75	18.39	~~35.91~~	1,000	964.09	2,080.29
Apr. 1	31	15.75	27.83	~~27.83~~	1,000	972.17	1,108.12
Apr. 23	22	15.75	10.52	10.52			1,108.12
May 1	8	16.25	3.95	~~14.47~~	1,000	985.53	122.59
June 1	31	16.25	1.69	~~1.69~~	124.28 ③	122.59	0

① $I = Prt = \$4000(0.15)\left(\frac{27}{365}\right) = \$44.38$.
② Principal portion = $\$1000 - \$44.38 = \$955.62$.
③ Final payment = $\$122.59 + \$1.69 = \$124.28$.

➡ **Check your understanding:** Redo the repayment schedule. This time, the prime rate was 3.75% on January 5, dropped to 3.5% effective February 15, and dropped again to 3.25% effective April 23. How much will the final payment be on June 1 if all other details about the loan remain the same? (Answer: Final payment on June 1 = $40.35)

▬▶ **Related problem:** #5 in Exercise 7.4

EXERCISE 7.4

Answers to the odd-numbered problems can be found in the end matter.

INTERMEDIATE PROBLEMS

Revolving Demand Loans

1. On the June 12 interest payment date, the outstanding balance on Delta Nurseries' revolving loan was $65,000. The floating interest rate on the loan stood at 6.25% on June 12, but rose to 6.5% on July 3, and to 7% on July 29. An additional $10,000 was drawn on June 30. What were the interest charges to Delta's bank account on July 12 and August 12?

2. Dr. Robillard obtained a $75,000 operating line of credit at prime plus 1%. Accrued interest up to but not including the last day of the month is deducted from his bank account on the last day of each month. On February 5 (of a non-leap-year) he received the first draw of $15,000. He made a payment of $10,000 toward principal on March 15, but took another draw of $7000 on May 1. Prepare a loan repayment schedule showing the amount of interest charged to his bank account on the last days of February, March, April, and May. Assume that the prime rate remained at 2.7% through to the end of May.

3. McKenzie Wood Products negotiated a $200,000 revolving line of credit with the Bank of Montreal at prime plus 2%. On the 20th of each month, interest is calculated (up to but not including the 20th) and deducted from the company's chequing account. If the initial loan advance of $25,000 on July 3 was followed by a further advance of $30,000 on July 29, how much interest was charged on July 20 and August 20? The prime rate was at 3% on July 3 and fell to 2.75% on August 5.

Fixed-Payment Demand Loans

4. A $5000 demand loan was advanced on June 3. Fixed monthly payments of $1000 were required on the first day of each month beginning July 1. Prepare the full repayment schedule for the loan. Assume that the interest rate remained at 8.75% for the life of the loan.

5. Keesha borrowed $7000 from her credit union on a demand loan on July 20 to purchase a motorcycle. The terms of the loan require fixed monthly payments of $1400 on the first day of each month, beginning September 1. The floating rate on the loan started at 8.75%, but rose to 9.25% on August 19, and to 9.5% effective November 2. Prepare a loan repayment schedule presenting the amount of each payment and the allocation of each payment to interest and principal.

ADVANCED PROBLEMS

Revolving Demand Loans

6. Mr. Michaluk has a $50,000 personal (revolving) line of credit with the Canadian Imperial Bank of Commerce (CIBC). The loan is on a demand basis at a floating rate of prime plus 1.5%. On the 15th of each month, a payment equal to the greater of $100 or 3% of the combined principal and accrued interest is deducted from his chequing account. The principal balance after a payment on September 15 stood at $23,465.72. Prepare the loan repayment schedule from September 15 up to and including the payment on January 15. Assume that he makes the minimum payments and the prime rate is 2.85% for the entire time.

7. Bronwyn's $15,000 line of credit is at prime plus 2.5%. The minimum payment (the greater of $100 or 3% of the combined principal and accrued interest) is automatically deducted from her chequing account on the 15th of each month. After the payment on August 15, her balance was $3589.80. To reduce the loan more quickly, she makes an additional discretionary payment of $300 on the last day of each month. Each $300 payment is applied entirely to principal. Prepare a repayment schedule for the August 15 to November 15 period. The prime rate was at 3.25% on August 15 but dropped 0.25% effective October 11.

Fixed-Payment Demand Loans

8. Giovando, Lindstrom & Co. obtained a $6000 demand loan at prime plus 1.5% on April 1 to purchase new office furniture. The company agreed to fixed monthly payments of $1000 on the first of each month, beginning May 1. Calculate the total interest charges over the life of the loan if the prime rate started at 3.00% on April 1, decreased to 2.85% effective June 7, and returned to 3.00% on August 27. Present a repayment schedule in support of your answer.

9. Dr. Chan obtained a $15,000 demand loan at prime plus 1.5% on September 13 from the Bank of Montreal to purchase a new dental X-ray machine. Fixed payments of $700 will be deducted from the dentist's chequing account on the 20th of each month, beginning October 20. The prime rate was 7.5% at the outset, dropped to 7.25% on the subsequent November 26, and rose to 7.75% on January 29. Prepare a loan repayment schedule showing the details of the first five payments.

7.5   Canada Student Loans

The first significant debt incurred by many who pursue post-secondary education is a student loan. All provincial governments and the federal government offer student loan programs. Only the federal government's Canada Student Loans Program (CSLP) is discussed in this section. Currently about 475,000 students (representing about one-third of full-time post-secondary enrollment) borrow over $2.6 billion per year under the program. Students in five provinces (British Columbia, Saskatchewan, Ontario, New Brunswick, and Newfoundland and Labrador) access Canada Student Loans in conjunction with the provincial student loan programs. In these "integrated" provinces, students receive one loan that is a combination of both federal and provincial funding. In the other provinces, students may access loans separately from both their province and the CSLP.

No interest is charged on Canada Student Loans as long as you retain full-time student status (at least 60% of a full course load) under the CSLP. Six months after you cease to be a student, you must begin to make monthly loan payments. For example, if final examinations end on May 7 and you do not return to college the following September, the six-month grace period runs from June 1 to November 30. Interest accrues at the floating rate of prime $+ 2\frac{1}{2}\%$ during this period. You may pay the accrued interest at the end of the grace period or have it *capitalized* (that is, converted to principal).

Before the end of the grace period, you must make arrangements with the National Student Loans Service Centre to consolidate all Canada Student Loans into a single loan. The first payment on a consolidated loan is due one month after the end of the grace period. In the preceding example, the first payment is due December 31.

At the time of consolidation, you choose either a *floating* interest rate of prime plus $2\frac{1}{2}\%$ or a *fixed* rate equal to the prime rate (at the time of consolidation) plus 5%. The choice may not be changed later. You also choose the amount of the *fixed* monthly payment subject to a maximum term of 114 months.

The interest portion of each monthly payment is calculated using the daily-interest method with the exact number of days since the previous payment. A loan repayment schedule can be constructed using the same format as for demand loans in Section 7.4. (Canada Student Loans are not demand loans from the lender's point of view. However, the borrower may prepay additional principal at any time without penalty.)

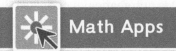

Math Apps

CANADA STUDENT LOANS: HOW TO MANAGE YOUR DEBT AFTER GRADUATION

Do you have a student loan? If so, you are certainly in the majority of post-secondary students across Canada. Most estimates agree that about 60% of all post-secondary students will have a debt load after graduation, with money owed on bank loans, lines of credit, credit cards, or on public loans under the Canada Student Loans Program (CSLP). If debt to family members is included, the estimate of 60% would likely be much higher, as many graduates report that they expect to repay loans from family members after graduation.

Student debt is an issue that concerns the Federation of Students. In a report titled "The Impact of Student Debt," the Federation points out that rising tuition costs are creating heavy loan burdens for graduates. The report estimates that, of those who do have debt when they graduate, the average debt load is over $28,000, and that the accumulated debt owed to the Canada Student Loans Program is a staggering $16 billion. This debt is usually repaid over many years after the student graduates, resulting in high interest costs. If, for example, a student with the average debt of $28,000 takes 10 years to repay a Canada Student Loan, the total interest paid could easily be in excess of $10,000 by the time the graduate is debt-free. The Federation points out that student debt can result in graduates delaying important life decisions like permanently moving out of their parents' home or buying a home of their own.

While many people agree that borrowing to fund your education is a smart investment that will result in long-term improvements in earning power, managing that debt upon graduation is very important. Being proactive and educated about your student loan repayment will help build your credit rating, and making smart choices will minimize the total time it will take to repay your debt. Here are some tips to keep in mind about how to manage your student debt load:

- *Thinking about not paying? Think again.* We have all heard stories of people who have gotten away with not repaying their student loans. It is estimated that, in the past, the Government of Canada wrote off up to $300 million each year of loans from people for whom up-to-date contact information was not available. But in 2015, the then-Conservative federal government changed processes to help government departments more easily share information. The likelihood of the government simply losing track of you has decreased! The Canada Revenue Agency has the authority to withhold tax returns, garnish your wages, or seize assets to get the money that you owe!

- *Make lump-sum payments.* Any small amount you can put toward your student loan over and above the regular repayment schedule will help you repay your debt faster, and will save you interest costs. So, when you graduate, if you find yourself with $100 left over at the end of the month, instead of going out for a fancy dinner, or buying a new pair of shoes, consider putting that extra money toward your student loan. These extra payments, over and above the regular monthly payments that are established, can significantly reduce the time it takes for you to become debt-free! Although we all like to treat ourselves to rewards for our hard work, repayment of your debt as quickly as possible will allow you bigger and better rewards in the future!

- *Increase your payment amount.* When you begin repaying your student loan, you will work with your loan provider to set up a repayment schedule. Consider "rounding up" your monthly payments. For example, if your required monthly payments are $128, consider increasing that to $150. Every extra dollar you pay each month goes straight to repaying the principal.

- *Apply for tax credits.* The interest paid on your student loans is eligible for a 15% tax credit every year. Ensure you are applying for that credit on every year's tax return.

- *Ask for help.* If you find yourself in financial difficulty, be proactive. Don't let your loan go into default or just choose not to make a payment. Contact the National Student Loans Service Centre to discuss your situation *before* things get out of hand. You may be eligible for temporary relief from your payments, or you may be offered various forms of assistance, depending upon your circumstances. Just remember that repayment assistance is not automatic; *you* must initiate the conversation. Waiting until your loan is in default can make you ineligible for repayment assistance. The problem will not go away by your ignoring it, so be proactive and explore your options well in advance of a financial crisis emerging.

| EXAMPLE 7.5A | Constructing a Repayment Schedule for a Canada Student Loan |

Heidi had Canada Student Loans totalling $10,600 when she graduated from college. Her six-month grace period ended on November 30, and she chose to have the grace period's accrued interest converted to principal. Heidi selected the floating-interest-rate option (prime plus 2.5%) when the prime rate was at 3.5%. Monthly payments beginning December 31 were set at $150.

Prepare a loan repayment schedule up to and including the payment on the following March 31. The intervening February had 29 days. The prime rate increased from 3.5% to 3.75% effective August 3, and rose another 0.5% effective January 14.

SOLUTION

The period from June 1 to August 3 has $215 - 152 = 63$ days, and the period from August 3 to (and including) November 30 has $334 + 1 - 215 = 120$ days. The accrued interest at the end of the grace period was

$$\begin{aligned}
I &= P_1 r_1 t + P_2 r_2 t \\
&= \$10,600(0.06)\left(\tfrac{63}{365}\right) + \$10,600(0.0625)\left(\tfrac{120}{365}\right) \\
&= \$109.78 + \$217.81 \\
&= \$327.59
\end{aligned}$$

The consolidated loan balance at the end of November was

$$\$10,600.00 + \$327.59 = \$10,927.59$$

Date	Number of days	Interest rate (%)	Interest ($)	Accrued interest ($)	Payment (advance) ($)	Principal portion ($)	Balance ($)
Dec. 1	—	6.25	—	—	—	—	10,927.59
Dec. 31	30	6.25	56.13 ①	~~56.13~~	150	93.87	10,833.72
Jan. 14	14	6.25	25.97	25.97			10,833.72
Jan. 31	17	6.75	34.06	~~60.03~~	150	89.97	10,743.75
Feb. 29	29	6.75	57.62	~~57.62~~	150	92.38	10,651.37
Mar. 31	31	6.75	61.06	~~61.06~~	150	88.94	10,562.43

① $I = Prt = \$10,927.59(0.0625)\left(\tfrac{30}{365}\right) = \$56.13$.

➡ **Check your understanding:** Redo the repayment schedule. This time, the prime rate was 5.5% when Heidi selected the floating-interest-rate option. The prime rate increased to 5.75% effective August 3, and fell to 5.65% effective January 14. What will be the balance on Heidi's loan on March 31? (Answer: $10,730.25)

▣▣▣➤ **Related problem:** #1 in Exercise 7.5

INTERMEDIATE PROBLEMS

1. Sarah's Canada Student Loans totalled $9400 by the time she graduated from Georgian College in May. She arranged to capitalize the interest on November 30 and to begin monthly payments of $135 on December 31. Sarah elected the floating-rate-interest option (prime plus 2.5%). The prime rate stood at 3.75% on June 1, dropped to 3.5% effective September 3, and then increased by 0.25% on January 17. Prepare a repayment schedule presenting details of the first three payments. February has 28 days.

2. Kari had Canada Student Loans totalling $3800 when she completed her program at Niagara College in December. She had enough savings at the end of June to pay the interest that had accrued during the six-month grace period. Kari made arrangements with the National Student Loans Service Centre to start end-of-month payments of $60 in July. She chose the fixed-interest-rate option (at prime plus 5%) when the prime rate was at 2.7%. Prepare a loan repayment schedule up to and including the September 30 payment.

3. Harjap completed his program at Nova Scotia Community College in December. On June 30, he paid all of the interest that had accrued (at prime plus 2.5%) on his $5800 Canada Student Loan during the six-month grace period. He selected the fixed-rate option (prime plus 5%) and agreed to make end-of-month payments of $95 beginning July 31. The prime rate was 2.7% at the beginning of the grace period and rose by 0.5% effective March 29. On August 13, the prime rate rose another 0.5%. The relevant February had 28 days.

   a. What amount of interest accrued during the grace period?

   b. Calculate the total interest paid in the first three regular payments, and the balance owed after the third payment. (*Hint:* Remember that the fixed-rate option means that the student is locking in the interest rate at the time the repayment schedule begins.)

ADVANCED PROBLEMS

4. Monica finished her program at New Brunswick Community College on June 3 with Canada Student Loans totalling $6800. She decided to capitalize the interest that accrued (at prime plus 2.5%) during the grace period. In addition to regular end-of-month payments of $200, she made an extra $500 lump payment on March 25 that was applied entirely to principal. The prime rate dropped from 5% to 4.75% effective September 22, and declined another 0.5% effective March 2. Calculate the balance owed on the floating-rate option after the regular March 31 payment. The relevant February had 28 days.

5. Seth had accumulated Canada Student Loans totalling $5200 by the time he graduated from Mount Royal College in May. He arranged with the National Student Loans Service Centre to select the floating-rate option (at prime plus $2\frac{1}{2}$%), to capitalize the grace period's accrued interest, and to begin monthly payments of $110 on December 31. Prepare a loan repayment schedule up to and including the February 28 payment. The prime rate was initially at 3.25%. It dropped by 0.25% effective January 31. Seth made an additional principal payment of $300 on February 14.

Key Terms

Commercial paper	Face value	Loan repayment schedule
Demand loan	Fair market value	Savings account
Discount rate	Guaranteed Investment	Treasury bill
Discounting a payment	Certificate (GIC)	

Summary of Notation and Key Formulas

Valuation Principle

The fair market value of an investment is the sum of the present values of the cash flows expected from the investment. The discount rate used in the present value calculations should be the prevailing market-determined rate of return on this type of investment.

Review Problems

Answers to the odd-numbered review problems can be found in the end matter.

BASIC PROBLEMS

1. **LO1** Seth has a savings account balance of $1834.38 on May 1. On May 8 his balance increased to $2400 and remained there until the end of the month. His account pays 1.85% per annum. Interest is calculated on the daily closing balance and paid on the first day of the next month. How much interest will be credited to Seth's account on June 1?

2. **LO2** An investment promises to pay $27,500 in 8 months from now. How much should an investor be willing to pay for this investment today if the market rate of return is 4.25%?

3. **LO3** Calculate the price of a $50,000, 91-day Province of Nova Scotia Treasury bill on its issue date when the market rate of return was 1.273%.

4. **LO3** A $100,000, 90-day commercial paper certificate issued by Bell Canada Enterprises was sold on its issue date for $98,950. What annual rate of return (to the nearest 0.001%) will it yield to the buyer?

5. **LO1** How much interest will be earned on a 91-day, $65,000 term deposit that pays an interest rate of 1.15%?

6. **LO1** What will be the maturity value of $5500 placed in a 120-day term deposit paying an interest rate of 2.75%?

INTERMEDIATE PROBLEMS

7. **LO2** An agreement stipulates payments of $4500, $3000, and $5500 in 4, 8, and 12 months, respectively, from today. What is the highest price an investor will offer today to purchase the agreement if he requires a minimum rate of return of 5.5%?

8. `LO1` An Investment Savings account offered by a trust company pays a rate of 0.50% on the first $1000 of daily closing balance, 1.00% on the portion of the balance between $1000 and $3000, and 1.5% on any balance in excess of $3000. What interest will be paid for the month of January if the opening balance was $3678, $2800 was withdrawn on the 14th of the month, and $950 was deposited on the 25th of the month?

9. `LO3` A $100,000, 182-day Province of New Brunswick Treasury bill was issued 66 days ago. What will it sell at today to yield the purchaser 2.48%?

10. `LO5` Mayfair Fashions has a $90,000 line of credit from the Bank of Montreal. Interest at prime plus 2% is deducted from Mayfair's chequing account on the 24th of each month. Mayfair initially drew down $40,000 on March 8 and another $15,000 on April 2. On June 5, $25,000 of principal was repaid. If the prime rate was 3.00% on March 8 and fell by 0.25% effective May 13, what were the first four interest deductions charged to the store's account?

11. `LO5` Ms. Wadeson obtained a $15,000 demand loan from TD Canada Trust on May 23 to purchase a car. The interest rate on the loan was prime plus 2%. The loan required payments of $700 on the 15th of each month, beginning June 15. The prime rate was 4.5% at the outset, dropped to 4.25% on July 26, and then jumped by 0.5% on September 14. Prepare a loan repayment schedule showing the details of the first four payments.

12. `LO5` Ruxandra's Canada Student Loans totalled $7200 by the time she finished Conestoga College in April. The accrued interest at prime plus 2.5% for the grace period was converted to principal on October 31. She chose the floating-interest-rate option and began monthly payments of $120 on November 30. The prime rate of interest was 3.5% on May 1, 3.25% effective July 9, and 4% effective December 13. Prepare a repayment schedule presenting details of the first three payments.

ADVANCED PROBLEMS

13. `LO1` Paul has $20,000 to invest for six months. For this amount, his bank pays 1.3% on a 90-day GIC and 1.5% on a 180-day GIC. If the interest rate on a 90-day GIC is the same three months from now, how much more interest will Paul earn by purchasing the 180-day GIC than by buying a 90-day GIC and then reinvesting its maturity value in a second 90-day GIC?

14. `LO1` Suppose that the current rates on 60- and 120-day GICs are 1.50% and 1.75%, respectively. An investor is weighing the alternatives of purchasing a 120-day GIC versus purchasing a 60-day GIC and then reinvesting its maturity value in a second 60-day GIC. What would the interest rate on 60-day GICs have to be 60 days from now for the investor to end up in the same financial position with either alternative?

15. `LO2` A conditional sale contract requires two payments three and six months after the date of the contract. Each payment consists of $1900 principal plus interest at 10.5% on $1900 from the date of the contract. One month into the contract, what price would a finance company pay for the contract if it requires a 16% rate of return on its purchases?

16. `LO3` A $25,000, 91-day Province of Newfoundland Treasury bill was originally purchased at a price that would yield the investor a 1.438% rate of return if the T-bill is held until maturity. Thirty-four days later, the investor sold the T-bill through his broker for $24,928.
    a. What price did the original investor pay for the T-bill?
    b. What rate of return will the second investor realize if she holds the T-bill until maturity?
    c. What rate of return did the first investor realize during his holding period?

17. **LO5** Duncan Developments Ltd. obtained a $120,000 line of credit from its bank to subdivide a parcel of land it owned into four residential lots and to install water, sewer, and underground electrical services. Amounts advanced from time to time are payable on demand to its bank. Interest at prime plus 4% on the daily principal balance is charged to the developer's bank account on the 26th of each month. The developer must apply at least $30,000 from the proceeds of the sale of each lot against the loan principal. Duncan drew down $50,000 on June 3, $40,000 on June 30, and $25,000 on July 17. Two lots quickly sold, and Duncan repaid $30,000 on July 31 and $35,000 on August 18. The initial prime rate of 3% changed to 3.25% effective July 5 and 3.5% effective July 26. Prepare a repayment schedule showing loan activity and interest charges up to and including the interest payment on August 26.

18. **LO5** George borrowed $4000 on demand from CIBC on January 28 for an RRSP contribution. Because he used the loan proceeds to purchase CIBC's mutual funds for his RRSP, the interest rate on the loan was set at the bank's prime rate. George agreed to make monthly payments of $600 (except for a smaller final payment) on the 21st of each month, beginning February 21. The prime rate was initially 3.75%, dropped to 3.5% effective May 15, and decreased another 0.25% on July 5. It was not a leap year. Construct a repayment schedule showing the amount of each payment and the allocation of each payment to interest and principal.

© moodboard/agefotostock RF

CHAPTER 8
Compound Interest: Future Value and Present Value

LEARNING OBJECTIVES
After completing this chapter, you will be able to:

LO1 Calculate the future value and present value in compound interest applications, by both the algebraic method and the preprogrammed financial calculator method

LO2 Calculate the maturity value of compound-interest Guaranteed Investment Certificates (GICs)

LO3 Calculate the redemption value of a compound-interest Canada Savings Bond

LO4 Calculate the price of strip bonds

LO5 Adapt the concepts and equations from compound interest to compound growth

LO6 Calculate the payment on any date that will create equivalence between alternate payment systems

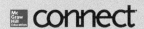 **connect** Throughout this chapter interactive charts and Help Me Solve It videos are marked with a ↗.

EXAMPLES OF COMPOUND INTEREST ARE easy to find. If you obtain a loan to purchase a car, interest will be compounded monthly. The advertised interest rates on mortgage loans are semiannually compounded rates. Interest is always compounded in long-term financial planning. So if you wish to take

control of your personal financial affairs or to be involved in the financial side of a business, you must thoroughly understand compound interest and its applications. The remainder of this textbook is devoted to the mathematics and applications of compound interest.

You will be able to hit the ground running! In Chapters 6 and 7, you learned the concepts of maturity value, time value of money, future value, and present value for the case of simple interest. These ideas transfer to compound interest. Now we just need to develop new mathematics for calculating future value and present value when interest is compounded. And there is good news in this regard! Most compound interest formulas are permanently programmed into financial calculators. After you become competent in the algebraic method for solving compound interest problems, your instructor may allow you to use a financial calculator to perform the computations. Before long, you will be impressed at the range of applications you can handle!

8.1 | Basic Concepts

The *simple* interest method discussed in Chapter 6 is restricted primarily to loans and investments having terms of less than one year. The *compound* interest method is employed in virtually all instances where the term exceeds one year. It is also used in some cases where the duration is less than one year.

In the **compound interest method**, interest is *periodically* calculated and *converted* to principal. "Converting interest to principal" means that the interest is added to the principal and is thereafter treated as principal. Consequently, interest earned in one period will itself earn interest in all subsequent periods. The time interval between successive interest conversion dates is called the **compounding period**. Suppose, for example, you invest $1000 at 10% compounded annually. "Compounded annually" means that "interest is compounded once per year." Therefore, the compounding period is one year. On each anniversary of the investment, interest will be calculated and converted to principal. The process is indicated in Figure 8.1. The original $1000 investment is represented by the column located at "0" on the time axis. During the first year, you will earn $100 interest (10% of $1000). At the end of the first year, this $100 will be converted to principal. The new principal ($1100) will earn $110 interest (10% of $1100) in the second year. Note that you earn $10 more interest in the second year than in the first year because you have $100 more principal invested at 10%. How much interest will be earned in the third year? Do you see the pattern developing? Each year you will earn more interest than in the preceding year—$100 in the first year, $110 in the second year, $121 in the third year, and so on. Consequently, the growth in value of the investment will accelerate as the years pass.

In contrast, if the $1000 earns 10% per annum *simple* interest, only the *original* principal will earn interest ($100) each year. A $1000 investment will grow by just $100 each year. After two years, your investment will be worth only $1200 (compared to $1210 with annual compounding).

In many circumstances, interest is compounded more frequently than once per year. The number of compoundings per year is called the **compounding frequency**. The commonly used frequencies and their corresponding compounding periods are listed in Table 8.1.

TABLE 8.1   Compounding Frequencies and Periods

Compounding frequency	Number of compoundings per year	Compounding period
Annually	1	1 year
Semiannually	2	6 months
Quarterly	4	3 months
Monthly	12	1 month

A compound interest rate is normally quoted with two components:
- A number for the annual interest rate
- Words stating the compounding frequency

FIGURE 8.1 Converting Interest to Principal at the End of Each Compounding Period

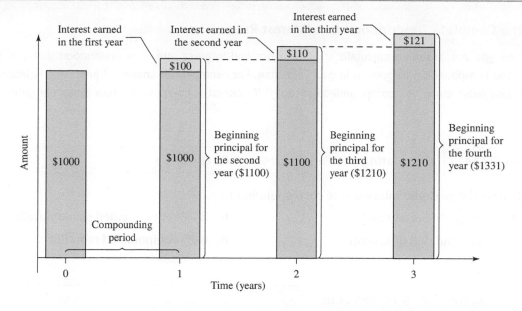

The two components together are called the **nominal interest rate**.[1] For example, an interest rate of 4% compounded semiannually means that 2% (half of the 4% nominal annual rate) is earned and compounded each six-month compounding period. A rate of 6% compounded monthly means that 0.5% (one-twelfth of 6%) is earned and compounded each month. We use the term **periodic interest rate** for the interest rate per compounding period. In the two examples at hand, the periodic interest rates are 2% and 0.5%, respectively. In general,

$$\text{Periodic interest rate} = \frac{\text{Nominal interest rate}}{\text{Number of compoundings per year}}$$

If we define the following symbols:

$$j = \text{Nominal interest rate}$$
$$m = \text{Number of compoundings per year}$$
$$i = \text{Periodic interest rate}$$

the simple relationship between the periodic interest rate and the nominal interest rate is

PERIODIC INTEREST RATE $$i = \frac{j}{m}$$ (8-1)

TRAP

"*m*" for Quarterly Compounding

What is the value of *m* for quarterly compounding? Sometimes students incorrectly use $m = 3$ with quarterly compounding because $\frac{1}{4}$ year = 3 months. But *m* represents the number of compoundings per year (4), not the length of the compounding period.

---

[1] As you will soon understand, you cannot conclude that $100 invested for one year at 4% compounded semiannually will earn exactly $4 of interest. Therefore, we use the word "nominal," meaning "in name only," to describe the quoted rate.

2. What is meant by the future value of an investment?

3. For a given nominal interest rate (say 10%) on a loan, would the borrower prefer it to be compounded annually or compounded monthly? Which compounding frequency would the lender prefer? Give a brief explanation.

4. For a six-month investment, rank the following interest rates (number one being "most preferred"): 6% per annum simple interest, 6% compounded semiannually, 6% compounded quarterly. Explain your ranking.

5. From a *simple inspection*, is it possible for an investor to rank the four rates of return in each of Parts (a) and (b)? If so, state the ranking. Give a brief explanation to justify your answer.

   a. 4.0% compounded monthly, 4.1% compounded quarterly, 4.2% compounded semiannually, 4.3% compounded annually.

   b. 4.0% compounded annually, 4.1% compounded semiannually, 4.2% compounded quarterly, 4.3% compounded monthly.

6. Why is $100 received today worth more than $100 received at a future date?

EXERCISE 8.2

Answers to the odd-numbered problems can be found in the end matter.

Note: In Section 8.4, you will learn how to use special functions on a financial calculator to solve compound-interest problems. Exercise 8.4 will invite you to return to this exercise to practise the financial calculator method.

BASIC PROBLEMS

1. What is the maturity value of $5000 invested at 6.0% compounded semiannually for 7 years?

2. What is the future value of $8500 after $5\frac{1}{2}$ years if it earns 1.2% compounded quarterly?

3. What was a $4400 investment worth after $6\frac{3}{4}$ years if it earned 5.4% compounded monthly?

4. Assume that a $10,000 investment can earn 4% compounded quarterly. What will be its future value

   a. after 15 years?   b. after 20 years?

   c. after 25 years?   d. after 30 years?

5. How much will $10,000 be worth after 25 years if it earns

   a. 3% compounded semiannually?   b. 4% compounded semiannually?

   c. 5% compounded semiannually?   d. 6% compounded semiannually?

6. To what amount will $10,000 grow after 25 years if it earns

   a. 6% compounded annually?   b. 6% compounded semiannually?

   c. 6% compounded quarterly?   d. 6% compounded monthly?

7. By calculating the maturity value of $100 invested for 1 year at each rate, determine which rate of return an investor would prefer for a 1-year investment.

   a. 8.0% compounded monthly   b. 8.1% compounded quarterly

   c. 8.2% compounded semiannually   d. 8.3% compounded annually

8. By calculating the maturity value of $100 invested for 5 years at each rate, determine which rate of return an investor would prefer for a 5-year investment.

   a. 2.28% compounded monthly

   b. 2.29% compounded quarterly

   c. 2.30% compounded semiannually

   d. 2.31% compounded annually

INTERMEDIATE PROBLEMS

9. What is the maturity value of a $12,000 loan for 18 months at 5.2% compounded quarterly? How much interest is charged on the loan?

10. What total interest will be earned by $5000 invested at 2.4% compounded monthly for $3\frac{1}{2}$ years?

11. How much more will an investment of $10,000 be worth after 25 years if it earns 5% compounded annually instead of 4% compounded annually? Calculate the difference in dollars and as a percentage of the smaller maturity value.

12. How much more will an investment of $10,000 earning 2% compounded annually be worth after 25 years than after 20 years? Calculate the difference in dollars and as a percentage of the smaller maturity value.

13. A $1000 investment is made today. Calculate its maturity values for the nine combinations of terms and annually compounded rates of return in the following table.

		Term	
Rate of return (%)	20 years	25 years	30 years
3	?	?	?
9	?	?	?
9	?	?	?

14. Interest rates were at historical highs in the early 1980s. In August of 1981, you could earn 17.5% compounded annually on a 5-year term deposit with a Canadian bank. Since then, the interest rate offered on 5-year term deposits has dropped dramatically. In February 2016, for example, major Canadian banks were offering 1.25% compounded annually on a 5-year term deposit. On a $10,000 deposit for a term of 5 years, how much more would you have earned at the historical high interest rate than at the more recent low rate?

15. Noori borrowed $5000 for $4\frac{1}{2}$ years. For the first $2\frac{1}{2}$ years, the interest rate on the loan was 8.4% compounded monthly. Then the rate became 5.5% compounded semiannually. What total amount was required to pay off the loan if no payments were made before the expiry of the $4\frac{1}{2}$-year term?

16. An investment of $2500 earned interest at 4.5% compounded quarterly for $1\frac{1}{2}$ years, and then 4.0% compounded monthly for 2 years. How much interest did the investment earn in the $3\frac{1}{2}$ years?

17. What amount today is equivalent to $10,000 four years ago, if money earned 3.5% compounded monthly over the past 4 years?

18. A $5000 payment due $1\frac{1}{2}$ years ago has not been paid. If money can earn 8.25% compounded quarterly, what amount paid today would be the economic equivalent of the missed payment?

19. A $2300 payment due $1\frac{1}{2}$ years ago has not been paid. If money can earn 6.25% compounded semiannually, what amount in 2 years from now would be the economic equivalent to the missed payment?

20. What amount 3 years from now is economically equivalent to $4000 due five months from now? Assume that money can earn 3% compounded monthly.

21. Stefan borrowed $12,000 at an interest rate of 6% compounded semiannually. On the 2nd and 4th anniversaries of the loan, he made payments of $3000. What payment made on the 6th anniversary of the loan will extinguish the debt?

22. Teresa borrowed $8500 at an interest rate of 8% compounded quarterly. Two years after the loan was advanced she made a payment of $3000. Five years after the loan was advanced she made a payment of $2000. What final payment made 8 years after the loan was advanced will extinguish the debt?

23. Payments of $1300 due today and $1800 due in $1\frac{3}{4}$ years from today are to be replaced by a single payment 4 years from now. What is the amount of that payment if money is worth 6% compounded quarterly?

24. Bjorn defaulted on payments of $2000 due 3 years ago and $1000 due $1\frac{1}{2}$ years ago. What would a fair settlement to the payee be $1\frac{1}{2}$ years from now if the money could have been invested to earn 4.2% compounded semiannually?

25. Sabrina invested $7200 three years ago, and an additional $2300 one year ago. Her investments have earned 3.5% compounded quarterly for the whole time.

    a. How much are Sabrina's investments worth today?

    b. How much interest has she earned altogether?

26. How much more interest would Aman earn on an investment of $150,000 for ten years if he is able to negotiate a rate of 6% compounded monthly instead of the advertised rate of 5.4% compounded monthly?

27. For a 15-year investment, would an investor prefer a rate of return of 3.27% compounded quarterly or 3.3% compounded semiannually? Show calculations to support your answer.

ADVANCED PROBLEMS

28. Alberto has just invested $60,000 in a 5-year Guaranteed Investment Certificate (GIC) earning 3% compounded semiannually. When the GIC matures, he will reinvest its entire maturity value in a new 5-year GIC. What will be the maturity value of the second GIC if it yields

    a. the same rate as the current GIC?

    b. 4% compounded semiannually?

    c. 2% compounded semiannually?

29. Faisal borrowed $3000, $3500, and $4000 from his father on January 1 of three successive years at college. Faisal and his father agreed that interest would accumulate on each amount at the rate of 5% compounded semiannually. Faisal is to start repaying the loan one year after the $4000 loan. What consolidated amount will he owe at that time?

30. A loan of $4000 at 4.5% compounded monthly requires three payments of $1000 at 6, 12, and 18 months after the date of the loan, and a final payment of the full balance after two years. What is the amount of the final payment?

31. Megan borrowed $1900, $3\frac{1}{2}$ years ago at 7% compounded semiannually. Two years ago she made a payment of $1000. What amount is required today to pay off the remaining principal and the accrued interest?

8.3 | Present Value

If money can earn 6% compounded annually, what amount *today* is equivalent to $1000 paid five years from now? This is an example of determining a payment's **present value**—an economically equivalent amount at an *earlier* date. In this instance, the present value is the (principal) amount you would have to invest at 6% compounded annually in order to end up with $1000 after five years. To calculate this initial investment, we need only rearrange $FV = PV(1 + i)^n$ to isolate PV, and then substitute the values for FV, i, and n. Dividing both sides of the formula by $(1 + i)^n$ leaves PV by itself on the right side. We thereby obtain a second version of formula (8-2):

$$PV = \frac{FV}{(1 + i)^n} = FV(1 + i)^{-n}$$

In summary, $PV = FV(1 + i)^{-n}$ applies to two types of problems:

- Calculating the initial investment needed to produce a particular maturity value, FV
- Calculating the present value of a scheduled payment, FV

TIP

Efficient Use of Your Calculator

Calculating PV using $FV(1 + i)^{-n}$ leads to a more efficient calculation than using $\frac{FV}{(1 + i)^n}$. To illustrate, we will evaluate $FV(1 + i)^{-n}$ for the values $FV = \$1000$, $n = 5$, and $i = 6\%$ (from the question posed at the beginning of this section). We have $PV = \$1000(1.06)^{-5}$. The number of keystrokes is minimized if we reverse the order of multiplication and evaluate $1.06^{-5} \times \$1000$. Enter the following keystroke sequence.

$$1.06 \boxed{y^x} \; 5 \boxed{+/-} \boxed{\times} \; 1000 \boxed{=}$$

The $\boxed{+/-}$ key must be pressed immediately after entering the number whose sign is to be reversed. After the $\boxed{\times}$ key is pressed, 0.747258173 (the value of 1.06^{-5}) appears in the display. The final $\boxed{=}$ keystroke executes the multiplication, giving $747.26 in the display.

The present value of a future payment will, of course, always be a smaller number than the payment. This is why the process of calculating a payment's present value is sometimes described as **discounting a payment**. The interest rate used in the present value calculation is then referred to as the **discount rate**.

The longer the time period before a scheduled payment, the smaller the present value will be. Figure 8.5 shows the pattern of decreasing present value for longer periods *before* the payment date. The decline is rapid in the first 10 years, but steadily tapers off at longer periods. With a discount rate of 10% compounded annually, the present value 7 years before the payment is about half the *numerical* value of the payment. Twenty-five years prior to the payment, the present value is less than one-tenth of the payment's size! In practical terms, payments that will be received more than 25 years in the future have little *economic* value today.

How would Figure 8.5 change for a discount rate of 8% compounded annually? And how would it differ for a discount rate of 12% compounded annually?

TIP

Numerical Values vs. Economic Values

In terms of numerical values, a present value is smaller than the payment, and a future value is larger than the payment. However, these *numerically different* amounts all have the *same economic* value. For example, suppose a $100 payment is due one year from now, and money can earn 10% compounded annually. Today's present value is $100(1.10)^{-1} = \$90.91$. The future value two years from now is $110.00. The three amounts all have the same economic value, namely the value of $90.91 *current* dollars.

FIGURE 8.5   The Present Value of $1000 (discounted at 10% compounded annually)

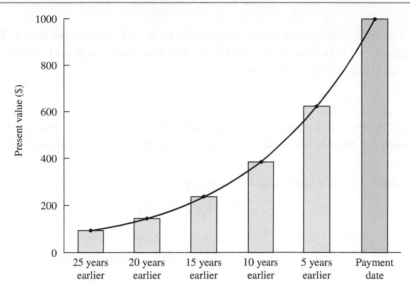

EXAMPLE 8.3A	The Investment Needed to Reach a Particular Future Value

If an investment can earn 4% compounded monthly, what amount must you invest now in order to accumulate $10,000 after $3\frac{1}{2}$ years?

SOLUTION

Given: $j = 4\%$, $m = 12$, $FV = \$10{,}000$, Term = 3.5 years

Then $\qquad i = \dfrac{j}{m} = \dfrac{4\%}{12} = 0.\overline{3}\%$ per month   and $n = m(\text{Term}) = 12(3.5) = 42$

Rearranging formula (8-2) to solve for PV,

$$PV = FV\,(1 + i)^{-n} = \$10{,}000(1.00333333)^{-42} = \$8695.61$$

You must invest $8695.61 now in order to have $10,000 after $3\frac{1}{2}$ years.

➡ **Check your understanding:** If an investment can earn 3% compounded semiannually, what amount must you invest now in order to accumulate $15,000 after 15 years? (Answer: $9596.44)

▬▬▶ **Related problem:** #1 in Exercise 8.3

TIP

Efficient Use of Your Calculator

If you use any fewer than six 3s in the value for *i* in Example 8.3A, you will have some round-off error in the calculated value for *PV*. For the fewest keystrokes and maximum accuracy in your answer, avoid manual re-entry of calculated values. The most efficient sequence of keystrokes resulting in the highest accuracy of *PV* in Example 8.3A is

0.04 $\div$ 12 $+$ 1 $=$ y^x 42 $+/-$ $\times$ 10000 $=$

When you employ the calculated value of *i* in this way, the calculator actually uses more than the seven 3s you see in the display (after pressing the first $=$ in the preceding sequence). The calculator maintains and uses two or three more figures than are shown in the display. In subsequent example problems, this procedure will be assumed but will not be shown.

EXAMPLE 8.3B	Calculating an Equivalent Payment at an Earlier Date

Mr. and Mrs. Espedido's property taxes, amounting to $2450, are due on July 1. What amount should the city accept if the taxes are paid eight months in advance and the city can earn 1.2% compounded monthly on surplus funds?

SOLUTION

The city should accept an amount that is equivalent to $2450, allowing for the rate of interest that the city can earn on its surplus funds. This equivalent amount is the present value of $2450, eight months earlier.

Given: $FV = \$2450, j = 1.2\%$ compounded monthly, $m = 12, n = 8$

Then
$$i = \frac{j}{m} = \frac{1.2\%}{12} = 0.1\% \text{ (per month)}$$

and   Present value, $PV = FV(1 + i)^{-n} = \$2450(1.001)^{-8} = \$2430.49$

The city should be willing to accept $2430.49 on a date eight months before the scheduled due date.

➡ **Check your understanding:** Suppose the Espedido's property taxes amounting to $3875 are due on July 1. What amount should the city accept if the taxes are paid nine months in advance and the city can earn 4% compounded quarterly on surplus funds? (Answer: $3761.04)

◼▶ **Related problem:** #9 in Exercise 8.3

EXAMPLE 8.3C	Calculating an Equivalent Value of Two Payments

Two payments of $10,000 each must be made one year and four years from now. If money can earn 6% compounded monthly, what single payment two years from now would be equivalent to the two scheduled payments?

SOLUTION

When more than one payment is involved in a problem, it is helpful to present the given information in a time diagram. Some of the calculations that need to be done may be indicated on the diagram. In this case, we can indicate the calculation of the equivalent values by constructing arrows from the scheduled payments to the date of the replacement payment. Then we write the relevant values for i $\left(\frac{6\%}{12} = 0.5\%\right)$ and n on each arrow.

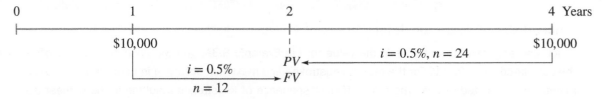

The single equivalent payment is equal to $PV + FV$.

$$FV = \text{Future value of } \$10,000, 12 \text{ months later}$$
$$= \$10,000(1.005)^{12}$$
$$= \$10,616.778$$

$$PV = \text{Present value of } \$10,000, \text{ 24 months earlier}$$
$$= \$10,000(1.005)^{-24}$$
$$= \$8871.857$$

The equivalent single payment is

$$\$10,616.778 + \$8871.857 = \$19,488.64$$

⮕ **Check your understanding:** Two payments of $8000 each must be made 3 years and 6 years from now. If money can earn 3.4% compounded quarterly, what single payment 5 years from now would be equivalent to the two scheduled payments? (Answer: $16,294.15)

▮▮▯▸ **Related problem:** #19 in Exercise 8.3

EXAMPLE 8.3D	Demonstrating Economic Equivalence

Show why the recipient of the payments in Example 8.3C should be indifferent between receiving the scheduled payments and receiving the replacement payment.

SOLUTION

If the recipient ends up in the same economic position with either alternative, then he should not care which alternative is used.

We will calculate how much money the recipient will have four years from now with each alternative, assuming that any amounts received are invested at 6% compounded monthly.

The two alternatives are presented in the two following time diagrams.

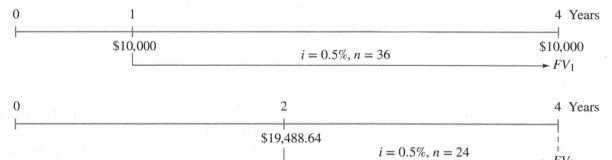

With the scheduled payments, the total amount that the recipient will have after four years is

$$FV_1 + \$10,000 = \$10,000(1.005)^{36} + \$10,000$$
$$= \$11,966.805 + \$10,000$$
$$= \$21,966.81$$

With the single replacement payment, the recipient will have

$$FV_2 = \$19,488.64(1.005)^{24} = \$21,966.81$$

With either alternative, the recipient will have $21,966.81 after four years. Therefore, the replacement payment is economically equivalent to the scheduled payments.

⮕ **Check your understanding:** Show why the recipient of the payments in the Check Your Understanding feature of Example 8.3C should be indifferent between receiving the scheduled payments and receiving the replacement payment. (Answer: With either alternative, the recipient will have $16,855.25 after six years.)

▮▮▯▸ **Related problem:** #23 in Exercise 8.3

A General Principle Regarding the Present Value of Loan Payments

Let us work through a problem that illustrates a very important principle. We will use the data and results from Example 8.2D. In that example, three payments of $1500 each were made on a $5000 loan at one-year intervals after the date of the loan. The interest rate on the loan was 5% compounded quarterly. The problem was to determine the additional payment needed to pay off the loan at the end of the fourth year. The answer was $1125.17.

We will now calculate the sum of the present values of all four payments at the date on which the loan was granted. Use the interest rate on the loan as the discount rate. The calculation of each payment's present value is given in the following table.

Payment	Amount, FV	N	i	PV = FV(1 + i)$^{-n}$
First	$1500.00	4	1.25%	$PV_1 = $ $1500(1.0125)^{-4} = $1427.29
Second	$1500.00	8	1.25%	$PV_2 = $ $1500(1.0125)^{-8} = $1358.10
Third	$1500.00	12	1.25%	$PV_3 = $ $1500(1.0125)^{-12} = $1292.26
Fourth	$1125.17	16	1.25%	$PV_4 = $1125.17(1.0125)^{-16} = $ $922.35
				Total: $5000.00

Note that the sum of the present values is $5000.00, precisely the original principal amount of the loan. *This outcome will occur for all loans.* The payments do not need to be equal in size or to be at regular intervals. The fundamental principle is highlighted below because we will use it repeatedly in later work.

Present Value of Loan Payments

The sum of the present values of all of the payments required to pay off a loan is equal to the original principal of the loan. The discount rate for the present-value calculations is the rate of interest charged on the loan.

EXAMPLE 8.3E	Calculating Two Unknown Loan Payments

Jenna borrowed $4000 from Liz at an interest rate of 5% compounded semiannually. The loan is to be repaid by three payments. The first payment, $1000, is due two years after the date of the loan. The second and third payments are due three and five years, respectively, after the initial loan. How much will the second and third payments be if the loan agreement requires that those two payments be equal in amount?

SOLUTION

In Example 8.2D, we solved a similar problem but only the last of four loan payments was unknown. In this problem, two payments are unknown and it would be difficult to use the approach of Example 8.2D. However, the fundamental principle developed in this section may be used to solve a wide range of loan problems (including Example 8.2D). Applying this principle to the problem at hand, we have

Sum of the present values of the three payments = $4000

The given data are presented on the time line below. If we let x represent the second payment, then the third payment must also be x. Notice how the idea expressed by the preceding word equation can (and should) be indicated on the diagram.

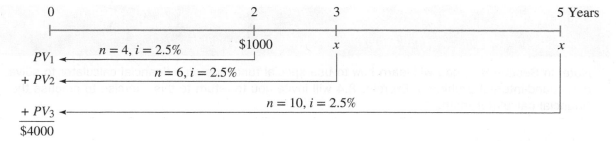

The second and third payments must be of sizes that will make

$$PV_1 + PV_2 + PV_3 = \$4000 \;\; ①$$

We can obtain a numerical value for PV_1, but the best we can do for PV_2 and PV_3 is to express them in terms of x. That is just fine—after we substitute these values into equation ①, we will be able to solve for x.

$$PV_1 = FV(1 + i)^{-n} = \$1000(1.025)^{-4} = \$905.951$$
$$PV_2 = x(1.025)^{-6} = 0.862296866x$$
$$PV_3 = x(1.025)^{-10} = 0.781198402x$$

Now substitute these values into equation ① and solve for x.

$$\$905.951 + 0.862296866x + 0.781198402x = \$4000$$
$$1.643495268x = \$3094.049$$
$$x = \frac{\$3094.049}{1.643495268}$$
$$x = \$1882.60$$

Jenna's second and third payments will be $1882.60 each.

▶ **Check your understanding:** Pete borrowed $5000 from Kenneth at an interest rate of 6% compounded quarterly. The 1st payment of $2000 was made 1 year after the date of the loan. The 2nd and 3rd payments are due 3 and 4 years, respectively, after the initial loan. Calculate the amount of the 2nd and 3rd payments if the loan agreement requires that these payments be equal in amount. (Answer: Each payment will be $1918.00.)

■■▶ **Related problem:** #31 in Exercise 8.3

 ## Checkpoint Questions

1. Circle "True" or "False" for each of the following:
   a. All else being equal, a smaller discount rate will result in a smaller present value.   True   False
   b. All else being equal, a longer term will result in a smaller present value.   True   False
   c. In practical terms, payments that will be received more than 25 years in the future have little economic value today in a compound interest environment.   True   False

2. What is the meaning of the term *discount rate*?

3. The process of discounting is the opposite of doing what?

4. Why does $100 due one year from now have less economic value than $100 has today? What do you need to know before you can determine the difference between the economic values of the two payments?

EXERCISE 8.3

Note: In Section 8.4, you will learn how to use special functions on a financial calculator to solve compound-interest problems. Exercise 8.4 will invite you to return to this exercise to practise the financial calculator method.

BASIC PROBLEMS

1. If money can be invested to earn 1.5% compounded annually, how much would have to be invested today to grow to $10,000 after

    a. 10 years?   **b.** 20 years?   **c.** 30 years?

2. What amount would have to be invested today for the future value to be $10,000 after 20 years if the rate of return is

    a. 4% compounded quarterly?   **b.** 6% compounded quarterly?

    c. 8% compounded quarterly?

3. What amount invested today would grow to $10,000 after 25 years if the investment earns

    a. 4% compounded annually?   **b.** 4% compounded semiannually?

    c. 4% compounded quarterly?   **d.** 4% compounded monthly?

4. What is the present value of $10,000 discounted at 4.5% compounded annually over 10 years?

5. What principal amount will have a maturity value of $4976.68 after 27 months if it earns 4.5% compounded quarterly?

6. The maturity value of an investment after 42 months is $8689.32. What was the original investment if it earned 4.25% compounded semiannually?

7. What amount today is economically equivalent to $8000 paid 18 months from now if money is worth 5% compounded monthly?

8. You owe $6000 payable three years from now. What alternative amount should your creditor be willing to accept today if she can earn 2.1% compounded monthly on a low-risk investment?

9. Sarah is scheduled to receive $6500 three years from now. What amount could Sarah accept today as an economically equivalent payment if her funds can earn 5% compounded semiannually?

10. When Rheal was born, her grandmother made a lump sum investment that would provide Rheal with $50,000 when she turned age 18. If the investment earned 5.5% compounded semi-annually during the entire 18-year period, how much did Rheal's grandmother invest on the day of Rheal's birth?

11. How much would you need to invest today in order to have a total of $200,000 in 20 years from now if your funds earn

    a. 3.6% compounded annually?

    b. 3.6% compounded monthly?

INTERMEDIATE PROBLEMS

12. Ross has just been notified that the combined principal and interest on an amount that he borrowed 27 months ago at 5% compounded quarterly is now $2012.93. How much of this amount is principal and how much is interest?

13. Jazrinder invested an amount 42 months ago that has now grown to be worth a total of $4200. How much did Jazrinder originally invest if she has earned 4.1% compounded semiannually during the entire term?

14. Mustafa can receive a $40 discount if he pays his property taxes early. Alternatively, he can pay the full amount of $2250 when payment is due in 9 months. Which alternative is to his advantage if he can earn 3% compounded monthly on short-term investments? In current dollars, how much is the advantage?

15. What amount, $1\frac{1}{2}$ years from now, is equivalent to $7000 due in 8 years if money can earn 5.2% compounded semiannually?

16. What amount 15 months ago is equivalent to $2600, $1\frac{1}{2}$ years from now? Assume money can earn 5.4% compounded monthly.

17. Alicia is considering two offers-to-purchase that she has received on a residential building lot she wishes to sell. One is a cash offer of $146,500. The other offer consists of three payments of $49,000—one now, one in six months, and one in twelve months. Which offer has the larger economic value if Alicia can earn 1.4% compounded quarterly on low-risk investments? How much more (in current dollars) is the better offer worth?

18. A payment of $1300 is scheduled for a date $3\frac{1}{2}$ years from now. What would be an equivalent payment 9 months from now if money is worth 3.5% compounded quarterly?

19. What single amount, paid 3 years from now, would be economically equivalent to the combination of $1400 due today and $1800 due in 5 years if funds can be invested to earn 6% compounded quarterly?

20. A bond pays $1000 interest at the end of every year for the next 30 years. What is the *current* economic value of each of the 15th and 30th payments if we discount the payments at

    a. 4% compounded semiannually?

    b. 8% compounded semiannually?

21. Mohinder has financial obligations of $1000 due in $3\frac{1}{2}$ years and $2000 due in $5\frac{1}{2}$ years. He wishes to settle the obligations sooner with a single payment 1 year from now. If money is worth 3.75% compounded semiannually, what amount should the payee be willing to accept?

22. Ramon wishes to replace payments of $900 due today and $500 due in 22 months by a single equivalent payment 18 months from now. If money is worth 5% compounded monthly, what should that payment be?

23. Maria was scheduled to pay Johann $6500 in two years from now, and an additional $8500 in six years from now.

    a. What single equivalent payment should Johann accept in three years from now instead of the two scheduled payments if he can earn 6% compounded quarterly on his investments?

    b. If Johann accepts the single payment calculated in Part (a), show calculations to prove that he will be in the same financial position six years from now as if Maria had made the two originally scheduled payments.

24. What payment $2\frac{1}{4}$ years from now would be a fair substitute for the combination of $1500 due (but not paid) 9 months ago and $2500 due in $4\frac{1}{2}$ years from now, if money can earn 3.5% compounded quarterly?

25. What single payment one year from now would be equivalent to $2500 due in three months, and another $2500 due in two years? Money is worth 7% compounded quarterly.

26. What single payment six months from now would be equivalent to payments of $500 due (but not paid) four months ago, and $800 due in 12 months? Assume money can earn 3.9% compounded monthly.

27. Joe Superstar has just signed a "four-year, $68-million deal" with the Toronto Blue Jays. The terms of the contract include a signing bonus of $4.8 million and salaries of $10 million, $17.2 million, $17.5 million, and $18.5 million in successive years of the contract. The news media always ignore the time value of money when they report the "value" of professional athletes' contracts. What is the economic value of Joe's contract on the date it was signed? Assume that the signing bonus was paid on that date, that the annual salaries will be paid in lump amounts $\frac{1}{2}$ year, $1\frac{1}{2}$ years, $2\frac{1}{2}$ years, and $3\frac{1}{2}$ years later, and that money is worth 5% compounded semiannually. Round the answer to the nearest $1000.

28. To motivate individuals to start saving at an early age, financial planners will sometimes present the results of the following type of calculation. Patrick and Leslie are exactly the same age. Patrick invested $1000 at age 25 and will leave his funds invested until age 55. If Leslie waits until age 30 to make her investment, how much will she need to deposit in order to have the same maturity value at age 55 as Patrick? Assume that both investments earn 3% compounded annually.

ADVANCED PROBLEMS

29. Teresita has three financial obligations to the same person: $2800 due in 1 year, $1900 due in $1\frac{1}{2}$ years, and $1100 due in 3 years. She wishes to settle the obligations with a single payment in $2\frac{1}{4}$ years, when her inheritance will be released from her mother's estate. What amount should the creditor accept if money can earn 2% compounded quarterly?

30. Michelle has just received an inheritance from her grandfather's estate. She will be entering college in $3\frac{1}{2}$ years, and wants to immediately purchase three compound-interest investment certificates having the following maturity values and dates: $4000 at the beginning of her first academic year, $5000 at the start of her second year, and $6000 at the beginning of her third year. She can obtain interest rates of 5% compounded semiannually for any terms between 3 and 5 years, and 5.6% compounded quarterly for terms between 5 and 7 years. What principal amount should she invest in each certificate?

31. A $4000 loan at 5% compounded monthly is to be repaid by two equal payments due 10 and 15 months from the date of the loan. What is the size of the payments?

32. A $15,000 loan at 5.5% compounded semiannually is advanced today. Two payments of $4000 are to be made 1 year and 3 years from now. The balance is to be paid in 5 years. What will the third payment be?

33. A $6000 loan at 6% compounded quarterly is to be settled by two payments. The first payment is due after nine months and the second payment, half the amount of the first payment, is due after $1\frac{1}{2}$ years. Determine the size of each payment.

8.4 | Using Financial Calculators

The formulas for many compound-interest calculations are permanently programmed into financial calculators. These calculators allow you to enter the numerical values for the variables into memory. Then you select the appropriate financial function to automatically perform the calculation.

Ideally, you should be able to solve compound-interest problems using both the algebraic method and the financial functions on a calculator. The algebraic approach strengthens your mathematical skills and provides more flexibility for handling non-standard cases. It helps prepare you to create spreadsheets for specific applications. Financial calculators make routine calculations more efficient and reduce the likelihood of making arithmetic errors. Most of the example problems from this point onward will present both algebraic and financial calculator solutions.

Key Definitions and Calculator Operation

The financial calculator instructions and keystrokes shown in the main body of this text and in the Student's Solutions Manual are for the Texas Instruments BA II PLUS. General instructions for two other models are provided in Appendices 8A and 10A.

The basic financial keys of the Texas Instruments BA II PLUS calculator are in the third row of its keyboard. The calculator's manual refers to them as the TVM (Time-Value-of-Money) keys. The definitions for these keys are as follows.

N	represents the number of compounding periods, n
I/Y	represents the nominal (annual) interest rate, j
PV	represents the principal or present value, PV
PMT	represents the periodic annuity payment (not used until Chapter 10)
FV	represents the maturity value or future value, FV

Each of the five keys has two uses:
1. Saving in memory a numerical value for the variable
2. Computing the value of the variable (based on previously saved values for all other variables)

As an example, let us compute the future value of $1000 invested at 5% compounded semiannually for 3 years. We must first enter values for N , I/Y , PV , and PMT. They may be entered in any order. To save $1000 in the PV memory, just enter the digits for 1000 and press PV . The display then shows[3]

> PV =   1,000.

Next enter values for the other variables in the same manner. (You do not need to clear your display between entries.) Note that the *nominal interest rate must be entered in percent form* (without the % symbol) rather than in its decimal equivalent form. For all compound interest problems in this chapter and Chapter 9, the value "0" must be stored in the PMT memory. (This tells the calculator that there is no regular annuity payment.) In summary, the keystrokes for entering these four known values are

> 1000 PV   6 N   5 I/Y   0 PMT

Do you think the calculator now has enough information to compute the future value? Note that we have not yet entered any information about the compounding frequency. To key in and save the value for the number of compoundings per year, you must first gain access to a particular list of internal settings. Note the *P/Y* symbol above the *I/Y* key. This indicates that the *P/Y* settings worksheet is the second function of the *I/Y* key. Therefore, to open this worksheet, press the key labelled "2nd" followed by the key labelled "*I/Y*." Hereafter, we will represent this keystroke combination by

> 2nd P/Y

After pressing these two keys, your calculator's display will show something like

> P/Y =   12.

This display is actually a "window" to the first item in a list of just two items as shown below.

> P/Y =   12.
> C/Y =   12.

---

[3] The assumption here is that the calculator has previously been set for "floating-decimal format." See the Appendix to this chapter for instructions on setting this format on the "Format worksheet."

You can scroll down to the second item by pressing the [↓] key. The definitions for these new symbols are:

P/Y represents the number of annuity payments per year

C/Y represents the number of compoundings per year

Therefore, C/Y corresponds to the algebraic symbol m.

If the calculation does not involve an annuity, P/Y must be given the same value as C/Y. This requirement does not come from any logic or line of reasoning. It is just a result of the particular way Texas Instruments has programmed the calculator. This requirement applies to all problems in this chapter and Chapter 9. In the current example, we have semiannual compounding. Therefore, we need to set both P/Y and C/Y equal to 2. To do that, scroll back up to the P/Y line in the list. Then press

2 [ENTER]

The calculator display now shows

$P/Y =$	2.

Next, scroll down to C/Y. Observe that its value has automatically changed to 2. Entering a new value for P/Y *always* causes C/Y to change automatically to the same value. So for all problems in this chapter and Chapter 9, we need only set $P/Y = m$. That will produce the desired result of making $C/Y = P/Y = m$. Later in Chapter 10, P/Y and C/Y will have differing values in some annuity problems. We will deal with this matter when needed.

Before we can compute the future value of the $1000, we must close the P/Y settings worksheet. Note that the second function of the key labelled CPT is QUIT. Pressing

[2nd] [QUIT]

will close whatever worksheet is open. Then, to execute the future value calculation, press

[CPT] [FV]

The calculator will display

$FV =$	−1,159.693418

Rounded to the nearest cent, the future value of the $1000 investment is $1159.69. The significance of the negative sign will be discussed in the next subsection.

Let's summarize the complete sequence of keystrokes needed for the future value calculation.

1000 [PV] 6 [N] 5 [I/Y] 0 [PMT]

[2nd] [P/Y] 2 [ENTER] [2nd] [QUIT] [CPT] [FV]

TIP

Efficient Use of Your Calculator

You can operate your calculator more efficiently if you take advantage of the following features.

1. After any computation, all internal settings and numbers saved in memory are retained until you change them or clear them. Therefore, you do not need to re-enter a variable's value if it is unchanged in a subsequent calculation.

2. Whenever you *accidentally* press one of the five financial keys, the number in the display at that moment will be saved as the value of that financial variable. At any time, you can check the value stored in a financial key's memory by pressing RCL followed by the key.

3. When you turn the calculator off, it still retains the internal settings and the values in memory. (When the calculator's battery becomes weak, this feature and other calculator operations are unreliable.)

Cash-Flow Sign Convention

Cash flow is a term frequently used in finance and accounting to refer to a cash payment. A cash inflow is a cash receipt; a cash outflow is a cash disbursement. A cash *inflow* should be saved in a financial calculator's memory as a *positive* value. A cash *outflow* should be entered as a *negative* number. These two simple rules have a rather overblown name in finance—the **cash-flow sign convention**.

Cash-Flow Sign Convention
Cash inflows (receipts) are positive.
Cash outflows (disbursements) are negative.

All financial calculators use the cash-flow convention. Finance courses and finance textbooks use it. The financial functions in spreadsheet software employ it. The greatest benefits from using the sign convention come in later chapters. However, we will introduce it now so you can become familiar with it before moving on to more complex cases.

To use the cash-flow sign convention, you must treat a compound interest problem as either an investment or a loan. The directions of the cash flows for these two cases are compared in the following table. When you invest money, you pay it (cash outflow) to some institution or individual. Later, you receive cash inflows from investment income and from the sale or redemption of the investment. In contrast, when you receive a loan, it is a cash inflow for you. The subsequent cash flows in the loan transaction are the loan payments (cash outflows).

Transaction	Initial cash flow	Subsequent cash flows
Investment	Outflow (negative)	Inflows (positive)
Loan	Inflow (positive)	Outflows (negative)

Now you can understand why your calculator gave a negative future value earlier in this section. Because we entered 1000 as a positive number in the PV memory, the calculator interpreted the $1000 as a loan. The computed future value represents the single payment required to pay off the loan. Since this payment is a cash outflow, the calculator displayed it as a negative number. To properly employ the sign convention for the initial $1000 investment, we should have entered 1000 in PV as a negative number. The calculator would then compute a positive future value—the cash inflow we will receive when the investment matures.

To illustrate the use of financial calculators, Examples 8.3A, 8.3C, and 8.3E will now be repeated as Examples 8.4A, 8.4B, and 8.4C, respectively.

EXAMPLE 8.4A | **The Investment Needed to Reach a Particular Future Value**

What amount must you invest now at 4% compounded monthly to accumulate $10,000 after $3\frac{1}{2}$ years?

SOLUTION

Given: $j = 4\%$, $m = 12$, $FV = \$10,000$, Term = 3.5 years

Then $n = m \times \text{Term} = 12(3.5) = 42$

Enter the known variables and then compute the present value.

42 [N] 4 [I/Y] 0 [PMT] 10000 [FV]

[2nd] [P/Y] 12 [ENTER] [2nd] [QUIT] [CPT] [PV]   *Answer:* −8,695.606596

Note that we entered the $10,000 as a positive value because it is the cash *inflow* you will receive 3.5 years from now. The answer is negative because it represents the investment (cash outflow) that must be made today. Rounded to the cent, the initial investment required is $8695.61.

➡ **Check your understanding:** If an investment can earn 3% compounded semiannually, what amount must you invest now in order to accumulate $15,000 after 15 years? Use a financial calculator to solve this problem. (Answer: $9596.44)

▮▮▷ **Related problem:** #1 in Exercise 8.3

EXAMPLE 8.4B | **Calculating an Equivalent Value of Two Payments**

Two payments of $10,000 each must be made one year and four years from now. If money can earn 6% compounded monthly, what single payment two years from now would be equivalent to the two scheduled payments?

SOLUTION

Given: $j = 6\%$ compounded monthly, making $m = 12$ and $i = \frac{j}{m} = \frac{6\%}{12} = 0.5\%$

Other data and the solution strategy are shown on the following time line. FV_1 represents the future value of the first scheduled payment and PV_2 represents the present value of the second payment.

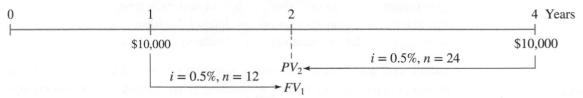

The single equivalent payment is $FV_1 + PV_2$. Before we start crunching numbers, let's exercise your intuition. Do you think the equivalent payment will be greater or smaller than $20,000? It is clear that FV_1 is greater than $10,000 and that PV_2 is less than $10,000. When the two amounts are added, will the sum be more than or less than $20,000? We can answer this question by comparing the time intervals through which we "shift" each of the $10,000 payments. The first payment will have one year's growth added, but the second payment will be discounted by two years' growth.[4] Therefore, PV_2 is farther below $10,000 than FV_1 is above $10,000. Hence, the equivalent payment will be less than $20,000. So if your equivalent payment turns out to be more than $20,000, you will know that your solution has an error. Returning to the calculations,

FV_1: 12 [N] 6 [I/Y] 10000 [PV] 0 [PMT]

      [2nd] [P/Y] 12 [ENTER] [2nd] [QUIT] [CPT] [FV] *Answer:* −10,616.778

PV_2: Do not clear the values and settings currently in memory. Then you need enter only those values and settings that change.

    24 [N] 10000 [FV] [CPT] [PV] *Answer:* −8,871.857

The equivalent payment two years from now is $10,616.778 + $8871.857 = $19,488.64.

➡ **Check your understanding:** Two payments of $8000 each must be made 3 years and 6 years from now. If money can earn 3.4% compounded quarterly, what single payment 5 years from now would be equivalent to the two scheduled payments? Use a financial calculator to solve this problem. (Answer: $16,294.15)

▮▮▮▶ **Related problem:** #19 in Exercise 8.3

Note: An equivalent payment problem is neither a loan nor an investment situation. Loans and investments always involve at least one cash flow in each direction. In contrast, an equivalent payment is a payment that can *substitute for* one or more other payments. The substitute payment will flow in the *same* direction as the payment(s) it replaces. So how should you apply the cash-flow sign convention to equivalent payment calculations? Just enter the scheduled payments as positive numbers and ignore the opposite sign on the calculated equivalent value.

EXAMPLE 8.4C	Calculating Two Unknown Loan Payments

Jenna borrowed $4000 from Liz at an interest rate of 5% compounded semiannually. The loan is to be repaid by three payments. The first payment, $1000, is due 2 years after the date of the loan. The second and third payments are due 3 and 5 years, respectively, after the initial loan. How much will the second and third payments be if the loan agreement requires that those two payments be equal in amount?

SOLUTION

Given: $j = 5\%$ compounded semiannually making $m = 2$ and $i = \frac{j}{m} = \frac{5\%}{2} = 2.5\%$

Let x represent the second and third payments. As indicated in the following diagram, PV_1, PV_2, and PV_3 represent the present values of the first, second, and third payments.

---

[4] You cannot conclude that the difference between PV_2 and $10,000 will be twice the difference between $10,000 and FV_2. To illustrate this sort of effect, consider that at 10% compounded annually, the future value of $100 one year later is $110 but the present value of $100 one year earlier is $90.91. We see that the increase ($10) when compounding ahead one year exceeds the decrease ($9.09) when discounting back one year.

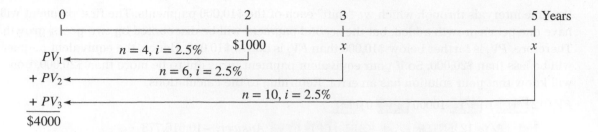

Since the sum of the present values of all payments equals the original loan, then

$$PV_1 + PV_2 + PV_3 = \$4000 \; ①$$

PV_1: 4 $\boxed{\text{N}}$ 5 $\boxed{\text{I/Y}}$ 0 $\boxed{\text{PMT}}$ 1000 $\boxed{\text{FV}}$

$\boxed{\text{2nd}}$ $\boxed{\text{P/Y}}$ 2 $\boxed{\text{ENTER}}$ $\boxed{\text{2nd}}$ $\boxed{\text{QUIT}}$ $\boxed{\text{CPT}}$ $\boxed{\text{PV}}$ *Answer:* −905.951

At first, we may be stumped as to how to proceed for PV_2 and PV_3. Let's think about the second payment of x dollars. We can compute the present value of just $1 from the x dollars.

6 $\boxed{\text{N}}$ 1 $\boxed{\text{FV}}$ $\boxed{\text{CPT}}$ $\boxed{\text{PV}}$ *Answer:* −0.862296866

The present value of $1 paid 3 years from now is $0.862296866 (about $0.86). Consider the following questions (Q) and their answers (A).

Q: What is the present value of $2?   A: It's about 2 × $0.86 = $1.72.

Q: What is the present value of $5?   A: It's about 5 × $0.86 = $4.30.

Q: What is the present value of x?   A: Extending the preceding pattern, the present value of x is about $x × $0.86 = $0.86x$. Precisely, it is
$PV_2 = \$0.862296866x$.

Similarly, calculate the present value of $1 from the third payment of x dollars. The only variable that changes from the previous calculation is $\boxed{\text{N}}$.

10 $\boxed{\text{N}}$ $\boxed{\text{CPT}}$ $\boxed{\text{PV}}$ *Answer:* −0.781198402

Hence, the present value of the third payment is

$$PV_3 = x(\$0.781198402) = \$0.781198402x$$

Now substitute the values for PV_1, PV_2 and PV_3 into equation ① and solve for x.

$$\$905.951 + 0.862296866x + 0.781198402x = \$4000$$
$$1.643495268x = \$3094.049$$
$$x = \frac{\$3094.049}{1.643495268}$$
$$x = \$1882.60$$

Jenna's second payment and third payments will be $1882.60 each.

⟹ **Check your understanding:** Pete borrowed $5000 from Kenneth at an interest rate of 6% compounded quarterly. The first payment of $2000 was made 1 year after the date of the loan. The second and third payments are due 3 and 4 years, respectively, after the initial loan. Using a financial calculator, calculate the amount of the second and third payments if the loan agreement requires that these payments be equal in amount. (Answer: Each payment will be $1918.00.)

▮▮▮▶ **Related problem:** #31 in Exercise 8.3

8.5   Other Applications of Compounding

Compound-Interest Investments

The two most common types of compound-interest investments owned by Canadians are Guaranteed Investment Certificates and Canada Savings Bonds.

LO2   Guaranteed Investment Certificates (GICs) GICs may be purchased from banks, credit unions, life insurance companies, trust companies, and caisses populaires (mostly in Quebec). When you buy a GIC from a financial institution, you are in effect lending money to it or to one of its subsidiaries. The financial institution uses the funds raised from selling GICs to make loans—most commonly, mortgage loans. The interest rate charged on mortgage loans is typically 1.5% to 2% higher than the interest rate paid to GIC investors. The word "Guaranteed" in the name of this investment refers to the *unconditional guarantee* of principal and interest by the parent financial institution. In addition to this guarantee, there is usually some form of government-regulated deposit insurance.

Most Guaranteed Investment Certificates are purchased with maturities in the range of one to five years. Longer maturities (up to 10 years) are available, but are not covered by deposit insurance. Normally, you earn higher interest rates for longer maturities. Early redemption restrictions apply to many types of GICs. You must accept lower interest rates for more generous redemption privileges. The following diagrams present typical alternatives for redemption privileges, the structure of interest rates, and the payment of interest.

Redemption Privileges

Non-redeemable: No portion of the principal may be withdrawn before maturity.	**Partially redeemable:** A limited portion of the principal may be withdrawn on the GIC's anniversary dates.	**Fully cashable:** The entire principal may be withdrawn on any date.

Structure of Interest Rates

Fixed rate: The interest rate does not change over the term of the GIC.	**Step-up rate:** The interest rate is increased every six months or every year according to a *predetermined* schedule.	**Variable rate:** The interest rate is adjusted every six months or every year to reflect prevailing market rates. There may be a minimum "floor," below which rates cannot drop.

Payment of Interest

Regular interest version: Interest only is paid periodically to the investor.	Compound interest version: Interest is periodically converted to principal and paid at maturity.

The regular interest versions of GICs are not mathematically interesting, as periodic interest is paid out to the investor instead of being converted to principal. For compound interest versions, there are two mathematically distinct cases:

1. If the interest rate is *fixed*, use $FV = PV(1 + i)^n$ to calculate the maturity value.
2. If the interest rate is either a *variable rate* or a *step-up rate*, the periodic rate i can differ for each compounding period. Then you must use a more general version of formula (8-2) that allows for a different $(1 + i)$ factor for each compounding period. That is, use

FUTURE VALUE (VARIABLE AND STEP-UP INTEREST RATES) $FV = PV(1 + i_1)(1 + i_2)(1 + i_3) \cdots (1 + i_n)$ **(8-4)**

EXAMPLE 8.5A   Calculating the Payment from a Regular Interest GIC

What periodic payment does an investor receive from a $9000, four-year, monthly payment GIC earning a nominal rate of 0.9% payable monthly? (Only the accrued interest is paid each month.)

SOLUTION

The interest rate per payment interval is

$$i = \frac{j}{m} = \frac{0.9\%}{12} = 0.075\%$$

The monthly payment is

$$PV \times i = \$9000 \times 0.00075 = \$6.75$$

➡ **Check your understanding:** What periodic payment does an investor receive from a $14,000, three-year, monthly payment GIC earning a nominal rate of 2% payable monthly? (Only the accrued interest is paid each month.) (Answer: $23.33)

▬▬▶ **Related problem:** #1 in Exercise 8.5

EXAMPLE 8.5B   Comparing GICS Having Different Nominal Rates

Suppose a bank quotes nominal annual interest rates of 3.6% compounded annually, 3.5% compounded semiannually, and 3.4% compounded monthly on five-year compound-interest GICs. Which rate should an investor choose?

SOLUTION

An investor should choose the rate that results in the highest maturity value. The given information may be arranged in a table.

j	m	$i = \dfrac{j}{m}$	n
3.6%	1	3.6%	5
3.5	2	1.75	10
3.4	12	$0.28\overline{3}$	60

Choose an amount, say $1000, to invest. Calculate the maturity values for the three alternatives.

$$FV = PV(1 + i)^n$$

$= \$1000(1.036)^5 = \$1193.44$ for $j = 3.6\%$ compounded annually

$= \$1000(1.0175)^{10} = \$1189.44$ for $j = 3.5\%$ compounded semiannually

$= \$1000(1.00283\overline{3})^{60} = \$1185.02$ for $j = 3.4\%$ compounded monthly

Let's now calculate these same maturity values using our financial calculator. We will switch to a vertical format for presenting the keystrokes. The case $j = 3.6\%$ compounded annually is shown in Box 1. A good habit to develop for calculations in later chapters is to enter the interest rate information first. The first five lines (after the title) do this. The fourth line is just a reminder that, when we enter a new value for P/Y, it also changes C/Y to the same value. The sequence for entering the remaining values does not matter.

Box 1
$j = 3.6\%$ cmpd. annually
3.6 I/Y
2nd P/Y
1 ENTER
(making $C/Y = P/Y = 1$)
2nd QUIT
5 N
1000 +/– PV
0 PMT
CPT FV
Ans: 1193.44

Box 2
$j = 3.6\%$ cmpd. annually
3.6 I/Y
P/Y 1 ENTER
(making $C/Y = P/Y = 1$)
5 N
1000 +/– PV
0 PMT
CPT FV
Ans: 1193.44

Every time we need to change the value of P/Y or C/Y, we will have the same keystrokes 2nd P/Y to access these variables and the same keystrokes 2nd QUIT to return to the calculation. To avoid this repetition in our calculator solutions, we will shorten the display hereafter as shown in Box 2. It is left to you to supply the missing keystrokes.

The keystrokes for calculating the maturity values at the other two interest rates are displayed in Boxes

Box 3
$j = 3.5\%$ cmpd. semiann.
Same *PV, PMT*
3.5 I/Y
P/Y 2 ENTER
(making $C/Y = P/Y = 2$)
10 N
CPT FV
Ans: 1189.44

Box 4
$j = 3.4\%$ cmpd. monthly
Same *PV, PMT*
3.4 I/Y
P/Y 12 ENTER
(making $C/Y = P/Y = 12$)
60 N
CPT FV
Ans: 1185.02

3 and 4. The calculator's memories retain the most recent values if you do not clear the TVM memories. Therefore, we show only those values that change from the preceding calculation.

Answering the initial question, the investor should choose the GIC earning 3.6% compounded annually since it produces the highest maturity value.

➡ **Check your understanding:** Suppose a credit union quotes nominal annual interest rates of 4.75% compounded annually, 4.7% compounded semiannually, and 4.66% compounded monthly on three-year compound-interest GICs. Which rate should an investor choose? (Answer: 4.66% compounded monthly)

▰▰▶ **Related problem:** #5 in Exercise 8.5

EXAMPLE 8.5C	Maturity Value of a Variable-Rate GIC

A chartered bank offers a five-year "Escalator Guaranteed Investment Certificate." In successive years it earns annual interest rates of 1%, 1.5%, 2%, 2.5%, and 3%, respectively, *compounded* at the end of each year. The bank also offers regular five-year GICs paying a fixed rate of 2% compounded annually. Calculate and compare the maturity values of $1000 invested in each type of GIC. (Note that 2% is the average of the five successive one-year rates paid on the Escalator GIC.)

SOLUTION

Using formula (8-4), the maturity value of the Escalator GIC is

$$FV = \$1000(1.01)(1.015)(1.02)(1.025)(1.03) = \$1103.95$$

Using formula (8-2), the maturity value of the regular GIC is

$$FV = \$1000(1.02)^5 = \$1104.08$$

The Escalator GIC will mature at $1103.95, but the regular GIC will mature at $1104.08 ($0.13 more). We can also conclude from this example that a series of compound interest rates does not produce the same future value as the *average* rate compounded over the same period.

▶ **Check your understanding:** A trust company offers a regular four-year GIC paying a fixed rate of 3.7% compounded semiannually. The trust company also offers a four-year "Stepper GIC" that earns successive annual interest rates of 3%, 3.5%, 4%, and 4.5%, respectively, *compounded* at the end of each year. Calculate and compare the maturity values of $5000 invested in each type of GIC. (Answer: The regular GIC matures at $5789.73, while the Stepper GIC matures at $5792.92.)

▶ **Related problem:** #13 in Exercise 8.5

LO3 **Canada Savings Bonds (CSBs)** The Government of Canada finances a small portion of the federal debt[5] by issuing Canada Savings Bond products. More than a million Canadians own a Canada Savings Bond product, making them lenders to the federal government.

Canada Savings Bonds (CSBs) are only available for purchase through the Payroll Savings Program. Approximately 10,500 participating employers across the country allow their employees to purchase CSBs through regular payroll deductions. Historically, all CSBs carried a 10-year term. Starting in the fall of 2012, however, all CSBs now carry a 3-year term—a change instituted by the federal government in an attempt to make CSBs more attractive to Canadian investors.

Each batch of bonds sold on a particular date is assigned a series number. For example, the CSBs issued on November 1, 2015 are referred to as Series 133 (S133). All CSBs have variable interest rates—the Finance Department changes the interest rate for a particular series on that series' anniversary date. The interest rate is adjusted to bring it into line with prevailing rates. The interest rates paid on CSBs issued on November 1 each year are presented in Table 8.2.

---

[5] At the end of March 2015, the total outstanding amount of Canada Savings Bonds products was $3.91 billion. This represented 0.6% of Canada's net federal debt.

TABLE 8.2 Interest Rates (%) on Canada Savings Bonds*

Interest rate effective Nov. 1 of:	S108 (issued Nov. 1, 2007)	S114 (issued Nov. 1, 2008)	S120 (issued Nov. 1, 2009)	S126 (issued Nov. 1, 2010)	S128 (issued Nov. 1, 2011)	S130 (issued Nov. 1, 2012)	S131 (issued Nov. 1, 2013)	S132 (issued Nov. 1, 2014)	S133 (issued Nov. 1, 2015)
2007	3.25	2008	2.00	2.00					
2009	0.40	0.40	0.40						
2010	0.65	0.65	0.65	0.65					
2011	0.50	0.50	0.50	0.50	0.50				
2012	0.50	0.50	0.50	0.50	0.50	0.50			
2013	0.50	0.50	0.50	0.50	0.50	0.50	0.50		
2014	0.50	0.50	0.50	0.50	0.50	0.50	0.50	0.50	
2015	0.50	0.50	0.50	0.50	0.50	—	0.50	0.50	0.50
Matures Nov. 1 of:	2017	2018	2019	2020	2021	2015	2016	2017	2018

Source: Canada Savings Bonds Annual Interest Rates. Government of Canada. http://www.csb.gc.ca/wp-content/uploads/2014/10/s92_outstanding_csb_oec_circulation.pdf

Canada Savings Bonds are issued in regular-interest versions (called R-bonds) and compound-interest versions (called C-bonds). R-bonds pay a full year's interest to their owners on each anniversary of the issue date. C-bonds convert interest to principal on each anniversary.

Canada Savings Bonds may be redeemed at any time.[6] The following rules apply to calculating the interest for the *partial* year since the most recent anniversary date.

- Interest is accrued to the first day of the month in which redemption occurs. (If you redeem a CSB partway through a month, you receive no interest for the partial month.)
- Interest is calculated on a simple interest basis. That is, the additional interest for the partial year is $I = Prt$, where

P = The principal (including converted interest on compound-interest bonds) at the preceding anniversary date

r = The prescribed annual interest rate for the current year

t = The number of months (from the preceding anniversary date up to the first day of the month in which redemption occurs) divided by 12

EXAMPLE 8.5D	Calculating the Redemption Value of a Compound-Interest Canada Savings Bond

A $1000-face-value Series S126 compound-interest Canada Savings Bond (CSB) was presented to a credit union branch for redemption. What amount did the owner receive if the redemption was requested on

a. November 1, 2015?

b. January 17, 2016?

---

[6] In 1998, the Government of Canada started to issue another type of savings bond called Canada Premium Bonds (CPBs). CPBs are issued for a three-year term with the interest rate for the three years fixed at the date of issue. They may be redeemed at any time, but *interest will be paid only up to the last anniversary date of the bond's issue.* The investor forfeits interest for any partial year that the bond has been held. Because of this forfeiture of interest for partial years, Canada Premium Bonds pay a higher interest rate than Canada Savings Bonds. Unlike Canada Savings Bonds, which are available only through the Payroll Savings Program, Canada Premium Bonds are sold through financial institutions such as banks, credit unions, caisses populaires, and trust companies.

SOLUTION

a. In Table 8.2, we note that Series S126 CSBs were issued on November 1, 2010. November 1, 2015 falls on the fifth anniversary of the issue date. Substituting the annual interest rates for S126 bonds from Table 8.2 into formula (8-4), we have

$$FV = PV(1 + i_1)(1 + i_2)(1 + i_3)(1 + i_4)(1 + i_5)$$
$$= \$1000(1.0065)(1.005)(1.005)(1.005)(1.005)$$
$$= \$1026.78$$

The owner received $1026.78 on November 1, 2015.

b. For a redemption that took place on January 17, 2016, the bond's owner would have been paid extra interest at the annual rate of 0.50% for November 2015 and December 2015 (but no interest for the days in January). The amount of the extra interest was

$$I = Prt = \$1026.78(0.005)\tfrac{2}{12} = \$0.86$$

Therefore, the total amount the owner received on January 17, 2016 was

$$\$1026.78 + \$0.86 = \$1027.64$$

▶ **Check your understanding:** A $1000-face-value Series S120 compound-interest CSB was presented to a bank branch for redemption on August 12, 2016. What amount did the owner receive? (Answer: $1034.76)

▬▶ **Related problem:** #10 in Exercise 8.5

Valuation of Investments

With many types of investments, the owner can sell the investment to another investor. Such investments are said to be transferable.[7] The key question is: What is the appropriate price at which the investment should be sold/purchased? We encountered the same question in Chapter 7 for investments earning simple interest. There we discussed the thinking behind the Valuation Principle (repeated below for ease of reference).

> ### Valuation Principle
> The fair market value of an investment is the sum of the present values of the expected cash flows. The discount rate used should be the prevailing market-determined rate of return on this type of investment.

For an investment with cash inflows extending beyond one year, the market-determined rate of return is almost always a compound rate of return. In this section, we will apply the Valuation Principle to two types of investments.

LO4 **Strip Bonds** Many investors choose to hold **strip bonds**[8] in their Registered Retirement Savings Plans (RRSPs). You need to know only a few essential features of strip bonds in order to handle strip-bond calculations. If you buy a strip bond, you will receive a *single* payment (called the face value of the bond) on the bond's maturity date. The maturity date could be as much as 30 years in the future. You will receive no interest payments in the interim. Consider a $1000 face-value strip bond that matures 18 years from now. Its owner will receive a single payment of $1000 18 years from now. What is the appropriate price to pay for the bond today? Clearly, it will be substantially less than $1000. The difference between the $1000 you will receive at maturity and the price you pay today represents the earnings on your initial investment (the purchase price). The situation is similar to the pricing of T-bills in Section 7.3.

---

[7] Guaranteed Investment Certificates and Canada Savings Bonds are normally not transferable.

[8] *Strip bonds* are created when investment dealers (brokers) break up marketable bonds into simple components that investors can purchase. Normally, investment dealers do this only with some of the marketable bonds issued by federal and provincial governments.

According to the Valuation Principle, the fair market price is the present value of the payment (of the face value) that will be received on the bond's maturity date. The discount rate you should use for "i" in $PV = FV(1 + i)^{-n}$ is the prevailing rate of return in financial markets for strip bonds of similar risk and maturity. Table 8.3 presents quotes for a few strip bonds in February 2016. The quoted "Prices" are per $100 of face value. The quoted "Yields" are understood in the financial world to be nominal rates with *semiannual* compounding. To simplify matters at this point, we have quoted strip bonds on a date in February 2016 that correspond exactly to either a February or an August maturity date. Consequently, the number of six-month compounding periods from the price quotation date until maturity is an integer in every case. (The more general circumstance where n is not an integer will be addressed in Section 9.2.)

TABLE 8.3   Strip Bond Price and Yield Quotations

Issuer	Maturity date	Price quotation date	Price ($)	Yield (%)
Nova Scotia Power Corp.	August 26, 2016	February 26, 2016	99.71	0.59
Newfoundland & Labrador Hydro	August 27, 2018	February 27, 2016	97.57	0.99
Hydro Quebec	August 26, 2020	February 26, 2016	93.56	1.49
Nova Scotia Power Corp.	February 26, 2021	February 26, 2016	89.68	2.20

Source: Perimeter Markets Inc., www.pfin.ca/canadianfixedincome/Default.aspx.

Consider the Hydro Quebec strip bond maturing on August 26, 2020. The market-determined rate of return (yield) on this bond late in the afternoon of February 26, 2016 was 1.49% compounded semiannually. This yield can vary by a few hundredths of a percent from hour to hour as investors react to events and economic forces.

We will now show that this market-determined yield is consistent with the quoted price of $93.56 (per $100 of face value). The price on February 26, 2016 should be the present value of the future $100 payment discounted at 1.49% compounded semiannually. With

$$FV = \$100, \ i = \tfrac{1.49\%}{2} = 0.745\%, \quad \text{and} \quad n = m(\text{Term}) = 2(4.5) = 9,$$
$$PV = FV(1 + i)^{-n} = \$100(1 + 0.00745)^{-9} = \$93.54$$

The quoted price is $93.56. Since the published yield was rounded to three figures, we can expect no better than two-figure accuracy in our calculated price. The quoted and calculated prices are consistent.

Note: In example problems from this point onward, we will present financial calculator procedures in a callout box adjacent to the algebraic solution. A curly bracket will indicate the algebraic calculations that the calculator procedure can replace.

EXAMPLE 8.5E	Calculating the Price of a Strip Bond

A $10,000-face-value strip bond has $15\tfrac{1}{2}$ years remaining until maturity. If the prevailing market rate of return is 1.5% compounded semiannually, what is the fair market value of the strip bond?

SOLUTION

Given: $FV = \$10,000, j = 1.5\%, m = 2$, Term $= 15\tfrac{1}{2}$ years

Therefore, $i = \dfrac{j}{m} = \dfrac{1.5\%}{2} = 0.75\%$ and $n = m(\text{Term}) = 2(15.5) = 31$

Fair market value = Present value of the face value
$$\left. \begin{aligned} &= FV(1 + i)^{-n} \\ &= \$10,000(1.0075)^{-31} \\ &= \$7932.38 \end{aligned} \right\}$$

The fair market value of the strip bond is $7932.38.

1.5 I/Y

P/Y 2 ENTER

(making $C/Y = P/Y = 2$)

31 N

10000 FV

0 PMT

CPT PV

Ans: 7932.38

➡️ **Check your understanding:** A $100,000-face-value strip bond has 18 years remaining until maturity. If the prevailing market rate of return is 1.8% compounded semiannually, what is the fair market value of the strip bond? (Answer: $72,429.92)

▰▰▶ **Related problem:** #17 in Exercise 8.5

Long-Term Promissory Notes A promissory note is a simple contract between a debtor and creditor setting out the amount of the debt (face value), the interest rate thereon, and the terms of repayment. A *long-term* promissory note is a note whose term is longer than one year. Such notes usually accrue compound interest on the face value.

The payee (creditor) on a promissory note may sell the note to an investor before maturity. The debtor is then obligated to make the remaining payments to the new owner of the note. To determine the note's selling/purchase price, we need to apply th7e Valuation Principle to the note's maturity value. The two steps are:

1. Determine the note's maturity value based on the contractual rate of interest on the note.
2. Discount (that is, calculate the present value of) the Step 1 result back to the date of sale/purchase. Since there is no "market" for private promissory notes, the seller and purchaser must negotiate the discount rate.

EXAMPLE 8.5F | **Calculating the Selling Price of a Long-Term Promissory Note**

A five-year promissory note with a face value of $3500, bearing interest at 5% compounded semiannually, was sold 21 months after its issue date to yield the buyer 4% compounded quarterly. What amount was paid for the note?

SOLUTION

We should find the maturity value of the note and then discount the maturity value (at the required yield) back to the date of the sale. These two steps are indicated on the following diagram.

```
0                           1¾                                    5  Years
├─────────────────────────────┼──────────────────────────────────────┤
$3500                          │       i = 5%/2 = 2.5%, n = 10      Maturity
└─                             │                                  ─┘ value
                               │          i = 4%/4 = 1%, n = 13
                          Price ◄
```

Step 1: Given: $PV = \$3500$, $j = 5\%$, $m = 2$, Term = 5 years

Therefore, $\quad i = \dfrac{j}{m} = \dfrac{5\%}{2} = 2.5\%$

and $\quad\quad\quad n = m(\text{Term}) = 2(5) = 10$

$\text{Maturity value} = PV(1 + i)^n$
$= \$3500(1.025)^{10}$
$= \$4480.30$

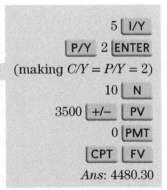

5 I/Y
P/Y 2 ENTER
(making C/Y = P/Y = 2)
10 N
3500 +/− PV
0 PMT
CPT FV
Ans: 4480.30

Step 2: Given: $j = 4\%$, $m = 4$, Term = 5 years − 21 months = 3.25 years

Therefore, $i = \dfrac{j}{m} = \dfrac{4\%}{4} = 1\%$

and $n = m(\text{Term}) = 4(3.25) = 13$

$$\left.\begin{aligned}
\text{Price paid} &= FV(1 + i)^{-n} \\
&= \$4480.30(1.01)^{-13} \\
&= \$3936.67
\end{aligned}\right\}$$

The amount paid for the note was $3936.67.

> Same *FV, PMT*
>
> 4 | I/Y |
>
> | P/Y | 4 | ENTER |
>
> (making *C/Y = P/Y = 4*)
>
> 13 | N |
>
> | CPT | PV |
>
> *Ans:* −3936.67

➡ **Check your understanding:** An eight-year promissory note with a face value of $8200, bearing interest at 7% compounded quarterly, was sold $5\frac{1}{2}$ years after its issue date to yield the buyer 6% compounded monthly. What amount was paid for the note? (Answer: $12,300.80)

▮▮▮▶ **Related problem:** #30 in Exercise 8.5

Compound Growth

LO5   The formula $FV = PV(1 + i)^n$ may be used in non-financial problems involving compound growth at a fixed periodic rate. Furthermore, you can use the financial functions of your calculator in such cases. Simply put the following interpretations on the variables.

If a quantity shrinks or contracts at a fixed periodic rate, it can be handled mathematically by treating it as *negative growth*. For example, suppose a firm's annual sales volume is projected to decline for the next four years by 5% per year from last year's level of 100,000 units. The expected sales volume in the fourth year may be obtained using $FV = PV(1 + i)^n$ with $n = 4$ and $i = (-5\%) = (-0.05)$. That is,

$$\begin{aligned}
\text{Sales (in Year 4)} &= 100{,}000[1 + (-0.05)]^4 \\
&= 100{,}000(0.95)^4 \\
&= 81{,}451 \text{ units}
\end{aligned}$$

In the financial-calculator approach, you would save "−5" in the I/Y memory. The decrease of 100,000 − 81,451 = 18,549 units represents an overall decline of $\frac{18{,}549}{100{,}000} \times 100\% = 18.55\%$ in the annual volume of sales. Note that the overall decline is less than 20%, an answer you might be tempted to reach by simply adding the percentage changes.

Inflation and Purchasing Power A useful application of compound growth in financial planning is using forecast rates of inflation to estimate future prices and the purchasing power of money. The rate of inflation measures the annual percent change in the price level of goods and services. By compounding the forecast rate of inflation over a number of years, we can estimate the level of prices at the end of the period.

When prices rise, money loses its purchasing power—these are "two sides of the same (depreciating) coin." If price levels double, a given nominal amount of money will purchase only half as much. We then say that the money has half its former purchasing power. Similarly, if price levels triple, money retains only one-third of its former purchasing power. These examples demonstrate that price levels and purchasing power have an inverse relationship. That is,

$$\frac{\text{Ending purchasing power}}{\text{Beginning purchasing power}} = \frac{\text{Beginning price level}}{\text{Ending price level}}$$

Let us push the reasoning one step further to answer this question: If price levels rise 50% over a number of years, what will be the percent *loss* in purchasing power? This gets a little tricky—the answer is *not* 50%. If the ending price level is 50% higher than the beginning price level, the ratio of price levels (on the right side of the preceding proportion) is

$$\frac{100}{150} \quad \text{or} \quad \frac{2}{3}$$

Therefore, money will *retain* $\frac{2}{3}$ of its purchasing power and *lose* the other $\frac{1}{3}$ or $33\frac{1}{3}\%$ of its purchasing power.

EXAMPLE 8.5G	The Long-Term Effect of Inflation on Purchasing Power

If the rate of inflation for the next 20 years is 2.5% per year, what annual income (rounded to the nearest $100) will be needed 20 years from now to have the same purchasing power as a $50,000 annual income today?

SOLUTION

The required income will be $50,000 compounded at 2.5% per year for 20 years.

Given: $PV = \$50,000$, $j = 2.5\%$, $m = 1$, Term = 20 years

Hence,
$$i = \frac{j}{m} = \frac{2.5\%}{1} = 2.5\%$$

and
$$n = m(\text{Term}) = 1(20) = 20$$

$$FV = PV(1 + i)^n$$
$$= \$50,000(1.025)^{20}$$
$$= \$81,930.82$$

After 20 years of 2.5% annual inflation, an annual income of $81,900 will be needed to have the same purchasing power as $50,000 today.

2.5 **I/Y**
P/Y 1 **ENTER**
(making $C/Y = P/Y = 1$)
20 **N**
50000 **PV**
0 **PMT**
CPT FV
Ans: −81,930.82

➡ **Check your understanding:** If the rate of inflation for the next 30 years is 1.5% per year, what annual income (rounded to the nearest $100) will be needed 30 years from now to have the same purchasing power as a $75,000 annual income today? (Answer: $117,200)

▬▬▶ **Related problem:** #25 in Exercise 8.5

EXAMPLE 8.5H	Compound Annual Decrease in Population

The population of a rural region is expected to fall by 2% per year for the next 10 years. If the region's current population is 100,000, what is the expected population 10 years from now?

SOLUTION

The 2% "negative growth" should be compounded for 10 years.

Given: $PV = 100,000$, $j = -2\%$, $m = 1$, Term = 10 years

Hence,
$$i = \frac{j}{m} = \frac{-2\%}{1} = -2\%$$

and
$$n = m(\text{Term}) = 1(10) = 10$$

$$FV = PV(1 + i)^n$$
$$= 100,000[1 + (-0.02)]^{10}$$
$$= 81,707$$

The region's population is expected to drop to about 81,707 during the next 10 years.

2 **+/− I/Y**
P/Y 1 **ENTER**
(making $C/Y = P/Y = 1$)
10 **N**
100000 **PV**
0 **PMT**
CPT FV
Ans: −81,707

➡️ **Check your understanding:** The population of a town is expected to fall by 3.5% per year for the next 8 years. If the town's current population is 43,000, what is the expected population 8 years from now? (Answer: 32,336)

◼◼◼▶ **Related problem:** #26 in Exercise 8.5

 Checkpoint Questions

1. Circle "True" or "False" for each of the following:

    a. The owner of a regular interest GIC will receive periodic interest payments   True   False
    throughout the term of the GIC.

    b. Canada Savings Bonds are a means for the federal government to borrow   True   False
    money from Canadian investors.

    c. The owner of a Canada Savings Bond must hold the bond until maturity.   True   False

    d. The owner of a strip bond will receive periodic interest payments throughout   True   False
    the term of the strip bond.

2. How, if at all, will the future value of a three-year variable-rate GIC differ if it earns 4%, 5%, and 6% in successive years instead of 6%, 5%, and 4% in successive years?

3. Why must the Finance Department keep the interest rates on existing CSBs at least as high as the rate on a new CSB issue?

4. Should we conclude that the owner of a strip bond earns nothing until the full face value is received at maturity? Explain.

5. If a quantity increases by x% per year (compounded) for two years, will the overall percent increase be more or less than $2x$%? Explain.

6. If a quantity declines by x% per year (compounded) for two years, will the overall percent decrease be more or less than $2x$%? Explain.

EXERCISE 8.5

Answers to the odd-numbered problems can be found in the end matter.

BASIC PROBLEMS

1. Krista invested $18,000 in a three-year regular-interest GIC earning 2.2% payable semiannually. What is each semiannual interest payment?

2. Eric invested $22,000 in a five-year regular-interest GIC earning 4.5% payable monthly. What is each monthly interest payment?

3. Mr. Dickson purchased a seven-year, $30,000 compound-interest GIC with funds in his RRSP. If the interest rate on the GIC is 1.75% compounded semiannually, what is the GIC's maturity value?

4. Mrs. Sandhu placed $11,500 in a four-year compound-interest GIC earning 3.75% compounded monthly. What is the GIC's maturity value?

5. A trust company offers three-year compound-interest GICs earning 1.8% compounded monthly or 1.9% compounded semiannually. Which rate should an investor choose?

6. If an investor has the choice between rates of 5.4% compounded quarterly and 5.5% compounded annually for a six-year GIC, which rate should she choose?

7. Sun Life Financial offers a five-year compound-interest GIC earning rates of 0.5%, 1%, 1.5%, 2.25%, and 3% in successive years. Manulife offers a similar GIC paying rates of 0.75%, 1.25%, 1.5%, 2%, and 3.25% in successive years. For a $10,000 investment, which GIC will have the greater maturity value after five years? How much greater?

INTERMEDIATE PROBLEMS

8. Stan purchased a $15,000 compound-interest Series S129 Canada Savings Bond on December 1, 2011. The interest rate in each year was 0.5%. What total interest did Stan receive when he redeemed the CSB on November 17, 2016?

9. Sabrina purchased a $5000 compound interest Series S127 Canada Savings Bond on December 1, 2010. The interest was 0.65% in the first year, and 0.5% in each subsequent year. What maturity value did Sabrina receive when she redeemed the CSB on September 27, 2016?

In Problems 10 to 12, use Table 8.2 to find the interest rates you need.

10. What amount did the owner of a $5000-face-value compound-interest Series S128 Canada Savings Bond receive when she redeemed the bond on

    a. November 1, 2015?   **b.** August 21, 2016?

11. What amount did the owner of a $10,000-face-value compound-interest Series S120 CSB receive when he redeemed the bond on

    a. November 1, 2015?   **b.** May 19, 2016?

12. What was the redemption value of a $300-face-value compound-interest Series S126 CSB on March 8, 2016?

13. The BMO Bank of Montreal advertised rates of 1.2%, 1.35%, 1.5%, 1.75%, and 2.25% for the five successive years of its five-year compound-interest RateRiser Plus GIC. At the same time, the bank was offering fixed-rate five-year compound-interest GICs yielding 1.25% compounded annually. What total interest would be earned during the five-year term on a $5000 investment in each type of GIC?

14. On the same date that the CIBC advertised rates of 1%, 1.1%, 1.15%, 1.25%, and 3% in successive years of its five-year compound-interest Escalating Rate GIC, it offered 1.25% compounded annually on its five-year fixed-rate GIC. How much more will a $10,000 investment be worth at maturity if the Escalating Rate GIC is chosen instead of the fixed-rate GIC?

15. Using the information given in Problem 14, calculate the interest earned in the fourth year from a $10,000 investment in each GIC.

16. Using the information given in Problem 14, how much would have to be initially invested in each GIC to have a maturity value of $20,000?

17. A $1000-face-value strip bond has 22 years remaining until maturity. What is its price if the market rate of return on such bonds is 3.95% compounded semiannually?

18. What price should be paid for a $5000-face-value strip bond with 19.5 years remaining to maturity if it is to yield the buyer 2.1% compounded semiannually?

19. Consider a $5000-face-value Hydro Quebec strip bond from the issue in Table 8.3 that matures on August 26, 2020. If the yield does not change as years go by, what is the bond's value on

    a. August 26, 2017?   **b.** August 26, 2018?   **c.** August 26, 2019?

20. Consider a $5000-face-value Newfoundland & Labrador Hydro strip bond from the issue in Table 8.3 that matures on August 27, 2018. If the yield does not change as years go by, what is the bond's value on

    a. August 27, 2015?   **b.** August 27, 2016?   **c.** August 27, 2017?

21. Mrs. Janzen wishes to purchase some 13-year-maturity strip bonds with the $12,830 in cash she now has in her RRSP. If these strip bonds are currently priced to yield 4.25% compounded semiannually, how many $1000 denomination bonds can she purchase?

22. How much will you need 20 years from now to have the purchasing power of $100 today if the (compound annual) rate of inflation during the period is

    a. 2%?   **b.** 3%?   **c.** 4%?

23. How much money was needed 15 years ago to have the purchasing power of $1000 today if the (compound annual) rate of inflation has been

    a. 2%?   **b.** 4%?

24. If the inflation rate for the next 10 years is 3.5% per year, what hourly rate of pay in 10 years will be equivalent to $15/hour today?

25. Mr. and Mrs. Rasuli would like to retire in 15 years at an annual income level that would be equivalent to $65,000 today. What is their retirement income goal if, in the meantime, the annual rate of inflation is

    a. 2%?   **b.** 3%?   **c.** 5%?

26. A city's population stood at 120,000 after five years of 3% annual growth. What was the population five years previously?

27. A college has targeted an enrollment increase of 8% per year. If the college has 18,000 full-time students today, what is the enrollment estimate in six years from now? Round your answer to the nearest 100 students.

ADVANCED PROBLEMS

28. In 2013 the number of workers in the forest industry was forecast to decline by 3% per year, reaching 205,000 in 2023. How many were employed in the industry in 2013?

29. An eight-year note for $3800 with interest at 6% compounded semiannually was sold after three years and three months to yield the buyer 4.2% compounded quarterly. What price did the buyer pay?

30. A four-year $8000 promissory note bearing interest at 6.6% compounded monthly was discounted 21 months after issue to yield 4.8% compounded quarterly. What were the proceeds from the sale of the note?

31. The late 1970s and early 1980s were years of historically high rates of inflation in Canada. For the years 1978, 1979, 1980, 1981, and 1982 the rates of inflation were 8.8%, 9.2%, 10.9%, 12.6%, and 10.0%, respectively.

    a. Suppose your hourly wage at the beginning of 1978 was $10 per hour. What wage did you need to earn at the end of 1982 just to keep pace with inflation?

    b. What percentage of its purchasing power did money lose over these five years?

32. The late 2000s and early 2010s were years of relatively low rates of inflation in Canada. For the years 2011, 2012, 2013, 2014, and 2015 the rates of inflation were 2.9%, 1.5%, 0.9%, 2.0%, and 1.1% respectively.

    a. Suppose your hourly wage at the beginning of 2011 was $12 per hour. What wage did you need to earn at the end of 2015 just to keep pace with inflation?

    b. What percentage of its purchasing power did money lose over these five years?

33. A pharmaceutical company had sales of $28,600,000 in the year just completed. Sales are expected to decline by 4% per year for the next three years until new drugs, now under development, receive regulatory approval. Then sales should grow at 8% per year for the subsequent four years. Rounded to the dollar, what are the expected sales for the final year of the seven-year period?

8.6   Equivalent Payment Streams

LO6   Sometimes a scheduled payment stream is replaced by another payment stream. This can happen, for example, in rescheduling payments on a loan. In this section we will learn how to make the new stream of payments economically equivalent to the stream it replaces. In this way, neither the payer nor the payee gains any financial advantage from the change.

The general principle we will develop is an extension of ideas from Sections 8.2 and 8.3. In those sections you learned how to obtain the equivalent value of a multiple-payment stream at a particular focal date. It was a two-step procedure:

1. Calculate the equivalent value of each payment at the focal date.
2. Add up the equivalent values to obtain the stream's equivalent value.

How, then, would you compare the economic values of two payment streams? Your intuition should be a good guide here. First calculate the equivalent value of each stream at the *same* focal date. Then compare the two equivalent values to rank them. For two payment streams to be economically equivalent, they must meet the following condition.

> **Criterion for the Equivalence of Two Payment Streams**
> A payment stream's equivalent value (at a focal date) is the sum of the equivalent values of all of its payments. Two payment streams are economically equivalent if they have the same equivalent value at the same focal date.

You must impose this requirement when designing a payment stream that is to be economically equivalent to a given payment stream. The criterion becomes the basis for an equation that enables us to solve for an unknown payment in the new stream.

> ### *TIP* ✔
>
> #### Choosing a Focal Date
>
> Any interest conversion date may be chosen for the focal date in an equivalent-payment stream problem. If two payment streams are equivalent at one conversion date, they will be equivalent at any other conversion date. Therefore, problems will generally not specify a particular focal date to be used in the solution. Calculations will usually be simplified if you locate the focal date at one of the unknown payments in the new stream. Then that payment's equivalent value on the focal date is simply its nominal value. But be careful to use the *same* focal date for *both* payment streams.

EXAMPLE 8.6A	Calculating an Unknown Payment in a Two-Payment Replacement Stream

Payments of $2000 and $1000 were originally scheduled to be paid one year and five years, respectively, from today. They are to be replaced by a $1500 payment due four years from today, and another payment due two years from today. The replacement stream must be economically equivalent to the scheduled stream. What is the unknown payment, if money can earn 7% compounded semiannually?

SOLUTION

The diagram below presents just the given information. Each payment stream has its own time line. The unknown payment is represented by x. We must calculate a value for x such that the two streams satisfy the Criterion for Equivalence.

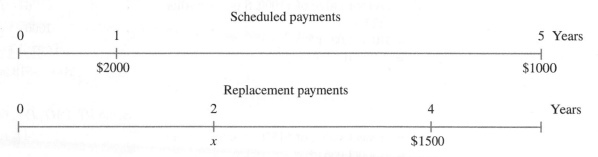

In the next diagram, the date of the unknown payment has been chosen as the focal date. Consequently, the unknown payment's equivalent value on the focal date is just x. The equivalent values of the other payments are represented by FV_1, PV_2, and PV_3.

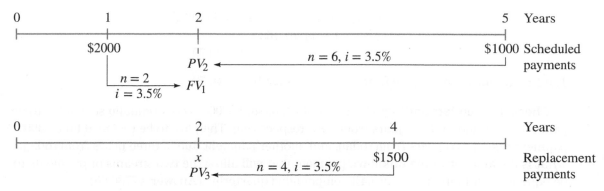

To satisfy the Criterion for Equivalence, we require

$$FV_1 + PV_2 = x + PV_3 \;\; \text{①}$$

The equivalent values of the individual payments are calculated in the usual way.

FV_1 = Future value of $2000, 1 year later
$$= PV(1 + i)^n$$
$$= \$2000(1.035)^2$$
$$= \$2142.450$$

```
                7  I/Y
           P/Y  2  ENTER
        (making C/Y = P/Y = 2)
                2  N
             2000  PV
                0  PMT
              CPT  FV
         Ans: −2142.450
```

PV_2 = Present value of $1000, 3 years earlier
$$= FV(1 + i)^{-n}$$
$$= \$1000(1.035)^{-6}$$
$$= \$813.501$$

```
        Same I/Y, PMT, P/Y, C/Y
                6  N
             1000  FV
              CPT  PV
          Ans: −813.501
```

PV_3 = Present value of $1500, 2 years earlier
$$= \$1500(1.035)^{-4}$$
$$= \$1307.163$$

```
        Same I/Y, PMT, P/Y, C/Y
                4  N
             1500  FV
              CPT  PV
         Ans: −1307.163
```

Substituting these amounts into equation ①, we have

$$\$2142.450 + \$813.501 = x + \$1307.163$$
$$\$2955.951 - \$1307.163 = x$$
$$x = \$1648.79$$

The first payment in the replacement stream must be $1648.79.

➡️ **Check your understanding:** Payments of $4000 and $7000 were originally scheduled to be paid one year ago and six years from now, respectively. They are to be replaced by a $3000 payment due in two years from today, and another payment due in three years from today. What is the amount of the unknown payment that will allow the two streams of payments to be equivalent if money can earn 4% compounded quarterly? (Answer: $7780.65)

▩▶ **Related problem:** #1 in Exercise 8.6

EXAMPLE 8.6B	Comparing Two Payment Streams

Mr. Huang has received two offers for a piece of property that he is selling. Offer 1 consists of a $20,000 down payment today, and an additional $180,000 in 3 years. Offer 2 consists of a $90,000 payment in 1 year from now, and an additional $113,000 payment in 5 years from now. Which offer should Mr. Huang accept if money can earn 4% compounded quarterly? In current dollars, what is the economic advantage of the preferred alternative?

SOLUTION

The diagram below presents just the given information. Note that each offer has its own time line.

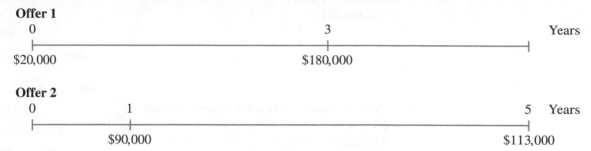

In order to compare the two offers, we must select a single focal point and find the equivalent value of each offer at that *same* focal point. The offer that provides the best economic value to Mr. Huang will emerge as the "winner" regardless of which focal point we choose. However, we must note that the last line of the question asks us to state *in current dollars* the economic advantage of the best offer. For this reason, we need to select "Year 0" as our focal point in order to be able to answer that portion of the question.

For offer 1, the $20,000 down payment is already at the focal point and no calculation is required for that payment. We need to find the PV of the $180,000 payment. The equivalent value of the $180,000 at the chosen focal point is represented by PV_1 in the diagram below.

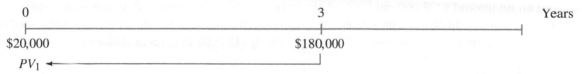

The equivalent value of the individual $180,000 payment is calculated in the usual way.

$$PV_1 = \text{Present value of }\$180,000, 3\text{ years earlier}$$
$$= FV(1 + i)^{-n}$$
$$= \$180,000(1.01)^{-12}$$
$$= \$159,740.861$$

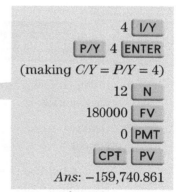

4 | I/Y

P/Y 4 ENTER

(making $C/Y = P/Y = 4$)

12 | N

180000 | FV

0 | PMT

CPT | PV

Ans: −159,740.861

To find the total value of offer 1 at the focal point, we add the $20,000 down payment to the PV_1 value. Offer 1 has an equivalent value of $20,000 + $159,740.86 = $179,740.86 in current dollars.

For offer 2, we must perform two calculations. We must find the PV of the $90,000 payment as well as the PV of the $113,000 payment. These are shown as PV_2 and PV_3 in the diagram below.

PV_2 = Present value of \$90,000, 1 year earlier
$$= FV(1 + i)^{-n}$$
$$= \$90,000(1 + 0.01)^{-4}$$
$$= \$86,488.231$$

Same *I/Y, P/Y, C/Y, PMT*

4 | N

90000 | FV

CPT | PV

Ans: −86,488.231

PV_3 = Present value of \$113,000, 5 years earlier
$$= FV(1 + i)^{-n}$$
$$= \$113,000(1 + 0.01)^{-20}$$
$$= \$92,608.525$$

Same *I/Y, P/Y, C/Y, PMT*

20 | N

113000 | FV

CPT | PV

Ans: −92,608.525

To find the total value of offer 2 at the focal point, we add PV_2 and PV_3. Offer 2 has an equivalent value of \$86,488.231 + \$92,608.525 = \$179,096.76.

Mr. Huang is the seller in this transaction, so he wants to select the offer that has the largest economic value. Therefore, he should select offer 1, since its economic value in current dollars is larger than that of offer 2. By selecting offer 1, Mr. Huang is better off by \$179,740.86 − \$179,096.76 = \$644.10 in current dollars.

➡ **Check your understanding:** Suppose offer 2 consisted of \$100,000 paid in 3 years from now, and an additional \$122,000 paid in 7 years from now. If money earns 4% compounded quarterly, which offer would Mr. Huang prefer? In current dollars, what is the economic advantage of the preferred alternative? (Answer: Offer 2 is better by \$1338.00 in current dollars.)

◼▶ **Related problem:** #8 in Exercise 8.6

 ## Checkpoint Questions

1. If two payment streams are equivalent at one discount rate, will they be equivalent at another discount rate?

2. Give two examples of advertisements or news items that routinely ignore the time value of money.

3. What would be the most convincing way to demonstrate that the replacement stream in Example 8.6A is economically equivalent to the given stream?

EXERCISE 8.6

Answers to the odd-numbered problems can be found in the end matter.

INTERMEDIATE PROBLEMS

1. Scheduled payments of \$3000 due today and \$2000 due in 15 months are to be replaced by two payments—\$1500 due in 15 months and a second payment of undetermined size due in 24 months. What must the second payment be for the two streams to be economically equivalent? Assume that money can earn 6% compounded quarterly.

2. Gandalf was scheduled to make payments of $4500 in $1\frac{1}{2}$ years from now, and $6000 in $3\frac{1}{2}$ years from now. He is proposing an alternative arrangement that would involve a payment in 6 months from now, followed by a payment of $10,000 in 3 years from now. How much would the payment in 6 months from now need to be in order for the two streams to be economically equivalent? Assume that money can earn 3% compounded semiannually.

3. A two-payment stream consisting of $1750 due today and $2900 due in 18 months is to be replaced by an economically equivalent stream comprised of an undetermined payment due in 9 months and a payment of $3000 due in 19 months. Calculate the unknown replacement payment if money is worth 4.2% compounded monthly.

4. Patrice defaulted on payments of $1000 due one year ago and $1500 due six months ago. A Small Claims Court orders her to make three payments—$800 one month from now, $900 four months from now, and a third payment seven months from now. The third payment is to be determined so that the creditor will end up in the same economic position as if the original payments had been made on time. The court set the fair rate of return at 2.4% compounded monthly. How much should the third payment be?

5. Miquel was supposed to make three payments of $2000 each—the first one year ago, the second one year from now, and the third three years from now. He missed the first payment and proposes to pay $3000 today and a second amount in two years. If money can earn 4.5% compounded semiannually, what must the second payment be to make the proposed payments equivalent to the scheduled payments?

6. CompuSystems was supposed to pay a manufacturer $19,000 on a date four months ago and another $14,000 on a date two months from now. Instead, CompuSystems is proposing to pay $10,000 today and the balance in five months, when it will receive payment on a major sale to the provincial government. What will the second payment be if money is worth 6% compounded monthly?

ADVANCED PROBLEMS

7. The owner of a residential building lot has received two purchase offers. Mrs. A is offering a $20,000 down payment plus $40,000 payable in one year. Mr. B's offer is $15,000 down plus two $25,000 payments due one and two years from now. Which offer has the greater economic value if money can earn 3.5% compounded quarterly? How much more is it worth in current dollars?

8. A lottery prize gives the winner a choice between (1) $10,000 now and another $10,000 in 5 years and (2) four $6000 payments—now and in 5, 10, and 15 years.

   a. Which alternative should the winner choose if money can earn 3% compounded annually? In current dollars, what is the economic advantage of the preferred alternative?

   b. Which alternative should the winner choose if money can earn 8.5% compounded annually? In current dollars, what is the economic advantage of the preferred alternative?

9. Henri has decided to purchase a $25,000 car. He can either liquidate some of his investments and pay cash, or accept the dealer's proposal that Henri pay $5000 down and $8000 at the end of each of the next three years.

   a. Which choice should Henri make if he can earn 3% compounded semiannually on his investments? In current dollars, what is the economic advantage of the preferred alternative?

   b. Which choice should Henri make if he can earn 11% compounded semiannually on his investments? In current dollars, what is the economic advantage of the preferred alternative?

   (*Hint:* When choosing among alternative streams of cash *inflows*, we should select the one with the greatest economic value. When choosing among alternative streams of cash *outflows*, we should select the one with the least economic value.)

10. The principal plus interest at 6% compounded quarterly on a $15,000 loan made $2\frac{1}{2}$ years ago is due in two years. The debtor is proposing to settle the debt by a payment of $5000 today and a second payment in one year that will place the lender in an equivalent financial position, given that money can now earn only 4% compounded semiannually.

  a. What should be the amount of the second payment?

  b. Demonstrate that the lender will be in the same financial position two years from now with either repayment alternative.

Key Terms

Cash flow	Discount rate	Nominal interest rate
Cash-flow sign convention	Discounting a payment	Periodic interest rate
Compound interest method	Equivalent payments	Present value
Compounding frequency	Future value	Strip bond
Compounding period	Maturity value	

Summary of Notation and Key Formulas

$$j = \text{Nominal annual interest rate}$$
$$m = \text{Number of compoundings per year}$$
$$i = \text{Periodic rate of interest}$$
$$PV = \text{Principal amount of a loan or investment; Present value}$$
$$FV = \text{Maturity value of a loan or investment; Future value}$$
$$n = \text{Number of compounding periods}$$

FORMULA (8-1) $i = \dfrac{j}{m}$ Obtaining the periodic interest rate from the nominal annual rate

FORMULA (8-2) $\begin{cases} FV = PV(1+i)^n & \text{Finding the maturity value or future value} \\ PV = FV(1+i)^{-n} & \text{Finding the principal or present value} \end{cases}$

FORMULA (8-3) $n = m \times (\textbf{Number of years in the term})$ Finding the number of compounding periods

FORMULA (8-4) $FV = PV(1+i_1)(1+i_2)(1+i_3) \dots (1+i_n)$
Finding the maturity value with compounding at a variable interest rate

Present Value of Loan Payments

The sum of the present values of all of the payments required to pay off a loan is equal to the original principal of the loan. The discount rate for the present-value calculations is the rate of interest charged on the loan.

Cash-Flow Sign Convention

Cash inflows (receipts) are positive.
Cash outflows (disbursements) are negative.

Criterion for the Equivalence of Two Payment Streams

A payment stream's equivalent value (at a focal date) is the sum of the equivalent values of all of its payments. Two payment streams are economically equivalent if they have the same equivalent value at the same focal date.

Review Problems

Answers to the odd-numbered review problems can be found in the end matter.

1. **LO1** By calculating the maturity value of $100 invested for three years at each rate, determine whether an investor would prefer to earn 3.9% compounded annually or 3.65% compounded quarterly for a three-year investment.

2. **LO1** Kate invested $5300 at 3.6% compounded monthly for seven years. What was the maturity value of her investment?

3. **LO1** How much would an investor need to deposit today into an investment earning 3.75% compounded quarterly if her goal is to have a total of $35,000 in eight years from now?

4. **LO2** Josie invested $24,000 in a five-year regular-interest GIC earning 4% payable semiannually. What is each semiannual interest payment?

5. **LO2** A five-year compound-interest GIC pays rates of 1%, 2%, 3%, 4%, and 5% in successive years. What will be the maturity value of $10,000 invested in this GIC?

6. **LO6** Sabina is scheduled to pay her sister $5000 in three years from now. How much should her sister accept as an economically equivalent payment today if money is worth 5% compounded semiannually?

7. **LO6** A contract requires Evan to pay $6,400 in $2\frac{1}{2}$ years from now. How much should his creditor be willing to accept today in settlement of this debt if money is worth

    a. 1.2% compounded monthly?

    b. 5.4% compounded monthly?

    c. 9.6% compounded monthly?

8. **LO4** A $1000-face-value strip bond has 19 years remaining until maturity. What is its price if the market rate of return on such bonds is 3.9% compounded semiannually?

9. **LO5** If the inflation rate for the next 10 years is 3% per year, what hourly rate of pay in 10 years will be equivalent to $15 per hour today?

10. **LO5** Meyers Enterprises sold 6700 units of product last year. If the company is projecting annual growth of 5.5%, what is the predicted annual unit sales in 4 years from now?

11. **LO1** Jacques has just been notified that the combined principal and interest on an amount he borrowed 19 months ago at 8.4% compounded monthly is now $2297.78. How much of this amount is principal and how much is interest?

12. **LO1** Accurate Accounting obtained a private loan of $25,000 for 5 years. No payments were required, but the loan accrued interest at the rate of 3% compounded monthly for the first $2\frac{1}{2}$ years and then at 4.25% compounded semiannually for the remainder of the term. What total amount was required to pay off the loan after 5 years?

13. **LO1** Isaac borrowed $3000 at 4.5% compounded quarterly $3\frac{1}{2}$ years ago. One year ago he made a payment of $1200. What amount will extinguish the loan today?

14. **LO6** What amount 3 years ago is equivalent to $4800 on a date $1\frac{1}{2}$ years from now if money earns 5% compounded semiannually during the intervening time?

15. **LO6** Jamil was scheduled to pay $3100 eight months ago, and an additional $5200 in 3 years from now. He did not make the $3100 payment. How much should his creditor be willing to accept in 18 months from now as full settlement of the entire debt if money can earn 6% compounded monthly?

16. **LO2** A credit union's Rate-Climber GIC pays rates of 2%, 3%, and 4% compounded semiannually in successive years of a three-year term.

    a. What will be the maturity value of $12,000 invested in this GIC?

    b. How much interest will be earned in the second year?

17. **LO2** If an investor has the choice between rates of 1.5% compounded semiannually and 1.6% compounded annually for a six-year GIC, which rate should be chosen?

18. **LO6** Donnelly Excavating has received two offers on a used backhoe that Donnelly is advertising for sale. Offer 1 is for $10,000 down and $30,000 in 18 months. Offer 2 is for $8000 down and $33,000 in two years from now. What is the economic value today of each offer if money is worth 4.25% compounded semiannually? Which offer should be accepted?

19. **LO2** On the same date that the Alberta Treasury Branches were advertising rates of 0.7%, 1%, 1.2%, 1.35%, and 2% in successive years of their five-year compound-interest Springboard GIC, they offered 1.6% compounded annually on their five-year fixed-rate compound-interest GIC. What will be the maturity values of $10,000 invested in each GIC?

20. **LO5** Due to the growth of free online buy-and-sell sites, a community newspaper anticipates that the number of classified ads in its publication will decline by 12% per year. If the newspaper published a total of 4800 classified ads in 2016, how many ads should it expect to sell in 2021?

21. **LO1** For the five-year period ended January 31, 2016, the Pender Small Cap Class F Opportunities Fund was one of the best performers of all Canadian mutual funds. It effectively earned a compound annual return of 19.3% for the five-year period. The RBC Canadian Index Fund, on the other hand, had a compound annual return over five years of only 1.2%. How much more would an initial $1000 investment in the Pender Fund have earned over the five-year period than a $1000 investment in the Canadian Index Fund?

22. **LO3** Use the data in Table 8.2 to determine the redemption value of a $500-face-value compound-interest Series S120 Canada Savings Bond on

    a. November 1, 2015

    b. April 15, 2016

23. **LO1** A $2400 payment was made on a $10,000 loan 30 months after the date of the loan. The interest rate was 6% compounded monthly for the entire load period. What amount was owed on the loan after three years?

24. **LO6** Scheduled payments of $2300 due 18 months ago and $3100 due in three years from now are to be replaced by two payments—$2000 due today and a second payment of undetermined size due in four years from now. What must the second payment be for the two streams to be economically equivalent? Assume that money can earn 4.75% compounded semiannually.

25. **LO3** A $1000-face-value compound-interest Series S126 Canada Savings Bond was redeemed on March 14, 2016. What amount did the bond's owner receive? (Obtain the issue date and the interest rates paid on the bond from Table 8.2.)

26. **LO6** Andrea was scheduled to pay Mike $1200 in 18 months from today and an additional $3000 in 33 months from today. What payment 6 months from now should Mike accept as a single equivalent payment if he can earn 6% compounded quarterly on his investments?

ADVANCED PROBLEMS

27. **LO1** A four-year $7000 promissory note bearing interest at 10.5% compounded monthly was sold 18 months after issue to yield the buyer 9.5% compounded quarterly. What were the proceeds from the sale of the note?

28. **LO1** On February 1 of three successive years, Roger contributed $3000, $4000, and $3500, respectively, to his RRSP. The funds in his plan earned 3% compounded monthly for the first year, 2.5% compounded quarterly for the second year, and 3.75% compounded semiannually for the third year. What was the value of his RRSP three years after the first contribution?

29. **LO1** Jarmila borrowed $3000, $3500, and $4000 from her grandmother on December 1 in each of three successive years at college. They agreed that interest would accumulate at the rate of 4% compounded semiannually. Jarmila is to start repaying the loan on June 1 following the third loan. What consolidated amount will she owe at that time?

30. **LO5** A study predicted that employment in base metal mining would decline by 3.5% per year for the next five years. What percentage of total base metal mining jobs was expected to be lost during the five-year period?

31. **LO2** A five-year, compound-interest GIC purchased for $1000 earns 2.25% compounded annually.

    a. How much interest will the GIC earn in the fifth year?

    b. If the rate of inflation during the five-year term is 1.1% per year, what will be the percent increase in the purchasing power of the invested funds over the entire five years?

32. **LO1** Loralyn borrowed $12,500 from her grandmother at an interest rate of 9% compounded semiannually. The loan is to be repaid by three payments. The first payment, $2000, is due three years after the date of the loan. The second and third payments are due seven and eight years, respectively, after the initial loan. How much will the second and third payments be if the loan agreement requires that those two payments be equal in amount?

33. **LO6** Carla has decided to purchase a $30,000 car. She can either liquidate some of her investments and pay cash, or accept the dealer's terms of $7000 down and successive payments of $10,000, $9000, and $8000 at the end of each of the next three years.

    a. Which choice should Carla make if she can earn 3% compounded semiannually on her investments? In current dollars, how much is the economic advantage of the preferred alternative?

    b. Which choice should Carla make if she can earn 10% compounded semiannually on her investments? In current dollars, how much is the economic advantage of the preferred alternative?

Appendix 8A: Instructions for Specific Models of Financial Calculators

SETTING THE CALCULATOR IN THE FINANCIAL MODE

Texas Instruments BA II PLUS	Sharp EL-738C	Hewlett Packard 10 bII+
Calculator is "ready to go" for financial calculations.	Press `MODE` 0	Calculator is "ready to go" for financial calculations.

SETTING THE NUMBER OF DECIMAL PLACES DISPLAYED AT 9

Texas Instruments BA II PLUS	Sharp EL-738C	Hewlett Packard 10 bII+
`2nd` `Format` 9 `ENTER` `2nd` `QUIT`	`SETUP` 0 0 9	▢ `DISP` 9

SETTING A FLOATING POINT DECIMAL[9]

Texas Instruments BA II PLUS	Sharp EL-738C	Hewlett Packard 10 bII+
Set for 9 decimal places as in the preceding table.	`SETUP` 0 2	▢ `DISP` `•`

CHECKING THE CONTENTS OF A FINANCIAL KEY'S MEMORY (USING THE PV KEY AS AN EXAMPLE)

Texas Instruments BA II PLUS	Sharp EL-738C	Hewlett Packard 10 bII+
`RCL` `PV`	`RCL` `PV`	`RCL` `PV`

---

[9] With this setting, the calculator will show all of the digits but no trailing zeros for a terminating decimal. Non-terminating decimals will be displayed with 10 digits on the BA II PLUS and the Sharp EL-738C, and 12 digits on the Hewlett Packard 10 bII+.

© Caia Image/Glow Images RF

CHAPTER 9

Compound Interest: Further Topics and Applications

LEARNING OBJECTIVES

After completing this chapter, you will be able to:

LO1 Calculate the interest rate and term in compound interest applications

LO2 Given a nominal interest rate, calculate its effective interest rate

LO3 Given a nominal interest rate, calculate its equivalent interest rate at another compounding frequency

 **connect**   Throughout this chapter interactive charts and Help Me Solve It videos are marked with a ↗.

IN ALL OF THE COMPOUND interest problems in Chapter 8, the interest rate and the term of the loan or investment were known. With a little reflection, you can think of many situations requiring the calculation of an interest rate, or a rate of return, or a rate of growth. For example, if you invest $1000 in a mutual fund, what rate of return must it earn to grow to $5000 over a 15-year period? If a stock's price rose from $15.50 to $27.40 over the past five years, what has been its equivalent annual percent increase in price?

   In other circumstances, we want to know the time required for an amount to grow from a beginning value to a target value. How long, for example, will it take an investment to double if it earns 10% compounded annually? By the end of Section 9.2, you will be able to answer such questions.

Compound interest rates on loans and investments may be quoted with differing compounding frequencies. This gives rise to questions such as: "How do we compare 7.9% compounded semiannually to 8% compounded annually? What semiannually compounded rate is equivalent to 6% compounded monthly?" The techniques you will learn in Sections 9.3 and 9.4 will enable you to answer these questions.

9.1 | Calculating the Periodic Interest Rate, i

 LO1   In cases where we know values for PV, FV, and n, the periodic and nominal rates of interest may be calculated.

Algebraic Method

Rearranging the basic equation $FV = PV(1 + i)^n$ to isolate i is more difficult than isolating PV. First divide both sides of the equation by PV and then interchange the two sides, giving

$$(1 + i)^n = \frac{FV}{PV}$$

Next take the nth root of both sides of the equation. This makes the left side simply $(1 + i)$, and we have

$$1 + i = \sqrt[n]{\frac{FV}{PV}}$$

Therefore,[1]

PERIODIC RATE OF INTEREST $$i = \sqrt[n]{\frac{FV}{PV}} - 1 = \left(\frac{FV}{PV}\right)^{1/n} - 1 \qquad (9\text{-}1)$$

Financial Calculator Method

Enter values for the known variables—PV, FV, n, and C/Y—into the appropriate memories. Then press CPT I/Y in sequence to compute j, the nominal annual rate of interest. If the value of i is required, calculate $i = \frac{j}{m}$.

TRAP

Sign Convention Now Mandatory

When you enter values for both FV and PV, it is imperative that you employ the cash-flow sign convention. If you fail to use it, an error message will appear in your calculator's display.

EXAMPLE 9.1A	Calculating the Periodic and Nominal Rates of Interest

The maturity value of a three-year, $5000 compound-interest GIC is $5788.13. To three-figure accuracy, calculate the nominal rate of interest paid on the GIC if interest is compounded

a. annually   **b.** quarterly

---

[1] It was pointed out in Section 2.2 that the nth root of a quantity is equivalent to raising it to the exponent $1/n$.

SOLUTION

Given: $PV = \$5000$, $FV = \$5788.13$

In Part (a), $m = 1$, $n = m(\text{Term}) = 1(3) = 3$ compounding periods.

In Part (b), $m = 4$, $n = m(\text{Term}) = 4(3) = 12$ compounding periods.

Formula (9-1) enables us to calculate the interest rate for one compounding period.

a. $i = \left(\dfrac{FV}{PV}\right)^{1/n} - 1$

$\qquad = \left(\dfrac{\$5788.13}{\$5000.00}\right)^{1/3} - 1$

$\qquad = (1.157626)^{0.\overline{3}} - 1$

$\qquad = 0.05000$

$\qquad = 5.000\%$

	P/Y 1 ENTER
	(making $C/Y = P/Y = 1$)
	3 N
	5000 +/− PV
	0 PMT
	5788.13 FV
	CPT I/Y
	Ans: 5.000

The nominal rate of interest on the GIC is

$j = mi = 1(5.000\%) = 5.00\%$ compounded annually.

b. $i = \left(\dfrac{\$5788.13}{\$5000.00}\right)^{1/12} - 1$

$\qquad = (1.157626)^{0.08\overline{3}} - 1$

$\qquad = 0.01227$

$\qquad = 1.227\%$

	Same PV, PMT, FV
	P/Y 4 ENTER
	king $C/Y = P/Y = 4$)
	12 N
	CPT I/Y
	Ans: 4.909

The nominal rate of interest on the GIC is

$j = mi = 4(1.227\%) = 4.91\%$ compounded annually.

➡ **Check your understanding:** The maturity value of a five-year, $10,000 compound-interest GIC is $14,532.94. To three-figure accuracy, calculate the nominal rate of interest paid on the GIC if interest is compounded monthly. (Answer: 7.50% compounded monthly)

▮▮▮▷ **Related problem:** #3 in Exercise 9.1

TIP

Don't Leave Out the Final Step

The calculation of i is usually not the last step in a problem. Formula (9-1) calculates the periodic interest rate, but typically you are asked to determine either the nominal interest rate or the effective interest rate (to be discussed in Section 9.3). Do not forget to complete the extra step needed to directly answer the question.

EXAMPLE 9.1B	Calculating a Semiannually Compounded Rate of Return

Mr. Dunbar paid $16,000 for a $40,000-face-value strip bond having $19\frac{1}{2}$ years remaining until maturity. (Recall that a strip bond is an investment that returns just one payment, the face value, at maturity.) What semiannually compounded rate of return will Mr. Dunbar earn on his investment?

SOLUTION

Given: $PV = \$16,000$, $FV = \$40,000$, Term $= 19\frac{1}{2}$ years, $m = 2$

Then
$$n = m(\text{Term}) = 2(19.5) = 39$$

$$
\left.
\begin{aligned}
i &= \left(\frac{FV}{PV}\right)^{1/n} - 1 \\
&= \left(\frac{\$40,000}{\$16,000}\right)^{1/39} - 1 \\
&= 2.5^{0.0256410} - 1 \\
&= 0.023773 \\
&= 2.3773\%
\end{aligned}
\right\}
$$

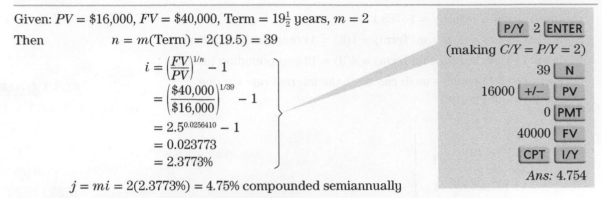

P/Y 2 ENTER
(making $C/Y = P/Y = 2$)
39 N
16000 +/− PV
0 PMT
40000 FV
CPT I/Y
Ans: 4.754

$j = mi = 2(2.3773\%) = 4.75\%$ compounded semiannually

Mr. Dunbar will earn 4.75% compounded semiannually on his strip bond investment.

➡ **Check your understanding:** Five years after it was issued, Mrs. Guo paid $14,599 for a $75,000-face-value, 30-year strip bond. What semiannually compounded rate of return will Mrs. Guo earn on her investment? (Answer: 6.65% compounded semiannually)

▨▶ **Related problem:** #4 in Exercise 9.1

EXAMPLE 9.1C	Calculating an Annually Compounded Rate of Return That Is Equivalent to a Series of Individual Annual Returns

In the years 2011, 2012, 2013, 2014, and 2015, the NEI Ethical Balanced Fund earned annual rates of return of –4.7%, –0.3%, 3.6%, 6.7%, and –0.8%, respectively. Calculate the fund's equivalent annually compounded rate of return for the five years. (This is the fixed annual rate of return that would produce the same overall growth.)

SOLUTION

The equivalent annually compounded rate of return for the three-year period cannot be obtained by simply averaging the five individual annual returns. Instead, we must use a two-step procedure:

Step 1: Use $FV = PV(1 + i_1)(1 + i_2)(1 + i_3) \dots (1 + i_n)$ to calculate how much an investment on December 31, 2010 was worth on December 31, 2015.

Step 2: Calculate the annually compounded rate of return that will produce the *same* growth in five years.

Step 1: For the initial investment, choose a "nice, round" amount such as $100 or $1000.

$$
\begin{aligned}
FV &= PV\left(1 + i_{2011}\right)\left(1 + i_{2012}\right)\left(1 + i_{2013}\right)\left(1 + i_{2014}\right)\left(1 + i_{2015}\right) \\
&= \$1000(1 - 0.047)(1 - 0.003)(1 + 0.036)(1 + 0.067)(1 - 0.008) \\
&= \$1041.89
\end{aligned}
$$

Step 2:
$$
\left.
\begin{aligned}
i &= \left(\frac{FV}{PV}\right)^{\frac{1}{n}} - 1 \\
&= \left(\frac{\$1041.89}{\$1000}\right)^{\frac{1}{5}} - 1 \\
&= 1.041893^{0.2} - 1 \\
&= 0.008241 \\
&= 0.82\%
\end{aligned}
\right\}
$$

P/Y 1 ENTER
(making $C/Y = P/Y = 1$)
5 N
1000 +/− PV
0 PMT
1041.89 FV
CPT I/Y
Ans: 0.82

$j = mi = 1(0.82\%) = 0.82\%$ compounded annually

The mutual fund's equivalent annually compounded rate of return for the 5-year period ended December 31, 2015 was 0.82% compounded annually.

▶ **Check your understanding:** In the years 2011 through 2015, the BMO Asset Allocation Fund earned annual rates of return of −1.5%, 5.9%, 10.5%, 9.0%, and 2.7%, respectively. Calculate the fund's equivalent annually compounded rate of return for the five years. (Answer: 5.23% compounded annually)

▬▶ **Related problem:** #21 in Exercise 9.1

Postscript: At the end of every month, the type of calculation in Example 9.1C is done for about 2000 mutual funds available in Canada. The equivalent compound annual rates of return are calculated for 3-year, 5-year, and 10-year periods terminating at the month-end. These returns are then published on Web sites of major newspapers and on investment sites that specialize in mutual funds. (In fact, these equivalent rates of return are easier to find than the year-by-year returns on which they are based.) You may have noticed that mutual fund advertisements commonly quote mutual fund performance in terms of the 3-year, 5-year, and 10-year compound annual returns. Now you know how they are obtained and how to interpret them.

EXAMPLE 9.1D	Calculating an Inflation-Adjusted (Real) Rate of Return

Over a 10-year period, Brooke's investment in Royal Bank stock grew in value from $11,465 to $18,535. During the same period, the Consumer Price Index (CPI) rose from 109.1 to 126.6. What was her *real* compound annual rate of return on the stock during the decade? (The real rate of return is the rate of return net of inflation. It represents the rate of increase in purchasing power.)

SOLUTION

With the CPI up from 109.1 to 126.6, Brooke needed $\frac{126.6}{109.1}$ times as many dollars at the end of the decade to purchase the same goods and services as at the beginning. The $11,465 value of the stock at the beginning had to grow to $11,465 \times \frac{126.6}{109.1} = \$13,304.02$ just to maintain her purchasing power. In fact, it grew to $18,535. In terms of end-of-decade dollars, her purchasing power rose from $13,304.02 to $18,535. Hence, to obtain the real rate of return, use $PV = \$13,304.02$, $FV = \$18,535$, and $n = 10$.

$$i = \left(\frac{\$18,535}{\$13,304.02}\right)^{\frac{1}{10}} - 1$$
$$= 1.393188^{0.1} - 1$$
$$= 0.03372$$
$$= 3.372\%$$

P/Y 1 ENTER
(making $C/Y = P/Y = 1$)
10 N
13304.02 +/− PV
0 PMT
18535 FV
CPT I/Y
Ans: 3.372

$j = mi = 1(3.372\%) = 3.37\%$ compounded annually

The real rate of return on the Royal Bank stock was 3.37% compounded annually.

▶ **Check your understanding:** Over a four-year period, Al's investment in Tim Horton's stock grew in value from $15,500 to $24,450. During the same period, the CPI rose from 113.0 to 121.3. What was his real annual compound rate of return on the stock during the four-year period? (Answer: 10.10% compounded annually)

▬▶ **Related problem:** #24 in Exercise 9.1

Postscript: Two points should be mentioned:

1. The same answer will be obtained if you choose to adjust for inflation by expressing $18,535 in terms of beginning-of-decade dollars.

2. An entirely different approach may have occurred to you. Suppose you separately calculate the rate of return on the stock, and the rate of inflation from the CPI data. (You would obtain 4.92% and 1.50% compounded annually, respectively.) You might think that

$$\text{Real rate of return} = \text{Actual rate of return} - \text{Rate of inflation}$$
$$= 4.92\% - 1.50\%$$
$$= 3.42\%$$

This is a slightly larger value (by 0.05%) than the strictly correct answer we obtained in the "official solution." The reason for the small difference is quite subtle and technical—we will spare you the details. However, real rates of return are, more often than not, calculated this way. Since nominal rates of return and inflation rates are easily obtained from published data, this approximation is an easier approach and is good enough for most purposes.

 Checkpoint Questions

1. Circle "True" or "False" for each of the following:

   a. If *FV* is less than *PV*, the value of *i* must be a negative number.   True   False

   b. If an investment has a negative rate of return, the *FV* value will be smaller   True   False
      than the *PV* value.

   c. If asked to solve for the nominal rate of compound interest in a problem, the   True   False
      solved value for *i* will be your final answer.

2. Which scenario had the higher periodic rate of return: "$1 grew to $2" or "$3 grew to $5"? The two investments were for the same length of time at the same compounding frequency. Justify your choice.

EXERCISE 9.1

Answers to the odd-numbered problems can be found in the end matter.

BASIC PROBLEMS

Calculate interest rates accurate to the nearest 0.01%.

1. No payments were made on a $3400 loan during its three-year term. What was the annually compounded nominal interest rate on the loan if the amount owed at the end of the term was $4297.91?

2. What was the annually compounded nominal rate of growth if an investment of $1000 grew to be worth $2321.06 after 20 years?

3. An initial $1800 investment was worth $2120.31 after two years and nine months. What quarterly compounded nominal rate of return did the investment earn?

4. A strip bond that will mature $7\frac{1}{2}$ years from now at its $13,000 face value can be purchased today for $9042. What rate of return (compounded semiannually) will this strip bond provide to an investor?

5. The amount owed on a promissory note for $950 after two years and five months is $1036.22. What monthly compounded nominal rate of interest was charged on the debt?

6. Philippe contributed $4300 to an RRSP eight years and six months ago. The money was invested in a Canadian Equity mutual fund. The investment is now worth $5537.82. Over the entire period, what monthly compounded nominal rate of return has the investment delivered?

7. When he died in 1790, Benjamin Franklin left $4600 to the city of Boston, with the stipulation that the money and its earnings could not be used for 100 years. The bequest grew to $332,000 by 1890. What (equivalent) compound annual rate of return did the bequest earn during the 100-year period?

8. Mr. and Mrs. Markovich note that the home they purchased 20 years ago for $70,000 is now appraised at $340,000. What was the (equivalent) annual rate of appreciation in the value of their home during the 20-year period?

9. A $1000 five-year compound-interest GIC matured at $1041.25. What semiannually compounded rate of interest did it earn?

10. The maturity value of a $5000 four-year compound-interest GIC was $5839.72. What quarterly compounded rate of interest did it earn?

11. Three years ago Mikhail invested $7000 in a three-year compound-interest GIC. He has just received its maturity value of $7321.99. What was the monthly compounded rate of interest on the GIC?

12. What annually compounded rate of interest will an investor need to earn if an investment of $100,000 is to grow to be worth $1,000,000 over a 25 year period?

13. Hussain's marketing business grew from only 36 active customers, to a total of 212 customers five years later. What annually compounded rate of growth has Hussain's business experienced over the five-year period?

INTERMEDIATE PROBLEMS

14. On December 31, 2015, the Templeton Growth Fund fact sheet reported that:

    $10,000 INVESTED IN TEMPLETON GROWTH FUND IN 1954 WOULD BE
    WORTH $10.43 MILLION TODAY.

    What compound annual rate of return did the fund realize over this period (December 31, 1954 to December 31, 2015)?

15. Anders discovered an old pay statement from 11 years ago. His monthly salary at the time was $2550 versus his current salary of $4475 per month. At what (equivalent) compound annual rate has his salary grown during the period?

16. The population of Canada grew from 24,820,000 in 1981 to 35,851,800 in 2015. What was the overall compound annual rate of growth in our population during the period?

17. For an investment to double in value during a 10-year period,
    a. What annually compounded rate of return must it earn?
    b. What monthly compounded rate of return must it earn?

18. The Consumer Price Index (based on a value of 100 in 2002) rose from 44.0 in 1980 to 78.4 in 1990. What was the (equivalent) annual rate of inflation in the decade of the 1980s?

19. The Consumer Price Index (based on a value of 100 in 2002) rose from 78.4 in 1990 to 95.4 in 2000. What was the (equivalent) annual rate of inflation in the decade of the 1990s?

20. The Consumer Price Index (based on a value of 100 in 2002) rose from 116.5 in 2010 to 126.6 in 2015. What was the (equivalent) annual rate of inflation in the five years from 2010 to 2015?

21. A portfolio earned annual rates of 20%, −20%, 0%, 20%, and −20% in five successive years. What was the portfolio's five-year equivalent annually compounded rate of return?

22. A portfolio earned annual rates of 20%, 15%, −10%, 25%, and −5% in five successive years. What was the portfolio's five-year equivalent annually compounded rate of return?

23. According to the Canadian Real Estate Association, the average selling price of Canadian homes rose from $67,000 in 1980 to $470,000 in 2016. What has been the overall compound annual appreciation of home prices?

24. An investor's portfolio increased in value from $100,000 to $193,000 over a seven-year period in which the Consumer Price Index rose from 114.1 to 125.2. What was the compound annual real rate of return on the portfolio during the period?

25. An investment grew in value from $14,380 to $21,570 during a five-year period. During that same period, the Consumer Price Index rose from 116.5 to 125.2. What was the compound annual real rate of return during the five years?

ADVANCED PROBLEMS

26. If the number of workers in the manufacturing sector in Canada declined by 9% from the end of 2008 to the end of 2016, what was the compound annual rate of attrition in the industry during the period?

27. A four-year promissory note for $3800 plus interest at 1.5% compounded semiannually was sold 18 months before maturity for $4000. What quarterly compounded nominal rate of return will the buyer realize on her investment?

28. According to Statistics Canada, undergraduate students paid an average of $6191 in tuition fees for the 2015/2016 academic year compared to fees of $4747 for the 2008/2009 year. During the same period, the Consumer Price Index rose from 114.1 to 126.6.

    a. What would have been the average tuition fees for the 2015/2016 year if tuition fees had grown just at the rate of inflation since the 2008/2009 year?

    b. What was the (equivalent) compound annual rate of increase of tuition fees during the period?

    c. What was the (equivalent) compound annual rate of inflation during the period?

29. An investment earned 3% compounded semiannually for two years and 5% compounded annually for the next three years. What was the equivalent annually compounded rate of return for the entire five-year period?

30. The Mawer Canadian Equity Fund won a 2015 Lipper Award for one of the best 10-year compound annual returns of any Canadian mutual fund. This fund invested in securities of larger Canadian companies. The fund's annual returns in successive years from 2005 to 2014 inclusive were 20.60%, 13.95%, 11.51%, −29.68%, 29.48%, 13.78%, 1.91%, 12.68%, 25.45%, and 15.83% respectively. For 3-year, 5-year, and 10-year periods ended December 31, 2015, what were the fund's equivalent annually compounded returns?

If we know values for PV, FV, and i, we can calculate the number of compounding periods and the term of the loan or investment.

Algebraic Method

You can take either of two approaches.
1. If you are familiar with the rules of logarithms, you can substitute the values for PV, FV, and i into $FV = PV(1 + i)^n$ and then solve for n.
2. If you are not comfortable manipulating logarithms, you can use formula (9-2). It is, in fact, just a "dressed-up" version of $FV = PV(1 + i)^n$ in which n is already isolated for you.

NUMBER OF COMPOUNDING PERIODS $$n = \frac{\ln(\frac{FV}{PV})}{\ln(1 + i)}$$ **(9-2)**

In Example 9.2A, we will demonstrate both algebraic methods. Thereafter, only the second approach will be used in the text.

Financial Calculator Method

Enter values for the four known variables—PV, FV, i, and m—into the appropriate memories. Then press
| CPT | N | in sequence to execute the calculation.

TIP

Don't Leave Out the Final Step

The calculation of n is usually not the last step in a problem. Typically you are asked to determine the total time in years and months (rather than the number of compounding periods). After solving for n, do not forget to complete the extra step necessary to directly answer the problem. Recall that formula (8-3) states that $n = m \times$ (Number of years in the term). A simple rearrangement of the formula is: Number of years in the term $= \frac{n}{m}$.

| **EXAMPLE 9.2A** | Calculating the Number of Compounding Periods |

What is the term of a compound-interest GIC if $4000 invested at 5.5% compounded annually earns interest totalling $1227.84?

SOLUTION

Given: $PV = \$4000$, $i = \frac{j}{m} = \frac{5.5\%}{1} = 5.5\%$, Total interest $= \$1227.84$

The maturity value of the GIC is

$$FV = PV + \text{Total interest} = \$4000 + \$1227.84 = \$5227.84$$

Method 1: Use the basic formula $FV = PV(1 + i)^n$ to calculate the number of compounding periods required for $4000 to grow to $5227.84. Substitute the known values for PV, FV, and i, giving

$$\$5227.84 = \$4000(1.055)^n$$

Therefore, $1.055^n = \dfrac{\$5227.84}{\$4000} = 1.30696$

Now take logarithms of both sides. On the left side, use the rule that: $\ln(a^n) = n(\ln a)$

Therefore, $n(\ln 1.055) = \ln 1.30696$

and $n = \dfrac{\ln(1.30696)}{\ln(1.055)} = \dfrac{0.267704}{0.0535408} = 5.000$

Since each compounding period equals one year, the term of the GIC is five years.

Method 2: Substitute the known values into the derived formula (9-2). The number of compounding periods required for \$4000 to grow to \$5227.84 is

$$n = \frac{\ln\left(\dfrac{FV}{PV}\right)}{\ln(1+i)} = \frac{\ln\left(\dfrac{\$5227.84}{\$4000}\right)}{\ln(1.055)}$$

$$= \frac{\ln(1.30696)}{\ln(1.055)}$$

$$= \frac{0.267704}{0.0535408}$$

$$= 5.000$$

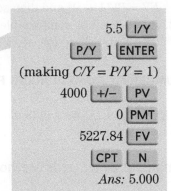

Since each compounding period equals one year, the term of the GIC is five years.

⇨ **Check your understanding:** What is the term of a compound-interest GIC if \$12,000 invested at 4.25% compounded semiannually earns interest totalling \$4,799.42? (Answer: 16 compounding periods; with semiannual compounding, the term is $\frac{16}{2}$ or 8 years.)

▮▮▶ **Related problem:** #3 in Exercise 9.2

TIP

Efficient Use of Your Calculator

The most efficient keystroke sequence for evaluating formula (9-2) in Method 2 of Example 9.2A is

5227.84 ÷ 4000 = LN ÷ 1.055 LN =

On the Sharp EL-738C calculator, the (natural) logarithm function LN is the second function of the 2 key.

Noninteger Values for n

If formula (9-2) or the financial calculator procedure gives a value for n that is not an integer, it means (as you would expect) that the term of the loan or investment includes a partial compounding period. In the final answer, we normally convert the fractional part of n to months, or to months and days (depending on the requested precision).

EXAMPLE 9.2B   **Calculating and Interpreting a Noninteger n**

Rounded to the nearest month, how long will it take a city's population to grow from 75,000 to 100,000 if the annual growth rate is 2%?

SOLUTION

In effect, we are given

$$PV = 75{,}000, FV = 100{,}000, \quad \text{and} \quad i = \frac{j}{m} = \frac{2\%}{1} = 2\% \text{ per year}$$

Using formula (9-2) to calculate the required number of compounding periods, we obtain

$$
\begin{aligned}
n &= \frac{\ln\!\left(\frac{FV}{PV}\right)}{\ln(1 + i)} \\
&= \frac{\ln\!\left(\frac{100{,}000}{75{,}000}\right)}{\ln(1.02)} \\
&= \frac{0.28768}{0.019803} \\
&= 14.527
\end{aligned}
$$

2 | I/Y
P/Y 1 ENTER
(making C/Y = P/Y = 1)
75000 | +/− | PV
0 | PMT
100000 | FV
CPT | N

Ans: 14.527

It requires 14.527 compounding periods for the population to grow from 75,000 to 100,000. Since a compounding period equals one year,

14.527 compounding periods = 14 years + 0.527 × 12 months = 14 years + 6.32 months

Rounded to the nearest month, it will take 14 years and 6 months for the city's population to reach 100,000.

▶ **Check your understanding:** A business is experiencing unit sales growth of 5% per year. Rounded to the nearest month, how long will it take sales to grow from 120,000 to 175,000 units per year? (Answer: 7 years and 9 months)

▶ **Related problem:** #10 in Exercise 9.2

EXAMPLE 9.2C | **Calculating an Investment's Doubling Time**

How long will it take an investment to double in value if it earns 6% compounded quarterly? Include accrued interest and round the answer to the nearest month.

SOLUTION

We require the maturity value of an investment to be twice the initial investment. Therefore, we can simply set $PV = \$1$ and $FV = \$2$.

We are given $i = \frac{j}{m} = \frac{6\%}{4} = 1.5\%$ per quarter.

Substituting in formula (9-2),

$$
\begin{aligned}
n &= \frac{\ln\!\left(\frac{FV}{PV}\right)}{\ln(1 + i)} \\
&= \frac{\ln(2)}{\ln(1.015)} \\
&= 46.556
\end{aligned}
$$

6 | I/Y
P/Y 4 ENTER
(making C/Y = P/Y = 4)
1 | +/− | PV
0 | PMT
2 | FV
CPT | N

Ans: 46.556

The doubling time is

$$\frac{46.556 \text{ quarters}}{4} = 11.667 \text{ years} = 11 \text{ years} + .667 \times 12 \text{ months} = 11 \text{ years and 8 months}$$

An investment earning 6% compounded quarterly will double in 11 years and 8 months (rounded to the nearest month).

⮕ **Check your understanding:** Rounded to the nearest month, how long will it take an investment to double in value if it earns 10% compounded semiannually? Include accrued interest. (Answer: 7 years and 1 month)

▬▶ **Related problem:** #13 in Exercise 9.2

Rule of 72

Investors have a rule of thumb to quickly *estimate* the number of years it will take an investment to double.[2] Known as the **Rule of 72**, it says:

$$\text{Doubling time (in years)} \approx \frac{72}{\text{Percent annual rate of return}}$$

For example, an investment earning 9% compounded annually will double in approximately $\frac{72}{9} = 8$ years. If the investment earns 12% compounded annually, it will double in about $\frac{72}{12} = 6$ years.

EXAMPLE 9.2D	Estimating Then Calculating an Investment's Doubling Time

How long will it take an investment to double in value if it earns 6.65% compounded annually? Begin by estimating the answer using the Rule of 72, then solve for a more precise answer. Include accrued interest and round the answer to the nearest month.

SOLUTION

Using the Rule of 72, the investment's doubling time is approximately $\frac{72}{6.65} = 10.827$ years, or 10 years and $0.827 \times 12 = 9.9$ months. Rounded to the nearest month, we estimate the investment's value will double in 10 years and 10 months.

Solving algebraically, we can set $PV = \$1$ and $FV = \$2$.

We are given $i = \frac{j}{m} = \frac{6.65\%}{1} = 6.65\%$ per year.

Substituting in formula (9-2),

$$n = \frac{\ln\left(\frac{FV}{PV}\right)}{\ln(1+i)}$$
$$= \frac{\ln(2)}{\ln(1.0665)}$$
$$= 10.766$$

The doubling time is

6.65 I/Y
P/Y 1 ENTER
(making $C/Y = P/Y = 1$)
1 +/− PV
0 PMT
2 FV
CPT N
Ans: 10.766

$$10.766 \text{ years} = 10 \text{ years} + 0.766 \times 12 \text{ months} = 10 \text{ years and } 9.2 \text{ months}$$

An investment earning 6.65% compounded annually will double in 10 years and 9 months (rounded to the nearest month), which is close to the estimate of 10 years and 10 months obtained using the Rule of 72.

[2] The approximation is very good for annual interest rates between 5% and 11%; the value estimated for the doubling time is within 2% of its true value.

⟹ **Check your understanding:** Use the Rule of 72 to estimate how long it will take an investment to double in value if it earns 9.2% compounded annually. Then, obtain a more exact answer by solving algebraically or using a financial calculator. Include accrued interest and round the answers to the nearest month. (Answer: Using Rule of 72: 7 years and 10 months; solved answer: 7 years and 11 months)

▭▶ **Related problem:** #12 in Exercise 9.2

Valuing Strip Bonds and Other Single-Payment Investments

Most loans and investments are structured so that the full term equals an integer multiple of the compounding period. However, an existing loan or investment contract may be sold and transferred to a new investor on a date that does not coincide with an interest-conversion date. The time remaining until maturity includes a partial compounding interval which must be taken into account in the price calculation. Consequently, n is not an integer in such cases.

In Table 9.1, consider the Province of British Columbia strip bond maturing on July 9, 2022. Let us see how the market's required rate of return (1.62% in the "Yield" column) on February 26, 2016 determines the $90.24 market price quoted on that date. (Recall that bond prices are quoted in the media as the price per $100 of face value, and that yields are understood to be annual rates with semiannual compounding.)

TABLE 9.1 Strip Bond Price and Yield Quotations (February 26, 2016)

Issuer	Maturity date	Price ($)	Yield (%)
Province of Saskatchewan	May 30, 2018	97.73	1.03
Province of Quebec	March 21, 2019	96.62	1.13
Government of Canada	September 15, 2020	97.09	0.65
Province of Nova Scotia	July 30, 2021	91.00	1.75
Province of British Columbia	July 9, 2022	90.24	1.62
Province of Manitoba	September 5, 2025	77.16	2.75
Province of Ontario	September 8, 2027	73.73	2.66

Source: Perimeter Markets Inc., http://www.pfin.ca/canadianfixedincome/Default.aspx.

As indicated on the following timeline, the quoted price should be the present value of the $100 face value discounted at 1.62% compounded semiannually all the way back from the maturity date (July 9, 2022) to February 26, 2016. For the present value calculation, we need to know the number of compounding periods in this interval. In general, this number will not be an integer. Determine the integer and fractional components of the number separately. Working back from the maturity date, there are 6 years (12 compounding periods) from July 9, 2022 back to July 9, 2016. Then there are an additional 134 days from July 9, 2016 back to February 26, 2016. This 134-day interval is the fraction $\frac{134}{182}$ of the full 182-day compounding period from January 9, 2016 to July 9, 2016.

Therefore, $n = 12\frac{134}{182} = 12.7363$ compounding periods, $i = \frac{1.62\%}{2} = 0.81\%$, and

$$\text{Price}, PV = FV(1 + i)^{-n} = \$100(1.0081)^{-12.7363} = \$90.24$$

This equals the quoted price.

EXAMPLE 9.2E	Calculating the Time Until Maturity of a Strip Bond

A \$10,000-face-value strip bond was purchased for \$4188.77. At this price, the bond provided the investor with a return of 5.938% compounded semiannually until the maturity date. To the nearest day, how long before the maturity date was the bond purchased? Assume that each half-year is exactly 182 days long.

SOLUTION

The purchase price of a strip bond equals the present value, on the date of purchase, of the bond's face value. The prevailing market rate of return should be used as the discount rate. In this example, \$4188.77 is the present value of \$10,000 discounted at 5.938% compounded semiannually. To determine the time interval used in the present value calculation, we must first calculate the number of compounding periods. We are given

$$PV = \$4188.77,\ FV = \$10,000,\quad \text{and}\quad i = \frac{j}{m} = \frac{5.938\%}{2} = 2.969\%$$

Substituting in formula (9-2),

$$
\left.
\begin{aligned}
n &= \frac{\ln\!\left(\dfrac{FV}{PV}\right)}{\ln(1 + i)} \\[2mm]
&= \frac{\ln\!\left(\dfrac{\$10,000}{\$4188.77}\right)}{\ln(1.02969)} \\[2mm]
&= 29.74176
\end{aligned}
\right\}
$$

5.938	I/Y
P/Y 2	ENTER

(making $C/Y = P/Y = 2$)

4188.77 +/-	PV
0	PMT
10000	FV
CPT	N

Ans: 29.74176

Since each compounding period is 0.5 year, the time remaining to maturity is

$$(0.50 \times 29)\ \text{years} + (0.74176 \times 182)\ \text{days} = 14.5\ \text{years} + 135.00\ \text{days}$$

Hence, the bond was purchased with 14 years, 6 months, and 135 days remaining until its maturity date.

▶ **Check your understanding:** A \$5000 strip bond was purchased for \$3054.29, providing the investor with a return of 3.9% compounded semiannually until the maturity date. To the nearest day, how long before the maturity date was the bond purchased? (Answer: 12 years, 6 months, and 95 days before maturity)

▩▶ **Related problem:** #17 in Exercise 9.2

EXAMPLE 9.2F	Solving for a Noninteger n in a Discounting Problem

A loan contract requires the payment of \$4000 plus interest two years after the contract's date of issue. The interest rate on the \$4000 face value is 9.6% compounded quarterly. Before the maturity date, the original lender sold the contract to an investor for \$4327.70. The sale price was based on a discount rate of 8.5% compounded semiannually from the date of sale. How many months before the maturity date did the sale take place?

SOLUTION

The selling price represents the present value (on the date of sale) of the loan's maturity value. In other words, $4327.70 was the present value of the maturity value, discounted at 8.5% compounded semiannually. Therefore, the solution requires two steps as indicated in the following time diagram.

1. Calculate the maturity value of the debt.

2. Determine the length of time over which the maturity value was discounted to give a present value of $4327.70.

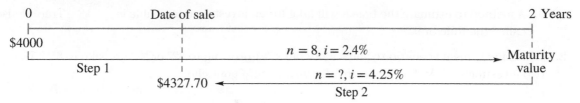

Step 1: For the maturity value calculation,

$$n = m(\text{Term}) = 4(2) = 8 \quad \text{and} \quad i = \frac{j}{m} = \frac{9.6\%}{4} = 2.4\%.$$

The maturity value of the contract is

$$\begin{aligned} FV &= PV(1 + i)^n \\ &= \$4000(1.024)^8 \\ &= \$4835.70 \end{aligned}$$

Step 2: For discounting the maturity value,

$$i = \frac{j}{m} = \frac{8.5\%}{2} = 4.25\%.$$

The number of compounding periods between the date of sale and the maturity date is

$$\begin{aligned} n &= \frac{\ln\!\left(\dfrac{FV}{PV}\right)}{\ln(1 + i)} \\ &= \frac{\ln\!\left(\dfrac{\$4835.70}{\$4327.70}\right)}{\ln(1.0425)} \\ &= 2.6666 \end{aligned}$$

Each compounding period is six months long. Therefore, the date of sale was

$$2.6666 \times 6 \text{ months} = 16.00 \text{ months before the maturity date}$$

Calculator panel (Step 1):
9.6 **I/Y**
P/Y 4 **ENTER**
(making $C/Y = P/Y = 4$)
8 **N**
4000 **+/−** **PV**
0 **PMT**
CPT **FV**
Ans: 4835.70

Calculator panel (Step 2):
Same *PMT, FV*
8.5 **I/Y**
P/Y 2 **ENTER**
(making $C/Y = P/Y = 2$)
4327.70 **+/−** **PV**
CPT **N**
Ans: 2.6666

➡ **Check your understanding:** A loan contract requires the payment of $12,000 plus interest five years after the contract's issue date. The interest rate on the $12,000 face value is 6% compounded monthly. The contract was later sold by the original lender to an investor for $13,895.80. The sale price was based on a discount rate of 4% compounded quarterly from the date of the sale. How many months before the maturity date did the sale take place? (Answer: 46 months before the maturity date)

◼◼▶ **Related problem:** #25 in Exercise 9.2

Checkpoint Questions

1. Circle "True" or "False" for each of the following:

   a. The solved value, n, is always equal to the number of years in the term of   True   False
   the loan or investment.

   b. If n is equal to the number of years in the term of the loan or investment,   True   False
   then the compounding frequency must be annual.

   c. A method to estimate the time it will take for an investment to double is   True   False
   called the Rule of 92.

2. Which investment scenario requires more time: "$1 growing to $2" or "$3 growing to $5"? The two investments earn the same rate of return. Justify your choice.

EXERCISE 9.2

Answers to the odd-numbered problems can be found in the end matter.

BASIC PROBLEMS

1. A $1100 investment earning 2.3% compounded annually grew to $1855.81. What was the term of the investment?

2. How long did it take $4625 earning 4.875% compounded annually to grow to $6768.42?

3. $5000 invested in a GIC earning 1.7% compounded semiannually earned interest of $350.29. What was the term of the GIC?

4. The current balance on a loan is $3319.59. If the interest rate on the loan is 5% compounded monthly, how long ago was the $2870 loan made?

5. How long did it take a $5000 investment earning 8% compounded quarterly to grow to be worth $17,067.92?

6. A few years ago Avtar invested $6000 in a compound-interest GIC that earned 2.5% compounded semiannually. He recently received the maturity value of $6626.92. What was the term of the GIC?

7. Marilyn was supposed to pay $1450 to Bernice on March 1. Some time later Marilyn paid Bernice an equivalent payment of $1528.01, allowing for a time value of money of 4.5% compounded monthly. When did Marilyn make the payment?

8. What is the remaining time until the maturity date of a $10,000 strip bond if it is purchased for $4011.33 to yield 6.4% compounded semiannually until maturity?

INTERMEDIATE PROBLEMS

9. Rounded to the nearest month, how long will it take a town's population to grow from 32,500 to 40,000 if the annual growth rate is 3%?

10. Rounded to the nearest month, how long will it take a business to grow from 400 customers per year to 550 customers per year if the business owner expects the customer base to grow by 12.5% per year?

11. Use the Rule of 72 to estimate how long it will take for an investment to double in value if it earns 4.65% compounded annually. Then, solve for the exact doubling time using the algebraic approach or a financial calculator. Round answers to the nearest month.

12. Marina deposited $1800 into an investment earning 6.4% compounded quarterly. When her investment is worth $2000, she will withdraw the money and make a down payment on a car. Rounded to the nearest month, how long will Marina wait until she will have a sufficient down payment to purchase the car?

13. Rounded to the nearest month, how long will it take an investment to double if it earns

    a. 8.4% compounded quarterly?

    b. 10.5% compounded semiannually?

14. Rounded to the nearest month, how long will it take an investment to triple if it earns

    a. 9% compounded annually?

    b. 8% compounded quarterly?

15. Rounded to the nearest month, how long before a scheduled payment of $10,000 would a payment of $5000 be an economically equivalent alternative? Assume money is worth 5% compounded annually.

16. How long before a future payment of $1000 would a payment of $100 be an economically equivalent alternative? Round your answer to the nearest month. Assume money can earn 4.8% compounded semiannually.

17. A $20,000-face-value strip bond was purchased for $10,045.94, providing the investor with a rate of return of 4.2% compounded semiannually. To the nearest day, how long before the maturity date was the bond purchased? Assume that each half-year is exactly 182 days long.

18. A $4000 loan at 4.8% compounded monthly was settled by a single payment of $5000 including accrued interest. Rounded to the nearest day, how long after the initial loan was the $5000 payment made? For the purpose of determining the number of days in a partial month, assume that a full month has 30 days.

19. If money is worth 3.6% compounded quarterly, how long (to the nearest day) before a scheduled payment of $6000 will $5000 be an equivalent payment? For the purpose of determining the number of days in a partial calendar quarter, assume that a full quarter has 91 days.

20. Wilf paid $557.05 for a $1000-face-value strip bond. At this price the investment will yield a return of 5.22% compounded semiannually. How long (to the nearest day) before its maturity date did Wilf purchase the bond? Assume that each half-year has exactly 182 days.

21. A $5000-face-value strip bond may be purchased today for $1073.36 yielding the purchaser 7.27% compounded semiannually. How much time (to the nearest day) remains until the maturity date? Assume that each half-year has exactly 182 days.

ADVANCED PROBLEMS

22. Rounded to the nearest month, how long will it take money to lose half of its purchasing power if the annual inflation rate is

    a. 2.5%?

    b. 3.5%?

23. Consider the Province of Nova Scotia strip bond in Table 9.1.

    a. Present calculations to verify, to the nearest dollar, the bond's price on February 26, 2016, based on the quoted yield of 1.75% compounded semiannually.

    b. What would the bond's price be on September 1, 2018 if the yield remains the same?

24. Consider the Province of Ontario strip bond in Table 9.1.

    a. Present calculations to verify, to the nearest dollar, the bond's price on February 26, 2016, based on the quoted yield of 2.66% compounded semiannually.

    b. What would the price be on January 1, 2020 if the bond's yield remains the same?

25. The proceeds from the sale of a $4500 five-year promissory note bearing interest at 5% compounded quarterly were $5277.81. How many months before its maturity date was the note sold if it was discounted to yield 6.3% compounded monthly?

26. When discounted to yield 7.98% compounded monthly, a $2600 three-year promissory note bearing interest at 9.25% compounded annually was priced at $3110.41. How many months after the issue date did the discounting take place?

27. $7500 was borrowed for a four-year term at 9% compounded quarterly. The terms of the loan allow prepayment of the loan based on discounting the loan's maturity value at 7% compounded quarterly. How long (to the nearest day) before the maturity date was the loan prepaid if the payout amount was $9380.24 including accrued interest? For the purpose of determining the number of days in a partial calendar quarter, assume that a full quarter has 91 days.

9.3 | Effective Interest Rate

LO2   The future value of $100 invested for one year at 10% compounded semiannually is $110.25. The future value of $100 invested for one year at 10.25% compounded annually is also $110.25. Therefore, an interest rate of 10% compounded semiannually has the *same effect* as a rate of 10.25% compounded annually. The **effective interest rate**, f, is defined as the *annually* compounded rate[3] that produces the *same* future value after one year as the given nominal rate. In the present example, 10% compounded semiannually has an effective rate of 10.25%. (When an effective rate is quoted or calculated, the compounding frequency does not need to be specified. Everyone understands from the definition of effective interest rate that "effective" implies "annual compounding.")

> ### TIP ✓
>
> **Intuitive Approach for Calculating f**
>
> Note in the preceding example that the effective interest rate (10.25%) is numerically equal to the actual amount of interest ($10.25) that $100 will earn in one year at the given nominal rate. This is a general result for all nominal interest rates. We can use this idea for our financial calculator method for determining f. That is, we can calculate the future value of $100 after one year at the given nominal rate. Then we can just inspect the future value to see the amount of interest earned (and thereby identify the value of f).

We can readily derive a formula for f. Suppose you invest $100 for one year at the effective rate f (compounded annually) and another $100 for one year at the nominal rate $j = mi$. Their future values are calculated in parallel columns below.

---

[3] There is a natural preference in business for discussing interest rates on the basis of annual compounding. This is because an *annually* compounded rate of return represents the *actual* percentage increase in a year. For example, at a return of 9% compounded annually, you can immediately say that $100 will grow by 9% ($9) in the next year. But at a return of 9% compounded monthly, you cannot say how much $100 will grow in a year without a short calculation. In the second case, the *actual* percentage increase will be more than 9%.

The first $100 will undergo just one compounding of the effective rate f.	The second $100 will undergo m compoundings of the periodic rate i.
$$\begin{aligned} FV &= PV(1+i)^n \\ &= \$100(1+f)^1 \end{aligned}$$	$$\begin{aligned} FV &= PV(1+i)^n \\ &= \$100(1+i)^m \end{aligned}$$

For f to be equivalent to the nominal rate j, these future values must be equal. That is,

$$\$100(1+f) = \$100(1+i)^m$$
$$1+f = (1+i)^m$$

EFFECTIVE INTEREST RATE $$f = (1+i)^m - 1$$ (9-3)

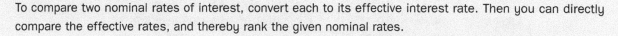

TIP

Comparing Nominal Rates of Interest

To compare two nominal rates of interest, convert each to its effective interest rate. Then you can directly compare the effective rates, and thereby rank the given nominal rates.

EXAMPLE 9.3A	Converting a Nominal Interest Rate to an Effective Interest Rate

What is the effective rate of interest corresponding to 4.5% compounded monthly?

SOLUTION

Given: $j = 4.5\%$, $m = 12$

For the financial calculator solution, we will use the intuitive approach described in the Tip box "Intuitive Approach for Calculating f." This approach is shown at the right.

Alternatively, we can use formula (9-3).

$i = \dfrac{j}{m} = \dfrac{4.5\%}{12} = 0.375\%$ per month and

$$\begin{aligned} f &= (1+i)^m - 1 \\ &= (1.00375)^{12} - 1 \\ &= 1.04594 - 1 \\ &= 0.04594 \\ &= 4.59\% \end{aligned}$$

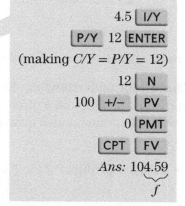

The effective interest rate is 4.59% (compounded annually).

➡ **Check your understanding:** What is the effective rate of interest corresponding to 8.4% compounded quarterly? (Answer: 8.67% effective rate)

▰▰▷ **Related problem:** #1 in Exercise 9.3

EXAMPLE 9.3B	Comparing Alternative Nominal Interest Rates

Which is the most attractive of the following interest rates offered on five-year GICs?

a. 5.70% compounded annually

b. 5.68% compounded semiannually

c. 5.66% compounded quarterly

d. 5.64% compounded monthly

SOLUTION

The preferred rate is the one having the highest effective rate. The algebraic calculations of the effective rates are presented in the following table.

	j	m	i	$f = (1 + i)^m - 1$
a.	5.70%	1	0.057	$f = j$ when $m = 1$; $f = 5.700\%$
b.	5.68%	2	0.0284	$f = (1.0284)^2 - 1 = 0.05761 = 5.761\%$
c.	5.66%	4	0.01415	$f = (1.01415)^4 - 1 = 0.05781 = 5.781\%$
d.	5.64%	12	0.0047	$f = (1.0047)^{12} - 1 = 0.05788 = 5.788\%$

In Appendix 9A, we describe and demonstrate the use of the Texas Instruments BA II PLUS's Interest Conversion Worksheet (ICONV). Let us now use that worksheet to calculate the effective interest rates in Parts (b), (c), and (d).

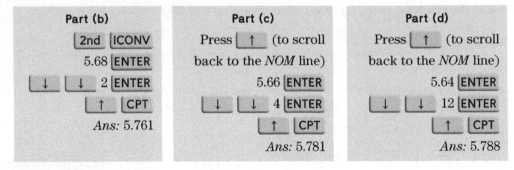

The most attractive rate is 5.64% compounded monthly since it has the highest effective rate.

➡ **Check your understanding:** An investor can earn 4.4% compounded quarterly or 4.35% compounded monthly on a three-year investment. Which is the most attractive interest rate? (Answer: 4.4% compounded quarterly is more attractive as it has a slightly higher effective rate.)

▮▮▮▶ **Related problem:** #4 in Exercise 9.3

Math Apps

BEWARE OF PAYDAY LOANS!

Every year, more than two million Canadians use a "payday loan"—a short-term loan designed to help a borrower cope with an occasional and unexpected cash-flow problem until their next paycheque arrives.

Payday loans are convenient. The lender generally does not do a credit check, so the transaction can be performed quickly. Such lenders typically offer extended hours and make no enquiries about the purpose of the loan. Online payday loan providers are even more convenient!

Most payday loans are in the range of $300 for a duration of about two weeks, and the lenders require that the borrower show proof of continuous employment for a minimum of three months, evidence of his or her address, and proof of having a chequing account.

The payday loan industry has been criticized for charging high rates to the people who can least afford them, and has come under scrutiny in many provinces. Most provincial governments have enacted legislation to limit the fees and rates payday lenders can provide.

Nevertheless, critics argue that even those regulated fees are too high. In Ontario, for example, payday loan charges are capped at $21 for every $100 borrowed. To many people (especially those who have not studied business math), it might seem that the payday lender is charging an interest rate of 21%; while that is indeed a high rate, it is in line with the rates consumers are used to seeing on credit cards. But you should have quickly seen the flaw in this thinking. The $21 fee is being charged on a short-term loan, not on a $100 loan for an entire year! If you pay $21 to borrow $100 for a two-week payday loan, the annualized rate of simple interest is $0.21 \times 26 \times 100 = 546\%$ per year.

In Ontario, legislation prevents a borrower from taking out another loan with a payday lender to immediately repay a previous one. This is designed to head off a situation in which interest begins to compound. However, there are no industry-wide databases or information sharing between payday loan companies that would prevent a borrower from securing a loan from a second payday loan company to repay a loan with an original lender.

Suppose, for example, that you borrow $300 for two weeks from an Ontario payday loan company that charges the maximum fee of $21 per $100 borrowed. At the end of the two weeks, you owe $300 + 3($21) = $363. If you don't have the money, you go to a second lender and borrow $400 for two weeks. You pay Lender 1 the $363 you owe, and buy some groceries with the $37 left over. At the end of two weeks, you owe $400 + 4($21) = $484 to Lender 2. If you still don't have the money, you are now off to Lender 3 to borrow $500. You see how this is spiralling out of control!

The Canadian Payday Loan Association (CPLA) was established in 2004, and represents about 950 licensed retail and online payday providers in Canada. According to their Web site (www.cpla-acps.ca), the mandate of the CPLA is "to work with federal and provincial governments to achieve a regulatory framework that protects customers and allows for a viable competitive industry." The association argues that licensed payday loan providers offer an important service, offering help for emergency situations, and filling a need for low-value, easily accessed, short-term loans—a niche that traditional banks and credit unions do not want to fill. Payday loans are, according to industry advocates, a viable alternative when infrequent cash-flow problems emerge, saving the borrower from, for example, having a rent cheque bounce or phone service cut off for lack of payment.

Despite the efforts of the CPLA, however, some cities are attempting to curb the growth of payday lenders in their communities, arguing that payday loan storefronts tend to be concentrated in low-income neighbourhoods, and create a cycle of debt and poverty. According the CPLA's Stan Keyes, however, without access to licensed payday loan providers, people will turn to unlicensed, online lenders that charge even higher rates. And "where is this unlicensed lender operating from? Belize, or the Cayman Islands? Is there protection against the borrower's bank account ... being drained by an unscrupulous lender? ... So be careful what you ask for."

Source: Quote, "where is this unlicensed lender operating from? ...," originally in "Payday Loans: Predatory Loan Sharks or Crucial Fix in a Pinch?" *The Globe and Mail*, Friday, May 15, 2015.

EXAMPLE 9.3C	Finding the Effective Rate Given the Principal and Maturity Value

Calculate the effective rate of interest if $100 grew to $150 in $5\frac{1}{2}$ years with quarterly compounding.

SOLUTION

The problem can be solved by first finding the quarterly compounded nominal rate that produces the given maturity value. Then the corresponding effective rate may be calculated. But this two-step solution is unnecessarily long.

The essential question (which may be answered in one step) is:
At what annually compounded rate will $100 grow to $150 after $5\frac{1}{2}$ years?

With $PV = \$100$, $FV = \$150$, $m = 1$, and $n = 5.5$, formula (9-1) gives

$$
\begin{aligned}
i &= \left(\frac{FV}{PV}\right)^{1/n} - 1 \\
&= \left(\frac{\$150}{\$100}\right)^{1/5.5} - 1 \\
&= 1.5^{0.\overline{18}} - 1 \\
&= 0.0.0765
\end{aligned}
$$

P/Y	1 ENTER

(making $C/Y = P/Y = 1$)

5.5	N
100 +/−	PV
0	PMT
150	FV
CPT	I/Y

Ans: 7.65

Since $100 will grow to $150 in $5\frac{1}{2}$ years at 7.65% compounded annually, the effective interest rate is 7.65%.

➡ **Check your understanding:** Calculate the effective rate of interest if $3600 grew to $4236.74 in $6\frac{1}{4}$ years with monthly compounding. (Answer: 2.64% effective rate)

▮▮▮➤ **Related problem:** #10 in Exercise 9.3

TIP ✔

Clarification of Terminology

Be clear on the distinction between the descriptions "compounded semiannually" and "per half-year." The former refers to the compounding *frequency*. The latter refers to the compounding *period*. For example, if you hear or read "6% compounded semiannually," you are being given the value for j. Then $i = \frac{j}{m} = \frac{6\%}{2} = 3\%$ (per half-year). On the other hand, if an interest rate is described as "6% per half-year," you are being given the value for i and the period to which it applies. Then $j = mi = 2(6\%) = 12\%$ compounded semiannually.

EXAMPLE 9.3D	Calculating the Effective Interest Rate on a Credit Card

A department store credit card quotes a rate of 1.75% per month on the unpaid balance. Calculate the effective rate of interest being charged.

SOLUTION

Since accrued interest is paid or converted to principal each month, we have monthly compounding with $i = 1.75\%$ per month, $m = 12$, and $j = mi = 12(1.75\%) = 21\%$ compounded monthly.

Therefore,

$$
\begin{aligned}
f &= (1 + i)^m - 1 \\
&= (1.0175)^{12} - 1 \\
&= 0.23144 \\
&= 23.14\%
\end{aligned}
$$

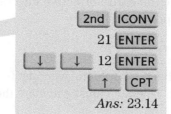

2nd ICONV
21 ENTER
↓ ↓ 12 ENTER
↑ CPT
Ans: 23.14

The effective rate on the credit card is 23.14%.

➡ **Check your understanding:** If a credit card quotes a rate of 2.2% per month on unpaid balances, what effective rate of interest is being charged? (Answer: 29.84% effective rate)

▰▰▷ **Related problem:** #14 in Exercise 9.3

EXAMPLE 9.3E | **Converting an Effective Interest Rate to a Nominal Interest Rate**

What monthly compounded (nominal) rate of interest has an effective rate of 10%?

SOLUTION

Given: $f = 10\%$, $m = 12$

Substitute these values into formula (9-3) and solve for i.

$$
\begin{aligned}
f &= (1 + i)^m - 1 \\
0.10 &= (1 + i)^{12} - 1 \\
1.10 &= (1 + i)^{12}
\end{aligned}
$$

2nd ICONV
↓ 10 ENTER
↓ 12 ENTER
↓ CPT
Ans: 9.57

Now use the rule that

If $x^m = a$, then $x = a^{1/m}$

Therefore,

$$
\begin{aligned}
1.1^{1/12} &= 1 + i \\
1 + i &= 1.1^{0.08\overline{3}} \\
i &= 1.007974 - 1 \\
&= 0.007974 \\
&= 0.7974\%
\end{aligned}
$$

Then $j = mi = 12(0.7974\%) = 9.57\%$ compounded monthly.

➡ **Check your understanding:** What nominal rate of interest compounded quarterly has an effective rate of 8%? (Answer: 7.77% compounded quarterly)

▰▰▷ **Related problem:** #19 in Exercise 9.3

EXAMPLE 9.3F	Converting an Interest Rate from Nominal to Effective and Back to Nominal

The department store mentioned in Example 9.3D has been charging 1.75% per month on its credit card. In response to lower prevailing interest rates, the board of directors has agreed to reduce the card's effective interest rate by 4%. To the nearest 0.01%, what will be the new periodic rate (per month)?

SOLUTION

To solve this problem, we must first calculate the effective rate corresponding to $i = 1.75\%$ per month. Then we must calculate the new monthly compounded rate whose effective rate is 4% lower.

Step 1: See the solution to Example 9.3D for this calculation. We obtained $f = 23.14\%$.

Step 2: The new effective rate must be $23.14\% - 4\% = 19.14\%$.

Substitute $f = 19.14\%$ and $m = 12$ into formula (9-3).

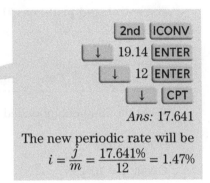

$$f = (1 + i)^m - 1$$
$$0.1914 = (1 + i)^{12} - 1$$
$$1.1914 = (1 + i)^{12}$$
$$1 + i = 1.1914^{1/12}$$
$$i = 1.1914^{0.08\overline{3}} - 1$$
$$= 1.01470 - 1$$
$$= 0.01470$$
$$= 1.47\%$$

2nd ICONV
↓ 19.14 ENTER
↓ 12 ENTER
↓ CPT
Ans: 17.641

The new periodic rate will be
$$i = \frac{j}{m} = \frac{17.641\%}{12} = 1.47\%$$

The new periodic interest rate on the credit card will be 1.47% per month.

➡ **Check your understanding:** A credit card company currently charging 2.2% per month wishes to raise the card's effective interest rate by 3%. To the nearest 0.01%, what will be the new periodic rate (per month)? (Answer: 2.39% per month)

▪▪▪▶ **Related problem:** #21 in Exercise 9.3

? Checkpoint Questions

1. What is meant by the effective rate of interest?

2. Circle "True" or "False" for each of the following:

   a. The effective rate of interest is always numerically smaller than the nominal interest rate.   True   False

   b. The effective interest rate is never equal to the nominal interest rate.   True   False

   c. A semiannually compounded nominal rate and a monthly compounded nominal rate have the same effective rate. The semiannually compounded rate must have a larger nominal value.   True   False

3. From a lender's point of view, would you rather disclose to borrowers the nominal interest rate or the effective interest rate?

EXERCISE 9.3

BASIC PROBLEMS

Calculate interest rates and growth rates accurate to the nearest 0.01%.

1. What is the effective interest rate corresponding to a nominal annual rate of
    a. 6% compounded semiannually?   **b.** 6% compounded quarterly?

2. What is the effective interest rate corresponding to a nominal annual rate of
    a. 3.6% compounded quarterly?   **b.** 3.6% compounded monthly?

3. What is the effective interest rate corresponding to a nominal annual rate of
    a. 9% compounded semiannually?   **b.** 9% compounded monthly?

4. Which of the following nominal interest rates has the highest effective rate: 12% compounded annually, 11.9% compounded semiannually, 11.8% compounded quarterly, or 11.7% compounded monthly?

5. Which interest rate would you prefer to earn on a three-year GIC: 6% compounded monthly, 6.1% compounded quarterly, 6.2% compounded semiannually, or 6.3% compounded annually?

6. Which interest rate would you prefer to pay on a loan: 9% compounded monthly, 9.1% compounded quarterly, 9.2% compounded semiannually, or 9.3% compounded annually?

7. Camille can obtain a residential mortgage loan from a bank at 5.5% compounded semiannually or from an independent mortgage broker at 5.4% compounded monthly. Which source should she pick if other terms and conditions of the loan are the same? Present calculations that support your answer.

8. Lisa is offered a loan from a bank at 4.2% compounded monthly. A credit union offers similar terms, but at a rate of 4.4% compounded semiannually. Which loan should she accept? Present calculations that support your answer.

9. Craig can buy a three-year compound-interest GIC paying 1.6% compounded semiannually or 1.56% compounded monthly. Which option should he choose? Present calculations that support your answer.

INTERMEDIATE PROBLEMS

10. After 27 months of quarterly compounding, a $3000 debt had grown to $3810. What effective rate of interest was being charged on the debt?

11. If a $5000 investment grew to $6450 in 30 months of monthly compounding, what effective rate of return was the investment earning?

12. Section 347 of the *Criminal Code* of Canada makes it illegal to charge more than 60% annual interest. Is a private lender who is charging a rate of 4.2% per month operating within the law? Provide calculations to support your answer.

13. An investment of $28,000 earned $7353.84 of interest in 4 years, 6 months of semiannual compounding.
     a. What nominal rate did the investor earn?
     b. What effective rate did the investor earn?

14. What is the effective rate of interest on a credit card that calculates interest at the rate of 1.8% per month?

15. If an invoice indicates that interest at the rate of 2% per month will be charged on overdue amounts, what effective rate of interest will be charged?

16. A company reports that its sales have grown 3% per quarter for the last eight fiscal quarters. What annual growth rate has the company been experiencing for the last two years?

17. If the nominal rate of interest paid on a savings account is 2% compounded monthly, what is the effective rate of interest?

18. ABC Ltd. reports that its sales are growing at the rate of 1.3% per month. DEF Inc. reports sales increasing by 4% each quarter. What is each company's effective annual rate of sales growth?

ADVANCED PROBLEMS

19. Belleville Credit Union has established interest rates on its three-year GICs so that the effective rate of interest is 2.6% on all three compounding options. What are the monthly, semiannually, and annually compounded rates?

20. Columbia Trust wants its annually, semiannually, and monthly compounded five-year GICs all to have an effective interest rate of 2.75%. What nominal annual rates should it quote for the three compounding options?

21. A department store chain currently charges 18% compounded monthly on its credit card. To what amount should it set the monthly compounded annual rate if it wants to add 2% to the effective interest rate?

22. An oil company wants to drop the effective rate of interest on its credit card by 3%. If it currently charges a periodic rate of 1.7% per month, at what amount should it set the periodic rate?

9.4 | Equivalent Interest Rates

LO3 The main purpose of this section is to prepare you for a routine calculation you will carry out for a broad category of annuities in Chapters 10, 11, 12, and 13. The concept behind the calculation is developed here because it is an extension of ideas from Section 9.3.

Equivalent interest rates are interest rates that produce the *same* future value after one year. For example, 8% compounded quarterly and 8.08% compounded semiannually are equivalent *nominal* interest rates. If you calculate the future value of $100 invested at either rate for one year, you will obtain $108.24. You can see that equivalent interest rates have *different numerical values* but produce the *same effect*.

If *nominal* rates are equivalent, so also are their respective *periodic* rates. From the preceding example, we can conclude that

$$i = \frac{8\%}{4} = 2\% \text{ per quarter is } equivalent \text{ to } i = \frac{8.08\%}{2} = 4.04\% \text{ per half-year}$$

They will both produce the same future value when compounded over a one-year term.

We want to be able to answer questions such as "What periodic rate per half-year is equivalent to 2.5% per quarter?" To answer this and similar questions, we will derive a formula that answers the general question "What i_2 with a specified m_2 is equivalent to a given i_1 with a given m_1?"

For equivalence, $100 invested at each rate for one year must have the same future value. The two investments are shown in the following diagrams. Both future values are obtained using $FV = PV(1 + i)^n$.

0	1 Year	0	1 Year

$$\$100 \xrightarrow{n = m_1, \ i = i_1} \$100(1 + i_1)^{m_1} \qquad \$100 \xrightarrow{n = m_2, \ i = i_2} \$100(1 + i_2)^{m_2}$$

We want to solve for the value of i_2 that makes the two future values equal. That is, solve for i_2 in

$$\$100(1 + i_2)^{m_2} = \$100(1 + i_1)^{m_1}$$
$$(1 + i_2)^{m_2} = (1 + i_1)^{m_1}$$

Divide both exponents by m_2, giving

$$1 + i_2 = (1 + i_1)^{m_1/m_2}$$

Hence,

EQUIVALENT PERIODIC RATE $\qquad\qquad i_2 = (1 + i_1)^{m_1/m_2} - 1$ $\qquad\qquad$ **(9-4)**

To answer the question "What periodic rate per half-year is equivalent to 2.5% per quarter?" substitute $m_2 = 2$, $i_1 = 2.5\% = 0.025$, and $m_1 = 4$ into formula (9-4).

$$i_2 = (1 + i_1)^{m_1/m_2} - 1 = (1.025)^{4/2} - 1 = 1.025^2 - 1 = 0.050625 = 5.0625\% \text{ per half-year}$$

EXAMPLE 9.4A	Calculation of Three Equivalent Interest Rates

For a given interest rate of 5% compounded quarterly, what is the equivalent nominal rate of interest with

a. annual compounding?

b. semiannual compounding?

c. monthly compounding?

SOLUTION

The given rate is $j_1 = 5\%$ with $m_1 = 4$. Therefore, $i_1 = 1.25\%$ per quarter.

In the following columns, we substitute the given values for m_1, m_2, and i_1 into formula (9-4).

a. $m_2 = 1$	**b.** $m_2 = 2$	**c.** $m_2 = 12$
$i_2 = (1.0125)^{4/1} - 1$	$i_2 = (1.0125)^{4/2} - 1$	$i_2 = (1.0125)^{4/12} - 1$
$= 0.05095$	$= 0.025156$	$= 0.0041494$
$= 5.095\%$ per year	$= 2.5156\%$ per half-year	$= 0.41494\%$ per month
$j_2 = m_2 \times i_2$	$j_2 = m_2 \times i_2$	$j_2 = m_2 \times i_2$
$= 1 \times 5.095\%$	$= 2 \times 2.5156\%$	$= 12 \times 0.41494\%$
$= 5.095\%$ compounded annually	$= 5.031\%$ compounded semiannually	$= 4.979\%$ compounded monthly

To use the ICONV worksheet, first compute the effective rate corresponding to the given nominal interest rate. Then compute the requested nominal rates that are equivalent to this effective rate.

Part (a)	Part (b)	Part (c)
2nd ICONV	Press ↓ (to scroll	Press ↓ (to scroll
5 ENTER	down to the *C/Y* line)	down to the *C/Y* line)
↓ ↓ 4 ENTER	2 ENTER	12 ENTER
↑ CPT	↑ ↑ CPT	↑ ↑ CPT
Ans: 5.095	*Ans:* 5.031	*Ans:* 4.979

a. $j = f = 5.095\%$ compounded annually

b. $j = 5.031\%$ compounded semiannually

c. $j = 4.979\%$ compounded monthly

➡️ **Check your understanding:** For a given interest rate of 6% compounded monthly, what is the equivalent nominal rate of interest with quarterly compounding? (Answer: 6.03% compounded quarterly)

▶ **Related problem:** #1 in Exercise 9.4

Checkpoint Questions

1. What is the significance of two nominal interest rates being equivalent?

2. Suppose the periodic rate for six months is 4%. Is the equivalent periodic rate for three months (pick one)

   (i) equal to $4\% \times \frac{3}{6} = 2\%$?

   (ii) less than 2%?

   (iii) greater than 2%?

   Answer the question without doing any calculations. Explain your choice.

3. Suppose the periodic rate for one month is 0.5%. Is the equivalent periodic rate for six months (pick one)

   (i) equal to $6(0.5\%) = 3\%$?

   (ii) less than 3%?

   (iii) greater than 3%?

   Answer the question without doing calculations. Explain your choice.

EXERCISE 9.4

Answers to the odd-numbered problems can be found in the end matter.

INTERMEDIATE PROBLEMS

Throughout this exercise, calculate interest rates accurate to the nearest 0.01%.

1. What semiannually compounded rate is equivalent to 4% compounded monthly?
2. What quarterly compounded rate is equivalent to 3.5% compounded semiannually?
3. What monthly compounded rate is equivalent to 6% compounded quarterly?
4. What semiannually compounded rate is equivalent to 8.5% compounded quarterly?
5. To be equivalent to 5.5% compounded annually, what must be the nominal rate with
   a. semiannual compounding?
   b. quarterly compounding?
   c. monthly compounding?
6. To be equivalent to 7% compounded quarterly, what must be the nominal rate with
   a. annual compounding?
   b. semiannual compounding?
   c. monthly compounding?

7. For a three-year GIC investment, what nominal rate compounded monthly would put you in the same financial position as 5.5% compounded semiannually?

8. A trust company pays 1.5% compounded semiannually on its three-year GIC. For you to prefer an annually compounded GIC of the same maturity, what value must its nominal interest rate exceed?

9. You are offered a loan at a rate of 9% compounded monthly. Below what nominal rate of interest would you choose semiannual compounding instead?

10. Banks usually quote residential mortgage interest rates on the basis of semiannual compounding. An independent mortgage broker is quoting rates with monthly compounding. What rate would the broker have to give to match 4.5% compounded semiannually available from a bank?

11. A credit union pays 5.25% compounded annually on five-year compound-interest GICs. It wants to set the rates on its semiannually and monthly compounded GICs of the same maturity so that investors will earn the same total interest. What should the rates be on the GICs with the higher compounding frequencies?

12. A bank offers a rate of 1.8% compounded semiannually on its four-year GIC. What monthly compounded rate should the bank offer on four-year GICs to make investors indifferent between the alternatives?

Key Terms

Effective interest rate	**Equivalent interest rates**	**Rule of 72**

Summary of Notation and Key Formulas

f = Effective rate of interest

FORMULA (9-1) $i = \sqrt[n]{\dfrac{FV}{PV}} - 1 = \left(\dfrac{FV}{PV}\right)^{1/n} - 1$ Finding the periodic interest rate (or periodic rate of return)

FORMULA (9-2) $n = \dfrac{\ln\left(\dfrac{FV}{PV}\right)}{\ln(1 + i)}$ Finding the number of compounding periods

FORMULA (9-3) $f = (1 + i)^m - 1$ Finding the effective rate of interest (or effective rate of return)

FORMULA (9-4) $i_2 = (1 + i_1)^{m_1/m_2} - 1$ Finding an equivalent periodic interest rate

Review Problems

Answers to the odd-numbered review problems can be found in the end matter.

Calculate percentages accurate to the nearest 0.01%.

BASIC PROBLEMS

1. **LO1** If a company's annual sales grew from $165,000 to $485,000 in a period of eight years, what has been the compound annual rate of growth of sales during the period?

2. **LO1** Maxine found an old pay statement from nine years ago. Her hourly wage at the time was $13.50 versus her current wage of $20.80 per hour. At what equivalent (compound) annual rate has her wage grown over the period?

3. **LO2** If an interest rate of 6.9% compounded semiannually is charged on a car loan, what effective rate of interest should be disclosed to the borrower?

4. **LO2** If the nominal rate of interest paid on a savings account is 1.2% compounded monthly, what is the effective rate of interest paid?

5. **LO1** How many months will it take for an investment of $1000 to grow to be worth $1072.44 at 3% compounded monthly?

6. **LO1** Jessica borrowed $5963 at an interest rate of 9% compounded annually. No payments have been made on the loan, and its current balance is $10,000. How many years ago did Jessica borrow the money? Round your answer to the nearest year.

7. **LO1** A strip bond that will mature 8 years from now at its $10,000 face value can be purchased today for $8630.18. What rate of return (compounded semiannually) will this bond provide to an investor?

8. **LO1** Liam invested $1800 at 4.15% compounded quarterly. The investment is now worth $2692.11. How long ago was the original investment made?

INTERMEDIATE PROBLEMS

9. **LO1** A community festival attracted 1354 people this year. If organizers expect attendance to grow at 5% per year, how many years will it take for the festival attendance to grow to 2000 people? Round your answer to the nearest year.

10. **LO1** If the Consumer Price Index rose from 111.5 to 125.8 over an $8\frac{1}{2}$-year period, what was the equivalent compound annual inflation rate during the period?

11. **LO1** The home the Bensons purchased 13 years ago for $115,000 is now appraised at $385,000. What has been the annual rate of appreciation of the value of their home during the 13-year period?

12. **LO1** What is the time remaining until the maturity date of a $50,000 strip bond if it has just been purchased for $33,839.92 to yield 2.38% compounded semiannually until maturity?

13. **LO1** A sum of $10,000 invested in the BirchLeaf Growth Fund at the end of 2004 would have declined to $5054.22 by the end of 2015. What compound annual rate of return did the fund realize during this 11-year period?

14. **LO1** To the nearest month, how long will it take an investment to double in value if it earns 3.75% compounded semiannually?

15. **LO2** Camille can obtain a residential mortgage loan from a bank at 4.75% compounded semiannually or from an independent mortgage broker at 4.68% compounded monthly. Which source should she pick if other terms and conditions of the loan are the same? Present calculations that support your answer.

16. LO3 What monthly compounded nominal rate would put you in the same financial position as 5.5% compounded semiannually?

17. LO1 Mutual funds with assets in precious metals have displayed high price volatility in recent years. For example, the Sentry Precious Metals Growth Fund had annual returns in successive years from 2010 to 2015 inclusive of 78.5%, −23.1%, −7.9%, −51.4%, 3.0% and −6.8%, respectively. What was the fund's equivalent compound annual return for the six years ended December 31, 2015?

18. LO2 Which of the following rates would you prefer for a loan: 7.6% compounded quarterly, 7.5% compounded monthly, or 7.7% compounded semiannually?

19. LO3 You are offered a loan at a rate of 4.5% compounded monthly. What semiannually compounded nominal rate would a competing bank need to offer in order to provide an equivalent rate?

20. LO1 An investor paid $6315.29 to purchase a $10,000 face value strip bond for her RRSP. At this price the investment will provide a return of 3.47% compounded semiannually. How long (to the nearest day) after the date of purchase will the bond mature? Assume that each half-year is exactly 182 days long.

21. LO2 A $10,000 investment grew to $12,000 after 39 months of semiannual compounding. What effective rate of return did the investment earn?

22. LO1 A portfolio earned −13%, 18%, 5%, 24%, and −5% in five successive years. What was the portfolio's five-year compound annual return?

23. LO1 Terry was supposed to pay $800 to Becky on March 1. At a later date, Terry paid Becky an equivalent payment in the amount of $895.67. If they provided for a time value of money of 8% compounded monthly, on what date did Terry make the payment?

24. LO3 A bank offers a rate of 2.3% compounded semiannually on its four-year GICs. What monthly and annually compounded rates should it quote in order to have the same effective interest rate at all three nominal rates?

25. LO1 To the nearest day, how long will it take a $20,000 investment to grow to $22,000 (including accrued interest) if it earns 3% compounded quarterly? Assume that a quarter-year has 91 days.

26. LO2 If a $15,000 investment grew to $21,805 in $4\frac{1}{2}$ years of quarterly compounding, what effective rate of return was the investment earning?

27. LO2 If an invoice indicates that interest at the rate of 1.2% per month will be charged on overdue amounts, what effective rate of interest will be charged?

28. LO3 A trust company pays 1.375% compounded annually on its five-year GICs. What semiannually compounded interest rate would produce the same maturity value?

29. LO1 The Lipper Fund Awards recognized mutual funds that have excelled in delivering strong performance. The Fidelity Canadian Growth Company Series B (managed by Pyramis Global Advisors) won a Lipper Award in 2015 for its five-year performance record. As of December 31, 2014, what three-year and five-year compound annual returns did the fund report if its annual returns in successive years from 2010 to 2014 inclusive were 17.56%, −8.76%, 14.51%, 44.24%, and 15.36%, respectively?

ADVANCED PROBLEMS

30. LO1 An investor's portfolio increased in value by 53% over a five-year period. At the same time, the Consumer Price Index rose from 119.9 to 126.6. What was the portfolio's annually compounded real rate of return?

31. LO1 When discounted to yield 3.5% compounded quarterly, a $4500 four-year promissory note bearing interest at 5.5% compounded semiannually was priced at $5169.10. How long after the issue date did the discounting take place?

32. LO1 The population of a mining town declined from 17,500 to 14,500 in a five-year period. If the population continues to decrease at the same compound annual rate, how long, to the nearest month, will it take for the population to drop by another 3000?

33. LO1 Rounded to the nearest month, how long will it take money to lose one-third of its purchasing power if the annual inflation rate is 3%?

34. LO1 An investor's portfolio increased in value from $35,645 to $54,230 over a six-year period. At the same time, the Consumer Price Index rose by 26.5%. What was the portfolio's annually compounded real rate of return?

Appendix 9A: The Texas Instruments BA II PLUS Interest Conversion Worksheet

Notice the letters **ICONV** above the [2] key. This means that the Interest Conversion Worksheet is the second function of the [2] key. You can access the worksheet by pressing [2nd] [2] in sequence. Hereafter, we will represent these keystrokes as [2] [ICONV]. The calculator's display then shows

NOM =	n.nn

where the n's represent numerical digits. (Your display may show more or fewer digits.)

You should think of a worksheet as a single column of items that you can view one at a time in the display. The Interest Conversion Worksheet's column consists of the following three items:

NOM =	n.nn
EFF =	n.nn
C/Y =	n

The solid line around the first item indicates that the calculator's display currently provides a "window" to the first item in the column. You can use the scroll keys [↓] and [↑] to move down or up the list. The three worksheet symbols are defined as follows:

$$NOM = \text{Nominal annual interest rate, } j$$
$$EFF = \text{Effective interest rate, } f$$
$$C/Y = \text{Number of compoundings per year, } m$$

The Interest Conversion Worksheet allows you to enter values for any two of these three variables and then compute the value of the remaining third variable. Close the worksheet by pressing [2nd] [QUIT]. (By the [QUIT] key, we mean the key showing QUIT as its second function.)

Let us use the worksheet to answer Example 9.3A, which asks us to calculate the effective interest rate corresponding to 4.5% compounded monthly.

[2nd] [ICONV]	⇒	Open the Interest Conversion Worksheet.
4.5 [ENTER]	⇒	Key in and save the value for *NOM*.
[↓] [↓] 12 [ENTER]	⇒	Scroll down to *C/Y*. Key in and save its value.
[↑] [CPT]	⇒	Scroll back up to *EFF*. Compute its value.

The effective interest rate appearing in the display is 4.59%.

CHAPTER 10
Annuities: Future Value and Present Value

LEARNING OBJECTIVES
After completing this chapter, you will be able to:

LO1 Define and distinguish between ordinary simple annuities, ordinary general annuities, simple annuities due, and general annuities due

LO2 Calculate the future value and present value of ordinary simple annuities

LO3 Calculate the fair market value of a cash flow stream that includes an annuity

LO4 Calculate the principal balance owed on a loan immediately after any payment

LO5 Calculate the future value and present value of ordinary general annuities

LO6 Calculate the future value and present value of annuities due

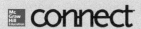 **connect** Throughout this chapter interactive charts and Help Me Solve It videos are marked with a ↗.

A LARGE NUMBER OF PERSONAL and business transactions involve an annuity—a series of equal regular payments. Examples are loan payments, wages, pensions, rent, installment savings plans, insurance premiums, mortgage payments, leases, bond interest, and preferred share dividends.

Many circumstances require the calculation of the future value or the present value of an annuity. For example, how much will you accumulate (future value) after 20 years if you invest $100 per month? What is the balance you owe on a loan (present value) that has 23 remaining monthly payments of $227?

In this chapter, you will learn the language of annuities and how to answer these questions. This chapter is also the foundation we will build upon throughout Chapters 11, 12, and 13. If you master the content of Chapter 10, you will be in an excellent position to comfortably handle the later chapters.

10.1 Introduction to Annuities

An **annuity** is a series of equal payments made or received at regular intervals. Many of us have annuities occurring in our financial lives, including payment of rent, loan payments, or automatic withdrawals from our bank accounts to be deposited into retirement savings plans. Similarly, businesses deal with annuities such as lease payments, insurance premiums, and preferred share dividends to name a few.

Identifying an Annuity

To determine whether a particular situation represents an annuity, ask yourself the following three questions:

1. Does the situation involve a *series* of payments (two or more)?
2. Are the payments *equal* in amount?
3. Are the payments made at *regular* intervals of time?

If the answer to *all three* questions is yes, then the situation does indeed represent an annuity.

From an individual's perspective, note that an annuity can be a series of payments being received (such as wages) or paid out (such as rent). For example, monthly rent payments represent an annuity being *paid* by the tenant, but represent an annuity being *received* by the landlord. Whether the annuity is a cash inflow or outflow depends upon which side of the transaction the individual or business is on.

Payment Interval

The time between successive payments in an annuity is called the **payment interval**. For example, if a loan is being repaid with a series of equal payments made quarterly, the payment interval is three months. Alternately, if an investment returns a series of equal payments made semiannually, the payment interval is six months. The payment interval of an annuity involving a series of rent payments would likely be one month, since most leases require payment of rent on a monthly basis. (We will simplify the discussion by assuming that all months have the same length, thereby meeting the requirement that the payments are being made at regular intervals.)

LO1 Classification of Annuities

Many situations involving annuities will first require that you identify the *type* of annuity before proceeding with any calculations. It is important that you classify the annuity carefully, as the way you handle the mathematics involved will vary depending upon the annuity type.

Do Payments Occur at the End or Beginning of the Payment Interval? Imagine you have obtained a personal loan to be repaid by a series of equal monthly payments. If the loan is advanced today, your first payment will be due at the *end* of the first payment interval, one month from today. When annuity payments occur at the *end* of each payment interval, the annuity is an **ordinary annuity**.

Now imagine you are renting an apartment and that rent payments are due monthly. When does the landlord require the rent payments to be made—at the start or end of each payment interval? Most rental agreements stipulate that the rent is due at the *start* of each month. The payment is made at the start of the payment interval (in this case, each month) and *then* you are permitted to occupy the apartment for the interval that follows the payment. When annuity payments occur at the *beginning* of each payment interval, the annuity is an **annuity due**. To summarize:

Ordinary Annuity → Payments at the end of each payment interval
Annuity Due → Payments at the beginning of each payment interval

---

TIP

Clues to the Type of Annuity

Information that helps you differentiate among ordinary annuities and annuities due may lie in subtle wording of a problem. Ordinary annuities are relatively easy to identify, because the question will almost always refer to payments that are made "at the end of" a given interval. Wording that indicates an annuity due may be more subtle. Look for a key word or phrase that provides the clue. Some examples of wording that indicates an annuity due are:

- "Payments at the beginning of ..."
- "Payments ... in advance"
- "First payment ... made today"
- "Payments ... starting now"

Does the Payment Interval Equal the Compounding Interval? Imagine you are receiving an annuity that pays you monthly payments. (Whether the payments are received at the start or end of each payment interval is, for the moment, not relevant.) Another way to classify an annuity requires you to compare the *payment interval* to the *interest compounding interval*. If you were able to deposit your monthly annuity payments into an account that earns 6% compounded monthly, the payment interval and the interest compounding interval are *equal*—they are both occurring monthly. When the payment interval matches the interest compounding interval, the annuity is classified as a **simple annuity**. If, on the other hand, you deposited the monthly annuity payments into an account that earns 8% compounded quarterly, the payment interval and the interest compounding interval are *not equal*. Payments would be made monthly, and interest would be compounding quarterly. When the payment interval and the interest compounding interval do not match, the annuity is classified as a **general annuity**. To summarize:

Simple Annuity → Payment interval and compounding interval are equal
General Annuity → Payment interval and compounding interval are not equal

Note that we now have two *independent* criteria for classifying annuities. Based on the timing of the payment within the payment interval, an annuity is classified as either an ordinary annuity or an annuity due. Based on whether or not the payment interval equals the compounding interval, an annuity is either a simple annuity or a general annuity. These two independent criteria result in four categories of annuities, which are summarized in Table 10.1.

TABLE 10.1   Distinguishing Characteristics of Annuity Categories

Annuity category	Is the payment at the *end* or at the *beginning* of each payment interval?	Compare the payment interval to the compounding interval.
Ordinary simple annuity	End	Equal
Ordinary general annuity	End	Not equal
Simple annuity due	Beginning	Equal
General annuity due	Beginning	Not equal

Before launching into any annuity problem, be careful to evaluate which of the four types of annuities you are dealing with. The flowchart presented in Figure 10.1 shows the questions you should be asking yourself in order to classify an annuity. With practice, classifying annuities will become a relatively easy (but essential) step in solving annuity problems.

FIGURE 10.1   Annuity Classification Flowchart

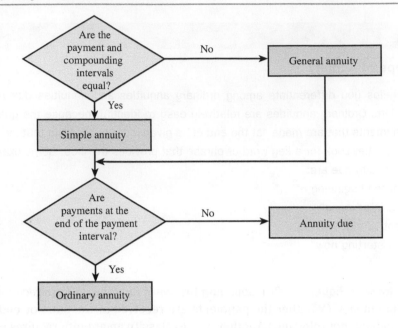

EXAMPLE 10.1A   **Classifying Annuities**

Identify the type of annuity described in each of the following scenarios.

a. An investor deposits $500 at the beginning of every month into an investment account earning 8% compounded quarterly.

b. A mortgage carrying an interest rate of 5.5% compounded semiannually will be repaid over 20 years with payments of $1500 at the end of every month.

c. A student repays $1200 at the end of every three months on a loan that carries interest of 4% compounded quarterly.

SOLUTION

a. Payments at the beginning of each payment interval   → Annuity due
Payment interval is monthly and interest compounds quarterly → General annuity
The annuity is a general annuity due.

b. Payments at the end of each payment interval   → Ordinary annuity
Payment interval is monthly and interest compounds semiannually → General annuity
The annuity is an ordinary general annuity.

c. Payments at the end of each payment interval   → Ordinary annuity
Payment interval is quarterly and interest compounds quarterly → Simple annuity
The annuity is an ordinary simple annuity.

> ➡ **Check your understanding:** A contract requires that monthly payments of $500 begin today, and continue at the start of every month for the next five years. The recipient of the payments will deposit them into an account earning 6% compounded monthly. What type of annuity is this? (Answer: The annuity is a simple annuity due.)
>
> ▰▰▷ **Related problem:** #1 in Exercise 10.1

The Term of an Annuity

The total time from the *beginning* of the first payment interval to the *end* of the last payment interval is the **term of the annuity**. For example, an annuity that consists of 15 quarterly payments would have a term of 15×3 months or 45 months from start to finish. As discussed in the following Trap boxes, be very careful when identifying the start of an annuity's term in relation to its first payment, and the end of the annuity's term in relation to its last payment. Depending upon whether the annuity is an ordinary annuity or an annuity due, the start and end of the annuity's term do not necessarily coincide with the first and last payments.

TRAP

"Where Do We Begin?"

Don't assume that the start of an annuity's term automatically coincides with the first payment. An annuity's term always begins at the start of the first payment *interval*. For an ordinary annuity, the first payment is made at the *end* of the first payment interval. So the term of an ordinary annuity begins *one period prior* to the first payment. For an annuity due, the first payment is made at the *start* of the first payment interval. So for an annuity due, the start of the annuity's term *is* the date of the first payment. Examples 10.1B and 10.1C illustrate this point.

TRAP

"Where Do We End?"

Don't assume that the end of an annuity's term automatically coincides with the last payment. An annuity's term always concludes at the end of the last payment *interval*. For an ordinary annuity, the last payment is made at the end of the final payment interval. So the term of an ordinary annuity does end on the date of the last payment. However, in the case of an annuity due, the final payment is made at the beginning of the last payment interval. The term of the annuity is not complete until the final payment interval has elapsed, one period after the final payment has been made. Examples 10.1B and 10.1C illustrate this point.

EXAMPLE 10.1B	Identifying the Start and End of the Term for an Ordinary Annuity

You have obtained a personal loan to be repaid by annual payments at the end of each of the next eight years. Draw a time diagram for this annuity. On the diagram, clearly label the date the loan was advanced, the first payment interval, the start of the annuity's term, each loan payment, the end of the annuity's term, and the total term of the annuity.

SOLUTION

Loan payments are made annually, so the payment interval is one year. The payments are made at the end of every payment interval. Therefore, the loan payments represent an ordinary annuity. The first payment is made at the end of the first payment interval, which is one year after the start of the annuity's term. The last payment, made at the end of the eighth payment interval, coincides with the end of the annuity's term. The term of the annuity is a total of eight years.

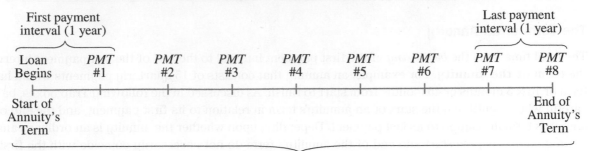

⮕ **Check your understanding:** Draw a similar time diagram to the one above for an ordinary annuity consisting of five quarterly payments. (Answer: Each payment interval will be three months long. The term of the annuity will be 5 intervals × 3 months = 15 months in total. Payment one will be made three months after the annuity begins, and the end of the annuity's term will coincide with payment five.)

▰▰▶ **Related problem:** #7 in Exercise 10.1

EXAMPLE 10.1C | **Identifying the Start and End of the Term for an Annuity Due**

You are going to contribute a series of eight equal payments to a retirement savings plan. The payments will be made at the start of each year, with the first payment being made today. Draw a time diagram for this annuity. On the diagram, clearly label the first payment interval, the start of the annuity's term, each payment, the end of the annuity's term, and the total term of the annuity.

SOLUTION

Payments are made annually, so the payment interval is one year. The payments are made at the beginning of every payment interval. Therefore, the loan payments represent an annuity due. The first payment is made immediately, at the start of the first payment interval. Therefore, the first payment coincides with the start of the annuity's term. The last payment is made at the start of the eighth payment interval. The annuity's term ends one payment interval (one year) after the final payment.

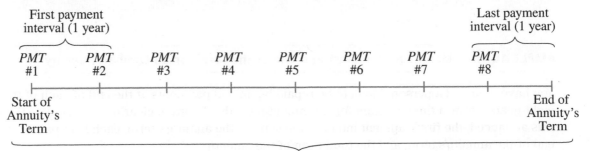

➡️ **Check your understanding:** Draw a time diagram similar to the one above for an annuity due consisting of five semiannual payments. The first payment is made today. (Answer: Each payment interval will be six months long. The first payment will coincide with the start of the annuity's term. The term of the annuity will be 5 intervals × 6 months = 30 months long and will end six months after payment five.)

▮▮▮▶ **Related problem:** #8 in Exercise 10.1

Checkpoint Questions

1. Circle "True" or "False" for each of the following:

   a. A contract requires a series three, $500 payments to be made in one month,   True   False
   six months, and ten months from today. The series of payments form an annuity.

   b. An annuity with payments at the beginning of each period is an   True   False
   ordinary annuity.

   c. An annuity in which the payment interval and the compounding interval   True   False
   are equal is a simple annuity.

   d. An annuity in which the payment interval and the compounding interval   True   False
   are different is a general annuity.

   e. You pay your car insurance premiums by a series of equal, preauthorized   True   False
   withdrawals at the beginning of every month from your chequing account.
   The payments form an ordinary annuity.

2. What distinguishes a simple annuity from a general annuity?

3. What distinguishes an ordinary annuity from an annuity due?

4. What is meant by the "term" of an annuity?

EXERCISE 10.1

Answers to the odd-numbered problems can be found in the end matter.

BASIC PROBLEMS

1. Kelli deposited $500 at the end of every month into an investment earning 5% compounded quarterly. What type of annuity is this?

2. Payments at the end of every three months are made on a loan carrying an interest rate of 8% compounded quarterly. What type of annuity is this?

3. A recent college graduate is going to begin making savings deposits of $100 at the start of every month into an investment earning 3.6% compounded monthly. What type of annuity is this?

4. Roham deposits $275 at the start of every month into an account that earns 4% compounded quarterly. What type of annuity is this?

5. An annuity consists of 42 payments made at the end of successive calendar quarters. How long is the term of the annuity?

6. An annuity consists of payments at the start of each six-month period. There are 27 payments in the annuity. How long is the term of the annuity?

7. You have obtained a personal loan to be repaid by a series of seven equal payments. The payments will be made at the end of every quarter. Draw a time diagram for this annuity. On the diagram, clearly label the date the loan was advanced, the first payment interval, the start of the annuity's term, each loan payment, the end of the annuity's term, and the total term of the annuity.

8. You are going to contribute a series of eight equal payments to a retirement savings plan. The payments will be made at the start of each six-month period, with the first payment being made today. Draw a time diagram for this annuity. On the diagram, clearly label the first payment interval, the start of the annuity's term, each payment, the end of the annuity's term, and the total term of the annuity.

9. On December 31, 2016 Jacob borrowed $15,000 from his mother. They agreed that the loan would carry interest at 9% compounded quarterly, and would be repaid with five equal payments made on December 31 of each year for the next five years.

   a. What type of annuity does the series of loan repayments represent?

   b. What are the dates of the first and last payments in the annuity?

   c. What are the start and end dates of the term of the annuity?

10. Melissa started a savings program on June 1, 2016 that involves a series of six $500 savings deposits at the start of every quarter. Her savings earned 6% compounded quarterly.

   a. What type of annuity does the series of savings deposits represent?

   b. What are the dates of the first and last deposit in the annuity?

   c. What are the start and end dates of the term of the annuity?

10.2 Future Value of an Ordinary Simple Annuity

LO2   The **future value of an annuity** is the sum of the future values of all the payments (evaluated at the end of the last payment interval). In this section, we will focus on future value calculations involving only ordinary simple annuities. In later sections, we will learn how to modify our approach to be able to calculate the future value of any type of annuity.

We introduce the techniques for calculating an ordinary annuity's future value by considering a specific case.

Future Value Using the Algebraic Method

Figure 10.2 is a time diagram showing the investment of $1000 at the *end* of every six months for two years. Suppose the invested money earns 8% compounded semiannually. Since we have semiannual payments and semiannual compounding, the four $1000 payments form an *ordinary simple* annuity. The only way we can calculate the annuity's future value at this stage is to use $FV = PV(1 + i)^n$ to calculate the future value of each payment, one at a time. Then, as indicated in the time diagram, we add these future values to obtain the future value of the annuity.

$$FV \text{ of annuity} = \$1000 + \$1000(1.04) + \$1000(1.04)^2 + \$1000(1.04)^3$$
$$= \$1000 + \$1040 + \$1081.60 + \$1124.86$$
$$= \$4246.46$$

The investments, including earnings, will amount to $4246.46 by the end of the annuity. If an annuity consists of many payments, this "brute force" approach to the future value calculation can become very time-consuming. Fortunately, there is a relatively compact formula for the future value of an ordinary simple annuity.

FIGURE 10.2 The Future Value of a Four-Payment Ordinary Simple Annuity

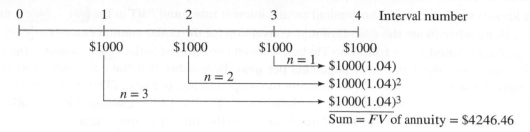

If we define the following symbols:

$$FV = \text{Future value of an ordinary annuity}$$
$$PMT = \text{Periodic payment in an annuity}$$
$$i = \text{(Given) periodic interest rate}$$
$$n = \text{Number of payments in the annuity}$$

then the future value of an ordinary simple annuity can be calculated using

FUTURE VALUE OF AN ORDINARY SIMPLE ANNUITY
$$FV = PMT\left[\frac{(1 + i)^n - 1}{i}\right]$$
(10-1)

Let us now use formula (10-1) to determine the future value of the annuity shown in Figure 10.2. We are given $PMT = \$1000$, $i = \frac{8\%}{2} = 4\%$ per half-year, and $n = 4$. Substituting these values into formula (10-1), we have

$$FV = \$1000\left[\frac{(1 + 0.04)^4 - 1}{0.04}\right] = \$1000\left(\frac{1.16985856 - 1}{0.04}\right) = \$4246.46$$

This is the same result obtained previously by the "brute force" approach. As the number of payments in an annuity increases, the time saved by employing formula (10-1) increases proportionately.

TIP

The Meaning of "*n*" Has Changed!

When working with any calculation involving an annuity, it is important to recognize that *n* represents the number of payments in the annuity. In Chapters 8 and 9, we were dealing with compound interest being applied to a single amount. In that case, *n* represented the number of interest compounding periods. For example, if a one-time, single investment earned interest compounded quarterly for 5 years, *n* would be 20, and we would use formula (8-2), $FV = PV(1 + i)^n$ to calculate the future value of that single deposit. When dealing with any formula involving an annuity (such as formula (10-1) and others that you will encounter in this chapter), *n* represents the number of payments in the annuity. It is easy to arrive at the correct *n* value for simple annuities, since the payment interval and the compounding interval are the same. However, when our work extends to general annuities, you will need to be very careful to arrive at the correct value for *n*. For example, if quarterly payments earn interest compounded semiannually for 10 years, what *n* value would you use in the calculation of the annuity's *FV*? Is $n = 10 \times 4 = 40$, or is $n = 10 \times 2 = 20$? Since *n* represents the number of payments in the annuity, the correct answer is $n = 40$. You can see how easy it could be to make an error. Slow down and think carefully about the meaning of *n*!

Future Value Using the Financial Calculator Functions

Save the known values for n, j (the nominal annual interest rate), and *PMT* in the N , I/Y , and PMT memories. Remember to use the cash-flow sign convention for the dollar amount entered in PMT . Except for the cases mentioned in the following Tip box, 0 should be entered in the PV memory. Open the *P/Y* worksheet and enter the number of payments per year. Remember that the calculator then *automatically* assigns the same value to *C/Y*, the number of compoundings per year. (This automatic feature is a convenience with *simple* annuities where, by definition, *C/Y* = *P/Y*.) After quitting the *P/Y* worksheet, the keystrokes CPT FV instruct the calculator to compute the annuity's future value.

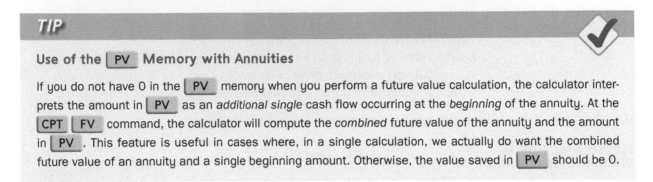

TIP

Use of the PV Memory with Annuities

If you do not have 0 in the PV memory when you perform a future value calculation, the calculator interprets the amount in PV as an *additional single* cash flow occurring at the *beginning* of the annuity. At the CPT FV command, the calculator will compute the *combined* future value of the annuity and the amount in PV . This feature is useful in cases where, in a single calculation, we actually do want the combined future value of an annuity and a single beginning amount. Otherwise, the value saved in PV should be 0.

To calculate the future value of the annuity represented in Figure 10.2, the keystrokes are:

4 N 8 I/Y 0 PV 1000 +/− PMT

2nd P/Y 2 ENTER 2nd QUIT CPT FV   *Answer:* 4246.46

In Example problems, we will present the keystroke sequence in a callout box as shown at the right. First we enter all of the information concerning the interest rate. This habit will help reduce the chance that inputs about payment and compounding intervals will be overlooked. To conserve space, we *represent* the actual keystroke sequence

2nd P/Y 2 ENTER 2nd QUIT

by the abbreviated sequence

P/Y 2 ENTER

You must supply the missing keystrokes.

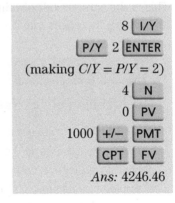

8 I/Y
P/Y 2 ENTER
(making *C/Y* = *P/Y* = 2)
4 N
0 PV
1000 +/− PMT
CPT FV
Ans: 4246.46

Contribution of Each Payment to an Annuity's Future Value

When you use formula (10-1) or a calculator's financial functions to calculate an annuity's future value, the amount each payment contributes to the future value is not apparent. Figure 10.3 helps us see the pattern. Five $10 investments are represented by columns at one-year payment intervals along the time axis. Assuming the investments earn 10% compounded annually, each payment's contribution to the $61.05 future value is indicated at the right side of the diagram. It is no surprise that an early payment contributes more to future value than any subsequent payment. The interesting feature is that the difference between the contributions from successive payments does not stay the same. The first payment contributes $1.33 more than the second payment, the second payment contributes $1.21 more than the third payment, and so on. Putting it another way, each payment's contribution to future value increases in an *accelerating* manner as we look at earlier payments. This reinforces the point made in Chapter 8 concerning the advantages of starting a savings plan as early in life as possible. Consider the following remarkable illustration of the relative effect of earlier versus later payments. Suppose you construct Figure 10.3 to include 30 annual investments of $10. You would find that the first seven payments (in combination) contribute *more* to the future value than the remaining 23 payments (in combination)! Can you think of a way to verify this outcome?

FIGURE 10.3   Contribution of Each Payment to an Annuity's Future Value

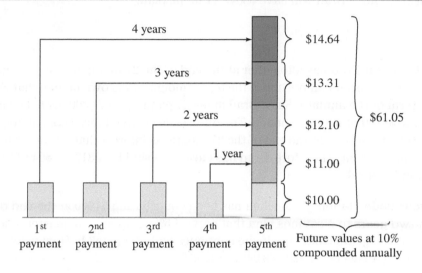

Applications of the Future Value of an Annuity

Most applications of the future value calculation fall into two categories (with the first being much more common):

- Determining the total amount of principal plus interest that will be accumulated at the end of a series of equal regular investments.
- Determining the single payment at the end of an annuity that is economically equivalent to the annuity. The interest rate that should be used in this case is the rate of return that can be earned on a low-risk investment. (A suitable value is the rate of return currently available on Government of Canada bonds whose time remaining until maturity is similar to the term of the annuity.)

EXAMPLE 10.2A	The Future Value of Periodic Investments Forming an Ordinary Simple Annuity

Brad has been contributing $300 at the end of each month for the past 15 months to a savings plan that earns 6% compounded monthly.

a. What amount will he have one year from now if he continues with the plan?

b. How much of the total from Part (a) is interest?

SOLUTION

a. The total amount will be the future value of $n = 15 + 12 = 27$ contributions of $PMT = 300 each. Payments are made at the end of each period. Payments and compounding both occur at one-month intervals.

Therefore, the payments form an *ordinary simple* annuity having $i = \frac{6\%}{12} = 0.5\%$ per month.

$$FV = PMT\left[\frac{(1+i)^n - 1}{i}\right]$$

$$= \$300\left[\frac{(1.005)^{27} - 1}{0.005}\right]$$

$$= \$300\left(\frac{1.14415185 - 1}{0.005}\right)$$

$$= \$8649.11$$

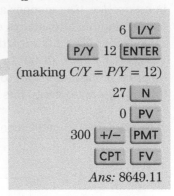

6 | I/Y

P/Y 12 ENTER

(making $C/Y = P/Y = 12$)

27 | N

0 | PV

300 | +/- | PMT

CPT | FV

Ans: 8649.11

One year from now, Brad will have $8649.11 in the plan.

b. The $8649.11 that Brad has altogether at the end of the 27-month period comprises principal and interest. The principal portion is the total amount of his own money that Brad has invested over the term of the annuity. Since Brad made 27 payments of $300 each, he has contributed $300 × 27 = $8100 of his own money. The difference between these contributions and the total value of the investment at the end of the 27 months is interest that has accumulated over the life of the investment. Therefore, Brad has earned $8649.11 − $8100 = $549.11 of interest over the 27-month period.

➡ **Check your understanding:** Angelina has been contributing $1000 at the end of each quarter for the past two years to a savings plan that earns 4.5% compounded quarterly. **a.** What amount will she have three years from now if she continues with the plan? **b.** How much of that total is earned interest? (Answers: **a.** $22,288.94; **b.** $2288.94)

▮▮▯▶ **Related problem:** #3 in Exercise 10.2

 ## Math Apps

TAX FREE SAVINGS ACCOUNTS (TFSAs)

In the 2008 federal budget, then–Finance Minister Jim Flaherty announced the introduction of the Tax Free Savings Account (TFSA). A TFSA is a registered, general-purpose savings vehicle that allows Canadians age 18 and older to earn tax-free income from their savings. In 2016, the TFSA annual contribution limit was $5500. Investment income earned is tax-free both within the TFSA and after it is withdrawn. Savings held in the TFSA can be invested in a wide range of investment vehicles, including cash, GICs, bonds, stocks, and mutual funds. Depending upon an investor's income tax rate, the tax savings from holding investments within a TFSA as compared to a non-registered account can be substantial.

Visit the federal government's TFSA Web site at www.cra-arc.gc.ca/tx/ndvdls/tpcs/tfsa-celi/menu-eng.html to learn more. There you can learn about how contributions to and withdrawals from a TFSA are handled, and how your annual contribution "room" is determined.

A TFSA can be one option for you to start taking advantage of the "magic" of compound interest. In this chapter, we will continue to demonstrate how, if you start early, relatively small investments can accumulate to large sums later in life. A TFSA can be an effective place to hold those funds and their compound-interest earnings.

EXAMPLE 10.2B	Calculating the Future Value of an Ordinary Simple Annuity When the Rate of Return Changes During the Term of the Annuity

How much would you accumulate altogether if you deposit $600 at the end of every six months for 16 years? The rate of return will be 4% compounded semiannually for the first $5\frac{1}{2}$ years and 5% compounded semiannually for the subsequent $10\frac{1}{2}$ years.

SOLUTION

Because the payments are made at the end of each period, and the compounding interval and the payment interval are both six months, we have an *ordinary simple* annuity with

$$i = \frac{j}{m} = \frac{4\%}{2} = 2\% \quad \text{and} \quad n = 2(5.5) = 11 \text{ for the first } 5\tfrac{1}{2} \text{ years, and}$$

$$i = \frac{5\%}{2} = 2.5\% \quad \text{and} \quad n = 2(10.5) = 21 \text{ for the subsequent } 10\tfrac{1}{2} \text{ years}$$

Since the rate of return changes during the term of the annuity, we must consider the first $5\frac{1}{2}$ years separately from the subsequent $10\frac{1}{2}$ years. The algebraic solution has three steps, as indicated in the following time diagram.

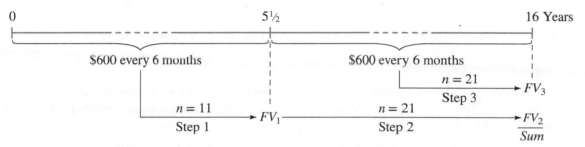

Step 1: Calculate the future value, FV_1, of the first 11 payments.

$$FV_1 = PMT\left[\frac{(1+i)^n - 1}{i}\right]$$

$$= \$600\left[\frac{(1.02)^{11} - 1}{0.02}\right]$$

$$= \$600\left[\frac{1.243374308 - 1}{0.02}\right]$$

$$= \$7301.229$$

4 I/Y
P/Y 2 ENTER
(making C/Y = P/Y = 2)
11 N
0 PV
600 +/– PMT *
CPT FV
Ans: 7301.229
*Invest the $600.
(Negative cash flow.)

Step 2: Determine the future value, FV_2, of $7301.229 after an *additional* $10\frac{1}{2}$ years earning the new rate of 5% compounded semiannually. Note that the $7301.229 is a single amount, PV, which is earning compound interest over time. Therefore, we use formula (8-2) to calculate the FV of the single amount after $10\frac{1}{2}$ years.

$$FV_2 = PV(1+i)^n$$
$$= \$7301.229(1.025)^{21}$$
$$= \$12{,}263.012$$

Step 3: Calculate the future value, FV_3, of the last 21 annuity payments. Then add FV_2 and FV_3.

$$FV_3 = \$600\left[\frac{(1.025)^{21} - 1}{0.025}\right]$$

$$= \$600\left[\frac{1.679581851 - 1}{0.025}\right]$$

$$= \$16,309.964$$

$$FV_2 + FV_3 = \$12,263.012 + \$16,309.964 = \$28,572.98$$

The future value of the annuity is $28,572.98.

> Same *PMT, P/Y, C/Y*
>
> 5 | I/Y
> 21 | N
> 7301.229 | +/- | PV *
> | CPT | FV
>
> *Ans: 28,572.98*
>
> *Re-invest the $7301.229. (Negative cash flow.)

⇒ **Check your understanding:** Calculate the future value of an ordinary annuity with payments of $100 each month for 20 years. The rate of return will be 3% compounded monthly for the first 8 years and 4.5% compounded monthly for the subsequent 12 years. (Answer: $37,621.04)

◼▶ **Related problem:** #15 in Exercise 10.2

EXAMPLE 10.2C	Calculating the Future Value of an Ordinary Simple Annuity After an Interruption of Payments

Mr. Cloutier, just turned 43, has already accumulated $34,500 in his Registered Retirement Savings Plan. He makes month-end contributions of $300 to the plan and intends to do so until age 60. He plans to retire then and cease further contributions. The RRSP will be allowed to continue to accumulate earnings until he reaches age 65. If the RRSP earns 4.2% compounded monthly for the next 22 years, what amount will his RRSP contain when he reaches age 65?

SOLUTION

The amount in the RRSP will be the combined future value of the $34,500 already accumulated and future contributions. The number of additional $300 contributions that Mr. Cloutier will make to his RRSP is

$$n = m(\text{Years of contributions}) = 12(17) = 204$$

Payments are made at the end of every month, and interest is compounding monthly. Therefore, we are dealing with an *ordinary simple* annuity.

The periodic rate is $i = \frac{j}{m} = \frac{4.2\%}{12} = 0.35\%$ per month. The following time diagram illustrates the three steps in the solution.

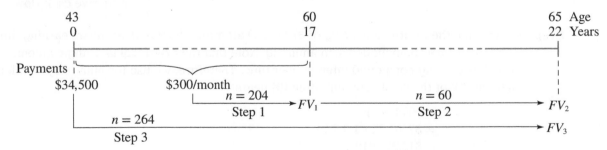

Step 1: Calculate FV_1, the future value at age 60 of the $300-per-month annuity.

$$FV_1 = PMT\left[\frac{(1 + i)^n - 1}{i}\right]$$

$$= \$300\left[\frac{(1 + 0.0035)^{204} - 1}{0.0035}\right]$$

$$= \$300\left(\frac{2.039599383 - 1}{0.0035}\right)$$

$$= \$300(297.0283952)$$

$$= \$89,108.519$$

4.2 | I/Y |

| P/Y | 12 | ENTER |

(making $C/Y = P/Y = 12$)

204 | N |

0 | PV |

300 | +/– | PMT |

| CPT | FV |

Ans: 89,108.519

Step 2: Calculate FV_2, the future value five years later, at age 65, of $89,108.519.

$$FV_2 = PV(1 + i)^n$$

$$= \$89,108.519(1.0035)^{60}$$

$$= \$109,890.927$$

Same *I/Y, P/Y, C/Y*

60 | N |

89108.519 | +/– | PV |

0 | PMT |

| CPT | FV |

Ans: 109,890.927

Step 3: Calculate FV_3, the future value at age 65 of the initial $34,500.

$$FV_3 = PV(1 + i)^n$$

$$= \$34,500(1.0035)^{264}$$

$$= \$86,777.389$$

Same *I/Y, P/Y, C/Y, PMT*

264 | N |

34500 | +/– | PV |

| CPT | FV |

Ans: 86,777.389

The total amount in the RRSP when Mr. Cloutier reaches age 65 will be

$$FV_2 + FV_3 = \$109,890.927 + \$86,777.389 = \$196,668.32$$

▶ **Check your understanding:** Mrs. Desjardins, just turned 52, has already accumulated $84,000 in her Registered Retirement Savings Plan. She makes end-of-quarter contributions of $750 to the plan and intends to do so until age 62. She then plans to retire and cease further contributions. The RRSP will be allowed to continue to accumulate earnings until she reaches age 65. If the RRSP earns 5% compounded quarterly for the next 13 years, what amount will her RRSP contain at age 65? (Answer: $205,083.50)

◼◼▶ **Related problem:** #19 in Exercise 10.2

 **Math Apps**

YOUR POTENTIAL TO BECOME A MILLIONAIRE!

One of the favourite themes of personal finance writers is to show you that, if you will only give up one or two of your wasteful habits and invest the money saved, you can become a millionaire. You can kick a filthy habit and become filthy rich! Attain better health and more wealth! Live longer and die richer!

Smoking is the primary target in these health-and-wealth scenarios. Suppose you give up a pack-a-day habit. At $12 per pack, that will save you about 30 × $12 = $360 per month.

Questions

1. If you invest the saving at the end of each month and earn 5% compounded monthly, how much (rounded to the nearest dollar) will you accumulate after
   a. 30 years?
   b. 40 years?
   c. 50 years?

While 5% compounded monthly may seem like an aggressive rate in the current low-interest-rate environment, viewed historically it is a realistic long-run rate of return, close to historical long-term rates of return achieved by diversified stock portfolios and equity mutual funds.

2. How much will your investment portfolio be worth after 40 years if it earns
   a. 4% compounded monthly?
   b. 6% compounded monthly?

Note the large difference an extra 1% rate of return over a long time frame makes to the value of a portfolio. While it would appear that you will be relatively well off, especially after 40 years of savings, how wealthy will you feel? Note that we have ignored inflation.

3. If the annual rate of inflation averages 2.4% compounded monthly, how many dollars will you need 50 years from now to have the same purchasing power as $1,000,000 today?

We have also ignored the fact that the price of a pack of cigarettes will also rise in the future. Consequently, the amount you save each month will rise from time to time over the years. (In Chapter 12, we will show you how to handle the case of a steadily growing payment.) These increases in the monthly saving rate will largely offset (or even more than offset) the effect of inflation on the purchasing power of your investment portfolio. Consequently, the answers in Question 1 can be viewed as reasonable estimates of the purchasing power in today's dollars of your portfolio.

If you are not a smoker, consider some other luxury you might forgo—a daily latte, a few of the drinks you buy each weekend, lunches you buy (instead of getting out of bed five minutes earlier to pack a bag lunch at half the cost), and so on.

Checkpoint Questions

1. Annuity A has the same n and i as Annuity B. A's *PMT* is double B's *PMT*. Will A's future value be (pick one) **(i)** double, **(ii)** more than double, or **(iii)** less than double the amount of B's future value? Give the reason for your choice.

2. Annuity G has the same i and *PMT* as Annuity H. G has twice as many payments as H. Will G's future value be (pick one): **(i)** double, **(ii)** more than double, or **(iii)** less than double the amount of H's future value? Give the reason for your choice.

EXERCISE 10.2

Answers to the odd-numbered problems can be found in the end matter.

BASIC PROBLEMS

1. What is the future value after $5\frac{1}{2}$ years of $100 invested at the end of every quarter if the funds earn 5% compounded quarterly?

2. $75 was invested at the end of every month for $2\frac{1}{2}$ years. Calculate the future value if the funds earned 3% compounded monthly.

3. Aaron has been contributing $2000 at the end of every half-year for the past four years to a savings plan that earns 6% compounded semiannually. What amount will he have in three years from now if he continues with the plan?

4. What will be the future value after 6 years and 7 months of regular month-end investments of $435 earning 3.6% compounded monthly?

5. Sabina plans to invest $175 at the end of every month for the next $8\frac{1}{4}$ years. What will her investment be worth at the end of the $8\frac{1}{4}$-year period if she earns 4.2% compounded monthly?

6. Jamal is saving for a trip that he'd like to take when he graduates from college in three years. If he invests $200 at the end of every three months for the next three years, how much will he have altogether if his funds earn 8% compounded quarterly?

7. Markus spends $200 per month on cigarettes. Suppose he quits smoking and invests the same amount at the end of each month for 20 years. If the invested money earns 3.6% compounded monthly, how much will Markus accumulate after 20 years?

INTERMEDIATE PROBLEMS

8. In 2016, the maximum contribution limit to a Tax Free Savings Account (TFSA) was $5500. Patrick has decided to make regular, end-of-month contributions to his TFSA for the next 20 years, which he estimates will earn 5.1% compounded monthly. How much will Patrick have altogether if his end-of-month contribution is

   a. $100?   **b.** $200?

   c. $458.33 (to take advantage of the full $5500 annual limit)?

9. You have decided to give up a $2-per-day coffee habit, and deposit the money that you saved at the end of every month into a Tax Free Savings Account (TFSA) that will earn 2.52% compounded monthly. For the purposes of this scenario, assume that each month has 30 days.

   a. How much will you have altogether in the TFSA when you graduate from college in exactly three years from now?

   b. How much of the total in Part (a) above is principal? How much is interest?

10. For the past five years, Ludmilla has been investing $500 at the end of every month into an investment earning 3% compounded monthly.

   a. How much is the investment worth today?

   b. How much of the answer in Part (a) represents interest earned over the course of the five years?

   c. How much more interest would Ludmilla have earned if her investment had earned 6% compounded monthly instead of 3% compounded monthly?

   d. Explain why the total interest earned at 6% compounded monthly in Part (c) is more than double the amount of interest earned at 3% compounded monthly in Part (b).

11. This problem demonstrates the dependence of an annuity's future value on the size of the periodic payment. Suppose a fixed amount will be invested at the end of each year and the funds will earn 5% compounded annually. What will be the future value of the investments after 25 years if the periodic investment is

   a. $1000 per year?

   b. $2000 per year?

   c. $3000 per year?

   Note that the future value of an annuity is proportional to the size of the periodic payment.

12. This problem demonstrates the dependence of the future value of an annuity on the interest rate. Suppose $1000 is invested at the end of each year for 20 years. Calculate the future value if the investments earn an annually compounded rate of return of

   a. 5%.   b. 6%.

   c. 7%.   d. 8%.

   Note that the future value increases proportionately *more* than the interest rate.

13. This problem demonstrates the dependence of the future value of an annuity on the number of payments. Suppose $1000 is invested at the end of each year. Assume the investments earn 5% compounded annually. Calculate the future value of the investments after each of the following numbers of payments:

   a. 5   b. 10

   c. 15   d. 20

   e. 25   f. 30

   Note that the future value increases proportionately *more* than n as n is increased.

14. Calculate the future value after 25 years in each of the following scenarios:

   a. $6000 is invested at the end of each year earning 6% compounded annually.

   b. $3000 is invested at the end of each half-year earning 6% compounded semiannually.

   c. $1500 is invested at the end of each quarter earning 6% compounded quarterly.

   d. $500 is invested at the end of each month earning 6% compounded monthly.

   Note that the same total amount ($6000) is invested each year and that the nominal interest rate (6%) is the same in each case. The combined beneficial effects of (i) smaller but earlier more frequent payments, and (ii) more frequent compounding are quite significant.

15. Calculate the future value of an ordinary annuity consisting of quarterly payments of $1200 for five years if the payments earn 10% compounded quarterly for the first two years and 9% compounded quarterly for the past three years.

Financial advisors stress the importance of starting a savings plan as early as possible in order to accumulate a substantial retirement fund. It is far better to make smaller contributions over a very long time, rather than trying to catch up by making larger payments over a short time. The following two questions reinforce that point.

16. Mary and Steve are both exactly 20 years old. Mary will deposit $1000 at the end of every year for the next 40 years, until age 60, into her retirement fund. Steve is going to wait until age 40 to begin his savings. In order to try to catch up to Mary, Steve will deposit $2000 at the end of every year from age 40 to 60. Note that by age 60, both Mary and Steve will have contributed $40,000 into their respective funds.

    a. Calculate how much Mary and Steve will each have at age 60 if they each earn 4% compounded annually on their investments.

    b. As a percentage of Steve's total, what percentage more does Mary have in her retirement fund at age 60?

17. You have decided that you can afford to save $100 at the end of every month. You predict that your investments will earn 4.8% compounded monthly.

    a. How much will you have when you retire at age 65 if you begin your end-of-month savings plan at age 25?

    b. How much will you have when you retire at age 65 if you begin your end-of-month savings plan at age 30?

    c. By delaying the savings program by 5 years, you have contributed only $6000 less than if you had begun investing at age 25, yet the difference in the accumulated savings at age 65 is quite dramatic. How much more do you have at age 65 when you start saving at age 25 instead of 30? Express your answer in both dollars, and as a percentage of the total in Part (b).

ADVANCED PROBLEMS

18. Nina, just turned 30, has already accumulated $10,000 in her Registered Retirement Savings Plan. She intends to continue to make deposits of $150 at the end of every month until age 62. She plans to retire then and cease further contributions. The RRSP will be allowed to continue to accumulate interest until she reaches age 65. If the RRSP earns 4.2% compounded monthly for the entire duration, what amount will her RRSP contain when she reaches age 65?

19. Dakota intends to save for major travel holidays by contributing $300 at the end of each month to an investment plan. At the end of every three years, she will withdraw $10,000 for a major trip abroad. If the plan earns 3% compounded monthly, what will be the plan's balance after seven years?

20. Marika has already accumulated $18,000 in her RRSP. If she contributes $2000 at the end of every six months for the next 10 years, and $300 at the end of each month for the subsequent five years, what amount will she have in her plan at the end of the 15 years? Assume that her plan will earn 3% compounded semiannually for the first 10 years, and 3% compounded monthly for the subsequent 5 years.

21. Sebastian has made contributions of $2000 to his RRSP at the end of every six months for the past eight years. The plan has earned 5.5% compounded semiannually. He has just moved the funds to another plan that earns 4% compounded quarterly. He will now contribute $1500 at the end of every three months. What total amount will Sebastian have in the plan seven years from now?

The **present value of an annuity** is the sum of the present values of all the payments (evaluated at the beginning of the first payment interval). In this section, we will focus on present value calculations involving only ordinary simple annuities. In later sections, we will learn how to modify our approach to be able to calculate the present value of any type of annuity.

We introduce the techniques for calculating an ordinary annuity's present value by considering a specific case.

Present Value Using the Algebraic Method

Figure 10.4 shows an ordinary annuity consisting of four semiannual payments of $1000. Suppose we want to find the present value of the annuity using a discount rate of 5% compounded semiannually. Since we have semiannual payments and semiannual compounding, the payments form an *ordinary simple annuity*. A "brute force" approach for determining the annuity's present value is shown in the diagram. In this approach, we calculate the present value of each payment using $PV = FV(1 + i)^{-n}$. Then we add the four present values to obtain the present value of the annuity.

FIGURE 10.4   The Present Value of a Four-Payment Ordinary Simple Annuity

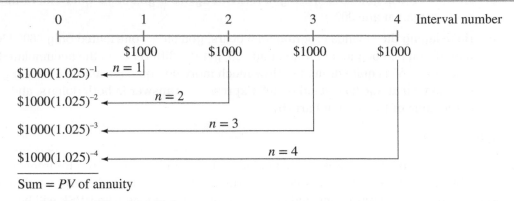

The present value of the annuity is

$$PV = \$1000(1.025)^{-1} + \$1000(1.025)^{-2} + \$1000(1.025)^{-3} + \$1000(1.025)^{-4}$$
$$= \$975.610 + \$951.814 + \$928.599 + \$905.951$$
$$= \$3761.97$$

As in the case of the future value calculation, there is a formula that makes the present value calculation more efficient.

PRESENT VALUE OF AN ORDINARY SIMPLE ANNUITY
$$PV = PMT\left[\frac{1 - (1 + i)^{-n}}{i}\right]$$
(10-2)

Substitute $PMT = \$1000$, $n = 4$, and $i = \frac{5\%}{2} = 2.5\%$ into formula (10-2) to obtain the present value of the preceding four-payment annuity.

$$PV = \$1000\left[\frac{1 - (1 + 0.025)^{-4}}{0.025}\right]$$
$$= \$1000\left(\frac{1 - 0.905950645}{0.025}\right)$$
$$= \$3761.97$$

This is the same result we obtained previously by the "brute force" approach. As the number of payments in an annuity increases, the time saved by employing formula (10-2) increases proportionately.

Present Value Using the Financial Calculator Functions

Save the known values for n, j (the nominal annual interest rate), and *PMT* in the $\boxed{\text{N}}$, $\boxed{\text{I/Y}}$, and $\boxed{\text{PMT}}$ memories. Remember to use the cash-flow sign convention for the dollar amount entered in $\boxed{\text{PMT}}$. Except for the cases mentioned in the following Tip box, 0 should be entered into the $\boxed{\text{FV}}$ memory. Open the *P/Y* worksheet and enter the number of payments per year. Remember that the calculator then *automatically* assigns the same value to *C/Y*, the number of compoundings per year. (This automatic feature is a convenience with *simple* annuities where, by definition, $C/Y = P/Y$.) After quitting the *P/Y* worksheet, the keystrokes $\boxed{\text{CPT}}$ $\boxed{\text{FV}}$ instruct the calculator to compute the annuity's present value.

TIP ✓

Use of the $\boxed{\text{FV}}$ Memory with Annuities

If you do not have 0 in the $\boxed{\text{FV}}$ memory when you perform a present value calculation, the calculator interprets the amount in $\boxed{\text{FV}}$ as an *additional single* cash flow occurring at the end of the annuity. At the $\boxed{\text{CPT}}$ $\boxed{\text{PV}}$ command, the calculator will compute the *combined* present value of the annuity *and* the amount in $\boxed{\text{FV}}$. This feature is useful in cases where, in a single calculation, we actually do want the combined present value of an annuity and an additional payment coming at the end of the annuity. Otherwise, the value saved in $\boxed{\text{FV}}$ should be 0.

To calculate the present value of the annuity represented in Figure 10.4, the keystrokes are:

$$4 \boxed{\text{N}} \quad 5 \boxed{\text{I/Y}} \quad 1000 \boxed{\text{PMT}} \quad 0 \boxed{\text{FV}}$$

$$\boxed{\text{2nd}} \boxed{\text{P/Y}} \ 2 \boxed{\text{ENTER}} \ \boxed{\text{2nd}} \boxed{\text{QUIT}} \ \boxed{\text{CPT}} \ \boxed{\text{PV}} \quad \textit{Answer: } -3761.97$$

In Example problems, we will present the keystroke sequence in a callout box as shown at the right. As we did for the future value calculation in Section 10.2, we again *represent* the actual keystroke sequence

$$\boxed{\text{2nd}} \boxed{\text{P/Y}} \ 2 \boxed{\text{ENTER}} \ \boxed{\text{2nd}} \boxed{\text{QUIT}}$$

by the abbreviated sequence

$$\boxed{\text{P/Y}} \ 2 \boxed{\text{ENTER}}$$

You must supply the missing keystrokes.

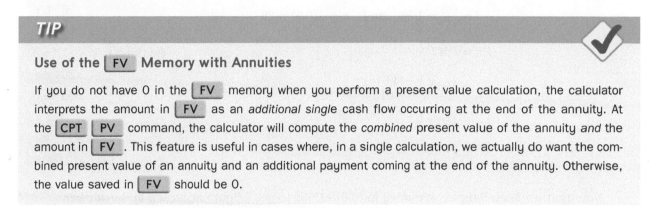

$5 \boxed{\text{I/Y}}$
$\boxed{\text{P/Y}} \ 2 \boxed{\text{ENTER}}$
(making $C/Y = P/Y = 2$)
$4 \boxed{\text{N}}$
$0 \boxed{\text{FV}}$
$1000 \boxed{\text{PMT}}$
$\boxed{\text{CPT}} \ \boxed{\text{PV}}$
Ans: −3761.97

Interpretation: The present value ($$3761.97) represents the initial investment required to generate the four $1000 payments. The computed value is negative because the initial investment is a cash outflow (negative) from the investor's point of view. The difference between the payments received and the initial investment is

$$4(\$1000) - \$3761.97 = \$238.03$$

This difference represents the earnings (at the rate of 5% compounded semiannually) on the balance that remains invested between payments.

EXAMPLE 10.3A	The Present Value of an Ordinary Simple Annuity

Determine the present value of $500 paid at the end of each calendar quarter for $6\frac{1}{2}$ years. Use a discount rate of 6% compounded quarterly.

SOLUTION

Given: $PMT = \$500$, Term $= 6\frac{1}{2}$ years, $j = 6\%$ compounded quarterly

Therefore,

$$i = \frac{6\%}{4} = 1.5\% \quad \text{and} \quad n = 4(6.5) = 26$$

$$PV = PMT\left[\frac{1 - (1 + i)^{-n}}{i}\right]$$

$$= \$500\left(\frac{1 - (1.015)^{-26}}{0.015}\right)$$

$$= \$500\left(\frac{1 - 0.67902052}{0.015}\right)$$

$$= \$10,699.32$$

Assume *PMT*s are inflows.

6 | I/Y
P/Y 4 | ENTER
(making $C/Y = P/Y = 4$)
26 | N
500 | PMT
0 | FV
CPT | PV
Ans: −10,699.32

Note that we keep 8-figure accuracy in "0.67902052 to get 7-figure accuracy in the answer. The present value of the annuity is $10,699.32.

➡ **Check your understanding:** Determine the present value of $1200 paid at the end of every six months for 20 years. Use a discount rate of 8% compounded semiannually. (Answer: $23,751.33)

▰▰▶ **Related problem:** #1 in Exercise 10.3

Contribution of Each Payment to an Annuity's Present Value

When you use formula (10-2) or a calculator's financial functions to calculate an annuity's present value, the amount each payment contributes to the present value is not apparent. Figure 10.5 helps us see the pattern. Five $10 payments are represented by columns at one-year intervals along the time axis. Using a discount rate of 10% compounded annually, each payment's contribution to the $37.91 present value is indicated at the left side of the diagram. Not surprisingly, each successive payment contributes a smaller amount to the present value. But notice that the *difference* between the contributions from two successive payments gets smaller as you look at later payments. For example, the second payment contributes $0.82 less than the first payment, the third payment contributes $0.76 less than the second payment, and so on. Eventually, distant payments contribute an insignificant amount to the present value. As an indication, suppose the annuity in Figure 10.5 is extended to 30 years. The total present value is $94.27, to which the thirtieth payment contributes only $0.57 (0.6%). If a further 20 payments are added (in Years 31 to 50), they will add only a combined $4.88 or 5.2% to the present value.

FIGURE 10.5   Contribution of Each Payment to an Annuity's Present Value

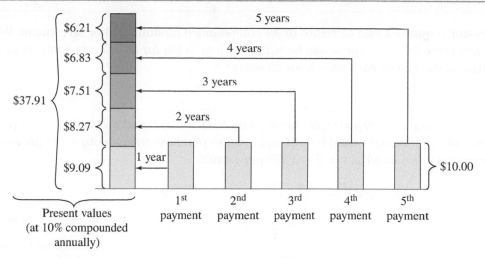

Applications of the Present Value of an Annuity

There are more applications of the present value calculation than of the future value calculation. Fundamentally, all present value applications are some form of *valuation*—putting a price tag on the "package" of annuity payments that are about to start. Three categories of applications are discussed in this section. A key issue in each category is how to choose the discount rate for the present value calculation.

LO3   **1. The Market Value of an Annuity** Clearly, the right to receive a series of future payments has value today. The *market* value of an annuity is the price at which it could be bought or sold among investors who are fully aware of investment alternatives. We look to the Valuation Principle (Section 7.2) for guidance in calculating the fair market value of any series of cash flows. It instructs us to calculate the present value of the cash flows, discounting them at the prevailing market rate of return (on investments of similar risk and duration). That is,

$$\begin{array}{c} \text{Fair market value} \\ \text{of an annuity} \end{array} = \left[\begin{array}{c} \text{Present value of the annuity payments} \\ \text{(discounted at the } market~rate~of~return) \end{array} \right]$$

Current market rates offered by insurance companies to purchasers of annuities are periodically reported in the major financial newspapers. Market rates on annuities of various terms may also be obtained from annuity brokers.

The present value calculation also allows you to estimate the amount you must have by the time you retire in order to purchase, for example, a 25-year annuity paying $3000 per month. (You would have to make an assumption about the market rate of return at the date of the annuity purchase.)

The cash flows from some investments include an annuity component. For example, some types of bonds pay a fixed dollar amount of interest every six months until the face value of the bond is repaid at maturity. Some preferred shares pay fixed quarterly dividends until the "par value" of the share is repaid on the redemption date. These two types of investments may be bought or sold in the financial markets on any business day. Consequently, valuation at *prevailing market* rates of return is important on a day-by-day basis. The fair market value is the present value of *all* remaining payments. The annuity *component* can be valued separately and added to the present value of the *other* expected payments.

EXAMPLE 10.3B | **Calculating the Purchase Price of an Ordinary Simple Annuity**

An investor requires a rate of return of 3% compounded monthly on her investment. What is the maximum price this investor would be willing to pay today for an annuity contract that will pay her $1000 at the end of each month for 20 years?

SOLUTION

The annuity is an *ordinary simple* annuity with $PMT = \$1000$ and $n = 12(20) = 240$ payments. The amount the investor would be willing to pay to purchase the annuity is the present value of the payments discounted at $i = \frac{3\%}{12} = 0.25\%$ per month.

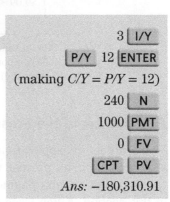

3 I/Y

P/Y 12 ENTER

(making $C/Y = P/Y = 12$)

240 N

1000 PMT

0 FV

CPT PV

$$PV = PMT\left[\frac{1 - (1 + i)^{-n}}{i}\right]$$

$$= \$1000\left[\frac{1 - (1.0025)^{-240}}{0.0025}\right]$$

$$= \$1000\left(\frac{1 - 0.549222714}{0.0025}\right)$$

$$= \$180,310.91$$

Note that we keep 9-figure accuracy in 0.549222714 to get 8-figure accuracy in the answer.

The maximum price the investor should be willing to pay today for the annuity is $180,310.91.

Ans: −180,310.91

▶ **Check your understanding:** What is the maximum price an investor would be willing to pay today to purchase an annuity paying $5000 at the end of each year for the next 20 years? Assume the investor requires a rate of return of 4% compounded annually. (Answer: $67,951.63)

▰▰▶ **Related problem:** #3 in Exercise 10.3

EXAMPLE 10.3C | **The Present Value of an Ordinary Simple Annuity and a Terminal "Lump" Payment**

A certain investment will pay you $50 at the end of every six months for 17 years. At the end of the 17 years, the investment will pay you an additional $1000 along with the last regular $50 payment. What is the fair market value of the investment if the prevailing rate of return on similar investments is 4.5% compounded semiannually?

SOLUTION

The fair market value of the investment is the present value of *all* of the payments discounted at the prevailing rate of return. The semiannual payments form an *ordinary simple* annuity having

$$PMT = \$50, \; n = 2(17) = 34 \text{ payments, and } i = \frac{4.5\%}{2} = 2.25\%$$

The combined present value of the annuity and the terminal lump payment is

Formula (10-2)   Formula (8-2)

$$PV = PMT\left[\frac{1 - (1 + i)^{-n}}{i}\right] + FV(1 + i)^{-n}$$

$$= \$50\left[\frac{1 - (1.0225)^{-34}}{0.0225}\right] + \$1000(1.0225)^{-34}$$

$$= \$50\left(\frac{1 - 0.469296411}{0.0225}\right) + \$1000(0.469296411)$$

$$= \$1179.341 + \$469.296$$

$$= \$1648.64$$

4.5	I/Y
P/Y 2	ENTER

(making $C/Y = P/Y = 2$)

34	N
50	PMT
1000	FV
CPT	PV

Ans: −1648.64

The fair market value of the investment is $1648.37.

⮕ **Check your understanding:** What is the fair market value today of an investment that will pay you $400 at the end of each month for the next $7\frac{1}{2}$ years, and a $5000 lump sum along with the last regular $400 payment? The prevailing rate of return on similar investments is 4.2% compounded monthly. (Answer: $34,486.34)

▬▬▶ **Related problem:** #15 in Exercise 10.3

EXAMPLE 10.3D	**The Present Value of two Ordinary Simple Annuities In Series**

How much will it cost to purchase a two-level retirement annuity that will pay $2000 at the end of each month for the first 10 years, and $3000 per month for the next 15 years? Assume that the payments represent a rate of return to the annuitant (the person receiving the payments) of 3.6% compounded monthly.

SOLUTION

The purchase price will be the present value of all of the payments. Since we have month-end payments and monthly compounding, the payments form two *ordinary simple* annuities in sequence. The given information and a three-step solution strategy are presented in the time diagram.

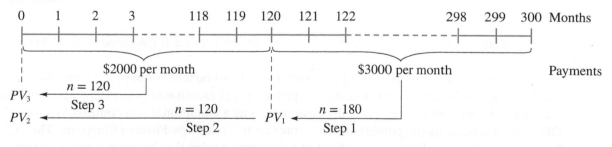

In Step 1, $n = 12(15) = 180$. In Steps 2 and 3, $n = 12(10) = 120$. In every step, $i = \frac{3.6\%}{12} = 0.3\%$.

Step 1: Calculate the present value, PV_1, of the $3000 annuity at its beginning.

$$PV_1 = PMT\left[\frac{1 - (1 + i)^{-n}}{i}\right]$$

$$= \$3000\left(\frac{1 - 1.003^{-180}}{0.003}\right)$$

$$= \$416,780.473$$

3.6	I/Y
P/Y	12 ENTER

(making $C/Y = P/Y = 12$)

180	N
3000	PMT
0	FV
CPT	PV

Ans: −416,780.743

Step 2: Calculate the present value, PV_2, of the Step 1 result at time 0.

$$PV_2 = FV(1 + i)^{-n}$$

$$= \$416,780.473(1.003)^{-120}$$

$$= \$290,934.618$$

Same I/Y, P/Y, C/Y

120	N
2000	PMT
416780.473	FV
CPT	PV

Ans: −492,233.004

Step 3: Calculate the present value, PV_3, of the $2000 annuity at time 0.

$$PV_3 = \$2000\left[\frac{1 - (1.003)^{-120}}{0.003}\right]$$

$$= \$201,298.386$$

The total present value will be

$$PV_2 + PV_3 = \$290,934.618 + \$201,298.386 = \$492,233.00$$

The purchase price of the two-level retirement annuity will be $492,233.00.

⇨ **Check your understanding:** How much would an investor be willing to pay to purchase a two-level annuity that will pay $5000 at the end of each six months for the first 10 years, and $6000 at the end of every six months for the subsequent 12 years? Assume that the investor requires a rate of return of 5.5% compounded semiannually. (Answer: $136,821.60)

▰▰▶ **Related problem:** #17 in Exercise 10.3

EXAMPLE 10.3E	Pricing an Ordinary Simple Annuity to Provide a Required Rate of Return

Crazy Ed's Furniture Mart is holding a "nothing down and no interest to pay" promotion on purchases exceeding $1000. Customers can pay six equal month-end payments with no interest charged. On such installment sales, the customer signs a conditional sale contract.[1] Crazy Ed's immediately sells the conditional sale contract to Conestoga Finance Company. The finance company purchases the contract at a discounted price that builds in a rate of return (on its purchase price) of 15% compounded monthly. What will Conestoga Finance pay for a $1200 contract (consisting of six payments of $200)?

---

[1] It is common for furniture retailers to sell such conditional sale contracts to a finance company. The retailer gets immediate cash from the sale of the contract and avoids having to set up a credit department. Rather than paying the retailer, the customer who bought the furniture is notified to submit payments directly to the finance company.

SOLUTION

The six installment payments form an *ordinary simple* annuity. To build the required rate of return into the purchase price, the payments must be discounted at the required rate of return. So we need to calculate the present value of $n = 6$ payments of $PMT = \$200$, discounted at $i = \frac{15\%}{12} = 1.25\%$ per month.

$$PV = PMT\left[\frac{1 - (1 + i)^{-n}}{i}\right]$$

$$= \$200\left[\frac{1 - (1 + 0.0125)^{-6}}{0.0125}\right]$$

$$= \$1149.20$$

15 I/Y
P/Y 12 ENTER
(making $C/Y = P/Y = 12$)
6 N
200 PMT
0 FV
CPT PV
Ans: −1149.20

Conestoga Finance will pay $1149.20 for the contract.

➡ **Check your understanding:** A customer just bought a $1800 dining room set from Crazy Ed's Furniture Mart and took advantage of the "nothing down and no interest to pay" promotion. The customer will pay six equal month-end payments with no interest charged. Conestoga Finance will buy the contract at a discounted price that builds in a rate of return of 12.6% compounded monthly. How much will Conestoga Finance pay for the contract? (Answer: $1735.66)

▶ **Related problem:** #18 in Exercise 10.3

LO4   **2. Loan Balance and Market Value of a Loan Contract** In Section 8.3 we established the general principle that

> Original loan = [Present value of *all* payments (discounted at the *contractual rate of interest* on the loan)]

The original loan is also the initial balance on the loan. The balance at any later time is the present value of the *remaining* payments.

> Principal balance = [Present value of the *remaining* payments (discounted at the *contractual rate of interest* on the loan)]

Both principles apply to any pattern of loan payments. However, most loans require equal periodic payments.[2] In these cases, we use formula (10-2) for the present value calculation.

EXAMPLE 10.3F	Calculating the Original Loan and a Subsequent Balance

The required monthly payment on a five-year loan bearing interest at 9% compounded monthly is $249.10.

a. What was the original principal amount of the loan?

b. What is the balance owed just after the 17th payment?

---

[2] As a technical point, the last payment in so-called equal-payment loans usually differs slightly from the others. In Section 13.1 you will learn how to calculate the exact amount of the final payment. Until then, we will make the assumption that the final payment is the same as the others. When you assume the final payment equals the others in the present value calculation for the "Original loan" or "Loan balance," your answer will have a small, immaterial error. To obtain strictly correct present values, you must use the strictly correct value for the final payment.

SOLUTION

The loan payments form an *ordinary simple* annuity having
$PMT = \$249.10$, $n = 12(5) = 60$, and $i = \frac{9\%}{12} = 0.75\%$ per month.

a. Original principal = Present value of all 60 payments

$$\text{Original principal} = PMT\left[\frac{1 - (1 + i)^{-n}}{i}\right]$$

$$= \$249.10\left(\frac{1 - 1.0075^{-60}}{0.0075}\right)$$

$$= \$249.10\left(\frac{1 - 0.63869970}{0.0075}\right)$$

$$= \$11,999.99$$

> Take borrower's viewpoint for the sign convention.
>
> 9 [I/Y]
> [P/Y] 12 [ENTER]
> (making $C/Y = P/Y = 12$)
> 60 [N]
> 249.10 [+/−] [PMT]
> 0 [FV]
> [CPT] [PV]
> *Ans:* 11,999.99

b. Balance after 17 payments = Present value of the remaining 43 payments

$$\text{Balance} = \$249.10\left(\frac{1 - 1.0075^{-43}}{0.0075}\right)$$

$$= \$249.10\left(\frac{1 - 0.72520810}{0.0075}\right)$$

$$= \$9126.76$$

> Same I/Y, PMT, FV, P/Y, C/Y
>
> 43 [N]
> [CPT] [PV]
> *Ans:* 9126.76

The original loan was $11,999.99 and the principal balance after 17 payments is $9126.76.

⮕ **Check your understanding:** An eight-year loan requires payments of $583.76 at the end of each quarter. The loan bears interest of 6% compounded quarterly. Calculate: **a.** the original principal amount of the loan and **b.** the loan balance owing just after the twenty-first payment. (Answer: **a.** $14,749.94, **b.** $5879.12.)

▰▰▰▶ **Related problem:** #21 in Exercise 10.3

Most loan contracts permit the lender to sell the contract to another investor at any time during the term of the loan. The investor/buyer is then entitled to receive subsequent loan payments from the borrower. To determine a price for the loan contract, the buyer and seller first agree upon the rate of return the buyer should earn. (Current interest rates offered by financial institutions on *new* loans provide a reference point for negotiating the buyer's rate of return.) Then this rate of return is "built in" or "locked in" by using it as the discount rate for calculating the present value of the remaining loan payments.

$$\text{Selling price of a loan contract} = \left(\begin{array}{c}\text{Present value of the remaining payments}\\\text{(discounted at the } \textit{negotiated rate} \text{ of return)}\end{array}\right)$$

EXAMPLE 10.3G	Calculating the Selling Price of a Loan Contract

Suppose the original lender in Example 10.3F wishes to sell the loan just after the 17th payment. What is the selling price if the negotiated rate of return to the buyer is to be

a. 7.5% compounded monthly?

b. 9% compounded monthly (the same as the interest rate on the loan)?

c. 10.5% compounded monthly?

SOLUTION

In each case,

$$\text{Selling price} = \binom{\text{Present value of the remaining 43 payments}}{\text{(discounted at the } \textit{negotiated rate of return}\text{)}}$$

$$\text{Selling price} = PMT\left[\frac{1-(1+i)^{-n}}{i}\right]$$

$$= \$249.10\left(\frac{1-1.00625^{-43}}{0.00625}\right)$$

$$= \$9367.20$$

Take buyer's viewpoint for the sign convention.

7.5 | I/Y

P/Y 12 | ENTER

(making $C/Y = P/Y = 12$)

43 | N

249.10 | PMT

0 | FV

CPT | PV

Ans: −9367.20

b. The periodic rate is $i = \frac{9\%}{12} = 0.75\%$

$$\text{Selling price} = \$249.10\left(\frac{1-1.0075^{-43}}{0.0075}\right)$$

$$= \$9126.76$$

Same *P/Y, C/Y, N, PMT, FV*

9 | I/Y

CPT | PV

Ans: −9126.76

c. The periodic rate is $i = \frac{10.5\%}{12} = 0.875\%$

$$\text{Selling price} = \$249.10\left(\frac{1-1.00875^{-43}}{0.00875}\right)$$

$$= \$8894.86$$

Same *P/Y, C/Y, N, PMT, FV*

10.5 | I/Y

CPT | PV

Ans: −8894.86

➡ **Check your understanding:** A five-year loan bearing interest of 5% compounded quarterly requires payments of $369.33 at the end of each calendar quarter. Just after the 15th payment, the loan contract was sold. What is the selling price if the negotiated rate of return to the buyer is to be 8% compounded quarterly? (Answer: $1740.82)

▭▶ **Related problem:** #24 in Exercise 10.3

 **Math Apps**

IS A CHEAP SMART PHONE A SMART CHOICE?

Like many consumers, you may have taken advantage of what appeared to be a cheap smart phone when signing up for a long-term contract with a mobile service provider. For example, in 2013, Bell Mobility offered a 16 GB iPhone 6S for only $398.99 when a customer signed up for a two-year contract. At the time, that model of iPhone was selling for $899 at major retailers. You "saved" $500.01 on the purchase of the phone. But is that deal really a deal? Now that you have some insight into annuities, you have the tools to do some important analysis and examine the cost of various options.

OPTION 1: Take advantage of Bell's offer and sign up for a two-year contract in order to purchase the phone for $398.99. The least expensive contract you could opt for at the time was an $80 per month voice and data plan that provided unlimited local calling, unlimited texts, and 500 MB of data usage per month. The total cost of this option was $398.99 paid at the start, plus $80 at the end of every month for two years.

OPTION 2: Buy the phone yourself from a major retailer for $899, then shop around for a competitive plan. For example, in 2016, Wind Mobile offered a voice and data plan with no fixed-term contract for $35 paid at the end of every month. This service provided unlimited Canada-wide minutes, unlimited texts, and 2 GB per month of data usage. Your total cost of this option would be $899 paid at the start, plus $35 at the end of every month for two years. (Note that since there is no contract, the cost of the plan could escalate in the future. For our purposes, we will assume that the $35 plan does not increase in price over the next two years.)

Which is a better deal? To evaluate how much each option is really costing, let's find the current economic value of the payment streams for each option. In today's dollars, how much is each really costing? To begin, we must select a rate of interest to use in our calculations. The rule of thumb when selecting a rate of interest to use in this type of analysis is to use the rate of return for the next best use of your funds. If you didn't buy the phone, what would you do with your money? Since you are a student and likely have debt, the rate of return we should select for this analysis is the current rate you are paying on outstanding debt. (If you were fortunate enough to have no debt, then the next-best use of your money would be to invest it, in which case you would use the rate of return you could be earning on your savings.) Let's assume you are currently paying 9% compounded monthly on your outstanding debt. Since the rate of return is compounded monthly, and the mobile fees are paid at the end of each month, each of the two options involves ordinary simple annuities, with $n = 24$, $i = \frac{j}{m} = \frac{9\%}{12} = 0.75\%$ per month.

Current economic value of Option 1

$=$ Cost of the phone $+ PV$ of the 24-month contract

$= \$398.99 + PMT\left[\dfrac{1 - (1 + i)^{-24}}{i}\right]$

$= \$398.99 + \$80\left[\dfrac{1 - (1 + 0.0075)^{-24}}{0.0075}\right]$

$= \$398.99 + \$1751.13 = \$2150.12$

Current economic value of Option 2

$=$ Cost of the phone $+ PV$ of the 24-month contract

$= \$899.00 + PMT\left[\dfrac{1 - (1 + i)^{-n}}{i}\right]$

$= \$899.00 + \$35\left[\dfrac{1 - (1 + 0.0075)^{-24}}{0.0075}\right]$

$= \$899.00 + \$766.12 = \$1665.12$

In today's dollars, you are paying $2150.12 − $1665.12 = $485 more for the "deal" than if you bought the phone yourself and opted for the cheaper monthly fee.

Postscript: Note that the answer in Part (b) of Example 10.3G equals the actual loan balance (which we calculated in Part (b) of Example 10.3F). Example 10.3G illustrates three scenarios summarized below.

Part	Rate of return vs. Interest rate on loan	Selling price vs. Balance on loan
a.	Rate of return < Interest rate on loan	Selling price > Balance on loan
b.	Rate of return = Interest rate on loan	Selling price = Balance on loan
c.	Rate of return > Interest rate on loan	Selling price < Balance on loan

Expressing the same relationships in another way,

- If the price you pay to purchase a loan is *equal* to the balance on the loan, the rate of return on your investment will be the *same* as the interest rate on the loan.
- Consequently, if you pay *more* than the loan balance, your rate of return will be *less* than the interest rate on the loan.
- Conversely, if you pay *less* than the loan balance, your rate of return will be *more* than the interest rate on the loan.

3. The Economic Value of an Annuity The *economic* value of a payment stream on a particular date (focal date) refers to a *single* amount that is an economic substitute for the payment stream. You will end up in the same financial position if you accept the economic value (on its focal date) instead of the scheduled payment stream.

The economic value of an annuity at the beginning of the annuity is just its present value. An appropriate value for the discount rate is the rate of return currently available on Government of Canada bonds (whose time until maturity is similar to the term of the annuity).

EXAMPLE 10.3H | **Comparing the Economic Values of Two Ordinary Simple Annuities**

An eligible individual may elect to start collecting the Canada Pension Plan monthly retirement pension at any time between the ages of 60 and 65. The payments are then reduced by 0.6% for each month the pension is collected before age 65. For example, if the pension starts five years early, at age 60, the monthly payment will be decreased by $(5 \times 12 \text{ months}) \times (0.6\%) = 36\%$. The reduction is permanent, extending to payments after age 65 as well.

The average life expectancy of a woman aged 60 is another 25 years. If a retired woman aged 60 lives just the expected 25 years, compare the economic values at age 60 of the following two alternatives:

- Collect a 100% pension from age 65.
- Collect a 64% pension from age 60.

Assume that money is worth 6% compounded monthly. Round your answers to the nearest dollar.

SOLUTION

The economic value at age 60 of a stream of pension payments will be the present value of the payments discounted at $i = \frac{6\%}{12} = 0.5\%$ per month.

The *relative* economic values of the pension alternatives will not depend on whether a 100% pension represents $500, $1000, or $1500 per month. Let's work on the basis of $1000 per month. Then the woman can choose either a full pension after age 65 of $1000 per month or a reduced pension after age 60 of $640 per month. The alternative pension payments are illustrated in the following time diagrams. In the first diagram, PV_1 represents the present value at age 60 of the reduced pension payments.

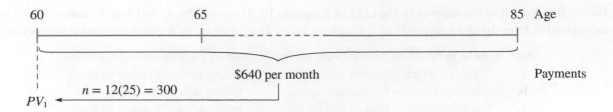

In the next diagram, PV_2 is the present value at age 65 of the full pension payments. PV_3 is the present value at age 60 of PV_2.

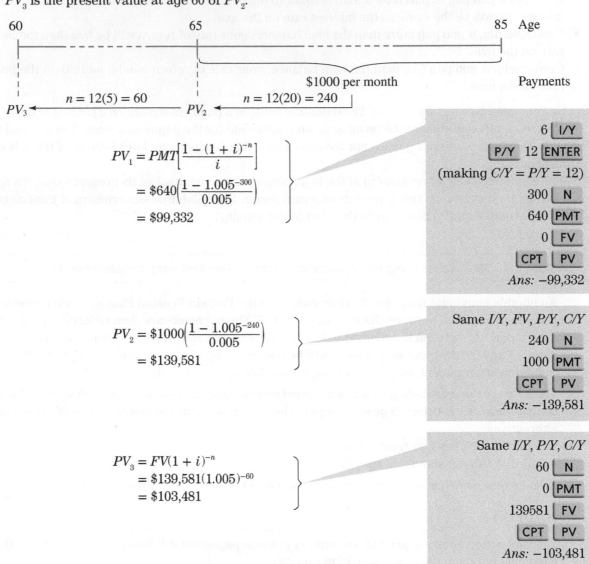

$$PV_1 = PMT\left[\frac{1 - (1 + i)^{-n}}{i}\right]$$

$$= \$640\left(\frac{1 - 1.005^{-300}}{0.005}\right)$$

$$= \$99{,}332$$

$$PV_2 = \$1000\left(\frac{1 - 1.005^{-240}}{0.005}\right)$$

$$= \$139{,}581$$

$$PV_3 = FV(1 + i)^{-n}$$
$$= \$139{,}581(1.005)^{-60}$$
$$= \$103{,}481$$

The economic value at age 60 of the early-pension option is $99,332. The economic value, also at age 60, of the full-pension option is $103,481. Based on our assumptions for life expectancy and the time value of money, the full-pension option is worth

$$\frac{\$103{,}481 - \$99{,}332}{\$99{,}332} \times 100\% = 4.18\%$$

more than the age-60 option. (We would get the same 4.18% advantage over the early-pension alternative for any dollar-amount assumptions used in our analysis, provided that the early-pension value is 64% of the full-pension value.)

⮕ **Check your understanding:** Suppose the average life expectancy of a woman aged 62 is another 20 years. If a retired woman aged 62 lives exactly the expected 20 years, compare the economic values at age 62 of collecting a 100% pension worth $1000 per month from age 65 versus collecting a 78.4% pension worth $784 per month from age 62. Assume that money is worth 9% compounded monthly. Round your answers to the nearest dollar. (Answer: At age 62, the economic value of the early-pension option is $87,138 and the economic value of the full-pension option is $79,698. The early-pension option is worth $7439.49 or 9.33% more than the age-65 option.)

◼️⮕ **Related problem:** #25 in Exercise 10.3

 ## Checkpoint Questions

1. Annuity A has the same n and i as Annuity B. A's *PMT* is double B's *PMT*. Will A's present value be (pick one) **(i)** double, **(ii)** more than double, or **(iii)** less than double the amount of B's present value? Give a reason for your choice.

2. Suppose the discount rate used to calculate the present value of an annuity is increased (leaving n and *PMT* unchanged). Will the annuity's present value be (pick one) **(i)** larger or **(ii)** smaller than before? Give a reason for your choice.

3. Annuity G has the same i and *PMT* as Annuity H. G has twice as many payments as H. Is G's present value (pick one) **(i)** double, **(ii)** more than double, or **(iii)** less than double the amount of H's present value? Give a reason for your choice.

4. Think of a 20-year annuity paying $2000 per month. If prevailing market rates decline over the next year, will the price to purchase a 20-year annuity increase or decrease? Explain.

EXERCISE 10.3

Answers to the odd-numbered problems can be found in the end matter.

BASIC PROBLEMS

1. An annuity consists of payments of $100 at the end of every quarter for $5\frac{1}{2}$ years. What is the annuity's present value, using a discount rate of 10% compounded quarterly?

2. Determine the present value of end-of-month payments of $75 continuing for $2\frac{1}{2}$ years. Use 8% compounded monthly as the discount rate.

3. What amount is needed to purchase an annuity paying $2500 at the end of every calendar quarter for the next 25 years? Assume the funds used to purchase the annuity will earn 6% compounded quarterly.

4. A contract requires end-of-month payments of $175 for the next $8\frac{1}{4}$ years. How much would an investor pay to purchase this contract if she requires a rate of return of 3% compounded monthly?

5. A new loan at 9% compounded quarterly requires payments of $727.88 at the end of every quarter for seven years. Rounded to the nearest dollar, what amount was borrowed?

6. Payments of $1240 at the end of every six months will pay off the balance owed on a loan in $9\frac{1}{2}$ years. If the interest rate on the loan is 5.9% compounded semiannually, what is the current balance on the loan?

7. Sabrina owns a loan contract that will provide her with payments of $350 at the end of every month for the next 11 years and 5 months. If Sabrina sells this loan contract today, what price would an investor be prepared to pay in order to "build in" a rate of return of 8.75% compounded monthly?

8. Determine the present value of payments of $100 at the end of each month for 20 years. Use a discount rate (interest rate) of 6% compounded monthly.

9. The rate of return offered by Reliance Insurance Co. on its 20-year annuities is 3.9% compounded monthly. Thom wishes to purchase an annuity from Reliance that will provide him with month-end payments of $1000 for the next 20 years. How much will Reliance charge Thom for this annuity?

INTERMEDIATE PROBLEMS

10. This problem demonstrates the dependence of an annuity's present value on the size of the periodic payment. Calculate the present value of 25 end-of-year payments of
    a. $1000.
    b. $2000.
    c. $3000.

    Use a discount rate of 5% compounded annually. After completing the calculations, note that present value is proportional to the size of the periodic payment.

11. This problem demonstrates the dependence of the present value of an annuity on the number of payments. Using 7% compounded annually as the discount rate, calculate the present value of an ordinary annuity paying $1000 per year for
    a. 5 years.
    b. 10 years.
    c. 20 years.
    d. 30 years.
    e. 100 years.
    f. 1000 years.

    Observe that the present value increases with increasing n, but at a diminishing rate. In this case, the 970 payments from Year 30 to Year 1000 cause the present value to increase by just 15%.

12. This problem demonstrates the dependence of the present value of an annuity on the discount rate. For an ordinary annuity consisting of 20 annual payments of $1000, calculate the present value using an annually compounded discount rate of
    a. 5%.
    b. 10%.
    c. 11%.
    d. 15%.

    Observe that the present value decreases as you increase the discount rate. However, the present value decreases proportionately *less* than the increase in the discount rate.

13. The Ottawa Senators fired their coach two years into his five-year contract, which paid him $90,000 at the end of each month. If the team owners buy out the remaining term of the coach's contract for its economic value at the time of firing, what will be the settlement amount? Assume that money can earn 3% compounded monthly.

14. The Montreal Canadiens have just announced the signing of Finnish hockey sensation Gunnar Skoroften to a 10-year contract at $3 million per year. The media are reporting the deal as being worth $30 million to the young Finn. Rounded to the dollar, what current economic value would you put on the contract if Skoroften will be paid $250,000 at the end of each month, and money can earn 6% compounded monthly?

15. Marika is shopping for a new cell phone and plan. She can get the phone she wants for an upfront payment of $299 if she signs up for a two-year plan with a major carrier. That plan will cost $75 at the end of every month for the duration of the two-year contract. Alternately, Marika can purchase the phone today for $639.99 and obtain service from a "no contract" service provider for $40 at the end of every month. Assume the "no contract" option does not escalate in price over the next two years. In current dollars, which option is economically preferable over the next two years if Marika uses a discount rate of 9% compounded monthly? In current dollars, how much will Marika save by selecting that alternative?

16. You want to buy a new laptop computer and have obtained pricing information from two major retailers. Retailer A is offering a "no money down no interest" event. You would pay $162.50 at the end of each month for the next 12 months. To purchase the same laptop from Retailer B, you will pay $500 today, and an additional $72.50 at the end of each month for the next 18 months. Which alternative is economically preferable if money is worth 6% compounded monthly? In current dollars, how much will you save by selecting the preferred alternative?

17. A Government of Canada bond will pay $50 at the end of every six months for the next 15 years, and an additional $1000 lump payment at the end of the 15 years. What is the appropriate price to pay if you require a rate of return of 6.5% compounded semiannually?

18. What is the maximum price you should pay for a contract guaranteeing month-end payments of $500 for the next 12 years if you require a minimum rate of return of 8% compounded monthly for the first five years and 9% compounded monthly for the remaining seven years?

19. Isaac wishes to purchase a 25-year annuity providing payments of $1000 at the end of each month for the first 15 years and $1500 at the end of each month for the remaining 10 years. If he requires a minimum rate of return of 3.6% compounded monthly, what is the maximum price Isaac will be willing to pay for the annuity?

20. A conditional sale contract between Classic Furniture and the purchaser of a dining room set requires month-end payments of $250 for 15 months. Classic Furniture sold the contract to Household Finance Co. at a discount to yield 19.5% compounded monthly. What price did Household pay Classic Furniture?

21. A 20-year loan requires semiannual payments of $808.15 including interest at 3.8% compounded semiannually.

    a. What was the original amount of the loan?
    b. What is the loan's balance $8\frac{1}{2}$ years later (just after the scheduled payment)?

22. The monthly payments on a five-year loan at 7.5% compounded monthly are $200.38.

    a. What was the original amount of the loan?
    b. What is the balance after the 30th payment?

23. Kent sold his car to Carolynn for $2000 down and end-of-month payments of $295.88 for $3\frac{1}{2}$ years, including interest at 7.5% compounded monthly. What was the selling price of the car?

24. The required payment on an eight-year loan (bearing interest of 8% compounded quarterly) is $385 at the end of every calendar quarter.

    a. What was the original principal amount of the loan?
    b. What is the balance owed on the loan just after the 10th payment?
    c. The original lender (the person who is receiving these loan payments) decides to sell the loan contract immediately after the 20th payment. What is the selling price if the negotiated rate of return to the buyer is 10% compounded quarterly?

25. You are selling a residential building lot. Mr. Seebach is offering $195,000 cash. Mrs. Chan is offering $100,000 down and payments of $6250 at the end of each calendar quarter for the next four years. Which offer should you accept if you use a discount rate of 5% compounded quarterly? In current dollars, how much more is the better offer worth to you?

ADVANCED PROBLEMS

26. A lottery offers the winner the choice between a $250,000 cash prize or month-end payments of $1000 for $12\frac{1}{2}$ years, increasing to $1500 per month for the subsequent $12\frac{1}{2}$ years. Which alternative would you choose if money can earn 3.66% compounded monthly over the 25-year period?

27. The British Columbia Teachers' Pension Plan allows a teacher to begin collecting a retirement pension before age 60, but the pension is reduced by 3% for each year the retiring teacher's age is under 60. For example, a teacher retiring at age 56 would receive 100% − 4(3%) = 88% of the monthly pension that she would receive at age 60 (with the same number of years of service). The reduction is permanent, extending to payments beyond age 60.

    Suppose that a female teacher will live the average life expectancy of 28 additional years for a woman aged 55. Compare the economic values at age 55 of the two alternatives of collecting an 85% pension from age 55 versus collecting a 100% pension from age 60. Assume that money is worth 4.8% compounded monthly.

28. An individual qualifying for Canada Pension Plan benefits may elect to start collecting the CPP monthly retirement benefit at any time between the ages of 60 and 70. If the retirement benefit starts after age 65, the pension payments are increased (from the amount that would otherwise be paid at age 65) by 0.7% for each month after age 65. For example, if the retiree chooses to begin receiving the benefit after turning 68, the CPP payments will be increased by (36 months) × (0.7%) = 25.2%.

    The average life expectancy of a man aged 65 is another 15 years. If a man aged 65 lives exactly the expected 15 years, compare the economic values at age 65 of the two alternatives of collecting a 100% pension from age 65 versus a 125.2% pension from age 68. Assume that money is worth 6% compounded monthly.

29. **Influence of Annuity Variables** There is an "Influence of Annuity Variables" interactive chart found in the Student Resources for Chapter 10. To access this chart, go to the Student Edition of the textbook's Connect. In the navigation bar, select "Chapter 10" in the drop-down box. In the list of resources for Chapter 10, select "Links in Textbook" and then click on the link named "Influence of Annuity Variables." This interactive chart enables you to observe and compare the effects of changes in the variables PMT, n, and i on both the future value and present value of an annuity.

    a. Enter $PMT = \$100$ and $i = 8\%$ for both Annuity A and Annuity B. Set $n = 20$ for Annuity A and $n = 40$ for Annuity B. This means that B contains twice as many payments as A. In percentage terms,

        (i) How much larger is the present value of B than the present value of A?

        (ii) How much larger is the future value of B than the future value of A?

    b. Enter $PMT = \$100$ and $n = 30$ for both annuities. Set $i = 8\%$ for Annuity A and $i = 9\%$ for Annuity B. In relative terms, the interest rate for B is $\frac{9\% - 8\%}{8\%} \times 100\% = 12.5\%$ larger than the rate for A. In percentage terms,

        (i) How much *smaller* is the present value of B than the present value of A?

        (ii) How much *larger* is the future value of B than the future value of A?

10.4 Future Value and Present Value of an Ordinary General Annuity

LO5   To this point, our calculations of the future and present values of annuities have been restricted to *ordinary simple* annuities. Each problem we have examined so far had payments made at the end of each payment interval (an ordinary annuity), and each question involved a situation in which the payment interval was *equal* to the compounding interval (a simple annuity). We will now learn how to handle *FV* and *PV* calculations for *ordinary general* annuities. Payments will still be occurring at the end of each payment interval, but now the payment interval will *differ* from the compounding interval. Actually, we have already covered all you need to know to calculate the future value and present value of an ordinary general annuity. We need only "link" two topics whose connection is not obvious.

Let us begin with formula (10-1) for the future value of an ordinary simple annuity.

$$FV = PMT\left[\frac{(1+i)^n - 1}{i}\right]$$ **(10-1)**

Keep in mind that this formula can be used *only* in cases where the compounding interval equals (or "matches") the payment interval. But if we can find a way to *transform* a general annuity into a simple annuity, then we can still use formula (10-1).

Sometimes an insight comes more easily if we consider a specific numerical example. Suppose we wish to find the future value of an ordinary annuity consisting of 12 payments of $100 at the end of every six months that earn 8% compounded quarterly. We are given

$$PMT = \$100 \text{ every six months, } i = \frac{8\%}{4} = 2\% \text{ per quarter, and } n = 12$$

Since the payment interval is six months but the compounding interval is three months, the payments form an *ordinary general* annuity. In order to use formula (10-1), we need the periodic rate for six months (the payment interval) that is *equivalent* to the given periodic rate of 2% per quarter. This is precisely the type of calculation for which formula (9-4) was derived in Section 9.4.

$$i_2 = (1+i_1)^{m_1/m_2} - 1$$ **(9-4)**

For the case at hand,

$$i_1 = \text{The } given \text{ periodic rate } (i = 2\%)$$
$$m_1 = \text{Number of compoundings per year (4) at the } given \text{ interest rate}$$
$$m_2 = \text{Number of compoundings per year at the } equivalent \text{ interest rate}$$
$$\text{(which will equal the number of payments per year (2))}$$
$$i_2 = \text{Periodic interest rate for a payment interval}$$

In this case, the exponent m_1/m_2 in formula (9-4) is

$$\frac{m_1}{m_2} = \frac{\text{Number of compoundings per year (at the given interest rate)}}{\text{Number of payments per year}} = \frac{4}{2} = 2$$

Substituting in formula (9-4), the periodic rate per payment interval (six months) is

$$i_2 = (1+i_1)^{m_1/m_2} - 1 = 1.02^{4/2} - 1 = 1.02^2 - 1 = 0.0404 = 4.04\%$$

Now substitute this value of i_2 for i in formula (10-1).

$$FV = PMT\left[\frac{(1+i)^n - 1}{i}\right] = \$100\left[\frac{(1.0404)^{12} - 1}{0.0404}\right] = \$1506.03$$

The future value of the general annuity is $1506.03.

Let us streamline formula (9-4) for use in general annuity problems. As noted in the preceding analysis,

$$i_1 = i \quad \text{and} \quad \frac{m_1}{m_2} = \frac{\text{Number of compoundings per year}}{\text{Number of payments per year}}$$

Since $\frac{m_1}{m_2}$ is a commonly occurring ratio in general annuities, we can simplify the appearance of formula (9-4) if we define a new symbol:

NUMBER OF COMPOUNDINGS PER PAYMENT INTERVAL	$c = \dfrac{\text{Number of compoundings per year}}{\text{Number of payments per year}}$	**(10-3)**

Then we can write formula (9-4) as

EQUIVALENT PERIODIC RATE FOR GENERAL ANNUITIES	$i_2 = (1 + i)^c - 1$	**(9-4c)**

TIP

Some Things Just Have to Be Memorized

You need to commit the definition of c to memory. The symbol "c" reminds us that "compoundings per year" comes first (in the numerator).

We have used the future value calculation to introduce the mathematics of general annuities. The same approach works in all types of general annuity calculations. It is summarized below.

Approach for Solving a General Annuity Problem

Transform the general annuity problem into a simple annuity problem by:

1. Using $i_2 = (1 + i)^c - 1$ to calculate the equivalent periodic rate that matches the payment interval.

2. Using this equivalent periodic rate as the value for *i* in the appropriate simple annuity formula.

Using the Texas Instruments BA II PLUS for General Annuities Recall that, when you enter a value for *P/Y*, the calculator automatically assigns the same value to *C/Y*. This is appropriate for simple annuities. But for general annuities, after entering the value for *P/Y* you must scroll down to *C/Y* and enter its different value. Then close the worksheet. The keystrokes for obtaining the future value of 12 semiannual payments of $100 earning 8% compounded quarterly are shown at right.

8	I/Y
P/Y 2	ENTER
C/Y 4	ENTER
12	N
0	PV
100 +/-	PMT
CPT	FV

Ans: 1506.03

TIP

Be Intentional About Identifying the Type of Annuity

A common error students make beyond this point in the course is to forget to make the necessary adjustments to the calculations when the annuity is *not* an *ordinary simple* annuity. To avoid this omission, immediately after your initial reading of the question, you should note the type of annuity at hand. If you intend to use your calculator's financial functions for the computation, you should also enter values for *I/Y*, *P/Y*, and *C/Y* at this early point. This is why we have been showing these values as being entered *first* in the callout boxes for the financial calculator solutions (even though we have been dealing only with calculations involving ordinary simple annuities prior to Section 10.4).

EXAMPLE 10.4A	Calculating the Equivalent Periodic Interest Rate

To five-figure accuracy, calculate the periodic interest rate that matches the payment interval for

a. semiannual payments earning 5% compounded annually.

b. monthly payments discounted at 6% compounded quarterly.

SOLUTION

a. $i = \dfrac{5\%}{1} = 5\%$ per *year* and $c = \dfrac{1 \text{ compounding per year}}{2 \text{ payments per year}} = 0.5$

Thus,

$$
\begin{aligned}
i_2 &= (1 + i)^c - 1 \\
&= 1.05^{0.5} - 1 \\
&= 0.024695 \\
&= 2.4695\% \text{ per half-year}
\end{aligned}
$$

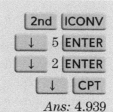

The periodic rate will be

$$i = \frac{j}{m} = \frac{4.939}{2}$$
$$= 2.4595\% \text{ per half-year.}$$

TIP

Estimating i_2

You can easily *estimate* the value of i_2, the periodic rate for a payment interval. It is a good idea to do this to check the "reasonableness" of the value you calculate for i_2. In Part (a), the interest rate for six months (the payment interval) will be *about* half the nominal annual rate of 5%; that is, $i_2 \approx 2.5\%$. (This number is only an approximation because it ignores compounding.) If formula (9-4c) does not give you a value close to 2.5%, you have made an error in your calculations. To estimate i_2 in general, simply divide the given nominal rate by the number of payments per year.

b. $i = \dfrac{6\%}{4} = 1.5\%$ per quarter and $c = \dfrac{4 \text{ compounding per year}}{12 \text{ payments per year}} = 0.\overline{3}$

Our estimate for i_2 is $\frac{6\%}{12} = 0.5\%$ per month. Using formula (9-4c) we obtain the more exact answer,

$$i_2 = (1 + i)^c - 1 = 1.015^{0.3} - 1 = 0.0049752 = 0.49752\% \text{ per month}$$

which is very near to our estimate.

To use the ICONV worksheet, first compute the effective rate corresponding to 6% compounded quarterly. Then compute the monthly compounded nominal rate that is equivalent to this effective rate.

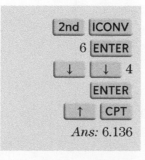

Press ↓ (to scroll down to the *C/Y* line)

12 ENTER

↑ ↑ CPT

Ans: 5.970

The periodic rate will be

$$i = \frac{j}{m} = \frac{5.970}{12} = 0.4975\% \text{ per month.}$$

➡ **Check your understanding:** Estimate the quarterly periodic interest rate (i_2) that is equivalent to 9% compounded monthly. Then, calculate the exact value to five-figure accuracy. (Answers: The estimate is 2.25% per quarter; to five-figure accuracy the calculated value is 2.2669% per quarter.)

■■➤ **Related problem:** #1 in Exercise 10.4

TIP ✔

Improving the Accuracy of Calculated Results

Sometimes the value for c is a *repeating* decimal. This happened in Part (b) of the preceding example, where we obtained $c = 0.\overline{3}$. In such cases, use your calculator in a way that optimizes the accuracy of the value you obtain for i_2. For example, immediately after dividing 4 by 12 in the preceding Part (b), save the quotient to memory. The calculator then retains at least two more digits than you see in the display. Later, when you need the exponent for the y^x function, recall the value for c from the memory.

Typically, the value you calculate for i_2 will be used in further calculations. Again, to optimize accuracy, i_2's value should be saved in memory immediately after you calculate it. The value in memory will have two or three more digits than you see in the display. Whenever i_2 is needed in a subsequent calculation, recall it from the memory. This procedure will improve both your efficiency in using the calculator and the accuracy of your results.

EXAMPLE 10.4B	Calculating the Future Value of an Ordinary General Annuity

If $1000 is invested at the end of every year at 5% compounded semiannually, what will be the total value accumulated in the investment after 25 years?

SOLUTION

Since the compounding period (six months) differs from the payment interval (one year), the regular investments at the end of each year form a *general annuity* having

$$PMT = \$1000, \ n = 1(25) = 25, \text{ and } i = \tfrac{5\%}{2} = 2.5\%$$

The total value of the investments will be their combined future value.

Before we can calculate this future value, we must determine the periodic interest rate for the one-year payment interval. (It will be *about* 8%.) Since

$$c = \frac{2 \text{ compoundings per year}}{1 \text{ payment per year}} = 2$$

then

$$i_2 = (1 + i)^c - 1$$
$$= 1.025^2 - 1 = 0.050625 \text{ per year}$$

Substitute this value for i in formula (10-1).

$$FV = PMT\left[\frac{(1 + i)^n - 1}{i}\right]$$

$$= \$1000\left[\frac{(1.050625)^{25} - 1}{0.050625}\right] = \$48,140.42$$

The total value after 25 years will be $48,140.42.

5	I/Y
P/Y 1	ENTER
C/Y 2	ENTER
25	N
0	PV
1000 +/–	PMT
CPT	FV

Ans: 48,140.42

➡ **Check your understanding:** If $50 is invested at the end of each month at 3% compounded semiannually, what will be the total value of the periodic investments after 30 years? (Answer: $29,044.28)

▪▪▪▶ **Related problem:** #4a in Exercise 10.4

TRAP ⚠

What Is the Correct Value for "*n*"?

In any annuity calculation, *n* represents the number of *payments*. Now that we are dealing with general annuities, you must be very careful about obtaining the correct value for *n*. Looking back to Example 10.4B, note that payments were made annually for 25 years, so $n = 1 \times 25 = 25$. If you were not careful, you might have mistakenly looked at the compounding frequency (semiannual) and concluded that $n = 2 \times 25 = 50$. To obtain the correct value for *n* in any annuity question, remember to ask yourself, "How many *payments* are there in this annuity?"

EXAMPLE 10.4C | Calculating the Present Value of an Ordinary General Annuity

Maureen turned 60 years old today and has today retired from teaching. While reviewing Maureen's personal net worth statement, her financial advisor points out that she has overlooked a significant asset—the current economic value of her pension. Now that she has retired, Maureen will be receiving pension payments of $3500 at the end of each month. Based on a 22-year life expectancy and money worth 8% compounded semiannually, calculate the current economic value of Maureen's pension. Round your answer to the nearest dollar.

SOLUTION

The current economic value of the pension can be calculated by finding the present value of the pension payments discounted at 8% compounded semiannually. With end-of-month payments and semiannual compounding, the pension constitutes an *ordinary general* annuity. We are given

$$PMT = \$3500, \; n = 12(22) = 264, \text{ and } i = \tfrac{8\%}{2} = 4\%$$

First we must calculate the periodic rate that matches the one-month payment interval. (It will be about $\tfrac{8\%}{12} = 0.67\%$.)

$$c = \frac{2 \text{ compoundings per year}}{12 \text{ payments per year}} = 0.1\overline{6}$$

Using formula (9-4c),

$$i_2 = (1 + i)^c - 1 = 1.04^{0.1\overline{6}} - 1 = 0.00655819692 \text{ per month}$$

Substitute this value for *i* in formula (10-2) to obtain the present value of the pension at age 60.

$$PV = PMT\left[\frac{1 - (1 + i)^{-n}}{i}\right]$$

$$= \$3500\left[\frac{1 - (1.006558197)^{-264}}{0.006558197}\right]$$

$$= \$438,662.91$$

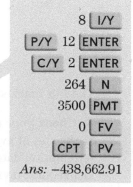

8 ⎣ I/Y

P/Y 12 ENTER

C/Y 2 ENTER

264 ⎣ N

3500 ⎣ PMT

0 ⎣ FV

CPT ⎣ PV

Ans: −438,662.91

The current economic value of Maureen's pension is $438,663. The significance of this number is that, if Maureen did not belong to the pension plan, she would need current savings of $438,663 in a personal RRSP earning 8% compounded semiannually in order to duplicate the pension benefits she will receive to age 82.

➡ **Check your understanding:** Fernando is exactly 62 years old and has just retired. He will receive a pension of $2600 at the end of every month. Assuming Fernando lives another 23 years, what is the current economic value of his pension if money is worth 8% compounded quarterly? Round your answer to the nearest dollar. (Answer: $329,096)

▬▶ **Related problem:** #14 in Exercise 10.4

EXAMPLE 10.4D | **Calculating the Fair Market Value of a Preferred Share**

The preferred shares of Dominion Trust Co. will pay a $0.75 per share dividend at the end of every calendar quarter until they are redeemed (that is, bought back by Dominion Trust) $8\frac{1}{2}$ years from now. On the redemption date, a shareholder will receive the $40 par value of each share in addition to the last regular dividend. What is the fair market value of a share if preferred shares of similar risk are currently generating a total rate of return of 6.5% compounded semiannually?

SOLUTION

This is a valuation application of present value. The fair market value of a share will be the combined present value of the dividends and the $40 payment of the par value. The dividend stream constitutes an *ordinary general* annuity having

$$PMT = \$0.75, \ n = 4(8.5) = 34, \text{ and } i = \tfrac{6.5\%}{2} = 3.25\%$$

Then

$$c = \frac{2 \text{ compoundings per year}}{4 \text{ payments per year}} = 0.5$$

and

$$i_2 = (1 + i)^c - 1 = 1.0325^{0.5} - 1 = 0.0161201 \text{ per quarter}$$

$$\text{Fair market value} = \left(\begin{array}{c} \text{Present value} \\ \text{of dividends} \end{array}\right) + \left(\begin{array}{c} \text{Present value} \\ \text{of par value} \end{array}\right)$$

$$= PMT\left[\frac{1 - (1 + i)^{-n}}{i}\right] + FV(1 + i)^{-n}$$

$$= \$0.75\left(\frac{1 - 1.0161201^{-34}}{0.0161201}\right) + \$40(1.0161201)^{-34}$$

$$= \$19.513 + \$23.224$$

$$= \$42.74$$

	6.5 I/Y
	P/Y 4 ENTER
	C/Y 2 ENTER
	34 N
	0.75 PMT
	40 FV
	CPT PV
	Ans: −42.74

The fair market value of a preferred share is $42.74.

➡ **Check your understanding:** Preferred shares of BCE Inc. will pay a $1.14 per share dividend at the end of every calendar quarter until they are redeemed $4\frac{1}{2}$ years from now. On the redemption date, a shareholder will receive the $25 par value of each share in addition to the last regular dividend. What is the fair market value of a share if investments of similar risk are currently generating a total rate of return of 3.5% compounded annually? (Answer: $40.34)

▬▶ **Related problem:** #19 in Exercise 10.4

Checkpoint Questions

1. What are the distinguishing characteristics of an ordinary general annuity?

2. An annuity with quarterly payments earns 6% compounded monthly. What is the value of c? What is the approximate value of the periodic rate of return for one payment interval? Will the correct value be larger or smaller than your estimate? Explain.

3. A loan at 6% compounded semiannually requires equal monthly payments. What is the value of c? What is the approximate value of the periodic interest rate for one payment interval? Will the correct value be larger or smaller than your estimate? Explain.

EXERCISE 10.4

Answers to the odd-numbered problems can be found in the end matter.

BASIC PROBLEMS

1. An ordinary general annuity earns a nominal rate of 4% compounded annually. Rounded to the nearest 0.001%, what is the corresponding periodic rate (i_2) if the annuity's payments are made semiannually?

2. An ordinary general annuity earns a nominal rate of 6% compounded monthly. Rounded to the nearest 0.001%, what is the corresponding periodic rate (i_2) if the annuity's payments are made quarterly?

3. An ordinary general annuity earns a nominal rate of 5% compounded semiannually. Rounded to the nearest 0.001%, what is the corresponding periodic rate (i_2) if the annuity's payments are made monthly?

4. An annuity consists of payments of $400 at the end of every calendar quarter for 11 years. If the annuity earns 3.5% compounded annually, calculate the annuity's

   a. future value   b. present value

5. An annuity consists of payments of $1000 made at the end of every year for 27 years. If the annuity earns 8% compounded semiannually, calculate the annuity's

   a. future value   b. present value

INTERMEDIATE PROBLEMS

6. Julianna has deposited $50 at the end of every month for the last 20 years. Her investment has earned 6% compounded quarterly. How much is Julianna's investment worth today?

7. Alejandro has graduated from college and obtained his first job. He plans to invest $3500 at the end of every year. If Alejandro can earn 4.5% compounded quarterly on his investments, how much will he have altogether in 10 years from now?

8. A loan will be repaid with $580 payments at the end of every month for 8 years. The loan carries an interest rate of 8% compounded quarterly. Rounded to the nearest dollar, how much was the original loan?

9. For the last five years, Larissa has been depositing $185 at the end of every month into a savings account that earns 5.5% compounded quarterly.

   a. If she continues this savings plan for another eight years, how much will she have in her savings account altogether?

   b.   How much of the total in Part (a) is interest?

10.   Mr. and Mrs. Krenz are contributing to a Registered Education Savings Plan (RESP) they have set up for their children. What amount will they have in the RESP after eight years of contributing $500 at the end of every calendar quarter if the plan earns 3% compounded monthly? How much of the total amount is interest?

11.   What amount will be required to purchase a 20-year annuity paying $2500 at the end of each month if the annuity provides a return of 6.75% compounded annually?

12.   How much larger will the value of a Tax Free Savings Account (TFSA) be at the end of 25 years if the TFSA earns 9% compounded monthly instead of 9% compounded annually? In both cases a contribution of $1000 is made at the end of every three months.

13.   What is the future value eight years from now of each of the following cash-flow streams if money can earn 5% compounded semiannually?

   a.   a single payment of $5000 today

   b.   a series of eight payments of $900 made at the end of each year for the next eight years

14.   Howard retired today and will receive pension payments of $2900 at the end of every month. If Howard collects this pension for the next 28 years, what is the current economic value of his pension if the payments are discounted at 4% compounded annually?

15.   Kent sold his car to Carolynn for $2000 down and monthly payments of $259.50 for $3\frac{1}{2}$ years, including interest at 7.5% compounded annually.

   a.   What was the selling price of the car?

   b.   How much is still owing on the loan immediately after the 12th payment?

16.   A loan contract will provide Lixin with payments of $4000 at the end of every six months. The contract has seven years to run. Lixin wants to sell the contract. How much will an investor pay for this loan contract if she wants to "build in" a rate of return of 8% compounded monthly?

17.   LeVero's end-of-month payments of $1167.89 will pay off his mortgage loan in 4 years and 7 months. The interest rate on his mortgage is 4.6% compounded semiannually. What is the current balance on the loan?

18.   How much larger will the value of an RRSP be at the end of 25 years if the contributor makes month-end contributions of $300 instead of year-end contributions of $3600? In both cases the RRSP earns 6.5% compounded semiannually.

19.   A particular issue of CIBC preferred shares will pay a $1.63 per share dividend at the end of every calendar quarter until they are redeemed (bought back by CIBC) $7\frac{1}{2}$ years from now. On the redemption date, a shareholder will receive the $25 par value of each share in addition to the last regular dividend. What is the fair market value of a share if preferred shares of similar risk are generating a total rate of return of 5.5% compounded semiannually?

ADVANCED PROBLEMS

20.   Year-end contributions of $1000 will be made to a Tax Free Savings Account (TFSA) for 25 years. What will be the future value of the account if it earns 3.6% compounded monthly for the first 10 years and 4% compounded semiannually thereafter?

21.   Micheline wishes to purchase a 25-year annuity providing payments of $1000 per month for the first 15 years and $1500 per month for the remaining 10 years. Sovereign Insurance Co. has quoted her a rate of return of 5% compounded annually for such an annuity. How much will it cost Micheline to purchase the annuity from Sovereign?

22. Gloria has just made her ninth annual $2000 contribution to her Tax Free Savings Account (TFSA). She now plans to make semiannual contributions of $2000. The first contribution will be made six months from now. How much will she have in her TFSA 15 years from now if the plan has earned and will continue to earn 5% compounded quarterly?

23. The Toronto Raptors announce the signing of one of their players to a "seven-year deal worth $43.2 million." The player will earn $400,000 at the end of each month for the first three years, and $600,000 at the end of each month for the subsequent four years. How do the Raptors get the $43.2 million figure? To the nearest $1000, what is the true current economic value of the deal if money can earn 4% compounded annually?

10.5 | Future Value and Present Value of an Annuity Due

LO6 Recall from Section 10.1 that an annuity due is an annuity whose payments are made at the *beginning* of each payment interval. If the payment interval and the interest compounding interval are *equal*, we have a *simple annuity due*. If the payment interval and the interest compounding interval *differ*, we have a *general annuity due*. In this section, we will learn how to calculate the future value and present value of annuities due. Much of what we have already learned about annuities in this chapter will be applied here with only slight modifications to account for the fact that payments are now being made at the beginning rather than end of each payment interval.

Future Value of an Annuity Due Using the Algebraic Method

The formula for the future value of an annuity due may be quickly derived from the formula for the future value of an ordinary annuity. To see the connection between them, let's consider a specific example. Consider an *ordinary annuity* consisting of equal payments at the *end* of every period for five periods. A time diagram for this annuity is shown in the upper part of Figure 10.6. Notice that the focal date for its future value, *FV*, is at the end of the annuity (coincident with the last payment).

FIGURE 10.6 The Relationship Between *FV* and *FV*(due)

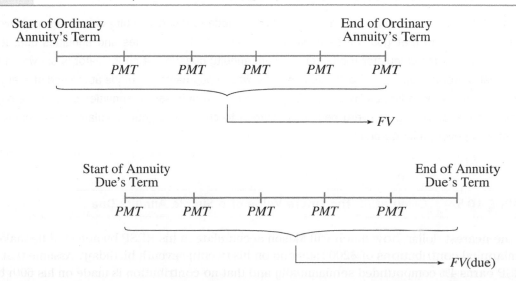

In the lower part of Figure 10.6, we have presented the same five payments, this time viewed as an annuity due. Since the payments are made at the *beginning* of every payment interval, the annuity's term has been adjusted. The annuity's term begins on the date of the first payment and ends one interval *after* the last payment. The focal date for its future value, labelled FV(due), is at the end of the annuity (one payment interval after the last payment).

Each of these values, FV and FV(due), is the future value of the same five payments. The only difference between them is that the FV(due) payments, by being made at the start of each interval have one additional interval to earn interest than the FV payments. Therefore, FV(due) equals the future value of FV, one payment interval later. That is,

$$FV(\text{due}) = FV \times (1 + i)$$

We see that the future value of an annuity due is simply $(1 + i)$ times the future value of an ordinary annuity. Substituting from formula (10-1) for FV, we obtain

FUTURE VALUE OF A SIMPLE ANNUITY DUE

$$FV(\text{due}) = FV \times (1 + i)$$
$$= PMT\left[\frac{(1 + i)^n - 1}{i}\right] \times (1 + i) \qquad \text{(10-4)}$$

If the beginning-of-period payments are made at an interval that is different from the interest compounding, the payments form a general annuity due. Use $i_2 = (1 + i)^c - 1$ to calculate the periodic interest rate that matches the payment interval. Then substitute this value for i in formula (10-4).

Future Value of an Annuity Due Using the Financial Calculator Functions

Since $FV(\text{due}) = FV \times (1 + i)$, the approach that probably occurs to you is to compute the annuity's future value as though it were an *ordinary* annuity, and then multiply the result by $(1 + i)$. The financial calculator will do this multiplication automatically if it is first "informed" that the annuity is an annuity *due*. Appendix 10A provides instructions for setting various financial calculator models in the annuity due mode. In example problems, "BGN mode" indicates that the calculator should be set to the annuity due mode.

TIP

Check the Calculator Mode Before Every Question

Most calculators remain in the most recently selected mode (ordinary annuity or annuity due) even after being turned off. Now that you will be dealing with both ordinary annuities and annuities due, it will be important to check the calculator mode before every annuity question. If no indicator is shown on the display, the calculator is prepared for ordinary annuities, whose payments are made at the end of every period. If the calculator screen indicates "BGN" or "Begin," the calculator is set for annuities due, whose payments are made at the beginning of every period. Be careful to check that your calculator is set appropriately before starting every annuity problem.

EXAMPLE 10.5A | Calculating the Future Value of a Simple Annuity Due

To the nearest dollar, how much will Mason accumulate in his RRSP by age 60 if he makes semiannual contributions of $2000 starting on his twenty-seventh birthday? Assume that the RRSP earns 4% compounded semiannually and that no contribution is made on his 60th birthday.

SOLUTION

The accumulated amount will be the future value of the contributions on Mason's 60th birthday. Viewed from the future value's focal date at his 60th birthday, the RRSP contributions are made at the *beginning* of every six months. Therefore, they form an *annuity due*. Since the payment interval equals the compounding interval, we have a *simple annuity due* with

$$PMT = \$2000, \ i = \tfrac{4\%}{2} = 2\%, \text{ and } n = 2(33) = 66 \text{ payments}$$

Substitute the preceding values into formula (10-4).

$$FV(\text{due}) = PMT\left[\frac{(1 + i)^n - 1}{i}\right] \times (1 + i)$$

$$= \$2000\left(\frac{1.02^{66} - 1}{0.02}\right) \times (1.02)$$

$$= \$2000\left(\frac{3.69497357 - 1}{0.02}\right)(1.02)$$

$$= \$274{,}887$$

BGN mode

4 I/Y
P/Y 2 ENTER
(making C/Y = P/Y = 2)
66 N
0 PV
2000 +/– PMT
CPT FV
Ans: 274,887.30

To the nearest dollar, Mason will have \$274,887 in his RRSP at age 60.

➧ **Check your understanding:** To the nearest dollar, how much will Dylan have in his RRSP by age 65 if he makes quarterly contributions of \$800 starting on his 30th birthday? Assume that the RRSP earns 5% compounded quarterly and that no contribution is made on his 65th birthday. (Answer: \$304,075)

▩▶ **Related problem:** #1 in Exercise 10.5

EXAMPLE 10.5B	Calculating the Future Value of a General Annuity Due

Repeat Example 10.5A with the change that the RRSP earns 4% compounded annually instead of 4% compounded semiannually.

SOLUTION

Payments are still being made at the beginning of every six-month period, so this is still an *annuity due*. However, since the compounding interval (one year) differs from the payment interval (six months), we now have a *general annuity due*. The value we must use for i in the FV formula is the periodic rate for the six-month payment interval. (It will be about $\tfrac{4\%}{2} = 2\%$.) Substitute

$$i = \frac{4\%}{1} = 4\% \quad \text{and} \quad c = \frac{\text{Number of compoundings per year}}{\text{Number of payments per year}} = \frac{1}{2} = 0.5$$

into formula (9-4c) giving

$$i_2 = (1 + i)^c - 1 = (1.04)^{0.5} - 1 = 0.019803903 \text{ per six months}$$

Use this value for i in formula (10-4) giving

BGN mode

4 I/Y
P/Y 2 ENTER
C/Y 1 ENTER
66 N
0 PV
2000 +/– PMT
CPT FV
Ans: 272,757

$$FV(\text{due}) = PMT\left[\frac{(1 + i)^n - 1}{i}\right] \times (1 + i)$$

$$= \$2000\left(\frac{1.019803903^{66} - 1}{0.019803903}\right) \times (1.019803903)$$

$$= \$2000\left(\frac{3.648381097 - 1}{0.019803903}\right)(1.019803903)$$

$$= \$272{,}757$$

Mason will have \$272,757 in his RRSP at age 60.

➡️ **Check your understanding:** Repeat the question in the Check Your Understanding portion of Example 10.5A with the change that the RRSP earns 5% compounded annually instead of 5% compounded quarterly. (Answer: $298,002)

▮▬✏️ **Related problem:** #5b in Exercise 10.5

EXAMPLE 10.5C	**Calculating the Future Value of an Annuity Due Where an Interest Rate Change Occurs During the Term of the Annuity**

Stephanie intends to contribute $2500 to her RRSP at the beginning of every six months, starting today, and continuing for a total of 40 contributions. If the RRSP earns 8% compounded semiannually for the first seven years and 7% compounded semiannually thereafter, what amount will she have in the plan in 20 years from now?

SOLUTION

The amount in the plan will be the future value of the contributions.

Note: The 40th contribution will occur $19\frac{1}{2}$ years from now. The 40 contributions form an annuity due when viewed from the future value's focal date 20 years from now. We are finding the FV(due) at the end of the term of the annuity, which is at a point one payment interval (6 months) after the last contribution.

The future value cannot be calculated in one step, because the interest rate changes after seven years. The solution strategy is indicated in the following time diagram. Since the payment interval equals the compounding interval throughout, the payments form a simple annuity in both segments of the 20 years.

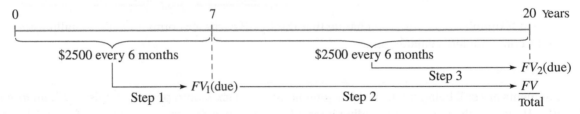

For the first 7 years, $i = \frac{8\%}{2} = 4\%$ and $n = 2(7) = 14$

For the next 13 years, $i = \frac{7\%}{2} = 3.5\%$ and $n = 2(13) = 26$

The future value, after seven years, of the first 14 contributions will be

$$FV_1(\text{due}) = PMT\left[\frac{(1+i)^n - 1}{i}\right] \times (1+i)$$

$$= \$2500\left(\frac{1.04^{14} - 1}{0.04}\right) \times (1.04)$$

$$= \$2500(18.291911)(1.04)$$

$$= \$47{,}558.969$$

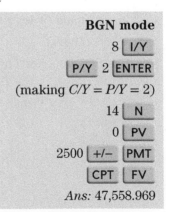

BGN mode

8 | I/Y |

| P/Y | 2 | ENTER |

(making $C/Y = P/Y = 2$)

14 | N |

0 | PV |

2500 | +/− | PMT |

| CPT | FV |

Ans: 47,558.969

The future value of $47,558.969 an additional 13 years later will be

$$FV = PV(1 + i)^n = \$47{,}558.969(1.035)^{26} = \$116{,}327.267$$

The future value, 20 years from now, of the last 26 payments will be

$$FV_2(\text{due}) = \$2500\left[\frac{(1.035)^{26} - 1}{0.035}\right] \times (1.035)$$

$$= \$2500(41.3131017)(1.035)$$

$$= \$106{,}897.651$$

The total amount in the RRSP after 20 years will be

$$FV + FV_2(\text{due}) = \$116{,}327.267 + \$106{,}897.651 = \$223{,}224.92$$

Stephanie will have $223,224.92 in her RRSP after 20 years.

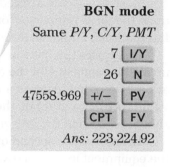

BGN mode
Same *P/Y, C/Y, PMT*

7	I/Y
26	N
47558.969 +/−	PV
CPT	FV

Ans: 223,224.92

➡️ **Check your understanding:** Peyton intends to contribute $750 to her RRSP at the beginning of every three months, starting today. If the RRSP earns 4% compounded quarterly for the first six years and 5% compounded quarterly thereafter, what amount will she have in the plan after 15 years? (Answer: $66,214.71)

▮▮▶ **Related problem:** #7 in Exercise 10.5

Present Value of an Annuity Due Using the Algebraic Method

The present value of an annuity due is the sum of the present values, at the beginning of the annuity, of all payments. Since payments occur at the *beginning* of each payment interval, the beginning of the annuity coincides with the first payment. We will use the symbol *PV*(due) for the present value of an annuity due.

The formula for *PV*(due) may be derived from the formula for the present value of an ordinary annuity. The line of reasoning is the same as used at the beginning of this section to derive the formula for *FV*(due). The outcome is that *PV*(due) is related to *PV* in the same way that *FV*(due) is related to *FV*. That is,

$$PV(\text{due}) = PV \times (1 + i)$$

Substituting from formula (10-2) for *PV*, we obtain

PRESENT VALUE OF A SIMPLE ANNUITY DUE

$$PV(\textbf{due}) = PV \times (1 + i)$$

$$= PMT\left[\frac{1 - (1 + i)^{-n}}{i}\right] \times (1 + i) \qquad \textbf{(10-5)}$$

If the beginning-of-period payments are made at an interval that is different from the interest compounding, the payments form a general annuity due. Use $i_2 = (1 + i)^c - 1$ to calculate the periodic interest rate that matches the payment interval. Then substitute this value for *i* in formula (10-5).

Present Value of an Annuity Due Using the Financial Calculator Functions

Set the calculator to the annuity due mode (so that "BGN" or "Begin" shows in the display). Then proceed as you would to compute the present value of an ordinary annuity.

Applications of the Present Value Calculation

As with ordinary annuities, most applications of the present value of an annuity due involve some aspect of valuation. Since the payments on most leases form an annuity due, we are now able to address an additional valuation topic.

The Book Value of a Lease When a business purchases equipment, its accountant records the acquisition of an asset (equipment). If instead, the business leases the equipment, you might think the accountant would just record the monthly lease payments as they are made. However, there is an additional issue.

Most leases for a fixed term are "non-cancellable." This means that the lessee is required to continue the lease payments for the full term of the lease, even if the leased equipment is no longer needed. International Financial Reporting Standards (IFRS) require this commitment to be recorded as a liability.[3]

This raises the question: "What amount should we use for this lease liability?" Should we simply add up all the payments for the entire term of the lease? No—that would place the same value on a dollar paid at the end of the lease as a dollar paid at the beginning. Instead, we should record the current economic value (present value) of the future lease payments. The follow-up question arises: "What discount rate should be used in the present value calculation?"

To answer this second question, consider that the usual alternative to leasing equipment is purchasing the equipment using borrowed funds. For this reason, IFRS will allow the discount rate to be the interest rate the business would pay to finance the purchase of the equipment.[4]

As time passes, the decreasing number of remaining payments represents a declining lease liability. In accordance with IFRS, the value of the lease liability is regularly reduced. At any point during the term of the lease, the present value of the *remaining* lease payments is known as the **book value of the lease** liability.

$$\text{Book value of a} \atop \text{long-term lease liability} = \left[{\text{Present value of the remaining payments} \atop \text{(discounted at the interest rate on debt financing)}} \right]$$

EXAMPLE 10.5D | **The Book Value of a Lease Liability**

National Engineering Services (NES) acquired a machine under a capital lease agreement. NES pays the lessor $2400 at the beginning of every three months for five years. If National can obtain five-year financing at 6% compounded quarterly,

a. what long-term lease liability will NES initially record?

b. what liability will be reported two years later?

SOLUTION

The initial liability (book value) is the present value of all of the lease payments. At any later date, the liability reported in the financial statements is the present value of the remaining payments. In both cases, the discount rate should be the interest rate at which the firm could have borrowed at the time of signing the lease. When viewed from the dates in either Part (a) or Part (b), the lease payments form a *simple annuity due* having $PMT = \$2400$ and $i = \frac{6\%}{4} = 1.5\%$.

a. $n = m(\text{Term}) = 4(5) = 20$ payments

The initial lease liability is

$$PV(\text{due}) = PMT\left[\frac{1-(1+i)^{-n}}{i}\right] \times (1+i)$$

$$= \$2400\left(\frac{1-1.015^{-20}}{0.015}\right)(1.015)$$

$$= \$41{,}822.80$$

> **BGN mode**
>
> 6 | I/Y
>
> P/Y 4 | ENTER
>
> (making $C/Y = P/V = 4$)
>
> 20 | N
>
> 2400 | +/– | PMT
>
> 0 | FV
>
> CPT | PV
>
> *Ans:* 41,822.80

---

[3]   A leasehold asset is also recorded. The lease represents a long-term asset in the sense that the right to use the equipment will produce benefits over the term of the lease.

[4]   If an interest rate is implicit in the lease and is practicable to calculate, IFRS requires that rate to be used to calculate the present value of the lease liability. If no implicit rate is available or is not practicable to obtain, the firm's incremental borrowing rate may be used.

b. After two years, $n = 4(3) = 12$ payments remain.
The book value of the lease liability will be

$$PV(\text{due}) = \$2400\left(\frac{1 - 1.015^{-12}}{0.015}\right)(1.015)$$

$$= \$26,570.68$$

BGN mode
Same I/Y, P/Y, C/Y
Same PMT, FV

| 12 | N |

| CPT | PV |

Ans: 26,570.68

➡ **Check your understanding:** Simpson Manufacturing acquired a machine under a capital lease agreement. Simpson pays $185 at the beginning of every month for four years to lease the machine. Simpson can obtain four-year financing at 6% compounded monthly. **a.** What long-term lease liability will Simpson initially record? **b.** What liability will be reported one year later? (Answer: **a.** $7916.75 **b.** $6111.54)

▮▮▶ **Related problem:** #13 in Exercise 10.5

| EXAMPLE 10.5E | Purchase or Lease a Piece of Equipment? |

Canadian Business Machines advertises a photocopier for $14,900. The same machine may be leased for 24 months at $700 per month (at the beginning of each month). At the end of the lease, the system may be purchased for 10% of the retail price. Would you recommend your company lease or purchase the photocopier if it can obtain a two-year loan at 8% compounded annually to purchase the photocopier?

SOLUTION

We cannot solve the problem by simply comparing the monthly loan payments to the monthly lease payments, for two reasons. Under the lease, you must pay an additional $1490 two years from now to own the system. Also, lease payments are made at the beginning of each month but loan payments are made at the end of each month.

We will compare the present values of the two alternatives. Since we are paying out money instead of receiving it, we should choose the alternative with the *lower* present value.

From basic principles, we know that the present value of the loan payments, discounted at the interest rate on the loan, equals the initial loan ($14,900). For a fair comparison, we should discount the lease payments (including the final payment to acquire ownership) using the same rate.

Since the payment interval (one month) differs from the compounding interval (one year), the lease payments form a *general annuity due* having

$$PMT = \$700 \text{ per month } n = 24 \text{ and } i = \tfrac{8\%}{1} = 8\% \text{ per year}$$

First calculate the periodic interest rate for the one-month payment interval. (It will be about $\frac{8\%}{12} = 0.\overline{6}\%$.)

$$c = \frac{\text{Number of compoundings per year}}{\text{Number of payments per year}} = \frac{1}{12} = 0.08\overline{3}$$

$$i_2 = (1 + i)^c - 1 = 1.08^{0.08\overline{3}} - 1 = 0.00643403 \text{ per month}$$

Substitute this value for i in subsequent calculations.

The present value of the monthly lease payments is

$$PV(\text{due}) = PMT\left[\frac{1 - (1 + i)^{-n}}{i}\right] \times (1 + i)$$

$$= \$700\left(\frac{1 - (1 + 0.00643403)^{-24}}{0.00643403}\right)(1.00643403)$$

$$= \$15,620.901$$

The present value of the end-of-lease purchase payment is

$$PV = FV(1 + i)^{-n} = \$1490(1.00643403)^{-24} = \$1277.435$$

The combined present value is $\$15,620.901 + \$1277.435 = \$16,898.34$.

The economic cost (in current dollars) of the lease is

$$\$16,898.34 - \$14,900 = \$1998.34$$

more than the economic cost of purchasing the photocopier using borrowed funds. Therefore, the photocopier should be purchased.

> **Check your understanding:** A machine can be purchased for $3500 or leased for 36 months for $95 per month, payable at the beginning of each month. At the end of the lease, the machine may be purchased for 15% of the retail price. If you can obtain a three-year loan at 8% compounded semiannually, should you lease or purchase it? (Answer: The economic cost (in current dollars) of leasing the machine is $27.73 less than the economic cost of purchasing it using borrowed funds. Therefore, the machine should be leased.)

> **Related problem:** #15 in Exercise 10.5

BGN mode

8	I/Y
P/Y 12	ENTER
C/Y 1	ENTER
24	N
700 +/–	PMT
1490 +/–	FV
CPT	PV

Ans: 16,898.34

EXAMPLE 10.5F	Finding the Economic Value of a Simple Annuity Due

The BC Lottery Corporation runs the "Millionaire Life" lottery. The winner of the Grand Prize can choose either $1,000,000 per year for 25 years or a single cash payment of $17,000,000. Which option should be chosen if the payments are made at the beginning of each year and, on low-risk investments, money can earn 3.2% compounded annually?

SOLUTION

The annuity option should be chosen if its economic value on the prize date exceeds $17,000,000. Its economic value is the present value of the 25 payments discounted at the rate of return money can earn. Since the first payment is received immediately and the payment interval (one year) equals the compounding interval (one year), the payments form a *simple annuity due* having

$$PMT = \$1,000,000, \quad n = 25,$$

$$j = 3.2\% \text{ compounded annually,} \quad \text{and} \quad i = \frac{3.2\%}{1} = 3.2\% \text{ per year}$$

Substituting in formula (10-5), we obtain

$$PV(\text{due}) = PMT\left[\frac{1 - (1 + i)^{-n}}{i}\right] \times (1 + i)$$

$$= \$1,000,000\left(\frac{1 - 1.032^{-25}}{0.032}\right)(1.032)$$

$$= \$1,000,000\left(\frac{1 - 0.45499599}{0.032}\right)(1.032)$$

$$= \$17,576,379 \text{ (rounded to the nearest dollar)}$$

> **BGN mode**
>
> 3.2 I/Y
> P/Y 1 ENTER
> (making $C/Y = P/Y = 1$)
> 25 N
> 1000000 PMT
> 0 FV
> CPT PV
>
> *Ans:* −17,576,379

Select the 25-year annuity because its current economic value is $576,379 more than the lump payment.

➡ **Check your understanding:** Redo the question, this time assuming that, on low-risk investments, money can earn 3.8% compounded annually. (Answer: Select the single lump payment option because it is worth $435,979 more than the economic value of the annuity.)

▰▰▰➤ **Related problem:** #10 in Exercise 10.5

 Checkpoint Questions

1. Circle "True" or "False" for each of the following:

   a. When calculating the *FV* of an annuity due, the focal date is at the same date as the final annuity payment.   True   False

   b. When calculating the *PV* of an annuity due, the focal date is at the same date as the first payment.   True   False

   c. The book value of a long-term lease liability is equal to the *FV* of the lease payments that have been made since the start of the lease.   True   False

2. Other things being equal (that is, *i*, *PMT*, *n*), why is

   a. the future value of an annuity due larger than the future value of an ordinary annuity?

   b. the present value of an annuity due larger than the present value of an ordinary annuity?

EXERCISE 10.5

Answers to the odd-numbered problems can be found in the end matter.

BASIC PROBLEMS

1. What is the future value of $100 invested at the beginning of every month for 25 years if the investments earn

   a. 6% compounded monthly?   **b.** 8% compounded monthly?

2. Money can earn 6% compounded monthly. What is the present value of beginning-of-month payments of $100 if the payments continue for

   a. 25 years? **b.** 30 years?

3. What is the present value of an annuity due consisting of semiannual payments of $1000 for 25 years, if money can earn

   a. 3% compounded semiannually? **b.** 4% compounded semiannually?

4. Svetlana intends to invest $1000 at the beginning of every six months. If the investments earn 7% compounded semiannually, what will her investments be worth (rounded to the nearest dollar) after

   a. 25 years? **b.** 30 years?

INTERMEDIATE PROBLEMS

5. Sergei celebrated his 22nd birthday today and made the first $2000 contribution to his RRSP. He will continue to contribute $2000 on each birthday until age 60. (No contribution is made on his 60th birthday). How much will Sergei have in his RRSP at age 60 if his contributions earn

   a. 4% compounded annually? **b.** 4% compounded quarterly?

6. Monarch Distributing Ltd. plans to accumulate funds for the purchase of a larger warehouse seven years from now. If Monarch contributes $10,000 at the beginning of each month to an investment account earning 4.5% compounded semiannually, what amount (rounded to the nearest dollar) will Monarch accumulate by the end of the seven years?

7. Starting today, Giorgio will contribute $2000 to his RRSP at the beginning of every six months. The plan will earn 4% compounded semiannually for the first 11 years and 3.5% compounded semiannually for the subsequent 14 years. What will be the value of his RRSP in 25 years from now?

8. Keiko has already accumulated $150,000 in her RRSP. She intends to continue to grow her RRSP by making contributions of $500 at the beginning of every month. How much will her RRSP be worth 15 years from now if the RRSP earns 6% compounded annually?

9. Salvatore will contribute $500 to a mutual fund at the beginning of each calendar quarter.

   a. What will be the value of his mutual fund after $6\frac{1}{2}$ years if the fund earns 4% compounded annually?

   b. How much of this amount represents investment earnings?

10. Alison wants to rent a storage locker to store her possessions while she travels in Europe for the next year. The storage operator has quoted her a price of $118.50 per month, payable at the start of each of the next 12 months. Alternately, Alison can make a single payment of $1350 at the start of the contract. Which alternative is economically preferable to Alison if she will be borrowing money at a rate of 8% compounded quarterly to fund the expense? In current dollars, how much will Alison save by selecting the preferred alternative?

11. How much interest will you have earned altogether at the end of a two-year period if you deposit $75 at the start of every month for 24 months? Assume your money will earn 6% compounded monthly.

12. Many people make their annual RRSP contribution for a taxation year close to the end of the year. Financial advisors encourage clients to contribute as early in the year as possible. How much more will there be in an RRSP at the end of 25 years if annual contributions of $5000 are made at the beginning of each year instead of at the end? Assume that the RRSP will earn

    a. 3.6% compounded annually. **b.** 3.6% compounded monthly.

13. The lease contract for a piece of manufacturing equipment requires quarterly payments of $2100 at the beginning of every three-month period for five years. The business would otherwise have to pay an interest rate of 8% compounded quarterly to borrow funds to purchase the equipment.

    a. What amount will the business initially report in its financial statements as the long-term lease liability?

    b. What will the liability be at the end of the fourth year?

14. Beaudoin Haulage has signed a five-year lease with GMAC on a new dump truck. Lease payments of $2700 are made at the beginning of each month. To purchase the truck, Beaudoin would have had to borrow funds at 9% compounded annually.

    a. What initial liability should Beaudoin report on its balance sheet?

    b. How much will the liability be reduced during the first year of the lease?

15. A piece of equipment sells for $20,000. Alternatively, the same piece of equipment can be leased for three years at $575 per month, payable at the beginning of each month. At the end of the lease, the equipment may be purchased for 20% of the retail price. You can obtain a three-year loan at 8% compounded quarterly to purchase the equipment. Should you buy or lease the equipment?

16. Carmella purchased a refrigerator under a conditional sale contract that required 30 monthly payments of $60.26 with the first payment due on the purchase date. The interest rate on the outstanding balance was 18% compounded monthly.

    a. What was the purchase price of the refrigerator?

    b. How much interest did Carmella pay during the entire contract?

17. Rino has just purchased a five-year term life insurance policy. For his premium payments, Rino can choose either beginning-of-month payments of $38.50 or beginning-of-year payments of $455. In current dollars, how much will Rino save during the five years by choosing the lower-cost option? Assume that money can earn 4.8% compounded monthly.

18. Under the headline "Local Theatre Project Receives $1 Million!" a newspaper article explained that the Theatre Project had just received the first of 10 annual grants of $100,000 from the Hinton Foundation. What is the current economic value of all of the grants if money is worth 4.5% compounded monthly?

19. You have received two offers on the used car you wish to sell. Mr. Lindberg is offering $8500 cash, and Rosie Senario's offer is five semiannual payments of $1900, including a payment on the purchase date. Which offer has the greater economic value at a discount rate of 5% compounded semiannually? What is the economic advantage (in current dollars) of the preferred alternative?

20. A rental agreement requires the payment of $900 at the beginning of each month.

    a. What single payment at the beginning of the rental year should the landlord accept instead of 12 monthly payments if money is worth 6% compounded monthly?

    b. Show that the landlord will be equally well off at the end of the year under either payment arrangement if rental payments are invested at 6% compounded monthly.

21. Karsten wants to have sufficient retirement savings at age 65 to be able to withdraw $40,000 at the beginning of each year for 16 years. If his savings earn 6% compounded annually, what amount must he have in savings at the time he turns 65?

22. What is the current economic value of an annuity due consisting of 22 annual payments of $700, if money is worth 6% compounded annually for the first three years, and 7% compounded annually thereafter?

ADVANCED PROBLEMS

23. What will be the amount in an RRSP after 25 years if contributions of $2000 are made at the beginning of each year for the first 10 years, and contributions of $4000 are made at the beginning of each year for the subsequent 15 years? Assume that the RRSP will earn 4% compounded quarterly.

24. Fay contributed $3000 per year to her RRSP on every birthday from age 21 to 30 inclusive. She then ceased employment to raise a family and made no further contributions. Her husband Fred contributed $3000 per year to his RRSP on every birthday from age 31 to 64 inclusive. Assuming that both plans earn 8% compounded annually over the years, calculate and compare the amounts in their RRSPs at age 65.

25. Bram must choose between two alternatives for $1,000,000 of life insurance coverage for the next 10 years. The premium quoted to him by Sun Life Insurance Co. is $51.75 per month. Atlantic Life will charge $44.25 per month for the first five years and $60.35 per month for the subsequent five years. In both cases, monthly premiums are payable at the beginning of each month. Which policy is "cheaper" if money can earn 4.8% compounded monthly? In current dollars, how much will Bram save by choosing the less costly policy?

10.6 Annuity Classification

This chapter introduced you to a variety of concepts related to annuities. You learned to distinguish between ordinary annuities and annuities due by checking whether annuity payments are made at the end or beginning of each payment interval. You learned to distinguish between simple and general annuities by checking whether the payment interval is the same as or different from the interest compounding interval. Finally, you learned that some annuity problems require you to calculate the future value of an annuity, while other problems require the calculation of the present value of an annuity.

While you have had an opportunity to practise solving a wide variety of annuity problems, the practice you have experienced so far has been missing one key component. Because each end-of-section set of problems was limited to *just* the ideas being presented in that section, you have not yet been challenged to fully demonstrate your ability to solve a mixed set of annuity problems. When you are dealing with real-world situations involving an annuity, you will first need to identify the type of annuity involved and decide upon the correct approach before you perform a single calculation. Accurately identifying the type of annuity and the approach required is an important step in the problem-solving process.

TIP

Identify the Type of Annuity at the Outset

Before doing any calculations for an annuity, you should write down the type of annuity involved. If you intend to use the financial calculator functions, set the calculator in the proper mode (ordinary or due) at this time. By doing these small steps at the outset, you are less likely to overlook them later when you become preoccupied with more complex aspects of the solution.

The end-of-chapter review problems will challenge you to differentiate among a wide variety of problems that involve all types of annuities presented in this chapter. The flowchart in Figure 10.7 presents a procedure for identifying the type of annuity and the relevant formulas. Even if you choose to use the financial calculator functions, this flowchart will remind you of some of the key questions to ask to ensure that you have your calculator set in the correct mode. The flowchart reminds you that you must take the time to identify the type of annuity before starting any annuity problem.

FIGURE 10.7 Annuity Classification Flowchart

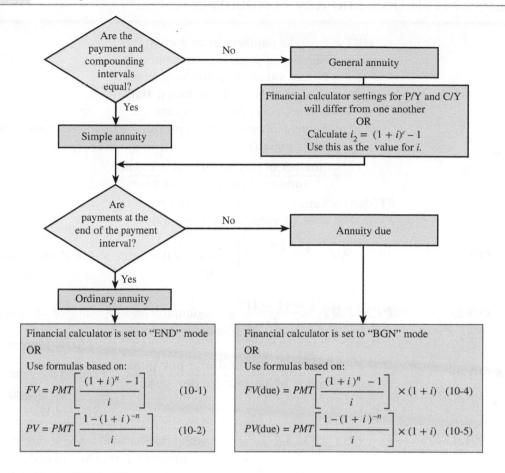

Key Terms

Annuity

Annuity due

Book value of a lease

Future value of an annuity

General annuity

General annuity due

Ordinary annuity

Ordinary general annuity

Ordinary simple annuity

Payment interval

Present value of an annuity

Simple annuity

Simple annuity due

Term of an annuity

Summary of Notation and Key Formulas

$$PMT = \text{Periodic payment in an annuity}$$
$$n = \text{Number of payments in the annuity}$$
$$FV = \text{Future value of an ordinary annuity}$$
$$PV = \text{Present value of an ordinary annuity}$$
$$i = \text{(Given) periodic interest rate}$$
$$i_2 = \text{Equivalent periodic interest rate (per payment interval for a general annuity)}$$
$$c = \frac{\text{Number of compoundings per year}}{\text{Number of payments per year}}$$
$$FV(\text{due}) = \text{Future value of an annuity due}$$
$$PV(\text{due}) = \text{Present value of an annuity due}$$

FORMULA (10-1) $\qquad FV = PMT\left[\dfrac{(1 + i)^n - 1}{i}\right]$ $\quad$ Finding the future value of an ordinary simple annuity

FORMULA (10-2) $\qquad PV = PMT\left[\dfrac{1 - (1 + i)^{-n}}{i}\right]$ $\quad$ Finding the present value of an ordinary simple annuity

FORMULA (10-3) $\qquad c = \dfrac{\textbf{Number of compoundings per year}}{\textbf{Number of payments per year}}$ $\quad$ Finding the number of compoundings per payment interval

FORMULA (9-4c) $\qquad i_2 = (1 + i)^c - 1$ $\quad$ Finding the periodic interest rate that matches the payment interval in a general annuity

FORMULA (10-4) $\qquad FV(\text{due}) = PMT\left[\dfrac{(1 + i)^n - 1}{i}\right] \times (1 + i)$ $\quad$ Finding the future value of an annuity due

FORMULA (10-5) $\qquad PV(\text{due}) = PMT\left[\dfrac{1 - (1 + i)^{-n}}{i}\right] \times (1 + i)$ $\quad$ Finding the present value of an annuity due

$$\text{Original loan} = \left[\begin{array}{c}\text{Present value of } \textit{all} \text{ payments} \\ \text{(discounted at the } \textit{contractual rate of interest} \text{ on the loan)}\end{array}\right]$$

$$\text{Principal balance} = \left[\begin{array}{c}\text{Present value of the } \textit{remaining} \text{ payments} \\ \text{(discounted at the } \textit{contractual rate of interest} \text{ on the loan)}\end{array}\right]$$

Approach for Solving a General Annuity Problem

Transform the general annuity problem into a simple annuity problem by:

1. Using $i_2 = (1 + i)^c - 1$ to calculate the equivalent periodic rate that matches the payment interval.

2. Using this equivalent periodic rate as the value for i in the appropriate simple annuity formula.

Review Problems

Answers to the odd-numbered review problems can be found in the end matter.

INTERMEDIATE PROBLEMS

1. **LO2** Calculate the amounts that will be accumulated after 20 years if
   a. $1000 is invested at the end of every six months at 3.5% compounded semiannually.
   b. $2000 is invested at the end of every year at 3.5% compounded annually.

2. **LO4** Rachelle purchased a motor home for $9000 down, with the balance to be paid by 60 monthly payments of $1176.40 including interest at 6% compounded monthly.
   a. What was the purchase price of the motor home?
   b. If the principal balance may be repaid at any time, what is the payout amount two years after the purchase date (not including the scheduled payment on that date)?

3. **LO6** Brunswick Trucking has signed a five-year lease with Ford Credit Canada Ltd. on a new truck. Lease payments of $1900 are made at the beginning of each month. To purchase the truck, Brunswick Trucking would have had to borrow funds at 5.85% compounded monthly.
   a. What initial liability should Brunswick report on its balance sheet?
   b. How much will the liability be reduced during the first year of the lease?

4. **LO6** Connor is exactly 27 years old today. Beginning today, he will deposit $2000 at the start of each year into a savings account that earns 4.75% compounded annually. How much will Connor have in his account on his 65th birthday? Note that no deposit is made on his 65th birthday.

5. **LO2 LO5** A retiree will receive retirement pension payments of $1000 at the end of every month for the next 12 years. What is the current economic value of the retiree's pension if money is worth
   a. 6% compounded monthly?   b. 6% compounded quarterly?

6. **LO5** How much will an investor have at the end of 20 years if he deposits $500 at the end of every month for the next 20 years? Assume money earns 3.5% compounded semiannually.

7. **LO6** How much will an investor have in 20 years from now if she deposits $500 at the start of every month? Assume money earns 5.16% compounded monthly.

8. **LO3** You can purchase a residential building lot for $64,000 cash, or for $10,000 down and month-end payments of $1000 for five years. If money is worth 4.56% compounded monthly, which option should you choose?

9. **LO3** Dr. Wilson is buying a 50% ownership in a veterinary practice by end-of-month payments of $714.60, including interest at 7% compounded semiannually for 15 years. Rounded to the nearest dollar,
   a. What valuation was placed on the partnership at the beginning of the payments?
   b. What total amount of interest will she pay over the 15 years?

10. **LO6** A lottery prize consists of annual payments of $5000 at the start of each year for 10 years. (The first payment will be made today.) What single lump sum payment today would represent an equivalent lottery prize in place of the scheduled 10 annual payments? Assume money earns 4.25% compounded annually.

11. **LO4** A 15-year loan requires month-end payments of $587.33 including interest at 8.4% compounded monthly.
    a. What was the original amount of the loan?

    b. What is the balance on the loan after half of the payments have been made?

12. **LO6** What is the current economic value of an inheritance that will pay $2500 to the beneficiary at the beginning of every three months for the next 20 years? Assume that money can earn 6% compounded monthly.

13. **LO6** Calculate the amount that will be accumulated after 20 years if

    a. $1000 is invested at the beginning of every six months at 3.5% compounded semiannually.

    b. $2000 is invested at the beginning of every year at 3.5% compounded annually.

14. **LO3** A Province of Ontario bond has $14\frac{1}{2}$ years remaining until it matures. The bond pays $231.25 interest at the end of every six months. At maturity, the bond repays its $5000 face value in addition to the final interest payment. What is the fair market value of the bond, if similar provincial bonds are currently providing investors with a return of 2.6% compounded semiannually?

15. **LO6** On the day their grandson Jeff was born, Mr. and Mrs. Zolob began an investment plan to help pay for his education. The grandparents contributed $50 at the start of every month, beginning on the day of Jeff's birth and continuing up to his 19th birthday. (Note that no contribution was made on his 19th birthday.) The investment earned 6% compounded quarterly. How much was the investment worth when it was presented to Jeff as his 19th birthday present?

16. **LO3** How much would an investor pay for a loan contract that guarantees payment of $249 at the end of each month for the next 12 months? Assume the investor requires a return of 10.2% compounded monthly.

17. **LO6** Mick contributed $5000 at the beginning of each year for 25 years to his TFSA. The funds earned 6% compounded annually. What was the TFSA's value after 25 years?

18. **LO2** Sylvia and Maclean are exactly the same age. From age 30 to age 60, Sylvia invested $3000 at the end of every six months. Maclean invested $6000 at the end of every six months from age 45 to age 60. How much does each investor have at age 60 if they each earn 5% compounded semiannually?

19. **LO6** A life insurance company quoted an annual premium of $387.50 (payable at the beginning of the year) for a $250,000 term insurance policy on a 35-year-old male nonsmoker. Alternatively, the insured can pay $33.71 at the beginning of each month by preauthorized electronic debit. Which payment plan would an applicant choose solely on the basis of money being worth 3.75% compounded monthly?

20. **LO4** Michael purchased a computer today during a "no money down" event. He will make payments of $226.51 at the end of each month for the next 12 months. These payments include interest at a rate of 16.5% compounded monthly. What was the original selling price of the computer?

21. **LO3** A mortgage broker offers to sell you a loan contract that would provide you with end-of-month payments of $900 for the next $2\frac{3}{4}$ years. In addition, at the end of the $2\frac{3}{4}$ year period, you will also receive a lump sum payment of $37,886. What should you pay for the contract, if you require a rate of return of 7.2% compounded monthly?

22. **LO6** A seven-year capital lease of an executive jet requires semiannual payments of $200,000 at the beginning of each six-month period. The company can borrow funds for seven years at 7.4% compounded semiannually.

    a. What long-term lease liability will the firm set up at the start of the term of the lease?

    b. What liability will remain halfway through the term of the lease?

23. **LO3** What is the appropriate price to pay for a contract guaranteeing payments of $1500 at the end of each quarter for the next 12 years? You require a rate of return of 6% compounded quarterly for the first five years, and 7% compounded quarterly for the next seven years.

24. **LO2** Calculate the future value of an ordinary annuity consisting of monthly payments of $300 for five years. The rate of return was 3% compounded monthly for the first two years, and will be 4.5% compounded monthly for the last three years.

25. **LO3 LO6** What amount is required to purchase an annuity that pays $4000 at the end of each quarter for the first five years and then pays $2500 at the beginning of each month for the subsequent 15 years? Assume that the annuity payments are based on a rate of return of 3.6% compounded quarterly.

26. **LO5** How much larger will the value of an RRSP be at the end of 20 years if the contributor makes month-end contributions of $500, instead of year-end contributions of $6000? In both cases the RRSP earns 4.5% compounded semiannually.

27. **LO2** Charlene has made contributions of $3000 to her RRSP at the end of every half-year for the past seven years. The plan has earned 7% compounded semiannually. She has just moved the funds to another plan earning 4.5% compounded quarterly, and will now contribute $2000 at the end of every three months. What total amount will she have in the plan five years from now?

ADVANCED PROBLEMS

28. **LO6** A rental agreement requires the payment of $1000 at the beginning of each month.
    a. What single payment at the beginning of the rental year should the landlord accept instead of 12 monthly payments if money is worth 6% compounded monthly?
    b. Show that the landlord will be equally well off at the end of the year under either payment arrangement if rental payments are invested at 6% compounded monthly.

29. **LO2** Dr. Krawchuk made deposits of $2000 to his RRSP at the end of each calendar quarter for six years. He then left general practice for specialist training and did not make further contributions for $2\frac{1}{2}$ years. What amount was in his RRSP at the end of this period, if the plan earned 5% compounded quarterly over the entire $8\frac{1}{2}$ years?

30. **LO5** Suppose Evan contributes $2000 to his RRSP at the end of every quarter for the next 15 years, and then contributes $1000 at each month's end for the subsequent 10 years. How much will he have in his RRSP at the end of the 25 years? Assume that the RRSP earns 6% compounded semiannually.

31. **LO6** Suppose you contribute $2500 to an RRSP at the beginning of every six months for the next 15 years, and then increase the contributions to $3000 at the beginning of every six months for the subsequent 10 years. How much will you have in your RRSP at the end of 25 years if your money earns 8% compounded quarterly?

32. **LO6** Suppose that Sam invests $5000 at the beginning of each year for 25 years to an RRSP that earns 6% compounded annually. Monika makes exactly the same contributions for the same amount of time, but her RRSP earns only 4% compounded annually. How much less does Monika have than Sam at the end of the 25 years?

33. **LO2** A court-ordered award for family support calls for payments of $800 at the end of each month for the next five years, followed by payments of $1000 at the end of each month for the subsequent ten years. If money is worth 6% compounded monthly, what is the current economic value of the award?

34. **LO2 LO5** Calculate the future value of investments of $800 at the end of each calendar quarter for seven years. The rate of return will be 7% compounded quarterly for the first 30 months and 6% compounded semiannually for the remainder of the annuity's term.

35. **LO6** What will be the amount in an RRSP after 30 years if contributions of $4000 are made at the beginning of each year for the first 10 years, and contributions of $6000 are made at the beginning of each year for the subsequent 20 years? Assume that the RRSP will earn 4.25% compounded annually.

Appendix 10A: Setting Your Calculator in the Annuity Due Mode

This appendix illustrates the keystrokes needed to set your calculator for annuity due calculations.

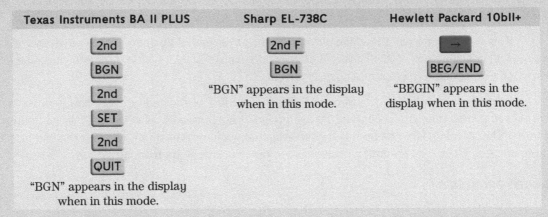

Texas Instruments BA II PLUS	Sharp EL-738C	Hewlett Packard 10bll+
2nd	2nd F	→
BGN	BGN	BEG/END
2nd	"BGN" appears in the display when in this mode.	"BEGIN" appears in the display when in this mode.
SET		
2nd		
QUIT		
"BGN" appears in the display when in this mode.		

When you repeat these keystrokes, your calculator will "toggle" or switch back to the ordinary annuity mode (no indicator in the display). The calculator remains in the most recently selected mode, even after being turned off.

© Caia Image/Glow Images RF

CHAPTER 11

Annuities: Periodic Payment, Number of Payments, and Interest Rate

LEARNING OBJECTIVES

After completing this chapter, you will be able to:

LO1 Calculate the periodic payment in ordinary annuities

LO2 Calculate the number of payments in ordinary annuities

LO3 Calculate the interest rate in ordinary annuities

LO4 Calculate the periodic payment, number of payments, and interest rate in annuities due

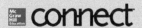 **connect**   Throughout this chapter interactive charts and Help Me Solve It videos are marked with a ↗.

IN CHAPTER 10, OUR DISCUSSION of annuities was restricted to applications of future value and present value calculations. But there are many circumstances in which one of the other variables must be determined. Consider the following questions:

- What is the monthly payment required to repay a $10,000 loan at 9% compounded monthly in four years?
- At a forecast rate of return, how long will it take to accumulate $500,000 in an RRSP if you contribute $300 per month?

- What rate of return is required for RRSP contributions of $400 per month to grow to $600,000 in 25 years?
- What interest rate are you being charged when you purchase cell phones, equipment, furniture, insurance, memberships, magazine subscriptions, etc., on an instalment plan instead of paying cash?

Clearly, the ability to answer such questions is important both in business and in your personal financial affairs.

In this chapter, you will learn how to answer these questions. The introduction to Chapter 10 stated that its contents would be "the foundation we will build upon throughout Chapters 11, 12, and 13." As you will soon discover, you already have the fundamentals in place for the topics in this chapter. You need only adapt familiar concepts and formulas to new situations.

11.1 Calculating the Periodic Payment in Ordinary Annuities

LO1 Some circumstances in which the periodic payment, *PMT*, must be calculated are
- determining the monthly payments on a loan
- determining the amount that must be saved on a regular basis to reach a savings goal
- determining the periodic payment from an annuity purchased with accumulated savings

In order to calculate *PMT*, you need to know the number of payments, *n*, and the periodic interest rate, *i* (or be able to readily determine them from the given information). In addition, you must know *either* the present value, *PV*, *or* the future value, *FV*, of the annuity.

Successful calculation of *PMT* requires that you pay careful attention to identify the type of annuity involved. Are the payment interval and interest compounding interval the same (*simple annuity*) or different (*general annuity*)? Are payments made at the beginning (*annuity due*) or end (*ordinary annuity*) of each payment interval? This section introduces the calculation of *PMT* for ordinary annuities, but later, in Section 11.4, we will modify our approach for annuities due. Therefore, identifying the annuity type at the outset of the question is a good habit to establish. You may find it useful to refer back to Figure 10.7, the annuity classification flowchart, for help with identifying the annuity type.

> **TIP**
>
> **Identify the Type of Annuity at the Outset**
>
> Before doing any calculations for an annuity, you should write down the type of annuity involved. If you intend to use the financial calculator functions, set the calculator in the proper mode (ordinary or due) at this time. By doing these small steps at the outset, you are less likely to overlook them later when you become preoccupied with more complex aspects of the solution.

Algebraic Method

The calculation of *PMT* may require up to four steps.

Step 1: If the payments form a *simple* annuity, go directly to Step 2.

If the payments form a *general* annuity, use $i_2 = (1 + i)^c - 1$ to calculate the periodic interest rate that matches the payment interval. Use i_2 as the value for *i* in Step 2.

Step 2: If the annuity's *FV* is known,
    substitute values of *FV*, *n*,
    and *i* into formula (10-1)

$$FV = PMT\left[\frac{(1+i)^n - 1}{i}\right]$$

Step 2: If the annuity's *PV* is known,
    substitute values of *PV*, *n*,
    and *i* into formula (10-2)

$$PV = PMT\left[\frac{1-(1+i)^{-n}}{i}\right]$$

Step 3: Calculate the quantity within the square brackets.

Step 4: Rearrange the equation to solve for *PMT*.

Financial Calculator Method (Texas Instruments BA II PLUS)

Set the calculator in the correct mode (ordinary annuity or annuity due). Enter the known values for $\boxed{\text{N}}$, $\boxed{\text{I/Y}}$, $\boxed{\text{PV}}$, $\boxed{\text{FV}}$, $\boxed{\text{P/Y}}$, and $\boxed{\text{C/Y}}$. Remember to use the cash-flow sign convention for amounts entered in $\boxed{\text{PV}}$ and $\boxed{\text{FV}}$. Then press $\boxed{\text{CPT}}$ $\boxed{\text{PMT}}$ to execute the computation.

EXAMPLE 11.1A	Calculating the Periodic Investment Needed to Reach a Savings Target

Markham Auto Body wishes to accumulate a fund of $300,000 during the next 18 months in order to open at a second location. At the end of each month, a fixed amount will be invested in a money market savings account with an investment dealer. What should the monthly investment be in order to reach the savings objective? The planning assumption is that the account will earn 3.6% compounded monthly.

SOLUTION

The savings target of $300,000 represents the future value of the fixed *monthly* investments. Since earnings are compounded *monthly*, the *end-of-month* investments form an *ordinary simple* annuity. We are given:

Step 1: $FV = \$300,000$, $n = 18$,   and $i = \frac{3.6\%}{12} = 0.3\%$ per month

Step 2:   Substitute the given values into formula (10-1).

$$FV = PMT\left[\frac{(1+i)^n - 1}{i}\right]$$

$$\$300,000 = PMT\left[\frac{1.003^{18} - 1}{0.003}\right]$$

Step 3: $\$300,000 = PMT(18.4664273)$

Step 4: $PMT = \dfrac{\$300,000}{18.4664273} = \$16,245.70$

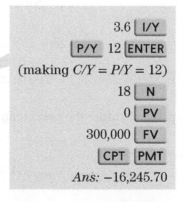

3.6 $\boxed{\text{I/Y}}$

$\boxed{\text{P/Y}}$ 12 $\boxed{\text{ENTER}}$

(making $C/Y = P/Y = 12$)

18 $\boxed{\text{N}}$

0 $\boxed{\text{PV}}$

300,000 $\boxed{\text{FV}}$

$\boxed{\text{CPT}}$ $\boxed{\text{PMT}}$

Ans: −16,245.70

Markham Auto Body should make monthly investments of $16,245.70 in order to accumulate $300,000 after 18 months.

➡ **Check your understanding:** Harpreet wishes to accumulate a total of $7000 to go on a European vacation planned for two years from now. If her savings earn 4.8% compounded monthly, how much will Harpreet need to deposit at the end of each month for the next two years in order to reach her savings goal? (Answer: $278.47/month)

▬▬▶ **Related problem:** #1a in Exercise 11.1

EXAMPLE 11.1B	Calculating the Periodic Investment Needed to Reach a Savings Target with a Beginning, Lump Sum Investment

Leila has already accumulated $14,000 of savings in her Tax Free Savings Account (TFSA). Her goal is to have a total of $40,000 in five years from now. How much will Leila need to deposit into her TFSA at the end of every month for the next five years to reach her savings target? Assume her funds will earn 5% compounded semiannually.

SOLUTION

The $14,000 that Leila has today in her savings account will earn compound interest for the next five years. Let's begin by calculating how much the $14,000 will be worth in five years from now. Note that the $14,000 is not a *PMT* in an annuity! It is a single amount, *PV*, that will grow to a future amount, *FV*, at 5% compounded semiannually for five years.

$$n = 2(5) = 10 \quad \text{and} \quad i = \frac{j}{m} = \frac{5\%}{2} = 2.5\% \text{ per half-year}$$

Substituting into formula (8-2) we obtain

$$\left.\begin{aligned} FV &= PV(1 + i)^n \\ &= \$14,000(1 + 0.025)^{10} \\ &= \$17,921.184 \end{aligned}\right\}$$

5	I/Y
P/Y 2	ENTER
(making C/Y = P/Y = 2)	
10	N
14000 +/–	PV
0	PMT
CPT	FV

Ans: 17,921.184

Leila's current savings of $14,000 will contribute $17,921.184 to her goal of $40,000 in five years from now. Therefore, her monthly deposits for the next five years must accumulate to $40,000 − $17,921.184 = $22,078.816. Since Leila will make *end-of-month* payments and earn *semiannual* compounding, the payments form an *ordinary general* annuity with

$$FV = \$22,078.816, \quad n = 12(5) = 60, \quad \text{and} \quad i = \frac{5\%}{2} = 2.5\% \text{ per half-year}$$

Step 1: Then,
$$c = \frac{\text{Number of compoundings per year}}{\text{Number of payments per year}} = \frac{2}{12} = 0.1\overline{6}$$

and

$$\begin{aligned} i_2 &= (1 + i)^c - 1 \\ &= (1 + 0.025)^{0.1\overline{6}} - 1 \\ &= 0.004123915 \text{ per month} \end{aligned}$$

Step 2: Substitute the preceding values into formula (10-1).

$$FV = PMT\left[\frac{(1 + i)^n - 1}{i}\right]$$

$$\$22,078.816 = PMT\left[\frac{(1 + 0.004123915)^{60} - 1}{0.004123915}\right]$$

5	I/Y
P/Y 12	ENTER
C/Y 2	ENTER
60	N
0	PV
22078.816	FV
CPT	PMT

Ans: −325.08

Solving for *PMT*,

$$67.91714005(PMT) = \$22,078.816$$
$$PMT = \frac{\$22,078.816}{67.91714005}$$
$$PMT = \$325.08$$

Combined with her current savings of $14,000, additional deposits of $325.08 at the end of every month will allow Leila to reach her savings target of $40,000 in five years from now.

Note: You could perform the entire question in one step using the financial calculator, as shown in the calculator callout to the right. Be very careful about cash flow! Leila's current savings of $14,000 are entered into the PV key as a negative amount, because this is money she is investing at the start.

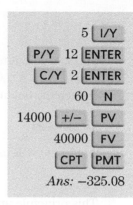

➡️ **Check your understanding:** Siobhan has already accumulated savings of $10,000. How much will she need to contribute at the end of every six months for the next 10 years if her goal is to have $75,000 in 10 years from now? Assume her investments earn 6% compounded quarterly. (Answer: $2111.24)

▮▮▷ **Related problem:** #18 in Exercise 11.1

EXAMPLE 11.1C	Calculating the Periodic Loan Payments That Form an Ordinary General Annuity

A $5000 loan requires payments at the end of each quarter for four years. If the interest rate on the loan is 9% compounded monthly, what is the size of each payment?

SOLUTION

The original loan equals the present value of all payments discounted at the loan's interest rate. Since interest is compounded *monthly* and payments are made at the *end* of each *quarter*, we have an *ordinary general* annuity with

$$PV = \$5000, \quad n = 4(4) = 16, \quad \text{and} \quad i = \frac{9\%}{12} = 0.75\% \text{ per month}$$

Step 1: Then, $$c = \frac{12 \text{ compoundings per year}}{4 \text{ payments per year}} = 3$$

and $$\begin{aligned} i_2 &= (1 + i)^c - 1 \\ &= (1.0075)^3 - 1 \\ &= 0.02266917 \text{ per quarter} \end{aligned}$$

Step 2: Substitute the preceding values into formula (10-2).

$$PV = PMT\left[\frac{1 - (1 + i)^{-n}}{i}\right]$$

$$\$5000 = PMT\left[\frac{1 - 1.02266917^{-16}}{0.02266917}\right]$$

Step 3: $$\$5000 = PMT(13.29497)$$

Step 4: $$PMT = \frac{\$5000}{13.29497} = \$376.08$$

The size of each quarterly payment is $376.08.

➡️ **Check your understanding:** A $20,000 loan requires payments at the end of each month for six years. If the interest rate on the loan is 9% compounded semiannually, what is the size of each payment? (Answer: $358.88)

▮▮▮▷ **Related problem:** #2b in Exercise 11.1

EXAMPLE 11.1D	Calculating the Periodic Loan Payment Required to Reach a Target Balance

Simon is about to purchase a new car. He plans to keep the car for three years, then trade it in. Simon will borrow $37,000 at 4.2% compounded monthly to purchase the car. What monthly payment will reduce the balance on the loan after three years to the expected trade-in value of $16,500?

SOLUTION

Again we will use the fundamental principle that

$$\text{Original principal} = \text{Present value of all payments}$$

This principle applies whether or not all payments are equal. (The $16,500 balance after three years can be viewed as the amount which, along with the last monthly payment, will pay off the loan.)

$$\$37{,}000 = \left(\begin{matrix} \text{Present value of the} \\ \text{loan payment annuity} \end{matrix} \right) + \left(\begin{matrix} \text{Present value of} \\ \text{the \$16,500 balance} \end{matrix} \right) \quad \text{①}$$

Since we have *end-of-month* payments and *monthly* compounding, the payments form an *ordinary simple* annuity. For both the annuity and the terminal payment,

$$n = 12(3) = 36 \quad \text{and} \quad i = \tfrac{4.2\%}{12} = 0.35\%$$

Using formulas (10-2) and (8-2) on the right side of equation ①, we obtain

$$PV = PMT\left[\frac{1 - (1 + i)^{-n}}{i} \right] + FV(1 + i)^{-n}$$

$$\$37{,}000 = PMT\left(\frac{1 - 1.0035^{-36}}{0.0035} \right) + \$16{,}500(1.0035)^{-36}$$

$$\$37{,}000 = PMT(33.768911) + \$14{,}549.845$$

Solving for *PMT*,

$$33.768911(PMT) = \$37{,}000 - \$14{,}549.845$$

$$33.768911(PMT) = \$22{,}450.155$$

$$PMT = \frac{\$22{,}450.155}{33.768911}$$

$$PMT = \$664.82$$

4.2	I/Y
P/Y 12	ENTER
(making C/Y = P/Y = 12)	
36	N
37000	PV
16500 +/−	FV
CPT	PMT

Ans: −664.82

Monthly payments of $664.82 will reduce the loan balance to $16,500 after three years.

➡ **Check your understanding:** Redo the question, this time assuming that the trade-in value of the car at the end of the three-year period will be $12,000. How much will Simon's end-of-month payments be for the next three years? (Answer: $782.33)

▌▌▌▶ **Related problem:** #16 in Exercise 11.1

EXAMPLE 11.1E	Calculating the Periodic Investment Required to Purchase a Specified Annuity on a Future Date

Douglas and Margaret Kuramoto want to retire in 15 years with enough funds in their RRSPs to purchase a 25-year annuity that will pay $3000 at the end of each month. They have already accumulated $125,000 in their RRSPs. In order to fulfill the plan, what RRSP contribution should they make at the end of each of the next 15 years? For the financial projections, they are assuming returns of 4% compounded annually on their RRSPs and 3% compounded monthly on the annuity purchased with their RRSP funds.

SOLUTION

The given information and the steps in the solution are presented in the following time diagram.

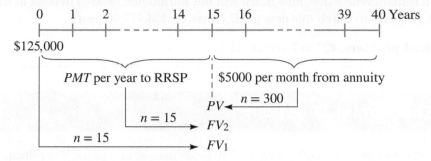

The total amount in the RRSPs 15 years from now will be the future value, FV_1, of the $125,000 already in the RRSPs *plus* the future value, FV_2, of 15 more annual contributions of size PMT. The amount needed to purchase the annuity paying $3000 per month will be the present value, PV, of the $12(25) = 300$ payments discounted at $i = \frac{3\%}{12} = 0.25\%$ per month. Each series of payments forms an *ordinary simple* annuity.

In order to have enough money in their RRSPs 15 years from now to purchase the desired annuity, the Kuramotos require

$$FV_1 + FV_2 = PV \; ①$$

The amount that will be needed to purchase the annuity is

$$PV = PMT\left[\frac{1 - (1 + i)^{-n}}{i}\right]$$

$$= \$3000\left(\frac{1 - 1.0025^{-300}}{0.0025}\right)$$

$$= \$632{,}629.36$$

3	I/Y
P/Y 12	ENTER
(making $C/Y = P/Y = 12$)	
300	N
3000	PMT
0	FV
CPT	PV
Ans: −632,629.36	

The future value of the $125,000 already saved is

$$FV_1 = PV(1 + i)^n$$
$$= \$125{,}000(1.04)^{15}$$
$$= \$225{,}117.94$$

The future value of the 15 annual contributions of PMT is

$$FV_2 = PMT\left[\frac{(1 + i)^n - 1}{i}\right]$$

$$= PMT\left(\frac{1.04^{15} - 1}{0.04}\right)$$

$$= 20.02358764(PMT)$$

4	I/Y
P/Y 1	ENTER
(making $C/Y = P/Y = 1$)	
15	N
125000 +/−	PV
632629.36	FV
CPT	PMT
Ans: −20,351.57	

Substituting these values into equation ①, we obtain

$$\$225{,}117.94 + 20.02358764(PMT) = \$632{,}629.36$$
$$20.02358764(PMT) = \$407{,}511.42$$
$$PMT = \$20{,}351.57$$

The Kuramotos must make annual RRSP contributions of $20,351.57.

➡️ **Check your understanding:** Suppose the Kuramotos decide that, when they retire in 15 years, they want to purchase a 20-year annuity that pays $4000 at the end of every month. If all other information remains the same, how much will the Kuramotos need to deposit at the end of each of the next 15 years to reach this new goal? (Answer: $24,777.06/year)

▶️ **Related problem:** #21 in Exercise 11.1

Checkpoint Questions

1. Suppose you choose to pay off a loan over 10 years instead of 5 years. The principal and interest rate are the same in both cases. Will the payment for the 10-year term be **(i)** half the payment for the 5-year term? **(ii)** more than half the payment? **(iii)** less than half the payment? Give the reasoning for your choice.

2. You intend to accumulate $100,000 in 10 years instead of 20 years by making equal monthly investment contributions. Will the monthly contribution for a 10-year plan be **(i)** twice the monthly contribution for a 20-year plan? **(ii)** less than twice the monthly contribution? **(iii)** more than twice the monthly contribution? Assume the same rate of return in both cases. Give the reasoning for your choice.

EXERCISE 11.1

Answers to the odd-numbered problems can be found in the end matter.

BASIC PROBLEMS

1. Marissa intends to make contributions to a Tax Free Savings Account (TFSA) such that the account will accumulate to $150,000 after 20 years. What end-of-quarter contributions must be made if the TFSA earns 4% compounded

    a. quarterly?   **b.** annually?

2. A $50,000 loan was advanced today. What payment is required at the end of every month for the next seven years to fully repay the debt if the interest rate on the loan is 7.5% compounded

    a. monthly?   **b.** quarterly?

3. John has $100,000 available to purchase an annuity. What end-of-month payments can he expect if the funds earn 4.2% compounded monthly and the payments run for

    a. 10 years?   **b.** 20 years?

4. How much would you need to deposit at the end of every month to reach your goal of having $5000 in two years from now? Assume your funds earn 6% compounded monthly.

5. Sarah has been making regular, equal deposits at the end of every three months into a Tax Free Savings Account (TFSA) for the last four years. Her funds have earned 4.2% compounded quarterly. Sarah's accumulated savings are $2858.44. How much has she deposited at the end of each quarter?

6. Aden is scheduled to make a lump payment of $25,000, 11 months from now, to complete a real estate transaction. What end-of-month payments for the next 11 months should the vendor be willing to accept instead of the lump payment if he can invest the funds at 5.4% compounded monthly?

7. Mr. Bean wants to borrow $7500 for three years. The interest rate is 9% compounded monthly. What end-of-quarter payments are required to fully repay the loan over the three-year period?

INTERMEDIATE PROBLEMS

8. In order to accumulate $500,000 after 25 years, calculate the amounts that must be invested at the end of each year if the invested funds earn

    a. 5% compounded annually.   **b.** 6% compounded annually.

    c. 7% compounded annually.   **d.** 8% compounded annually.

    Also, calculate the total earnings in each case. (Note that the total earnings increase proportionately more than the rate of return from one case to the next.)

9. A 20-year annuity is purchased for $400,000. What payment will it deliver at the end of each quarter if the funds in the annuity earn

    a. 4% compounded quarterly?   **b.** 5% compounded quarterly?

    c. 6% compounded quarterly?   **d.** 7% compounded quarterly?

    In each case, also calculate the total earnings distributed over the life of the annuity. (Note that the total earnings increase proportionately more than the rate of return from one case to the next.)

10. The interest rate on a $100,000 loan is 4.8% compounded monthly. What end-of-month payment amount will repay the loan in

    a. 5 years?   **b.** 10 years?

    c. 15 years?   **d.** 20 years?

    Also calculate the total interest paid in each case. (Note that a doubling of the term more than doubles the total interest paid over the life of the loan.)

11. Assume that the investments within an RRSP will earn 6% compounded annually. What contribution must be made at the end of each month in order for the RRSP to grow to $750,000 in

    a. 15 years?   **b.** 20 years?

    c. 25 years?   **d.** 30 years?

    Also calculate the total earnings within the RRSP in each case. (Note that the total earnings increase proportionately more than the duration of the contributions.)

12. Calculate the amount that must be invested at the end of each year at 5% compounded annually in order to accumulate $500,000 after

    a. 25 years.   **b.** 30 years.

    In each case, also determine what portion of the $500,000 represents earnings on the annual investments.

13. Karen obtained a $20,000 loan at 8% compounded semiannually. What end-of-month payment will repay the loan in $7\frac{1}{2}$ years? How much interest will Karen pay over the life of the loan?

14. Brenda and Tom want to save $30,000 over the next four years for a down payment on a house. What amount must they regularly save from their month-end pay if their savings can earn 5.5% compounded semiannually?

15. Henrick can buy a rural property from a family member for $700,000 with terms of $100,000 down and the balance payable over 20 years by payments at the end of each quarter including interest at 5% compounded annually. What will be the size of the payments? How much interest will Henrick pay over the life of the loan?

16. Sofia has been approved for a RBC Royal Bank four-year $25,000 car loan at 7.5% compounded monthly. What end-of-month payments will reduce the balance on the loan after four years to the expected trade-in value of $4000?

17. In order to purchase another truck, Beatty Transport recently obtained a $50,000 loan for five years at 5.8% compounded semiannually. The loan is structured to reduce the balance owing to $10,000 at the end of the five-year period. How much are Beatty's end-of-month loan payments?

18. Owen has just received an inheritance of $20,000. He has deposited the funds into an account that will earn 5% compounded quarterly. Owen plans to add to his savings by making end-of month deposits to the account for the next five years. If Owen's goal is to have a total of $50,000 at the end of five years, how much do his regular, monthly deposits need to be?

19. On the day she was born, Ella's grandparents deposited $2500 into a savings account to help fund her education. To that account they made equal deposits on each of Ella's birthdays, including her 18th birthday today. If the investment has earned 4% compounded quarterly, and the balance in the account today is $24,458.81, how much did her grandparents deposit on each of Ella's birthdays?

ADVANCED PROBLEMS

20. The interest rate on a $200,000 loan is 8% compounded quarterly.

    a. What payments at the end of every quarter will reduce the balance to $150,000 after $3\frac{1}{2}$ years?

    b. If the same payments continue, what will be the balance seven years after the date that the loan was received?

    c. How much interest will be paid during the first seven years?

21. Louise wants to retire in 20 years with enough savings in her RRSP to be able to purchase a 25-year annuity that will pay her $4000 at the end of every month. She has already accumulated $50,000 in her RRSP. In order to meet her goal, what RRSP contribution should Louise make at the end of each of the next 20 years? Assume she earns 4% compounded annually on her RRSP, and 3.6% compounded monthly on the annuity purchased with her RRSP funds.

22. Ken and Belinda have a five-year-old daughter. At the end of every six months for the next $12\frac{1}{2}$ years, they wish to contribute equal amounts to a Registered Education Savings Plan (RESP). Six months after the last RESP contribution, the first of 12 semiannual withdrawals of $5000 will be made. If the RESP earns 8.5% compounded semiannually, what must be the size of their regular RESP contributions?

23. Four years from now, Tim and Justine plan to take a year's leave of absence from their jobs and travel through Asia, Europe, and Africa. They want to accumulate enough savings during the next four years so they can withdraw $3000 at each month-end for the entire year of leave. What amount must they pay into the fund at the end of every calendar quarter for the next four years to reach their goal? The planning assumptions are that their savings will earn 4% compounded quarterly for the next four years and 3% compounded monthly during the fifth year.

24. Beth and Nelson want to accumulate a combined total of $600,000 in their RRSPs by the time Beth reaches age 60, which will be 30 years from now. They plan to make equal contributions at the end of every six months for the next 30 years. For planning purposes, assume that their RRSPs will earn 5% compounded semiannually for the next 30 years.

    a. What should be their combined semiannual RRSP contributions?

    b. What monthly amount can they expect to receive if they use the $600,000 in their RRSPs 30 years from now to purchase an annuity that will provide end-of-month payments for 25 years? Assume that the funds used to purchase the annuity will earn 3% compounded monthly.

25. Dr. Collins wants the value of her RRSP 30 years from now to have the purchasing power of $500,000 in current dollars.

    a. Assuming an inflation rate of 2% per year, what nominal dollar amount should Dr. Collins have in her RRSP after 30 years?

    b. Assuming her RRSP will earn 4.5% compounded semiannually, what contributions should she make at the end of every three months to achieve the goal?

26. **Using the "Cool Million" Chart** An interactive "Cool Million" (found in the"Interactive Charts" under the Student Resources for Chapter 11) enables you to visualize the growth of your retirement savings over several years. Another feature allows you to determine what changes you would need to make to your investment plan for you to attain nominal "millionaire" status on your 65th birthday.

    Enter data for an investment plan that will be reasonable for you after you gain full-time employment. Note that the "Expected rate of return" and the "Expected inflation rate" are both *annually* compounded rates. Click on the "Calculate" button to generate a new chart. The series of blue bars show the growth of your investments. If you move your cursor over any bar, the numerical value (in $000s) will be displayed.

    The series of purple bars represent the inflation-adjusted value, or purchasing power, of the investments in terms of dollars at the very beginning—the "Your age" date.

    If you click on the "View Report" button, a window containing a bulleted list of three suggested changes will appear. *Any one* of these changes to your savings plan will enable you to accumulate (a nominal) $1,000,000 at your target retirement age. Adjust one or more items in your input data to arrive at a plan that represents your best chance of entering retirement as a millionaire. What will be the purchasing power of your nominal $1,000,000 in beginning dollars?

11.2 Calculating the Number of Payments in Ordinary Annuities

LO2 Circumstances in which the number of payments, n, must be calculated include
- determining the time required for periodic payments to pay off a loan.
- determining the time required for a periodic savings plan to reach a savings target.
- determining how long a single investment can sustain periodic withdrawals.

In order to calculate the number of annuity payments, you need to know *PMT* and i (or be able to determine them from the given information). In addition, you must know either the *PV* or the *FV* of the annuity.

As with the calculation of *PMT*, calculating n requires that you pay careful attention to identify the type of annuity involved. This section introduces the calculation of n in ordinary annuities, in which payments are being made at the end of every payment interval. In Section 11.4, we will modify our approach for annuities due. Therefore, identifying the annuity type at the outset of the question continues to be a good practice. You may find it useful to refer back to Figure 10.7, the annuity classification flowchart, for help with identifying the annuity type.

Suppose you substitute known values for *FV*, *PMT*, and i in formula (10-1) for the future value of an annuity, and then proceed to solve for n. The procedure is more complex than it was in Section 11.1 for isolating *PMT*—it requires some familiarity with manipulating logarithms. Similar comments apply to formula (10-2) for the present value of an annuity. For these reasons, we present the following versions of formulas (10-1) and (10-2) rearranged to calculate n.

$$n = \frac{\ln\left(1 + \frac{i \times FV}{PMT}\right)}{\ln(1 + i)} \qquad \text{(10-1}n\text{)}$$

$$n = -\frac{\ln\left(1 - \dfrac{i \times PV}{PMT}\right)}{\ln(1 + i)} \tag{10-2n}$$

Since these are merely new versions of formulas (10-1) and (10-2), we will refer to them as (10-1n)[1] and (10-2n). If the payments form a general annuity, the periodic interest rate that matches the payment interval (that is, i_2) must be substituted for i.

TIP

Interpretation of "n" When It Is Not an Integer

The value obtained for n will not necessarily be an integer. To illustrate the interpretation of a non-integer value, suppose $n = 21.3$ in a particular case. This means that there are 22 payments, but the last payment is smaller than the others. Prevailing business practice is to allow a full payment interval for the final reduced payment. Even though the fractional part of n in this case is 0.3, it is only an approximation to say that the last payment is 30% of the size of the others. The method for calculating the exact size of the final payment will be presented in Chapter 13.

TIP

Obtaining the Term of an Annuity from the Value of n

A problem may ask for the *term* of the annuity rather than the number of payments. Let's consider a specific numerical example before addressing the general case. Suppose a question has asked you to determine the term of an annuity in which there are four payments per year. Suppose you obtained $n = 34.5$ payments. This means the annuity consists of 35 payments. (Remember the preceding "tip.") Since there are four payments per year, the annuity's term in years is

$$\frac{35 \text{ payments}}{4 \text{ payments per year}} = 8.75 \text{ years}$$

In general,

$$\text{Term of annuity (in years)} = \frac{i \text{ (rounded upward)}}{\text{Number of payments per year}}$$

The common practice is to convert the fractional part of a year to months. Since

$$0.75 \text{ years} = 0.75(12 \text{ months}) = 9 \text{ months}$$

the term in our numerical example would normally be expressed as "8 years and 9 months."

EXAMPLE 11.2A	Calculating n Given the Future Value of an Ordinary General Annuity

One month from now, Maurice will make his first monthly contribution of $250 to a Tax Free Savings Account (TFSA). Over the long run, he expects to earn 5% compounded annually. How long will it take for the contributions and accrued earnings to reach $100,000? (Round n to the next larger integer.)

---

[1] The derivation of formula (10-1n) from formula (10-1) is presented in the textbook's Web site. In Connect, select "Chapter 11" in the drop-down box. In the list of resources, select "Additional Material" in the navigation bar. After the page loads, click on the link named "Appendix 11A."

SOLUTION

Since compounding occurs *annually*, the *end-of-month* contributions form an *ordinary general annuity* having

$$FV = \$100{,}000, \quad PMT = \$250, \quad \text{and} \quad i = \tfrac{5\%}{1} = 5\%$$

To obtain the periodic rate matching the monthly payment interval, first calculate

$$c = \frac{1 \text{ compounding per year}}{12 \text{ payments per year}} = 0.08\overline{3}$$

Then

$$i_2 = (1 + i)^c - 1 = 1.05^{0.08\overline{3}} - 1 = 0.004074124 \text{ per month}$$

Substitute these values into formula (10-1n).

$$
\begin{aligned}
n &= \frac{\ln\!\left(1 + \dfrac{i \times FV}{PMT}\right)}{\ln(1 + i)} \\[2mm]
&= \frac{\ln\!\left[1 + \dfrac{0.004074124\,(\$100{,}000)}{\$250}\right]}{\ln(1.004074124)} \\[2mm]
&= \frac{2.629649514}{0.004065847} \\[2mm]
&= 237.80
\end{aligned}
$$

```
        5  I/Y
  P/Y  12  ENTER
  C/Y   1  ENTER
        0  PV
  250  +/-  PMT
100000  FV
    CPT    N
  Ans: 237.80
```

The annuity has 238 payments taking 238 months. We need to express the time required in years and months.

238 months $= \frac{238}{12}$ years $= 19.833$ years $= 18$ years $+ \left(0.8333 \times 12 \text{ months}\right) = 19$ years, 10 months

It will take 19 years and 10 months for Maurice to accumulate $100,000 in the TFSA.

➡ **Check your understanding:** Three months from now, Stephen will make his first quarterly contribution of $1000 to a TFSA. If the TFSA earns a return of 7.2% compounded monthly, how long will it take for the TFSA value to reach $250,000? (Round n to the next-larger integer.) (Answer: 24 years)

▮▮▮▶ **Related problem:** #2 in Exercise 11.2

TRAP

Interpretation of "*n*" in a General Annuity

In an annuity, n represents the number of payments. When you calculate n for a general annuity (in which the payment interval and the compounding interval are not the same), it is important that you remember this fact so that you avoid a common pitfall. Suppose, for example, that you are asked how long it would take for a $20,000 loan at 9% compounded monthly to be repaid by end-of-quarter payments of $1000. The answer is $n = 26.95$ which, rounded up, would be 27 payments. If you mistakenly refer to the compounding interval (instead of the payment interval), you might conclude that the loan will be repaid in 27 *months*. This is, of course, not correct. Referring to the payment frequency, we see that payments are *quarterly*, so the loan will be repaid in 27 quarters. Since $\frac{27}{4} = 6.75$ years, the loan will be repaid in 6 years and 9 months.

EXAMPLE 11.2B	Calculating the Time Required to Pay Off a Loan

Robson and Lynn are discussing the terms of a $28,000 home improvement loan with their bank's lending officer. The interest rate on the loan is 7.5% compounded monthly.

a. How long will it take to repay the loan if the end-of-month payments are $220?

b. How long will it take to repay the loan if they pay an extra $20 per month?

c. Calculate the approximate total nominal interest savings over the life of the loan as a result of making payments of $240 instead of $220 at the end of each month.

SOLUTION

The original loan equals the present value of all the payments. The payments form an *ordinary simple* annuity with $PV = \$28,000$ and $i = \frac{7.5\%}{12} = 0.625\%$. In Part (a), $PMT = \$220$, and in Part (b), $PMT = \$240$.

a. Substitute $PV = \$28,000$, $i = 0.625\%$, and $PMT = \$220$ into formula (10-2n).

$$n = -\frac{\ln\left(1 - \dfrac{i \times PV}{PMT}\right)}{\ln(1 + i)}$$

$$= -\frac{\ln\left[1 - \dfrac{0.00625(\$28,000)}{\$220}\right]}{\ln(1.00625)}$$

$$= 254.71$$

7.5	I/Y
P/Y 12	ENTER
(making $C/Y = P/Y = 12$)	
28000	PV
220 +/−	PMT
0	FV
CPT	N
Ans: 254.71	

It will take 255 payments, requiring 255 months to pay off the loan.

255 months $= \frac{255}{12}$ years $= 21.25$ years $= 21$ years $+ (0.25 \times 12)$ months $= 21$ years, 3 months

Therefore, it will take 21 years and 3 months to pay off the loan. (The last payment will be *approximately* $0.71 \times \$220 \approx \$156$.)

b. Again, we can substitute $PV = \$28,000$, $i = 0.625\%$, and $PMT = \$240$ into formula (10-2n).

$$n = -\frac{\ln\left(1 - \dfrac{i \times PV}{PMT}\right)}{\ln(1 + i)}$$

$$= -\frac{\ln\left[1 - \dfrac{0.00625(\$28,000)}{\$240}\right]}{\ln(1.00625)}$$

$$= 209.65$$

Same *I/Y, P/Y, C/Y*	
Same *PV, FV*	
240 +/−	PMT
CPT	N
Ans: 209.65	

It will take 210 months (17 years and 6 months) to pay off the loan. The last payment will be *approximately* $0.65(\$240) \approx \$156$.

With monthly payments of $220, the total of all payments is approximately

$$254.71(\$220) \approx \$56,036$$

With monthly payments of $240, the total of all payments is approximately

$$209.65(\$240) \approx \$50,316$$

Ignoring the time value of money, the saving of interest is approximately

$$\$56,036 - \$50,316 \approx \$5720$$

Postscript: By increasing their monthly payments by less than 10%, Robson and Lynn will pay off the loan in about 18% less time ($17\frac{1}{2}$ years instead of $21\frac{1}{4}$ years). Their total interest costs on the $28,000 loan will be reduced by over 20% (from $28,036 to $22,316). This outcome is typical of long-term debt. It is one of the main reasons why financial planners encourage us to make even slightly larger payments on long-term debt.

➡ **Check your understanding:** How much less time will it take to repay a $25,000 loan with end-of-quarter payments of $1500 than with end-of-quarter payments of only $1000? The loan carries interest of 6% compounded quarterly. (Answer: The loan will be repaid three years sooner with the $1500 per quarter payments.)

▮▮▮➤ **Related problem:** #16 in Exercise 11.2

EXAMPLE 11.2C	Calculating the Time Required to Reach a Savings Goal and the Length of Time a Fund Will Sustain Regular Withdrawals

a. Annual contributions of $5000 will be made at every year-end to an RRSP. Rounding n upward, how long will it take for the funds in the RRSP to grow to $500,000 if they earn 5.75% compounded annually?

b. If the $500,000 will be used to purchase an annuity earning 4% compounded quarterly and paying $10,000 at the end of each quarter, how long after the purchase date will the annuity payments continue?

SOLUTION

In Part (a), the future value of the contributions is to be $500,000. The contributions form an *ordinary simple* annuity with $PMT = \$5000$ and $i = \frac{5.75\%}{1} = 5.75\%$.

In Part (b), the accumulated $500,000 becomes the *present value* of an *ordinary simple* annuity having $PMT = \$12,000$ and $i = \frac{4\%}{4} = 1\%$.

a. Substitute the known values into formula (10-1n).

$$n = \frac{\ln\left(1 + \dfrac{i \times FV}{PMT}\right)}{\ln(1 + i)}$$

$$= \frac{\ln\left[1 + \dfrac{0.0575(\$500,000)}{\$5000}\right]}{\ln(1.0575)}$$

$$= 34.15531$$

5.75	I/Y
P/Y	1 ENTER
(making $C/Y = P/Y = 1$)	
0	PV
5000 +/-	PMT
500000	FV
CPT	N

Ans: 34.16

Rounding n upward, it will take 35 years for the RRSP to accumulate $500,000. (In this particular case, the interest earned during the 35th year will allow the RRSP to reach $500,000 before[2] the 35th contribution is actually made.)

---

[2] The calculation is actually telling us that the RRSP will reach $500,000 after 34.15531 years if a 35th payment of (essentially) 0.15531 × $5000 is paid into the plan after only 0.15531 of the 35th year. This is not what actually happens—no contribution will be made before the end of the 35th year. To calculate precisely when the RRSP will reach $500,000 (including accrued interest), calculate the amount in the RRSP after 34 contributions (years). Then, use formula (9-2) to calculate the fraction of a year required for the preceding amount to grow to $500,000 through the accrual of interest.

b. Substitute the known values into formula (10-2n).

$$n = -\frac{\ln\left(1 - \frac{i \times PV}{PMT}\right)}{\ln(1 + i)}$$

$$= -\frac{\ln\left[1 - \frac{0.01(\$500,000)}{\$10,000}\right]}{\ln(1.01)}$$

$$= 69.66$$

	4 I/Y
	P/Y 4 ENTER
	(making $C/Y = P/Y = 4$)
	500000 +/− PV
	10000 PMT
	0 FV
	CPT N

Ans: 69.66

There will be 70 quarterly payments, with the last payment being about 34% smaller than the others. Therefore, the annuity payments will run for

$$\frac{70 \text{ quarters}}{4 \text{ quarters per year}} = 17.5 \text{ years} = 17 \text{ years and 6 months}$$

 Check your understanding: a. Quarterly contributions of $1500 will be made at the end of every three months to an RRSP. Rounding n upward, how long will it take for the funds in the RRSP to grow to $350,000 if they earn 4.2% compounded quarterly? **b.** If the $350,000 is used to purchase an annuity earning 3% compounded semiannually and paying $17,000 at the end of every six months, how long after the purchase date will the annuity payments continue? (Answer: **a.** 29 years, 9 months **b.** 12 years, 6 months)

Related problem: #23 in Exercise 11.2

? Checkpoint Questions

1. If you double the size of the monthly payment you make on a loan, will you pay it off in (pick one) **(i)** half the time? **(ii)** less than half the time? **(iii)** more than half the time? Give the reason for your choice.

2. If you contribute $250 per month to an RRSP instead of $500 per month, will the time required to reach a particular savings target be (pick one) **(i)** twice as long? **(ii)** less than twice as long? **(iii)** more than twice as long? Give the reason for your choice.

EXERCISE 11.2

Answers to the odd-numbered problems can be found in the end matter.

BASIC PROBLEMS

1. An annuity earning 3.5% compounded semiannually has a present value of $50,000. How many payments of $3425.81 at the end of every six months will the annuity sustain?

2. The future value of an annuity is $100,000. To achieve this total, an investor made end-of-year investments of $1658.87 earning 5.2% compounded annually. How many annual investments were made?

3. If money in a new Tax Free Savings Account earns 2.25% compounded monthly, how long will it take for the plan to reach a future value of $30,000 based on end-of-month contributions of $273.03?

4. Thaya will make end-of-quarter payments of $642.73 to repay a $10,000 loan. How many loan payments will he make in total if he is being charged interest at 6% compounded quarterly?

5. Halima will deposit $500 at the end of every six months into a savings plan that earns 3% compounded semiannually. After how many deposits will Halima have surpassed her savings goal of $7000?

INTERMEDIATE PROBLEMS

6. For $200,000, Jamal purchased an annuity that delivers end-of-quarter payments of $3341.74. If the funds in the annuity earn 4.5% compounded quarterly, what is the term of the annuity?

7. An endowment fund is set up with a donation of $100,000. If it earns 3% compounded monthly, for how long will it sustain end-of-month withdrawals of $1000? (Include the final, smaller withdrawal.)

8. Rounding up the number of contributions to the next integer, how long will it take an RRSP to surpass $100,000 if the investor makes end-of-quarter contributions of $3500 and the plan earns 5% compounded semiannually?

9. For how long has Vickram been making end-of-quarter contributions of $1200 to an RESP for his son's education if the RESP has earned 4.75% compounded annually and is presently worth $60,727?

10. End-of-month payments of $315.49 are required on a $20,000 loan at 5.5% compounded quarterly. What is the term of the loan?

11. Rounded to the next-higher month, how long will it take end-of-month deposits of $500 to accumulate to $100,000 in an investment account that earns 5.25% compounded monthly?

12. Silas is about to begin regular month-end contributions of $500 to a bond fund. The fund's long-term rate of return is expected to be 3% compounded semiannually. Rounded to the next-higher month, how long will it take Silas to accumulate $250,000?

13. How long will $500,000, in an investment account that earns 5.25% compounded monthly, sustain month-end withdrawals of $3000?

14. Farah has $600,000 in her RRSP and wishes to retire. She is considering using the funds to purchase an annuity that earns 3% compounded annually and pays her $3500 at the end of each month. If she buys the annuity, for how long will she receive payments? Include the final, smaller annuity payment in the total.

15. If $300,000 is used to purchase an annuity earning 4.5% compounded monthly and paying $2500 at the end of each month, what will be the term of the annuity? Include the final, smaller annuity payment in the total.

16. Suppose that you contribute $425 per month to your RRSP. Rounding up to the nearest month, how much longer will it take for the RRSP's value to reach $500,000 if it earns 4.2% compounded annually than if it earns 4.2% compounded monthly?

17. How much longer will it take month-end RRSP contributions of $500 to accumulate $500,000 than month-end contributions of $550? Assume that the RRSP earns 3.75% compounded monthly. Round the time required in each case to the next-higher month.

18. How much longer will it take monthly payments of $1000 to pay off a $100,000 loan if the monthly compounded rate of interest on the loan is 5.25% instead of 4.875%?

19. What duration of annuity paying $5000 at the end of every quarter can be purchased with $200,000 if the invested funds earn 3.5% compounded semiannually? Include the final, smaller annuity payment in the total.

20. Bonnie and Clyde want to take a six-month leave of absence from their jobs to travel extensively in South America. Rounded to the next-higher month, how long will it take them to save $40,000 for the leave if they make month-end contributions of $700 to a savings plan that earns 3.5% compounded semiannually?

21. Ernie's Electronics sells an HD LED television priced at $2395 for $100 down and payments of $100 per month, including interest at 9.6% compounded monthly. How long after the date of purchase will the final payment be made?

22. **a.** How long will it take monthly payments of $400 to repay a $50,000 loan if the interest rate on the loan is 8% compounded semiannually?

    b. How much will the time to repay the loan be reduced if the payments are $40 per month larger?

23. **a.** Mrs. Gobi will make end-of-quarter deposits of $850 to her RRSP. The fund earns 4% compounded semiannually. Rounding n upward, how long will it take for the funds in the RRSP to grow to $250,000?

    b. If Mrs. Gobi uses $250,000 to purchase an annuity earning 3% compounded semiannually and paying $2500 at the end of every month, how long after the purchase date will the annuity payments continue? Round the answer up to the next-highest integer.

ADVANCED PROBLEMS

24. Rashid wants to use $500,000 from his RRSP to purchase an annuity that pays him $2000 at the end of each month for the first 10 years and $3000 per month thereafter. Global Insurance Co. will sell Rashid an annuity of this sort with a rate of return of 4.8% compounded monthly. For how long will the annuity run?

25. A 65-year-old male can purchase either of the following annuities from a life insurance company for $50,000. A 25-year term annuity will pay $307 at the end of each month. A life annuity will pay $408 at the end of every month until the death of the annuitant. To what age must the man survive for the life annuity to have the greater economic value? Assume that money can earn 6% compounded monthly.

26. Twelve years ago, Mr. Lawton rolled a $17,000 retiring allowance into an RRSP that subsequently earned 7% compounded semiannually. Three years ago he transferred the funds to a Registered Retirement Income Fund (RRIF). Since then, he has been withdrawing $1000 at the end of each quarter. If the RRIF earns 4.2% compounded quarterly, how much longer can the withdrawals continue?

27. Harold's RRSP is already worth $56,000. Rounded to the next-highest month, how long will it take the RRSP to reach $250,000 if additional contributions of $2000 are made at the end of every six months? Assume the RRSP earns 3.9% compounded monthly.

11.3 | Calculating the Interest Rate in Ordinary Annuities

 LO3 Circumstances in which you need to calculate the interest rate include
- determining the rate of return required for periodic savings to reach a goal in a particular length of time.
- determining the rate of return earned on money used to purchase an annuity.
- determining the interest rate implied by specified loan payments.
- determining the interest rate being charged when an installment payment plan is offered as an alternative to a "cash" payment.
- determining the interest rate built into the payments on a vehicle or equipment lease.

The interest rate most readily calculated is the periodic interest rate, i. To determine i, you must know the values for PMT, n, and either FV or PV.

As with the calculation of PMT and n, calculating i requires that you pay careful attention to identify the type of annuity involved. This section introduces the calculation of i in ordinary annuities, where payments are being made at the end of every payment interval. In Section 11.4, we will modify our approach for annuities due. Therefore, identifying the annuity type at the outset of the question continues to be a good practice.

Problems requiring the calculation of i pose some special difficulties for an algebraic approach. Formulas (10-1) for FV and (10-2) for PV cannot be rearranged through algebraic manipulations to isolate i. Consequently, no formulas can be given for i (corresponding to those for n in Section 11.2).

Appendix 11B presents an approximation technique called the "trial-and-error method," a systematic but time-consuming procedure for *improving an estimate* of an equation's solution. With each repetition or *iteration* of the procedure, the approximation gets closer to the correct solution. We illustrate the method in Appendix 11B by using it to solve Example 11.3A a second time.

In this section, we will show only the financial-calculator method for the solutions to example problems. For the interest rate computation, the financial calculator also uses a repetitive iterative procedure when you press CPT I/Y . But the only evidence you may notice of this happening is that it takes the calculator slightly longer to compute *I/Y* than it takes to compute one of the other financial variables.

EXAMPLE 11.3A | **Finding the Rate of Return on Funds Used to Purchase an Ordinary Annuity**

A life insurance company advertises that $50,000 will purchase a 20-year annuity paying $341.13 at the end of each month. What monthly compounded nominal rate of return and effective rate of return does the annuity investment earn?

P/Y 12 ENTER
(making $C/Y = P/Y = 12$)
240 N
50000 +/- PV
341.13 PMT
0 FV
CPT I/Y
Ans: 5.400

SOLUTION

The purchase price of an annuity equals the present value of all payments. Hence, the rate of return on the $50,000 purchase price is the discount rate that makes the present value of the payments equal to $50,000. The payments form an ordinary annuity with

$$PV = \$50,000, \quad PMT = \$341.13, \quad m = 12, \quad \text{and} \quad n = 12(20) = 240$$

Same N, PMT,
PV, FV

P/Y 12 ENTER
C/Y 1 ENTER
CPT I/Y
Ans: 5.536

Enter these values in your calculator as indicated in the box at upper right. The nominal rate of return we obtain is 5.40% compounded monthly. Then $i = \frac{j}{m} = \frac{5.4\%}{12} = 0.450\%$ and the corresponding effective interest rate is

$$f = (1 + i)^m - 1 = 1.00450^{12} - 1 = 0.05536 = 5.54\%$$

➡ **Check your understanding:** A life insurance company advertises that $125,000 will purchase a 25-year annuity paying $1860.62 at the end of every quarter. What quarterly compounded nominal rate of return and effective rate of return does the annuity investment earn? (Answer: 3.40% compounded quarterly or an effective (annually compounded) rate of 3.44%)

▪▪▪▶ **Related problem:** #1 in Exercise 11.3

EXAMPLE 11.3B | **Calculating the Rate of Return Required to Reach a Savings Goal in a Specified Time Period**

What annually compounded rate of return must Rachel earn in her RRSP in order for month-end contributions of $500 to accumulate to $300,000 after 25 years?

SOLUTION

The contributions form an *ordinary* annuity whose future value after 25 years is to be $300,000. That is,

$$FV = \$300{,}000, \quad PMT = \$500, \quad m = C/Y = 1, P/Y = 12,$$
$$\text{and} \quad n = 12(25) = 300$$

Enter these values in your calculator as indicated in the box at upper right. The nominal rate of return we obtain is 5.17% compounded annually.

Rachel's RRSP must earn 5.17% compounded annually to reach her savings goal.

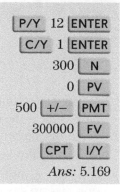

P/Y 12 ENTER
C/Y 1 ENTER
300 N
0 PV
500 +/− PMT
300000 FV
CPT I/Y
Ans: 5.169

➡ **Check your understanding:** What annually compounded rate of return must Suhanna earn in her RRSP in order for end-of-quarter contributions of $2000 to accumulate to $300,000 after 20 years? (Answer: 5.98% compounded annually)

▦▶ **Related problem:** #4 in Exercise 11.3

EXAMPLE 11.3C	**Calculating the Implied Interest Rate for an Installment Payment Option**

Rolling Meadows Golf and Country Club allows members to pay the annual membership fee by a single payment of $2400 at the beginning of the year, or by payments of $220 at the beginning of each month. What effective rate of interest is paid by members who choose to pay by the month?

SOLUTION

The first monthly payment is due on the same date as the full annual fee. In effect, the golf club initially lends $2400 - $220 = $2180 to a member choosing the monthly payment option. The member then repays the "loan" by 11 month-end payments of $220.

Again we use the fundamental principle that the original "loan" equals the present value of all payments. We need to calculate the discount rate that makes $2180 the present value of 11 payments of $220. We have

$$PV = \$2180, \quad PMT = \$220, \quad P/Y = 12, \quad \text{and} \quad n = 11$$

Since we are asked for the effective rate, set $C/Y = m = 1$. Enter these values in your calculator as indicated in the box at upper right to obtain

$$I/Y = 23.62\% \text{ compounded annually}$$

Hence, members on the monthly payment plan are paying an effective rate of 23.62%.

P/Y 12 ENTER
C/Y 1 ENTER
11 N
2180 PV
220 +/− PMT
0 FV
CPT I/Y
Ans: 23.615

➡ **Check your understanding:** A health club allows members to pay the annual membership fee of $850 by a single payment at the beginning of the year, or by payments of $75 at the beginning of each month. What effective rate is the club charging members who choose to pay by the month? (Answer: 13.44%)

▦▶ **Related problem:** #14 in Exercise 11.3

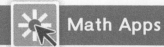

Math Apps

SHOULD YOU CHOOSE A CASH DISCOUNT INCENTIVE OR LOW INTEREST RATE FINANCING?

To promote vehicle sales, it is common for automobile manufacturers to offer the purchaser of a new vehicle the choice between
- a discount (or incentive) on a "cash" purchase, or
- financing at a lower interest rate than may be available from conventional lenders.

For example, in mid-2016, Toyota Canada offered buyers of a new Toyota Tundra 4 × 4 Crewmax SR5 (MSRP $42,995) the choice of a $2000 cash incentive (deducted from the MSRP) or financing at 1.99% compounded monthly on an 84-month loan from Toyota Canada Finance. How do you decide which alternative to choose?

Your initial reaction may be that your personal financial condition will determine your choice. That is, if you have sufficient financial resources on hand, you will pay cash and take the $2000 discount. On the other hand, if you need financing, you will choose the below-market interest rate.

Let's think more carefully about the second scenario. Assume that you have cash on hand of $2995 that you will use as a down payment. You will, therefore, need to finance the remaining $42,995 − $2995 = $40,000 of the purchase price. There is likely another option open to you. Instead of borrowing $40,000 at 1.99% compounded monthly through Toyota Canada Finance, you can approach a bank or credit union for a loan of only

$$\$40,000 - \$2000 = \$38,000$$

With the $2995 down payment of your own, this loan would give you enough to pay cash and qualify for the $2000 cash incentive. Now it is apparent that you must regard forgoing the $2000 incentive as an *additional* cost of the "cheap" 1.99% financing.

The following questions lead you through an analysis of the two financing alternatives. For the easiest comparison, let us assume the $38,000 bank loan has an 84-month (or seven-year) term.

Questions

1. What will the monthly payment be if you borrow $40,000 for 84 months through Toyota Canada Finance at 1.99% compounded monthly?

2. If, by a remarkable coincidence, the monthly payment on the $38,000 bank loan is exactly the same amount, what interest rate is the bank charging?

3. What, then, should be your decision rule for whether to choose the bank loan and take the cash discount incentive, or to choose the 1.99% financing?

4. Now consider the other scenario in which you have sufficient financial resources to pay cash without borrowing. Suppose you have investments that you could sell and use the proceeds to purchase the vehicle. Nevertheless, you may still choose to borrow at the below-market rate of 1.99% because your investments are generating a high rate of return. What should be your rule for deciding whether to liquidate investments or to use the Toyota financing to purchase the vehicle?

EXERCISE 11.3

BASIC PROBLEMS

Calculate all interest rates accurate to the nearest 0.01%.

1. The present value of an annuity paying $500 at the end of every month for $8\frac{3}{4}$ years is $43,295. What monthly compounded nominal rate and effective rate were earned?

2. An annuity of $800 deposited at the end of every quarter for 20 years had a future value of $125,052.91. What quarterly compounded nominal rate and effective rate were earned during the 20-year term of the annuity?

3. A car loan with a present value of $28,000 will be repaid with end-of-month payments of $472.01 for six years. What monthly compounded nominal rate and effective rate were paid on this loan?

4. Montel is checking potential outcomes for the growth of his RRSP. He plans to make contributions of $500 at the end of each month. What monthly compounded nominal rate and effective rate of return must his RRSP earn for its future value after 25 years to be

   a. $400,000?   **b.** $500,000?   **c.** $600,000?

   (Note that a modest increase in the rate of return over a long period produces substantially larger future values.)

5. What nominal rate of interest compounded semiannually would allow deposits of $500 at the end of every six months for the next 10 years to grow to be worth $13,685?

INTERMEDIATE PROBLEMS

6. An annuity purchased for $50,000 sustained quarterly withdrawals of $1941.01 for 7 years and 9 months. What nominal rate of return and effective rate of return did the funds in the annuity earn?

7. RRSP contributions of $4345.11 at the end of every six months are projected to grow to be worth $400,000 in 25 years. What nominal and effective rates of return were used in the forecast?

8. With end-of-month contributions of $329.80, a Tax Free Savings Account is forecast to pass $100,000 in value after 15 years and 5 months. Determine the nominal and effective rates of return used in the forecast.

9. Morgan has $500,000 accumulated in her RRSP and intends to use the amount to purchase a 20-year annuity. She is investigating the size of annuity payment she can expect to receive, depending on the rate of return earned by the funds in the annuity. What monthly compounded nominal rate of return must the funds earn for the end-of-month payment to be

   a. $3000?   **b.** $3500?   **c.** $4000?

10. If $100,000 will purchase a 20-year annuity paying $830 at the end of each month, what monthly compounded nominal rate and effective rate of interest will the invested funds earn?

11. After $10\frac{1}{2}$ years of contributions of $2000 at the end of every six months to an RESP, the accumulated amount stood at $65,727.82. What semiannually compounded nominal rate of return and effective annual rate of return were earned by the funds in the RESP?

12. What quarterly compounded nominal rate and effective rate of interest are being charged on a $5000 loan if quarterly payments of $302.07 will repay the loan in $5\frac{1}{2}$ years?

13. A $9000, four-year term loan requires monthly payments of $220.77. What are the monthly compounded nominal rate and the effective rate of interest on the loan?

14. A major daily newspaper charges $260 (paid in advance) for an annual subscription, or $26 per month payable at the end of each month. What is the effective interest rate being charged to the monthly payment subscribers?

15. In an insurance settlement for bodily injury, a court awarded Mr. Goodman $103,600 for two years' loss of wages of $4000 per month plus interest on the lost wages to the end of the two years. What effective rate of interest has the court allowed on the lost wages?

16. A national wireless provider sells for $200 a phone worth $650 to customers who sign up for a two-year service contract priced at $75 payable at the end of every month. Yasmin has determined that if she buys outright the same phone herself, she can purchase identical service from a different provider for only $45 payable at the end of every month. Yasmin has determined, therefore, that she is really paying an additional $75 − $45 = $30 a month for two years to repay the $450 she "saved" on the discounted phone. What monthly compounded nominal rate of interest is the national provider "charging" on the "loan" that is buried in its two-year service contract?

ADVANCED PROBLEMS

17. Another type of sales promotion for vehicles is to advertise the choice between a "Cash Purchase Price" and "0% Purchase Financing." The tiny print at the bottom of a GM Canada full-page advertisement included the statement: "The GMAC purchase finance rates are not available with and are not calculated on the 'Cash Purchase Price' shown. The difference between the price for the GMAC purchase finance offer and the 'Cash Purchase Price' offer is deemed under provincial laws to be a cost of financing." In other words, there are two prices for a vehicle—a lower price if you pay cash and a higher price if you want to take advantage of the "0% financing." Another disconcerting aspect of this type of promotion is that the higher price for the 0% financing is usually not quoted in the advertisement. Rather, it must be negotiated with the dealer.

    Suppose the "Cash Purchase Price" of a car is $23,498, and the price that qualifies for full 0% financing (with 48 monthly payments) turns out to be $26,198. What effective interest rate will you be paying for the "0% financing?"

18. Vijay purchased a Province of Nova Scotia bond for $1050. The bond will pay $35 interest to Vijay at the end of every six months until it matures in seven years. On the maturity date the bond will pay back its $1000 face value (as well as the interest payment due on that date). What semiannually compounded rate of return will Vijay earn during the seven years?

19. A car dealer offered "$1250 cash back or 1.9% factory financing over 60 months" to purchasers of selected new vehicle models. A customer financed $30,000 at the low interest rate instead of paying $28,750 cash (after the $1250 rebate). What was the effective rate of interest on the loan if the forgone cash rebate was treated as part of the cost of financing? (The 1.9% interest rate was a monthly compounded nominal rate.)

20. An advertisement for new vehicles offered "1.9% 48-month financing or $2000 cash back." A car buyer financed $25,000 at the low interest rate instead of paying $23,000 cash (after the $2000 rebate). What was the effective rate of interest on the loan if the forgone cash rebate was treated as part of the cost of financing? (The 1.9% interest rate was a monthly compounded nominal rate.)

11.4 Calculating the Periodic Payment, Number of Payments, and Interest Rate in Annuities Due

LO4   To calculate any one of these three quantities for an annuity due, follow the same procedure you would for an ordinary annuity, but with one change. You must use the annuity due formula that is the counterpart of the ordinary annuity formula. These counterparts are listed in the following table. Formulas (10-4n) and (10-5n) have not been presented before. They are versions of formulas (10-4) and (10-5), respectively, rearranged to isolate n.

Ordinary annuity formula		Annuity due formula	
$FV = PMT\left[\dfrac{(1+i)^n - 1}{i}\right]$	(10-1)	$FV(\text{due}) = PMT\left[\dfrac{(1+i)^n - 1}{i}\right] \times (1+i)$	(10-4)
$PV = PMT\left[\dfrac{1-(1+i)^{-n}}{i}\right]$	(10-2)	$PV(\text{due}) = PMT\left[\dfrac{1-(1+i)^{-n}}{i}\right] \times (1+i)$	(10-5)
$n = \dfrac{\ln\left(1 + \dfrac{i \times FV}{PMT}\right)}{\ln(1+i)}$	(10-1n)	$n = \dfrac{\ln\left[1 + \dfrac{i \times FV(\text{due})}{PMT(1+i)}\right]}{\ln(1+i)}$	(10-4n)
$n = -\dfrac{\ln\left(1 - \dfrac{i \times PV}{PMT}\right)}{\ln(1+i)}$	(10-2n)	$n = -\dfrac{\ln\left[1 - \dfrac{i \times PV(\text{due})}{PMT(1+i)}\right]}{\ln(1+i)}$	(10-5n)

Calculating i algebraically requires the trial-and-error method described in Appendix 11B. We will use only the financial-calculator method to solve for the interest rate in Example problems.

The Mathematics of Vehicle Leasing

In recent years, 20% to 25% of new vehicles were leased. The main elements of a typical lease contract are as follows:

- The lessee makes fixed beginning-of-month payments for the term of the lease. The most common term is four years.
- The lessee is responsible for all vehicle operating costs (including insurance) during the term of the lease. In this respect, leasing does not differ from owning a vehicle.
- Most leases are "closed-end" or "walk-away" leases. At the end of the term, the lessee can simply return the vehicle to the car dealer. Alternatively, at the option of the lessee, the vehicle may be purchased for a *predetermined* amount (called the **residual value**). The residual value represents the dealer's estimate of the market value of the vehicle at the end of the lease.

We will use a particular example to develop your understanding of the economics and mathematics of leasing. Suppose your down payment on a three-year lease is $3000. The car's purchase price is $30,000 and its residual value after three years is $15,000. We will now explain how the lease payment is calculated.

From the car dealer's point of view, the $27,000 "balance" is paid by 36 beginning-of-month payments plus a projected final payment of $15,000 after three years. This final payment will come either from you (if you exercise the purchase option) or from the sale of the vehicle at the end of the lease. Since the future selling price can only be estimated, the amount of the final payment is not known with certainty. The lease payments are calculated on the assumption that the final payment will be $15,000.

Except for the uncertainty in the amount of the final payment, the situation is similar to repaying a $27,000 loan by 36 beginning-of-month payments plus a final payment of $15,000 after three years. In that case, we know that the present value of all loan payments and the $15,000 final payment (discounted at the interest rate on the loan) is \$27,000. Similarly, the present value of all lease payments and the residual value (discounted at the interest rate charged on the lease) is \$27,000. In general,

$$\begin{pmatrix}\text{Purchase}\\\text{price}\end{pmatrix} - \begin{pmatrix}\text{Down}\\\text{payment}\end{pmatrix} = \begin{pmatrix}\text{Present value of}\\\text{the lease payments}\end{pmatrix} + \begin{pmatrix}\text{Present value of}\\\text{the residual value}\end{pmatrix}$$

The interest rate on a lease is applied as a monthly compounded rate. Therefore, the monthly lease payments form a *simple annuity due*.

There are six variables embedded in this mathematical relationship. They are: the purchase price, the down payment, the residual value, the number of payments, the amount of the monthly payment, and the interest rate on the lease. If five of the variables are given, you can calculate the sixth. In the advertisements that car dealers place in newspapers, you may not find the values for all six variables. The most commonly omitted variable is the "residual value" (which may be called the "option to purchase at lease end"). If its value is given at all, it will be found among the details in the tiny print at the bottom of the advertisement.

EXAMPLE 11.4A	**Calculating the Size of Lease Payments**

A lease that has $2\frac{1}{2}$ years to run is recorded on a company's books as a liability of \$27,369. If the company's cost of borrowing was 6% compounded monthly when the lease was signed, what is the amount of the lease payment at the beginning of each month?

SOLUTION

The "book value" of the lease liability is the present value of the remaining lease payments. The discount rate employed should be the interest rate the company would have paid to borrow funds. The lease payments constitute a *simple annuity due* with

$$PV(\text{due}) = \$27{,}369, \quad n = 12(2.5) = 30, \quad \text{and} \quad i = \tfrac{6\%}{12} = 0.5\% \text{ per month}$$

Substitute the given values into formula (10-5) and solve for *PMT*.

$$PV(\text{due}) = PMT\left[\frac{1 - (1 + i)^{-n}}{i}\right] \times (1 + i)$$

$$\$27{,}369 = PMT\left(\frac{1 - 1.005^{-30}}{0.005}\right)(1.005)$$

$$= PMT(27.79405)(1.005)$$

$$= PMT(27.93302)$$

$$PMT = \$979.81$$

BGN mode

6 │ I/Y

│ P/Y │ 12 │ENTER

(making *C/Y* = *P/Y* = 12)

30 │ N

27369 │ PV

0 │ FV

│ CPT │ PMT

Ans: −979.81

The monthly lease payment is \$979.81.

➡ **Check your understanding:** A lease that has $3\frac{3}{4}$ years to run is recorded on a company's books as a liability of \$22,823.44. If the company's cost of borrowing was 5.1% compounded monthly when the lease was signed, what is the amount of the lease payment at the beginning of each month? (Answer: \$555.94)

▇▇▶ **Related problem:** #15 in Exercise 11.4

EXAMPLE 11.4B | **Calculating the Payment Needed to Attain a Savings Goal**

Mr. Walters has already accumulated $104,000 in his Registered Retirement Savings Plan (RRSP). His goal is to build it to $175,000 with equal contributions at the beginning of each six-month period for the next seven years. If his RRSP earns 4.5% compounded semiannually, what must be the size of further contributions?

SOLUTION

Since earnings are compounded *semiannually*, the *semiannual* investments at the *beginning* of every six month period form a *simple annuity due*. The $175,000 target will be the combined future value of the $104,000 already in the RRSP and the future value of the simple annuity due. That is,

$$\$175,000 = \text{Future value of } \$104,000 + FV(\text{due}) \quad \text{①}$$

with $n = 2(7) = 14$ and $i = \frac{4.5\%}{2} = 2.25\%$ per half-year

The future value of the $104,000 will be

$$FV = PV(1 + i)^n = \$104,000(1.0225)^{14} = \$142,010.28$$

Substitute the given values into formula (10-4). The future value of the 14 contributions will be

$$FV(\text{due}) = PMT\left[\frac{(1 + i)^n - 1}{i}\right] \times (1 + i)$$

$$= PMT\left(\frac{1.0225^{14} - 1}{0.0225}\right)(1.0225)$$

$$= PMT(16.60919)$$

Substituting these amounts into equation ①, we obtain

$$\$175,000 = \$142,010.28 + PMT(16.60919)$$

$$PMT = \frac{\$175,000 - \$142,010.28}{16.60919} = \$1986.23$$

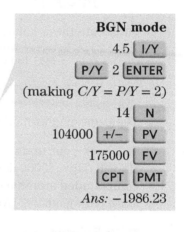

BGN mode

4.5 I/Y

P/Y 2 ENTER

(making $C/Y = P/Y = 2$)

14 N

104000 +/− PV

175000 FV

CPT PMT

Ans: −1986.23

Mr. Walters must make semiannual contributions of $1986.23 to reach the $175,000 target in seven years.

➡ **Check your understanding:** Mrs. Banerjee has already accumulated $128,000 in her RRSP. Her goal is to build it to $500,000 by the time she retires in 20 years from now. If her RRSP earns 6% compounded monthly, how much must Mrs. Banerjee deposit at the beginning of each month for the next 20 years in order to reach her goal? (Answer: $164.30)

▣▶ **Related problem:** #12 in Exercise 11.4

EXAMPLE 11.4C | **Calculating the Payment on a Car Lease**

An automobile manufacturer is calculating the lease payments to charge on a compact vehicle, which has a selling price of $27,900. During a month-long promotion, the manufacturer will offer an interest rate of only 1.8% compounded monthly on a three-year lease. If the residual value is $14,500, what will be the lease payments, assuming a $2500 down payment?

SOLUTION

Earlier in this section, we developed the leasing equation:

$$\left(\begin{array}{c}\text{Purchase}\\\text{price}\end{array}\right) - \left(\begin{array}{c}\text{Down}\\\text{payment}\end{array}\right) = \left(\begin{array}{c}\text{Present value of}\\\text{the lease payments}\end{array}\right) + \left(\begin{array}{c}\text{Present value of}\\\text{the residual value}\end{array}\right)$$

For the lease on this vehicle,

$$\$27{,}900 - \$2500 = \left(\begin{array}{c}\text{Present value of}\\\text{the lease payments}\end{array}\right) + \left(\begin{array}{c}\text{Present value}\\\text{of }\$14{,}500\end{array}\right) \quad ①$$

The lease payments form a *simple annuity due* with $i = \frac{1.8\%}{12} = 0.15\%$ and $n = 36$.
The present value of the lease payments is

$$PV(\text{due}) = PMT\left[\frac{1-(1+i)^{-n}}{i}\right] \times (1+i)$$

$$= PMT\left[\frac{1-1.0015^{-36}}{0.0015}\right](1.0015)$$

$$= PMT(35.07224)$$

The present value of the $14,500 residual value is

$$PV = FV(1+i)^{-n} = \$14{,}500(1.0015)^{-36} = \$13{,}738.32$$

Substitute these values into equation ① and solve for *PMT*.

$$\$25{,}400 = PMT(35.07224) + \$13{,}738.32$$

$$PMT = \frac{\$25{,}400 - \$13{,}738.32}{35.07224} = \$332.50$$

The beginning-of-month lease payment is $332.50.

> **BGN mode**
>
> 1.8 `I/Y`
>
> `P/Y` 12 `ENTER`
>
> (making $C/Y = P/Y = 12$)
>
> 36 `N`
>
> 25400 `+/−` `PV`
>
> 14500 `FV`
>
> `CPT` `PMT`
>
> *Ans:* 332.50

➡ **Check your understanding:** Bob is leasing a vehicle that has a selling price of $35,895. He will pay a $5000 down payment. The manufacturer is offering an interest rate of 3.9% compounded monthly on a four-year lease. If the residual value is $16,000, what will Bob's lease payments be? (Answer: $386.39/month)

▬▶ **Related problem:** #23 in Exercise 11.4

EXAMPLE 11.4D	Calculating *n* Given the Future Value of a Simple Annuity Due

Rounding *n* upward to the next integer, how long will it take to accumulate $500,000 in an RRSP if the first quarterly contribution of $2000 is made today? Assume the RRSP earns 5% compounded quarterly.

SOLUTION

First, we need to find the number of contributions required for the future value to reach $500,000. Since payments are made at the beginning of each period and the compounding interval equals the payment interval, the contributions form a *simple annuity due* having

$$PMT = \$2000, \quad i = \frac{5\%}{4} = 1.25\%, \quad \text{and} \quad FV(\text{due}) = \$500{,}000$$

Substitute these values into formula (10-4n).

$$n = \frac{\ln\left[1 + \dfrac{i \times FV(\text{due})}{PMT(1 + i)}\right]}{\ln(1 + i)}$$

$$= \frac{\ln\left[1 + \dfrac{0.0125 \times \$500{,}000}{\$2000(1.0125)}\right]}{\ln(1.0125)}$$

$$= \frac{1.40767}{0.0124225}$$

$$= 113.32$$

BGN mode	
5	I/Y
P/Y	4 ENTER
(making $C/Y = P/Y = 4$)	
0	PV
2000 +/−	PMT
500000	FV
CPT	N
Ans: 113.32	

The 114th contribution is required to reach $500,000. The time to the end of the 114th payment interval is

$$114 \text{ quarters} = \tfrac{114}{4} = 28.5 \text{ years} = 28 \text{ years and 6 months}$$

With n rounded to the next higher integer, it will take 28 years and 6 months to accumulate $500,000 in the RRSP. (Including accrued earnings, the $500,000 is actually reached quite early in the 114th interval.)

▶ **Check your understanding:** Rounding n upward to the next integer, how long will it take to accumulate $40,000 to use as the down payment on a house if the first monthly contribution of $500 is made today? Assume the savings plan earns 6% compounded monthly. (Answer: 5 years and 8 months)

▰▰▶ **Related problem:** #3 in Exercise 11.4

EXAMPLE 11.4E	Calculating *n* Given the Present Value of a General Annuity Due

An investment fund is worth $210,000 and earns 4% compounded semiannually. If $2000 is withdrawn at the beginning of each month starting today, when will the fund become depleted?

SOLUTION

The initial amount in the account equals the present value of the future withdrawals. Since the first withdrawal occurs today, and the payment interval differs from the compounding interval, the withdrawals form a *general annuity due* having

$$PV(\text{due}) = \$210{,}000, \ PMT = \$2000, \quad \text{and} \quad i = \tfrac{4\%}{2} = 2\%$$

The value we must use for i in formula (10-5n) is the periodic rate for the one-month payment interval.

Substitute

$$c = \frac{\text{Number of compoundings per year}}{\text{Number of payments per year}} = \frac{2}{12} = 0.1\overline{6}$$

into

$$i_2 = (1 + i)^c - 1 = (1.02)^{0.1\overline{6}} - 1 = 0.00330589 \text{ per month}$$

Substitute the known values into formula (10-5n).

$$n = -\frac{\ln\left[1 - \frac{i \times PV(\text{due})}{PMT(1 + i)}\right]}{\ln(1 + i)}$$

$$= -\frac{\ln\left[1 - \frac{0.00330589(\$210,000)}{\$2000(1.00330589)}\right]}{\ln(1.00330589)}$$

$$= 128.65$$

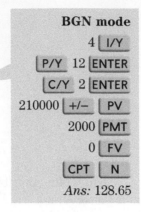

BGN mode

4 | I/Y
P/Y 12 ENTER
C/Y 2 ENTER
210000 +/- PV
2000 PMT
0 FV
CPT N

Ans: 128.65

The fund will permit 129 monthly withdrawals. The final withdrawal, smaller than $2000, will occur at the *beginning* of the 129th payment interval. But that will be 128 months from now. So the fund will be depleted at the time of the 129th payment, which is 128 months or 10 years and 8 months from now.

➡ **Check your understanding:** An investment fund is worth $178,000 and earns 6% compounded quarterly. If $2500 is withdrawn at the beginning of each month starting today, when will the fund become depleted? (Answer: 7 years and 3 months from now)

▬▬► **Related problem:** #19 in Exercise 11.4

EXAMPLE 11.4F	Calculating the Interest Rate for an Annuity Due

SOLUTION

Therese intends to contribute $3000 at the beginning of each six-month period to an RRSP. What semiannually compounded rate of return must her RRSP earn in order to reach $400,000 after 25 years?

The payments form an *annuity due* whose future value after 25 years is to be $400,000. That is,

$$FV(\text{due}) = \$400,000, \quad PMT = \$3000,$$
$$\text{and} \quad n = m(\text{Term}) = 2(25) = 50$$

If we set $P/Y = C/Y = 2$, we will obtain the semiannually compounded rate of return. Enter these values and compute I/Y.

Therese's RRSP must earn 6.89% compounded semiannually.

➡ **Check your understanding:** Maurice deposited $1200 at the start of every three-month period to a savings plan. After 15 years, the savings plan was worth $105,810.50. What rate of return compounded quarterly did the plan earn? (Answer: 4.80% compounded quarterly)

▬▬► **Related problem:** #5 in Exercise 11.4

BGN mode

P/Y 2 ENTER
(making $C/Y = P/Y = 2$)
50 N
0 PV
3000 +/- PMT
400000 FV
CPT I/Y

Ans: 6.89

EXAMPLE 11.4G	Calculating the Interest Rate Built into an Installment Payment Option

A $100,000 life insurance policy requires an annual premium of $420 or a monthly premium of $37. In either case, the premium is payable at the beginning of the period of coverage. What is the effective rate of interest policyholders pay when they choose the monthly payment plan?

SOLUTION

In effect, the insurance company lends the $420 annual premium to policyholders choosing the monthly payment option. These policyholders then repay the "loan" with 12 beginning-of-month payments of $37. Hence, $420 is the present value of the 12 payments that form an annuity *due*. We have

$$PV(\text{due}) = \$420, \quad PMT = \$37, \quad n = 12, \quad \text{and} \quad P/Y = 12$$

The effective interest rate is the same as the annually compounded rate ($C/Y = 1$). Enter these values and compute I/Y.

The effective interest rate on the monthly payment plan is 13.04%.

BGN mode

P/Y	12	ENTER
C/Y	1	ENTER
	12	N
	420	PV
37	+/−	PMT
	0	FV
CPT		I/Y

Ans: 13.04

➡ **Check your understanding:** A health club allows members to pay the annual membership fee of $1250 by a single payment at the beginning of the year, or by payments of $118 at the beginning of each month. What effective rate of interest do members pay when they choose the monthly payment plan? (Answer: 32.19%)

▰▰▷ **Related problem:** #22 in Exercise 11.4

EXAMPLE 11.4H	Calculating the Interest Rate Built into Lease Payments

A car dealer advertised the Hyundai Santa Fe GL AWD sport utility vehicle for sale at $33,610. The same vehicle could also be leased for five years at $379 per month, based on a $4310 down payment. At the end of the lease, the lessee could purchase the vehicle for $10,711. What monthly compounded interest rate was built into the lease?

SOLUTION

Mathematically, the problem is the same as calculating the interest rate charged on a loan where the balance is reduced from $29,300 (= $33,610 − $4310) to $10,711 by 60 beginning-of-month payments of $379. That is, $29,300 is the combined present value of 60 payments of $379 and a terminal payment of $10,711. In effect, we are given

$$PV(\text{due}) = \$29,300, \quad PMT = \$379, \quad n = 60, \quad \text{and} \quad FV = \$10,711$$

The interest rate built into the lease was 4.13% compounded monthly.

BGN mode

| P/Y | 12 | ENTER |

(making $C/Y = P/Y = 12$)

	60	N
	29300	PV
379	+/−	PMT
10711	+/−	FV
CPT		I/Y

Ans: 4.13

➡ **Check your understanding:** Suppose that, at the end of the lease, the lessee in the question above could purchase the vehicle for $15,000. If all other information about the lease remains the same, what monthly compounded interest rate was built into the lease? (Answer: 7.56% compounded monthly)

▰▰▷ **Related problem:** #26 in Exercise 11.4

Checkpoint Questions

1. An ordinary annuity and an annuity due have the same future value, n, and i. Which annuity has the larger payment? Give the reasoning for your answer.

2. Other variables being the same, how will the size of the residual value affect the size of the car lease payments?

3. The term of the lease on a vehicle is about to expire. Answer Parts (a) and (b) strictly on financial considerations.

   a. If the market value of the vehicle is less than the residual value, what should the lessee do?

   b. If the market value of the vehicle exceeds the residual value, what should the lessee do?

   c. In view of your answers to (a) and (b), will the interest rate on a lease contract tend to be higher or lower than the interest rate on a loan to purchase the same vehicle? Explain.

EXERCISE 11.4

Answers to the odd-numbered problems can be found in the end matter.

INTERMEDIATE PROBLEMS

Calculate all interest rates accurate to the nearest 0.01%.

1. How much must be invested at the beginning of each year in order to accumulate $750,000 after 25 years? The invested funds earn 6% compounded annually.

2. What beginning-of-month withdrawals can a $400,000 RRIF (Registered Retirement Income Fund) sustain for 20 years if the investments within the RRIF earn 3.6% compounded monthly?

3. Rounding up to the next integer, how long will it take an RRSP to grow to $600,000 if an investor contributes $2500 at the beginning of each quarter and the RRSP earns 4% compounded quarterly?

4. Rounding up to the next month, for how long will a $100,000 fund sustain beginning-of-month withdrawals of $700 if the fund earns 6% compounded monthly?

5. Ichiro is checking potential outcomes for the growth of his RRSP. He plans to make contributions of $500 at the beginning of each month. What monthly compounded nominal rate of return must his RRSP earn for its future value after 25 years to be

   a. $300,000?   **b.** $500,000?

6. Gina has $500,000 accumulated in her RRSP and intends to use the amount to purchase a 20-year annuity. She is investigating the size of quarterly payments she can expect to receive, depending upon the rate of return earned by the funds. What quarterly compounded nominal rate of return must the funds earn for the beginning-of-quarter payment to be

   a. $8000?   **b.** $10,000?

7. To accumulate $200,000 after 20 years, what amount must be invested each year if the investment earns 6% compounded annually and the contributions are made

   a. at the beginning of each year?

   b. at the end of each year?

8. What maximum annual withdrawals will a $200,000 fund earning 5% compounded annually sustain for 20 years if the withdrawals are made
   a. at the beginning of each year?
   b. at the end of each year?

9. Triex Manufacturing wants to accumulate $500,000 for an expansion planned to begin in five years. If today Triex makes the first of equal quarterly payments into a fund earning 3.6% compounded monthly, what size should these payments be?

10. An insurance company wishes to offer customers a monthly installment alternative to the annual premium plan. All premiums are payable at the beginning of the period of coverage. The monthly payment plan is to include an interest charge of 12% compounded monthly on the unpaid balance of the annual premium. What will be the monthly premium for a policy that would cost $1800 if paid in full at the start of the year?

11. Advance Leasing calculates the monthly payments on its three-year leases on the basis of recovering the capital cost of the leased equipment and earning a 6.3% compounded monthly rate of return on its capital investment. What will be the monthly lease payment on equipment that costs $8500?

12. Shane is about to have his 25th birthday. He has set a goal of retiring at age 55 with $600,000 in an RRSP. For planning purposes he is assuming that his RRSP will earn 6% compounded annually.
    a. What contribution on each birthday from age 25 to 54 inclusive will be required to accumulate the desired amount in his RRSP?
    b. If he waits five years before starting his RRSP, what contribution on each birthday from age 30 to 54 inclusive will be required to accumulate the target amount?

13. Wendy will soon turn 33. She wants to accumulate $300,000 in an RRSP by her 60th birthday. How much larger will her annual contributions have to be if they are made at the end of each year (from age 33 to age 59 inclusive) instead of at the beginning of each year? Assume that her RRSP will earn 4% compounded annually.

14. CompuLease leases computers and peripheral equipment to businesses. What lease payments must CompuLease charge at the beginning of each quarter of a five-year lease if it is to recover the $40,000 capital cost of a system and earn 9% compounded quarterly on its investment?

15. Island Water Taxi has decided to lease another boat for five years rather than finance the purchase of the boat at an interest rate of 7.5% compounded monthly. It has set up a long-term lease liability of $43,000. What is the lease payment at the beginning of each month?

16. Rentown advertised a computer at a cash price of $1699 and at a rent-to-own rate of $129 at the beginning of each month for 24 months. What effective rate of interest is a customer paying to acquire the computer in a rent-to-own transaction?

17. Kent wants to save half of the $30,000 purchase price of a new car by making monthly deposits of $700, beginning today, into a T-bill savings account earning 3.3% compounded monthly. How long will it take him to reach his goal?

18. Central Personnel's accountant set up a long-term lease liability of $11,622.73 to recognize a new contract for the lease of office furniture. She used the firm's 4.8% monthly compounded cost of borrowing as the discount rate. If the lease payment at the beginning of each month is $265.55, what is the term of the lease?

19. How much longer will a $100,000 fund earning 4% compounded semiannually sustain beginning-of-month withdrawals of $900 than beginning-of-month withdrawals of $1000?

20. How many fewer deposits will it take to accumulate savings of $100,000 with beginning-of-month deposits of $220 than with beginning-of-month deposits of $200? The savings earn 5.4% compounded monthly.

21. An RRSP is now worth $130,000 after contributions of $2500 at the beginning of every six months for 16 years. What effective rate of return has the plan earned?

22. Pembroke Golf Club's initiation fee is $5500. It offers an installment payment alternative of $1000 down and $1000 at the end of each year for five years. What effective rate of interest is being charged on the installment plan?

ADVANCED PROBLEMS

23. The MSRP on a Nissan Maxima 3.5 SV is $38,625. The interest rate on a 48-month lease is 1.9% compounded monthly. What is the monthly lease payment, assuming a down payment of $5400 and a residual value of $11,990?

24. The $298.28 monthly payment on a 48-month lease of a Kia SOUL was based on a down payment of $2500, an interest rate of 3.9% compounded monthly, and a residual value of $9600. What is the full price (MSRP) for the car?

25. A Smart ForTwo cabriolet (MSRP $23,900) can be leased for $258.89 per month. This payment is based on an interest rate of 3.9% compounded monthly, a down payment of $1425, and a residual value of $12,794. What is the term of the lease?

26. What monthly compounded nominal rate of interest is being charged if the payment on a 36-month lease of a Jaguar XF (MSRP $66,400) is $899 at the start of each month? The down payment is $4999 and the residual value is $35,295.

27. Mr. and Mrs. Friedrich have just opened a Registered Education Savings Plan (RESP) for their daughter. They want the plan to pay $3000 at the beginning of each half year for four years, starting nine years from now when their daughter will enter college or university. What semiannual contributions, including one today, must they make for the next nine years if the RESP earns 3.25% compounded semiannually?

28. Ambleside Golf Club's board of directors has set next year's membership fee at $1900, payable at the beginning of the year. The board has instructed its accountant to calculate beginning-of-quarter and beginning-of-month payment plans that provide a 15% semiannually compounded rate of return on the unpaid balance of the annual fee. What will be the amounts of the quarterly and monthly payments?

29. If you contribute $1000 to an RRSP at the beginning of every three months for 25 years and then use the accumulated funds to purchase an annuity paying $2000 at the beginning of each month, what will be the term of the annuity? Include the final, smaller payment. Assume that the RRSP earns 4.5% compounded quarterly, and the funds invested in the annuity earn 3.6% compounded monthly.

30. Jamal borrowed $350 from his mother at the beginning of every month for $2\frac{1}{2}$ years while he attended Seneca College.

    a. If the interest rate on the accumulating debt was 6% compounded semiannually, what amount did he owe his mother at the end of the $2\frac{1}{2}$-year period?

    b. If he made the first monthly payment of $175 on the loan at the end of the first month following the $2\frac{1}{2}$-year period, how long after the date he entered college will he have the loan repaid?

Key Terms

Residual value

Summary of Notation and Key Formulas

FORMULA (10-1n) $n = \dfrac{\ln\left(1 + \dfrac{i \times FV}{PMT}\right)}{\ln(1 + i)}$ Finding the number of annuity payments, given FV, PMT, and i

FORMULA (10-2n) $n = -\dfrac{\ln\left(1 - \dfrac{i \times PV}{PMT}\right)}{\ln(1 + i)}$ Finding the number of annuity payments, given PV, PMT, and i

FORMULA (10-4n) $n = \dfrac{\ln\left[1 + \dfrac{i \times FV(\text{due})}{PMT(1 + i)}\right]}{\ln(1 + i)}$ Finding the number of payments, given $FV(\text{due})$, PMT, and i

FORMULA (10-5n) $n = -t\,\dfrac{\ln\left[1 - \dfrac{i \times PV(\text{due})}{PMT(1 + i)}\right]}{\ln(1 + i)}$ Finding the number of payments, given $PV(\text{due})$, PMT, and i

Review Problems

The following Review Problems represent a wide range of annuity problems. Before attempting each, be sure to write down the type of annuity. This small step will help you to select the proper approach for solving the problem. You may find it useful to refer back to Figure 10.7, the annuity classification flowchart, for help in identifying the annuity type.

Interest rates should be calculated accurate to the nearest 0.01%.

Answers to the odd-numbered review problems can be found in the end matter.

INTERMEDIATE PROBLEMS

1.   **LO1** Calculate the amount that must be invested at the end of every six months at 4.75% compounded semiannually in order to accumulate $500,000 after 20 years.

2.   **LO2** If $400,000 accumulated in an RRSP is used to purchase an annuity earning 3.9% compounded monthly and paying $3750 at the end of each month, what will be the term of the annuity?

3.   **LO1** What end-of-month payments for 15 years will pay off a $50,000 loan at 8.25% compounded monthly?

4.   **LO3** What semiannually compounded rate and effective rate of interest are being charged on a $12,000 loan if payments of $1022.89 at the end of every six months will repay the loan in seven years?

5. **LO3** or **LO4** A furniture retailer offers a financing plan on a $1500 purchase. The customer will pay four equal quarterly payments of $400 to pay for the purchase. The first of the four payments is made on the date of purchase. What effective rate of interest is the retailer charging on the loan?

6. **LO2** The interest rate on a $100,000 loan is 6% compounded monthly. How much longer will it take to pay off the loan with end-of-month payments of $1000 than with end-of-month payments of $1050?

7. **LO3** For $100,000, Royal Life Insurance Co. will sell a 20-year annuity paying $802.76 at the end of each month. What monthly compounded nominal rate and effective rate of return does the annuitant (the buyer of the annuity) earn on the invested funds?

8. **LO4** Heather wants to accumulate $4000 for a trip to Hong Kong that she will take in two years from now. Her investment account earns 4.2% compounded monthly. What amount must Heather deposit at the beginning of each month for the next two years to reach her savings target?

9. **LO1** Howardson Electric obtained a $90,000 loan at 9.75% compounded monthly. What size of payments at the end of every six months will repay the loan in 10 years?

10. **LO2** An annuity purchased for $175,000 pays $4000 at the end of every quarter. How long will the payments continue if the funds earn 3% compounded semiannually?

11. **LO3** After contributing $2000 at the end of each quarter for $13\frac{3}{4}$ years, Foster has accumulated $151,147.22 in his RRSP. What effective rate of return was earned by the RRSP over the entire period?

12. **LO4** RRSP contributions of $500 are made at the beginning of every six months. How many more contributions will it take to reach $750,000 if the RRSP earns 4% compounded semiannually than if it earns 5% compounded semiannually?

13. **a. LO2** How long will it take payments of $600 at the end of every month to repay a $65,000 loan if the interest rate on the loan is 9.5% compounded semiannually?

    b. LO2 How much will the time to repay the loan be reduced if the payments are $50 more per month?

14. **LO3** If $100,000 will purchase a 20-year annuity paying $632.65 at each month's end, what monthly compounded nominal rate and effective rate of interest are earned by the funds?

15. **LO3** A finance company paid a furniture retailer $1934 for a conditional sale contract requiring 12 end-of-month payments of $175. What effective rate of return does the finance company earn on the purchase?

16. **LO3** or **LO4** The annual membership dues in the Rolling Meadows Golf and Country Club can be paid by four payments of $898.80 at the beginning of each calendar quarter, instead of by a single payment of $3428 at the beginning of the year. What effective rate of interest is the club charging its members who select the quarterly installment plan?

17. **LO1** The interest rate on a $30,000 loan is 4.5% compounded monthly. What end-of-month payments are required to pay off the loan in eight years?

18. **LO2** How much sooner will a $65,000 loan at 7.2% compounded monthly be paid off if the end-of-month payments are $625 instead of $600? What will be the approximate saving in (nominal) interest costs over the life of the loan?

19. **LO1** Anne has already saved $6,400. She will deposit this into a savings account that earns 4.1% compounded semiannually. Anne's goal is to have a total of $75,000 in six years from now. How much will she need to deposit to her savings account at the end of every month for the next six years in order to reach her goal?

20. **LO4** Fletcher Machine Shop has decided to lease a piece of equipment for eight years rather than finance the purchase of the equipment at an interest rate of 7.2% compounded monthly. It has set up a long-term lease liability of $84,000. What is the lease payment at the beginning of each month?

21. **LO1** What payments must be made at the end of each quarter to an RRSP earning 4.2% compounded annually so that its value $8\frac{1}{2}$ years from now will be $15,000?

22. **LO3** $3500 will be contributed to an RRSP at the end of every six months for 20 years. What effective rate of return must the plan earn if it is to be worth $250,000 at the end of the 20 years?

23. **LO4** Mr. Schwartz used the $245,000 available in his RRSP to purchase an annuity that will pay him $2000 at the beginning of every month. If the funds in the annuity earn interest at 6% compounded quarterly, for how long will Mr. Schwartz receive annuity payments?

24. **LO3 or LO4** Continental Life Insurance Company of Canada offered $250,000 of term life insurance to a 40-year-old female non-smoker for an annual premium of $447.50 (payable at the start of the year). Alternatively, the policyholder can pay $38.82 at the start of each month. What effective rate of interest is charged to those who pay monthly?

25. **LO1 LO2** The McGowans are arranging a $220,000 mortgage loan from their bank. The interest rate on the loan will be 4.9% compounded semiannually.

    a. What will the end-of-month payments be if the loan has a 20-year term?

    b. If the McGowans choose to pay $1500 at the end of each month, how long will it take to pay off the loan?

26. **LO1** By the time he turns 60, Justin (just turned age 31) wants to have $250,000 in his RRSP. What annual contributions on his 32nd through 60th birthdays (inclusive) are required to meet this goal if the RRSP earns 4% compounded annually?

ADVANCED PROBLEMS

27. **LO1** The interest rate on a $100,000 loan is 7.5% compounded quarterly.

    a. What end-of-quarter payments will reduce the balance to $75,000 after five years?

    b. If the same payments continue, what will be the balance 10 years after the date that the loan was received?

28. **LO2** Dana's RRSP investment account currently has a balance of $21,963.32. She intends to continue to deposit $700 at the end of every quarter. If her investments earn 5% compounded semiannually, how long will it take Dana to accumulate a total of $100,000?

29. **LO2** A 70-year-old man can purchase either of the following annuities for the same price from a life insurance company. A 20-year-term annuity will pay $394 at each month-end. A life annuity will pay $440 at the end of each month until the death of the annuitant. To what age must the man survive for the life annuity to have the greater economic value? Assume that money can earn 3.3% compounded monthly.

30. **LO3** An advertisement for Ford trucks offered "2.9% financing (for 48 months) or $4000 cash back." A truck buyer financed $40,000 at the low interest rate instead of paying $36,000 cash (after the $4000 rebate). What was the effective rate of interest on the loan if the forgone cash rebate is treated as part of the cost of financing? (The 2.9% interest rate is a monthly compounded nominal rate.)

31. **LO3 or LO4** A magazine offers a one-year subscription rate of $63.80 and a three-year subscription rate of $159.80, both payable at the start of the subscription period. Assuming that you intend to continue the subscription for three years and that the one-year rate does not increase over the next two

years, what effective rate of "return on investment" will be "earned" by paying for a three-year subscription now instead of three consecutive one-year subscriptions?

32. **LO1** Mr. Braun wants the value of his RRSP 25 years from now to have the purchasing power of $400,000 in current dollars.

   a. Assuming an inflation rate of 2.5% per year, what nominal dollar amount should Mr. Braun have in his RRSP after 25 years?

   b. What contributions should he make at the end of every three months to achieve the goal if his RRSP earns 5.5% compounded semiannually?

33. **LO2** Georgina is about to retire with $188,000 in her RRSP. She will use the funds to purchase an annuity providing payments of $6000 at the end of each quarter. What will be the annuity's term if the funds invested in the annuity earn 4.8% compounded monthly?

34. **LO1** Noreen's RRSP is currently worth $125,000. For the next 10 years, she will make contributions at the end of every six months. How much does Noreen need to contribute at the end of every six months for the next 10 years to reach her goal of having a total of $300,000 when she retires? Her RRSP earns 4% compounded annually.

35. **LO1** A conditional sale contract for a $1450 transaction required a 10% down payment with the balance to be paid by 12 equal monthly payments. The first payment is due one month after the date of the purchase. The retailer charges an interest rate of 13% compounded semiannually on the unpaid balance. What is the monthly payment?

© Peathegee Inc. RF

CHAPTER 12
Annuities: Special Situations

LEARNING OBJECTIVES
After completing this chapter, you will be able to:

LO1 Calculate the present value, period of deferral, periodic payment, and number of payments for deferred annuities

LO2 Calculate the present value and payment of a perpetuity and a deferred perpetuity

LO3 Calculate the present value and future value of an annuity whose payment size grows at a constant rate

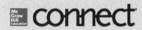 **connect** Throughout this chapter interactive charts and Help Me Solve It videos are marked with a ↗.

THREE SPECIAL CASES OF ANNUITIES are examined in this chapter. The first is deferred annuities. A deferred annuity is an annuity that does not begin until a time interval has passed. We will learn how to adapt what we already know about annuities to take into consideration the delayed, or "deferred," start.

The second is perpetuities—annuities whose payments continue forever. For example, a college might receive a $200,000 gift or bequest to offer an annual scholarship in perpetuity. The mathematics of perpetuities turn out to be surprisingly simple.

The third special case is constant-growth annuities—annuities whose payments increase at a steady rate. We often make a "constant-growth assumption" in long-term financial planning. A growing annuity is usually a better approximation of our saving pattern than a constant payment annuity. As wages increase over time (even if only through inflation), most people are able to save more each year. Many pension plans index or link pension payments to the Consumer Price Index. The payments increase over time by the same percentage as the CPI. Again, a growing annuity is a good representation of this payment pattern.

12.1 | Deferred Annuities

LO1 A **deferred annuity** may be viewed as an *ordinary* annuity that does not begin until a time interval (named the **period of deferral**) has passed. Figure 12.1 shows a deferred annuity on a time line. In the figure,

$$d = \text{Equivalent number of payment intervals in the period of deferral}$$

Note that the period of deferral ends one payment interval *before* the first payment. Viewed from the *end* of the period of deferral, the payments then form an ordinary annuity.

FIGURE 12.1 Time Diagram for a Deferred Annuity

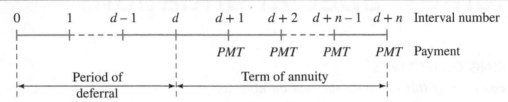

The future value of a deferred annuity is the future value of all of the payments at the end of the last payment interval. Can you see what needs to be done to determine the future value? Looking back from the end of the final payment interval, the payments appear as they would for an ordinary annuity. So it is a simple matter of doing the same future value calculation you learned in Section 10.2 for ordinary annuities.

The present value of a deferred annuity is the present value of all of the payments at the *beginning* of the period of deferral. How can the present value be calculated, using ideas you have already learned? The two regions identified in Figure 12.1 suggest a two-step procedure indicated in Figure 12.2.

1. Calculate the present value, PV_1, of the payments at the *end* of the period of deferral—this is just the present value of an ordinary annuity.
2. Calculate the present value, PV_2, of the Step 1 amount at the *beginning* of the period of deferral.

FIGURE 12.2 The Present Value of a Deferred Annuity

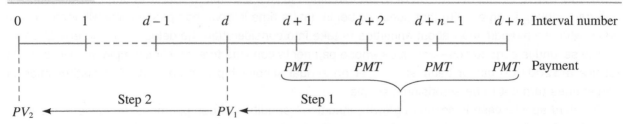

EXAMPLE 12.1A | **Calculating the Present Value of a Deferred Annuity**

Mr. and Mrs. Templeton are setting up a fund to help finance their granddaughter's college education. They want her to be able to withdraw $3000 every three months for three years after she starts college. Her first withdrawal will be $5\frac{1}{2}$ years from now. If the fund can earn 3.2% compounded quarterly, what single amount contributed today will provide for the withdrawals?

SOLUTION

The money the Templetons invest now will have $5\frac{1}{2}$ years to grow before withdrawals start. Thereafter, further earnings of money still in the fund will help support the periodic withdrawals. The one-time "up front" contribution is the present value of the withdrawals.

The time diagram is presented as follows. Viewed from today, the withdrawals form a deferred annuity. In order to have an *ordinary* annuity following the period of deferral, the period of deferral must end three months before the first payment. This makes the period of deferral only $5\frac{1}{4}$ years.

Since payments and compounding both occur quarterly, we have a deferred *simple* annuity with

$$PMT = \$3000, \; n = 4(3) = 12, \; d = 4(5.25) = 21, \quad \text{and} \quad i = \tfrac{3.2\%}{4} = 0.8\%$$

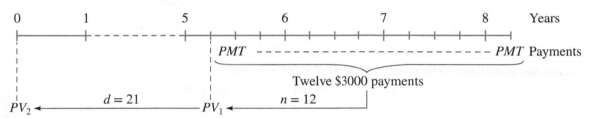

The present value of the payments $5\frac{1}{4}$ years from now is

$$PV_1 = PMT\left[\frac{1 - (1 + i)^{-n}}{i}\right]$$

$$= \$3000\left(\frac{1 - 1.008^{-12}}{0.008}\right)$$

$$= \$34{,}195.844$$

3.2 **I/Y**
P/Y 4 **ENTER**
(making $C/Y = P/Y = 4$)
12 **N**
3000 **PMT**
0 **FV**
CPT **PV**
Ans: −34,195.844

The present value of the payments today is

$$PV_2 = FV(1 + i)^{-n}$$
$$= \$34{,}195.844(1.008)^{-21}$$
$$= \$28{,}926.92$$

Same *I/Y, P/Y, C/Y*
21 **N**
0 **PMT**
34195.844 **FV**
CPT **PV**
Ans: −28,926.92

The Templetons can provide the desired financial support for their granddaughter by putting $22,926.92 into the fund today.

➡ **Check your understanding:** Suppose Mr. and Mrs. Templeton want their granddaughter to be able to withdraw $3800 every three months for three years after she starts college, and her first withdrawal will be eight years from now. If the fund can earn 4.2% compounded quarterly, what single amount contributed today will provide for the withdrawals? (Answer: $30,841.48)

▬▬▶ **Related problem:** #3 in Exercise 12.1

EXAMPLE 12.1B	Calculating the Length of the Deferral Period

Mrs. Sevard purchased a deferred annuity from an insurance company for $10,971. The money used to purchase the annuity will earn 6% compounded quarterly. The annuity will provide 16 quarterly payments of $1000. If the first payment is to be received on October 1, 2020, when did Mrs. Sevard purchase the deferred annuity?

SOLUTION

The key idea on which we base the solution is that the purchase price is the present value, on the date of purchase, of all 16 annuity payments. The payments form a deferred simple annuity with $PMT = 1000, $n = 16$, and $i = \frac{6\%}{4} = 1.5\%$. The data and solution steps are presented in the following diagram.

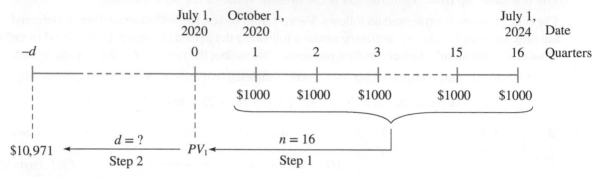

For the payments to be treated as an *ordinary* annuity, the period of deferral must end on July 1, 2020 (one payment interval before the first payment).

The present value of the payments on July 1, 2020 is

$$PV_1 = PMT\left[\frac{1 - (1 + i)^{-n}}{i}\right]$$

$$= \$1000\left(\frac{1 - 1.015^{-16}}{0.015}\right)$$

$$= \$14,131.26$$

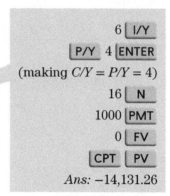

6 | I/Y

P/Y 4 ENTER

(making $C/Y = P/Y = 4$)

16 | N

1000 | PMT

0 | FV

CPT | PV

Ans: −14,131.26

This amount is the future value, at the end of the period of deferral, of the $10,971 purchase price. We must now use formula (9-2) to calculate the number of compounding periods required for $10,971 to grow to $14,131.26.

$$d = \frac{\ln\left(\frac{FV}{PV}\right)}{\ln(1 + i)}$$

$$= \frac{\ln\left(\frac{\$14,131.26}{\$10,971}\right)}{\ln 1.015}$$

$$= 17.00$$

Same *I/Y, P/Y, C/Y*

10971 +/− | PV

0 | PMT

14131.26 | FV

CPT | N

Ans: 17.00

Therefore, the period of deferral is 17 calendar quarters (4 years, 3 months) before July 1, 2020. That puts the purchase date of the deferred annuity at April 1, 2016.

➡ **Check your understanding:** Mr. Bellarose purchased a deferred annuity for $16,301.86. The money used to purchase the annuity will earn 6% compounded semiannually. The annuity will provide nine semiannual payments of $2500, beginning on July 1, 2019. When did Mr. Bellarose purchase the deferred annuity? (Answer: January 1, 2016)

▰▰▰▶ **Related problem:** #5 in Exercise 12.1

EXAMPLE 12.1C | **Calculating the Periodic Payment in a Deferred Annuity**

Budget Appliances has a promotion on a washer-dryer combination selling for $1750. Buyers will pay "no money down and no payments for six months." The first of 12 equal monthly payments is required six months from the purchase date. What should the monthly payments be if Budget Appliances is to earn 15% compounded monthly on its account receivable during both the deferral period and the repayment period?

SOLUTION

Viewed from the date of the sale, the payments form a *deferred simple* annuity—a 12-payment *ordinary simple* annuity following a five-month period of deferral. That is,

$$n = 12, d = 5, \quad \text{and} \quad i = \frac{15\%}{12} = 1.25\%$$

In effect, Budget Appliances makes a $1750 loan to the customer on the date of the sale. As indicated on the following time line, the balance owed on the loan will increase to *FV* over the next five months as interest accrues. Then the 12 monthly payments will pay off this balance. Hence,

$$\left(\begin{array}{c}\text{Future value of \$1750}\\\text{at the end of Month 5}\end{array}\right) = \left(\begin{array}{c}\text{Present value of the payments}\\\text{at the end of Month 5}\end{array}\right)$$

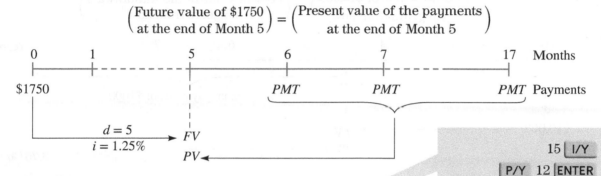

The amount owed after five months will be

$$\begin{aligned}FV &= PV(1 + i)^n\\&= \$1750(1.0125)^5\\&= \$1862.14\end{aligned}$$

This amount is the present value of the 12-payment ordinary simple annuity. Substituting in formula (10-2),

$$PV = PMT\left[\frac{1 - (1 + i)^{-n}}{i}\right]$$

$$\$1862.14 = PMT\left[\frac{1 - (1.0125)^{-12}}{0.0125}\right]$$

$$\$1862.14 = PMT(11.07931)$$

Hence,

$$PMT = \frac{\$1862.14}{11.07931} = \$168.07$$

Monthly payments of $168.07 will provide Budget Appliances with a return of 15% compounded monthly on its account receivable.

➡ **Check your understanding:** Suppose a washer-dryer combination selling for $2300 is sold during a "no money down" promotion. The first of 12 equal monthly payments is required eight months after the date of purchase. How much will the monthly payments be if the retailer is to earn 18% compounded monthly during both the deferral period and the repayment period? (Answer: $234.03/month)

▪▬▶ **Related problem:** #18 in Exercise 12.1

EXAMPLE 12.1D	Calculating the Number of Payments in a Deferred Annuity

$10,000 is invested in a fund earning 3.75% compounded semiannually. Five years later, the first semiannual withdrawal of $1000 will be taken from the fund. After how many withdrawals will the fund be depleted? (The final payment that extinguishes the fund will be smaller than $1000. Include it in the count.)

SOLUTION

Viewed from the date of the investment, the withdrawals form a deferred *simple* annuity. The period of deferral is $4\frac{1}{2}$ years long. We have

$$PMT = \$1000, \quad d = 2(4.5) = 9, \quad \text{and} \quad i = \frac{3.75\%}{2} = 1.875\%$$

In effect, the accumulated funds after 4.5 years purchase a "home-made" annuity. As indicated in the following diagram,

$$\left(\begin{array}{c} \text{Future value of \$10,000} \\ \text{4.5 years from now} \end{array} \right) = \left(\begin{array}{c} \text{Present value of the withdrawals} \\ \text{4.5 years from now} \end{array} \right)$$

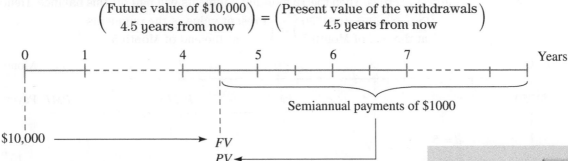

The future value of $10,000 after $4\frac{1}{2}$ years will be

$$FV = PV(1 + i)^n$$
$$= \$10,000(1 + 0.01875)^9$$
$$= \$11,819.76$$

Now use formula (10-2n) to obtain n.

$$n = -\frac{\ln\left[1 - \frac{i \times PV}{PMT}\right]}{\ln(1 + i)}$$

$$= -\frac{\ln\left[1 - \frac{0.01875 \times \$11,819.76}{\$1000}\right]}{\ln(1.01875)}$$

$$= 13.49$$

The fund will be depleted after 14 withdrawals. (There will be 13 full withdrawals of $1000, and a final, 14th withdrawal that will be less than $1000.)

3.75 I/Y
P/Y 2 ENTER
(making C/Y = P/Y = 2)
9 N
10000 +/– PV
0 PMT
CPT FV
Ans: 11,819.76

Same I/Y, P/Y, C/Y
11819.76 +/– PV
1000 PMT
0 FV
CPT N
Ans: 13.49

➡ **Check your understanding:** $25,000 is invested in a fund earning 5% compounded quarterly. Ten years later, the first quarterly withdrawal of $5000 will be taken from the fund. After how many withdrawals will the fund be depleted? (Include the final, smaller payment in the count.) (Answer: 9 withdrawals)

▨▶ **Related problem:** #21 in Exercise 12.1

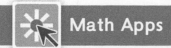 **Math Apps**

CARD TRICKS: THE "NO INTEREST, NO PAYMENTS FOR A YEAR" TRAP

"No interest and nothing to pay for a six-month or one-year grace period" is a common type of promotion offered by home improvement stores, and by department stores on the sale of furniture, major appliances, home electronics, and other "big ticket" items. In most cases, you must put the purchase on the store's own credit card in order to qualify for the deferral of payment.

But here's the catch. If you don't pay the purchase price *before* the no-interest grace period ends, you are likely to be charged interest for the *entire* grace period at the credit card's full rate (typically 28.8%). Since this circumstance proves highly profitable for the retailer, you can't expect to receive a reminder from the retailer as you approach the end of your "interest-free" period.

Suppose you try to argue that "no interest" ought to mean "no interest payable for the grace period regardless of whether you pay during the grace period." You are then likely to be referred to the fine print in the purchase or credit card agreement where it indicates that interest actually accrues during the grace period, but this interest will be cancelled if you pay the principal within the grace period. So technically it's not an "interest-free" period, but rather a grace period during which the retailer will cancel or rebate the interest if the principal is paid on time.

Question

On a $5000 purchase (including sales taxes) under a "no interest and nothing to pay for one year" promotion, how much interest will you be charged for the grace period if you are one day late on your payment of the principal? Use an interest rate of 28.8% compounded monthly.

 Checkpoint Questions

1. What is meant by a deferred annuity?

2. How long is the period of deferral if the first quarterly payment of a deferred annuity will be paid $3\frac{1}{2}$ years from today?

3. Why do we terminate the period of deferral one payment interval before the first payment?

4. For the same n, *PMT*, and i, would it cost more or less to purchase a deferred annuity than an ordinary annuity? Explain.

EXERCISE 12.1

Answers to the odd-numbered problems can be found in the end matter.

INTERMEDIATE PROBLEMS

1. The first of six semiannual payments of $2000 will be made $5\frac{1}{2}$ years from today. What is the present value of this deferred annuity using a discount rate of 3% compounded semiannually?

2. Jie wishes to purchase a five-year annuity that will pay quarterly payments of $750. The first payment will be paid 3 years and 9 months from today. How much will Jie pay today for this annuity if it is priced to provide a rate of return of 4.2% compounded quarterly?

3. What minimum initial amount of money, invested today to earn 6% compounded monthly, will support a monthly payout of $500 for $3\frac{1}{2}$ years if the first payment occurs 2 years and 10 months from now?

4. What amount of money invested now will provide monthly payments of $200 for five years, if the ordinary annuity is deferred for $3\frac{1}{2}$ years and the money earns 3.75% compounded monthly?

5. A deferred annuity is comprised of eight annual payments of $1500. What is the period of deferral if the present value of the payments, discounted at 4.9% compounded annually, is $8037.87?

6. For $30,000, Manny purchased a deferred annuity from an insurance company that will pay him quarterly payments of $852.48 for $12\frac{1}{2}$ years. The payments are based upon the purchase amount earning 4.1% compounded quarterly. When will Manny receive the first payment?

7. Ronelda has accumulated $49,248.55 in her RRSP. If she makes no further contributions and her RRSP continues to earn 4.5% compounded monthly, for how long a period of deferral must she wait before her RRSP can sustain month-end withdrawals of $400 for 15 years?

8. Mr. Haddit plans to retire eight years from today. He projects that he will need $30,000 per year in his retirement, which he assumes will be for 15 years. The first payment will be nine years from today. To fund his retirement, Mr. Haddit will invest a lump amount today and later use it to sustain the 15 withdrawals. If his investment earns 6% compounded annually, how much must he invest today?

9. Marion's grandfather's will established a trust that will pay her $1500 every three months for 11 years. The first payment will be made 6 years from now, when she turns 19. If money is worth 3.5% compounded quarterly, what is today's economic value of the bequest?

10. Using an inheritance he recently received, Sam wants to purchase a deferred annuity that will pay $5000 every three months between age 60 (when he plans to retire) and age 65 (when his permanent pension will begin). The first payment is to be three months after he reaches 60, and the last is to be on his 65th birthday. If Sam's current age is 50 years and 6 months, and the invested funds will earn 4.4% compounded quarterly, what amount must he invest in the deferred annuity?

11. A conditional-sale contract requires the debtor to make six quarterly payments of $569, with the first payment due in six months. What amount will a finance company pay to purchase the contract on the date of sale if the finance company requires a rate of return of 16% compounded quarterly?

12. If money can earn 6.5% compounded annually for the next 20 years, which of the following annuities has the greater economic value today: $1000 paid at the end of each of the next 10 years, or 10 annual payments of $2000 with the first payment occurring 11 years from today?

13. Negotiations between Delco Manufacturing and the union representing its employees are at an impasse. The union is seeking a 3% wage increase. Delco's offer is 1%. The employees have passed a vote authorizing job action. Suppose the union succeeds in winning the 3% increase after a two-month strike. For an employee 15 years from retirement, will there be any economic gain? Compare the current economic values of (1) 10 years' end-of-month wages at the employer's offer (101% of last year's wages) vs. (2) wages including a 3% increase to the same time horizon but after a two-month strike. Assume money is worth 5.4% compounded monthly.

14. A $35,000 loan bearing interest at 10% compounded quarterly was repaid, after a period of deferral, by quarterly payments of $1573.83 over 12 years. What was the time interval between the date of the loan and the first payment?

15. A $20,000 investment will be allowed to grow at 4.5% compounded semiannually until it can support semiannual withdrawals of $1000 for 20 years. Rounded to the nearest month, how long before the first withdrawal must the investment be allowed to grow?

16. Mrs. Corriveau has just retired at age 58 with $299,317 in her RRSP. She plans to live off other savings for a few years and allow her RRSP to continue to grow on a tax-deferred basis until there is an amount sufficient to purchase a 25-year annuity paying $2000 at the end of each month. If her RRSP and the annuity each earn 3.75% compounded monthly, how much longer must she let her RRSP grow (before she buys the annuity)?

17. Kenneth borrowed $5000 today at a rate of 6.6% compounded quarterly. The loan will be repaid with equal quarterly payments for two years. The first payment will occur in nine months from today. Interest begins accruing today. How much will the quarterly payments be during the two-year repayment period?

18. During a one-week promotion, Al's Appliance Warehouse is planning to offer terms of "nothing down and nothing to pay for four months" on major appliances priced above $500. Four months after the date of sale, the first of eight equal monthly payments is due. If the customer is to pay interest at the rate of 12% compounded monthly on the outstanding balance from the date of sale, what will be the monthly payments on a dishwasher priced at $995?

19. As of Brice's 54th birthday, he has accumulated $154,000 in his Registered Retirement Savings Plan (RRSP). What size of end-of-month payments in a 20-year annuity will these funds purchase at age 65 if he makes no further contributions? Assume that his RRSP and the investment in the annuity will earn 4.2% compounded monthly.

20. Nancy borrowed $8000 from her grandfather to buy a car when she started college. The interest rate being charged is 4.5% compounded monthly. Nancy is to make the first $200 monthly payment on the loan three years after the date of the loan. How long after the date of the initial loan will she make the final payment?

21. $10,000 was invested in a fund earning 2.4% compounded monthly. How many monthly withdrawals of $300 can be made if the first occurs $3\frac{1}{2}$ years after the date of the initial investment? Count the final smaller withdrawal.

ADVANCED PROBLEMS

22. You have just received a $35,000 gift from your parents, representing your share of the sale of the family cottage. You will invest this money, then use it to fund a round the world trip that you plan to commence in exactly two years from now. In exactly two years from now, when you begin your trip, you will make the first of a series of monthly withdrawals of $4000. When the $4000 per month withdrawals have depleted your savings, you will come home. How long will your trip last if your money earns 4% compounded monthly during the entire time? Include the final, smaller withdrawal, as you will budget carefully during your last month of travel.

23. Twelve years ago, Mr. Lawton rolled a $17,000 retiring allowance into an RRSP that subsequently earned 10% compounded semiannually. Today he will transfer the funds to a Registered Retirement Income Fund (RRIF) earning 5% compounded quarterly from which he will receive $2000 at the end of every quarter. How long will the withdrawals continue? Include the last, smaller withdrawal in the count.

24. Leslie received a settlement when her employer declared her job redundant. Under special provisions of the *Income Tax Act*, she was eligible to put $22,000 of the settlement in an RRSP. Fifteen years from now, she intends to transfer the money from the RRSP to a Registered Retirement Income Fund (RRIF). Thereafter, Leslie will make equal withdrawals at the end of each quarter for 20 years. If both the RRSP and the RRIF earn 4.5% compounded quarterly, what will be the amount of each withdrawal?

25. Novell Electronics recently bought a patent that will allow it to bring a new product to market in $2\frac{1}{2}$ years. Sales forecasts indicate that the product will increase the quarterly profits by $18,000. If the patent cost $150,000, how long after the date of the patent purchase will it take for the additional profits to repay the original investment along with a return on investment of 4.5% compounded quarterly? Assume that the additional profits are received at the end of each quarter.

26. Dave and Morley borrowed $20,000 from Dave's father to make a down payment on a house. The interest rate on the loan is 4% compounded annually, but no payments are required for two years. The first monthly payment of $325 is due on the second anniversary of the loan. How long after the date of the original loan will the last payment be made?

27. A property development company obtained a $2.5 million loan to construct a commercial building. The interest rate on the loan is 5% compounded semiannually. The lender granted a period of deferral until rental revenues become established. The first quarterly payment of $100,000 is required 21 months after the date of the loan. How long after the date of the original loan will the last payment be made?

28. Bernice is about to retire with $139,000 in her RRSP. She will make no further contributions to the plan, but will allow it to accumulate earnings for another six years. Then she will purchase an annuity providing payments of $5000 at the end of each quarter. Assume that the RRSP will earn 4.5% compounded annually and the funds invested in the annuity will earn 3.6% compounded monthly. How long after the purchase of the annuity will its payments continue?

12.2 | Perpetuities

LO2 Suppose a $100,000 investment can earn 5% compounded annually. It will earn $5000 in the first year. If the $5000 is paid out from the investment account at the end of the year, the principal will remain at $100,000. As long as the investment continues to earn 5% compounded annually, $5000 can be paid out at the end of every year forever. The value of the investment (principal plus accrued interest) will rise steadily from $100,000 to $105,000 during any year, and then abruptly fall back to $100,000 when the $5000 is paid out on the last day of the year. Consequently, a graph of the investment's "Value" vs. "Time" has the sawtooth pattern shown in Figure 12.3.

FIGURE 12.3   Value of $100,000 Investment That Pays Out Only Its Interest Earnings

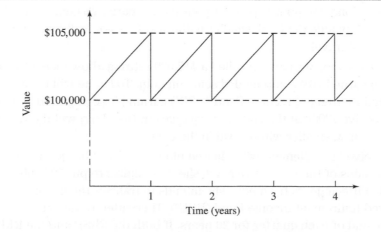

If more than $5000 is paid out at the end of each year, a portion of it will be principal. As the years go by, the principal balance will be eroded in an accelerating fashion because less and less interest is earned in each successive year. The trend is illustrated in Figure 12.4[1] where $6000 is paid each year. In conclusion, $5000 is the *maximum* amount that can be paid out at the end of every year *in perpetuity*.

FIGURE 12.4   Value of $100,000 Investment That Pays Out More Than Its Interest Earnings

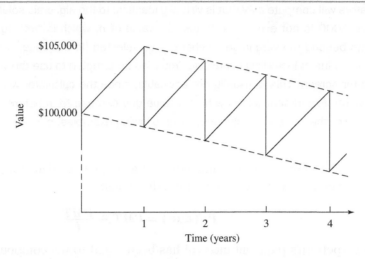

An annuity whose payments continue forever is called a **perpetuity**. Figure 12.5 presents a time diagram for an **ordinary perpetuity** with payments of size *PMT* at the *end* of each payment interval. In a **perpetuity due**, the payments will occur at the *beginning* of each payment interval.

FIGURE 12.5   Time Diagram for the Payments of an Ordinary Perpetuity

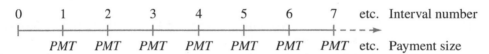

Let us use formula (10-2) to calculate the present value of annual payments of $5000 in perpetuity, discounting at 5% compounded annually. (Do you have any hunch what the present value will be?) We have *PMT* = $5000 and i = 5% = 0.05. But what value shall we use for *n*? To answer this question, recall that payments far in the future make a negligible contribution to present value. So let us just use $n = 1000$. (If you have any doubts about doing this, calculate the present value of the 1000th payment by itself. You'll find the 1000th payment is worth an infinitesimally small fraction of a cent today!) We obtain

$$PV = PMT\left[\frac{1 - (1 + i)^{-n}}{i}\right] = \$5000\left[\frac{1 - (1.05)^{-1000}}{0.05}\right] = \$100,000$$

We could have anticipated this result from our knowledge that the present value of an annuity is the amount required to purchase the annuity. If money can earn 5% compounded annually, $100,000 can purchase a perpetuity paying

$$0.05 \times \$100,000 = \$5000$$

at the end of every year. Since "0.05" is the value of i, "$100,000" is the value of *PV*, and "$5000" is the value of *PMT*, the general relationship among these three variables for an ordinary perpetuity is

$$i(PV) = PMT$$

That is,

PRESENT VALUE OF AN ORDINARY PERPETUITY $$PV = \frac{PMT}{i}$$ (12-1)

---

[1]   Figures 12.3 and 12.4 were suggested by Oded Tal of Conestoga College.

TIP

Using a Financial Calculator to Solve Perpetuity Questions

A perpetuity is an annuity with an infinite number of payments. To use the preprogrammed functions of a financial calculator to solve perpetuity questions, enter a very large value for n. For example, if you use $n = 5000$, most financial calculators will compute a PV that is virtually identical to the algebraic solution. You may wonder why this is true, since 5000 is not even close to the real value of n, which is "infinity." The answer lies in the fact that payments beyond the very large number you've selected (in this case, 5000) are so far in the future that their present value is incredibly minuscule. You may be tempted to use the very largest n you can fill up on your calculator screen. This is usually not advisable, since the calculator will often not be able to handle such a large value. Experiment with how high a value you can use for n before the calculator returns an "ERROR" message. For the calculator solutions in the following examples, $n = 5000$ has been chosen.

A perpetuity due may be viewed as the combination of a single immediate payment and an ordinary perpetuity. Therefore, the present value of a perpetuity due is just

PRESENT VALUE OF A
PERPETUITY DUE
$$PV(\text{due}) = PMT + \frac{PMT}{i} \qquad\qquad \textbf{(12-2)}$$

To this point, the perpetuity's payment interval has been equal to the compounding interval. If this is not the case, we are dealing with an ordinary *general* perpetuity or a *general* perpetuity due. Then we must make the same adjustment that we did for annuities. That is, we must use the formula $i_2 = (1 + i)^c - 1$ to calculate the periodic interest rate that matches the payment interval, and substitute this value of i_2 for i in the PV formula. Alternately, if using a financial calculator, the P/Y and C/Y values we enter will differ from one another.

EXAMPLE 12.2A	Calculating the Endowment and Rate of Return Required to Sustain an Ordinary Perpetuity

A chartered bank is considering the establishment in perpetuity of a Visiting Professor Chair in Public Policy at a university. The ongoing cost will be $11,250 at the end of each month.

a. If money can earn 5.4% compounded monthly in perpetuity, what endowment is required to fund the position?

b. What monthly compounded nominal rate of return must an endowment of $2.25 million earn to fully fund the position?

SOLUTION

a. The payments form an *ordinary simple* perpetuity having

$$PMT = \$11{,}250 \quad \text{and} \quad i = \tfrac{5.4\%}{12} = 0.45\% \text{ per month}$$

The required endowment is

$$PV = \frac{PMT}{i}$$
$$= \frac{\$11{,}250}{0.0045}$$
$$= \$2{,}500{,}000$$

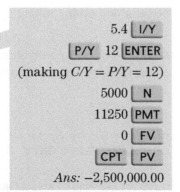

5.4 I/Y

P/Y 12 ENTER

(making $C/Y = P/Y = 12$)

5000 N

11250 PMT

0 FV

CPT PV

Ans: −2,500,000.00

b. With $PV = \$2,250,000$ and $PMT = \$11,250$ per month, the required interest rate per payment interval is

$$i = \frac{PMT}{PV} = \frac{\$11,250}{\$2,250,000} = 0.005 = 0.5\% \text{ per month}$$

The required nominal rate of return is

$$j = mi = 12(0.5\%) = 6\% \text{ compounded monthly}$$

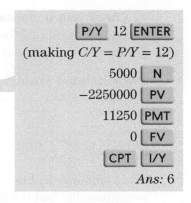

P/Y 12 ENTER
(making $C/Y = P/Y = 12$)
5000 N
−2250000 PV
11250 PMT
0 FV
CPT I/Y
Ans: 6

➡ **Check your understanding:** Suppose the ongoing cost of the position will be $15,400 at the end of every month. **a.** If money can earn 3% compounded monthly in perpetuity, what endowment is required to fund the position? **b.** What monthly compounded rate of return must an endowment of $3.36 million earn to fully fund the position? (Answer: **a.** $6,160,000 **b.** 5.5% compounded monthly)

▮▮▶ **Related problem:** #7 in Exercise 12.2

EXAMPLE 12.2B	Calculating the Price of a Perpetual Preferred Share

Some preferred shares promise a fixed periodic dividend in perpetuity.

What is the fair market value of a perpetual preferred share just after payment of a quarterly $0.50 dividend? The market requires a dividend yield of 5% compounded annually on preferred shares of similar risk.

SOLUTION

According to the Valuation Principle, the fair market value of a share is the present value of the expected dividend payments (discounted at the rate of return required in the financial market). Since a dividend has just been paid, the first dividend the purchaser will receive will be three months from now. Viewed from the purchase date, the dividend payments form an *ordinary* perpetuity. Since the payment interval is three months but the compounding interval is one year, the dividend payments form a *general* perpetuity.

Given: $PMT = \$0.50$, $i = \frac{5\%}{1} = 5\%$

We must first calculate the equivalent periodic rate for the three-month payment interval. (It will be *about* $\frac{5\%}{4} = 1.25\%$ per quarter.)

$$c = \frac{\text{Number of compoundings per year}}{\text{Number of payments per year}} = \frac{1}{4} = 0.25$$

Then

$$i_2 = (1 + i)^c - 1 = 1.05^{0.25} - 1 = 0.0122722 = 1.22722\% \text{ per quarter}$$

and

$$PV = \frac{PMT}{i_2} = \frac{\$0.50}{0.0122722} = \$40.74$$

Thus, the fair market value of a share is $40.74.

5 I/Y
P/Y 4 ENTER
C/Y 1 ENTER
5000 N
0.50 PMT
0 FV
CPT PV
Ans: −40.74

⇨ **Check your understanding:** Redo the problem, this time assuming the market requires a dividend yield of 3.6% compounded semiannually on preferred shares of similar risk. (Answer: $55.80 per share)

▰▰▶ **Related problem:** #9 in Exercise 12.2

EXAMPLE 12.2C | **Calculating the Initial Endowment for a General Perpetuity**

What amount must be placed in a perpetual fund today if it earns 4.8% compounded semiannually, and the first monthly payment of $500 in perpetuity will be made

a. one month from today?

b. one year from today?

SOLUTION

In both cases, the required initial amount is the present value of the payments. Since payments are made monthly but compounding takes place semiannually, the payments form a *general perpetuity* having

$$PMT = \$500 \text{ per month} \quad \text{and} \quad i = \tfrac{4.8\%}{2} = 2.4\% \text{ per six months}$$

We must calculate the equivalent periodic rate for the one-month payment interval. (It will be *approximately* $\frac{4.8\%}{12} = 0.4\%$ per month.)

$$c = \frac{\text{Number of compoundings per year}}{\text{Number of payments per year}} = \frac{2}{12} = 0.1\overline{6}$$

and

$$
\begin{aligned}
i_2 &= (1 + i)^c - 1 \\
&= (1.024)^{0.1\overline{6}} - 1 \\
&= 0.00396057687 \\
&= 0.396057687\% \text{ per month}
\end{aligned}
$$

a. The required initial endowment is

$$PV = \frac{PMT}{i_2} = \frac{\$500}{0.00396057687} = \$126{,}244.24$$

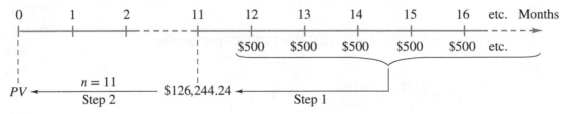

4.8 I/Y
P/Y 12 ENTER
C/Y 2 ENTER
5000 N
500 PMT
0 FV
CPT PV
Ans: −126,244.24

The initial amount required to fund the perpetuity is $126,244.24.

b. The perpetuity is shown on a time line in the following diagram. Viewed from a date 11 months from now, the payments form an ordinary perpetuity. Viewed from today, the payments form a deferred ordinary perpetuity with an 11-month period of deferral.

0	1	2	11	12	13	14	15	16	etc. Months

$500 $500 $500 $500 $500   etc.

PV ← n = 11 — $126,244.24 ← Step 1
      Step 2

The calculation of today's present value of payments must be done in two steps. First determine the present value, 11 months from today, of the ordinary perpetuity. (This is the same as the $126,244.24 amount we calculated in Part (a).) The amount that must be placed in the fund today is the present value of $126,244.24 eleven months earlier. Using formula (8-2), this present value is

$$PV = FV(1 + i_2)^{-n}$$
$$= \$126,244.24(1.00396057687)^{-11}$$
$$= \$120,872.73$$

4.8	I/Y
P/Y 2	ENTER

(making $C/Y = P/Y = 2$)

1.833333333	N
0	PMT
126244.24	FV
CPT	PV

Ans: −120,872.73

▶ **Check your understanding:** What amount must be placed in a perpetual fund today if it earns 3.6% compounded monthly, and the first quarterly payment of $1000 in perpetuity will be made three years from today? (Answer: $100,351.64)

▶ **Related problem:** #11 in Exercise 12.2

EXAMPLE 12.2D	Calculating the Payment in a Deferred General Perpetuity

Mrs. Paquette is setting up a trust fund with an initial contribution of $150,000. The funds are to be immediately invested, and the first semiannual payment of a perpetuity is to be made five years from now. The payments are to be used for the care of her son for the rest of his life, and then are to be paid to the Canadian Foundation for Multiple Sclerosis. If the funds in trust earn 5% compounded annually, what is the maximum payment the trust can make in perpetuity?

SOLUTION

The data and solution idea are shown in the following time diagram. Viewed from a focal date $4\frac{1}{2}$ years from now, the payments form an *ordinary* perpetuity. Since the payment interval (six months) does not equal the compounding interval (one year), the payments form a *general* perpetuity.

The future value of the $150,000 contribution after $4\frac{1}{2}$ years will be the amount (present value) sustaining the perpetuity. That is,

$$\left(\begin{array}{c} FV \text{ of } \$150,000 \\ 4.5 \text{ years from now} \end{array}\right) = \left(\begin{array}{c} PV \text{ of the ordinary general} \\ \text{perpetuity, 4.5 years from now} \end{array}\right) ①$$

Since

$$i = \frac{5\%}{1} = 5\% \quad \text{and} \quad c = \frac{\text{Number of compoundings per year}}{\text{Number of payments per year}} = \frac{1}{2} = 0.5$$

then

$$i_2 = (1 + i)^c - 1 = 1.05^{0.5} - 1 = 0.024695077 = 2.4695077\% \text{ per 6 months}$$

The left side of equation ① is

$$FV = PV(1 + i_2)^n$$
$$= \$150{,}000(1.024695077)^9$$
$$= \$186{,}828.49$$

The right side is

$$PV = \frac{PMT}{i_2} = \frac{PMT}{0.024695077}$$

Substitute these values into ① giving

$$\$186{,}828.49 = \frac{PMT}{0.024695077}$$

Hence,

$$PMT = 0.024695077 \times \$186{,}828.49$$
$$= \$4613.74$$

The trust can make semiannual payments of $4613.74 in perpetuity.

5	I/Y
P/Y	1 ENTER
4.5	N
−150000	PV
0	PMT
CPT	FV

(making $C/Y = P/Y = 1$)

Ans: 186,828.49

5	I/Y
P/Y	2 ENTER
C/Y	1 ENTER
5000	N
−186828.49	PV
0	FV
CPT	PMT

Ans: 4,613.74

➡ **Check your understanding:** Redo the question, this time assuming that the funds in trust earn 8% compounded quarterly. What is the maximum payment the trust can make at the end of every six months in perpetuity? (Answer: $8655.17)

▬▶ **Related problem:** #14 in Exercise 12.2

Checkpoint Questions

1. Circle "True" or "False" for each of the following:

   a. A perpetuity and an annuity both have the same values for *PMT* and *i*.   True   False
      The perpetuity will have a smaller *PV* than the annuity.

   b. If market interest rates rise, it will require a larger endowment to sustain a   True   False
      perpetuity with a particular payment size.

   c. If the rate of return (dividend yield) required by investors declines, the   True   False
      market value of a perpetual preferred share (paying a fixed periodic dividend)
      will rise.

EXERCISE 12.2

Answers to the odd-numbered problems can be found in the end matter.

BASIC PROBLEMS

1. Mrs. O'Reilly donated $500,000 to Medicine Hat College for a perpetual scholarship fund for women in business studies. What amount can be awarded on each anniversary, if the scholarship fund earns $4\frac{1}{2}\%$ compounded annually?

2. What amount is required to fund a perpetuity that pays $10,000 at the beginning of each quarter? The funds can be invested to earn 5% compounded quarterly.

3. A perpetuity is to pay $10,000 at the end of every six months. How much money is required to fund the perpetuity if the money can be invested to earn 4% compounded semiannually?

4. A charitable organization is raising money to fund an animal shelter. The organization would like to donate $2000 at the end of every month in perpetuity to help offset the shelter's operating costs. How much must be raised to fund the perpetuity if money can earn

   a. 4.5% compounded monthly?

   b. 6.5% compounded monthly?

INTERMEDIATE PROBLEMS

5. How much more money is required to fund an ordinary perpetuity than a 30-year ordinary annuity if both pay $5000 quarterly and money can earn 5% compounded quarterly?

6. Ranger Oil recently donated $750,000 to the Northern Alberta Institute of Technology (NAIT) to fund (in perpetuity) five annual bursaries for students in Petroleum Engineering Technology. If the first five bursaries are to be awarded immediately, what is the maximum amount of each bursary? Assume that the bursary fund earns 4.9% compounded semiannually.

7. An old agreement requires a town to pay $500 per year in perpetuity to the owner of a parcel of land for a water well dug on the property in the 1920s. The well is no longer used, and the town wants to buy out the contract, which has become an administrative nuisance. What amount (including the regular scheduled payment) should the landowner be willing to accept on the date of the next scheduled payment if long-term low-risk investments now earn 3.8% compounded annually?

8. The alumni association of Niagara College is initiating a one-year drive to raise money for a perpetual scholarship endowment fund. The goal is to offer 10 scholarships per year, each worth $5000.

   a. How large a fund is required to begin awarding the scholarships one year after the funds are in place if the funds can be invested to earn 5% compounded annually in perpetuity?

   b. Suppose that, during its fund-raising year, the alumni association finds an insurance company that will pay 5.5% compounded annually in perpetuity. How much less money does the association need to raise?

   c. What dollar amount in scholarships can be awarded annually if the alumni association raises only $750,000? Use the interest rate from Part (b).

9. A city sells plots in its cemetery for $1000 plus an amount calculated to provide for the cost of maintaining the grounds in perpetuity. This cost is figured at $25 per plot due at the end of each quarter. If the city can invest the funds to earn 3.8% compounded annually in perpetuity, what is the price of a plot?

10. A company's preferred shares pay a $2 dividend every six months in perpetuity. What is the fair market value of the shares just after payment of a dividend if the dividend yield required by the market on shares of similar risk is

    a. 4% compounded semiannually?

    b. 5% compounded semiannually?

11. Mr. O'Connor set up a trust account paying $500 per month in perpetuity to the local hospital. These payments consume all of the interest earned monthly by the trust. Between what amounts does the balance in the trust account fluctuate if it earns 3% compounded monthly?

ADVANCED PROBLEMS

12. What sum of money, invested today in a perpetual fund earning 5.5% compounded semiannually, will sustain quarterly perpetuity payments of $1000 if the first payment is made

    a. three months from today?

    b. one year from today?

13. The common shares of Unicorp. are forecast to pay annual dividends of $2 at the end of each of the next five years, followed by dividends of $3 per year in perpetuity. What is the fair market value of the shares if the market requires an 5% annually compounded rate of return on shares having a similar degree of risk?

14. Mr. Chan has donated $1 million to a college to set up a perpetuity for the purchase of books and journals for a new library to be built and named in his honour. The donation will be invested and earnings will compound for three years, at which time the first of the quarterly perpetuity payments will be made. If the funds earn 6% compounded quarterly, what will be the size of the payments?

15. A wealthy benefactor has donated $1,000,000 to establish a perpetuity that will be used to support the operating costs of a local heritage museum scheduled to open in three years' time. If the funds earn 2.4% compounded monthly, what monthly payments, the first occurring three years from now, can the museum expect?

16. A legal dispute delayed for 18 months the disbursement of a $500,000 bequest designated to provide quarterly payments in perpetuity to a hospice. While under the jurisdiction of the court, the funds earned interest at the rate of 5% compounded semiannually. The hospice has just invested the $500,000 along with its earnings in a perpetual fund earning 5.2% compounded semiannually. What payments will the hospice receive beginning three months from now?

12.3 Constant-Growth Annuities

LO3   In many situations in real life, regular payments that we make or receive do not remain constant. As a result of inflation and wage growth, we pay more for rent, memberships, insurance, etc., as the years go by. Usually we are able to increase our saving rate and RRSP contributions from time to time. Some pension plans (including the Canada Pension Plan, the Quebec Pension Plan, and the Old Age Security program) provide annual cost-of-living increases. Many businesses grow their revenue, profit, and dividends through real economic growth as well as through inflation.

For long-range financial projections and planning, it is natural to want to incorporate some sort of growth pattern in future payments. The constant-payment annuities we have been considering so far may not provide an adequate approximation of many patterns of increasing payments. In this section we consider the case of **constant-growth annuities**—annuities in which the payments change by the *same percentage* from one payment to the next. Let

$$g = \text{Rate of growth in payment size between successive payments}$$

For example, if each quarterly payment is 1.5% larger than the preceding payment, then $g = 1.5\% = 0.015$. In general, if we let PMT represent the amount of the *first* payment, then

$$\begin{aligned} \text{Second payment} &= PMT + g \times PMT \\ &= PMT(1 + g) \end{aligned}$$

$$\begin{aligned} \text{Third payment} &= (\text{Second payment}) + g \times (\text{Second payment}) \\ &= (\text{Second payment}) \times (1 + g) \\ &= PMT(1 + g) \times (1 + g) \\ &= PMT(1 + g)^2 \end{aligned}$$

You can now see the pattern. Each payment is a factor $(1 + g)$ larger than the preceding payment. In other words, the payment's growth rate, g, compounds every payment interval.

The formulas for the future value and the present value of a constant-growth ordinary simple annuity are:

FUTURE VALUE OF A CONSTANT-GROWTH ORDINARY ANNUITY
$$FV = PMT\left[\frac{(1 + i)^n - (1 + g)^n}{i - g}\right] \tag{12-3}^2$$

PRESENT VALUE OF A CONSTANT-GROWTH ORDINARY ANNUITT
$$PV = PMT\left[\frac{1 - (1 + g)^n(1 + i)^{-n}}{i - g}\right] \tag{12-4}$$

Valuation of Common Shares

According to the Valuation Principle, the fair market value of common shares is the present value of all future dividends (discounted at the market's required rate of return). The further we look into the future, the more difficult it becomes to forecast the dividends. Because of this high degree of uncertainty, the rate of return at which investors discount the future dividends is appropriately high.

One approach to stock valuation is to forecast separate dividend growth rates for the short run (three to five years during which forecasts are more reliable) and the long run (where the "crystal ball" becomes cloudy). For example, an analyst might forecast dividends growing at 15% per year for four years and 5% per year thereafter. During the first four years we have a growing annuity; thereafter we have a growing perpetuity. However, at the high discount rates employed in common stock valuation, dividends beyond 30 years contribute little to the present value of the dividend stream.

---

[2] Formulas (12-3) and (12-4) are not programmed into financial calculators. However, there is a way to trick your calculator into using its financial functions (designed for fixed-payment annuities) to calculate the future value or present value of a constant-growth annuity. It doesn't save much time, but if you find it satisfying to make a device do something for which it was not intended, here is what you do. Make the following "adjustments" to the values entered for I/Y and PMT.

FV Calculation: In the I/Y memory, enter the "adjusted" nominal annual rate: $m\left(\frac{1+i}{1+g} - 1\right) \times 100\%$. In the PMT memory, enter the "adjusted" payment: $PMT \times (1 + g)^{n-1}$.

PV Calculation: Use the same I/Y value as for the FV calculation above. In the PMT memory, enter the "adjusted" payment: $\frac{PMT}{1+g}$.

EXAMPLE 12.3A | **Future Value of Growing RRSP Contributions**

Monica intends to make RRSP contributions on February 28 of each year. She plans to contribute $3000 in the first year and increase the contribution by 3% every year thereafter.

a. Rounded to the nearest dollar, how much will she have in her RRSP at the time of her 30th contribution if the plan earns 5% compounded annually?

b. What will be the amount of her last contribution?

SOLUTION

a. The amount in the RRSP will be the future value of the 30 contributions. Viewed from the date of the 30th payment, the contributions form a constant-growth *ordinary simple* annuity having

$$PMT = \$3000, \quad i = 5\%, \quad n = 30, \quad \text{and} \quad g = 3\%$$

Substitute these values into formula (12-3).

$$FV = PMT\left[\frac{(1 + i)^n - (1 + g)^n}{i - g}\right]$$

$$= \$3000\left(\frac{1.05^{30} - 1.03^{30}}{0.05 - 0.03}\right)$$

$$= \$3000\left(\frac{4.3219424 - 2.4272625}{0.02}\right)$$

$$= \$284{,}202$$

Rounded to the nearest dollar, Monica will have $284,202 in her RRSP at the time of her 30th contribution.

b. The final contribution will be the future value of $3000 after 29 compoundings at 3%.

$$\text{Final contribution} = \$3000(1.03)^{29} = \$7069.70$$

➡ **Check your understanding:** Manon plans to contribute $1000 to her RRSP in the first year, and increase the contributions by 2% every year thereafter. Rounded to the nearest dollar, how much will she have in her RRSP at the time of her 25th contribution if the plan earns 4.5% compounded annually? (Answer: $54,593)

▰▰▰▶ **Related problem:** #1 in Exercise 12.3

EXAMPLE 12.3B | **Amount Required to Purchase an Indexed Annuity**

If money accumulated in an RRSP is used to purchase a fixed payment annuity, the payments will steadily lose purchasing power due to inflation. For this reason, some retirees purchase indexed annuities in which the payments increase at a predetermined rate.

Rounded to the nearest dollar, how much will it cost to purchase a 20-year ordinary annuity making semiannual payments that grow at the rate of 2% compounded semiannually? The first payment is $10,000 and the funds used to purchase the annuity earn 3.5% compounded semiannually.

SOLUTION

The cost will be the present value of the payments.

The payments form a constant-growth *ordinary simple* annuity having

$PMT = \$10,000$, $i = \frac{3.5\%}{2} = 1.75\%$ per half-year, $n = 2(20) = 40$, and $g = \frac{2\%}{2} = 1\%$ per half-year

Substitute these values into formula (12-4).

$$PV = PMT\left[\frac{1 - (1+g)^n(1+i)^{-n}}{i-g}\right]$$

$$= \$10,000\left[\frac{1 - (1.01)^{40}(1.0175)^{-40}}{0.0175 - 0.01}\right]$$

$$= \$341,550$$

To the nearest dollar, the indexed annuity will cost $341,550.

➡ **Check your understanding:** Rounded to the nearest dollar, how much will it cost to purchase a 25-year ordinary annuity making quarterly payments that grow at the rate of 2% compounded quarterly? The first payment is $1500 and the funds used to purchase the annuity earn 6% compounded quarterly. (Answer: $94,269)

▮▮▮▶ **Related problem:** #3 in Exercise 12.3

EXAMPLE 12.3C	Calculating the Initial Payment in a Constant-Growth Annuity

Derek is 30 years old and intends to accumulate $1 million in his RRSP by age 60. He expects his income and annual RRSP contributions to keep pace with inflation, which he assumes will be 2% per year. Rounded to the nearest dollar, what will be his initial contribution one year from now if he assumes the RRSP will earn 5% compounded annually?

SOLUTION

$1 million is the future value of a constant-growth *ordinary simple* annuity having

$$FV = \$1,000,000, \quad i = 5\%, \quad n = 30, \quad \text{and} \quad g = 2\%$$

Substitute these values into formula (12-3).

$$FV = PMT\left[\frac{(1+i)^n - (1+g)^n}{i-g}\right]$$

$$\$1,000,000 = PMT\left(\frac{1.05^{30} - 1.02^{30}}{0.05 - 0.02}\right)$$

$$\$1,000,000 = PMT(83.686)$$

$$PMT = \frac{\$1,000,000}{83.686} = \$11,949$$

Rounded to the nearest dollar, Derek's initial contribution one year from now will be $11,949.

➡ **Check your understanding:** Shelley is 20 years old and intends to accumulate $1.5 million in her RRSP by age 65. She expects her income and annual RRSP contributions to keep pace with inflation, which she assumes will be 2% per year. Rounded to the nearest dollar, what will be her initial contribution one year from now if she assumes the RRSP will earn 6% compounded annually? (Answer: $5297)

▮▮▮▶ **Related problem:** #4 in Exercise 12.3

Checkpoint Questions

1. In this section, does constant growth mean that each successive payment increases by the same dollar amount? If not, what does it mean?

2. How would you handle cases where successive annuity payments decrease by the same percentage every payment interval?

EXERCISE 12.3

Answers to the odd-numbered problems can be found in the end matter.

INTERMEDIATE PROBLEMS

1. Suppose year-end contributions to an RRSP start at $3000 and increase by 2.5% per year thereafter. What amount will be in the RRSP after 25 years if the plan earns 6% compounded annually?

2. Chantal will make year-end contributions for 30 years to an RRSP earning 5% compounded annually.

   a. How much will she have after 30 years if the annual contribution is $2000?

   b. How much more will she have after 30 years if she increases the contributions by 2% every year?

3. How much will it cost to purchase a 20-year indexed annuity in which the end-of-quarter payments start at $5000 and grow by 2% compounded quarterly? Assume that the money used to purchase the annuity earns 6% compounded quarterly.

4. Randall wants to accumulate $750,000 in his RRSP by the end of his 30-year working career. What should be his initial year-end contribution if he intends to increase the contribution by 3% every year and the RRSP earns 5.25% compounded annually?

5. Ken Tuckie is about to buy a 25-year annuity that will deliver end-of-month payments. The first payment will be $1000. How much more will it cost to index the annuity so that payments grow at the rate of 2.4% compounded monthly? Assume the money used to purchase the annuity earns 5.4% compounded monthly.

6. Mrs. Kirkpatrick (age 65) is about to begin receiving a CPP retirement pension of $11,000 per year. This pension is indexed to the Consumer Price Index (CPI). Assume that the annual pension will be paid in a single year-end payment, the CPI will rise 3% per year, and money is worth 5% compounded annually. What is the current economic value of

   a. 20 years of pension benefits?

   b. 25 years of pension benefits?

7. Ida Ho is about to retire from a government job with a pension that is indexed to the Consumer Price Index (CPI). She is 60 years old and has a life expectancy of 25 years. Estimate the current economic value of her pension, which will start at $20,000 per year. For the purpose of this estimation, assume that Ida will draw the pension for 25 years, the annual pension will be paid in a single year-end payment, the CPI will rise 2.5% per year, and money is worth 5% compounded annually.

8. Maritime Bank recently announced that its next semiannual dividend (to be paid six months from now) will be $1 per share. A stock analyst's best estimate for the growth in future dividends is 4% compounded semiannually.

   a. If you require a rate of return of 5.8% compounded semiannually on the stock, what maximum price should you be willing to pay per share? Ignore the present value of dividends beyond a 50-year time horizon.

   b. What price do you obtain if you do not ignore dividends beyond 50 years? (*Hint:* Use a large value, say 1000, for n in the present value calculation.)

ADVANCED PROBLEMS

9. The dividends on the common shares of Mosco Inc. are forecast to grow at 10% per year for the next five years. Thereafter, the best guess is that the annual dividend will grow at the same 3% annual rate as the nominal GNP. A $2.00 dividend for the past year was recently paid. Assume that the required rate of return is 6% compounded annually. What is the fair market value of the shares if we ignore all dividends beyond a 30-year time horizon?

10. Dean has already implemented the first stage of his financial plan. Over a 30-year period, he will continue to increase his annual year-end RRSP contributions by 2% per year. His initial contribution was $2000. At the end of the 30 years, he will transfer the funds to an RRIF and begin end-of-month withdrawals that will increase at the rate of 1.8% compounded monthly for 25 years. Assume that his RRSP will earn 6% compounded annually and his RRIF will earn 3% compounded monthly. What will be the size of his initial RRIF withdrawal?

Key Terms

Constant-growth annuity	Ordinary perpetuity	Perpetuity
Deferred annuity	Period of deferral	Perpetuity due

Summary of Notation and Key Formulas

d = Equivalent number of payment intervals in the period of deferral
g = Rate of growth in payment size between successive payments

FORMULA (12-1) $PV = \dfrac{PMT}{i}$ Finding the present value of an ordinary perpetuity

FORMULA (12-2) $PV(\text{due}) = PMT + \dfrac{PMT}{i}$ Finding the present value of a perpetuity due

FORMULA (12-3) $FV = PMT\left[\dfrac{(1+i)^n - (1+g)^n}{i-g}\right]$ Finding the future value of a constant-growth ordinary annuity

FORMULA (12-4) $PV = PMT\left[\dfrac{1-(1+g)^n(1+i)^{-n}}{i-g}\right]$ Finding the present value of a constant-growth ordinary annuity

Review Problems

Answers to the odd-numbered problems can be found in the end matter.

1. **LO1** What amount of money invested now will provide payments of $500 at the end of every month for five years following a four-year period of deferral? The money will earn 3.8% compounded monthly.

2. **LO2** If money can earn 4% compounded annually, how much more money is required to fund an ordinary perpetuity paying $1000 at the end of every year, than to fund an ordinary annuity paying $1000 per year for 25 years?

3. **LO2** A company's preferred shares pay a $1.25 dividend every three months in perpetuity. What is the fair market value of a share just after payment of a dividend if the rate of return required by the market on shares of similar risk is

   a. 4% compounded quarterly?

   b. 5% compounded quarterly?

4. **LO3** How much will it cost to purchase a three-year annuity that provides end-of-month payments that start at $2000 and grow by 1.5% compounded monthly? The funds in the annuity earn 6% compounded monthly.

5. **LO1** What amount of money invested now will provide quarterly payments of $1350 for eight years, if the ordinary annuity is deferred for $2\frac{1}{2}$ years and the money earns 4.2% compounded monthly?

6. **LO2** Mr. Larsen's will directed that $200,000 be invested to establish a perpetuity making payments at the end of each month to his wife for as long as she lives and subsequently to the Canadian Heart Foundation. What will the payments be if the funds can be invested to earn 4.8% compounded monthly?

7. **LO2** Mrs. McTavish wants to establish an annual $5000 scholarship in memory of her husband. The first scholarship is to be awarded two years from now. If the funds can earn 4% compounded annually, what amount must Mrs. McTavish pay now to sustain the scholarship in perpetuity?

8. **LO1** A $65,000 loan, bearing interest at 8% compounded quarterly was repaid, after a period of deferral, by quarterly payments of $3821.85 over 10 years. What was the time interval between the date of the loan and the first payment?

9. **LO1** A firm obtained a $3 million loan from a government agency to build a factory in an economically depressed region. The loan is to be repaid in semiannual payments over 15 years, and the first payment is due three years from today. What will the payments be if the interest on the loan is 6% compounded semiannually?

10. **LO3** Arif used $300,000 of RRSP savings to purchase a 25-year annuity from which he will receive end-of-month payments. The money used to purchase the annuity will earn 4.8% compounded monthly. The annuity payments will grow by 3% compounded monthly in order to keep pace with expected inflation. What will be the initial payment in the annuity?

11. **LO2** What minimum amount will have to be dedicated today to a fund earning 3.6% compounded quarterly, if the first quarterly payment of $2000 in perpetuity is to occur

    a. three months from now?

    b. five years from now?

12. **LO2** How much more money is required to fund an ordinary perpetuity than a 25-year ordinary annuity, if the funds can earn 4% compounded quarterly, and both pay $500 monthly?

13. **LO3** Tarin will make savings deposits at the end of every year for 10 years. The first deposit will be $1000. Subsequent deposits will increase by 2% annually, to match her expected annual wage increases. If her funds earn 4.75% compounded annually, how much will Tarin have at the end of 10 years?

14. **LO2** What percentage more money is required to fund an ordinary perpetuity than to fund a 30-year ordinary annuity, if the funds can earn 5.8% compounded semiannually? The perpetuity and the annuity each pay $1000 semiannually.

ADVANCED PROBLEMS

15. **LO2** Dr. Pollard donated $100,000 to the Canadian National Institute for the Blind. The money is to be used to make semiannual payments in perpetuity (after a period of deferral) to finance the recording of audiobooks. The first perpetuity payment is to be made five years from the date of the donation. If the funds are invested at 5% compounded semiannually, what will be the size of the payments?

16. **LO2** The common shares of Bancorp Ltd. are forecast to pay annual dividends of $3 at the end of each of the next five years, followed by dividends of $2 per year in perpetuity. What is the fair market value of the shares if the market requires a 5% annually compounded rate of return on shares having a similar degree of risk?

17. **LO1** Cynthia currently has $185,000 in her RRSP. She will make no further contributions, but will allow this fund to accumulate interest at 6% compounded semiannually for the next 10 years. At that point, she will purchase an annuity that will pay end-of-month payments for 20 years. If the funds in the annuity earn 6% compounded monthly, how much will the annuity payments be?

© BananaStock/Jupiterimages RF

CHAPTER 13

Loan Amortization; Mortgages

LEARNING OBJECTIVES

After completing this chapter, you will be able to:

LO1   Construct a loan's amortization schedule

LO2   Calculate the principal balance after any payment using the Retrospective Method

LO3   Calculate the final loan payment when it differs from the others

LO4   Calculate the principal and interest components of any payment or group of payments

LO5   Calculate mortgage payments for the initial loan and its renewals

LO6   Calculate mortgage loan balances and amortization periods to reflect prepayments of principal

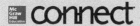 **connect**   Throughout this chapter interactive charts and Help Me Solve It videos are marked with a ↗.

LOAN AMORTIZATION IS THE PROCESS of repaying the original principal by equal periodic payments. (The final payment may differ from the others.) Although all payments are the same size, each one consists of a different combination of principal and interest. There are several applications in which we need to separate the principal and interest components of one or more payments. In Sections 13.1 and 13.2, you will learn the concepts needed to do these calculations.

The largest single amount most of us will ever borrow is a mortgage loan for the purchase of a home. At the end of 2015, Statistics Canada reported that total residential mortgage debt in Canada was $1.3 trillion—over $46,000 for every person over the age of 19. This represented 71% of total household debt (mortgage loans, personal loans, line-of-credit loans, and credit-card debt). Mortgage financing is also very common in the commercial sector. In fact, a higher proportion of commercial properties and residential rental properties have mortgage loans against them than owner-occupied dwellings do. Good management of mortgage debt is a key factor in growing your net worth.

13.1 | Loan Amortization

A loan for a major purchase such as a vehicle, machinery, or real estate is usually set up as a term loan. In a **term loan**, the periodic payment and usually the interest rate are fixed for the term or duration of the loan. If the loan is for the purchase of a vehicle or equipment, the term of the loan is typically three to five years. The payments are calculated so that the loan will be fully repaid (or amortized) at the end of the term.

A loan obtained to finance the purchase of real estate is typically too large for the borrower to repay within five years. Payments are usually calculated to repay the loan over a longer time period (up to 30 years) called the **amortization period**. But most lenders will agree to fix the interest rate for a maximum period of only 5 to 10 years. Typically, loans secured by real estate (mortgage loans) are set up for a *term* of up to 5 years, and an *amortization period* of up to 25 or 30 years. At the end of the loan's term, the principal balance becomes due. Lenders will normally renew the loan (for the amount of the loan balance) at a new market-based interest rate for another term. Usually, the loan payment is recalculated to maintain the loan on its original amortization path.

LO1   Amortization Schedules

A **loan amortization schedule** is a table that
- breaks down each payment into its interest and principal components, and
- gives the principal balance outstanding after each payment.

Typical headings for the columns of an amortization schedule are presented in Table 13.1.

TABLE 13.1   Column Headings for an Amortization Schedule

Payment number	Payment ($)	Interest portion ($)	Principal portion ($)	Principal balance ($)
0	—	—	—	Original loan
1				
etc.	etc.			

Each payment occupies a row in the schedule. The values entered in the last three columns are calculated as follows:

1. Calculate the "Interest portion" of the payment using

$$\text{Interest portion} = i \times \text{Principal balance after the previous payment}$$

where i is the periodic interest rate for one payment interval.

2. Calculate the "Principal portion" of the payment from

$$\text{Principal portion} = PMT - \text{Interest portion}$$

3. Calculate the new "Principal balance" from

$$\text{Principal balance} = \text{Previous principal balance} - \text{Principal portion}$$

EXAMPLE 13.1A	Constructing a Full Amortization Schedule

Marpole Carpet Cleaning borrowed $7600 from Richmond Credit Union at 8% compounded quarterly. The loan is to be repaid by equal payments at the end of every quarter over a two-year term. Construct the amortization schedule for the loan.

SOLUTION

The loan payments form an *ordinary simple* annuity having

$$PV = \$7600, \quad n = 4(2) = 8, \quad \text{and} \quad i = \tfrac{8\%}{4} = 2\%$$

The payment amount must be calculated before beginning the amortization schedule. Substitute these values into formula (10-2) and solve for *PMT*.

$$PV = PMT\left[\frac{1 - (1 + i)^{-n}}{i}\right]$$

$$\$7600 = PMT\left[\frac{1 - (1.02)^{-8}}{0.02}\right]$$

$$PMT = \frac{\$7600}{7.32548144}$$

$$= \$1037.47$$

8 | I/Y |
| P/Y | 4 | ENTER |
(making $C/Y = P/Y = 4$)
8 | N |
7600 | PV |
0 | FV |
| CPT | PMT |
Ans: −1037.47

Rounded to the nearest cent, Marpole's quarterly payment will be $1037.47. Now construct the amortization schedule.

Payment number	Payment ($)	Interest portion ($)	Principal portion ($)	Principal balance ($)
0	—	—	—	7600.00
1	1037.47	152.00 ①	885.47 ②	6714.53 ③
2	1037.47	134.29	903.18	5811.35
3	1037.47	116.23	921.24	4890.11
4	1037.47	97.80	939.67	3950.44
5	1037.47	79.01	958.46	2991.98
6	1037.47	59.84	977.63	2014.35
7	1037.47	40.29	997.18	1017.17
8	1037.47	20.34	1017.13	0.04

① Step 1: Interest portion = $i \times$ Previous balance
$\qquad = 0.02(\$7600) = \$152.00$

② Step 2: Principal portion = *PMT* − Interest portion
$\qquad = \$1037.47 - \$152.00 = \$885.47$

③ Step 3: Balance after payment = Previous balance − Principal portion
$\qquad = \$7600.00 - \$885.47 = \$6714.53$

The balance after two years does not turn out to be zero. We will address this point after this example.

➡ **Check your understanding:** Suppose Marpole Carpet Cleaning paid an interest rate of 5% compounded quarterly on the loan described above. Construct a full amortization schedule for the loan at this new rate. (Answer: Your new schedule will contain eight payments of $1004.21. As a way to verify your work, check your schedule against the following values for Payment 5: Interest portion of Payment 5 = $48.68; Principal portion of Payment 5 = $955.53; Principal balance = $2938.87)

▮▮▶ **Related problem:** #1 in Exercise 13.1

The Final Payment in a Loan Amortization Schedule In Example 13.1A, the loan balance at the end of the two-year term was not exactly zero (even though we calculated the payment so that it would pay off the loan after two years). The 4 cent balance is not a significant amount, but we should aim for utmost precision in financial calculations. Why didn't we get a zero balance? (Give this question some thought before reading on.)

When we make payments in everyday commerce, we do not deal in fractions of a cent. We acknowledged this fact in Example 13.1A when we rounded the loan payment to the nearest cent. But the mathematics tells us that the quarterly payment must be $1037.474473 for eight payments to pay off the loan. Therefore, each payment was actually

$$\$1037.474473 - \$1037.47 = \$0.004473$$

(or 0.4473¢) too small. That shortfall will leave a balance after eight payments of *approximately*

$$8(\$0.004473) = \$0.03578$$

The *precise* balance will be the future value of the eight shortages. That is,

$$\text{Balance} = PMT\left[\frac{(1 + i)^n - 1}{i}\right] = \$0.004473\left[\frac{(1.02)^8 - 1}{0.02}\right] = \$0.03839$$

which appears in the amortization table as $0.04 because all dollar amounts are rounded to the nearest cent.

In a case where the calculated payment is rounded *up* to the nearest cent, each actual payment includes a small *over*payment. The balance in the amortization schedule at the end of the loan's term will be a negative amount (equal to the future value of the individual overpayments). This negative balance represents a refund owed to the borrower.

In practice, lenders adjust the size of the *final* payment to make the final balance precisely zero. In Example 13.1A, the lender would increase the final payment by $0.04 to $1037.51, making the principal portion $1017.17 and the final balance $0.00.

In general, Steps 2 and 3 of the three-step procedure presented earlier in this section must be altered as follows for the *final* payment.

2. The principal portion of the *final* payment is simply the previous principal balance (in order to reduce the new balance to zero).

3. Calculate the final payment using

$$\text{Final payment} = \text{Interest portion} + \text{Principal portion}$$

Using the Texas Instruments BA II PLUS Amortization Worksheet This worksheet streamlines the calculation of the interest and principal components of a payment in the amortization schedule. Appendix 13A provides instruction on the use of the Amortization Worksheet. (Appendix 13B demonstrates the amortization functions on the Sharp EL-738C calculator.) We will employ the BA II PLUS Amortization Worksheet in the next example.

EXAMPLE 13.1B	Constructing a Full Amortization Schedule Where the Payments Form a General Annuity

Healey Fishing obtained a $40,000 loan for a major refit of a trawler. The loan contract requires seven equal annual payments including interest at 6.5% compounded semiannually. Construct the full amortization schedule for the loan. Calculate the total interest paid over the life of the loan.

Checkpoint Questions

1. Circle "True" or "False" for each of the following:

   a. A loan's balance at the midpoint through its amortization period will be   True   False
      less than half of the original principal.

   b. A loan has a 10-year amortization period. If the interest rate is fixed, the   True   False
      principal repaid in the third year will be less than the principal repaid in
      the seventh year.

   c. Loan A is for $20,000 and Loan B is for $10,000. Both have the same interest   True   False
      rate and amortization period. The total interest paid on Loan A will be twice
      the total interest paid on Loan B.

2. If the loan payments and interest rate remain unchanged, will it take longer to reduce a loan's
   balance from $20,000 to $10,000 than to reduce the balance from $10,000 to $0? Explain briefly.

3. The calculated monthly payment on a loan amortized over five years is rounded up by 0.2 cents
   to get to the nearest cent.

   a. Will the adjusted final payment be more than or less than the regular payment?

   b. Will the difference between the regular and the final payment be (pick one) **(i)** more than
      (ii) less than or **(iii)** equal to 0.2 cents × 60 = 12 cents? Explain.

EXERCISE 13.2

Answers to the odd-numbered problems can be found in the end matter.

In problems throughout this exercise, round the calculated loan payments to the nearest cent
before going on to calculate loan balances and/or interest and principal components.

INTERMEDIATE PROBLEMS

1. A $40,000 loan at 3.6% compounded monthly will be repaid by monthly payments over 10 years.

   a. Calculate the interest component of Payment 35.
   b. Calculate the principal component of Payment 63.
   c. Calculate the reduction of principal in Year 1.
   d. Calculate the reduction of principal in Year 10.

2. The interest rate on a $14,000 loan is 5.4% compounded semiannually. Semiannual payments
   will pay off the loan in seven years.

   a. Calculate the interest component of Payment 10.
   b. Calculate the principal component of Payment 3.
   c. Calculate the interest paid in Year 6.
   d. How much do Payments 3 to 6 inclusive reduce the principal balance?

3. A five-year loan of $25,000 at 5.2% compounded quarterly requires quarterly payments.

   a. Calculate the interest component of Payment 10.
   b. Calculate the principal component of Payment 13.
   c. Calculate the total interest in Payments 5 to 10 inclusive.
   d. Calculate the principal paid in Year 4.

4. A $125,000 loan at 6.0% compounded semiannually will be repaid by monthly payments over a 20-year amortization period.
   a. Calculate the interest component of Payment 188.
   b. Calculate the principal component of Payment 101.
   c. Calculate the reduction of principal in Year 1.
   d. Calculate the reduction of principal in Year 20.

5. The interest rate on a $50,000 loan is 7.6% compounded semiannually. Quarterly payments will pay off the loan in 10 years.
   a. Calculate the interest component of Payment 8.
   b. Calculate the principal component of Payment 33.
   c. Calculate the total interest in Payments 21 to 30 inclusive.
   d. Calculate the reduction of principal in Year 3.

6. A five-year loan of $20,000 at 4.8% compounded quarterly requires monthly payments.
   a. Calculate the interest component of Payment 47.
   b. Calculate the principal component of Payment 21.
   c. Calculate the interest paid in Year 2.
   d. How much do Payments 40 to 45 inclusive reduce the principal balance?

7. The monthly payments on a $15,000 loan at 6.0% compounded monthly are $275.
   a. Calculate the interest component of Payment 13.
   b. Calculate the principal component of Payment 44.
   c. Calculate the final payment.

8. Quarterly payments of $3000 are required on an $80,000 loan at 6.0% compounded quarterly.
   a. Calculate the interest component of Payment 30.
   b. Calculate the principal component of Payment 9.
   c. Calculate the final payment.

9. The interest rate on a $100,000 loan is 7.2% compounded semiannually. The monthly payments on the loan are $700.
   a. Calculate the interest component of Payment 221.
   b. Calculate the principal component of Payment 156.
   c. Calculate the final payment.

10. A $37,000 loan at 8.2% compounded semiannually is to be repaid by equal semiannual payments over 10 years.
    a. What will be the principal component of the 6th payment?
    b. What will be the interest component of the 16h payment?
    c. How much will Payments 6 to 15 inclusive reduce the principal?
    d. How much interest will be paid in the third year?
    e. What will be the final payment?

11. A 10-year annuity providing a rate of return of 3.6% compounded quarterly was purchased for $25,000. The annuity makes payments at the end of each quarter.
    a. How much of the 25h payment is interest?
    b. What is the principal portion of the 13th payment?
    c. What is the total interest in Payments 11 to 20 inclusive?
    d. How much is the principal reduction in the second year?
    e. What is the final payment?

12. Guy borrowed $8000 at 7.8% compounded monthly and agreed to repay the loan in equal quarterly payments over four years.
    a. How much of the 5th payment will be interest?
    b. What will be the principal component of the 11th payment?
    c. How much interest will be paid by Payments 5 to 12 inclusive?
    d. How much will the principal be reduced in the second year?
    e. What will be the final payment?

Problems 13 to 15 are variations of Problems 10 to 12 respectively. The size of the regular payment is given instead of the duration of the loan or investment annuity.

13. A $37,000 loan at 8.2% compounded semiannually is to be repaid by semiannual payments of $2500 (except for a smaller, final payment).
    a. What will be the principal component of the 16th payment?
    b. What will be the interest portion of the 6th payment?
    c. How much will Payments 8 to 14 inclusive reduce the principal balance?
    d. How much interest will be paid in the fifth year?
    e. What will be the final payment?

14. An annuity providing a rate of return of 5.6% compounded quarterly was purchased for $25,000. The annuity pays $800 at the end of each quarter (except for a smaller, final payment).
    a. How much of the 16th payment is interest?
    b. What is the principal portion of the 33rd payment?
    c. What is the total interest in Payments 20 to 25 inclusive?
    d. How much will the principal be reduced by payments in the sixth year?
    e. What will be the final payment?

15. Guy borrowed $8000 at 7.8% compounded monthly and agreed to make quarterly payments of $500 (except for a smaller, final payment).
    a. How much of the 11th payment will be interest?
    b. What will be the principal component of the 6th payment?
    c. How much interest will be paid by Payments 3 to 9 inclusive?
    d. How much will the principal be reduced in the third year?
    e. What will be the final payment?

16. An annuity paying $1400 at the end of each month (except for a smaller final payment) was purchased with $225,000 that had accumulated in an RRSP. The annuity provides a semiannually compounded rate of return of 3.2%.
    a. What amount of principal will be included in Payment 137?
    b. What will be the interest portion of Payment 204?
    c. How much will the principal be reduced by Payments 145 to 156 inclusive?
    d. How much interest will be paid in the 15th year?
    e. What will be the final payment?

17. Ms. Esperanto obtained a $40,000 home equity loan at 4.5% compounded monthly.
    a. What will she pay monthly if the amortization period is 15 years?
    b. How much of the payment made at the end of the fifth year will go toward principal and how much will go toward interest?
    c. What will be the balance on the loan after five years?
    d. How much interest did she pay during the fifth year?

18. Elkford Logging's bank will fix the interest rate on a $60,000 loan at 4.2% compounded monthly for the first four-year term of an eight-year amortization period. Monthly payments are required on the loan.

    a. If the prevailing interest rate on four-year loans at the beginning of the second term is 6% compounded monthly, what will be the monthly payments for the last four years?

    b. What will be the interest portion of the 23rd payment?

    c. Calculate the principal portion of the 53rd payment.

19. Christina has just borrowed $12,000 at 7% compounded semiannually. Since she expects to receive a $10,000 inheritance in two years when she turns 25, she has arranged with her credit union to make monthly payments that will reduce the principal balance to exactly $10,000 in two years.

    a. What monthly payments will she make?

    b. What will be the interest portion of the 9th payment?

    c. Determine the principal portion of the 16th payment.

20. **Composition of Loan Payments Chart** An interactive chart for investigating the composition of loan payments is provided in the textbook's Connect. Go to the Student Edition of Connect. In the navigation bar, select "Chapter 13" in the drop-down box. In the list of resources for Chapter 13, select "Links in Textbook" and then click on the link named "Composition of Loan Payments." The chart provides cells for entering the essential information about a loan (PV, j, m, PMT, and payments/year). You can then compare the composition (interest and principal components) of any two payments. Simply enter the serial numbers of the two payments and then click on the "Submit" button. Two bar diagrams provide a visual comparison of the interest and principal components. The actual numerical values are also displayed. Consider a $120,000 mortgage loan at 4.5% compounded semiannually. Monthly payments of $800 will pay off the loan in 25 years and 4 months.

    a. How much more interest is paid by the 20th payment than the 220th payment?

    b. How long does it take before the interest component of a payment drops below 50%?

    c. Which payment number is closest to being made up of (i) 75% interest? (ii) 25% interest?

    d. Which payment number comes closest to having a mix of principal and interest that is the opposite of the first payment's mix?

    e. Which payment number comes closest to having double the principal component of the 5th payment?

    f. Which payment number comes closest to having half the interest component of the 10th payment?

13.3 Mortgage Loans: Fundamentals

Basic Concepts and Definitions

A mortgage loan is a loan secured by some *physical* property. Often the borrowed money is used to purchase the property. If the property securing the loan is not real estate, the mortgage is called a *chattel* mortgage. This section will deal only with mortgage loans secured by real property.

The **face value** of the mortgage is the original principal amount that the borrower promises to repay. In legal language, the borrower is called the **mortgagor** and the lender is called the **mortgagee**. The mortgage contract sets out the terms and conditions of the loan. It also specifies the lender's remedies, should the borrower default on repayment of the loan. The key remedy is the ultimate power to foreclose on the property and cause it to be sold to recover the amounts owed. At the time a mortgage loan is granted, the lender registers the mortgage on the title of the property at the provincial government's land titles office. Anyone can search the title to determine potential claims against the property.

Even though a homeowner may already have a mortgage loan, the remaining equity in the home can sometimes be used as security for another mortgage loan. The second lender's claim will rank behind the existing claim of the first lender. If the borrower defaults on the first mortgage loan, the first lender's claim must be satisfied before any claim of the second lender. Because of this ranking of the claims, the existing mortgage is referred to as the *first mortgage* and the additional mortgage as the *second mortgage*. Since a second mortgage lender is exposed to greater risk, the interest rate on a second mortgage is significantly higher than the rate on a first mortgage. Loans advertised by financial institutions as "home equity loans" or "home improvement loans" will often be secured by a second mortgage.

The most common amortization periods for mortgage loans are 25 and 30 years. However, a lender will usually commit to a fixed interest rate for only a shorter period or term. The **term** of a mortgage loan is the length of time from the date on which the loan is advanced to the date on which the remaining principal balance is due and payable. Most institutional lenders offer terms of six months to seven years. At the expiry of the loan's term, the lender will normally renew the loan for another term, but at the prevailing market rate of interest on the date of renewal. The payments are adjusted so that the borrower continues with the original amortization period but at the new interest rate.

↗ LO5   Calculating the Payment and Balance

The federal *Interest Act* requires that the mortgage contract "contains a statement showing … the rate of interest chargeable, calculated yearly or half-yearly, not in advance." In our terminology, the interest rate must be disclosed as the equivalent semiannually compounded nominal rate or the equivalent annually compounded rate.[1] The semiannually compounded rate has become the industry standard for disclosure in the mortgage contract. Mortgage interest rates advertised by most financial institutions are also semiannually compounded rates (even though the compounding frequency is not usually stated). Most mortgage loans are set up for monthly payments. With interest compounded semiannually, the monthly payments form an *ordinary general* annuity having

$$c = \frac{\text{Number of compoundings per year}}{\text{Number of payments per year}} = \frac{2}{12} = \frac{1}{6} = 0.1\overline{6}$$

The mortgage interest rates quoted by a minority of credit unions and a majority of independent mortgage brokers are monthly compounded rates. Monthly payments then form an *ordinary simple* annuity.

Most mortgage lenders will agree to semimonthly, biweekly, or weekly payments instead of monthly payments. For the *same dollar total* of mortgage payments in a year, you will pay off more principal if you spread the total over more frequent smaller payments than over less frequent larger payments. With more frequent smaller payments, money is (on average) paid *sooner* resulting in *earlier* reduction of principal and *lower* subsequent interest charges.

Usually the borrower chooses a standard amortization period of 15, 20, 25, or 30 years. The payments for the initial term are then calculated *as though* the interest rate is fixed for the *entire* amortization period. Occasionally, the borrower has a preference for a particular payment size. As long as the resulting amortization period is no more than 30 years, most mortgage lenders will agree to such a proposal.

The principal balance on the mortgage loan after any payment may be calculated using either the Prospective Method or (preferably) the Retrospective Method. The balance at the end of a mortgage's

---

[1]   The *Interest Act* makes the lender liable for a very severe penalty for failing to disclose the rate of interest as required by the Act. In that event, the Interest Act states that "no interest whatever shall be chargeable, payable, or recoverable, on any part of the principal money advanced." The borrower would be entitled to a refund of any interest already paid and consequently would have the loan on an interest-free basis.

term becomes, in effect, the beginning loan amount for the next term. The lender calculates a new payment size on the basis of current interest rates and (normally) a continuation of the original amortization period. Part (b) of Example 13.3A demonstrates this procedure.

The principal and interest components of any mortgage payment may be calculated as described in Section 13.2 for other term loans. Particularly when the amortization period is more than 20 years, the payments in the first few years are primarily interest. Consider a mortgage loan at 6% compounded semiannually with a 25-year amortization period. Figure 13.3 shows how the interest and principal components of the fixed monthly payments change over the lifetime of the loan.

FIGURE 13.3   The Composition of Mortgage Payments During a 25-Year Amortization

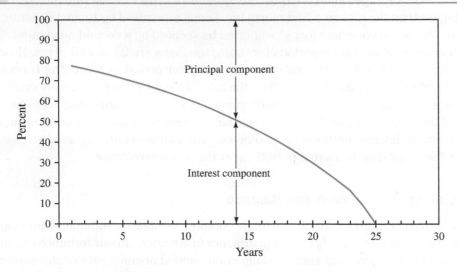

At any point in the 25-year amortization, the interest portion of a payment is the vertical distance below the curve. The principal portion of the payment is the remainder of the 100%, that is, the vertical distance above the curve. For example, the payment at the end of Year 14 is about 50% interest and 50% principal. During the first five years, at least 70% of every payment is interest. Consequently, the principal balance declines very slowly during the early years (as you will see in Figure 13.4).

FIGURE 13.4   A Mortgage's Declining Balance During a 25-Year Amortization

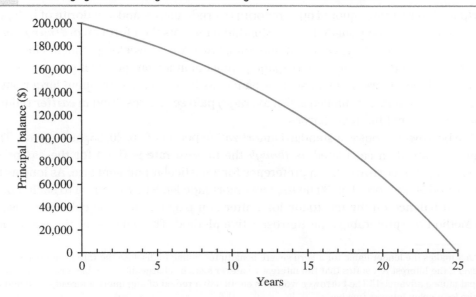

Figure 13.4 illustrates how the balance owed on a $200,000 mortgage loan at 5% compounded semi-annually declines during its 25-year amortization period. As expected from the preceding discussion, the balance decreases slowly in the early years. It takes about 20% of the amortization period to pay off the first $20,000 (10% of the original loan). Almost *two-thirds* of the amortization period are required to reduce the balance to *one-half* of the original principal. The principal declines at an accelerating rate in later years as an ever-increasing portion of each payment is applied to the principal.

EXAMPLE 13.3A	Calculating the Payments on a Mortgage Loan at Its Beginning and at Renewal

A $250,000 mortgage loan is written with a 25-year amortization period, a three-year term, and an interest rate of 5.6% compounded semiannually. Payments are made monthly. Calculate

a. the balance at the end of the three-year term.

b. the size of the payments upon renewal for a five-year term at 6.2% compounded semiannually (with the loan maintaining its original 25-year amortization).

SOLUTION

a. Before the balance can be calculated, we must obtain the monthly payment. Use the amortization period rather than the term of the mortgage when calculating the payment. That is, calculate the monthly payment that will repay the loan in 25 years if the interest rate remains at 5.6% compounded semiannually. The mortgage payments constitute an *ordinary general annuity* having

$$PV = \$250{,}000, \quad n = 12(25) = 300, \quad i = \tfrac{5.6\%}{2} = 2.8\%, \quad \text{and} \quad c = \tfrac{2}{12} = 0.1\overline{6}$$

The periodic interest rate that matches the one-month payment interval is

$$i_2 = (1 + i)^c - 1 = 1.028^{0.1\overline{6}} - 1 = 0.004613136 \text{ per month}$$

Solve formula (10-2) for *PMT*.

$$\$250{,}000 = PMT\left[\frac{1 - (1 + 0.004613136)^{-300}}{0.004613136}\right]$$

$$\$250{,}000 = PMT(162.2783675)$$

$$PMT = \frac{\$250{,}000}{162.2783675}$$

$$PMT = \$1540.56$$

5.6	I/Y
P/Y 12	ENTER
C/Y 2	ENTER
300	N
250000	PV
0	FV
CPT	PMT

Ans: −1540.56

Using the Retrospective Method, the balance after three years will be

$$\binom{\text{Balance after}}{\text{36 payments}} = \binom{\text{Future value of \$250,000}}{\text{after 36 months}} - \binom{\text{Future value of the 36}}{\text{payments already made}}$$

$$= \$250{,}000(1.004613136)^{36} - \$1540.56\left[\frac{(1.004613136)^{36} - 1}{0.004613136}\right]$$

$$= \$295{,}052.091 - \$60{,}180.713$$

$$= \$234{,}871.38$$

Same *I/Y, P/Y, C/Y, PV*

36	N
1540.56 +/−	PMT
CPT	FV

Ans: −234,871.38

The balance after the initial three-year term will be $234,871.38.

b. The renewal is handled in the same way as a new mortgage whose original principal equals the balance from Part (a), but with a 22-year amortization period and an interest rate of 6.2% compounded semiannually. That is,

$$PV = \$234{,}871.38, \quad n = 12(22) = 264, \quad i = \frac{6.2\%}{2} = 3.1\%, \quad \text{and} \quad c = \frac{2}{12} = 0.1\overline{6}$$

The periodic interest rate that matches the one-month payment interval is

$$i_2 = (1 + i)^c - 1 = 1.031^{0.1\overline{6}} - 1 = 0.005101168 \text{ per month}$$

Solve formula (10-2) for *PMT.*

$$\$234{,}871.38 = PMT\left[\frac{1 - (1 + 0.005101168)^{-264}}{0.005101168}\right]$$

$$\$234{,}871.38 = PMT(144.8713526)$$

$$PMT = \frac{\$234{,}871.38}{144.8713526}$$

$$PMT = \$1621.24$$

> Same *P/Y, C/Y*
>
> 6.2 | I/Y
> 264 | N
> 234871.38 | PV
> 0 | FV
> CPT | PMT
>
> *Ans:* −1621.241

Upon renewal of the mortgage at 6.2% compounded semiannually, the payments will increase to $1621.24 per month.

➡ **Check your understanding:** Suppose the loan above had been written with a 20-year amortization period at 4.8% compounded semiannually for a three-year term. Calculate **a.** the balance at the end of the three-year term. **b.** the size of the payments upon renewal for a five-year term at 5.5% compounded semiannually (with the loan maintaining its original 20-year amortization). (Answer: **a.** $225,837.84 **b.** $1698.84)

▰▰▶ **Related problem:** #7 in Exercise 13.3

EXAMPLE 13.3B	Calculations Where the Mortgage Payment Is Rounded up

The monthly payments for the first five-year term of a $120,000 mortgage loan were based on a 10-year amortization and an interest rate of 6% compounded semiannually. The payments were rounded up to the next higher $10.

a. Calculate the size of the monthly payments.

b. What is the principal balance at the end of the five-year term?

c. If the interest rate at renewal is 7.8% compounded semiannually for a second five-year term, calculate the new monthly payments also rounded to the next higher $10.

d. Calculate the size of the final payment.

SOLUTION

a. The payments form an *ordinary general* annuity with

$$PV = \$120{,}000, \quad n = 12(10) = 120, \quad i = \tfrac{6.0\%}{2} = 3.0\%, \quad \text{and} \quad c = \tfrac{2}{12} = 0.1\overline{6}$$

The periodic rate for the one-month payment interval is

$$i_2 = (1 + i)^c - 1 = 1.03^{0.1\overline{6}} - 1 = 0.004938622$$

Solve formula (10-2) for *PMT*.

$$\$120{,}000 = PMT\left[\frac{1 - (1 + 0.004938622)^{-120}}{0.004938622}\right]$$

$$\$120{,}000 = PMT(90.3742467)$$

$$PMT = \frac{\$120{,}000}{90.3742467}$$

$$PMT = \$1327.81$$

Rounded to the next higher \$10, the monthly payment is \$1330.

6	I/Y
P/Y 12	ENTER
C/Y 2	ENTER
120	N
120000	PV
0	FV
CPT	PMT

Ans: −1327.81

b. The balance after five years is

$$\begin{pmatrix}\text{Balance after} \\ \text{60 payments}\end{pmatrix} = \begin{pmatrix}\text{Future value of \$120,000} \\ \text{after 60 months}\end{pmatrix} - \begin{pmatrix}\text{Future value of the 60} \\ \text{payments already made}\end{pmatrix}$$

$$= \$120{,}000(1.004938622)^{60} - \$1330\left[\frac{(1.004938622)^{60} - 1}{0.004938622}\right]$$

$$= \$161{,}269.966 - \$92{,}618.706$$

$$= \$68{,}651.26$$

Same *I/Y, P/Y, C/Y, PV*

60	N
1330 +/−	PMT
CPT	FV

Ans: −68,651.26

c. The balance from Part (b) becomes the initial loan amount for the second five-year term. With

$$PV = \$68{,}651.26, \; n = 60, \text{ and } i = \frac{7.8\%}{2} = 3.9\%, \text{ we obtain}$$

$$i_2 = (1 + i)^c - 1 = 1.039^{0.1\overline{6}} - 1 = 0.006396825$$

and

$$\$68{,}651.26 = PMT\left[\frac{1 - (1 + 0.006396825)^{-120}}{0.006396825}\right]$$

$$\$68{,}651.26 = PMT(49.69739566)$$

$$PMT = \frac{\$68{,}651.26}{49.69739566}$$

$$PMT = \$1381.39$$

Same *P/Y, C/Y*

7.8	I/Y
60	N
68651.26	PV
0	FV
CPT	PMT

Ans: −1381.39

Rounded to the next higher \$10, the monthly payment on renewal will be \$1390.

d. Since the payment size has been rounded up, it will require slightly less than 60 full payments to pay off the debt, and the final payment will be less than \$1390. We must begin by finding the exact number of "rounded up" payments that will be required to pay off the loan. The number of payments is

$$n = -\frac{\ln\left(1 - \dfrac{i \times PV}{PMT}\right)}{\ln(1 + i)}$$

$$= -\frac{\ln\left(1 - \dfrac{0.006396825 \times \$68{,}651.26}{\$1390}\right)}{\ln(1.006396825)}$$

$$= 59.55$$

Same *I/Y, P/Y, C/Y, PV*

1390 +/−	PMT
0	FV
CPT	N

Ans: 59.55

There will still be 60 payments in the second term, but the 60th payment will be smaller than $1390. The final payment will be the balance after 59 payments plus one month's interest. That is,

Final payment = Balance after 59 payments × $(1 + i)$

$$\begin{pmatrix} \text{Balance after} \\ \text{59 payments} \end{pmatrix} = \begin{pmatrix} \text{Future value of \$68,651.26} \\ \text{after 59 months} \end{pmatrix} - \begin{pmatrix} \text{Future value of the 59} \\ \text{payments already made} \end{pmatrix}$$

$$= PV(1 + i)^n - PMT\left[\frac{(1 + i)^n - 1}{i}\right]$$

$$= \$68,651.26(1.006396825)^{59} - \$1390\left[\frac{(1.006396825)^{59} - 1}{0.006396825}\right]$$

$$= \$100,007.998 - \$99,250.498$$

$$= \$757.50$$

Same *I/Y, P/Y, C/Y*
Same *PV, PMT*

59 | N
CPT | FV
Ans: −757.50

Hence,

$$\text{Final payment} = \$757.50 \times 1.006396825 = \$762.35$$

▶ **Check your understanding:** The monthly payments for the first five-year term of a $115,000 mortgage loan were based on a 10-year amortization and an interest rate of 5% compounded semiannually. The payments were rounded up to the next higher $10. **a.** Calculate the size of the monthly payments. **b.** What is the principal balance at the end of the five-year term? **c.** If the interest rate at renewal is 7% compounded semiannually for a second five-year term, calculate the new monthly payments also rounded to the next higher $10. (Answer: **a.** Rounded payment = $1220. **b.** $64,350.81 **c.** Rounded payment = $1280).

◀▶ **Related problem:** #12 in Exercise 13.3

Qualifying for a Mortgage Loan

Mortgage lenders must determine whether a mortgage loan is adequately secured by the property, and whether the borrower has the financial capacity to make the mortgage payments. To do this, they calculate and set upper limits on three ratios:[2]

1. *Loan-to-Value Ratio* $= \dfrac{\text{Principal amount of the loan}}{\text{Lending value of the property}} \times 100\% \leq 80\%$

The 80% *maximum* for this ratio means the borrower's *minimum* down payment is 20% of the "lending value." (The lending value is the lesser of the purchase price and the market value as determined by a certified appraiser.) Note that buyers who have less than a 20% down payment may still qualify for a mortgage, but they will be required to pay for mortgage insurance through the Canada Mortgage and Housing Corporation (CMHC).

2. *Gross Debt Service Ratio* (GDS ratio):

$$\text{GDS ratio} = \frac{\begin{pmatrix} \text{Total monthly payments for mortgage,} \\ \text{condo fees, property taxes, and heat} \end{pmatrix}}{\text{Gross monthly income}} \times 100\% \leq 32\%$$

The upper limit on this ratio means that the major costs of home ownership should not require more than 32% of the borrower's gross income.

---

[2] The indicated upper limits are typical for what are called "conventional first mortgages."

3. *Total Debt Service Ratio* (TDS ratio):

$$\text{TDS ratio} = \frac{\left(\begin{array}{c}\text{Total monthly payments for mortgage,}\\ \text{condo fees, property taxes, and other debt}\end{array}\right)}{\text{Gross monthly income}} \times 100\% \leq 32\%$$

The upper limit on this ratio means that payments related to home ownership *and all other debt* should not require more than 40% of the borrower's gross income.

A borrower must qualify on *all* three ratios. The upper limits for the GDS and TDS ratios vary somewhat from one lender to another. Depending on the lender, the maximum GDS ratio can range from 30% to 33% and the maximum TDS ratio from 37% to 42%.

In addition to the ratios imposed by mortgage lenders, borrowers are also affected by mortgage rules set out by the federal government. Through the Office of the Superintendent of Financial Institutions, the government continues to keep a close eye on the mortgage market in Canada, to try to ensure that Canadians are not taking on unmanageable levels of debt. The combination of high home prices and low interest rates has raised the concern that Canadians are stretching their finances to buy homes that they won't be able to afford should interest rates increase in the future. In 2012, the government reduced the allowable amortization period of CMHC-insured mortgages from 30 years to 25 years. While the maximum amortization period for non-insured mortgages (those in which the borrower is making a down payment of at least 20%) remained at 30 years, there is speculation that the government may move to reduce that at some point in the future. A reduced amortization period results in higher monthly payments for a given level of debt. Because of the limitations placed by the GDS and TDS ratios, the maximum mortgage that a borrower would qualify for would be reduced if the maximum amortization period is reduced. In 2016, the federal government introduced stricter down payment rules for CMHC-insured mortgages. While the minimum down payment for "affordable" homes remains at 5% of the purchase price, borrowers will need to accumulate a minimum down payment of 10% on the portion of any CMHC-backed mortgage that exceeds $500,000.

EXAMPLE 13.3C	**Determining the Maximum Mortgage Loan for Which a Borrower Qualifies**

The Schusters have saved $60,000 for the down payment on a home. Their gross monthly income is $6300. They want to know the maximum conventional mortgage loan for which they can qualify in order to determine the highest price they can pay for a home. They have 18 payments of $600 per month remaining on their car loan. Their bank has upper limits of 32% for the GDS ratio and 40% for the TDS ratio.

a. Allowing for property taxes of $300 per month and heating costs of $225 per month, what maximum monthly mortgage payment do the GDS and TDS ratios permit?

b. What is the maximum mortgage loan for which the Schusters can qualify? (Use a 25-year amortization and an interest rate of 5.2% compounded semiannually for a five-year term. Round the answer to the nearest $100.)

c. Based on a $60,000 down payment and the maximum loan from Part (b), what is the highest price they can pay for a home? Round the answer to the nearest $100.

SOLUTION

a. The GDS ratio allows

$$\frac{\left(\begin{array}{c}\text{Maximum mortgage payment}\\ + \text{ property taxes} + \text{heating costs}\end{array}\right)}{\text{Gross income}} = 0.32$$

That is,

$$\frac{\text{Maximum mortgage payment} + \$300 + \$225}{\$6300} = 0.32$$

Hence,

$$\text{Maximum mortgage payment} + \$300 + \$225 = 0.32(\$6300)$$
$$\text{Maximum mortgage payment} = 0.32(\$6300) - \$525 = \$1491$$

The TDS ratio allows

$$\frac{\left(\begin{array}{c}\text{Maximum payments on all debt}\\ + \text{ property taxes} + \text{heating costs}\end{array}\right)}{\text{Gross income}} = 0.40$$

Hence,

$$\text{Maximum mortgage payment} + \$600 + \$300 + \$225 = 0.40(\$6300)$$
$$\text{Maximum mortgage payment} = 0.40(\$6300) - \$1125 = \$1395$$

For the Schusters' situation, the TDS ratio is the more restrictive ratio. It limits the maximum mortgage payment to $1395 per month.

b. The TDS ratio restricts the Schusters to a maximum mortgage payment of $1395 per month. For a loan at 5.2% compounded semiannually with a 25-year amortization,

$$n = 12(25) = 300, \quad i = \tfrac{5.2\%}{2} = 2.6\%, \quad c = 0.1\overline{6}, \quad \text{and} \quad i_2 = (1 + 0.026)^{0.1\overline{6}} = 0.004287121$$

The maximum loan permitted by the TDS ratio is

$$PV = \text{Present value of 300 payments of } \$1395$$
$$= \$1395\left[\frac{1 - 1.004287121^{-300}}{0.004287121}\right]$$
$$= \$235{,}200 \text{ rounded to the nearest } \$100$$

c. Combining the maximum loan with the $60,000 down payment, the Schusters would have

$$\$235{,}200 + \$60{,}000 = \$295{,}200$$

available to purchase a home, subject to satisfying the criterion for a conventional mortgage. If they purchase a home for $295,200, the loan-to-value[3] would be

$$\frac{\$235{,}200}{\$295{,}200} \times 100\% = 79.67\%$$

Since the ratio is less than 80%, the Schusters meet the loan-to-value criterion for a conventional mortgage loan. Therefore, $295,200 is the maximum price they can pay for a home, without requiring CMHC mortgage insurance.

▶ **Check your understanding:** Suppose the Schusters do not have the $600-per-month car loan. What would be the maximum conventional mortgage they could qualify for, given that all other information above remains the same? (Answer: The GDS is now more restrictive than the TDS ratio. The GDS ratio limits the maximum monthly mortgage payment to $1491, which would support a mortgage of $251,400 and a total price of $251,400 + $60,000 = $311,400; however, that would slightly exceed the loan-to-value criterion for a conventional mortgage. Therefore, the loan-to-value criterion limits the maximum home price the Schusters can afford. Since their $60,000 down payment is 20% of a total home value of $300,000, the maximum conventional mortgage they qualify for is $300,000 − $60,000 = $240,000.)

▬▶ **Related problem:** #13 in Exercise 13.3

---

[3] Mortgage lenders usually base the loan-to-value ratio on the lesser of the purchase price and the market value of the property by an independent appraiser. In this example, the appraised value would have to be at least $235,200 ÷ 0.8 = $294,000 for the Schusters to qualify for a $235,200 conventional mortgage loan.

   The Schusters also need to keep in mind that they will have significant legal, appraisal, survey, and registration costs in connection with the purchase of the home. A rule of thumb is to allow 1.5% of the purchase price for these "closing costs."

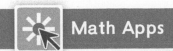 **Math Apps**

AN ANALYSIS OF THE INTEREST "SAVINGS" FROM CHOOSING A SHORTER AMORTIZATION PERIOD

Many financial planners and commentators emphasize the large amount of interest that can be saved by choosing a shorter mortgage amortization period. Their typical analysis goes as follows. (We will use monthly compounding rather than semiannual compounding to simplify the math.)

Suppose you obtain a $200,000 mortgage loan at 4.8% compounded monthly. The following table compares 20- and 25-year amortizations.

Amortization period	Monthly payment ($)	Total of all payments ($)	Total interest ($)
25 years	1145.99	343,797.00	143,797.00
20 years	1297.91	311,498.40	111,498.40
Difference:	(151.92)	32,298.60	32,298.60

By choosing a 20-year amortization, you will have "interest savings" of $32,298.60. The "savings" result from eliminating payments of $1145.99 per month during Years 21 to 25 by spending an extra $151.92 per month during Years 1 to 20. That is,

$$\text{Interest savings} = (5 \times 12 \times \$1145.99) - (20 \times 12 \times \$151.92) = \$32,298.60$$

It seems quite astounding—increasing the monthly mortgage payment by just over 13% reduces the total interest costs by over 22%! The usual conclusion is that reduction of your mortgage's amortization period should be one of your highest financial priorities because of the amazing "interest savings." In the present example, you will be "$32,298.60 ahead" by choosing the 20-year amortization.

Do you see any flaws in this conventional analysis? Is it complete? Does it violate any basic concept you have learned? (Clearly, the analysis must be problematic—otherwise, we would not be making an issue of it. But before reading on, cover up the remainder of the discussion and take five minutes to see if you can identify the error made by so many "experts.")

The main flaw in the analysis is that a basic concept in finance—the time value of money—has been ignored. Whenever you add nominal dollar amounts that are paid on different dates, you are ignoring the time value of money. The longer the time frame over which the payments are spread, the more serious the resulting error will be. In the preceding analysis, a dollar in Year 25 is treated as having the same value as a dollar in Year 1. In fact, individual dollars saved in Years 21 to 25 have, on average, significantly less economic value than extra dollars spent in Years 1 to 20.

Let us do a rigorous analysis to determine the amount of the economic advantage of the shorter amortization period.

Questions

1. For the first 20 years, the monthly payments on the 25-year amortization are $151.92 lower than the payments on the 20-year amortization loan. Suppose you invest this difference each month to earn the same rate of interest that you pay on either mortgage. How much will you accumulate after 20 years?

2. What will be the balance owed after 20 years on the 25-year mortgage? Compare this balance to the Question 1 result. Which mortgage alternative puts you in a better financial position 20 years from now? Where did all of the "interest savings" go?

3. How will the outcome differ if the rate of return on your investments is higher than the interest rate you pay on your mortgage?

4. Write a "decision rule" that your friends (who have not had the good fortune to take this course) can use to decide whether to select a longer or a shorter mortgage amortization period.

Postscript: We do agree with the fundamental advice that paying off your mortgage as fast as possible should be a high financial priority. We merely make the point that the usual analysis is flawed and overstated. Legitimate reasons for the advice are:

- When you use extra money to reduce the principal on your mortgage, you are *certain* of earning an *after-tax* rate of return equal to the interest rate on the mortgage. After you adjust returns from alternative investments for their *risk* and *tax exposure*, the mortgage "investment" is usually very attractive in comparison.
- Human nature is such that we are more readily motivated to accelerate mortgage repayment than to undertake some other investment plan.
- Reduction of household debt improves our ability to absorb financial shocks such as loss of income due to sickness or job loss.

Post-postscript: In the next section, you will learn about other possibilities for accelerating the repayment of a mortgage loan. Some books present calculations of the resulting "interest savings." We play down this fundamentally flawed perspective for the reasons discussed.

LO6 Common Prepayment Privileges and Penalties

Any payments other than the regular contractual payments on a mortgage loan are called **prepayments**. Unless they include a penalty, prepayments are applied entirely to the reduction of principal, since the regular payments already cover interest charges. Mortgages that place no restrictions or penalties on extra payments by the borrower are called **open mortgages**. At the other extreme are **closed mortgages**, which do not allow any prepayment without a penalty. A borrower must pay a higher interest rate on an open mortgage than on a closed mortgage having the same term—about 2% higher for a one-year-term open mortgage.

Between the two extremes just described are closed mortgages with prepayment options. These mortgages grant limited penalty-free prepayment privileges. The more common prepayment options are one or more of the following.

- *Individual (or lump) payments.* Once each year the borrower can prepay without penalty up to 15% of the original amount of the mortgage loan. Mortgage "years" are measured from the date of the loan.
- *Increasing the regular payment.* Once each year, the borrower can permanently increase the size of the regular payments. There is usually an upper limit (such as 15%) on the increase in any year.
- *"Doubling up."* On any payment date, the borrower can pay up to twice the regular monthly payment. Taken to the extreme, the borrower could double *every* payment.

If the mortgage contract allows more than one of these options, the borrower can take advantage of two or more simultaneously. However, unused privileges cannot be carried forward. For example, if you do not use a 15% lump prepayment privilege in the first year, you cannot carry it forward to enable you to prepay up to 30% in the second year.

Details of these prepayment privileges vary among lending institutions. For example, single prepayments may be permitted only once each year or several times (subject to the 10% or 15% annual limit).

Another increasingly common feature of mortgages is a "skip a payment" provision, which allows the borrower to miss one monthly payment each year. Whereas a prepayment will shorten the time required to ultimately pay off a mortgage, skipping a payment will lengthen the time.

It is not unusual for homeowners to sell their house partway through the term of a closed mortgage. If a mortgage has a *portability* clause, the balance owed may be transferred to the next property purchased by the borrower. Some mortgages are *assumable*. An assumable mortgage loan may be transferred to (or "assumed by") the purchaser of the property securing the mortgage *if* the purchaser satisfies the lender's GDS and TDS ratios. The most typical scenario, however, is for the vendor to "pay out" the balance owed on the mortgage. The mortgage contract provides for a financial penalty on any prepayment not specifically permitted by the contract. The most common prepayment penalty is the *greater* of
- three months' interest on the amount prepaid
- the lender's reduction in interest revenue from the prepaid amount (over the remainder of the mortgage's term)[4]

EXAMPLE 13.3D	The Consequences of a Lump Prepayment

The interest rate for the first five-year term of a $200,000 mortgage loan is 5.5% compounded semiannually. The mortgage requires monthly payments over a 25-year amortization period. The mortgage contract gives the borrower the right to prepay up to 15% of the original mortgage loan, once each year, without interest penalty. Suppose that, at the end of the second year of the mortgage, the borrower makes a prepayment of $30,000.

a. How much will the amortization period be shortened?

b. What will be the principal balance at the end of the five-year term?

SOLUTION

a. The $10,000 prepayment at the time of the 24th regular monthly payment will be applied entirely to reducing the principal. To answer Part (a), we must take the following steps:

Step 1: Calculate the payments based on a 25-year amortization.

Step 2: Calculate the balance after 24 payments.

Step 3: Reduce this balance by $30,000.

Step 4: Calculate the number of monthly payments needed to pay off this new balance.

Step 5: Calculate the reduction in the original 25-year amortization period.

Step 1: The periodic rate for the one-month payment interval is

$$i_2 = (1 + i)^c - 1 = 1.0275^{0.1\overline{6}} - 1 = 0.004531682 \text{ per month}$$

Solve formula (10-2) for *PMT*.

$$\$200,000 = PMT\left[\frac{1 - 1.004531682^{-300}}{0.004531682}\right]$$

$$PMT = \$1220.78$$

The monthly payment is $1220.78.

5.5	I/Y
P/Y 12	ENTER
C/Y 2	ENTER
300	N
200000	PV
0	FV
CPT	PMT

Ans: −1220.783

---

[4]   The following is an extract from a mortgage contract describing this penalty. "The amount, if any, by which interest at the rate on this mortgage exceeds interest at the current reinvestment interest rate, calculated on the amount prepaid by you, for the remaining term of the mortgage. The 'current reinvestment interest rate' at the time of prepayment means the rate at which we would lend to you on the security of a similar mortgage of your property for a term starting on the date of prepayment and ending on the balance due date of the mortgage."

Step 2: $\begin{pmatrix}\text{Balance after}\\24\text{ payments}\end{pmatrix}$

$= \begin{pmatrix}\text{Future value of \$200,000}\\\text{after 24 months}\end{pmatrix}$

$\quad - \begin{pmatrix}\text{Future value of the 24}\\\text{payments already made}\end{pmatrix}$

$= \$200,000(1.004531682)^{24}$

$\quad - \$1220.78\left[\dfrac{(1.004531682)^{24} - 1}{0.004531682}\right]$

$= \$192,046.68$

> Same *I/Y, P/Y, C/Y, PV*
> 24 N
> 1220.78 +/− PMT
> CPT FV
> *Ans:* −192,046.677

The balance after 24 payments is $192,046.68.

Step 3: The balance after the $30,000 prepayment is $162,046.68.

Step 4: Calculate the number of payments of $1220.78 required to pay off the balance of $162,046.68.

$$n = -\dfrac{\ln\!\left(1 - \dfrac{i \times PV}{PMT}\right)}{\ln(1 + i)}$$

$$= -\dfrac{\ln\!\left(1 - \dfrac{0.004531682 \times \$162,046.68}{\$1220.78}\right)}{\ln(1.004531682)}$$

$$= 203.51$$

> Same *I/Y, P/Y, C/Y, PMT*
> 162046.68 PV
> 0 FV
> CPT N
> *Ans:* 203.51

After the $30,000 prepayment, 204 additional payments will pay off the loan.

Step 5: With the prepayment, a total of 24 + 204 = 228 monthly payments are required. Therefore, the $30,000 prepayment reduces the amortization period by

$$300 - 228 = 72 \text{ months} = 6 \text{ years}$$

b. Beginning with the balance of $162,046.68 after the $30,000 prepayment, calculate the new balance after another 36 payments.

$\begin{pmatrix}\text{Balance after}\\36\text{ payments}\end{pmatrix}$

$= \begin{pmatrix}\text{Future value of \$162,046.68}\\\text{after 36 months}\end{pmatrix} - \begin{pmatrix}\text{Future value of the 36}\\\text{payments already made}\end{pmatrix}$

$= \$162,046.68(1.004531682)^{36} - \$1220.78\left[\dfrac{(1.004531682)^{36} - 1}{0.004531682}\right]$

$= \$143,072.16$

> Same *I/Y, P/Y, C/Y*
> Same *PV, PMT*
> 36 N
> CPT FV
> *Ans:* −143,072.16

The balance at the end of the five-year term will be $143,072.16.

▶ **Check your understanding:** Redo Parts (a) and (b) above, this time assuming that the borrower makes a prepayment of $15,000 at the end of the second year of the mortgage. (Answer: **a.** 5 years and 3 months **b.** $160,723.68)

▶ **Related problem:** #18 in Exercise 13.3

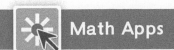 **Math Apps**

MORTGAGE CHOICES: UNDERSTANDING THE OPTIONS

When negotiating a residential mortgage, a potential homeowner has many decisions to make. Banks and other mortgage lenders offer a staggering array of choices when it comes to mortgage loans. A borrower must understand these options, and be prepared to select the mortgage best suited to his or her situation and long-term financial goals. The choices a borrower will be confronted with include:

- *The amortization period.* We have seen in previous examples that longer amortization periods make payments more affordable, but result in a longer period of time before the loan will be fully repaid. Being in debt longer means that more interest is paid over the life of the loan. Typical amortization periods for new mortgages are 20, 25, or 30 years, although (as discussed earlier), if the mortgage requires Canada Mortgage and Housing Corporation insurance because the down payment is less than 20%, the maximum amortization period allowed is 25 years.

- *The payment frequency.* Most mortgages allow a choice among weekly, biweekly, semimonthly, or monthly payments. The more frequent the payment, the more often the principal balance is being reduced, and the lower the total interest will be overall. Many borrowers find it convenient to choose a payment frequency that matches how frequently they are paid by their employer.

- *Open versus closed.* An open mortgage can be repaid either in part or in full at any time in the future, without prepayment penalties. With a closed mortgage, you will pay a prepayment charge if you wish to renegotiate your interest rate, prepay more than your mortgage allows, or pay off your mortgage balance before the end of the negotiated closed term. You will typically pay a higher rate for an open mortgage than a closed mortgage, because of the greater flexibility the open mortgage provides. Nevertheless, if you anticipate a financial windfall and want the flexibility to pay off your mortgage in the near future, an open mortgage might be the better choice, despite the higher interest rate.

- *Variable versus fixed rate.* Perhaps the most difficult choice a borrower must make is between a fixed versus variable rate. With a fixed rate, the interest rate is "locked in" for the duration of the negotiated term (usually up to five years). With a variable rate, however, the interest rate the borrower pays moves up and down depending upon fluctuations in the bank's prime lending rate. While a borrower might like the stability that a fixed rate provides, that peace of mind comes with a cost. A bank's fixed mortgage rate is almost always higher than the advertised variable rate for the same period.

To see the range of choices a borrower has to select from, examine the various rate options below, as quoted by CIBC in April 2016:

Term	Open fixed	Closed fixed	Open variable	Closed variable
6 month	6.95%			
1 year	6.35%	2.84%		
3 year		3.39%		2.70%
5 year		4.79%	4.00%	2.70%

Questions

Here is a chance to practise wading through these various rates. Read the following scenarios, and decide whether you would recommend an open or closed mortgage, and whether you think each borrower should select a fixed or variable rate. Be prepared to explain your recommendations.

1. Rasheed thinks that interest rates are going to rise dramatically within the very near term. He has a substantial mortgage and is more than 20 years away from paying it off. He expects to receive substantial annual bonuses at his job, and wishes to use those funds to pay down his mortgage as quickly as possible. These bonuses might be a very significant percentage of his original mortgage amount.

2. Mariam is convinced that interest rates are going to drop dramatically within the very near term. She has a substantial mortgage that is many years away from being repaid. She does not expect to be able to make any additional payments toward her mortgage other than her regular monthly payments.

3. Conor has a substantial mortgage. He thinks interest rates are going to rise sharply in the near term. He is in the process of searching for jobs overseas, and expects to sell his home immediately upon securing the right job opportunity.

4. Jemma is a first-time home buyer. She is on a strict budget and does not consider herself very educated about the complexities of the mortgage market. She has established an absolute monthly maximum that she can afford to contribute toward mortgage payments, and she cannot afford to go beyond that amount.

EXAMPLE 13.3E	The Consequences of an Increase in the Payment Size

Two-and-one-half years ago the Simpsons borrowed $190,000 secured by a mortgage against the home they purchased at the time. The monthly payments, based on an interest rate of 5.25% compounded semiannually for a five-year term, would amortize the debt over 25 years. The mortgage has a prepayment clause that allows the Simpsons to increase the monthly payments by up to 15% once in each year. Any increase is to be a permanent increase. If the Simpsons increase payments by 10% starting with the 31st payment:

a. How much will the amortization period be shortened?

b. What will be the principal balance at the end of the first five-year term?

SOLUTION

a. The following steps are required to answer the question.

Step 1: Calculate the original size of the payments.

Step 2: Calculate the balance after $2\frac{1}{2}$ years (30 payments).

Step 3: Calculate the size of the payments after a 10% increase.

Step 4: Calculate the number of the new larger payments needed to amortize the balance from Step 2.

Step 5: Calculate the reduction from the original 25-year amortization period.

Step 1:   The periodic rate for the one-month payment interval is

$$i_2 = (1 + i)^c - 1 = 1.02625^{0.1\overline{6}} - 1 = 0.004327902 \text{ per month}$$

Solve formula (10-2) for *PMT*.

$$\$190,000 = PMT\left[\frac{1 - (1 + 0.004327902)^{-300}}{0.004327902}\right]$$

$$\$190,000 = PMT(167.8083175)$$

$$PMT = \frac{\$190,000}{167.8083175}$$

$$PMT = \$1132.24$$

The monthly payment is $1132.24.

5.25	I/Y
P/Y 12	ENTER
C/Y 2	ENTER
300	N
190000	PV
0	FV
CPT	PMT

Ans: −1132.24

Step 2: $\begin{pmatrix}\text{Balance after} \\ \text{30 payments}\end{pmatrix}$

$$= \begin{pmatrix}\text{Future value of } \$190,000 \\ \text{after 30 months}\end{pmatrix} - \begin{pmatrix}\text{Future value of the 30} \\ \text{payments already made}\end{pmatrix}$$

$$= PV(1 + i)^n - PMT\left[\frac{(1 + i)^n - 1}{i}\right]$$

$$= \$190,000(1.004327902)^{30} - \$1132.24\left[\frac{(1.004327902)^{30} - 1}{0.004327902}\right]$$

$$= \$216,281.539 - \$36,187.4736$$

$$= \$180,094.07$$

The balance after 30 payments is $180,094.07.

Same *I/Y, P/Y, C/Y, PV*

30	N
1132.24	+/−
	PMT
CPT	FV

Ans: −180,094.07

Step 3:   The higher payment is 1.1($1132.24) = $1245.46.

Step 4:   Calculate the number of payments of $1245.46 required to pay off the balance of $180,094.07.

$$n = -\frac{\ln\left(1 - \frac{i \times PV}{PMT}\right)}{\ln(1 + i)}$$

$$= -\frac{\ln\left(1 - \frac{0.004327902 \times \$180,094.07}{\$1245.46}\right)}{\ln(1.004327902)}$$

$$= 227.62$$

Same *I/Y, P/Y, C/Y*

180094.07	PV
1245.46 +/−	PMT
0	FV
CPT	N

Ans: 227.62

There are 228 additional payments needed to pay off the loan.

Step 5:   The total time to amortize the loan will be 30 + 228 = 258 months instead of the original 300 months. Therefore, the amortization period will be shortened by

$$300 - 258 = 42 \text{ months, or 3 years and 6 months}$$

b. By the end of the five-year term, the balance in Step 2 will be reduced by an additional 30 payments of $1245.46.

$$\begin{pmatrix} \text{Balance after 30} \\ \text{more payments} \end{pmatrix}$$

$$= \begin{pmatrix} \text{Future value of } \$180{,}094.07 \\ \text{after 30 months} \end{pmatrix} - \begin{pmatrix} \text{Future value of the 30} \\ \text{additional payments made} \end{pmatrix}$$

$$= PV(1+i)^n - PMT\left[\frac{(1+i)^n - 1}{i}\right]$$

$$= \$180{,}094.07(1.004327902)^{30} - \$1245.46\left[\frac{(1.004327902)^{30} - 1}{0.004327902}\right]$$

$$= \$205{,}005.382 - \$39{,}806.0931$$

$$= \$165{,}199.29$$

Same *I/Y, P/Y, C/Y*
Same *PV, PMT*

30 [N]

[CPT] [FV]

Ans: −165,199.29

The balance at the end of the five-year term will be $165,199.29.

➡ **Check your understanding:** Redo Parts (a) and (b) above, this time assuming that the Simpsons increase payments by 15% starting with the 35th payment. (Answer: **a.** 4 years, 9 months **b.** $165,154.70)

▰▰▰▶ **Related problem:** #20 in Exercise 13.3

EXERCISE 13.3

Answers to the odd-numbered problems can be found in the end matter.

INTERMEDIATE PROBLEMS

1. A $145,000 mortgage loan carries an interest rate of 5.2% compounded semiannually, a five-year term, and a 30-year amortization period. Payments will be made at the end of every month.

   a. Calculate the balance owing on the mortgage at the end of the five-year term.

   b. What will be the monthly payments if the loan is renewed for another five-year term at 7% compounded semiannually and the original amortization period is continued?

2. The interest rate on a $200,000 mortgage loan is 5% compounded semiannually.

   a. Calculate the monthly payment for each of 15-year, 20-year, 25-year, and 30-year amortizations.

   b. By what percentage must the monthly payment be increased for a 20-year amortization instead of a 25-year amortization?

   c. By what percentage must the monthly payment be increased for a 20-year amortization instead of a 30-year amortization?

   d. For each of the four amortization periods in Part (a), calculate the total interest paid over the entire amortization period. Assume that the interest rate and payments do not change and the final payment equals the others.

3. A $200,000 mortgage loan has a 25-year amortization.

   a. Calculate the monthly payment at interest rates of 6%, 7%, and 8% compounded semiannually.

   b. By what percentage does the monthly payment on the 8% mortgage exceed the monthly payment on the 7% mortgage?

   c. Calculate the total interest paid over the entire 25-year amortization period at each of the three interest rates. (Assume the final payment equals the others.)

4. The Graftons can afford a maximum mortgage payment of $1500 per month. The current interest rate is 5.2% compounded semiannually. What is the maximum mortgage loan they can afford if the amortization period is

   a. 15 years?   **b.** 20 years?

   c. 25 years?   **d.** 30 years?

5. The Tarkanians can afford a maximum mortgage payment of $1000 per month. What is the maximum mortgage loan they can afford if the amortization period is 25 years and the interest rate is

   a. 5.5% compounded semiannually?   **b.** 6.5% compounded semiannually?

   c. 7.5% compounded semiannually?

6. A $200,000 mortgage loan at 6.6% compounded semiannually has a 25-year amortization period.

   a. Calculate the monthly payment.

   b. If the interest rate were 1% lower (that is, 5.6% compounded semiannually), what loan amount would result in the same monthly payment? Round your answer to the nearest dollar.

7. The Switzers are nearing the end of the first five-year term of a $200,000 mortgage loan with a 25-year amortization. The interest rate has been 6.5% compounded semiannually for the initial term. How much will their monthly payments increase if the interest rate upon renewal is 7.5% compounded semiannually and the original amortization period is continued?

8. The Melnyks are nearing the end of the first three-year term of a $250,000 mortgage loan with a 20-year amortization. The interest rate has been 6.7% compounded semiannually for the initial term. How much will their monthly payments decrease if the interest rate upon renewal is 5.7% compounded semiannually and the original amortization period is continued?

9. The interest rate for the first three years of an $280,000 mortgage loan is 4.8% compounded semiannually. Monthly payments are calculated using a 25-year amortization.

   a. What will be the principal balance at the end of the three-year term?

   b. What will be the monthly payments if the loan is renewed at 6% compounded semiannually and the original amortization period is continued?

ADVANCED PROBLEMS

10. Five years ago, Ms. Halliday received a mortgage loan from Scotiabank for $260,000 at 6.8% compounded semiannually for a five-year term. Monthly payments were based on a 25-year amortization. The bank is agreeable to renewing the loan for another five-year term at 4.8% compounded semiannually. Calculate the principal reduction that will occur in the second five-year term if

    a. the payments are recalculated based on the new interest rate and a continuation of the original 25-year amortization.

    b. Ms. Halliday continues to make the same payments as she made for the first five years (resulting in a reduction of the amortization period).

11. A $190,000 mortgage loan charges interest at 6.6% compounded *monthly* for a four-year term. Monthly payments were calculated for a 15-year amortization and then rounded up to the next-higher $10.

    a. What will be the principal balance at the end of the first term?

   b. What will be the monthly payments on renewal for a three-year term if they are calculated for an interest rate of 7.2% compounded monthly and an 11-year amortization period, but again rounded to the next-higher $10?

12. The interest rate for the first five years of a $187,000 mortgage loan was 7.25% compounded semiannually. The monthly payments computed for a 15-year amortization were rounded to the next-higher $10.

   a. Calculate the principal balance at the end of the first term.

   b. Upon renewal at 6.5% compounded semiannually, monthly payments were calculated for a five-year amortization and again rounded up to the next $10. What will be the amount of the monthly payments?

13. The Delgados have a gross monthly income of $6000. Monthly payments on personal loans total $500. Their bank limits the gross debt service ratio at 33% and the total debt service ratio at 42%.

   a. Rounded to the nearest $100, what is the maximum 25-year mortgage loan for which they can qualify on the basis of their income? Assume monthly heating costs of $200 and property taxes of $220 per month. Current mortgage rates are 6.8% compounded semiannually.

   b. Rounded to the nearest $100, what minimum down payment must they have to qualify for the maximum conventional mortgage (80% loan-to-value ratio) on a new home?

14. Marge and Homer Sampson have saved $95,000 toward the purchase of their first home. Allowing $7000 for legal costs and moving expenses, they have $88,000 available for a down payment.

   a. Based only on a loan-to-value ratio of 80%, what is the maximum purchase price they can consider?

   b. After thorough investigation, the Sampsons made a $360,000 offer on a townhouse subject to arranging financing. Next they met with their banker. With an $88,000 down payment, the Sampsons will need a mortgage loan of $272,000. The current interest rate on a five-year-term fixed-rate mortgage with a 25-year amortization is 5.4% compounded semiannually. The banker gathered data for calculating the Sampsons' GDS and TDS ratios. Annual property taxes will be $3000. Annual heating costs will be about $2400. The Sampsons make monthly payments of $800 on a car loan ($14,000 balance). Their gross monthly income is $7000. Calculate the GDS and TDS ratios for the Sampsons.

   c. Note that the Sampsons meet the GDS criterion ($\leq$ 32%) but exceed the TDS limit (40%). The item causing the problem is the $800-per-month car payment. Suppose the Sampsons use $14,000 of their down-payment savings to pay off the car loan. They will still have enough to make the minimum down payment (0.20 × $360,000 = $72,000) but will have to increase the mortgage loan by $14,000 to $286,000. Recalculate the GDS and TDS ratios. Do the Sampsons satisfy all three ratios by taking this approach?

15. A $200,000 mortgage at 6.6% compounded semiannually with a 25-year amortization requires monthly payments. The mortgage allows the borrower to prepay up to 10% of the original principal once each year. How much will the amortization period be shortened if, on the first anniversary of the mortgage, the borrower makes (in addition to the regular payment) a prepayment of

   a. $10,000?   **b.** $20,000?

16. A $200,000 mortgage at 4.9% compounded semiannually with a 25-year amortization requires monthly payments. The mortgage entitles the borrower to increase the amount of the regular payment by up to 15% once each year. How much will the amortization period be shortened if, after the 12th payment, the payments are increased by

    a. 7.5%?   **b.** 15%?

17. A $100,000 mortgage at 6.2% compounded semiannually with a 25-year amortization requires monthly payments. The mortgage allows the borrower to "double up" on a payment once each year. How much will the amortization period be shortened if the borrower doubles the 10th payment?

18. Monthly payments on a $150,000 mortgage are based on an interest rate of 4.9% compounded semiannually and a 30-year amortization. If a $5000 prepayment is made along with the 32nd payment,

    a. how much will the amortization period be shortened?

    b. what will be the principal balance after four years?

19. After three years of the first five-year term at 6.3% compounded semiannually, Dean and Cindy decide to take advantage of the privilege of increasing the payments on their $200,000 mortgage loan by 10%. The monthly payments were originally calculated for a 30-year amortization.

    a. How much will the amortization period be shortened?

    b. What will be the principal balance at the end of the five-year term?

20. The MacLellans originally chose to make payments of $2600 per month on a $275,000 mortgage written at 7.4% compounded semiannually for the first five years. After three years they exercised their right under the mortgage contract to increase the payments by 10%.

    a. If the interest rate does not change, when will they extinguish the mortgage debt?

    b. What will be the principal balance at the end of the five-year term?

21. **Mortgage Payoff Chart** To access this chart, go to the Student Edition of the textbook's Connect. In the navigation bar, select "Chapter 13" in the drop-down box. In the list of resources for Chapter 13, select "Links in Textbook" and then click on the link named "Mortgage Payoff Chart." Over the full amortization period, the chart plots graphs of both the mortgage balance and the cumulative interest paid. Note the "Definitions" section below the chart. You can select from a variety of accelerated payment and prepayment options. If you enter a non-zero "Prepayment amount," the chart presents additional graphs for the balance and cumulative interest under the prepayment plan. (Round prepayment amounts to the nearest dollar before entry.) These graphs enable you to see how much the prepayments reduce both the cumulative interest cost and the time required to pay off the loan. Use this chart (and its associated report) to answer the following problem. A $225,000 mortgage loan with an amortization period of 25 years carries interest at 5.5% compounded semiannually for a five-year term. At the end of the term, the borrower made a one-time prepayment of $10,000. If the interest rate does not change for the remainder of the loan, how much is the amortization period shortened as a result of the prepayment?

Key Terms

Amortization period	**Mortgagee**	**Prospective Method**
Closed mortgage	**Mortgagor**	**Retrospective Method**
Face value	**Open mortgage**	**Term**
Loan amortization schedule	**Prepayments**	**Term loan**

Summary of Notation and Key Formulas

In all but the last of the following equations, the relevant interest rate or discount rate is the loan's contractual rate of interest.

We frequently use the following concept to calculate the payment size or the amortization period.

$$\text{Original loan} = \begin{bmatrix} \text{Present value of all payments} \\ \text{(discounted at the } \textit{contractual rate of interest} \text{ on the loan)} \end{bmatrix}$$

Prospective Method for calculating a loan's balance:

$$\text{Balance} = \begin{bmatrix} \text{Present value of the remaining payments} \\ \text{(discounted at the } \textit{contractual rate of interest} \text{ on the loan)} \end{bmatrix}$$

Retrospective Method for calculating a loan's balance:

$$\text{Balance} = \begin{pmatrix} \text{Future value of} \\ \text{the original loan} \end{pmatrix} - \begin{pmatrix} \text{Future value of the} \\ \text{payments already made} \end{pmatrix}$$

The final loan payment usually differs from the others.

$$\text{Final payment} = (1 + i) \times \begin{pmatrix} \text{Balance after the} \\ \text{second-to-last payment} \end{pmatrix}$$

The interest and principal components of a loan payment may be calculated from nearby balances.

$$\text{Interest component} = i \times \text{Balance after the previous payment}$$

$$\text{Principal component} = PMT - \text{Interest component}$$

$$\text{Principal component} = \begin{pmatrix} \text{Balance after the} \\ \text{previous payment} \end{pmatrix} - \begin{pmatrix} \text{Balance after the} \\ \text{current payment} \end{pmatrix}$$

Review Problems

Answers to the odd-numbered review problems can be found in the end matter.

INTERMEDIATE PROBLEMS

1. **LO1** Jessica bought a $1150 television for 25% down and the balance to be paid with interest at 11.25% compounded monthly in six equal monthly payments. Construct the full amortization schedule for the debt. Calculate the total interest paid.

2. **LO1** Givens, Hong, and Partners obtained a $7000 term loan at 8.5% compounded annually for new boardroom furniture. Prepare a complete amortization schedule in which the loan is repaid by equal semiannual payments over three years.

3. **LO1 LO3** Metro Construction received $60,000 in vendor financing at 6.5% compounded semiannually for the purchase of a loader. The contract requires semiannual payments of $7500 until the debt is paid off. Construct the complete amortization schedule for the debt. How much total interest will be paid over the life of the loan?

4. **LO1 LO3** Suppose that the loan in Problem 3 permits an additional prepayment of principal on any scheduled payment date. Prepare another amortization schedule that reflects a prepayment of $5000 with the third scheduled payment. How much interest is saved as a result of the prepayment?

5. **LO1 LO2 LO3** Niagara Haulage obtained an $80,000 loan at 5.4% compounded monthly to build a storage garage. Construct a partial amortization schedule for payments of $1000 per month showing details of the first two payments, Payments 41 and 42, and the last two payments.

6. **LO1 LO2** The interest rate on a $6400 loan is 5% compounded semiannually. If the loan is to be repaid by monthly payments over a four-year term, prepare a partial amortization schedule showing details of the first two payments, Payments 34 and 35, and the last two payments.

7. **LO2 LO4** A $28,000 loan at 8% compounded quarterly is to be repaid by equal quarterly payments over a seven-year term.

   a. What will be the principal component of the 6th payment?

   b. What will be the interest portion of the 22nd payment?

   c. How much will the loan's balance be reduced by Payments 10 to 15 inclusive?

   d. How much interest will be paid in the second year?

8. **LO2 LO4** A 20-year annuity was purchased with $180,000 that had accumulated in an RRSP. The annuity provides a semiannually compounded rate of return of 5% and makes equal month-end payments.

   a. What will be the principal portion of Payment 134?

   b. What will be the interest portion of Payment 210?

   c. How much will the annuity's balance be reduced by Payments 75 to 100 inclusive?

   d. How much interest will be paid in the sixth year?

9. **LO2 LO3 LO4** An annuity providing a rate of return of 3.9% compounded monthly was purchased for $45,000. The annuity pays $400 at the end of each month.

   a. How much of Payment 37 will be interest?

   b. What will be the principal portion of Payment 92?

   c. How much interest will be paid by Payments 85 to 96 inclusive?

   d. How much principal will be repaid in the fifth year?

   e. What will be the amount of the final payment?

10. **LO2 LO5** The interest rate for the first five years of a $265,000 mortgage loan is 4.25% compounded semiannually. Monthly payments are calculated using a 20-year amortization.

    a. What will be the principal balance at the end of the five-year term?

    b. What will be the new payments if the loan is renewed at 5.5% compounded semiannually and the original amortization period is continued?

11. `LO2` `LO3` `LO4` A $255,000 amount from an RRSP is used to purchase an annuity paying $6000 at the end of each quarter. The annuity provides an annually compounded rate of return of 6%.

  a. What will be the amount of the final payment?

  b. What will be the interest portion of the 27th payment?

  c. What will be the principal portion of the 53rd payment?

  d. How much will the principal balance be reduced by Payments 14 to 20 inclusive?

  e. How much interest will be received in the sixth year?

12. `LO2` `LO5` `LO6` Madeline obtained a $225,000 mortgage at 5.25% compounded semiannually for a five year term. Monthly payments are calculated using a 25-year amortization. At the outset, Madeline decided to round up her monthly payments to the next higher $100. How much less will Madeline owe at the end of the five-year term as a result of rounding up her payments than if she had not rounded them up?

13. `LO5` Through persuasive negotiation, Russ has obtained an interest rate of 4.8% compounded semi-annually for the first five-year term of his mortgage, rather than the 5.1% compounded semiannually the bank was advertising. If Russ borrows $200,000 for a 25-year amortization, how much less will his monthly payments be during the first five-year term as a result of his negotiation of the lower interest rate?

ADVANCED PROBLEMS

14. `LO2` `LO5` A $25,000 home improvement (mortgage) loan charges interest at 6.6% compounded monthly for a three-year term. Monthly payments are based on a 10-year amortization and rounded up to the next $10.

  a. What will be the principal balance at the end of the first term?

  b. How much interest will be paid over the life of the loan?

15. `LO2` `LO5` `LO6` The interest rate for the first five years of a $280,000 mortgage is 4.8% compounded semiannually. Monthly payments are based on a 25-year amortization. If a $5000 prepayment is made at the end of the third year,

  a. how much will the amortization period be shortened?

  b. what will be the principal balance at the end of the five-year term?

16. `LO2` `LO5` `LO6` The interest rate for the first three years of a $163,000 mortgage is 5.4% compounded semiannually. Monthly payments are based on a 20-year amortization. If a $4000 prepayment is made at the end of the 16th month,

  a. how much will the amortization period be shortened?

  b. what will be the principal balance at the end of the three-year term?

17. `LO2` `LO5` `LO6` After two years of the first five-year term at 6.7% compounded semiannually, Dan and Laurel decide to take advantage of the privilege of increasing the payments on their $210,000 mortgage loan by 10%. The monthly payments were originally calculated for a 25-year amortization.

  a. How much will the amortization period be shortened?

  b. What will be the principal balance at the end of the five-year term?

18. `LO2` `LO5` A mortgage contract for $245,000 written 10 years ago is just at the end of its second five-year term. The interest rates were 6% compounded semiannually for the first term and 5% compounded semiannually for the second term. If monthly payments throughout have been based on the original 25-year amortization, calculate the principal balance at the end of the second term.

Appendix 13A: The Texas Instruments BA II PLUS Amortization Worksheet

The Amortization Worksheet enables you to quickly obtain the interest and principal components of any loan payment, or to quickly obtain the total of the interest components and the total of the principal components in a group of consecutive payments.

Let us use an example to demonstrate the use of the Amortization Worksheet. A $10,000 loan at 6% compounded monthly is repaid by monthly payments over a five-year term. Suppose we want to determine the total interest and total principal in Payments 11 to 20 inclusive.

The basic information about the loan must be entered in the usual manner in the $\boxed{\text{I/Y}}$, $\boxed{\text{P/Y}}$, $\boxed{\text{C/Y}}$, $\boxed{\text{PV}}$, $\boxed{\text{N}}$, and $\boxed{\text{PMT}}$ memories. In the present example, we do not know the value for $\boxed{\text{PMT}}$ at the outset. Therefore, we must first calculate it. Then we must re-enter the *rounded* value in the $\boxed{\text{PMT}}$ memory *before* accessing the Amortization Worksheet.

Find "AMORT" located above the $\boxed{\text{PV}}$ key. To access the Amortization Worksheet, press $\boxed{\text{2nd}}$ $\boxed{\text{AMORT}}$. Recall that a worksheet can be thought of as a column of items that you can view one at a time in the calculator's display. The "AMORT" worksheet's column contains the five items listed below. You see the top item when you first access the worksheet. Other items may be viewed using the scroll keys $\boxed{\downarrow}$ and $\boxed{\uparrow}$.

P1 =	nn
P2 =	nn
BAL =	n,nnn.nn
PRN =	n,nnn.nn
INT =	n,nnn.nn

$6\boxed{\text{I/Y}}$

$\boxed{\text{P/Y}}\ 12\boxed{\text{ENTER}}$

(making $C/Y = P/Y = 12$)

$60\boxed{\text{N}}$

$10000\boxed{\text{PV}}$

$0\boxed{\text{FV}}$

$\boxed{\text{CPT}}\ \boxed{\text{PMT}}$

Ans: -193.3280

$193.33\boxed{+/-}\ \boxed{\text{PMT}}$

P1 represents the serial number of the *first* payment in the group of consecutive payments. *P2* represents the serial number of the *last* payment in the group. *BAL* represents the principal balance *after* Payment number *P2*. *PRN* and *INT* represent the total principal and total interest in Payments *P1* to *P2* *inclusive*. Where the letters nn and n,nnn.nn are indicated above, you will see numerical values in your display.

We want the total interest and total principal in Payments 11 to 20 inclusive. After accessing the worksheet,

Press		11	$\boxed{\text{ENTER}}$	to set $P1 = 11$
Press	$\boxed{\downarrow}$	20	$\boxed{\text{ENTER}}$	to scroll down and set $P2 = 20$
Press	$\boxed{\downarrow}$			to scroll down and view "$BAL = 6{,}993.06$"
Press	$\boxed{\downarrow}$			to scroll down and view "$PRN = -1{,}540.95$"
Press	$\boxed{\downarrow}$			to scroll down and view "$INT = -392.35$"
Press	$\boxed{\text{2nd}}$	$\boxed{\text{QUIT}}$		to exit from the worksheet

The balance after Payment 20 is $6993.06, the total principal in Payments 11 to 20 inclusive is $1540.95, and the total interest in the same group of payments is $392.35.

The computation took place at the moment you pressed the $\boxed{\downarrow}$ key after entering the value for *P2*. The calculator uses the Retrospective Method. Consequently, it ignores whatever value may be residing in the $\boxed{\text{FV}}$ memory.

If you want the interest and principal components of a *single* payment (and the balance after that payment), enter the payment's serial number for *both P1* and *P2*.

Answers to Odd-Numbered Problems

CHAPTER 1

Review and Applications of Basic Mathematics

Exercise 1.1

1. 4
3. 24
5. 20
7. 49
9. 0.5
11. 6
13. −26
15. 255
17. 9
19. 42,875
21. 6
23. 44
25. $100.74
27. $570.68
29. 84

Checkpoint Questions (Section 1.2)

1. **a.** False. The leading zeros are inserted to properly position the decimal point, as opposed to adding precision to the measurement. The value 0.00312 has three figures of accuracy, not five.
   b. True. In this case, each zero comes from a decision about what the digit should be, rather than where the decimal point should be. The value 1.000047 has seven-figure accuracy.
   c. False. The number 100.38 has five-figure accuracy.
   d. True. To test, divide the numerator of the second fraction, $\frac{156}{637}$, by the numerator of the first fraction, $\frac{12}{49}$, to get $156 \div 12 = 13$. Now multiply the denominator of the first fraction, $\frac{12}{49}$, by 13. Since $13 \times 49 = 637$, which is equal to the denominator of the second fraction, we can conclude that the two fractions are indeed equivalent.
   e. False. To test, divide the numerator of the second fraction, $\frac{126}{240}$, by the numerator of the first fraction, $\frac{9}{16}$, to get $126 \div 9 = 14$. Now multiply the denominator of the first fraction, $\frac{9}{16}$, by 14. Since $14 \times 16 = 224$, which is NOT equal to the denominator of the second fraction, we can conclude that the two fractions are not equivalent.
   f. False. The fraction 8/3 is an improper fraction. True. The value 2 1/3 is a mixed number.

3. We want six-figure accuracy in the answer. Therefore, values used in the calculations must be accurate to at least seven figures.

5. To be accurate to the nearest 0.01%, an interest rate greater than 10% must have four-figure accuracy. Therefore, five figures must be retained in numbers used in the calculations.

Exercise 1.2

1. $\frac{3}{8} = \frac{12}{32} = \frac{45}{120}$
3. $\frac{8}{9} = \frac{248}{279} = \frac{488}{549}$
5. $2.3500 = 235.00\%$
7. $-1.4000 = -140.00\%$
9. $0.025000 = 2.5000\%$
11. $12.625 = 1262.5\%$
13. $-2.\overline{6} = -266.\overline{6}\%$
15. $1.\overline{370} = 137.\overline{037}\%$
17. 9.646
19. 1000
21. 0.03041
23. 0.009091
25. $0.016667 = 1.6667\%$
27. $0.0079167 = 0.79167\%$
29. $6.0588 = 605.88\%$
31. $1.0029 = 100.29\%$
33. $195.64
35. $3384.52
37. $720.04
39. $439.79
41. $7159.48
43. $18,705.01

Exercise 1.3

1. $44.44
3. 2.00%
5. 200%
7. $1.24
9. $215.69
11. 62.1%

13. 17.9%

15. $495.00

17. $2000.00

19. a. 168%   **b.** 50.1%

21. 80

23. $6.3 million

25. $34.7 billion

27. $84,000.00

29. a. 5.05%   **b.** 6.68%

    c. 9.42%

31. $138,500

33. a. 170   **b.** 41

Exercise 1.4

1. $754.67

3. $2474.06

5. $616.50

7. $530.00

9. $7239.03

11. $4200/month from Supreme
    $4050/month from Buy-Right

13. a. $3694.00   **b.** 1.6468%

15. $110,833.33

Checkpoint Questions (Section 1.5)

1. a. False. The weights can sum to any number. The weighting values are dictated by the relative importance of the various values. Those weights do not need to sum to 1.

    b. True. The weighted average value of the trucks that were purchased is
$$\frac{(6 \times \$28,000) + (4 \times \$32,000) + (10 \times \$46,000)}{20} = \$37,800$$

    c. True. If Shelley drove exactly the same number of kilometres in both the city and highway, her average gasoline consumption would be equal to the simple weighted average of the city and highway consumption ratings. The simple average of city and highway mileage is $\frac{6.8 + 4.9}{2} = 5.85$ litres per 100 kilometres. Since Shelley's actual average gasoline consumption of 5.7 litres per 100 kilometres is lower than the simple average, we know that Shelley must drive relatively more kilometres in the city where her car consumes more fuel than on the highway where it consumes less.

3. The weighted average will equal the simple average when the items being averaged all have the same weighting factor. This will happen when each of the values being averaged has the same importance, or occurs the same number of times.

Exercise 1.5

1. 1.13

3. 7.65%

5. 3.50

7. $2.22 per litre

9. 3.04

11. 2.30%

13. a. $10.67   **b.** $10.66

    c. $2547.74

15. $170,167

17. 25.5

Exercise 1.6

1.

Quarter	GST remittance (refund)
1	$7,768.25
2	(17,015.25)
3	20,432.40
4	8,240.90

3. a. $41,475.00   **b.** $45,415.13

    c. $44,240.00

5. $3827.88

7. $64.57

9. a. $0.01 per $100   **b.** $30.00

11. a. 7.4837   **b.** 7.1273

Review Problems

1. a. 23   **b.** −40

    c. 29   **d.** $205.39

3. $125.00

5. $945.63

7. a. $2275.40   **b.** $343.08

    c. $619.94

9. $2.97

11. a. $10,225.00   **b.** 3.54%

13. $2231.25

15. $2667

17. a. $1295.88   **b.** $208.62

    c. $3735.16

19. $81,308.33

CHAPTER 2

Review and Applications of Algebra

Exercise 2.1

1. 0

3. $6x^2y$

5. $7x^2 - 4y^2 + 7xy$

7. $4.92y + 7$

9. $12a^2b - 20a^2 + 24ab$

11. $-10x^3y + 5x^2y^2 + 15xy^3$

13. $2a^2 + 34a + 99$

15. $6x$

17. $x - y$

19. $\frac{x^2 - 2x + 3}{4}$

21. 23.75

23. -44.8

25. 0.250

27. $776.12

29. $1378.42

31. $-0.7x + 3.45$

33. $18.8x - 8.5$

35. $1794.22

37. $1071.77

Exercise 2.2

1. $500.00

3. $3500.00

5. 0.175

7. $15.00

9. $2400.00

11. $V_i = \$1728.97$

13. x^2

15. h^{11}

17. $(1 + i)^{n+1}$

19. y^9

21. n^4

23. x^{21}

25. $\dfrac{(1 + i)^3}{27i^3}$

27. -9

29. 0.299070

31. 1.05822

33. 0.985149

35. 1.00816

37. $-4r^{11}$

39. $54\,x^{10}y^4$

41. 3.16049

43. 20.1569

45. 0.00896339

Exercise 2.3

1. 2

3. 43

5. 200

7. 0.5

9. 9

11. $(x, y) = (4, 2)$

13. $(p, q) = (2, -3)$

15. $(c, d) = (500, 1000)$

17. $(v, w) = \left(\frac{3}{2}, -\frac{1}{3}\right)$

19. $(x, y) = (17.0, 6.24)$

21. $286.66

23. $699.47

25. $391.01

Exercise 2.4

1.

x:	−3	0	6
y:	−6	0	12

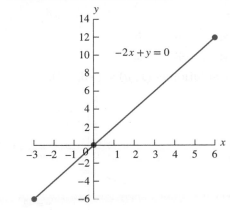

3.

x:	−8	0	12
y:	−3	3	12

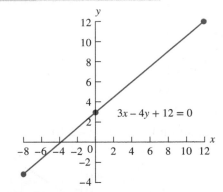

5.

x:	0	3000	6000
y:	5000	18,500	32,000

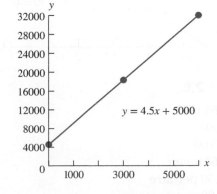

7. Slope = $80
C-intercept = $100

9. a. Slope = $\frac{9}{5}$
F-intercept = 32
18 Fahrenheit
b. Slope = $\frac{5}{9}$
C-intercept = $-17\frac{7}{9}$

11. $x - 3y = 3$

x:	-6	3
y:	-3	0

$y = -2$

x:	-6	3
y:	-2	-2

The solution is $(x, y) = (-3, -2)$.

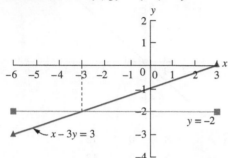

13. $y - 3x = 11$

x:	-4	2
y:	-1	17

$5x + 30 = 4y$

x:	-4	2
y:	2.5	10

The solution is $(x, y) = (-2, 5)$.

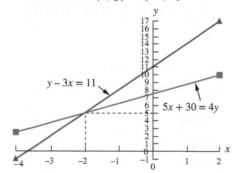

Exercise 2.5

1. 2065 hits
3. $4.60
5. $25.00
7. $125\frac{3}{4}$ hours
9. $1.59 per litre
$2.89 per dozen

11. 24 two-bedroom homes
60 three-bedroom homes
12 four-bedroom homes
13. 55 parking spaces for customers with
physical disabilities
550 small-car spaces
770 regular parking spaces
15. 17.67 tonnes from pile A
14.83 tonnes from pile B
17. 75%
19. CGA: 18 hours
Clerk: 23 hours
21. George's share: $30,128.81
Robert's share: $37,661.02
Sven's share: $21,090.17
23. 1340 seats in the red section
3120 seats in the blue section
25. 1057
27. 238 student members
345 regular members
29. $19.00 per hour plus $0.35 per km
31. 30 to Stage A
48 to Stage B
36 to Stage C

Exercise 2.6

1. 5.26%
3. 18.18%
5. $118.26
7. $25.00
9. 11.11%
11. $80.00
13. 0.62% less
15. $111.11
17. $90.00
19. $150.00
21. 1140
23. 17.19%
25. 34,344,000
27. a. 181.82%   **b.** −51.61%
c. 36.36%
29. 6.04%
31. $498.00
33. $595,308,000
35. −16.67%
37. 1.52%
39. 12.36%
41. $80,000
43. 17.65% increase
45. 24.24% less

Review Problems

1. a. $8x + 3y$ **b.** $25x - 16$
3. 6.26%
5.

x:	−3	0	6
y:	−2	4	16

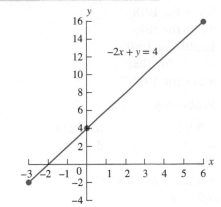

7. 89 children
   37 adults
9. a. $34.58   **b.** $500.00
   c. $117.65   **d.** $199.50
   e. $562.00   **f.** $350.00
   g. $210.00
11. $-22a^2 + 21ab + 16b^2$
13. $0.120 = 12.0\%$
15. $-\frac{9}{x}$
17. a. $(a, b) = (5, -2)$
   b. $(x, y) = (11.40, -6.32)$
19. Slope = $2.75
   B-intercept = $28
21. Kajsa: $12,203.39
   Grace: $14,644.07
   Mary Anne: $9152.54
23. $3.55 per kg for lingcod
   $4.10 per kg for red snapper
25. a. 238.24%   **b.** $7.48
27. a. 79.27%   **b.** −79.27%
29. $-\frac{5}{8x^2}$
31. $4505.14
33. $288,889
35. $10.92 in the "reds"
   $7.80 in the "blues"

CHAPTER 3

Ratios and Proportions

Exercise 3.1

1. a. 3:45   **b.** 1:15
   c. $\frac{1}{15}\ \frac{3}{15}$ **d.** $0.0\overline{6}$
   e. $6.\overline{6}\%$

3. 3:16
5. 3:1:2
7. 2:3
9. 3:5:7
11. 8:13:5
13. 1:6
15. 4:1
17. 8:9:10
19. 2.53:1
21. 1:4.58
23. 1:2.61
25. 3.35:1:1.78
27. 1:1.54:2.29
29. 1:2.47:1.37
31. 5:7:8
33. 3.36:1:2.18
35. 8:7:5
37. 20:1

Exercise 3.2

1. 42.0
3. 233
5. 28.7
7. 0.0155
9. $\frac{1}{3}$
11. $4723.06
13. 40 hours
15. $32,602.50
17. $x = 1.50$ and $y = 2.00$
19. $a = 81.6$ and $b = 61.4$
21. $x = 6375$ and $y = 10,625$
23. General Motors: 4.86 million vehicles
   Ford: 3.10 million vehicles
25. Wholesale costs: $2.95 million
   Overhead expenses: $1.55 million
27. 29 outlets
   $43.13 million

Exercise 3.3

1. $1411.67
3. Vendor's share = $1709.40;
   Purchaser's share = $1139.60
5. a. $3184.00   **b.** $3444.98
7. a. A's premium = $168,750
      B's premium = $450,000
      C's premium = $281,250
   b. A's premium = $168,750
      B's premium = $450,000
      C's premium = $281,250

9. **a.** Harry: $80,000
   Draco: $108,000
   Hermione: $68,000
   b. $25,920
11. Kevin's allocation: $39,619.51
    Lyle's allocation: $36,741.98
    Marnie's allocation: $36,098.51
13. **a.** $542,500
    b. W: 443 shares
    Y: 517 shares
    Z: 590 shares
    c. W's contribution: $50,050
    Y's contribution: $58,450
    Z's contribution: $66,500

Exercise 3.4

1. C$2428.20
3. ¥1,337,638.05
5. C$4696.39
7. C$167.89
9. C$334.05
11. Krona 6.23 = C$1.00
13. C$1723.50
15. C$10,325.77
17.

	Royal	**Kiosk**
a.	5.99%	10.24%
b.	6.66%	20.17%
c.	8.19%	19.76%

19. C$6.81 less
21. Direct conversion: €796.03
    Indirect conversion: €796.10
    These are equal to three-figure accuracy.
23. Personally designed travel is C$526.35 cheaper.
25. Minnesota ore is C$17.59 per tonne more expensive.

Exercise 3.5

1. C$ has depreciated.
3. US$ has appreciated.
5. C$0.85 decrease
7. C$5.32 increase
9. C$1.2927 per US$1.00
   US$0.7736 per C$1.00
11. Decrease of £0.0025
13. C$486.97 increase

Exercise 3.6

1. 6387.55
3. 122.20
5. $1010.33

7. **a.** $1157.02   **b.** $1209.03
   c. The cost of services rose 5.20% more than the cost of goods.
9. Portfolio increased by 63.78%.
   Consumer prices increased by 28.75%.
11. **a.** $160.978.5
    b. 8.55% for 1978
    9.71% for 1979
    12.20% for 1980
    11.30% for 1981
    8.24% for 1982

Review Problems

1. **a.** 6:20:15   **b.** 3:2:4
   c. 3:6:2   **d.** 5:4:7
3. **a.** 18.06
   b. $a = 332.8$ and $b = 205.4$
5. 95,025 units
7. Gain of C$5.76
9. 194 nurses
   97 aides
11. Wife to receive $148,798.17
    Son to receive $106,284.40
    Stepson to receive $75,917.43
13. $3777.36 to A
    $11,392.03 to B
    $4646.75 to C
    $8783.86 to D
15. Health care allocation: $35.26 billion
    Social services allocation: $9.94 billion
17. C$33.95 increase
19. **a.** 9.86%   **b.** $109.86
21. Alberta coal is C$6.29 per tonne cheaper.

CHAPTER 4

Mathematics of Merchandising

Exercise 4.1

1. Amount of discount = $83.00
   Net price = $166.00
3. Amount of discount = $21.33
   Discount rate = 16.67%
5. $83.70
7. List price = $3256.00
   Amount of discount = $407.00
9. $371.90
11. 17.80%
13. 22.50%
15. $57.48

17. Net price = $56.31
Amount of discount = $42.69
19. $290,303
21. 26.55%
23. a. $286.23   **b.** 38.26%
25. 6%
27. a. $5197.50   **b.** $374.00
29. 236 points
31. a. $300.00   **b.** $105.00
33. 9.72%

Exercise 4.2

1. $2317.70
3. $799.18
5. a. $4975.11   **b.** $5025.87
   c. $5025.87
7. a. $8772.37   **b.** $8684.65
9. Amount credited = $3092.78
   Balance owing = $2352.22
11. $475.50
13. a. $3778.78   **b.** April 20
15. $1557.67
17. a. May 28   **b.** $4200
19. $374.90
21. $2127.35

Exercise 4.3

1. $3765.25
3. $1450.61
5. a. May 15   **b.** June 4
   c. $788.00   **d.** $1066.32
   e. $262.33
7. a. $8163.27   **b.** $6608.73
9. Amount credited = $510.20
   Balance owed = $305.29
11. Amount credited = $709.46
   Discount rate = $1.\overline{3}\%$
13. $15,828.35

Checkpoint Questions (Section 4.4)

1. a. False. Markup includes overhead or
   operating expenses per unit, E, in addition
   to operating profit per unit, P.
   b. False. If price is set equal to unit cost,
   the retailer will suffer a loss equal to the
   amount of E, per unit operating expenses.
   c. True. In the absence of any regulations
   or licensing agreements, retailers are free
   to set pricing in accordance with what
   the "market will bear", and markup can
   indeed exceed cost.

   d. True. A simple example proves the
   point. Rate of markup based on cost
   is calculated as $\frac{M}{C} \times 100\%$. For rate of
   markup on cost to be equal to 100%, M and
   C would need to be equal. For example,
   if $M = \$100$ and $C = \$100$, rate of markup
   based on cost would be 100%, and selling
   price, S, would be $C + M = \$100 + \$100 =$
   $\$200$, which is indeed double the cost, C.
3. No. Because S is always greater than M, rate
   of markup on selling price cannot exceed
   100%

Exercise 4.4

1. a. Markup = $11,200
   Selling price = $39,200
   b. 40%   **c.** 28.57%
3. $27.25
5. Rate of markup on cost = 106.19%
   Rate of markup on selling price = 51.50%
7. $0.55
9. a. $32.00   **b.** $24.00
   c. $8.00   **d.** 50.00%
   e. 33.33%
11. a. $12.25   **b.** $8.75
   c. $3.50   **d.** 70.00%
   e. 41.18%
13. Rate of markup on cost = 209.52%
   Rate of markup on selling price = 67.69%
15. a. $527.40   **b.** 23.11%
   c. 18.77%   **d.** $487.40
17. a. $37.90   **b.** 31.03%
19. a. $17.33   **b.** 47.37%
21. $0.35
23. $7.80
25. $33.25
27. $108.90

Checkpoint Questions (Section 4.5)

1. No. Since $C < S$, a 40% markup on cost
   represents a smaller dollar amount than
   a 40% markdown on the same item. A
   40% markup on cost followed by a 40%
   markdown will give a reduced selling price
   that is *less* than C.

Exercise 4.5

1. a. $285   **b.** $36.\overline{6}\%$
3. a. $277.50   **b.** 21.62%
5. a. 39.40%   **b.** 39.40%
7. a. $200.60   **b.** 32.00%

9. $398.08
11. a. Rate of markup on cost = 100.0%
   b. Rate of markup on selling price = 50%
   c. Rate of markdown = 50%
13. a. Selling price = $29.62
   b. Rate of markup on cost = 53.87%
   c. Markdown = $7.41
   d. Reduced price = $22.21
15. No. The actual rate of markdown is only 47.17%, which is lower than the 55% discount being advertised.
17. 15.63%

Exercise 4.6

1. a. $216.00   **b.** $259.20
   c. $118.80   **d.** $475.20
   e. $285.12   **f.** 32.00%
   g. Loss of $49.68
3. $108.00
5. 34.00%
7. Regular price = $59.60
   Rate of markdown = 30.00%
   Reduced profit = $2.98 loss
9. Rate of markup on selling price = $33.\overline{3}$%
   Reduced selling price = $122.50
   Reduced profit = $1.96 loss
11. a. $467.50   **b.** Loss of $28.46
13. a. 15.00%   **b.** Loss of $19.76
15. 23.61%
17. a. 25.00%   **b.** Loss of $6.12
   c. 25.00%

Review Problems

1. Source B is $1.30 cheaper
3. $1886.18
5. $352.08
7. a. $20.65   **b.** 76.50%
   c. $18.59
9. a. $46.75   **b.** $38.25
11. $3350.71
13. $3314.54
15. a. $780.48   **b.** $720.00
   c. 34.69%   **d.** $34.38
17. a. $67.30   **b.** $61.24
19. $574.00
21. $3089.25
23. 24.32%
25. a. $427.14   **b.** $65,447.33
27. 1.75%
29. $2725.10
31. 119 points
33. a. $59.63   **b.** 26.83%

35. a. 153.33% of cost   **b.** 6.52%

CHAPTER 5

Cost-Volume-Profit Analysis

Exercise 5.1

1. a. Variable cost   **b.** Fixed cost
   c. Mixed cost   **d.** Variable cost
   e. Fixed cost   **f.** Mixed cost
   g. Variable cost   **h.** Fixed cost
3. a. Fixed costs:
   Cell phone
   Business licence
   Advertising
   Business liability insurance
   Sarah's wages
   Car insurance and licence
   Variable costs:
   Cleaning supplies
   Oil changes
   Fuel
   Tires
   Friend's wages
   Depreciation
   b. Total monthly fixed costs = $1842.50/month
   Total variable cost per home = $43.15/home
5. $4,112,500
7. $224,392,000

Exercise 5.2

1. a. 5000 toys/year   **b.** $150,000/year
3. a. 1500 jars/year   **b.** $3000
5. a. 150 units/week
   b. (i) Loss of $240/week
   (ii) Profit of $800/week
7. a. 6000 copies/month **b.** $50/month
9. a. 75%   **b.** $1,125,000/year
   c. (i) $50,000 profit
   (ii) $50,000 loss
   (iii) $90,000 profit
   d. 43,000 units/year
   e. Break-even volume increases by 5000 units.
   Break-even revenue increases by $125,000.
11. a. 75% of capacity   **b.** $666,667 loss
13. a. 12.719 tonnes/hectare
   b. (i) Profit of $260/hectare
   (ii) Loss of $310/hectare
   c. 11.694 tonnes/hectare
15. a. 28 participants   **b.** $400
   c. 20 participants
17. a. $40.97   **b.** $40.58

19. a. 72% **b.** $266,667
  c. $4,650,000 **d.** $0.67
  e. $1.50

21. Unit selling price = $75 per tire
  Total revenue in Q2 = $3,750,000
  Unit variable cost = $55 per tire
  Fixed costs = $300,000 per quarter

Exercise 5.3

1. $TR = (S)X = \$2.50$
  $XTC = (VC)X + FC = \$1.00X + \$60,000$

X:	20,000	60,000
TR:	$50,000	$150,000
TC:	$80,000	$120,000

  a. 40,000 packages/month
  b. 45,000 packages/month

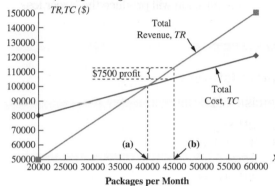
Packages per Month

3. $TR = (S)X = \$10$
  $XTC = (VC)X + FC = \$7.5X + \$100,000$

X:	20,000	60,000
TR:	$200,000	$600,000
TC:	$250,000	$550,000

  a. 40,000 bags/year **b.** $50,000
  c. 64,000 bags/year **d.** 36,000 bags/year

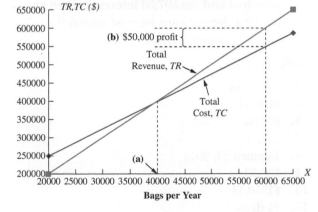
Bags per Year

5. $TR = (S)X = \$0.10$
  $XTC = (VC)X + FC = \$0.05X + \$300$

X:	4000	8000
TR:	$400	$800
TC:	$500	$700

  a. 6000 copies/month
  b. $50/month

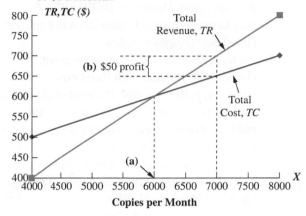
Copies per Month

Exercise 5.4

1. a. 5000 toys/year **b.** $150,000/year
3. a. 1500 jars/year **b.** $3000
5. a. 150 units/week
  b. **(i)** Loss of $240/week
    (ii) Profit of $800/week
  c. 200 units/week
7. a. 6000 copies/month **b.** $50/month
9. a. 75% **b.** $1,125,000
  c. **(i)** $50,000 profit
    (ii) $50,000 loss
    (iii) $90,000 profit
  d. 43,000 units/year
  e. Break-even volume increases by 5000 units
    Break-even revenue increases by $125,000
11. a. 75% of capacity **b.** $666,667 loss
13. a. 12.719 tonnes/hectare
  b. **(i)** Profit of $260/hectare
    (ii) Loss of $310/hectare
  c. 11.694 tonnes/hectare
15. a. 28 participants **b.** $400
  c. 20 participants
17. a. $40.97 **b.** $40.58
19. a. 72% **b.** $266,667
  c. $4,650,000 **d.** $0.6\overline{6}$
  e. $1.50
21. Unit selling price = $75 per tire
  Total revenue in Q2 = $3,750,000
  Unit variable cost = $55 per tire
  Fixed costs = $300,000 per quarter

Checkpoint Questions (Exercise 5.5)

1. **a.** False. A fixed cost can, at some point, change. What makes it a fixed cost, however, is the fact that the cost is changing for a reason other than a change in sales volume. For example, rent is a fixed cost. At the renewal of a rental agreement, the rent may increase. However, rent is still a fixed cost because its total value does not change based on changes in sales.
   b. False. A fixed cost can, at some point, change. What makes it a fixed cost, however, is the fact that the cost is changing for a reason other than a change in sales volume. For example, rent is a fixed cost. At the renewal of a rental agreement, the rent may increase. However, rent is still a fixed cost because its total value does not change based on changes in sales.
   c. True   **d.** True
   e. False. All else being equal, lower fixed costs will result in a *lower* break-even point.

3. At the break-even point, all fixed costs and all variable costs are covered and NI = 0. Production beyond the break-even point results in additional variable costs. Therefore, only the difference between additional revenue ($1) and additional variable costs [$1 × (1 — CR)] contributes to net income.

Exercise 5.5

1. **a.** 80%   **b.** $850 per month
   c. 34 lawns per month
3. **a.** 75% of capacity   **b.** $666,666.67 loss
5. **a.** $800,000 per year
   b. $90,000 increase in net income
   c. $40,000 increase in net income
   d. $60,000 reduction in net income

Review Problems

1. **a.** variable cost   **b.** fixed cost
   c. fixed cost   **d.** variable cost
3. **a.** $3.25 per dog   **b.** $5225
5. **a.** 18,000 units   **b.** $3,240,000
   c. If $X = 20,000$ units, profit is $140,000
       If $X = 17,500$ units, loss is $35,000
7. **a.** 2400 seats per year **b.** $36,000 loss
9. **a.** 2479 books   **b.** $56,160
   c. Select the $35 price **d.** 323 books

11. **a.** 5000 units   **b.** 7500 units
    c. $120,000
    d. (i) $10,000 lower   (ii) $20,000 higher
    e. (i) $48,000 lower   (ii) $24,000 higher
    f. (i) $40,000 higher (ii) $80,000 lower
    g. $28,000 lower
13. **a.** Plan 1: Break-even point is 2500 people
        Plan 2: Break-even point is 2500 people
    b. (i) Plan 1: Profit = $3000;
            Plan 2: Profit = $2000
        (ii) Plan 1: Loss = $1800;
            Plan 2: Loss = $1200
    c. If attendance surpasses the break-even point, the 30% commission rate generates the higher profit. However, if attendance falls short of the 2500 break-even point, the 30% commission will produce the larger loss.

CHAPTER 6

Simple Interest

Exercise 6.1

1. $21.88
3. 8 months
5. 8.75%
7. $27,906.98
9. $198.00
11. $169.20
13. 1.75% per month
15. 2.0%
17. Interest on the first term deposit = $97.50. Interest on the second term deposit = $98.45. The interest earned on the second deposit is larger because both the original $10,000 principal and the $97.50 interest earned on the first deposit earn interest during the second 3-month period.

Exercise 6.2

1. 227 days
3. $108.54
5. $22.09
7. 1.50%
9. January 27, 2016
11. $28.53
13. $1550.11
15. 41 days
17. January 29, 2014
19. $196.03
21. $7649.90

Exercise 6.3

1. $3027.44
3. $780.00
5. $18,301.58
7. $14,100.00 of principal; $1279.58 of interest
9. 10.70%
11. 18.50%
13. 8 months
15. 59.46%
17. Save $11.23 in current dollars by buying the tires today.
19. 7.82%

Checkpoint Questions (Section 6.4)

1. "Equivalent payments" are alternative payments (on different dates) that will put the recipient in the same economic position.
3. **a.** True. An earlier amount, P, will grow to a larger value, S, over time at a positive rate of interest. Therefore, an earlier value, P, will always be smaller than an equivalent future value, S, provided that the rate of return is positive.
   b. False. If the interest rate increases, the investor can deposit an amount smaller than $1000 today and have it grow to be equal to the future scheduled payment. The difference will be made up with additional dollars of interest earned due to the higher interest rate.
   c. True. If the investor received the payment scheduled for today and invested it, he would earn less interest over the course of six months at the new rate, 6%, than he would have at the old rate, 9%. Therefore, a payment in six months that is smaller than $1500 will be economically equivalent to the payment scheduled today.

Exercise 6.4

1. $555.95
3. $5360.89
5. $994.44
7. $455.27
9. 7.25%
11. 90 days late
13. $1591.36
15. **a.** $560 today   **b.** 10.86%
17. The two options are essentially equivalent.
19. **a.** Save $661.92 by selecting the September 30 installation date.
    b. 12.24%

21. **a.** Smith's offer: $142,799.51
        Kim's offer: $143,832.54
    b. Kim's offer is worth $1033.03 more.

Checkpoint Questions (Section 6.5)

1. The economic value of a nominal amount of money depends on the date when it is paid. This property of money is called the time value of money.
3. **a.** True   **b.** False
   c. False

Exercise 6.5

1. $793.04
3. $1923.57
5. $2974.83
7. Rocca Roofing quote is $773.82 cheaper.
9. $4442.98
11. $3115.85
13. **a.** $5877.97   **b.** $5889.79
15. $2719.68

Exercise 6.6

1. $1037.79
3. $1589.92
5. **a.** $5455.29
   b. $25,455.29 repaid altogether; $455.29 is interest.
7. $1533.72
9. $1291.81

Review Problems

1. $636.90
3. $7236.32
5. **a.** $17,413.66   **b.** $416.66
7. 4.75%
9. $9873.40
11. $70.96
13. September 8
15. $59,729.01
17. $8459.14
19. $7384.25
21. $13,106.48
23. March 24, 2014
25. **a.** Offer A: $193,846.15
        Offer B: $193,235.29
    b. Offer A is worth $610.86 more
    c. Offer A: $190,943.40
        Offer B: $191,650.49
        Accept Offer B. It is worth $707.09 more.
27. $3106.16

the $20,000 principal into two halves. Each half of loan A is identical to loan B.

3. a. Each regular payment includes a 0.2¢ overpayment. Therefore, the adjusted final payment will be less than the regular payment.

  b. The reduction in the final payment will be the future value of the 60 overpayments of 0.2¢. This will be (i) more than 60(0.2¢) = 12¢.

Exercise 13.2

1. a. $171.57   **b.** $331.91
  c. $2922.10   **d.** $5283.96
3. a. $267.20   **b.** $1300.12
  c. $1922.45   **d.** $5342.60
5. a. $822.74   **b.** $1542.15
  c. $4474.70   **d.** $4055.64
7. a. $62.66   **b.** $247.84
  c. $233.79
9. a. $302.03   **b.** $271.30
  c. $562.08
11. a. $163.64   **b.** $555.92
  c. $2444.55   **d.** $2031.80
  e. $820.60
13. a. $1796.03   **b.** $1298.27
  c. $10,317.16   **d.** $2233.04
  e. $584.80
15. a. $83.43   **b.** $377.99
  c. $852.07   **d.** $1650.55
  e. $197.28
17. a. $370.80
  b. $196.33 toward interest
    $174.47 toward principal
  c. $31,238.73   **d.** $2426.05
19. a. $146.95   **b.** $65.34
  c. $84.95

Exercise 13.3

1. a. $133,422.34
  b. $934.51
3. a. $1279.61 at 6% compounded semiannually
    $1400.83 at 7% compounded semiannually
    $1526.43 at 8% compounded semiannually
  b. 8.97%
  c. $183,883 at 6% compounded semiannually
    $220,249 at 7% compounded semiannually
    $257,929 at 8% compounded semiannually
5. a. $163,829.28
  b. $149,293.00
  c. $136,695.14

7. $105.11 increase
9. a. $170,746.97   **b.** $1158.91
11. a. $114,809.84   **b.** $1270.00
13. a. $226,700   **b.** $56,700
15. a. 2 years and 8 months
  b. 4 years and 1 months
17. 4 months
19. a. 5 years and 4 months
  b. $183,476.71

Review Problems

1.

Payment number	Payment	Interest portion	Principal portion	Principal balance
0	—	—	—	$862.50
1	$148.50	$8.09	$140.41	722.09
2	148.50	6.77	141.73	580.36
3	148.50	5.44	143.06	437.30
4	148.50	4.10	144.40	292.90
5	148.50	2.75	145.75	147.15
6	148.53	1.38	147.15	0.00
	Total:	$28.53		

3.

Payment number	Payment	Interest portion	Principal portion	Principal balance
0	—	—	—	$60,000.00
1	$7500.00	$1950.00	$5550.00	54,450.00
2	7500.00	1769.63	5730.37	48,719.63
3	7500.00	1583.39	5916.61	42,803.02
4	7500.00	1391.10	6108.90	36,694.12
5	7500.00	1192.56	6307.44	30,386.68
6	7500.00	987.57	6512.43	23,874.25
7	7500.00	775.91	6724.09	17,150.16
8	7500.00	557.38	6942.62	10,207.54
9	7500.00	331.75	7168.25	3039.29
10	3138.07	98.78	3039.29	0.00
	Total:	$10,638.07		

5.

Payment number	Payment	Interest portion	Principal portion	Principal balance
0	—	—	—	$80,000.00
1	$1000.00	$480.00	$520.00	79,480.00
2	1000.00	476.88	523.12	78,956.88
⋮	⋮	⋮	⋮	⋮
40	—	—	—	56,570.72
41	1000.00	339.42	660.58	55,910.14
42	1000.00	335.46	664.54	55,245.60
⋮	⋮	⋮	⋮	⋮
108	—	—	—	1305.32
109	1000.00	7.83	992.17	313.15
110	315.03	1.88	313.15	0.00

7. a. $834.36   **b.** $170.31
 c. $5697.14   **d.** $1891.34
9. a. $146.00   **b.** $16.37
 c. $1025.91   **d.** $3268.88
 e. $303.33
11. a. $497.92   **b.** $2702.05
 c. $4816.51   **d.** $19,964.68
 e. $11,643.57
13. $34.08 less
15. a. 11 months
 b. $123,841.35
17. a. 4 years and 2 months
 b. $96,786.36

Glossary

Algebraic expression A statement of the mathematical operations to be carried out on a combination of numbers and variables.

Amortization period The total length of time over which equal regular payments will repay a loan.

Annuity A series of equal payments at regular intervals.

Annuity due An annuity in which the periodic payments occur at the beginning of each payment interval.

Base (1) The quantity that is multiplied by itself in a power. (2) The initial amount to which a percent change is applied.

Binomial An expression containing two terms.

Book value of the lease The present value of the remaining lease payments (discounted at the interest rate on debt financing).

Break-even chart A graph presenting both total costs and total revenue as a function of sales volume so that the break-even point may be determined.

Break-even point The sales volume at which net income is zero; the intersection of the total cost and total revenue lines on a break-even chart.

Buy rate The exchange rate a currency dealer uses when buying a currency from you.

Cash discount A discount allowed for a payment within the discount period.

Cash flow A cash disbursement (cash outflow) or a cash receipt (cash inflow).

Cash-flow sign convention A set of rules for using an algebraic sign to indicate the direction of cash movement. Cash *inflows* (receipts) are positive, and cash *outflows* (disbursements) are negative.

Closed mortgage A mortgage that does not permit any penalty-free prepayments.

Commercial paper Promissory notes issued by large corporations to borrow funds for a short term.

Common factor An integer that divides two or more other integers evenly.

Complex fraction A fraction containing one or more other fractions in its numerator or denominator.

Compound interest Interest calculated on the original principal and on previously calculated interest.

Compound interest method The procedure for calculating interest wherein interest is *periodically* calculated and *added* to principal.

Compounding frequency The number of compoundings that take place per year.

Compounding period The time interval between two successive conversions of interest to principal.

Constant-growth annuities Annuities in which the payments increase by the *same percentage* from one payment to the next.

Contribution margin The amount by which the unit selling price exceeds the unit variable cost.

Contribution rate The contribution margin expressed as a percentage of the unit selling price.

Cost function The total costs expressed in terms of the number of units sold.

Cost-volume-profit analysis A procedure for estimating a firm's *operating profit* (or net income before taxes) at any sales *volume* given the firm's *cost* structure.

Credit period The time period granted to a customer for paying an invoice.

Deferred annuity An annuity where the start of the periodic payments is delayed by more than one payment interval.

Demand loan A loan wherein the lender is entitled to demand full repayment at any time without notice.

Denominator The number under a division line in a fraction. The denominator is also known as the divisor.

Discount period The time period within which a payment on an invoice qualifies for a prompt payment discount.

Discount rate The interest rate used in calculating the present value of future cash flows.

Discounting a payment The process of calculating a payment's present value.

Effective interest rate The equivalent annually compounded rate of interest.

End-of-month dating Dating system for payment in which the discount and credit periods *both* begin at the end of the month in the invoice date.

Equation A statement of the equality of two algebraic expressions.

Equivalent discount rate The single discount rate that gives the same net price as the combined effect of multiple discounts.

Equivalent fractions Fractions that have the same value.

Equivalent interest rates Different nominal interest rates that produce the same maturity value of a given principal after one year.

Equivalent payments Alternative payments that will result in the same future value at a later date.

Equivalent ratio A ratio obtained from another ratio by multiplying each term by the same number, or by dividing each term by the same number.

Exchange rate The amount of one currency required to purchase one unit of another currency.

Exponent The number of times that the base is used in repeated multiplication.

Face value (1) The amount paid at maturity of a Treasury bill or commercial paper. (2) The initial principal amount of a mortgage.

Factors The components of a term in an algebraic expression that are separated by multiplication or division signs; the components of a product.

Fair market value A price established by competitive bidding among many buyers and sellers.

Fixed cost A cost that does not change with the volume of sales.

Focal date The date selected for the calculation of equivalent values.

Future value (1) A payment's equivalent value at a *subsequent* date, allowing for the time value of money. (2) The total of principal plus interest due on the maturity date of a loan or investment.

Future value of an annuity The single amount, at the end of the annuity, that is economically equivalent to the annuity.

General annuity An annuity in which the payment interval does not equal the compounding interval.

General annuity due An annuity in which the payment interval does *not* equal the compounding interval, and payments occur at the *beginning* of each payment interval.

Gross profit The difference between the selling price and the unit cost of an item of merchandise. (Also called *markup*.)

Guaranteed Investment Certificates (GICs) Fixed-term deposit investments that earn a predetermined rate of interest.

Improper fraction A fraction in which the numerator is larger than the denominator.

Interest The fee or rent that lenders charge for the use of their money.

Like terms Terms having the same literal coefficient.

Linear equation An equation in which the variable is raised only to the first power.

List price The price quoted by a supplier of a product before any trade discounts.

Literal coefficient The non-numerical factor in a term.

Loan amortization schedule A table presenting details of the interest and principal components of each payment, and the balance after each payment.

Loan repayment schedule A table presenting details of interest charges, payments, and outstanding balances on a loan.

Lowest terms The equivalent ratio having the smallest possible integers for its terms.

Markdown The amount that the price of an item is reduced from the regular selling price.

Markup The difference between the selling price and the unit cost of an item of merchandise. (Also called *gross profit*.)

Maturity date The date on which the principal and accrued interest on an investment or loan are due.

Maturity value The total of principal plus interest due on the maturity date of a loan or investment.

Mid-rate The exchange rate when no charge is embedded in the exchange rate. It is approximately midway between the buy rate and the sell rate.

Mill rate The amount of property tax per $1000 value.

Mixed number A number consisting of a whole number plus a fraction.

Monomial An expression containing only one term.

Mortgagee The party lending money on the security of a mortgage.

Mortgagor The party borrowing money and giving a mortgage as security on the loan.

Net price The price paid after the deduction of trade discounts.

Nominal interest rate The stated *annual* interest rate on which the compound-interest calculation is based.

Nonlinear equation An equation in which the variable appears with an exponent other than "1," or appears as part of a mathematical function.

Numerator The number above the division line in a fraction. The numerator is also known as the dividend.

Numerical coefficient The numerical factor in a term.

Open mortgage A mortgage loan that places no restrictions or penalties on extra payments by the borrower.

Ordinary annuity An annuity in which the payments are made at the *end* of each payment interval.

Ordinary dating Dating system for payment in which the credit period and the discount period start on the date of the invoice.

Ordinary general annuity An annuity in which the payment interval does *not* equal the compounding interval, and payments are made at the *end* of each payment interval.

Ordinary perpetuity A perpetuity in which the payments are at the end of each payment interval.

Ordinary simple annuity An annuity in which the payment interval *equals* the compounding interval, and payments are made at the *end* of each payment interval.

Partial payment Any payment that is smaller than the amount required to fully settle an invoice.

Payment interval The length of time between successive payments in an annuity.

Payment stream A series of two or more payments required by a single transaction or contract.

Period of deferral The time interval before the beginning of the first payment *interval* in a deferred annuity.

Periodic interest rate The rate of interest earned in one compounding period.

Perpetuity An annuity whose payments continue forever.

Perpetuity due A perpetuity in which the payments are at the beginning of each payment interval.

Polynomial An expression containing more than one term.

Power A mathematical operation indicating the multiplication of a quantity (the *base*) by itself a certain number (the *exponent*) of times.

Prepayments Any loan payments in addition to the regular contractual payments.

Present value A payment's economically equivalent amount at a *prior* date, allowing for the time value of money.

Present value of an annuity The single amount, at the beginning of the annuity, that is economically equivalent to the annuity.

Prime rate of interest A chartered bank's lowest lending rate.

Principal The original amount borrowed or invested.

Proper fraction A fraction in which the numerator is less than the denominator.

Proportion A statement of the equality of two ratios.

Proration A procedure in which an amount is subdivided and allocated on a proportionate basis.

Prospective Method A method for calculating a loan's balance based on payments still to be made.

Rate of interest The percentage of the principal that will be charged for a particular period of time, normally one year.

Rate of markdown The markdown expressed as a percentage of the regular selling price.

Rate of markup on cost The markup expressed as a percentage of the cost of the merchandise.

Rate of markup on selling price The markup expressed as a percentage of the selling price of the merchandise.

Ratio A comparison, by division, of the relative size of two or more quantities.

Receipt-of-goods dating Dating system for payment in which the discount and credit periods start on the date of receipt of the goods.

Residual value The amount for which the lessee can purchase a leased vehicle at the end of the term of the lease.

Retrospective Method A method for calculating a loan's balance based on payments already made.

Revenue function The total revenue expressed in terms of the number of units sold.

Root A particular numerical value for the variable that makes the two sides of the equation equal.

Rule of 72 A rule of thumb for a quick estimation of the number of years it will take an investment to double at a known compound annual rate of return.

Savings accounts Deposit accounts that offer essentially unrestricted withdrawal privileges.

Sell rate The exchange rate a currency dealer uses when selling a currency to you.

Simple annuity An annuity in which the payment interval equals the compounding interval.

Simple annuity due An annuity in which the payment interval *equals* the compounding interval, and payments occur at the *beginning* of each payment interval.

Simple interest Interest calculated only on the original principal and paid only at the maturity date.

Slope The change in the y-coordinate per unit change in the x-coordinate.

Spread The difference between the sell and buy rates for a currency.

Strip bond An investment instrument entitling its owner to receive only the face value of a bond at maturity.

Substitution Assigning a numerical value to each of the algebraic variables in an expression.

Tax rate The percentage of a price or taxable amount that is payable as tax.

Term The time period for which a loan or investment is made.

Term loan A loan that must be repaid over a predetermined time period.

Term of an annuity The total time from the beginning of the first payment interval to the end of the last payment interval.

Terms The components of an algebraic expression that are separated by addition or subtraction signs.

Terms of a ratio The numbers being compared in the ratio.

Terms of payment The specifications on an invoice of the length of the credit period, any cash discount offered and the corresponding discount period, and the date on which the credit and discount periods start.

Time diagram A time axis showing the dollar amounts and the dates of payments.

Time value of money The property that a given *nominal* amount of money has different economic values on different dates.

Trade discount A discount granted by the supplier to a purchaser of goods for resale.

Treasury bills Promissory notes issued (at a discount to face value) by the federal government or a provincial government to borrow money for a short term.

Trinomial An expression containing three terms.

Unit variable cost The cost of producing one more unit of output.

Variable cost A cost that grows in direct proportion to the volume of output or sales.

y-intercept The value for y (the ordinate) where the line crosses the y-axis ($x = 0$).

Index